GLOBAL COMMERCIAL CONTRACTS

GLOBAL COMMERCIAL CONTRACTS

CISG, PICC, AND OTHER INTERNATIONAL INSTRUMENTS

INGEBORG SCHWENZER
EDGARDO MUÑOZ

OXFORD
UNIVERSITY PRESS

Great Clarendon Street, Oxford, OX2 6DP,
United Kingdom

Oxford University Press is a department of the University of Oxford.
It furthers the University's objective of excellence in research, scholarship,
and education by publishing worldwide. Oxford is a registered trade mark of
Oxford University Press in the UK and in certain other countries.

Public sector information reproduced under Open Government Licence v3.0
(https://www.nationalarchives.gov.uk/doc/open-government-licence/)

Published in the United States of America by Oxford University Press
198 Madison Avenue, New York, NY 10016, United States of America.

British Library Cataloguing in Publication Data
Data available

Library of Congress Control Number: 2025946496

ISBN 978–0–19–882651–4 (pbk.)
ISBN 978–0–19–882650–7 (hbk.)

DOI: 10.1093/law/9780198826507.001.0001

Printed and bound by
CPI Group (UK) Ltd., Croydon, CR0 4YY

The manufacturer's authorized representative in the EU for product safety is
Oxford University Press España S.A. of Parque Empresarial San Fernando de Henares,
Avenida de Castilla, 2 – 28830 Madrid (www.oup.es/en or product.safety@oup.com).
OUP España S.A. also acts as importer into Spain of products made by the manufacturer.

Preface

This book provides a comprehensive overview of the practical challenges in international commercial contracts. It begins by addressing conflicts of laws in cross-border agreements and then focuses primarily on comparing the CISG and PICC, highlighting key differences between them. The book also explores other essential international instruments, including the UN Convention on the Use of Electronic Communications in International Commercial Contracts, the UN Convention on Limitation, Incoterms© 2020, UCP 600, and the URDG 750, offering readers a well-rounded picture of the legal frameworks governing international commerce. Comparing unified solutions with their domestic counterparts facilitates a thorough understanding of uniform law.

This resource is ideal for practitioners and scholars seeking clarity in international contract law. It is indispensable for students who envisage taking part in the Vis International Commercial Arbitration Moot as it provides the necessary background knowledge for a successful participation in this global competition.

We wish to express our sincere gratitude to the many individuals who contributed to the preparation of Global Commercial Contracts. In particular, we extend our deepest thanks to Andrea Cointa Lamas Bernal, who served as our main research assistant. We are also grateful to the team of research assistants whose efforts enriched our analysis and facilitated the completion of this project. We thank Aastha Gupta, Aditya Gopikrishnan, Ananya Jaria, Antonio Ochoa Quintana, Jesús Tlacaelel Covarrubias Miranda, José Centeotl Covarrubias Miranda, Kavya Gupta, Luz Ximena Castañeda Ibarra, Paulina Meza Barocio, and Vihaan M.N.

A textbook thrives on the interaction with its readers. We therefore invite any comments and suggestions.

Ingeborg Schwenzer and Edgardo Muñoz
Muellheim/Guadalajara, July 2025

Contents

Table of Cases

AUSTRIA

BELGIUM

BOSNIA AND HERZEGOVINA

BULGARIA

Parties	Date	Source	Page Numbers
Isola P EOOD v Nordmann, Rassmann Handelsgesellschaft mbH	2021	Апелативен съд София (Court of Appeal Sofia) 2139/2020, CISG-online 5583	176n.4, 177n.12
Metal lockers case	2019	ВАРНЕНСКИ ОКРЪЖЕН СЪД (District Court Varna) 972/2016, CISG-online 5588	202n.6

CANADA

Parties	Date	Source	Page Numbers
Diversitel Communications, Inc v Glacier Bay Inc	2003	Superior Court of Justice of Ontario 03-CV-23776 SR, CISG-online 1436	257n.25
Hewlett-Packard France v Matrox Graphics Inc.	2020	Cour supérieure du Québec/ Superior Court of Québec, 2020 QCCS 78/500-05-070786-023, CISG-online 4876	329n.361
Oz Optics Ltd v Timbercon Inc	2011	Court of Appeal (Ontario) 2011 ONCA 714	95n.163
Solea International BVBA v Bassett & Walker International Inc.	2018	Superior Court of Justice of Ontario, CV-15-527848/2018 ONSC 4261, CISG-online 4194	331n.390
Solea International BVBA v Bassett & Walker International Inc	2019	Court of Appeal of Ontario C66182/2019 ONCA 617, CISG-online 4505	222n.3, 235n.2

CHINA

Parties	Date	Source	Page Numbers
Hama GmbH & Co KG v Yongkang Kangteng Film Equipment Co, Ltd	2018	Intermediate People's Court Jinhua, Zhejiang Province (2018) Zhejiang 07 Minzhong No. 361, CISG-online 4782	230n.35

CZECH REPUBLIC

Parties	Date	Source	Page Numbers
KT MOTORSPORT spol s.r.o. v Garage Vandecasteele NV	2022	Court: Nejvyšší soud Ceské republiky (Supreme Court of the Czech Republic) 23 Cdo 1062/2021, CISG-online 6766	59n.16
Manufactured paint case	2008	Nejvyšší soud Ceské republiky (Supreme Court of the Czech Republic) 32 Odo 824/2007, CISG-online 1848	73n.11
Solarpower GmbH v Servis FVE a. s. et al.	2018	Nejvyšší soud České republiky (Supreme Court of the Czech Republic) 32 Cdo 2978/2016, CISG-online 4197	303n.147
VÚB a.s. v LITOZ s.r.o.	2019	Nejvyšší soud České republiky (Supreme Court of the Czech Republic) 23 Cdo 427/2017-336, CISG-online 4867	331n.389
ZEVETA Bojkovice, a.s. v FAGOR ARRASATE S COOP	2019	Nejvyšší soud Ceské republiky (Supreme Court of the Czech Republic) 23 Cdo 3439/2018, CISG-online 5670	51n.39

DENMARK

Parties	Date	Source	Page Numbers
Attianese S.p.A. v P. S. Import ApS	2024	Sø- og Handelsretten (Maritime and Commercial Court) BS-40411/2023-SHR, CISG-online 7177	292n.48
Dominion Denmark A/S v Polytex Composite s.r.o.	2023	Sø- og Handelsretten (Maritime and Commercial Court) BS-48358/2019-SHR, CISG-online 6331	230n.34, 240n.35
Production line for the production of cellulose products case	2018	Østre Landsret (Court of Appeal for the Eastern Circuit) B-424-17, CISG-online 4581	98n.185

EGYPT

Parties	Date	Source	Page Numbers
AWB v General Company for Silos and Storage	2020	Court of Cassation (Egyptian Supreme Court) 2490 of Judicial Year 81, CISG-online 5708	241n.40

ESTONIA

Parties	Date	Source	Page Numbers
Albrecht & Dill Trading GmbH v ERST Finance AS et al.	2023	Tallinna Ringkonnakohus (Court of Appeal Tallinn) 2-21-10111, CISG-online 6841	239n.22
Wiesenhof International GmbH v Estonian Meat House OÜ	2023	Tartu Maakohus (County Court Tartu) 2-22-11320, CISG-online 6648	229n.30

FINLAND

Parties	Date	Source	Page Numbers
Albrecht & Dill Trading GmbH v ERST Finance AS et al.	2023	Tallinna Ringkonnakohus (Court of Appeal Tallinn) 2-21-10111, CISG-online 6841	239n.22
Skin care products case	1998	Helsingin hovioikeus (Court of Appeal Helsinki) S 96/1215, CISG-online 1304	278n.131
Tönnies Lebensmittel GmbH & Co KG v Polarica Oy	2016	Lapin käräjäoikeus (District Court Lapland) 8040, CISG-online 5517	62n.31

FRANCE

Parties	Date	Source	Page Numbers
[...] Sà.r.l. v Emerito SL	2024	Cour d'appel de Montpellier (Court of Appeal Montpellier) 22/01909, CISG-online 6846	267n.76

FRANCE (CONT)

GERMANY (CONT)

GERMANY (CONT)

LATVIA

LITHUANIA

NETHERLANDS

NETHERLANDS (CONT)

RUSSIA

SERBIA

SLOVAKIA

SOUTH KOREA

SPAIN

Parties	Date	Source	Page Numbers
Carlos Soto S.A. v Don Emiliano	2015	Audiencia Provincial de Pontevedra (Court of Appeal Pontevedra) 681/2014/531/2015, CISG-online 2730	152n.126
Dcoop Sociedad Cooperativa Andaluza v Patano s.r.l.	2023	Audiencia Provincial de Jaén (Court of Appeal Jaén) 1697/2021/1323/2023, CISG-online 6896	141n.42, 269n.80
Dye for clothes case	1997	Audiencia Provincial de Barcelona (Court of Appeal Barcelona) 755/95-C, CISG-online 338	322n.304
Gimex, SA v Basque Imagen Grafica y Textil, SL	2003	Audiencia Provincial de Navarra (Court of Appeal Navarra) 73/2002, CISG-online 811	343n.47
Hoogendik Import/Export B.V. et al. v Bluemarine Fish International, S.L.	2014	Audiencia Provincial de Pontevedra (Court of Appeal Pontevedra) 251/2013/569/2014, CISG-online 2576	152n.126
Krane-Maschinen-Service GmbH & Co Handels-KG v Grúas Andaluza, SA	2010	Audiencia Provincial de Murcia (Court of Appeal Murcia) 408/2010, CISG-online 2130	309–10n.200
OKWIND v TGB Group Technologies, S.L.	2024	Audiencia Provincial de Barcelona (Court of Appeal Barcelona), 749/2022/981/2024, CISG-online 7300	346n.5
SMR Automotive Systems Spain, SAU v Bühler Motor GmbH	2013	Juzgado de Primera Instancia e Instrucción No 2 de La Almunia de Dona Godina (Court of First Instance No 2 of La Almunia de Dona Godina) 107/2013, CISG-online 2532	204n.19
Sunprojuice DK A/S v San Sebastián SCA	2007	Audiencia Provincial de Madrid (Court of Appeal Madrid) 92/2007, CISG-online 1637	103n.210
VSL Middle East LLC v Trenzas y Cables de Acero PSC SL	2013	Audiencia Provincial de Cantabria (Court of Appeal Cantabria) 400/2013, CISG-online 2487	302n.138

SWEDEN

Parties	Date	Source	Page Numbers
CeDe Group AB v KAN Sp z.o.o.	2020	Högsta domstolen (Swedish Supreme Court) T 6032-16, CISG-online 5500	45n.8, 59n.15

SWITZERLAND

Parties	Date	Source	Page Numbers
Art books case	1999	Handelsgericht des Kantons Zürich (Commercial Court Canton Zurich) HG 970238.1, CISG-online 488	295n.82, 296n.85
Business cards case	2006	Cour de Justice de Genève (Court of Appeal Canton Geneva) ACJC/47/2006, CISG-online 1504	218n.118
Cables and wires case	2004	Bundesgericht/Tribunal fédéral (Swiss Federal Supreme Court) (2004) 4C.144/2004, CISG-online 848	154n.136
Chinese wire rod case II	2015	Bundesgericht/Tribunal fédéral (Swiss Federal Supreme Court) 4A_614/2014, CISG-online 2592	265n.66
Clothes case II	1997	Kantonsgericht St. Gallen (Court of Appeal Canton St Gallen) 3 ZK 96-145, CISG-online 330	190n.92
Electronic electricity meters case	2018	Appellationsgericht Basel-Stadt (Court of Appeal Canton Basel-Stadt) ZB.2017.20 (AG.2018.557), CISG-online 3906	46n.16, 58n.10, 58n.11, 59n.16
FCF SA v Adriafil Commerciale S.r.l. (Egyptian cotton case II)	2000	Bundesgericht/Tribunal fédéral (Swiss Federal Supreme Court) 4C.105/2000, CISG-online 770 25	257n.25, 257n.26
Filling and packaging plant case	2006	Zivilgericht Basel-Stadt (Court of First Instance Basel-Stadt) P 2004 152, CISG-online 1731	98n.185, 99n.189

UNITED STATES

UNITED STATES (CONT)

ARBITRATION AND TRIBUNAL (CONT)

Table of International Instruments

Table of European Union

Table of National Legislation

1

Introduction

I. The Development of International Trade

As general statistics demonstrate, the sustained overall development of international trade over the last half-century is startling. World Trade Organization (WTO) figures indicate that worldwide merchandise export and import trade has increased and recovered from the slowdown of the COVID-19 pandemic.[1] These figures are roughly 300 times more than those in the 1950s, and more than ten times the level of the 1980s.[2] The highest growth is no longer found in North America, Europe, and Japan; instead, it is found in the transition economies from different points of the globe—particularly China, Latin America, and some African countries.[3]

Even recent protectionist measures—such as tariffs on foreign goods imposed by countries that once championed free trade—are unlikely to reverse this trend. On the contrary, they may spur the emergence of new trade alliances and regional agreements, highlighting the resilience and adaptability of global commerce.

The growth in trade is partly attributable to containerization, which has revolutionized the efficiency and scale of global cargo shipping. It has been suggested that approximately 90 per cent of non-bulk cargo is moved worldwide in containers on

---

[1] World Trade Organization, *World Trade Statistical Review 2024* (Geneva, WTO 2023) < https://www.wto.org/english/res_e/statis_e/world_trade_statistics_e.htm> accessed 23 November 2025.

[2] World Trade Organization (ed), *World Trade Report 2024: Trade and inclusiveness* (WTO 2024) < https://www.wto.org/english/res_e/booksp_e/wtr24_e/wtr24_e.pdf> accessed 24 November 2025; World Trade Organization, 'Evolution of Trade under the WTO: Handy Statistics' <https://www.wto.org/english/res_e/statis_e/trade_evolution_e/evolution_trade_wto_e.htm#fnt-1> accessed 23 November 2025.

[3] World Trade Organization, *World Trade Report 2024* (n 2); World Trade Organization, *World Trade Statistical Review 2024* (n 1).

cargo ships.[4] Anecdotally, today it is said to be cheaper to ship a bottle of wine from Melbourne, Australia to Hamburg, Germany (by sea, approximately 21,046 kilometres (km)) than to take it from Hamburg to Munich (approximately 776 km).

In recent times, international trade in merchandise has been surpassed by international trade in services. Today, the service sector accounts for more than 70 per cent of global Gross Domestic Product (GDP), and this share may even increase in the future.[5]

II. The Applicable Law in General

In an international contract, two core questions are to be answered: first, where will a dispute arising from the international contract be resolved; and second, which law or rules of law will be applied.[6] Ideally, parties to an international contract provide for both, by inserting a dispute resolution clause as well as a choice of law clause.

1. Dispute resolution

Parties may choose the form of dispute resolution in their contract.[7] By a forum selection clause, they may agree on which country's state courts should hear a possible dispute arising from the contract.[8] They may choose not only the forum of one of the parties but also a third neutral forum.[9] However, it is not certain whether the courts of a certain country, a country of one of the parties, will respect such a forum selection clause.[10] The Hague Convention on Choice of Court

---

[4] Jihong Chen and others, 'Identifying Factors Influencing Total-Loss Marine Accidents in the World: Analysis and Evaluation Based on Ship Types and Sea Regions' (2019) 191 *Ocean Engineering* <https://www.sciencedirect.com/science/article/pii/S0029801819306377> accessed 23 November 2025.

[5] Worldbank and World Trade Organization (eds), *Trade in Services for Development: Fostering Sustainable Growth and Economic Diversification* (World Trade Organization 2023) 14 <https://www.wto.org/english/res_e/booksp_e/trade_in_services_and_development_e.pdf> accessed 24 November 2025.

[6] Gary Born, *International Arbitration and Forum Selection Agreements: Drafting and Enforcing* (6th edn, Kluwer Law International BV 2021) 163; Cyril Emery, 'International Commercial Contracts' (*GlobaLex | Foreign and International Law Research*) para 2.2 <https://www.nyulawglobal.org/globalex> accessed 23 September 2024.

[7] Born, *International Arbitration and Forum Selection Agreements* (n 6) 1.

[8] Ibid 2.

[9] Gary Born, *International Arbitration: Law and Practice* (3rd edn, Kluwer Law International 2021) 10;

'2021 International Arbitration Survey: Adapting Arbitration to a Changing World | White & Case LLP' (6 May 2021) <https://www.whitecase.com/publications/insight/2021-international-arbitration-survey> accessed 23 November 2025.

[10] Born, *International Arbitration and Forum Selection Agreements* (n 6) 141–6.

Agreements 2005 has entered into force in the European Union Member States, Mexico, Montenegro, Moldova, Singapore, Ukraine, and the United Kingdom.[11] This means that, for example, a Brazilian court seized by a Brazilian contract partner will not, and does not have to acknowledge a choice of court clause contained in the parties' contract that provides for jurisdiction of the courts of the State of New York, United States of America, in a dispute between the parties.[12] Furthermore, even if one party obtains a court judgment in its favour, its enforcement must be sought in a country different from the one where it has been rendered. In many countries, this still requires a bilateral or multilateral convention between the states involved; or at least reciprocity, which means that court decisions are enforced in both states and vice versa.[13] Today, the Hague Convention on the Recognition and Enforcement of Foreign Judgments in Civil or Commercial Matters 2019 seeks to facilitate the effective international circulation of judgments. However, this Convention still has limited application as it has entered into force only in the European Union Member States, Albania, Montenegro, Ukraine, the United Kingdom, and Uruguay.[14]

This is the main reason why parties to an international contract today prefer international arbitration as the method of dispute resolution. The obstacles that still exist with relation to state courts and enforcement of their judgments, are far less in international arbitration. This is due to the United Nations (UN) Convention on the Recognition and Enforcement of Foreign Arbitral Awards, commonly known as the New York Convention, 1958. The New York Convention has 172 Member States,[15] and is thus the most successful international convention in the field of private law. On the one hand, it ensures that courts in Member States

---

[11] Hague Conference on Private International Law (HCCH), 'Status Table—Convention of 30 June 2005 on Choice of Court Agreements' <https://www.hcch.net/en/instruments/conventions/status-table/?cid=98> accessed 24 November 2025; Andrea Schulz, 'The Hague Convention of 30 June 2005 on Choice of Court Agreements', *Yearbook of Private International Law* (Sellier de Gruyter 2009) 1-3.

[12] For problems related to the validity of choice-of-law and choice-of-forum clauses: Dana Stringer, 'Choice of Law and Choice of Forum in Brazilian International Commercial Contracts: Party Autonomy, International Jurisdiction, and the Emerging Third Way' (2006) 44 *Columbia Journal of Transnational Law* 959.

[13] Regulation (EU) No 1215/2012 of the European Parliament and of the Council of 12 December 2012 on jurisdiction and the recognition and enforcement of judgments in civil and commercial matters (recast) [2012] OJ L351; Yuliya Zeynalova, 'The Law on Recognition and Enforcement of Foreign Judgments: Is It Broken and How Do We Fix It?' (2013) 31 *Berkeley Journal of International Law* 150; for a survey of the regime of recognition and enforcement of foreign judgments in 15 Asian jurisdictions see Anselmo Reyes (ed), *Recognition and Enforcement of Judgments in Civil and Commercial Matters* (Hart 2019).

[14] Francisco Garcimartín and Geneviève Saumier, *Explanatory Report on the Convention of 2 July 2019 on the Recognition and Enforcement of Foreign Judgments in Civil or Commercial Matters: HCCH 2019 Judgments Convention* (HCCH 2020). See also Membership Status at https://www.hcch.net/en/instruments/conventions/status-table/?cid=137, accessed 27 November 2025.

[15] 'Status: Convention on the Recognition and Enforcement of Foreign Arbitral Awards' (New York, 1958) (the 'New York Convention') (United Nations Commission On International Trade Law) <https://uncitral.un.org/en/texts/arbitration/conventions/foreign_arbitral_awards/status2> accessed 25 November 2025.

deny jurisdiction if the contract contains a valid arbitration clause; on the other hand, it ensures that a foreign arbitral award can easily be enforced in any other Member State of the New York Convention.[16]

International commercial arbitration today is widely harmonized. Many countries have modelled their arbitration laws on the United Nations Commission on International Trade Law (UNCITRAL) Model Law on International Commercial Arbitration 1985 and 2006 (MAL 2006).[17] The UNCITRAL Arbitration Rules for ad hoc arbitration 2021 as well as institutional rules today are more or less comparable and produce largely similar effects.[18]

Increasingly, parties are opting for mediation, be it as a sole dispute resolution mechanism or as a preliminary stage before turning to arbitration (multi-tier dispute resolution clauses). On an international level, mediation clauses and mediated settlements do not yet yield the same use as arbitral agreements. However, this might be about to change with the recent adoption of the UN Convention on International Settlement Agreements resulting from Mediation, or the Singapore Convention on Mediation, 2018. The Convention establishes a harmonized legal framework for the right to invoke settlement agreements resulting from mediation, as well as for their enforcement. It currently has 18 Member States.[19]

2. The applicable substantive law

Party autonomy is recognized in a majority of the States, allowing parties to select the substantive law governing their contract.[20] If parties, however, fail to choose the applicable law, the court or arbitral tribunal deciding the dispute will have to determine which law is to be applied to the contract.[21]

---

[16] Dirk De Meulemeester and Paul Lefebvre, 'The New York Convention: An Autopsy of Its Structure and Modus Operandi' (2018) 35 *Journal of International Arbitration* 413; Vereinte Nationen and Vereinte Nationen (eds), *UNCITRAL Secretariat Guide on the Convention on the Recognition and Enforcement of Foreign Arbitral Awards (New York, 1958)* (2016 edn, United Nations 2016) 1-3.

[17] Ilias Bantekas and others, *UNCITRAL Model Law on International Commercial Arbitration: A Commentary* (Cambridge University Press 2020) 1-5.

[18] UNCITRAL, 'Arbitration Centres that Follow UNCITRAL Arbitration Rules' <https://uncitral.un.org/en/texts/arbitration/contractualtexts/arbitration/centres> accessed 20 November 2025.

[19] 'Status: United Nations Convention on International Settlement Agreements Resulting from Mediation | United Nations Commission On International Trade Law' <https://uncitral.un.org/en/texts/mediation/conventions/international_settlement_agreements/status> accessed 27 November 2025.

[20] See in arbitration: English Arbitration Act 2025, s 46(1); Law of the Russian Federation on International Commercial Arbitration 1993, s 28; Brazilian Arbitration Act 1996, s 2; French Code of Civil Procedure, art 1511. Born, *International Arbitration* (n 9) 279 ff.

[21] Stephan W Schill (ed), 'ICC 2023-3. Partial Award in Case No. ICC-PA-2023-052', *ICC Awards Series*, vol I (ICCA & Kluwer Law International 2023) in said case, when dispute arose, one of the issues was the determination of the law applicable to the substance, since the parties did not come to an agreement, the arbitral tribunal decided in a preliminary award.

If there is no uniform law that applies to the contract, State courts turn to their own domestic rules on conflict of laws or private international law. Usually, these private international law rules designate the law with the closest connection to the contract.[22] However, the outcomes achieved vary significantly across domestic legal systems. For an international contract for the sale of goods, many countries provide for the law of the seller's place of business to govern the contract.[23] However, there may be numerous other possibilities for domestic law to determine the applicable law; for example, the place of conclusion of the contract, the place of the execution of the contract, etc.[24] Thus, simple reliance on the private international law rules of the forum State can make the outcome highly unpredictable.

Arbitral tribunals are not bound by the domestic rules of international private law of the State where they have their seat.[25] In cases where the parties have not made a choice of law, most arbitration laws and rules provide that the tribunal shall apply the substantive law or rules of law most closely connected to the contract.[26] Thereby, the arbitrators may fall back on conflict of law rules but, in general, they are not obliged to do so, albeit according to MAL Article 28(2) 'the arbitral tribunal shall apply the law determined by the conflict of laws rule which it considers applicable'. In many instances, the arbitral tribunal may even apply a uniform law if its prerequisites for automatic application are not fulfilled.[27]

---

[22] Inter-American Convention on the Law Applicable to International Contracts 1994, art 8; Regulation (EC) No 593/2008 of the European Parliament and of the Council of 17 June 2008 on the law applicable to contractual obligations (Rome I) [2008] OJ L 177/6, art 4(1); Ingeborg Schwenzer and Edgardo Muñoz, *Global Sales and Contract Law* (2nd edn, Oxford University Press 2022) para 4.01 ff.

[23] Switzerland's Federal Act on International Private Law, art 117 (2); for international instruments see Convention on the Law Applicable to Contracts for the International Sale of Goods 1955, art 3(1); Regulation (EC) No 593/2008 of the European Parliament and of the Council of 17 June 2008 on the law applicable to contractual obligations (Rome I) [2008] OJ L 177/6, art 4(1).

[24] Schwenzer and Muñoz (n 22) para 4.26 ff.

[25] Gary Born, *International Commercial Arbitration* (3rd edn, Kluwer Law International 2022) s 19.03[B][1]; Michał König, 'Non-State Law in International Commercial Arbitration' (2015) 35 *Polish Yearbook of International Law* 278.

[26] See e.g. Swiss Arbitration Rules art 35(1): '[I]n the absence of a choice of law, by applying the rules of law with which the dispute has the closest connection'; Cairo Regional Centre for International Commercial Arbitration (CRCICA) Rules 2011, art 35(1): 'Failing such designation by the parties, the arbitral tribunal shall apply the law which has the closest connection to the dispute'; German Arbitration Institute (DIS) Rules 1998, art 23(2): 'Failing any designation by the parties, the arbitral tribunal shall apply the law of the State with which the subject matter of the proceedings is most closely related.' Compared to DIS Rules 2018, art 24(2): 'If the parties have not agreed upon the rules of law to be applied to the merits of the dispute, the arbitral tribunal shall apply the rules of law that it deems to be appropriate.' Born, *International Arbitration* (n 9) 288.

[27] For insights into the application of the CISG by arbitral tribunals, see Born, *International Commercial Arbitration* (n 25) s 19.03 [A][4].

III. Who Needs Uniform and Harmonized Law and Why?

As mentioned above, most legal systems today recognize party autonomy and allow the parties to choose the governing law for their contract. However, in practice, this may not always yield satisfactory results. Different laws have always been perceived to be an obstacle to international trade. In the nineteenth and twentieth centuries, this prompted harmonization and unification on the nation state level. With the Austrian *Allgemeines Bürgerliches Gesetzbuch* and the French *Code Civil*, codification started in civil law jurisdictions around the world, in Europe, Latin America, and Asia.[28] In common law countries, core areas of trade were laid down in statutes like the Sale of Goods Act in England, or the Uniform Sales Act in the United States, which was later followed by the Uniform Commercial Code. Since the middle of the twentieth and twenty-first centuries, the trend of harmonization and unification of private law continues, on the global level.[29]

Before turning to the different international instruments, we will first discuss which parties trading internationally need uniform law and why it is not sufficient to grant them party autonomy. In practice, we can distinguish three different groups of parties.

In the first group, we have two parties from countries where the same language is spoken; for example, an Indian party and an English party, or an Australian party and one from New Zealand. Likewise, this would also apply to a German and a Swiss or Austrian party, or a French and a Belgian party. Not only do these parties speak the same language but they also share the same legal tradition, with similar legal terms and rules that are easily accessible for each of them.[30] It is highly probable that these parties would be able to agree on the law of one of their countries, or on a third law of the same legal tradition. For example, a US and an Australian party may agree on English law. These cases come close to purely domestic cases; the outcome is more or less predictable and the transaction costs in ascertaining the applicable law and the outcome in case of dispute are relatively low. It is conceded that these parties do not really need a uniform law, and they may well opt out from the otherwise existing uniform law in favour of some domestic law familiar to both.

The second group is characterized by an inequality of bargaining power. One party has such overwhelming bargaining power that it may force upon the other party, whatever terms it deems appropriate and serve its own interests. Let us

---

[28] See generally Uwe Kischel, 'The Basic Context of Civil Law' in Andrew Hammel (tr), *Comparative Law* (Oxford University Press 2019); Schwenzer and Muñoz (n 22) para 2.63 ff.

[29] Christoph Brunner, 'Introduction' in Christoph Brunner and Benjamin Gottlieb (eds), *Commentary on the UN Sales Law (CISG)* (Kluwer Law International BV 2019) 1 ff; Ingeborg Schwenzer, 'Introduction' in Ingeborg Schwenzer and Ulrich G Schroeter (eds), *Schlechtriem & Schwenzer Commentary on the UN Convention on the International Sale of Goods (CISG)* (5th edn, Oxford University Press 2022).

[30] Schwenzer and Muñoz (n 22) para 3.01 ff.

assume there is a contract between a globally acting US agricultural company and a Brazilian farmers' association. The American party would most probably insist on its own courts, let us say New York courts, and likewise, its own law, let us say New York law. The reason for this decision is that the US party trusts US courts to rule in its favour, and it knows New York law. The Brazilian party does not have enough bargaining power to oppose these terms. However, if a conflict arises, the Brazilian party may well turn to the Brazilian state courts. In the first place, the Brazilian courts will not recognize the choice of court agreement but will assume jurisdiction.[31] And second, they will not recognize the choice of law clause but will rather apply their own law instead.[32] Thus, the American party finds itself before a court it does not know and did not want to litigate in, confronted with an applicable law it does not know and did not want to submit to. It is true that US courts would probably not recognize and enforce a judgment by Brazilian courts in the United States under such circumstances. If, however, the US party has assets in Brazil or in some other country, the judgment may be enforced there. In such a case, even for the party with overwhelming bargaining power, arbitration and a uniform law governing the contract might be preferable.

In the third group, we find parties from countries where different languages are spoken, parties with a different legal background, and who are dealing at arm's length with one another. These may be two parties from civil law countries, such as a Chinese party contracting with a Mexican party; or a party from a civil law legal system and a party from a common law legal system, such as a Spanish party contracting with a US party. Under these circumstances, neither party would agree to choose the other party's law; otherwise, each might lose its face. Most probably, they would not agree to choose English law either, albeit in certain trade sectors such as oil and gas, this is done on a regular basis.

Rather, parties tend to choose a third, a so-called neutral law.[33] More often than not, this boils down to the choice of Swiss law.[34] Very often, the main reason for this choice is that parties tend to confuse political neutrality with the suitability of the law chosen for international contracts,[35] or simply because they do not really care. Just like dispute resolution clauses, choice of law clauses are typically called 'champagne clauses' or 'midnight clauses'. They are agreed upon at the end of a long

---

[31] See Brazilian Code of Civil Procedure (BCCP) in Portuguese *LEI Nº 13.105, DE 16 DE MARÇO DE 2015 Código de Processo Civil* 2015, arts 25 and 63 which first allows forum selection but also embodies the reasons to object if any parties were to select a forum different from Brazil.

[32] Anelize Slomp Aguiar, 'The Law Applicable to International Trade Transactions with Brazilian Parties: A Comparative Study of the Brazilian Law, the CISG, and the American Law About Contract Formation' (2012) IX *Revista Brasileira de Arbitragem* 33.

[33] Luiz Gustavo Meira Moser, 'Inside Contracting Parties' Minds: The Decision Making Processes in Cross-Border Sales' (2017) 8 *Journal of International Dispute Settlement* 250; Born, *International Commercial Arbitration* (n 25) s 19.04[D][4].

[34] Swiss law is one of the most commonly chosen laws by parties in ICC proceedings, see '2024 ICC Dispute Resolution Statistics' (2025) 2 *ICC Dispute Resolution Bulletin*.

[35] Born, *International Commercial Arbitration* (n 25) s 19.04.

bargaining process, just before the champagne bottles are opened to celebrate the successful deal. In this euphoric situation, parties do not consider a later dispute, and at least, they are convinced that in their detailed contract, they have provided for any difficulties that may arise at some later stage. The disillusion follows in case a conflict arises. If parties have chosen to arbitrate, the language of the arbitration would most probably be English.[36] If they have chosen Swiss law, they are confronted with the fact that Swiss law is mostly in German, some in French, and little in Italian. Thus, they find themselves facing a foreign law, in a foreign language. In the first place, in addition to their own domestic lawyer or an English or US law firm, they need a lawyer in the country of the law chosen. For the purposes of the arbitration, all legal texts, case law, and scholarly writing must be translated into English to accompany the submissions as exhibits. Most probably, they will need a legal expert to explain the law to the arbitrators as at least not all of them will be knowledgeable in the law chosen.[37] More often than not, the outcome of the case will depend on whose legal expert is better in cross-examination. Furthermore, the law chosen may be highly unpredictable. This is especially true for Swiss law. With only 8 million inhabitants, Switzerland is a very small country. The Swiss Civil Code and the Code of Obligations that govern contract law are more than 100 years old. Still, questions relating to the core areas of contract law have not yet been decided by the Supreme Court, or there may be decisions rendered more than 50 years ago. Usually, there is, however, a lot of conflicting scholarly writing, leaving ample room for legal arguments. Finally, the law chosen may not be suitable for international contracts.[38] Domestic law is intended to solve domestic conflicts, whereas international contracts pose distinct problems. Furthermore, many domestic laws—especially in civil law countries—are still firmly rooted in nineteenth-century dogmatism.[39]

IV. The Benefits of Uniform Law

The first benefit of uniform law relates to language. All UNCITRAL instruments are drawn up in the six official languages UN; Arabic, Chinese, English, French,

---

[36] According to statistics for 2020, well over 40 per cent of SCC proceedings were conducted in English, and ICC statistics for 2019 record that 79 per cent of awards were rendered in English; see Daniel Greineder, 'Arbitrators Don't Speak Esperanto: The Difficulties and Dominance of English as a Procedural Language in Arbitration' (*Kluwer Arbitration Blog*, 7 November 2021) <https://arbitrationblog.kluwerarbitration.com/2021/11/07/arbitrators-dont-speak-esperanto-the-difficulties-and-dominance-of-english-as-a-procedural-language-in-arbitration/> accessed 27 November 2025.

[37] ICC Commission Reports, 'Issues for Arbitrators to Consider Regarding Experts (2021 Update)' (2021) 2 *ICC Dispute Resolution Bulletin* 63 ff, s 2.

[38] See e.g. Swiss sales law differentiates meticulously between 'delivery' and 'non-delivery' of the ordered goods, and differs from the internationally established standard, see *M v H* [1995] BGer BGE 121 III 453.

[39] Schwenzer and Muñoz (n 22) para 2.31 ff.

Russian, and Spanish. Whenever an UNCITRAL instrument is adopted by a country, it is usually translated into the language of the respective country. Thus, at least the text of the instrument is available for everyone in his or her own mother tongue. Although due to historic reasons, UNIDROIT's working languages are generally only English and French, UNIDROIT instruments are often translated into other languages. Thus, the UNIDROIT Principles of International Commercial Contracts 2016, have been published in five original versions, including German, Italian, and Spanish, and further translated into 11 languages.[40]

Case law, or at least abstracts of cases dealing with uniform law, are translated into English. These translations as well as their originals are easily available on freely accessible databases. For case law on UNCITRAL instruments, the official database is CLOUT (Case Law on UNCITRAL Texts);[41] for UNIDROIT instruments, it is Unilex, which additionally covers some UNCITRAL instruments.[42] There are many other databases around the world gathering case law on uniform law and making it freely available to the public.[43]

Most scholarly writing on uniform law today is in English. Many English legal publications are translated into other languages, such as Chinese, Japanese, or Portuguese. There exist English article-by-article commentaries that are again translated into different languages.[44] Thus, a Mexican lawyer can rely on the same text as an opposing counsel from Australia or Germany, in his or her respective languages.

Finally, whereas arbitrators can usually not be expected to know more than a handful of legal systems that are traditionally related to the one they have been educated in, nowadays many are also knowledgeable in uniform law. This thus allows an informed discussion on legal problems between counsel and tribunal, without being obliged to rely on legal experts.

---

[40] Arabic, Chinese, Greek, Hungarian, Japanese, Persian, Portuguese, Romanian, Russian, Turkish, and Ukrainian. See also, 'UNIDTROIT Principles 2016, Official Languages' <https://www.unidroit.org/instruments/commercial-contracts/unidroit-principles-2016/> accessed 6 May 2025.

[41] 'CLOUT Network (Contributors to the CLOUT System) | United Nations Commission On International Trade Law' <https://uncitral.un.org/en/cloutnetwork> accessed 24 November 2025.

[42] 'UNILEX Case Database' <https://www.unilex.info/instrument/principles> accessed 25 November 2025.

[43] See e.g. http://www.cisg-online.org and Jean Davis, 'LibGuides: International Commercial Arbitration & International Commercial Law Research: Databases: Int'l. Commercial Law' <https://guides.brooklaw.edu/commercial/commercial_law_databases> accessed 24 November 2024; 'CISG Database' (*Institute of International Commercial Law*, 9 May 2015) <https://iicl.law.pace.edu/cisg/cisg> accessed 24 April 2024.

[44] See e.g. Schlechtriem & Schwenzer (eds), *Commentary on the UN Convention on the International Sale of Goods* (5th edn, Oxford University Press 2022), which is also available in German, Spanish, Portuguese, Turkish, Polish, Japanese, and soon French.

2

Harmonization and Unification of International Commercial Law

The harmonization and unification of private law began to take shape in the aftermath of the First World War, around the 1920s. This period marked a growing recognition of the need for legal consistency in cross-border commercial and civil relations. Early efforts laid the groundwork for institutions and instruments that would later shape modern transnational private law.

I. The CISG—a Bit of History

Efforts to unify the law on the international sale of goods began in the 1920s. In 1926 the International Institute for the Unification of Private Law (UNIDROIT) was founded in Rome and inaugurated in 1928. It was the Austrian-born eminent scholar Ernst Rabel, the founder of modern comparative law, who suggested work should begin on the unification of sales law. Already one year later, he presented the first provisional report on the possibilities of sales law unification. One year later, a committee of representatives from different legal systems was founded. The first draft of a uniform sales law was published in 1935. In 1936, Rabel published the first volume of his seminal work *Das Recht des Warenkaufs*.[1]

After the Second World War, unification efforts were resumed. UNIDROIT was the catalyst in this process. Finally, the so-called Hague Conventions on the sale of goods, the Uniform Law on International Sale of Goods (ULIS) and the Uniform Law on the Formation of Contracts for the International Sale of Goods (ULF) were drawn up at the Hague Conference in 1964.[2]

Measured against the expectation that they would bring about a worldwide unification of international sales law, the Hague Sale of Goods Conventions were a disappointment. Even before the finalization of the Hague Sale of Goods Conventions, it was clear that countries such as France, the United States, and the Nordic countries would not become Contracting States.[3] Socialist and developing countries perceived ULIS and ULF to favour sellers from industrialized Western economies and thus also refused to participate. In the end, the Hague Sale of Goods Conventions only had nine Contracting States.[4] Despite this number, the practical relevance of the Hague Sale of Goods Conventions should not be underestimated.

The limited success of the Hague Sale of Goods Conventions prompted further intense work in the field of unification of sales law.

In 1966, the UNCITRAL was established as a permanent commission of the United Nations to 'further the progressive harmonization and modernization of the law of international trade'.[5] UNCITRAL started working on the unification of sales law in 1968 using the Hague Sale of Goods Conventions as its starting point. In 1977, the so-called Vienna draft of a uniform sales law was finalized, supplemented in 1978 and thus forming the so-called New York draft that was finally circulated among the governments of the UN Member States.[6] The CISG was finalized at a diplomatic conference in Vienna in March and April 1980. A total of 62 countries participated in the Conference, 42 of which voted for the adoption of the final instrument that became the CISG.[7] As established in Article 99 CISG,

---

[1] Ingeborg Schwenzer, 'Introduction' in Ingeborg Schwenzer and Ulrich G Schroeter (eds), *Schlechtriem & Schwenzer Commentary on the UN Convention on the International Sale of Goods (CISG)* (5th edn, Oxford University Press 2022) 1.

[2] Ibid.

[3] Michael G Bridge, *The International Sale of Goods* (4th edn, Oxford University Press 2017) para 10.06; Christoph Brunner, 'Introduction' in Christoph Brunner and Benjamin Gottlieb (eds), *Commentary on the UN Sales Law (CISG)* (Kluwer Law International BV 2019) para 3.

[4] 'ULIS and ULF entered into force in Belgium on August 1972, Gambia on 5 September 1974, Germany on 16 April 1974, Israel on 18 August 1972 (ULIS) and 30 December 1980 (ULF), Italy on 23 August 1972, Luxembourg on 6 August 1979, the Netherlands on 18 August 1972, San Marino on 18 August 1972, and Great Britain (although with the reservation that the uniform law must be chosen by the parties) on 18 August 1972.' See Schwenzer, 'Introduction' (n 1) 1 fn 6.

[5] United Nations Commission On International Trade Law, 'Frequently Asked Questions - Mandate and History' (*Origin, Mandate and Composition of UNCITRAL*) <https://uncitral.un.org/en/about/faq/mandate_composition/history> accessed 24 November 2025.

[6] Schwenzer, 'Introduction' (n 1) 2.

[7] Brunner (n 3) para 4.

the CISG was to enter into force on the first day of the month following the twelfth month after the submission of the last of the ten necessary ratification documents. This threshold was met on 11 December 1986 when China, Italy, and the United States ratified the Convention. Accordingly, the CISG entered into force on 1 January 1988.

The CISG may truly be called a worldwide success. At the time of writing, UNCITRAL lists 97 Contracting States.[8] According to WTO trade statistics, nine of the ten largest export and import nations are contracting States, with the United Kingdom being the sole exception.[9] Today, more than 80 per cent of world trade is potentially governed by the CISG.

The greatest success is probably the strong influence the CISG has exerted at both the international as well as the domestic level. The Uniform Act on General Commercial Law 2010[10] enacted by the Organization for the Harmonization of Business Law in Africa (OHADA) States in Africa is, in many respects, practically a transcript of the CISG. The UNIDROIT Principles on International Commercial Contracts (PICC) were all modelled on the CISG. Furthermore, the EC Consumer Sales Directive heavily drew on the Convention.[11] Similarly, the Sale of Goods Acts in the Nordic countries, recent East Asian codifications, the modernized German law of obligations and sales law, the majority of post-Soviet codifications in Eastern Europe, Central Asia, two of the Baltic states, the Hungarian Civil Code, the Argentine Civil and Commercial Code, the French Civil Code reform to the law of obligations, the new Japanese Civil Code, and the new Chinese Civil Code are built on the CISG.[12] In sum, during the last 20 years, every international and domestic legislator turned to the CISG when planning a reform or new enactment of the law of obligations and contracts. There is only one exception and that is the Turkish revision of its Code of Obligations in 2012. Finally, anecdotally, the CISG is used in developing countries to teach traders and farmers the basic structures of contract law so as to improve their level of sophistication.

---

[8] See CISG Ratification status in 'Status: United Nations Convention on Contracts for the International Sale of Goods (Vienna, 1980) (CISG) | United Nations Commission On International Trade Law' <https://uncitral.un.org/en/texts/salegoods/conventions/sale_of_goods/cisg/status> accessed 24 November 2025.

[9] 'CISG Contracting and Non-Contracting States by Foreign Trade Volume | CISG-Online.Org' <https://cisg-online.org/cisg-contracting-states/contracting-states-by-foreign-trade-volume> accessed 24 November 2025.

[10] *Acte Uniforme Portant sur le Droit Commercial Général* 2010.

[11] Ingeborg Schwenzer, 'The CISG Advisory Council' in MG Bridge, Ulrich G Schroeter, and Ingeborg Schwenzer (eds), *The CISG Advisory Council opinions* (2nd edn, Eleven International Publishing 2021). For an analysis see Elias Van Gool and Anaïs Michel, 'The New Consumer Sales Directive 2019/771 and Sustainable Consumption: A Critical Analysis' (2021) 10 *Journal of European Consumer and Market Law* 136.

[12] Ingeborg Schwenzer and Edgardo Muñoz, *Global Sales and Contract Law* (2nd edn, Oxford University Press 2022) para 2.31 ff.

II. Further UNCITRAL Endeavours

In addition to the CISG, UNCITRAL has embarked upon the unification and harmonization of many other areas of international trade. This includes conventions, model laws and rules, as well as legal and legislative guides and recommendations.

In the field of the international sale of goods, there are primarily worth mentioning the UN Convention on the Limitation Period in the International Sale of Goods, 1974 (LC), the UNCITRAL Uniform Rules on Contract Clauses for an Agreed Sum Due Upon Failure of Performance, 1983, and the UNCITRAL Legal Guide on International Countertrade Transactions. However, there are still core areas of general contract law that have not been tackled by UNCITRAL. In 2012, Switzerland made a proposal to UNCITRAL to consider the desirability and feasibility of further unification of contract law on a global level. Although there was strong support for this proposal from many countries, such as Japan, China, and Singapore, it finally failed due to fierce opposition from the United States, followed by Canada and Israel.[13]

Closely related to contract law is the field of electronic commerce. Besides the UN Convention on the Use of Electronic Communications in International Contracts (2005), there are the UNCITRAL Model Laws on Electronic Commerce (1996), Electronic Signatures (2001), and Electronic Transferable Records (2017).

Other provisions directly linked to the international sale of goods are the rules for the international transport of goods. However, the latest version of the UN Convention on Contracts for the International Carriage of Goods Wholly or Partly by Sea (2008, 'Rotterdam Rules') has not entered into force. The 'Hamburg Rules', the UN Convention on the Carriage of Goods by Sea (1978), on the other hand, are still in force in 35 Member States.

In addition, the UN Convention on International Bills of Exchange and International Promissory Notes (1988) and the Convention on Independent Guarantees and Stand-by Letters of Credit (1995) had the aim of unifying international payments, albeit with little success. The first has not entered into force, and the second attracted only eight Member States.

UNCITRAL also has developed many activities in the field of security interests. This finally culminated in the UNCITRAL Model Law on Secured Transactions (2016). Whether it will be welcomed and implemented by domestic legislators remains to be seen. Likewise, insolvency has been an important area of activity by UNCITRAL. The UNCITRAL Model Law on Cross-Border Insolvency (1997) has been implemented in quite a few legal systems.

---

[13] Note by the Secretariat of the General Assembly's UNCITRAL, 'Proposal by Switzerland on possible future work by UNCITRAL in the Area of International Contract Law' (2012) UN Doc A/CN.9/758.

The probable most prominent and successful area of unification and harmonization initiated by UNCITRAL is international arbitration. As already mentioned, long before UNCITRAL was established the New York Convention was finalized by the UN in 1958. In 1976, UNCITRAL published its own set of arbitration rules, which were revised in 2010. In 1980, the UNCITRAL Conciliation Rules were finalized. In 1985, UNCITRAL issued the Model Law on International Arbitration (MAL) —amended in 2006— which has exercised extraordinary influence on the arbitration laws of domestic legal systems thus having a tremendous harmonizing effect worldwide.[14] In 2002, a model law on international commercial conciliation followed. International commercial mediation is now addressed by the Singapore Convention. The work on online dispute resolution up to now has only led to Technical Notes (2016), but not yet to any uniform instrument.

III. The UNIDROIT Principles on International Commercial Contracts (PICC)

Among the existing uniform projects, the PICC have received the most attention on a global scale. The first suggestions to develop a restatement of international commercial law date back to 1968 after the 1964 Hague Sale of Goods Conventions had been finalized but before they entered into force in 1972. The final decision to embark on this project was taken in 1971. It took until 1980 to establish the Working Group. In 1985, the initial task for the Working Group, namely the 'Progressive Codification of International Trade Law', was changed to the 'Preparation of Principles for International Commercial Contracts'.

In 1994, the Governing Council of UNIDROIT authorized the first version of the PICC to be published but did not formally approve them. Whereas UNCITRAL had a truly global representation, the comparative basis for the PICC was exclusively provided by Western legal systems of both common law and civil law tradition. However, the Official Comments to the PICC never reveal the source of inspiration for a particular concept or that the solutions adopted were the result of comparative research. The only hint that this might have been the case is the fact that the members of the Working Group came from different legal systems with diverse legal traditions.

The UNIDROIT Governing Council initiated preparations for a second edition in 1997. The final version was approved and published in 2004. Whereas the 1994 version more or less covered the same subjects as the CISG, five new topics were added in the 2004 version. These were agency, contracts for the benefit of third

---

[14] Ilias Bantekas and others, *UNCITRAL Model Law on International Commercial Arbitration: A Commentary* (Cambridge University Press 2020) 10.

parties, set-off, limitation of actions, assignments of rights and contracts, and the transfer of obligations. In total, the original 120 articles were extended to 185.

In 2010 the third version of the PICC was published. The extensions were not as many as between the first and the second version. However, a chapter on illegality was added in 2010.[15] The rules on rescission of the contract, termed 'avoidance' by the PICC, were amended and so were the rules on avoidance of the contract, termed 'termination' by the PICC.[16]

Finally, in 2016 the fourth edition of the PICC took into account the special needs of long-term contracts which, however, required only marginal alteration of the 2010 version.[17] This last version is now a comprehensive set of rules on contract law. For the time being, no further versions of the PICC are considered.

The PICC pursue different objectives and may assume different functions. These have been explicitly laid down in the Preamble of the PICC. First, they are intended to set forth general rules for international commercial contracts, a common core of international contract law. However, some of their rules cannot be regarded as being part of such a common core but were rather modelled directly on a domestic concept that the drafters preferred. A prominent example is the judicial penalty,[18] which is only found in French legal systems but neither in common law nor in the Germanic legal systems. In their presentation, the PICC follow the concept of restatement of law as it is found in the United States. The second purpose of the PICC is to serve as a model law for national and international legislators and as a guide for contracts between parties.[19] Finally, the PICC also encourage parties to an international contract to choose the PICC as the rules of law applicable to their contract. However, whether such a choice of law is possible under the applicable conflict of laws rules is a different question.[20]

Little is known about the actual relevance of the PICC in practice. Whereas some praise them as being the ideal regime for any international contract,[21] others remain rather sceptical.[22] There are three main concerns about the suitability of PICC for international practice: as will be seen, they have been greatly influenced

---

[15] Michael Joachim Bonnell, 'The New Provisions on Illegality in the UNIDROIT Principles 2010' (2011) 16 *Uniform Law Review* 517, 518.

[16] Reinhard Zimmermann, 'The Unwinding of Failed Contracts in the UNIDROIT Principles 2010' (2011) 16 *Uniform Law Review* 563, 564.

[17] Michael Joachim Bonell, 'The Law Governing International Commercial Contracts and the Actual Role of the UNIDROIT Principles' (2018) 23 *Uniform Law Review* 15.

[18] PICC 2016, art 7.2.4.

[19] Stefan Vogenauer (ed), *Commentary on the UNIDROIT Principles of International Commercial Contracts (PICC)* (2nd edn, Oxford University Press 2015) Preamble, para 5.

[20] Eckart Brödermann, *UNIDROIT Principles of International Commercial Contracts: An Article-by-Article Commentary* (2nd edn, Nomos 2023) 1 et seq.

[21] Ibid.

[22] Giuditta Cordero-Moss, 'UNIDROIT' in Petra Butler (ed), *International Commercial Contracts: Law and Practice* (2013); International Bar Association, *Perspectives in Practice of the UNIDROIT Principles 2016* (2019) <https://www.ibanet.org/MediaHandler?id=D266F2AF-3E0B-4DC0-AFCE-662E5D49BB7E> accessed 24 November 2025.

by civil law legal tradition; closely related to this is the abundant use of the principle of good faith; and finally as the PICC are mostly applied in arbitration and, thus, there is yet few published case law one could rely on.[23]

IV. Further UNIDROIT Endeavours

UNIDROIT has embarked on many other areas of harmonization and globalization of international private law. The most successful UNIDROIT convention is the Convention on International Interests in Mobile Equipment 2001, the so-called Cape Town Convention, with currently 88 Member States.[24] Most noteworthy, furthermore, are the UNIDROIT Convention on Stolen or Illegally Exported Cultural Objects 1995, which now has 56 Member States,[25] the UNIDROIT Convention on International Financial Leasing 1988 with 11 Member States,[26] the UNIDROIT Convention on International Factoring 1988 with only nine Member States,[27] and the Model Franchise Disclosure Law 2002.

Furthermore, UNIDROIT moved into the field of harmonization of procedural law. Together with the American Law Institute (ALI), the ALI/UNIDROIT Principles on Transnational Civil Procedure were published in 2006, while together with the European Law Institute (ELI), the ELI/UNIDROIT Principles on Transnational Civil Procedure aimed at the specificities of the European legal market were adopted in 2020. UNIDROIT is currently working with the ICC Institute of World Business Law on a project on International Investment Contracts.

V. The Hague Conference

The purpose of the Hague Conference is to work for the progressive unification of the rules on conflict of laws.[28] Thus, the aim is slightly different from those envisaged by UNIDROIT and UNCITRAL, whose purpose is the harmonization and unification of substantive private law matters.[29]

---

[23] Sarah Lake, 'An Empirical Study of the UNIDROIT Principles—International and British Responses' (2011) 16 *Uniform Law Review* 669 et seq.

[24] See Member States 'States Parties Cape Town Convention' <https://www.unidroit.org/instruments/security-interests/cape-town-convention/states-parties/> accessed 27 June 2025.

[25] See Member States in 'States Parties' <https://www.unidroit.org/instruments/cultural-property/1995-convention/status/> accessed 27 June 2025.

[26] See Member States in 'Status of the Convention' <https://www.unidroit.org/instruments/leasing/convention/status/> accessed 27 June 2025.

[27] See Member States in 'Status of the Convention' <https://www.unidroit.org/instruments/factoring/convention/status/> accessed 27 June 2025.

[28] Statute of the Hague Conference on Private International Law 1955, art 1.

[29] Bantekas and others (n 14); Vogenauer (n 19).

Although the earlier work of the Hague Conference comprised contract and sales law issues, most of the Hague Conventions deal with international private law matters in the area of family, inheritance, or tort law. However, there are two recent instruments with great relevance for international commercial contracts: the first is the Hague Convention on Choice of Court Agreements (2005),[30] and the second is the Hague Principles on Choice of Law in International Commercial Contracts (2015).[31] Whereas the former recognizes party autonomy with relation to the choice of forum clauses, the latter does so for the choice of law in international contracts. Thus, both instruments significantly promote the general principle of party autonomy on the international level, an indispensable cornerstone for global trade. More recently, Hague adopted the Convention on the Recognition and Enforcement of Foreign Judgments in Civil or Commercial Matters 2019 that seeks to facilitate the effective international circulation of judgments.[32]

VI. UNCITRAL, UNIDROIT, and the Hague Conference Legal Guide to Uniform Legal Instruments in the Area of International Commercial Contracts (with a Focus on Sales) 2020

A constant matter of debate is the use of the PICC to interpret provisions of the CISG. The question is a general one and affects all uniform projects. The Legal Guide to Uniform Legal Instruments in the Area of International Commercial Contracts, with a focus on sales, which was published jointly by UNCITRAL, UNIDROIT, and the Hague Conference in 2020, provides an institutional approach to understanding the relationship among existing uniform law texts such as PICC, the CISG, and the HCCH Principles. The Guide places emphasis on the fact that these instruments are complementary in nature when more than one instrument applies to a transaction. Accordingly, it offers some basic guidelines on their interaction.[33] On the one hand, the Guide recalls that parties could choose both the CISG and the PICC as the governing laws of their contracts. In that case, the CISG will be regarded as a body of rules of law.[34] Depending on the choice made

---

[30] See Member States in 'Status Table of the Convention of 30 June 2005 on Choice of Court Agreements' <https://www.hcch.net/en/instruments/conventions/status-table/?cid=98> accessed 19 November 2025.

[31] 'Status Table—Principles on Choice of Law in International Commercial Contracts' <https://www.hcch.net/en/instruments/conventions/publications1/?dtid=41&cid=135> accessed 24 November 2025.

[32] 'Convention of 2 July 2019 on the Recognition and Enforcement of Foreign Judgments in Civil or Commercial Matters' <https://www.hcch.net/en/instruments/conventions/specialised-sections/judgments> accessed 24 November 2025.

[33] UNCITRAL, 'Legal Guide to Uniform Legal Instruments in the Area of International Commercial Contracts (with a focus on sales)' (53rd session, 2020) UN Doc A/CN.9/1029 V.20-01178, para 16 ff.

[34] A choice which is possible under many arbitration laws and rules as well as the Hague Conference on Private International Law Principles on Choice of Law in International Commercial Contracts

by the parties, the PICC may play the limited role of supplementing the CISG on matters that are not covered by the latter.

On the other hand, the Adjustments to the Guide recognize the common understanding that the PICC are not, as such, considered to be the general principles of the CISG but rather that they can serve to corroborate the existence of a given general principle, and, thus, they can be a tool to interpret the CISG (Article 7(1) CISG)[35] or to fill its gaps (Article 7(2) CISG),[36] whenever there is no collision between the two instruments. In particular, the Guide proposes that the PICC may be used to determine the meaning of rules and concepts of the CISG. It suggests that recourse to the PICC in interpreting the CISG is generally accepted because Article 7(1) CISG stipulates that, in its interpretation, 'regard is to be had to its international character',[37] and case law has taken note of this argument.[38] The Guide also asserts that recourse to the PICC can be made to fill gaps in the CISG because Article 7(2) CISG stipulates that questions concerning matters governed by the Convention which are not expressly settled in it 'are to be settled in conformity with the general principles on which it is based'.[39] It argues that, in spite of the fact that the PICC were published only 14 years after the CISG was adopted, at least some of their rules are restatements of general principles of international commercial law on which, among others, the CISG is based. The Guide supports this view with the argument that UNCITRAL has formally commended the use of the PICC for their intended purposes and these purposes, as set out in the Preamble to the PICC, include the use of the PICC 'to supplement international uniform law instruments'.[40]

Irrespective of the PICC Preamble and its rules on the scope of application, the issue whether the PICC may be taken into account for the purposes of interpretation or gap filling of another contract law regime depends on the rules and principles of interpretation and gap-filling of that particular regime. In the next chapter, we address the question of whether and to what extent the PICC may be used to interpret or fill in the CISG gaps.

(HCCH Principles) art 3. Also under HCCH Principles art 2(2), the parties may choose more than one law to govern their contract. See UNCITRAL (n 33) paras 125–126.

[35] As noted in some case law, see *Genfoot Inc v SCHENKERocean Ltd* [2019] Noregs Høgsterett (Norwegian Supreme Court) HR-2019-231-A (sak nr. 18-051892SIV-HRET), CISG-online 4318.

[36] As noted in some case law, see *Chilean Sea Bass Inc v Kendell Seafood Imports, Inc* [2024] US District Court for the District of Rhode Island 21-cv-337-JJM-LDA, CISG-online 6990.

[37] See UNCITRAL (n 33) para 351.

[38] *Busrel Inc v Dotton et al.* [2022] US District Court for the Western District of New York 1:20-cv-01767, CISG-online 6111.

[39] See UNCITRAL (n 33) para 352.

[40] See UNCITRAL (n 33) para 352, referring to UNGA Official Records, 'Report of the United Nations Commission on International Trade Law (67th Session 2012) UN Doc (A/67/17) Supplement No 17, paras 137–140.

VII. Regional Endeavours

Around the world, many regional attempts to harmonize or unify contract law can be discerned. Some come in the form of binding instruments, others are mere uniform projects that aim at unification at a later stage.

1. Africa—OHADA

On the African continent, to this day uniform law is primarily associated with the *Organisation pour l'Harmonisation en Afrique du Droit des Affaires* (OHADA). Currently, OHADA has 17 Member States, most of them former French colonies.[41] In the area of sales law, the *Acte Uniforme Relatif au Droit Commercial Général* (Uniform Act on General Commercial Law—AUDCG), in addition to general commercial law, also contains rules on sales law. The first version of AUDCG entered into force in 1998; in 2011 a new version entered into force. The main structure and legal concepts for sales law on the whole have been taken over from the CISG. However, French law continued to have a strong influence, both on the 1998 Act as well as on its revision in 2011.[42]

In 2002, the OHADA Council of Ministers decided to approach UNIDROIT and seek the assistance of its expertise in drafting a uniform act on contract law. In conjunction with UNIDROIT a draft act which used the PICC as a model was presented in 2005. However, this project was not pursued further and is no longer listed on OHADA's list of drafts or new subjects.[43]

2. Europe

In the European Union, many areas of private law have been harmonized and unified by directives and regulations. A number of uniform projects aim at further harmonization and unification.

a.) Directives and regulations

Based on Article 288 of the Treaty on the Functioning of the European Union, the European Union operates with essentially two instruments: directives and regulations.[44] Directives do not apply directly, rather they establish a minimum standard with which Member States must comply. Hence, Member States must enact

---

[41] See 'State Members—OHADA' <https://www.ohada.org/en/state-members/> accessed 6 February 2025.

[42] Schwenzer and Muñoz (n 12) para 3.40.

[43] Ibid para 3.41.

[44] Treaty on the Functioning of the European Union 1957, art 288.

legislation that complies with these standards. Thus directives do not unify the law, but they harmonize it. Regulations, on the other hand, are directly applicable uniform law that must be applied by any Member State.

In the area of contract law and sales law, the European Union primarily works with directives. Prominent examples are the Consumer Sales Directive,[45] the Consumer Rights Directive,[46] and the Late Payment Directive.[47] The Consumer Sales Directive is largely based upon the CISG. A Digital Content Directive was issued in 2019.[48]

As regards private international law, however, regulations prevail. Most notably, the Rome I Regulation provides for the law that governs contracts in the European Union.[49] The Brussels I Regulation contains a jurisdictional regime; it rules which courts of EU Member States have jurisdiction in cases with links to more than one country in the European Union.[50]

b.) Uniform projects

At the European level, the Principles of European Contract Law (PECL) were developed in a similar fashion as the PICC. Yet, as the name indicates, the focus is on Europe and more specifically on the members of the European Union. However, they also took into account the US Uniform Commercial Code as well as the Restatements. Hence, there is no significant difference between PICC and PECL. This is also due to the fact that the PECL, just like the PICC, are largely built on the CISG.

The Draft Common Frame of Reference (DCFR) was the last uniform project in Europe.[51] It was drafted and published by the Study Group on a European Civil Code and the Research Group on Existing EC Private Law. In contrast to PICC and PECL, the DCFR addressed not only contract law but virtually all matters typically addressed in civil codes to the exclusion of family law and inheritance law.

The Common European Sales Law (CESL)[52] contained provisions on contract formation, contract interpretation, including unfair contract terms, and—as its

---

[45] Council Directive 2019/771/EU of the European Parliament and of the Council of 20 May 2019 on Certain Aspects Concerning Contracts for the Sale of Goods [2019] OJ L 136/28.

[46] Council Directive 2011/83/EU of the European Parliament and of the Council of 25 October 2011 on Consumer Rights [2011] OJ L 304/64.

[47] Council Directive 2011/7/EU of the European Parliament and of the Council of 16 February 2011 on Combating Late Payment in Commercial Transactions (Recast) [2011] OJ L 48/1.

[48] Council Directive 2019/770/EU of the European Parliament and of the Council of 20 May 2019 on Certain Aspects Concerning Contracts for the Supply of Digital Content and Digital Services [2019] L136/1.

[49] Council Regulation (EC) No 593/2008 of the European Parliament and of the Council of 17 June 2008 on the Law Applicable to Contractual Obligations (Rome I) [2008] OJ L 177/6.

[50] Council Regulation (EU) No 1215/2012 of the European Parliament and of the Council of 12 December 2012 on Jurisdiction and the Recognition and Enforcement of Judgments in Civil and Commercial Matters (Recast) [2012] OJ L 351/1.

[51] Schwenzer and Muñoz (n 12) para 3.60.

[52] Ingeborg Schwenzer and Lisa Spagnolo (eds), *Globalization versus Regionalization: 4. Annual MAA Schlechtriem CISG Conference, 18 March 2012, Hong Kong* (Eleven Publishing 2013).

core part—obligations and remedies of the parties to a sales contract. Furthermore, provisions on damages and interest, and restitution as well as prescription, could be found. Thus, the sphere of application of the CESL was more or less identical with the CISG with the exception of unfair contract terms. CESL was meant to be an optional instrument; this means that it would not apply automatically but rather that parties had to choose its application by opting in. Finally, in 2014 the idea was abandoned and CESL was withdrawn.

3. Asia

Following the European model, as of 2009, a group of academics in Eastern Asia started to work on Principles of Asian Contract Law (PACL). The drafters want them to mirror specific features of contract law common to the Asian countries involved. Up to now, the areas of performance and non-performance have been covered.[53]

4. Latin America

The Principles of Latin American Contract Law (PLACL) provide a model for Latin American legislatures for any possible revision of their civil codes. A first version of the PLACL was launched in 2017. As the South American civil codes are more or less based on the French Code Civil it does not come as a great surprise that the PLACL have been heavily influenced by French legal concepts, such as, for example, the requirement of cause which interestingly was abandoned in the French Civil Code by the 2016 amendment.[54]

5. Criticism

Although any endeavours for harmonization and unification as such can be welcome, and comparative studies enhance our knowledge of different legal cultures, the practical use of regional uniform projects is very doubtful.[55] Practice needs a

---

[53] Shiyuan Han, 'Principles of Asian Contract Law: An Endeavor of Regional Harmonization of Contract Law in East Asia' (2014) 58 *Villanova Law Review*.

[54] Rodrigo Andres Momberg Uribe, 'The Process of Harmonisation of Private Law in Latin America: An Overview' in Rodrigo Momberg and Stefan Vogenauer (eds), *The Future of Contract Law in Latin America: The Principles of Latin American Contract law* (Hart Publishing 2020); Christina Ramberg, 'Principles of Latin American Contract Law: Conference Notes' (2016) 21 *Uniform Law Review—Revue de droit uniforme* 129.

[55] Bruno Zeller, 'Regional Harmonisation of Contract Law—Is It Feasible?' (2016) 3 *Journal of Law, Society and Development* 85.

simple uniform law for all international and domestic contracts. This is why many domestic legislators modelled their domestic contract law according to the CISG. If one propagates regional harmonization, one adds another layer, thus forcing parties to adapt their contracts to three different situations, domestic, regional, and global. If such a regional instrument is optional, at best parties do not opt into it; if it is binding they will rather opt out and choose a different governing law. Thus the solution, considering the interests of the parties involved, is global rather than any regional unification of contract law.

VIII. Uniform Trade Terms and Trade Practices

Numerous institutions are actively involved in drafting international contracts and standardizing trade terms and practices. Their efforts aim to promote legal certainty, reduce transaction costs, and facilitate cross-border commerce. These bodies include intergovernmental organizations, private associations, and industry-specific standard setters.

The International Chamber of Commerce (ICC) plays a very important role in this task. The ICC was founded in 1919 to promote international trade. One of its first projects was the development of general trade terms. In 1936, the first version of Incoterms® was published. Since then the terms have been regularly updated to keep pace with international trade.[56] The latest version, Incoterms® 2020, came into force in January 2020. In the field of letters of credit, the ICC developed the Uniform Customs and Practice for Documentary Credit (UCP) which also were continuously updated over the decades. Since 2007, the UCP 600 have been in force.[57] Furthermore, the ICC offers different model contracts as well as contract clauses that parties can use as a blueprint for their respective contracts.

Several trade associations provide model contracts specifically tailored to the needs of the members of the trade. Among them are the International Federation of Consulting Engineers (commonly known as FIDIC, acronym for its French name *Fédération Internationale Des Ingénieurs-Conseils*), which addresses all kinds of construction contracts worldwide. Also noteworthy are the Grain and Feed Trade Association (GAFTA), as well as the Federation of Oils, Seeds and Fats Associations (FOSFA). It is said that more than 80 per cent of contracts involving these commodities are based on the contract templates of these associations.

---

[56] See the process of updates throughout time in 'Incoterms® Rules History' (ICC—International Chamber of Commerce) <https://iccwbo.org/business-solutions/incoterms-rules/incoterms-rules-history/> accessed 25 November 2025.

[57] *ICC Uniform Customs and Practice for Documentary Credits: 2007 Revision (UCP 600)* (International Chamber of Commerce 2007).

IX. *Lex Mercatoria*

The *lex mercatoria* is a body of law that originally developed in medieval times completely independently of sovereign control. It was based on pragmatism and the universal realities of trade. The understanding of *lex mercatoria* has considerably evolved over time. In its modern incarnation, it is said to be found in uniform projects, such as the PICC.[58]

Today, the discussion focuses on the question of whether the parties may choose *lex mercatoria* as the law applicable to their contract.[59]

---

[58] Vogenauer (n 19) preamble, 64–7.

[59] Horia Ciurtin, 'A Quest for Deterritorialisation: The "New" Lex Mercatoria in International Arbitration' (2019) 85 *Arbitration: The International Journal of Arbitration, Mediation and Dispute Management* 123; Michael Mustill, 'The New Lex Mercatoria: The First Twenty-Five Years' (2017) XIV *Revista Brasileira de Arbitragem* 205; Anthony Connerty, 'Lex Mercatoria: Reflections from an English Lawyer' (2014) 30 *Arbitration International* 701.

3

Scope of Application of the CISG, the PICC, and Other International Instruments

I. Legal Nature of the Different Instruments

The CISG is a convention. A convention is designed to unify law by establishing a binding international instrument. Once a State has joined the convention by ratification or accession under public international law it becomes binding on the courts of that Member State. If the prerequisites for the application of the CISG are given, courts must apply the Convention and may not resort to their domestic law. Therefore, a Convention is often called 'hard law'.

In contrast, the PICC are not a convention; they are mere principles not binding on State courts. Instead, they only apply if the parties to an international contract have chosen them as the governing law. They are therefore called 'soft law'. It is disputed whether the parties can choose soft law as the governing law when litigating in a State court. For example, the EU Rome I Regulation on the Law Applicable to

Contractual Obligations[1] does not allow the parties to select sets of rules that are not State laws. It is possible, however, that parties incorporate transnational instruments of soft law into their contract, the soft law thus being given the status of a contract term. The difference is that mandatory rules of the otherwise applicable State law are not affected. In arbitration, however, things are different. Most arbitration laws and institutional rules allow the parties to choose not only State law but also 'rules of law', a category which encompasses soft law.[2]

II. International Contracts

Both the CISG and the PICC only relate to international contracts, excluding purely domestic transactions.

Article 1(1) CISG defines in a clear-cut manner when a contract is 'international', namely if the parties have their respective places of business in different States.[3] The term 'place of business' is to be interpreted autonomously. In line with case law and scholarly writing, a place of business exists if a party uses it openly to participate in trade and if it displays a certain degree of duration, stability, and independence.[4] If a party has more than one place of business, the relevant place of business is that which has the closest relationship to the contract and its performance (Article 10 CISG).[5] The fact that a party has its place of business in a foreign country must have been apparent at the time of the conclusion of the contract,

---

[1] Council Regulation (EC) 593/2008 of the European Parliament and of the Council of 17 June 2008 on the law applicable to contractual obligations (Rome I) [2008] OJ L 177/6, art 3.

[2] See e.g. UNCITRAL Model Law on International Commercial Arbitration 1985 and 2006 (MAL 2006) art 28(1); Swiss Private International Law Act 1987 art 187(1); ICC Rules of Arbitration 2021 (ICC Rules) art 21(1).

[3] *LS v JS* [2020] Viši privredni sud u Banjaluci (High Commercial Court Banja Luka) 57 0 Ps 123777 19 Pž, CISG-online 5724; *R&R Manufacturing SAS v Everestt International Industries Ltd* [2023] Cour d'appel de Besançon (Court of Appeal Besançon) 21/01330, CISG-online 6643; *Garage Door Systems, LLC v Blue Giant Equipment Corp* [2024] US District Court for the Southern District of Indiana 1:23-cv-02223-JMS-KMB, CISG-online 7026.

[4] Pascal Hachem, 'Article 1 CISG: Sphere of Application' in Ingeborg Schwenzer and Ulrich G Schroeter (eds), *Schlechtriem & Schwenzer Commentary on the UN Convention on the International Sale of Goods (CISG)* (5th edn, Oxford University Press 2022) para 24; Simon Manner and Moritz Schmitt, 'Article 6 (The Contract and the Convention (Primacy of the Contract))' in Christoph Brunner and Benjamin Gottlieb (eds), *Commentary on the UN Sales Law (CISG)* (Wolters Kluwer 2019) para 6; Harry M Flechtner, *Honnold's Uniform Law for International Sales Under the 1980 United Nations Convention* (5th edn, Wolters Kluwer 2021) 39; *Triage Matériel Professionnel S.a.r.l. v JGB-2 Sp z.o.o.* [2023] Cour d'appel de Paris (Court of Appeal Paris) 21/19946, CISG-online 6569: holding that TMP could not prove that JGB-2's liaison office in France constituted a stable and independent place of business.

[5] *Target Corp v JJS Developments Ltd* [2018] US District Court for the District of Minnesota 16-cv-1184 (JNE/TNL), CISG-online 3046; *Artificial fish (violation of intellectual property) case* [2018] Cour d'appel de Paris (Court of Appeal Paris) 16/21302, CISG-online 5622; *Zodiac Seats US LLC v Synergy Aerospace Corp* [2019] US District Court for the Eastern District of Texas 4:17-cv-00410-ALM-KPJ, CISG-online 4234: where the court made a thorough analysis of the closest relationship to the contract and its performance;

otherwise this fact is to be disregarded and the contract is to be treated as a domestic one (Article 1(2) CISG). The respective nationality or legal domicile of the parties is irrelevant[6] (Article 1(3) CISG), as well as the place of performance of the contract when the parties are from two Contracting States.[7]

In contrast to the CISG, the PICC do not clearly define what is meant by an international contract. Instead, they intend to give the concept of 'internationality' the broadest possible interpretation, excluding situations where all relevant elements are connected with only one country. This illustrates a fundamental difference between the CISG and the PICC; the PICC are generally more open to interpretation than the CISG.[8]

III. B2B versus B2C

Again both the CISG as well as the PICC only envisage commercial contracts, business to business (B2B) transactions, whereas business to consumer (B2C) transactions are excluded.

The CISG autonomously defines what is to be considered a consumer sale. Domestic distinctions, especially those relating to the civil or commercial character of the parties that can be found in many civil law jurisdictions, are discarded (Article 1(3) CISG).[9] In its Article 2(a), the CISG draws a clear line between B2B and B2C transactions. A consumer sale is one where the goods are bought for personal, family, or household purposes. However, the seller must have known or could not have been unaware of the fact that the buyer was acting as a consumer at the time of the conclusion of the contract. Thus, in a case where the Finnish buyer was buying a used car via the Internet, the court held that the intention of private use was not discernible for the seller.[10]

The exclusion of B2C contracts under the PICC is simply expressed in their Preamble setting forth rules for international 'commercial' contracts. A definition of a B2C transaction, as in the CISG, is missing in the PICC.

---

[6] *Transportes Peñón Blanco SAPI de CV et al. v Volvo Group North America, LLC et al.* [2024] US District Court for the Middle District of North Carolina 1:23CV176, CISG-online 6909: holding that the fact that a business is incorporated in a particular country does not mean that its place of business is necessarily in that country for the purposes of a contract under the CISG.

[7] *INTRAVAL SL v ECOM Industries GmbH* [2020] Tribunal Supremo (Spanish Supreme Court) 3133/2017/398/2020, CISG-online 5370: where the Spanish Supreme Court found that the fact that the contract was intended to be performed in the United Kingdom was irrelevant for determining the application of the CISG.

[8] Eckart Brödermann, *UNIDROIT Principles of International Commercial Contracts: An Article-by-Article Commentary* (2nd edn, Kluwer Law International BV 2023) 75, 76, art 1.6.

[9] *Used Car Case III* [2017] Oberlandesgericht Köln (Court of Appeal Cologne) 19 U 101/16, CISG-online 2946.

[10] *Used Car Case II* [2009] Oberlandesgericht Hamm (Court of Appeal Hamm) 28 U 107/08, CISG-online 1978.

The reasons for excluding B2C transactions in international instruments are manifold. In various legal systems consumer protection nowadays is achieved by special rules. The level of consumer protection thereby differs significantly between the countries.[11] The international instruments do not want to meddle with these national endeavours.[12] Moreover, consumer protection widely has to rely on mandatory rules whereas the international contract instruments are characterized by the principle of freedom of contract. Ultimately, it is questionable whether efficient consumer protection—especially at the international level—should rely on substantive contract law and not rather on procedural mechanisms such as class actions and/or online dispute resolution. At any rate, the time for harmonizing or even unifying rules on consumer protection at the international level is not ripe.

IV. Sphere of Application of the CISG

1. Parties having their places of business in two contracting states

According to Article 1(1)(a) CISG, the CISG applies if the parties have their places of business in different States and both States are Contracting States, that is, if at the time of the conclusion of the contract, the CISG was in force in both States. This kind of application of the CISG is called direct application because no recourse to any rules of private international law is necessary. With more and more States acceding to the CISG, application via Article 1(1)(a) CISG becomes more and more regular.

Which State is a Contracting State can easily be found out by consulting the UNCITRAL website.[13] Doubts, however, can exist in cases of succession of states.[14] Thus, to this very day, it remains disputed whether Macao, as a special administrative region of China, is a Contracting State. Macao was restored to China—after having been part of non-contracting states—in 1997 at the time when China was already a Contracting State to the CISG. China did not make a reservation according to Article 93 CISG by which it could have exempted the special administrative regions from the applicability of the CISG. Nevertheless, neither was the

---

[11] Ingeborg Schwenzer and Edgardo Muñoz, *Global Sales and Contract Law* (2nd edn, Oxford University Press 2022) para 6.18.

[12] *Dodge Grand Caravan case* [2020] Landgericht Landshut (District Court Landshut) 73 O 3793/19, CISG-online 5282: holding that the CISG is not intended to apply to international B2C contracts in order to prevent conflicts with national consumer protection regulations.

[13] CISG, 'Status: United Nations Convention on Contracts for the International Sale of Goods (Vienna, 1980) (CISG) | United Nations Commission on International Trade Law' <https://uncitral.un.org/en/texts/salegoods/conventions/sale_of_goods/cisg/status> accessed 26 November 2025.

[14] Ulrich G Schroeter, 'Article 93 CISG: Multi-Territorial States' in Schwenzer and Schroeter (eds) (n 4) paras 41–45.

CISG explicitly mentioned to be applicable to these regions—unlike other international instruments. Most recently, however, some courts have found that if a Contracting State makes no declaration under Article 93(1) CISG, the Convention is to extend to all territorial units of that State.[15] In any event, lingering doubts regarding the status of Hong Kong—a territory returned to China after the latter had already become a Contracting State to the CISG—were resolved when China filed a declaration on 5 May 2022 extending the territorial application of the CISG to Hong Kong. As of 1 December 2022, the CISG also applies to Hong Kong as part of a Contracting State.[16]

2. Conflict of laws rules lead to the law of a contracting state

If the two parties do not have their places of business in Contracting States, the CISG is still applicable if the rules of private international law lead to the application of the law of a Contracting State (Article 1(1)(b) CISG).[17] This is the so-called indirect application of the CISG as at first, the rules of private international law of the forum must be consulted. Article 1(1)(b) CISG is only applicable where the forum is in a Contracting State because courts of non-Contracting States or arbitral tribunals are under no international public law duty to apply Article 1(1)(b) CISG. They may still apply the CISG if the rules of their private international law or the applicable arbitration law and institutional arbitration rules provide.

Article 1(1)(b) CISG was heavily criticized at the Vienna Conference for extending the application of the CISG considerably. These concerns led to the introduction of Article 95 CISG, allowing a reservation permitting a State to declare that it will not be bound by Article 1(1)(b) CISG.[18] The most prominent States making use of this reservation are China and the United States.

It has been debated whether a court in a Contracting State that has not made a declaration according to Article 95 CISG has to apply the CISG if its rules of private international law lead to the application of the law of a reservation State. For example, a German court is called upon to decide a case between a US-based seller (Contracting State with Article 95 reservation) and an Indian-based buyer (non-Contracting State) whereby the German rules of private international law lead to

---

[15] *Pulse Electronics, Inc v UD Electronic Corp* [2021] US District Court for the Southern District of California 18-cv-00373-BEN-MSB, CISG-online 5547; Schroeter, 'Article 93 CISG: Multi-Territorial States' in Schwenzer and Schroeter (eds) (n 4) para 54.

[16] CISG-online.org, 'CISG by Jurisdiction Hong Kong SAR (China)' <https://cisg-online.org/CISG-by-jurisdiction?command=detail&detail=100> accessed 26 November 2025.

[17] *Stolen wheel loader case* [2023] Obergericht des Kantons Zug (Court of Appeal Canton Zug) Z1 2022 6, CISG-online 6313; *Punching line case* [2023] Bezirksgericht Willisau (Court of First Instance Willisau) 1A4 18 9, CISG-online 7179.

[18] *AM PNEU s.r.o. v N[.]* [2019] Okresný súd Malacky (District Court Malacky) 10Cb/161/2017, CISG-online 6144.

the application of US law (assuming the CISG is an integral part of United States law for international sales). Although such a scenario will not happen very often, in such a case one should apply the CISG.[19]

3. Choice of the CISG by the parties

Whether the parties can choose the CISG as the governing law for their contract is not dealt with by the CISG but by the rules of private international law of the forum or arbitral seat.

In most legal systems, under the principle of freedom of contract, the parties may use the CISG as contract terms. This is called a substantive choice of law. The otherwise applicable law determines whether such derogation from its rules is possible and/or whether mandatory provisions of this law prevail.

Whether the CISG may be chosen just as a national law to the exclusion of an otherwise applicable national law is a different question. In such a case, the same rules apply as if the parties want to choose so-called soft law. Most jurisdictions do not allow such a choice.

4. Contract of sale

The CISG applies to contracts of sale, which are traditionally defined as an exchange of goods against money.

Whether barter contracts—exchange of goods against goods—are covered by the CISG is disputed. Several authors answer this question in the negative.[20] However, this approach seems to be very formalistic. The suitability of the CISG to these contracts is uncontested. In domestic legal settings, barter contracts are regularly put on the same footing as contracts for sale. Therefore, the CISG should also apply to international barter contracts.[21] Both parties are to be treated as sellers in regard to the goods they deliver and as buyers in regard to the goods they receive.

Sales contracts with special financing agreements, such as hire-purchase agreements, may also be covered by the CISG, at least where the economic result is the buyer's final acquisition of the goods or where the value of the goods is completely

---

[19] Hachem, 'Article 1 CISG: Sphere of Application' in Schwenzer and Schroeter (eds) (n 4) para 38; *Bruno Rimini (Furniture) Ltd v Connor Marketing, Inc* [2015] US District Court for the Eastern District of California 1:14-01906 WBS SAB, CISG-online 2662: holding that the CISG was erroneously not applied.

[20] Christoph Brunner, Fabian Meier, and Marco Stacher, 'Article 2 (Exclusions from the Convention)' in Brunner and Benjamin (eds), (n 4) para 9.

[21] Hachem, 'Article 1 CISG: Sphere of Application' in Schwenzer and Schroeter (eds) (n 4) para 12.

exhausted at the end of the contract.[22] On the other hand, operating and financial leasing contracts will typically be excluded from the CISG.

Today, it is generally held that framework contracts, such as distributorship agreements, as such are not covered by the CISG although the individual supply orders may well be.[23] Increasingly, some also advocate that if the sales obligations in the distribution agreement form the preponderant part of the contract, not only the individual supply orders should be subject to the CISG but also the entire distributorship agreement.[24] Thus, coherent results can be achieved with regard to the individual supply orders and the overarching agreement, for example, in cases where an individual supply contract is affected by hardship, and the question must be answered how this in turn affects the framework agreement.

5. Contracts for goods to be manufactured and mixed contracts

a.) Contracts for goods to be manufactured

In many legal systems, there is a clear distinction between contracts for sale and contracts for work and labour. Under the CISG, Article 3(1) CISG deals with contracts for goods to be manufactured. Basically, a contract for goods to be manufactured is a contract of sale. It does not matter whether the goods to be manufactured are generic goods or specific customized goods. The only exception applies if the buyer itself undertakes to supply a substantial part of the materials necessary for the manufacture or production of the goods (Article 3(1) CISG). Mere processing of the client's goods, such as dyeing or tailoring of clothing from the client's materials, converting crude oil into gasoline, or repairing, restoring, overhauling etc., are not covered by the CISG.

b.) Mixed contracts

In many areas of international trade, 'pure' sales contracts today are an exception rather than the rule. Take for example the sale of wind turbines. Usually, the seller

---

[22] Ibid para 14; Brunner, Meier, and Stacher, 'Article 2 (Exclusions from the Convention)' in Brunner and Gottlieb (eds) (n 4) para 9.

[23] See e.g. Stephan W Schill (ed), *'Distributor (Xanadu) v Supplier (Utopia) (Final Award)* [2022] SCC No. 2023-5' 1 ICCA Awards Series 1, 4–5: the arbitral tribunal rejected the application of the CISG in the Supply Agreement on the grounds that the distributorship agreement did not cover the sale of specific goods and did not contain definite terms regarding quantity and price; *Cast v Festilight* Cour d'appel de Reims (Court of Appeal Reims) 11/01950, CISG-online 2479: holding that distributorship agreements are not governed by the CISG but individual supply orders are; *Reecon North America, LLC v Du-Hope Int'l Group et al.* [2019] US District Court for the Western District of Pennsylvania 2:18-CV-00234-JFC, 2:18-CV-00631-JFC, CISG-online 4425.

[24] See analysis proposed by Pilar Perales Viscasillas, 'Extending the Scope of the 1980 Vienna Convention on the International Sale of Goods to Framework Distribution Contracts' in Ingeborg Schwenzer (ed), *35 Years CISG and Beyond*, Vol 19 (Eleven International Publishing 2016) 131, s 7.3.3; Hachem, 'Article 1 CISG: Sphere of Application' in Schwenzer and Schroeter (eds) (n 4) para 15.

will not only be responsible for designing, manufacturing, and supplying the turbines but it also will undertake to erect, install, and complete them. The seller may additionally be obliged to train the buyer's personnel and provide particular operation and maintenance services even after the completion of the project. Most domestic legal systems struggle to find suitable solutions for such a situation. They may apply different sets of rules depending on which obligation is breached. On the international level, such an approach would lead to undesirable friction between uniform and domestic law. The CISG has found a simple and pragmatic answer in Article 3(2) CISG dealing with these so-called mixed contracts.[25]

If both obligations—the delivery as well as the services obligation—are contained in one single contract, then it is again decisive which of the obligations constitutes the preponderant part. If the service obligations are the preponderant part, the whole contract is outside the CISG.[26]

c.) Preponderant part

What is the preponderant part of the obligation must first and foremost be decided by having regard to the contract itself. Thus, in many contracts, the parties themselves stipulate, expressly or tacitly, that a certain percentage of the price relates to the delivery obligation and a certain percentage to the services obligation. A contract might provide for a payment schedule that shows that a certain percentage is due up to delivery and the rest upon having rendered the services.

In assessing the 'preponderant part of the obligations of the party who furnishes the goods', some case law compares the economic value of the goods and services separately.[27] This comparison is often based on the hypothetical prices each component would command under distinct contracts. Such an approach helps determine whether the contract primarily concerns the sale of goods or the provision of services. However, this approach may oversimplify the assessment in economic terms as one could consider that if the service part of the contract represents more than 50 per cent its value, the latter is the preponderant part.

---

[25] CISG Advisory Council, 'CISG-AC Opinion No 4, Contracts for the Sale of Goods to Be Manufactured or Produced and Mixed Contracts (Article 3 CISG), 24 October 2004, Rapporteur: Professor Pilar Perales Viscasillas, Universidad Carlos III de Madrid [2004]' (2004) Black Letter Rule 7.

[26] Ibid para 3.1 ff; Pascal Hachem, 'Article 7 CISG: Interpretation of the Convention and Gap-Filling' in Schwenzer and Schroeter (eds) (n 4) para 18.

[27] See [...] v Tarkett Sports BV [2024] Rechtbank Oost-Brabant (District Court Oost-Brabant) C/01/388535/HA ZA 22-678, CISG-online 7150: the court decided that the CISG was not applicable due to the fact that the services portion of the contract represented two-thirds of the value; Punching line case [2023] Bezirksgericht Willisau (Court of First Instance Willisau) 1A4 18 9, CISG-online 7179; Park Plus Inc v Sotefin SA [2023] Swiss Arbitration Centre 500146-2022 (Final Award), CISG-online 7020; RGB LED neon signs case [2020] Visoki trgovački sud Republike Hrvatske (High Commercial Court of the Republic of Croatia) 57 Pž-59/2019-2, CISG-online 7296; Prada S.pA v Caporicci USA Corp [2019] Camera Arbitrale Milano (CAM) (Milan Chamber of Arbitration) ARB/17/00120 (Final Award), CISG-online 5573.

As a rule of thumb, the applicability or non-applicability of the CISG to services must 'significantly' exceed 50 per cent of the contract value.[28] In any case, there must be an overall assessment of the value of the entire contract at the time of its conclusion, including the combined price for goods and services and any other price components, not to the price of the goods only.

However, the economic value approach should (only) be the starting point. No fixed percentage should be considered as a strict rule. The intention and interest of the parties must prevail in the assessment.[29] The parties could have afforded greater importance to the delivery of the goods early in the negotiations and the service obligations could have only come as a convenient addition after some considerations. Moreover, the value test can be misleading: if a car is repainted in gold, this does not become a sale because the paint to be supplied by the painter is more expensive than the paint job. A hard and fast rule based only on a comparison of values, therefore, is not desirable.

Turnkey contracts—such as a contract for the installation of a hydro power plant where the seller designs, manufactures, and delivers the plant, and undertakes to install it, test it, and to supervise its operation—must also be judged by applying Article 3(2) CISG. If the services part of the contract does not prevail then the whole contract is governed by the CISG.

Article 3(2) CISG thus is a powerful provision that facilitates dealing with mixed contracts. An open question, however, is whether the provisions of the CISG must be adapted if the services part of the obligation has been breached. With regard to services, one distinguishes between obligations of result and obligations of means. Whereas the CISG can directly be applied to the former, some adaptation—for example with regard to Article 79 CISG—may be necessary.

V. Sphere of Application of the PICC

Although the PICC were enacted to govern international contracts, nothing prevents their application to domestic transactions, so long as the freedom of contract in the default governing system endorses such choice by the parties. The PICC apply to both one-time contracts as well as to long-term contracts thanks to the new rules added to the 2016 edition.[30]

---

[28] CISG-AC Opinion No 4 (n 25) para 2.7; Hachem, 'Article 7 CISG: Interpretation of the Convention and Gap-Filling' in Schwenzer and Schroeter (eds) (n 4) para 20.

[29] CISG-AC Opinion No 4 (n 25) para 3.4; Hachem, 'Article 1 CISG: Sphere of Application' in Schwenzer and Schroeter (eds) (n 4) para 19; *Potato chips plant case* [2017] Bundesgerichtshof (German Supreme Court) VII ZR 101/14, CISG-online 2961.

[30] Brödermann (n 8) para 11.

1. Application by the parties' express choice

As stated above in section I, PICC are an instrument of soft law. They are not part of any national legal system and they do not have the binding character of an international treaty or convention. Their application results, primarily, from the parties' agreement to have their contract governed by their rules and principles. UNIDROIT proposes four categories of Model Clauses for parties wishing that their agreement be governed by the PICC.[31] Under the first category, the parties may choose the PICC as the rule of law governing the contract. This opting in at the level of conflict of laws is possible under different arbitration rules and the arbitration law, where the parties may choose the 'rules of law', not only a 'law' of a given country to govern their contract.[32] The second category of model clauses proposes the incorporation of the PICC as terms of the contract. Such opting in of the PICC at the level of the substantive law does not present any problem as the parties in this case incorporate by reference the whole PICC rules into their contract instead of inserting every single provision into its text. The mandatory provisions of the otherwise applicable domestic law remain applicable to the contract and might impose limits on the choice of specific provisions in the PICC. The third category refers to the PICC to interpret and supplement the CISG when the latter applies by operation of its own scope of application rules or where it is opted in by the parties. Considering that the CISG has its own rules of interpretation and supplementation of internal gaps, the PICC's application, in that case, should be limited to filling in the external gaps pursuant to Articles 4 and 7(2) CISG. Finally, the fourth category refers to the PICC to interpret and supplement the applicable domestic law, including any international uniform law instrument incorporated into that law. The aim of this type of clause is to ensure the interpretation and supplementation of the applicable domestic law in accordance with the internationally accepted principles and rules set forth in the PICC.

2. Application by the parties' implicit choice

The PICC Preamble states that they may be applied when the parties have agreed that their contract be governed by general principles of law, the *lex mercatoria* or the like. In this case, the PICC will apply by reference to the concept associated with the PICC, that is, by virtue of an implicit choice. The concepts of *lex mercatoria* or 'the like' are not defined within the PICC. Comment 4(b) to the Preamble states that parties 'sometimes provide that [the contract] shall be governed by the

---

[31] UNIDROIT, 'UPICC Model Clauses—UNIDROIT' (19 June 2021) <https://www.unidroit.org/instruments/commercial-contracts/upicc-model-clauses/> accessed 27 November 2025.
[32] See e.g. MAL, art 28; ICC Rules of Arbitration art 21.

'general principles of law', by the 'usages and customs of international trade', by the '*lex mercatoria*, etc'.[33] The reference to 'usages' in the Official Comments for the Preamble could suggest that such a term fits within the definition of something 'similar to *lex mercatoria*'. The Official Comments criticize the vagueness of such concepts; it advises that explicit reference be made to the PICC.[34] However, the Official Comments appear to conclude that despite the uncertainty carried out by the vague reference to *lex mercatoria* or 'international usages', such might be enough to trigger the PICC's application by virtue of the Preamble.[35]

It is doubtful whether the PICC might be considered *lex mercatoria*, 'a somewhat vague and very contentious concept'.[36] The concept of *lex mercatoria* describes a body of non-national and transnational rules created within the realm of businesses, whereas the PICC are drawn largely on state and international law and only to a limited extent on business practices.[37] Ultimately, whether the PICC can or cannot be viewed as an accurate codification of *lex mercatoria* must be determined in each rule.[38]

The concept of *lex mercatoria* has also been associated to the notion of 'general principles of law',[39] which is different to usages of trade.[40] *Lex mercatoria* and 'the like' are extensive and imprecise open-ended terms. This has led some arbitral tribunals to maintain that the PICC are a reflection of international usages pursuant to Article 9(2) CISG and thus to fill in some gaps in the contract according to the PICC provisions.[41] Others have also decided to apply the PICC as usages of trade under MAL 2006, Article 28(4) or International Chamber of Commerce Arbitration Rules (ICC Rules) Article 13(5) in order to integrate the contract over any domestic law.[42] However, the PICC can

---

[33] International Institute for the Unification of Private Law (ed), *UNIDROIT Principles of International Commercial Contracts* (UNIDROIT International Institute for the Unification of Private Law 2017) 3–4, Preamble, off cmt 4(b).

[34] Ibid 4.

[35] Ibid.

[36] Ralf Michaels, 'Preamble I: Purposes, Legal Nature, and Scope of the PICC; Applicability by Courts; Use of the PICC for the Purpose of Interpretation and Supplementation and as a Model' in Stefan Vogenauer (ed), *Commentary on the UNIDROIT Principles of International Commercial Contracts (PICC)* (2nd edn, Oxford University Press 2015) para 79.

[37] Ibid.

[38] Ibid.

[39] Matthias Scherer, 'Preamble II: The Use of the PICC in Arbitration' in Vogenauer (ed), (n 36) para 18.

[40] Ibid para 21.

[41] See also Djakhongir Saidov, 'Cases on CISG Decided in the Russian Federation' (2003) 7(1) *Vindobona Journal of International Commercial Law and Arbitration* 59–60.

[42] *NoriDane Foods A/S v Anexo Comercial Ltda* [2017] Tribunal de Justiça do Estado do Rio Grande do Sul (Court of Appeal of the State of Rio Grande do Sul) 70072362940, CISG-online 2818; Arbitral Award, 10 December 1997, Ad-Hoc Arbitration, seat Buenos Aires, abstract available at <http://www.unilex.info/principles/case/646> accessed 22 April 2025; Arbitral Award, November 1996, ICC International Court of Arbitration, seat Paris, Case No. 8502, published in the ICC International Court of Arbitration Bulletin, Vol. 10, No. 2, Fall 1999, 7, abstract available at <http://www.unilex.info/princip les/case/655> accessed 22 April 2025.

hardly be considered, *in toto*, as an expression of a sort of consolidated set of usages.[43]

3. In the absence of any choice by the parties

The PICC Preamble states that the PICC may be applied when the parties have not chosen any law to govern their contract. This is possible pursuant to some conflict of laws provisions in arbitration rules that allow arbitrators, in the absence of any choice by the parties, to apply 'the rules of law which they determine to be appropriate'.[44] Arbitrators will normally apply a particular domestic law as the proper law of the contract, yet exceptionally they may resort to non-national or supranational rules such as the PICC.[45]

4. As an instrument to interpret and supplement national and international laws

Paragraphs four and five of the PICC's Preamble state that the PICC may be used to interpret or supplement international uniform law instruments or domestic laws. The PICC's application under this ground will depend on whether the same is possible pursuant to the underlying applicable law. As discussed in more detail in Chapter 5.V.5, the CISG and many national and international laws[46] have their own rules of interpretation and supplementation of both the contract and the statutory rules. Article 7 CISG requires an autonomous interpretation and to fill in

---

[43] 'ICC Award Case No. 9029 in ICC International Court of Arbitration Bulletin, Vol. 10, No. 2, Fall 1999, 88–96: in this case, the arbitral tribunal rejected the application of the PICC because 'although the UNIDROIT Principles constitute a set of rules theoretically appropriate to prefigure the future lex mercatoria should they be brought into line with international commercial practice, at present there is no necessary connection between the individual [provisions of the] Principles and the rules of the lex mercatoria, so that recourse to the Principles is not purely and simply the same as recourse to an actually existing international commercial usage'. At the end it did make reference to two articles of the PICC, showing how some of the individual provisions can be applied if the case has a resemblance, but the PICC as a whole does not necessarily reflect trade usages in all regions. .

[44] ICC Rules of Arbitration art 21; International Institute for the Unification of Private Law (n 33) 4, off cmt 4(c).

[45] Ibid.

[46] The appropriateness of self-contained rules of interpretation and gap-filling for uniform law like CISG art 7 has been recognized by the adoption of the same wording, or at least very similar provisions, in subsequent conventions, model laws, and uniform projects. For example MAL, art 2A(2); Convention on the Use of Electronic Communications in International Contracts 2005, art 5(2); UNCITRAL Model Law on Commercial Conciliation 2002, art 2(2); UNCITRAL Model Law on Electronic Signatures 2001, art 4(2); UN Convention on the Assignment of Receivables in International Trade 2001, art 7(2); UNIDROIT Convention on International Interests in Mobile Equipment 2001, art 5(2); UNIDROIT Convention on International Financial Leasing (Ottawa) 1988, art 6(2); UNIDROIT Convention on International Factoring (Ottawa) 1988, art 4(2); UNIDROIT Convention on Agency in the International Sale of Goods (Geneva) 1983, art 6(2). Cf also PICC 2004, art 1.6(2).

the CISG internal gaps in accordance with its principles. Thus, all solutions developed must be based on the Convention itself and resorting to the PICC may violate the autonomy of the Convention.[47] The PICC were drafted and published in 1994, after the CISG's entry into force.[48] Provisions in the PICC were largely based on the CISG and, hence, they may express some of the CISG principles in more detail. However, the PICC include provisions on matters that were expressly or implicitly excluded from the Convention, like fraud and duress, and that, in some instances, depart from the express provisions of the CISG, for example hardship remedies under Article 79 CISG.

VI. Sphere of Application of Other International Instruments

UNCITRAL uses several instruments to aim at harmonization and unification; for instance, conventions, model laws, rules, and guidelines. A model law is a legislative text that is recommended to States for enactment as part of their national law. The States are free to change the text of the model law, thus retaining much more flexibility than with a convention.

The ICC has also undertaken significant private unification efforts in this area in the form of soft law or *lex mercatoria* instruments. These instruments require the parties to agree to them in order for their contract to be governed by them.

Below we present a few examples of instruments that form part of the rules for international commercial contracts and a brief description of their scope of application.

1. International bank guarantees

Independent guarantees have been a creation of the practice of international trade.[49] Most national systems have not enacted law dealing with independent guarantees expressly.[50] The validity and binding effect of an independent guarantee therefore directly rests on the general principle of freedom of contract and sanctity of contracts. Their terms are negotiated between the guarantor—usually a bank—and its customer (the principal) pursuant to what was agreed in the underlying contract by the seller/buyer or owner/contractor, and are interpreted and construed by courts and arbitrators in accordance with the provisions of the

---

[47] Schwenzer and Muñoz (n 11) para 3.54.
[48] Ibid para 3.55.
[49] Filip De Ly, 'The UN Convention on Independent Guaranteed and Stand-by Letters of Credit' 33 *The International Lawyer* 833.
[50] With two notable exceptions: French Civil Code, art 2321, and United States of America (USA) Uniform Commercial Code (UCC) art 5 with provisions on Stand-By Letters of Credit.

applicable rules, if any, or of the proper law of the guarantee, usually domestic laws on agency.[51]

In light of the absence of specific regulation at a national level, some international treaties purporting to harmonize international practice have seen the day, for instance, the UN Convention on Independent Guarantees and Stand-By Letters of Credit (1995) (the 'UN Convention on Independent Guarantees').[52] In addition, uniform contract terms to which the parties may agree[53] have also flourished and enhanced the use and utility of independent guarantees. The ICC has issued four major texts on independent guarantees: the ICC Uniform Rules for Contract Guarantees (URCG) (1978),[54] the ICC Uniform Rules for Demand Guarantees (URDG 458) (1992), the ICC Uniform Rules for Contract Bonds (URCB) (1994) and the ICC Uniform Rules for Demand Guarantees (URDG 758) (2010). Finally, the American Institute of International Banking Law & Practice has issued the International Standby Practices (ISP98).[55]

2. Documentary credits

Letters of credit are a creation of international trade practice, which works as the primary legal source. The private codification and standardization of documentary credits have so far been based on uniform soft law rules. Their application thus requires an agreement of the parties to that respect. The parties may agree upon the buyer's obligation to have a bank open a letter of credit for the seller's benefit. In such a case, the contract of sale may determine the terms and characteristics of the letter of credit that the buyer is expected to open.[56]

The most important source in this area is the Uniform Customs and Practice for Documentary Credits published by the ICC, the latest version of which was published by the ICC in 2007 (UCP 600).[57] The UCP 600 are generally accepted and

---

[51] In spite of the fact that practice is not entirely uniform considering the multiple fora which are available and the various systems of law which may apply in each forum, this state of affairs does not appear to have given rise to major difficulties.

[52] The UN Convention on Independent Guarantees and Stand-By Letters of Credit (1995) has been ratified by eight States to date (Belarus, Ecuador, El Salvador, Gabon, Kuwait, Liberia, Panama, and Tunisia) and signed, but not ratified, by the United States). The UN Convention contains interesting and useful provisions in spite of the fact that it has not gained widespread acceptance yet.

[53] ICC Uniform Rules for Demand Guarantees 2010 (URDG 758) art 1(a) states that the rules 'apply to any demand guarantee or counter-guarantee that expressly indicates it is subject to them'. And where a guarantee issued on or after 1 July 2010 states that it is subject to the URDG without stating whether the 458 1992 version or the 758 2010 version is to apply, the guarantee will be subject to the 758 2010 version (see URDG 758, art 1(d)).

[54] Christopher R. Seppala, 'The ICC Uniform Rules for Demand Guarantees ("URDG") in Practice: A Decade of Experience' *A Contractor's View of the URDG* (2001).

[55] Also published as ICC Publication No. 590.

[56] Michael G Bridge, *The International Sale of Goods* (4th edn, Oxford University Press 2017) para 6.30 ff; Jan Ramberg (ed), *International Commercial Transactions* (4th edn, ICC 2011) 47.

[57] Federico Santacruz and Jorge Oria, 'Documentary Credits' (2008) 27 *International Financial Law Review* 64.

widely used.[58] The first edition of the UCP goes back to 1933.[59] Certain commentators point out that the application of the UCP 600 is almost universal.[60] The UCP 600 play an important part in governing documentary credits since domestic law is not uniform in the various jurisdictions and, as is often the case, the same question of law may have a different answer, depending on the jurisdiction one has to consider.[61] In Chapter 10, we deal with documentary credits, as a mode of payment, in more detail.

3. International commercial terms

The Parties' reference to an ICC Incoterms 2020 in their sales contract will define, by reference to the three-letter acronym, obligations such as place of delivery; risk of or damage to the goods; cost and arrangement of transport and customs clearance; any required insurance, inspection, and packing obligations, etc.; thereby reducing the potential of uncertainty and legal disputes.[62] The ICC Incoterms 2020 are expressed in 11 groups and divided into two categories. First, the Incoterms for multimodal transport (Ex Works (EXW), Free Carrier (FCA), Carriage Paid To (CPT), Carriage and Insurance Paid To (CIP), Delivered at Place Unloaded (DPU), Delivered at Place (DAP), Delivered Duty Paid (DDP)) and, second, the ICC Incoterms 2020 for maritime and inland waterway transport (Free On Board (FOB), Free Alongside Ship (FAS), Cost, Insurance and Freight (CIF), Cost and Freight (CFR)). Although initially conceived for the international sale of goods, they might also be used in domestic transactions.

The ICC Incoterms 2020 are not by themselves a sales contract. They are not conceived to reflect trade practice for a particular type of goods or means of payment, despite the fact that some of them, for instance FOB and CIF, have historically been used in documentary credits and in the sale of commodities. The ICC Incoterms 2020 do not deal with matters such as goods' description, quality, or quantity; the time or the method of payment; the remedies that might follow from

---

[58] Florian Mohs, 'Article 53 CISG: General Obligations of the Buyer' in Schwenzer and Schroeter (eds) (n 4) para 31.

[59] Report of the Secretary-General, 'Uniform Customs and Practice for Documentary Credits' (1994) UN Doc A/CN.9/395; Roy Goode, 'Rule, Practice, and Pragmatism in Transnational Commercial Law' (2005) 54 *International and Comparative Law Quarterly* 550.

[60] Jurgen Basedow, 'The State's Private Law and the Economy: Commercial Law as an Amalgam of Public and Private Rule-Making' (2008) 56 *The American Journal of Comparative Law* 709; Ramberg (n 56) 142.

[61] Basedow (n 60) 709; William Patrick Cronican, 'Buyer Beware: Electronic Letters of Credit and the Need for Default Rules' (2013) 45 *McGeorge Law Review* 383, 386. In the United States, letters of credit are regulated in art 5 (5-101 to 5-118) UCC. In Mexico the documentary credits were only recently regulated in 2008 in Mexico Credit Institutions Act (Ley de Instituciones de Crédito) art 71; cf Santacruz and Oria (n 57) 63.

[62] Chambre de commerce internationale (ed), *Incoterms 2020: ICC Rules for the Use of Domestic and International Trade Terms* (International Chamber of Commerce 2019) 2.

a breach of contract; the effects of commercial sanctions or embargoes; the imposition of tariffs; intellectual property rights; title over the goods; or the applicable law or jurisdiction of courts and arbitral tribunals. All these are matters that the parties should make specific provision for in their contract or, in the absence of such provisions, that are dealt with by the applicable law, most commonly the CISG, English law, etc.[63]

The ICC Incoterms® 2020 are explained in more detail in Chapters 8, 10, and 11 of this work relating to the obligations covered by these rules.

4. Electronic communications

The UNCITRAL Model Law on Electronic Commerce of 1996 (MLEC) set forth rules for the use of electronic means in commerce for adoption by national legislation. Its goal is to provide legally for equal treatment to paper-based and electronic information, which is essential for fostering efficiency in international trade. The MLEC provisions are based on the principles of non-discrimination, technological neutrality, and functional equivalence that are widely regarded as the founding elements of modern electronic commerce law.

On the other hand, UN Convention on the Use of Electronic Communications in International Contracts 2005 (Electronic Communications Convention) pursues similar goals and is based on the same principles as the MLEC. The Electronic Communications Convention applies to all electronic communications exchanged between parties whose places of business are in different States when at least one party has its place of business in a Contracting State.[64] It may also apply by virtue of the parties' choice. B2C contracts, as well as certain financial transactions, negotiable instruments, and documents of title, are excluded from the Convention's scope of application.[65] Finally, the Convention allows contractual parties to exclude its application or vary its terms within the limits allowed by otherwise applicable legislative provisions.[66]

5. Limitation period in the international sale of goods

The UN Convention on the Limitation Period in the International Sale of Goods 1974 (LC) establishes uniform rules governing the period of time within which a party under a contract for the international sale of goods must commence legal

---

[63] Ibid 2–3.
[64] UN Convention on Electronic Communications 2005, art 1.
[65] UN Convention on Electronic Communications 2005, art 2.
[66] UN Convention on Electronic Communications 2005, art 3.

proceedings against another party to assert a claim arising from the contract or relating to its breach, termination or validity. It was intended to be a sister convention to the CISG. It has not received, however, as much approval as the CISG. The LC has been ratified by 30 Member States in its original version and by 23 Member States as amended by the Protocol of 11 April 1980.[67]

Similar to the CISG, the LC applies to contracts for the sale of goods between parties whose places of business are in different States if both of those States are Contracting States or when the rules of private international law lead to the application to the contract of sale of goods of the law of a Contracting State. It may also apply by virtue of the parties' opt-in. The LC applies only to international transactions and avoids the recourse to rules of private international law for those contracts falling under its scope of application. International contracts falling outside the scope of application of the LC, as well as contracts subject to a valid choice of other law, would not be affected by the LC. Purely domestic sales contracts are not affected by the LC and are regulated by domestic law.

The relevant limitation provisions in the LC are addressed in Chapter 17.

---

[67] UNCITRAL, 'Status: Convention on the Limitation Period in the International Sale of Goods (New York, 1974)' <https://uncitral.un.org/en/texts/salegoods/conventions/limitation_period_inte rnational_sale_of_goods/status> accessed 27 June 2025.

4

Party Autonomy and Freedom of Contract

Party autonomy and freedom of contract entail that the parties are free to decide to enter into contracts and with whom they might contract.[1] Moreover, and most importantly, these principles entail that the parties are autonomous in shaping the content of their contract—this includes the liberty to formulate a type of contract which is not necessarily described in statute or to mix and match different and already recognized categories of contracts. Finally, it might also mean that the parties enjoy the freedom to choose the underlying law governing their contract and to derogate from its provisions, as far as these are not mandatory.[2]

I. Opting In—Opting Out

1. Opting in

a.) At the level of the substantive law

Opting into an international convention such as the CISG or an instrument of soft law, such as the PICC or the ICC Incoterms 2020, is part of the parties' freedom of contract and does not typically present any problems. The parties' intent to incorporate by reference into their contract the whole or part of the provisions of

---

[1] Ingeborg Schwenzer and Edgardo Muñoz, *Global Sales and Contract Law* (2nd edn, Oxford University Press 2022) para 4.48 ff.

[2] Ibid para 4.01 ff. See also *Niederreiter GmbH v DEVON Medical Inc* [2016] ICC International Court of Arbitration ICC Case 21196/FS, CISG-online 5988.

any of those instruments will be recognized by most substantive laws as part of the freedom of private parties to tailor-make their agreements.

An effective opting in at this level will depend on how clear the parties are in making such incorporation into their contract pursuant to the proper rules of interpretation; Article 8 CISG, Article 4.1 PICC, and other interpretation provisions are thus relevant. For the ICC Incoterms 2020, the drafters suggest the following formula: '[the chosen Incoterms rule] [name port, place or point] Incoterms 2020'.[3] UNIDROIT also proposes some model clauses for the effective incorporation of the UNIDROIT PICC as contractual terms. The proposal includes the wording '[t]he UNIDROIT Principles of International Commercial Contracts (2016) are incorporated in this contract to the extent that they are not inconsistent with the other terms of the contract'.[4] UNCITRAL has not made any express suggestion for the incorporation of the CISG in that sense. However, reference to 'the Vienna Sales Convention is incorporated by reference', 'the 1980 UN Sales Convention provisions apply as terms of the contract', or 'the CISG rules are part of this contract' should be regarded as sufficiently clear. This may, however, not be the case where the parties merely refer to 'international law provisions'.[5]

b.) At the level of the conflict of laws

The possibility of opting into a law or rules of law, which in principle should not be applicable by default, depends on the conflict of laws rules of the competent court or arbitral tribunal.

In arbitration proceedings, the parties are allowed to opt in the application of 'rules of law' to the substance of the dispute under MAL Article 28 and, for example, ICC Arbitration Rules Article 21.[6] It might be argued thus that this type of provision would recognize the application (at the conflict of laws level) of a-national or supranational legal instruments such as the CISG, the PICC, or the like, and not only the law of a State.

The same solution may follow from some conflict of laws rules directed to State courts where the parties' choice of a-national and supranational laws to govern their contracts is recognized. Nevertheless, traditionally, the choice of law applicable to international contracts is limited to a particular domestic law, yet this traditional approach will suffice to make the CISG applicable in some scenarios. For

---

[3] Chambre de commerce internationale (ed), *Incoterms 2020: ICC Rules for the Use of Domestic and International Trade Terms* (International Chamber of Commerce 2019) 3.

[4] See 'UPICC Model Clauses—UNIDROIT' (19 June 2021) <https://www.unidroit.org/instruments/commercial-contracts/upicc-model-clauses/> accessed 24 November 2025.

[5] *German equipment case* [2000] Tribunal of International Commercial Arbitration at the Russian Federation Chamber of Commerce and Industry (MKAC) 356/1999, CISG-online 1077: the Tribunal then applied the Convention on account of art 1(1)(a).

[6] See other rules examples: Singapore International Arbitration Centre Rules 2016, art 31; Permanent Court of Arbitration Rules, art 35; Hong Kong International Arbitration C Administered Arbitration Rules 2024, art 36.

example, where 'Swiss law' is chosen by two parties not located in Contracting States, the CISG applies on account of its Article 1(1)(b) as part of Swiss law.[7] It is then also clear that Swiss law applies to matters not governed by the Convention and that the mandatory provisions of Swiss law apply. Problems, however, do arise where two parties not located in CISG Contracting States, for example, stipulate 'this contract is governed by the 1980 United Nations Convention on Contracts for the International Sale of Goods'. If one assumes that the Convention can be chosen at the level of conflict of laws, this would mean that the CISG applies to the contract but that it remains unclear which law applies to matters not governed by the Convention and the mandatory rules of the law which would have applied by default are also not applicable.

The relevant question may be whether the CISG makes sufficient clear provision for the law applicable to those areas not covered. The answer is positive under the CISG scope of application provisions, in particular Article 4 CISG.[8] The parties are therefore not subjected to an unforeseeable law, in particular, since some modern conflict of laws rules point to the law of the place of the seller.[9]

Eventually, even if a choice of law at the level of conflict of laws is not recognized, the principle of *favor negotii* calls for interpreting the parties' opting into the CISG as a valid choice of law at the level of substantive law.[10] Thus, the general debate about the possibility of choosing the CISG at the level of conflict of laws is not of practical effect regarding the application of the Convention but only with regard to the applicable mandatory domestic rules.[11]

2. Opting out

The exclusion—also called opting out—of the law or rules of law applicable in the area of international commercial transactions is relevant for treaties, like the CISG, that have a direct application under their scope of application rules or other 'conflict of laws' provisions. In the case of soft law instruments, such as the PICC or the Incoterms, which application primarily depends upon the parties' choice, the issue of exclusion is somehow less significant. PICC and ICC Incoterms are legal

---

[7] *Stolen wheel loader case* [2023] Obergericht des Kantons Zug (Court of Appeal Canton Zug) Z1 2022 6, CISG-online 6313; Pascal Hachem, 'Article 1 CISG: Sphere of Application' in Ingeborg Schwenzer and Ulrich G Schroeter (eds), *Schlechtriem & Schwenzer Commentary on the UN Convention on the International Sale of Goods (CISG)* (5th edn, Oxford University Press 2022) para 31.

[8] *CeDe Group AB v KAN Sp z.o.o.* [2020] Högsta domstolen (Swedish Supreme Court) T 6032-16, CISG-online 5500; Ulrich G Schroeter, 'Contract Validity and the CISG' (2017) 22 *Uniform Law Review* 47, 50 ff.

[9] Council Regulation (EC) No 593/2008 of the European Parliament and of the Council of 17 June 2008 on the law applicable to contractual obligations (Rome I) [2008] OJ L 177/6, art 4(1)(a).

[10] Pascal Hachem, 'Article 7 CISG: Interpretation of the Convention and Gap-Filling' in Schwenzer and Schroeter (eds) (n 7) para 37.

[11] Ibid.

frameworks for international trade. Judges or arbitrators may apply them as part of 'international principles', *lex mercatoria*, or trade usages.[12] However, despite their widespread use, parties can choose to exclude them and Article 1.5 PICC clarifies this exclusion possibility. Parties retain the freedom to exclude these soft law instruments from their agreements if they wish.[13]

Article 6 CISG states that the CISG applies subject to the parties' contrary agreement. The agreement to exclude the Convention can relate to the CISG as a whole or only in part.[14]

The exclusion of the CISG will typically take place when Parties opt in favour of the application of the law of a non-Contracting State, including its mandatory provisions.[15] Because Article 6 CISG recognizes the freedom of the parties to choose a system of law for their sales contract, the default application of the CISG and the national law otherwise applicable to questions not governed by the Convention will be pre-empted. The question whether the CISG has been effectively excluded has to be determined pursuant to its own rules of formation (Articles 14–24 CISG) and interpretation (Article 8 CISG).[16] On the other hand, the question whether a different legal system applies should be decided in accordance with the law designated by the conflict of laws rules of the forum judge or arbitrator.[17] This will

---

[12] See e.g. Inter-American Convention on the Law Applicable to International Contracts (1994), art 9: 'If the parties have not selected the applicable law, or if their selection proves ineffective, the contract shall be governed by the law of the State with which it has the closest ties. The Court will take into account all objective and subjective elements of the contract to determine the law of the State with which it has the closest ties. It shall also take into account the *general principles of international commercial law* recognized by international organizations' (emphasis added); *NoriDane Foods A/S v Anexo Comercial Ltda* [2017] (Tribunal de Justiça do Estado do Rio Grande do Sul (Court of Appeal of the State of Rio Grande do Sul)) 70072362940, CISG-online 2818.

[13] Gilles Cuniberti and Stefan Vogenauer, 'Article 1.5' in Stefan Vogenauer (ed), *Commentary on the UNIDROIT Principles of International Commercial Contracts (PICC)* (2nd edn, 2015) para 3.

[14] *Diammonium phosphate case* [2023] Cairo Regional Centre for International Commercial Arbitration (CRCICA) 1527/2021 (Final Award), CISG-online 6272; *Horse case VII* [2024] Rechtbank Noord-Nederland (District Court Northern Netherlands) C/18/231001/KG ZA 24-7, CISG-online 6902: where the choice of law provided for the complete exclusion of the CISG; Hachem, 'Article 7 CISG: Interpretation of the Convention and Gap-Filling' in Schwenzer and Schroeter (eds) (n 7) para 2; Loukas A Mistelis, 'Article 6' in Stefan M Kröll, Loukas A Mistelis, and Pilar Perales Viscasillas (eds), *UN Convention on Contracts for the International Sale of Goods (CISG): A Commentary* (2nd edn, CH Beck 2018) para 11.

[15] *Citroen Type C 5 case* [2006] Oberlandesgericht Linz (Court of Appeal Linz) 6 R 160/05z, CISG-online 1377; *Construction materials case IV* [2004] Tribunal Cantonal du Jura (Court of Appeal Canton Jura) Ap 91/04, CISG-online 965. See *Winches case* [2019] Landgericht Koblenz (District Court Koblenz) 1 O 38/19, CISG-online 4529: holding erroneously that a choice of law in favour of English law (a non-Contracting State of the CISG) does not amount to an exclusion of the Convention under art 6 CISG; Franco Ferrari and Marco Torsello, *International Sales Law—CISG in a Nutshell* (2nd edn, West Academic Publishing 2018) 42.

[16] *Electronic electricity meters case* [2018] Appellationsgericht Basel-Stadt (Court of Appeal Canton Basel-Stadt) ZB.2017.20 (AG.2018.557), CISG-online 3906; *Ground mace case* [2020] Bundesgerichtshof (German Supreme Court) I ZR 245/19, CISG-online 5488; Hachem, 'Article 7 CISG: Interpretation of the Convention and Gap-Filling' in Schwenzer and Schroeter (eds) (n 7) paras 4–6.

[17] Hachem, 'Article 7 CISG: Interpretation of the Convention and Gap-Filling' in Schwenzer and Schroeter (eds) (n 7) para 5.

include questions of interpretation, formation, but also validity of choice of law clauses. Some legal systems, for example Brazil, would not recognize the choice of a foreign law under the judge's 'conflict of laws' provisions.[18]

Exclusion of the CISG may be either express or implied. An express exclusion occurs when the parties clearly state that their contract shall not be governed by the Convention. Common examples include clauses such as 'this contract shall be governed by [X] law to the exclusion of the CISG' or references to a specific domestic statute of a Contracting State, such as 'this contract shall be governed by the Swiss Code of Obligations'. These formulations constitute typical instances of an express exclusion of the CISG.[19] An implied exclusion can be inferred from a choice of law clause designating the law of a non-Contracting State, for example India.[20] On the other hand, clauses designating the law of a Contracting State in broad terms, for instance 'this contract is governed by French law', might not sufficiently indicate the parties' intention to impliedly exclude the CISG, as the Convention is part of that law. State courts and arbitral tribunals have upheld the application of the CISG where the parties have chosen the law of a Contracting State without further specifications.[21]

These principles also apply in cases of government contracts, that is, where one party is a State or a State-owned entity. The reference to the law of the State or to a Public Procurement Statute cannot be regarded as an implied exclusion of the CISG.

Regarding the PICC, Article 1.5 recognizes that the parties may completely exclude their application too.[22] The PICC and other soft law do not automatically apply in the first place. Accordingly, the parties' express provision for the application of another legal regime will most likely be assumed as an exclusion of the PICC and similar instruments under the proper rules of interpretation, yet the

---

[18] Brazilian Civil Code 1942, Decree-Law 4.657, art 2.

[19] *Cybernetix SA v CD Systems de Columbia SA* [2011] Cour de Cassation (French Supreme Court) 09-70305, CISG-online 2311: the CISG was not applied because parties had chosen internal French law; *Horse case VII* [2024] Rechtbank Noord-Nederland (District Court Northern Netherlands) C/18/231001/KG ZA 24-7, CISG-online 6902; *Ersanlar Tarim SMS v F.lli Rinaldi s.n.c.* [2021] Tribunale di Foggia (District Court Foggia) 5410/2014, CISG-online 5787; *Coffee roasters case* [2023] Rechtbank Gelderland (District Court Gelderland) C/05/413314/HZ ZA 23-2, CISG-online 6394; Hachem, 'Article 7 CISG: Interpretation of the Convention and Gap-Filling' in Schwenzer and Schroeter (eds) (n 7) para 18.

[20] CISG Advisory Council, 'CISG-AC Opinion No. 16, Exclusion of the CISG under Article 6, Rapporteur: Doctor Lisa Spagnolo, Monash University, Australia. Adopted by the CISG Advisory Council Following Its 19th Meeting, in Pretoria, South Africa on 30 May 2014' (2014) comment 4.2; Mistelis, 'Article 6' in Kröll, Mistelis, and Perales Viscasillas (eds) (n 14) para 12.

[21] *Czech Insurer v Russian Buyer* [2020] ICC International Court of Arbitration ICC Case No. FA-2020-225, CISG-online 5553; *Dongguan Jianqun Shoes Company, Ltd v Consolidated Shoe Company, Inc et al.* [2022] US District Court for the Western District of Virginia 6:21-cv-00048, CISG-online 6092; *Salzgitter Flachstahl GmbH v Riveco Generai Sider S.pA* [2022] Corte Suprema di Cassazione (Italian Supreme Court) 36144/2022, CISG-online 6009; *Boxmark Leather GmbH & Co KG v Sals Leather Services S.r.l* [2024] Tribunal de Apelaciones en lo Civil de Segundo Turno (Court of Appeal for the Second Circuit) 171/2024/2-19258/2022, CISG-online 7035.

[22] Cuniberti and Vogenauer, in Vogenauer (ed) (n 13) para 3.

express exclusion of their application might be advisable in two scenarios. First, when the parties make an express provision for the application of *lex mercatoria*, international principles, usages of trade, or similarly terms that have been associated in the past with the PICC and other soft law instruments but the parties do not wish that such designation be interpreted as an implicit choice of the PICC, etc.[23] Second, where the parties may not wish to designate a specific legal regime, they might nevertheless want to clarify that they do not expect the adjudicator to decide the application of the PICC under their own scope of application rules or the relevant 'conflict of laws' provisions.[24]

II. Derogation, Variation, and Mandatory Rules

1. Derogation and variation

Both Article 6 CISG and Article 1.5 PICC recognize that the Parties may derogate from or vary particular provisions.[25] The parties would generally decide to depart from or change certain solutions of the applicable rules of law mechanically, through negotiated contracts or standard terms.[26] The French maxim, 'the contract is the law of the parties', is a reflection of the implicit freedom in most legal systems to vary the otherwise default contractual provisions. Accordingly, the parties' specific terms will usually be understood, under the relevant rules of interpretation (Article 8 CISG and Article 4.1 PICC), as an implicit derogation or deviation from the default legal system.

It follows that the Parties can, for example, determine the standard of fundamental breach or fundamental non-performance in Article 25 CISG and Article 7.3.1(2) PICC, respectively; exclude the right to cure under Article 48 CISG and Article 7.1.4 PICC; or eliminate or fix a time for the duty to notify non-conformity

---

[23] Ibid.
[24] Ibid.
[25] Brooke Marshall, 'The Hague Choice of Law Principles, CISG, and PICC: A Hard Look at a Choice of Soft Law' (2018) 66 *The American Journal of Comparative Law* paras 201–202; International Institute for the Unification of Private Law (ed), *UNIDROIT Principles of International Commercial Contracts* (UNIDROIT International Institute for the Unification of Private Law 2016) 14, s 3; Hachem, 'Article 7 CISG: Interpretation of the Convention and Gap-Filling' in Schwenzer and Schroeter (eds) (n 7) para 28.
[26] *Bunker Partner OU et al. v Golden Arrow Olieproducten Amsterdam BV* [2024] Rechtbank Rotterdam (District Court Rotterdam) C/10/656674/HA ZA 23-392, CISG-online 7118; *Magna Automotive (CZ) s.r.o. v Faurecia Sièges d'Automobile SAS* [2022] Cour d'appel de Versailles (Court of Appeal Versailles) 21/03438, CISG-online 6160; *United Auto Enterprises BVBA v OC Group BV* [2023] Gerechtshof Den Haag (Court of Appeal The Hague) 200.308.899/01, CISG-online 6429; Hachem, 'Article 7 CISG: Interpretation of the Convention and Gap-Filling' in Schwenzer and Schroeter (eds) (n 7) para 28; Simon Manner and Moritz Schmitt, 'Article 6 (The Contract and the Convention (Primacy of the Contract))' in Christoph Brunner and Benjamin Gottlieb (eds), *Commentary on the UN Sales Law (CISG)* (Wolters Kluwer 2019) para 8.

under Article 39 CISG. The parties can also limit the type and amount of damages for breach of contract under Articles 74 to 77 CISG and Articles 7.4.1 to 7.4.8 PICC.

The ICC Incoterms have the effect of derogating the default rules on risk transfer, place of delivery, transport costs, etc. in the CISG. The ICC Incoterms® 2020 rules can also be modified in themselves but there are dangers in doing so. Alteration should therefore be extremely clear and conscious choices in the contract to avoid surprises. For instance, if the allocation of transportation costs in the ICC Incoterms® 2020 is altered by other clauses in the contract, the parties should clearly state whether they intended to vary the point at which delivery and the risk transfers take place.[27]

2. Mandatory rules

Some conflict of laws rules, such as Article 11 Mexico City Convention, state the pre-eminence of the mandatory provisions of the forum over the law chosen by the parties.[28] Some conflict of laws provisions, such as Article 3(3) Rome Regulation I, also require the judge to apply the mandatory provisions of the country to which the contract is most connected, irrespective of the law chosen by the parties.[29]

When parties incorporate the CISG or the PICC into their contract at the level of substantive law, the legal system's mandatory rules that would have applied by default are applicable.[30] Therefore, some mandatory rules will impose limits on parties' incorporation of the PICC and CISG provisions, in particular when there is any conflict with the underlying domestic law.[31]

If the parties opt into the CISG at the level of the conflict of laws rules stating, for example, 'the contract is governed by Swiss law', the law of Switzerland, including its mandatory provisions, will apply. In addition, as stated above, the conflict of law rules of the forum might require the application of the judge's own mandatory rules or of a closest connected third country, irrespective of the choice of Swiss law.

A different question is whether the CISG and the PICC themselves contain mandatory provisions that the parties cannot derogate from or vary. Article 1.5 PICC anticipates a positive answer; the parties' freedom of contract is guaranteed, except as otherwise provided in the PICC. For example, Article 1.7. PICC requires the parties to act in good faith and fair dealing, and such duty may not be excluded

---

[27] Chambre de commerce internationale (ed) (n 3) 17, para 78.

[28] Inter-American Convention on the Law Applicable to International Contracts 1994, art 11.

[29] Rome I 2008, art 3(3).

[30] Hachem, 'Article 7 CISG: Interpretation of the Convention and Gap-Filling' in Schwenzer and Schroeter (eds) (n 7) para 6.

[31] Clayton P Gillette and Steven D Walt, 'Judicial Refusal to Apply Treaty Law: Domestic Law Limitations on the CISG's Application' (2017) 22 *Uniform Law Review* 452; Michael Joachim Bonell, 'The Law Governing International Commercial Contracts and the Actual Role of the Unidroit Principles' (2018) 23 *Uniform Law Review* 15, 16.

or limited. The mandatory provisions that expressly prohibit derogation in the PICC are: Article 1.7 on good faith and fair dealing; provisions on Chapter 3 on impossibility; Articles 5.1.7(2) and 7.4.13(2) on the reasonableness requirement on price determination and penalties for breach; Article 7.1.6 on the test of gross unfairness for exemption clauses; and Article 10.3(2) on restriction over limitation periods. However, given the soft law nature of the PICC, the rest of the PICC provisions might be modified or derogated. The CISG does not contain mandatory provisions, except for Article 12 CISG.

III. Freedom of Form

1. General principle

Articles 11 CISG and Article 1.2 PICC provide that a contract does not need to be made in writing or in any particular form and it may be proved by any means, including witnesses. These provisions, also included in other B2B international law instruments, are the reflection of the freedom of form principle in contracts.[32] They may not surprise most lawyers since in many jurisdictions,[33] although not in all, business deals are not subject to any form requirements either.[34]

The freedom of form principle is particularly appropriate in the context of international commercial contracts where, in light of modern means of communication, many transactions are concluded rapidly and by a convened use of instantaneous communication channels such as software applications, telephones, mobiles, etc. Other transactions take longer by means of non-instantaneous means like e-mail, post services, by paper or digitally signed documents, etc.[35]

However, some CISG Contracting States were opposed to any CISG contract's conclusion, modification, or termination be made in writing when a party to the contract has its place of business in the reservation Contracting State

---

[32] *4work SIA v DND Talis UAB* [2022] Rīgas pilsētas tiesa (District Court City of Riga) C-2279-22/72, CISG-online 6925; CISG Advisory Council, 'CISG-AC Opinion No. 23, Mistake, Fraud, Misrepresentation and Initial Impossibility in CISG Contracts, Rapporteur: Professor Hugh Beale, Universities of Warwick (Em.) and Oxford, United Kingdom. Adopted Unanimously by the CISG Advisory Council Following its 47th Meeting, in Kopaonik, Serbia, on December 12–14, 2023' (2023) comments 13.1–13.3.

[33] For instance, Switzerland Federal Act on the Amendment of the Swiss Civil Code 1911, art 11; German Civil Code (BGB), art 125; Russian Federation Civil Code, art 434(1).

[34] Harry M Flechtner, *Honnold's Uniform Law for International Sales under the 1980 United Nations Convention* (5th edn, Wolters Kluwer 2021) 226; for Latin American law countries see Edgardo Muñoz, *Modern Law of Contracts and Sales in Latin-America, Spain and Portugal* (Eleven International Publishing 2011) 76; in England the Sale of Goods Act s 4(1) embodies the principle of freedom of form, see Michael G Bridge, *The International Sale of Goods* (4th edn, Oxford University Press 2017) 542.

[35] Martin Schmidt-Kessel, 'Article 11 CISG: Freedom of Form' in Schwenzer and Schroeter (eds) (n 7) para 4.

(Article 12 CISG and Article 96 CISG).[36] The reason behind the in-writing requirement goes back to the exact requirement in the domestic laws of the reservation Contracting States.[37] In most of these States' laws, the in-writing requirement is a means of proof rather than a formal validity requirement. China withdrew this CISG reservation later on.[38] Argentina should follow suit since its most recent civil and commercial code no longer requires the in-writing form for the sale of goods contract.

Whenever a party to a CISG contract has its place of business in a Contracting State that has made the above-mentioned reservation, or when the contract itself requires its conclusion or any modification be made in writing, Article 13 CISG becomes applicable. The notion of 'in writing' under this provision is interpreted broadly within the framework of the Convention. Article 13 CISG states that the term 'writing' in the CISG includes telex and telegram. These two means of communication are no longer used today. However, under the principles of functional equivalence underlying the CISG, other equivalent means of communication will also meet the in-writing requirement.[39] Revised Opinion No. 1 of the CISG AC has developed the meaning of the term 'writing' to include 'any electronic communication provided that the information contained therein is accessible so as to be usable for subsequent reference'.[40] The same opinion proposes that the prerequisite of 'writing' is met as long as the electronic communication is able to fulfil the same functions as a paper message, by saving (retrieving) and understanding (perceiving) the message.[41] A similar approach is followed in Article 1.11 PICC,

---

[36] CISG art 96 reads: 'a Contracting State whose legislation requires contracts of sale to be concluded in or evidenced by writing may at any time make a declaration in accordance with article 12 CISG that any provision of article 11, article 29, or Part II of this Convention, that allows a contract of sale or its modification or termination by agreement or any offer, acceptance, or other indication of intention to be made in any form other than in writing, does not apply where any party has his place of business in that State'; See e.g. the case of Chile and Russia. *Chilean Sea Bass Inc v Kendell Seafood Imports, Inc* [2024] US District Court for the District of Rhode Island 21-cv-337-JJM-LDA, CISG-online 6990; *Pharmaceutical products case IV* [2021] Oberlandesgericht Hamburg (Court of Appeal Hamburg) 6 Sch 3/21, CISG-online 5767.

[37] These States include Argentina, Armenia, Belarus, Chile, Democratic People's Republic of Korea, Paraguay, Russia, Ukraine, and Vietnam.

[38] CISG, 'Status of Reservations in Accordance with Art. 96 CISG' <https://cisg-online.org/cisg-article-by-article/part-4/art.-96-cisg> accessed 24 November 2025.

[39] See functional equivalence principle in CISG art 20 stating: 'A period of time for acceptance fixed by the offeror by telephone, telex or other means of instantaneous communication'; *Pomeranian puppies case* [2022] Rechtbank Limburg (District Court Limburg) C/03/293528/HA ZA 21-320, CISG-online 5920: holding that WhatsApp messages qualified as 'in writing'; *ZEVETA Bojkovice, a.s. v FAGOR ARRASATE S COOP* [2019] Nejvyšší soud České republiky (Supreme Court of the Czech Republic) 23 Cdo 3439/2018, CISG-online 5670: holding that the written form requirement under the CISG is met when the contract is concluded via e-mail.

[40] CISG Advisory Council, 'CISG-AC Opinion No. 1 (Revised), Electronic Communications under CISG (14 October 2024). Rapporteur: Professor Christina Ramberg, Gothenburg, Sweden. Adopted unanimously by the CISG Advisory Council during its 53th meeting, in Pavia (Italy), 14–17 October 2024' (2024) Black Letter Rule 3.

[41] Ibid comment 3.2.

where 'writing' is defined as any kind of communication that can be replicated in tangible form while maintaining a record of the information it contains.[42]

2. Domestic requirements

Different domestic laws typically specify which contracts must be concluded in writing or executed by public deed in order to be valid.[43] However, most B2B contracts, including the sale of goods, are not typically included in such category. On the other hand, some civil law jurisdictions consider the in-writing form as the only means of evidence for some contracts. In particular, contracts beyond a certain amount cannot be proven by witnesses but need the written record or form.[44]

In the common law, the Statute of Frauds of some countries imposes the written form on a wide variety of transactions.[45] Section 2-201 UCC, for example, provides that a contract for the sale of goods for a price of US$ 500 or more is not enforceable by way of action or defence unless there is some writing sufficient to indicate that a contract for sale has been made between the parties and signed by the party against whom enforcement is sought.[46]

Under the above-mentioned cases, the conclusion of the contract in writing is a means of evidence rather than validity or enforceability requirement for the contract. This means that the form is imposed with a view to strengthening evidence. Its omission does not affect the contract itself. However, the effect is similar as it renders the rights acquired ineffective.

Article 11 CISG and Article 1.2 PICC take into account this distinction in domestic laws. The second sentence in both provisions is intended to make it clear that to the extent that the principle of freedom of form applies, it implies the admissibility of oral evidence in judicial and arbitral proceedings.

Lastly, doctrines such as consideration in the common law tradition or *causa* in the civil law tradition that may be labelled under domestic law as validity matters are pre-empted by the CISG and PICC provisions on the formation on contract.[47]

---

[42] See PICC art 1.11: '"writing" means any mode of communication that preserves a record of the information contained therein and is capable of being reproduced in tangible form'.

[43] Schwenzer and Muñoz (n 1) para 22.06 ff. For instance, the sale of real estate is often subject to strict formalities like the in-writing form and the registry in the registry of land or estates in many jurisdictions.

[44] Ibid.

[45] In the United Arab Emirates, Federal Decree by Law No. (35) of 2022 Promulgating the Law of Evidence in Civil and Commercial Transactions, art 35 (500 Dirhams); in Australia, only in Tasmania Sales of Goods Act 1895 s 9, and in Western Australia Sales of Goods Act 1895, s 4 (AUS$ 20).

[46] Larry A DiMatteo, *International Contracting: Law and Practice* (3rd edn, Wolters Kluwer Law & Business 2013).

[47] Pilar Perales Viscasillas, 'Comments on the Draft Digest Relating to Articles 14–24 and 66–70' in Franco Ferrari and others (eds), *The Draft UNCITRAL Digest and Beyond: Cases, Analysis and Unresolved Issues in the U.N. Sales Convention: Papers of the Pittsburgh Conference Organized by the Center for International Legal Education (CILE)* (Sweet & Maxwell 2004) 260–1.

Under the above provisions, there is no need of consideration or *causa* to create or modify a contract.

3. Form agreed by the parties

The freedom of form also includes the ability of the parties to agree upon a form requirement for their contract. This is the case at the domestic[48] and international levels for instruments such as the CISG and the PICC.[49] In determining whether the parties set specific form requirements for the conclusion of their contract, the interpretation provisions in the applicable law, like Article 8 CISG and Article 4.1 PICC, are relevant. For instance, the parties may have stipulated in drafts of their contract previously exchanged by e-mail that its conclusion as well as any modification thereof should be made in writing. The requirement may also be inferred from the presence of signatures spaces, such as those found in draft versions of the contract exchanged during negotiations, or simply from the high value of the transaction—for instance, contracts involving several million US dollars. In assessing the meaning of 'in writing' (and in the absence of a provision to that effect), one may consider all relevant circumstances and reach the conclusion that such a concept includes the record of their agreements in the form of electronic communications used during negotiations.[50]

A different question may be what the effect of the parties' failure to comply with the agreed form requirement is. Does lack of the form agreed upon by the parties result in the non-existence of the contract, a curable nullity, or ineffective evidence in future trials? The parties' background and jurisdiction may also assist in finding what a reasonable person in their same position should have expected on that matter.

Prior practices between the parties or international usages under Article 9 CISG and Article 1.9 PICC might also integrate a form requirement, a particular meaning and effect into the parties' contract.

4. Form for modification

A fundamental question for international commercial contracts is the role of form requirements in the modification or termination of the parties' commercial

---

[48] See e.g. Joseph Chitty, *Chitty on Contracts* (35th edn, Sweet & Maxwell 2023) para 4-001.

[49] *4work SIA v DND Talis UAB* [2022] Rīgas pilsētas tiesa (District Court City of Riga) C-2279-22/72, CISG-online 6925: holding that art 11 CISG is not mandatory, as the parties may agree on different requirements; Pilar Perales Viscasillas, 'Article 11' in Kröll, Mistelis, and Perales Viscasillas (eds) (n 14) para 19; Flechtner (n 34) 226.

[50] Schwenzer and Muñoz (n 1) paras 22.15–22.16.

relationship. As a general rule, contracts can be modified or terminated by the mere agreement of the parties, without any further form requirement (Article 29 CISG and Article 3.1.2. PICC).[51]

However, written contracts often contain provisions (so-called no oral modification clauses or NOM clauses) stating that any modification or termination shall be made in writing in order to be effective or that oral modification or termination is invalid. Parties wish to have certainty about what their agreement consists of during the different stages of performance; NOM clauses seem to promote the parties' behaviour in that direction.[52] The default provisions in international treaties confirm the freedom of the parties to provide for NOM clauses in their contracts. Article 29(2) CISG and Article 2.1.18 PICC state that a contract in writing which contains a clause requiring any modification or termination by agreement to be in a particular form, such as in writing, may not be otherwise modified or terminated. As explained above, whether the parties intended to require a specific form for modifying or terminating their contract must be determined through interpretation under the applicable rules—namely Article 8 CISG and Article 4.1 PICC. The mere fact that the contract is in writing does not necessarily imply an agreement to exclude oral modifications.[53] Similarly, the legal effect of failing to follow a NOM clause must also be assessed through interpretation. In addition, prior practices between the parties or international trade usages, as referred to in Article 9 CISG and Article 1.9 PICC, may establish a form requirement for modifications or terminations.

However, a party may be precluded from asserting a non-oral modification clause to the extent that the other party has relied upon the first party's conduct or statements that it would not invoke the clause (Article 29(b) CISG and Article 2.1.18 PICC). For instance, suppose Party X and Party Y have a written contract containing a NOM clause. During the course of their business relationship, Party X verbally agrees to extend the delivery deadline, and Party Y relies on this extension by delaying shipment and reorganizing its logistics accordingly. Later, Party X attempts to terminate the contract, invoking the original deadline and the NOM clause. In this scenario, Party X may be precluded from relying on the NOM clause under Article 29(2)(b) CISG and Article 2.1.18 PICC, because Party Y reasonably relied on Party X's conduct and would be unfairly prejudiced. This outcome is based on the principle of estoppel (or *venire contra factum proprium*), which prevents a party from acting inconsistently with its prior conduct.

---

[51] See CISG art 29(2) sentence 2: 'However, a party may be precluded by his conduct from asserting such a provision to the extent that the other party has relied on that conduct'; see also PICC art 3.1.2: 'A contract is concluded, modified or terminated by the mere agreement of the parties, without any further requirement'; *Raw sugar case* [2017] Sąd Apelacyjny w Białymstoku (Court of Appeal Bialystok) I ACa 715/16, CISG-online 4415.

[52] Ulrich Schroeter, 'Article 29 CISG: Modification of Contract: "No Oral Modifications" Clauses' in Schwenzer and Schroeter (eds) (n 7) para 22 ff.

[53] Flechtner (n 34) 407.

5

Interpretation and Gap Filling of the Applicable Law

I. General: Uniform Application and Interpretation

The statutory provisions governing international commercial contracts are not always clear or comprehensive. Interpretation is needed to elucidate the effect and scope of some statements and concepts. Gap-filling exercises are also required to address matters that are not expressly dealt with by these texts. The drafters of uniform law instruments, like the CISG and the PICC, did not provide specific rules for each and every issue of the sales or commercial contracts they intended to govern; occasionally they also used vague concepts that many regard as shortcomings. In most instances, those broad concepts and possible internal gaps were necessary to achieve consensus among the countries' delegates.

The CISG and the PICC contain rules for the interpretation and gap-filling of their provisions. Article 7 CISG and Article 1.6. PICC require that, in the CISG's and the PICC's interpretation, regard is to be given to their international character (and of the need to promote the observance of good faith in international trade, in the CISG case). They also require that questions concerning matters governed by those instruments, but which are not expressly settled by their provisions, be solved in conformity with the general principles on which they are based. These rules are instrumental for developing uniform law and adjusting to the new realities.[1]

---

[1] Pascal Hachem, 'Article 7 CISG: Interpretation of the Convention and Gap-Filling' in Ingeborg Schwenzer and Ulrich G Schroeter (eds), *Schlechtriem & Schwenzer Commentary on the UN Convention on the International Sale of Goods (CISG)* (5th edn, Oxford University Press 2022) para

The appropriateness of such self-contained rules of interpretation and gap-filling for uniform law has been recognized by the adoption of the same wording, or at least very similar provisions, in subsequent conventions, model laws, and uniform projects.[2]

II. Interpretation

Article 7(1) CISG and Article 1.6. PICC focus on two principles of interpretation: the origin of the rules (their 'international character') and the aim of promoting uniformity. Article 7(1) CISG also requires to consider the principle of 'good faith' in its interpretation.

1. Independent interpretation

The reference to the international nature of the CISG and the PICC suggests that the character of their rules should be taken into account when adopting any interpretative approach. It upholds the principle of autonomous interpretation, meaning that the terms in these instruments should be understood without relying on any domestic conceptions. However, in rare exceptional cases, it might be possible to demonstrate that a specific term was chosen precisely because of its meaning under domestic law, or that its position within the context of the CISG's or the PICC's rules has not given it a new functional meaning. It is often said that the 'reasonable person' concept in Article 8(2) CISG and Article 4.1(2) PICC of contract interpretation is rooted in the common law tradition.[3] Also the system of remedies in both the CISG and the PICC reflects the unitary approach of strict

---

30; Pilar Perales Viscasillas, 'Article 7' in Stefan M Kröll, Loukas A Mistelis, and Pilar Perales Viscasillas (eds), *UN Convention on Contracts for the International Sale of Goods (CISG): A Commentary* (2nd edn, CH Beck 2018) para 2.

[2] See United Nations Convention on the Use of Electronic Communications in International Contracts 2005, art 5(2); UNCITRAL Model Law on Commercial Conciliation 2002, art 2(2) (no reference to domestic law); UNCITRAL Model Law on Electronic Signatures 2001, art 4(2); UN Convention on the Assignment of Receivables in International Trade 2001, art 7(2); UNIDROIT Convention on International Interests in Mobile Equipment 2001, art 5(2); UNIDROIT Convention on International Financial Leasing (Ottawa) 1988, art 6(2); UNIDROIT Convention on International Factoring (Ottawa) 1988, art 4(2); UNIDROIT Convention on Agency in the International Sale of Goods (Geneva) 1983, art 6(2); cf also PICC art 1.6(2); Stefan Vogenauer, 'Article 1.6' in Stefan Vogenauer (ed), *Commentary on the UNIDROIT Principles of International Commercial Contracts (PICC)* (2nd edn, Oxford University Press 2015) para 2.

[3] Larry A DiMatteo, *International Contracting: Law and Practice* (3rd edn, Wolters Kluwer Law & Business 2013) 232; E Allan Farnsworth, *Contracts* (4th edn, Aspen Publishers 2004) 80–1; Nicole Kornet, *Contract Interpretation and Gap Filling: Comparative and Theoretical Perspectives* (Intersentia; 2006) 116.

liability inspired by the common law systems:[4] a party is liable for breaching its contractual promise irrespective of any fault and the type of obligation breached.[5] Even in these situations, domestic doctrine and case law cannot be used simply to interpret their articles. Instead, it must be interpreted independently, considering its role within the CISG's or the PICC's framework.

The CISG and the PICC were born from multinational negotiations that ended in compromises to achieve what the country delegates deemed the minimum necessary for the contracting parties particular interests. A convention created under such circumstances must be interpreted with its own international character as its starting point.

Accordingly, the methods and techniques of interpretation must also be generated independently. Those methods that have been particularly developed for civil law codes and other domestic statutes should not apply in the interpretation of international instruments like the CISG or the PICC automatically. Neither should one make recourse to methods of interpretation that are proper of international law treaties such as the Vienna Convention on the Law of Treaties of 1969 (VCLT),[6] in particular for the PICC that constitute soft law. The CISG is a treaty of direct application in Contracting States, which becomes part of their national law applicable to international sales and, thus, is directly binding upon their State courts.[7] As other uniform law treaties, the methods used for the interpretation of its provisions should take into account the particular matters that it governs, that is, international sales (and certain mixed contracts under Article 3(2) CISG). The same follows for the PICC; their international origin and purpose requires that

---

[4] Richard Posner, 'Let Us Never Blame a Contract Breaker' in Omri Ben-Shahar and Ariel Porat (eds), *Fault in American Contract Law* (Cambridge University Press 2010) 5: This does not necessary mean that the injured party will be redressed with all remedies stipulated under the law, since specific outcomes may follow according to the degree of breach and the nature of the obligation broken; cf Ingeborg Schwenzer and Edgardo Muñoz, *Global Sales and Contract Law* (2nd edn, Oxford University Press 2022) para 41.04.

[5] Posner (n 4) 4; Barry Nicholas, 'Fault and Breach of Contract' in J Beatson and Daniel Friedmann (eds), *Good faith and fault in contract law* (Clarendon 1997) referring to the endorsement of this principle in *Paradine v Jane* (1647) Aleyn 26, 82 ER 897 and Introductory note to Chapter 11 of the United States Restatement Second Contracts; Peter De Cruz, *Comparative Law in a Changing World* (3rd edn, Routledge-Cavendish 2007) 346.

[6] In any event, the VCLT provisions may not be appropriate to interpret the provisions on the seller's and the buyer's obligations under the CISG as they are too vague.

[7] *Kumpers Composites GmbH & Co KG v TPI Composites Inc* [2025] US District Court for the District of Arizona CV-23-00214-PHX-SMB, CISG-online 7294; *Vanport International, Inc v DFC Wood Products Pty Ltd* [2024] US District Court for the District of Oregon 3:22-cv-01041-HZ, CISG-online 6778; Simon Cornelius Manner and Moritz Schmitt, 'Article 1 (Basic Rules of Application; Relation to Contracting State)' in Christoph Brunner and Benjamin Gottlieb (eds), *Commentary on the UN Sales Law (CISG)* (Wolters Kluwer Law International 2019) para 8; Pascal Hachem, 'Introduction to Articles 1–6 CISG: General Questions Regarding the Sphere of Application' in Schwenzer and Schroeter (eds) (n 1) para 15.

they are applied uniformly in a broad range of international commercial contracts across parties from multiple jurisdictions.[8]

2. Uniform interpretation

Article 7(1) CISG and Article 1.6. PICC, and similar provisions modelled by the former, require that in the interpretation of the international instrument, regard is to be had to the need to promote uniformity in their application. In the CISG case, the mandate of Article 7 is binding upon State courts.[9] The rule follows the unification purpose of binding or non-binding international uniform law. Since there is no global body to decide as a last instance court on the divergent interpretation from different jurisdictions, as there is for example in the European Union or in OHADA, the aim of uniformity, and thus equality, predictability, and efficiency of a reliable system of precedents, can only be achieved if courts and arbitral tribunals have regard of the well-reasoned and supported decisions of other jurisdictions and thereby develop a common interpretation of such texts, just as they do at the national level.[10]

Several efforts have been made to gather the information required for achieving uniform interpretation and application. For UNCITRAL texts, the UNCITRAL Secretariat has established an information system 'CLOUT',[11] that aims to enable the collection of decisions and their dissemination through abstracts concerning UN Conventions and model laws. Today, a number of other databases, including CISG-online, and UNILEX, further contribute to the gathering, systematization, and diffusion of case law on the CISG and the PICC.[12]

In addition to the above case law websites, UNCITRAL's *Digest* on the CISG offers the compilation of selected cases organized by articles of the Convention but

---

[8] Ralf Michaels, 'Preamble I: Purposes, Legal Nature, and Scope of the PICC; Applicability by Courts; Use of the PICC for the Purpose of Interpretation and Supplementation and as a Model' in Vogenauer (ed) (n 2) para 22.

[9] Christoph Brunner and Philipp K Wagner, 'Article 7 (Interpretation of the Convention and Gap-Filling)' in Brunner and Gottlieb (eds) (n 7) para 4.

[10] *Electronic electricity meters case* [2018] Appellationsgericht Basel-Stadt (Court of Appeal Canton Basel-Stadt) ZB.2017.20 (AG.2018.557), CISG-online 3906; *Italian wooden products case* [2019] Okresný súd Dunajská Streda (District Court Dunajská Streda) 19Cb/67/2018/6118256517, CISG-online 5661: holding that uniformity can be ensured by having regard to the existing case law on the CISG interpreting its provisions; *4work SIA v DND Talis UAB* [2022] Rīgas pilsētas tiesa (District Court City of Riga) C-2279-22/72, CISG-online 6925: relying on the compiled case law in order to uphold the uniform application of the CISG; *Diammonium phosphate case* [2023] Cairo Regional Centre for International Commercial Arbitration (CRCICA) 1527/2021 (Final Award), CISG-online 6272.

[11] UNCITRAL, 'Case Law on UNCITRAL Texts (CLOUT) | United Nations Commission on International Trade Law' <https://uncitral.un.org/en/case_law> accessed 22 November 2025; *Electronic electricity meters case* (n 10); *Brands International Corporation v Reach Companies, LLC* [2024] US Court of Appeals (8th Circuit) 23-2164, CISG-online 7006.

[12] 'CISG-Online | CISG-Online.Org' <https://cisg-online.org/home> accessed 22 November 2025; 'UNILEX DATABASE' <https://www.unilex.info/> accessed 22 November 2025.

abstains from critical comments or analysis.[13] The opinions of the CISG Advisory Council,[14] a private initiative by a number of scholars, take on controversial topics of the CISG, critically analysing cases and academic contributions on these topics, with the aim of finding a uniform line of understanding and application of the CISG under Article 7(1) CISG. The opinions of the CISG Advisory Council, which up to now count 24 plus two declarations, are considered persuasive authority and have already been referred to as such by State courts, arbitral tribunals, and scholarly opinion.[15]

In addition to these materials, the contributions of academic jurists on the laws applicable to international commercial contracts should not be neglected. The *Schlechtriem & Schwenzer: Commentary on the UN Convention on the International Sale of Goods (CISG)*, for instance, has been translated into different languages, including German, Spanish, Portuguese, Polish, Japanese, French, and Turkish. It has become the leading commentary on the CISG frequently cited by tribunals and courts all over the world.[16] It analyses and references all major literature and case law on the CISG from courts and arbitral tribunals across the globe.

3. Good faith

In contract law, the principle of 'good faith' is viewed differently in common law systems compared to civil law systems. In common law systems, the principle of good faith historically had a limited role in contract law. The prevailing view was

---

[13] 'United Nations Commission on International Trade Law |' <https://uncitral.un.org/> accessed 22 November 2025; see also Spiros V Bazinas, 'Uniformity in the Interpretation and the Application of the CISG: The Role of CLOUT and the Digest' in *Celebrating Success: 25 Years United Nations Convention on Contracts for the International Sale of Goods' Collation of Papers at UNCITRAL SIAC Conference 22–23 September 2005, Singapore, Singapore International Arbitration Centre*, 18.

[14] CISG Advisory Council <https://cisgac.com/> accessed 22 November 2025.

[15] See e.g. *Turkish-Indian sales contract case* [2018] ICC International Court of Arbitration 18981 (Final award), CISG-online 3838 where an ICC Tribunal relied on CISG-AC No. 6 'Calculation of Damages under CISG Article 74'; *CeDe Group AB v KAN Sp z.o.o.* [2020] Högsta domstolen (Swedish Supreme Court) T 6032-16, CISG-online 5500 paras 27, 44–45, relying on CISG-AC Opinion No. 18 on 'Set off under CISG'; *MaRa Medical-Technical-Aid GmbH v Ningbo Laida Automotive Technology Co Ltd* [2021] Intermediate People's Court Ningbo, Zhejiang Province (2021)浙02民初824号, CISG-online 6203; *The North Face t-shirts case* [2023] Rechtbank Noord-Holland (District Court Noord-Holland), C/15/331571/HA ZA 22-544, CISG-online 6736, paras 4.11, 4.13, 4.14, and 4.16 relying on CISG-AC Opinion 22: 'The seller's liability for goods infringing intellectual property rights under Article 42 CISG.'

[16] See e.g. *Forestal Guarani SA v Daros Int'l, Inc* [2010] US Court of Appeals (3rd Circuit) 08-4488, CISG-online 2112 para 12: Referring to the commentary, the Court observed 'a court must at the outset conduct a choice-of-law analysis based on private international law principles to determine which state's law governs contract formation, and then apply that law to a party's claim ... Our study of the available sources on the subject establishes this position as the clear majority view'; *Electronic electricity meters case* [2018] Appellationsgericht Basel-Stadt (Court of Appeal Canton BaselStadt) ZB.2017.20 (AG.2018.557), CISG-online 3906; *KT MOTORSPORT spol s.r.o. v Garage Vandecasteele NV* [2022] Court: Nejvyšší soud České republiky (Supreme Court of the Czech Republic) 23 Cdo 1062/2021, CISG-online 6766.

that parties were generally free to pursue their own interests and were not required to act in good faith towards each other.[17] This approach was often summarized by the Latin phrase '*caveat emptor*', meaning 'let the buyer beware'. In contrast, civil law systems, particularly those influenced by Roman law, have traditionally placed a greater emphasis on good faith in contracts. The principle of good faith, or 'bona fides', was seen as a fundamental principle underlying all contractual relationships. Parties were expected to act honestly and fairly towards each other, and contracts could be invalidated if one party acted in bad faith.[18]

However, in recent years, there has been a convergence between common law and civil law approaches to good faith in contract law. Many common law jurisdictions, influenced by developments in civil law and international trade, have recognized a more limited duty of good faith in contracts.[19] Similarly, some civil law jurisdictions have expanded the scope of good faith to encompass a broader range of contractual obligations.[20]

The role of good faith in international commercial contracts is not uniform. Article 7(1) CISG provides that in the interpretation of the Convention, regard is to be had to the observance of good faith in international trade. The principle of good faith in Article 7(1) CISG is not defined and its meaning is controversial. Three questions arise in connection with this provision. First, what does good faith mean? Second, does that principle apply to the interpretation of the Convention's text only or also to the contractual relationship between the parties? Third, can the principle of good faith modify the literal effects of some of the CISG provisions?

As to the first question, the contours of the good faith notion can be drawn from provisions of the Convention relating to the parties' statements, rights, and obligations.[21] For instance, Article 16(2)(b) CISG prevents a party from revoking an offer where it was reasonable for the other party to rely upon the offer being irrevocable.[22] Article 29 CISG allows a party to deviate from an agreed non-oral modification clause to the extent that it relied on the other party's conduct that the latter would not assert its rights under that clause.[23] Moreover, Article 40 CISG bars the

---

[17] Schwenzer and Muñoz (n 4) paras 18.09 and 31.03 ff.
[18] Nadia Nedzel, 'A Comparative Study of Good Faith, Fair Dealing, and Precontractual Liability' 12 Tulane European and Civil Law Forum 97, 97–130; Ayse Nihan Karadayi Yalim, *Interpretation and Gap Filling in International Commercial Contracts* (Intersentia 2019) 97–130.
[19] Nedzel (n 18) 103.
[20] Nedzel (n 18) 103; Hachem, 'Article 7 CISG: Interpretation of the Convention and Gap-Filling' in Schwenzer and Schroeter (eds) (n 1) para 17.
[21] Bruno Zeller, 'Good Faith—The Scarlet Pimpernel of the CISG' [2000] *International Trade and Business Law Review* Part 2, (ii) (iv).
[22] *Asia Telco Technologies v Brightstar Int'l Corp* [2015] US District Court for the Southern District of Florida 15-20608-Civ-Scola, CISG-online 3056; Zeller (n 21) part 2.
[23] *Rock Advertising Limited (Respondent) v MWB Business Exchange Centres Limited (Appellant)* [2018] Supreme Court of the United Kingdom UKSC 24, CISG-online 3078; Zeller (n 21); Christoph Brunner, 'Article 29 (Modification of Contract; Writing Requirement)' in Brunner and Gottlieb (eds) (n 7) para 15; Ulrich G Schroeter, 'Article 29 CISG: Modification of Contract; "No Oral Modifications" Clauses"' in Schwenzer and Schroeter (eds) (n 1) para 69.

seller from relying on the buyer's failure to examine the goods and give notice of non-conformity under Articles 38 and 39 of the CISG, if the seller knew or could have not been unaware of that lack of conformity.[24] Consequently, the concept of good faith should lead to interpretations resulting in fairness, fair conduct, reasonable standards of fair dealing, a common ethical sense, and honesty in fact.

With regard to the second question, it must be noted that the principle of good faith applies only to the interpretation of the CISG. It is not intended to integrate new obligations to the parties' contract or to interpret the parties' statements and conduct.[25] The criteria in Articles 8 and 9 CISG apply to the latter task. The wording of Article 7(1) CISG and its drafting history confirm that the principle of good faith cannot be applied to the interpretation or integration of contracts.[26] On the other hand, the PICC, although modelled on the CISG, took a different view by omitting the notion of good faith in Article 1.6 PICC and providing a specific rule in Article 1.7 PICC which directly obliges the parties to act in good faith.[27]

Regarding the third question, it has been recognized—particularly from courts in civil law jurisdictions—that when interpreting the provisions of the CISG under the principle of good faith, said principle may affect the parties' rights and obligations.[28] Some courts and scholars have made use of the principle of good faith to uphold that, for example, the declaration of avoidance required by Article 75 and 76 CISG is unnecessary where the debtor has finally and definitely refused to perform.[29] Also, an Austrian arbitral tribunal decided that a seller that had repeatedly made statements to the buyer from which the latter could reasonably infer that the seller would not raise the defence of late notice in Article 39 CISG was barred from invoking such provision pursuant to Articles 7(1) CISG and, by analogy, the reliance concept expressed in Articles 16(2)(b) and 29(2) CISG. The Tribunal referred to this as the prohibition of *venire contra factum proprium*: 'a special application

---

[24] *Ets André Bondet SA v Eco Tendance S.a.r.l. et al.* [2021] Cour d'appel de Grenoble (Court of Appeal Grenoble) 18/02617, CISG-online 5780; *Bois & Matériaux v Ceramiche Marca Corona* [2021] Cour d'appel de Bourges (Court of Appeal Bourges) 21/00343, CISG-online 5861; *Shenzen Synergy Digital Co, Ltd v Mingtel, Inc* [2022] US District Court for the Eastern District of Texas 4:19-cv-00216, CISG-online 5845; Zeller (n 21) part 2.

[25] Zeller (n 21) part 2.

[26] Hachem, 'Article 7 CISG: Interpretation of the Convention and Gap-Filling' in Schwenzer and Schroeter (eds) (n 1) para 7.

[27] Ibid.

[28] Francesco G Mazzotta, 'Good Faith Principle: Vexata Quaestio' in Larry A DiMatteo (ed), *International Sales Law: A Global Challenge* (Cambridge University Press 2014). Therefore, despite the limiting wording of Article 7(1), the good faith concept has been applied, de facto, to the conduct of the contracting parties.

[29] *Iron molybdenum case* [1997] Oberlandesgericht Hamburg (Court of Appeal Hamburg) 1 U 167/95, CISG-online 261; *Metallurgical sand case* [2006] Sąd Najwyższy (Supreme Court of Poland) III CSK 103/05, CISG-online 1399; Hachem, 'Article 7 CISG: Interpretation of the Convention and Gap-Filling' in Schwenzer and Schroeter (eds) (n 1) para 19; See also, citing CISG-online 261 *PVC foil case* [2019] Oberlandesgericht Naumburg (Oberlandesgericht des Landes Sachsen-Anhalt) (Court of Appeal Naumburg) 12 U 152/18, CISG-online 4506: holding that the requirement of prior contract avoidance can only be waived if it is certain that the obligor will not perform under any circumstances.

of the general principle of good faith, one of the general principles on which the Convention is based'.[30] In another case, an Appellate Court in Germany found that after two and a half years since the breach of contract, a buyer had lost its right to declare its avoidance. As a consequence, the Court dismissed the buyer's claim for damages against the seller under Articles 45(1)(b), 45(2), and 49(1)(a) CISG. The Court found that allowing the buyer to declare the contract avoided after such a long time would violate the principle of good faith contained in Article 7(1) of the Convention.[31]

This tendency to invoke the principle of good faith as a basis for creating obligations is prevalent in civil law jurisdictions but is less prominent in common law systems. Such divergence may hinder the uniform application of the CISG, as common law courts remain resistant to employing good faith as a doctrinal foundation for imposing obligations on the parties.

III. Methods of Interpretation

The principle of autonomous interpretation also applies to the methods used in interpreting the CISG and other international instruments, like the PICC, that enshrine the same principle. Provisions modelled on Article 7(1) CISG do not lay down the methods to be used in the Convention's interpretation. Automatic recourse to domestic law techniques of interpretation should be avoided. However, since legal systems have now gained experience in this area, in part thanks to legislative work and scholarly writings in search for objective rules, their methods no longer differ from each other and may be considered in the interpretation of uniform law instruments for international commercial contracts. The following methods can be considered as common ground.

1. Wording and systematic position

The first element to be taken into account in the interpretation of legal provisions is the wording and position within the international instrument. Textual interpretation must take into account that most international instruments call for autonomous interpretation (Article 7(1) CISG, Article 1.6(1) PICC, etc.). Accordingly, the literal meaning afforded by a domestic legal dictionary to the same term or word

---

[30] *Cold-rolled metal sheets case I* [1994] Vienna International Arbitral Centre of the Austrian Federal Economic Chamber (VIAC) SCH-4318, CISG-online 120.

[31] *BMW 3 Series case* [1995] Oberlandesgericht München (Court of Appeal Munich) 7 U 1720/94, CISG-online 143; Similarly, see *Tönnies Lebensmittel GmbH & Co KG v Polarica Oy* [2016] Lapin käräjäoikeus (District Court Lapland) 8040, CISG-online 5517: holding that respondent lost its right to claim damages from claimant in accordance with the *venire contra factum proprium* principle.

might not be considered an authentic interpretation. In addition, literal interpretation of international instruments could only be made about text drafted in the official languages in which they were enacted. UNCITRAL texts are produced in six official languages, while UNIDROIT official languages are five.[32] The wording of one version could shed light on the meaning of some provisions in a different language version.[33] In case of contradiction between versions, the working languages must be consulted, which for the CISG and the PICC were English and French, as they might reflect the intention of the delegates better.[34] In some instances, the language in which the instrument was first drafted, usually English, may be given more credit in terms of meaning accuracy.[35]

In the interpretation of international instruments, reference should also be made to the position that a given provision, concept, or statement has within a particular section, chapter or the whole framework. Also, the structure of a particular article, its character as a rule, that is, obligation, duty, remedy, exception, must be considered in the interpretation task. In the PICC's case, the Official Comment to the Black Letter Rule, together with illustrations, form a significant part of the context in which a provision was conceived and of its relationship with other rules.[36] In cases of conflict between the Black Letter Rule and the Official Comment, the former should prevail.

2. Drafting history

The drafting history reflected in the so-called *travaux préparatoires* could also be used to unveil the particular meaning or the scope that the drafters of international uniform law conceived for a specific provision.[37] Most international institutions focused on the creation of binding or non-binding uniform law, such as UNCITRAL, UNIDROIT, the Hague Conference, etc., make available the official records of discussions that lead to the enactment of a given instrument. These records often include preliminary commentaries prepared by the institution.

---

[32] UNCITRAL official languages are Arabic, Chinese, English, French, Russian, and Spanish, while UNIDROIT official languages are English, French, German, Italian, and Spanish.

[33] Ingeborg Schwenzer and Cesar Pereira, 'Lost in Translation: Interpreting Diverging but Equally Authentic CISG Texts' (2025) 43 *Journal of Law and Commerce* 129, 137–8.

[34] Ibid 137–9; *Used textile cleaning machine case* [2003] Bundesgericht/Tribunal fédéral (Swiss Federal Supreme Court) 4C.198/2003, CISG-online 840: considering primarily the English version and secondly the French text in regard to the German nonbinding translation of the CISG. Ulrich Magnus, 'Tracing Methodology in the CISG: Dogmatic Foundations' in André Janssen and Olaf Meyer (eds), *ISG Methodology* (European Law Publishers 2009) 53; Vogenauer, 'Article 1.6' in Vogenauer (ed) (n 2) para 22.

[35] Schwenzer and Pereira (n 33) 138–9.

[36] Vogenauer, 'Article 1.6' in Vogenauer (ed) (n 2) para 24.

[37] Perales Viscasillas, 'Article 7' in Kröll, Mistelis, and Perales Viscasillas (eds) (n 1) para 35; Hachem, 'Article 7 CISG: Interpretation of the Convention and Gap-Filling' in Schwenzer and Schroeter (eds) (n 1) para 22.

However, historical interpretation through official records is not binding and becomes less persuasive the longer a model law, convention, or soft law has been in force.[38] This is due to the fact that the practice of international commercial contracts is subject to fast-paced developments around the world. The drafters of uniform law may not have foreseen the new type of goods and services that were to be traded just a few years ahead. The drafters were also unable to forecast how new technologies might affect the way business would be done or the understanding of different notions. For that reason, the interpretation of uniform law for international commercial contracts should not represent the type of trade practice that prevailed decades ago, where the players, ideologies, and technology might have been completely different than today.

3. Methods of public international law

The rules of interpretation applicable to public international law instruments, like those in the VCLT, are not appropriate for use in the understanding of private international law. They are intended for interpretation of obligations acquired by States *vis á vis* their sovereign counterparts, and thus they place too much emphasis on the intentions of Contracting States.[39] Therefore, private international law instruments of direct application, for example the CISG, need to draw their own rules of interpretation from their nature and purpose (Article 7(1) CISG and similar rules).[40] That does not exclude that the rules in the VCLT might be used in the interpretation of the final provisions in uniform law treaties addressed to the signatory States rather than to private parties, for instance, Part IV of the CISG.

4. Comparative law

The value of interpreting the laws of international commercial contracts in light of its comparative law background cannot be underestimated, although it has to be used with great caution. Uniform law instruments are regarded as a compromise between the laws on commercial transactions in different legal systems. Not every single provision in legal bodies like the CISG, the PICC, etc., represents a new *sui generis* rule that came out of the blue, or that was enacted in order to find a

---

[38] Hachem, 'Article 7 CISG: Interpretation of the Convention and Gap-Filling' in Schwenzer and Schroeter (eds) (n 1) para 22.
[39] Odile Ammann, *Domestic Courts and the Interpretation of International Law: Methods and Reasoning Based on the Swiss Example* (Brill 2020) 191.
[40] Bruno Zeller, 'Interpretation of the United Nations Convention on Contracts for the International Sale of Goods According to Principles of International Law' (2003) 1 *Journal of International Commercial Law* 273.

middle-ground solution between the commercial laws of these legal traditions. On the contrary, some provisions embody doctrines and principles rooted in legal systems belonging to the common law, the civil law, and other law traditions.[41] The objective of uniform law instruments has been to find, by comparison, the best solution for each trade matter at an international level.

Legal scholars are primarily responsible for using the comparative law method in interpreting uniform law; they intend to provide courts and arbitral tribunals with orientation by studying the relevant uniform commercial law on a truly comparative basis.[42] There are different ways in which comparative law can be used for this purpose. One approach is to compare the text of the CISG with the laws of different countries to see how similar issues are addressed. This historical background can help clarify ambiguous provisions. For example, if the CISG uses a term that is unclear, comparing it with how similar terms have been historically understood in other legal systems can provide insight into its meaning. Another approach is to compare the overall structure and system of the CISG with that of other legal systems. This can help to understand the underlying principles and policies behind the CISG. For example, comparing the remedies available under the CISG with those available in common law systems can provide a better understanding of the CISG's approach to remedies for breach of contract. A third approach is to compare the functional outcomes of the CISG with those of other legal systems. This can involve comparing how the CISG and other legal systems address similar practical problems or achieve similar goals. For example, comparing how the CISG and some law systems deal with the issue of damages calculations can provide insights into new ways to understand Article 74 CISG, including compensation through the disgorgement of profits.[43]

By using comparative law in these ways, interpreters of the CISG can gain a deeper understanding of its provisions and how they may be applied in practice. But one should keep in mind that uniform law was created as an autonomous system with its own principles and rules of interpretation. Despite the background of their provisions and their comparative law nature, it is strongly discouraged to automatically interpret those instruments with the lenses of a similar domestic law since such approach is likely to result in a wrong application.[44]

---

[41] Irrespective of its origin, art 7 CISG provides that in the interpretation of the CISG regard is to be had of its international character and to the need to promote uniformity in its application and the observance of good faith in international trade; cf Hachem, 'Article 7 CISG: Interpretation of the Convention and Gap-Filling' in Schwenzer and Schroeter (eds) (n 1) paras 1–3.

[42] Hachem, 'Article 7 CISG: Interpretation of the Convention and Gap-Filling' in Schwenzer and Schroeter (eds) (n 1) para 24.

[43] Ingeborg Schwenzer, 'Article 74 CISG: Calculation of Damages in General' in Schwenzer and Schroeter (eds) (n 1) para 6 ff.

[44] Franco Ferrari, 'Homeward Trend: What, Why and Why Not' in André U Janssen and Olaf Meyer (eds), *CISG Methodology* (Sellier 2009) 185–201, providing some case law examples that evidence some mistakes made by courts misinterpreting the CISG on the basis of a domestic law.

5. Other international uniform law

Some State courts, arbitral tribunals, and scholars have used uniform soft law, such as the PICC, to interpret related binding treaties, such as the CISG. In particular, as discussed in Chapter 2, the 2020 Guide jointly prepared by UNCITRAL, UNIDROIT, and the Hague Conference recognizes the complementary nature of instruments such as the CISG and the PICC, and offers guidance on their coordinated application—specifically emphasizing the role of the PICC in interpreting and supplementing the CISG pursuant to Articles 7(1) and 7(2) of the Convention. However, one should bear in mind that international institutions like UNCITRAL, UNIDROIT, or the Hague Conference pursue different goals and have diverse political interests for each of their uniform law projects. The CISG was mainly conceived as an instrument to enhance international trade globally; it was created by experts and delegates with different backgrounds and legal traditions.[45] Other projects, like the PICC, also have a uniform law nature and are the product of comparative law works and discussions.[46] However, compared to other set of rules such ICC Incoterms or the UCP 600, whose regular updates are expected to incorporate the best and up-to-date practices or conduct developed by a particular traders' community,[47] the PICC had the purpose of reflecting principles that would last over time, irrespective of their general observance.[48] Most of the delegates involved in the PICC's creation were law academics and there was no consultations with traders.[49]

In addition, the PICC first edition was drafted and published in 1994, after the CISG's entry into force.[50] Some provisions in the PICC were largely based on the CISG and, hence, they may express some of the CISG principles in more detail. However, specific PICC provisions contradict the CISG rules or principles. For instance, the role of good faith in the PICC as a principle to interpret and integrate the contract, fault (*culpa*) as one of the criteria to determine fundamental breach,[51]

---

[45] Angelo Chianale, 'The "CISG" as a Model Law: A Comparative Law Approach' [2016] *Singapore Journal of Legal Studies* 29.

[46] Stefan Vogenauer, 'Introduction' in Stefan Vogenauer (ed), *Commentary on the UNIDROIT Principles of International Commercial Contracts (PICC)* (2nd edn, Oxford University Press 2015) para 23: 'The drafters drew inspiration from a wide variety of sources. They analysed the contract laws of the major jurisdictions of the world.'

[47] Ibid para 25: 'Despite the assertion that the drafters give "special attention" to non-legislative instruments, such as standardized trade terms and model contracts elaborated by international organizations, the influence of such instruments is barely visible, so the PICC do not live up to the claim of being an 'authentic expression of what is usually called *lex mercatoria*.'

[48] Ibid para 36: 'The style of drafting of the PICC resembles that of the civilian codes, rather than that of the Anglo-American statutes ... They were aim at formulating rules.'

[49] Ibid paras 18–20: 'The Working Group was composed of distinguished lawyers representing the major legal systems of the world, but all sitting in their personal capacity ... All of them were experts in Contract law and international trade. Most of them were academics; only the Australian participant was practitioner ... However, the Working Group did not adhere to formal consultation mechanisms, such as hearings with interest groups, lobbyists, or other stakeholders.'

[50] Schwenzer and Muñoz (n 4) para 3.55.

[51] PICC 2016, art 7.3.1(2)(c).

the remedies in case of hardship, etc. The mandate of Article 7(1) CISG should not be forgotten: all solutions developed must be based on the relevant uniform treaty itself and resorting to instruments like the PICC, automatically, may violate the autonomy principle.[52]

IV. Gap Filling: General Principles, Private International Law

Uniform law instruments governing international commercial contracts are not complete or exhaustive statutes. On the one hand, the production of soft law at this level has focused on specific matters of what sometimes are complex transactions. For instance, with regard to the international sale of goods, the ICC offers optional rules to govern specific issues of risk transfer, delivery and transport by means of the ICC Incoterms®; it also proposes rules concerning matters of payment and credit by means of the UPC 600 and provisions for questions regarding independent bank guarantees through the URDG 760. All these soft law rules have gaps that should be filled in accordance with the agreement of the parties or the applicable law.

On the other hand, more 'comprehensive' instruments, like the PICC or the CISG—which might apply by virtue of the parties' agreement or by determination of the adjudicator,[53] also have legal gaps; some questions arising out of an international sales or commercial contract might not be expressly or impliedly answered by their provisions. The starting point to fill in those legal lacunae should be answered by the proper rules of supplementation. The first part of Article 7(2) CISG states that '[q]uestions concerning matters governed by this Convention which are not expressly settled in it are to be settled in conformity with the general principles on which it is based'. These questions, which are not expressly but rather impliedly settled, are called 'internal gaps' because their answers can be found reading between the text lines of the treaty. Article 1.6 PICC has a similar provision, which is repeated after the CISG in different model laws and uniform projects. All those issues that cannot be solved by looking into the express or implicit rules of the uniform law are usually known as 'external gaps'.

The mechanism proposed by Article 7(2) CISG and Article 1.6 PICC is simple. In order to supplement the statutory rules, a two-step procedure is required. The first step calls for determining whether the issue at stake is governed by the uniform

---

[52] Larry A DiMatteo and Andre Janssen, 'Interpretive Methodologies in the Interpretation of the CISG' in DiMatteo (ed) (n 28) 95 ff: 'If the interpretation and application of the CISG is to be truly autonomous, referencing soft law is more an obstacle than a facilitator to autonomous interpretation'; Schwenzer and Muñoz (n 4) para 3.54.

[53] See Chapter 3. It is explained that the PICC could also be applicable by virtue of a conflict of laws rule of the judge and the arbitrator. See also, *Intraval SL v Econ Industries GmbH* [2020] Tribunal Supremo (Spanish Supreme Court) 3133/2017/398/2020, CISG-online 5370.

law applicable. If the answer is positive: that is, the instrument deals impliedly with that matter. The second step requires identifying the 'general principles upon which the [legal text] is based' and apply them to the issue at hand.[54] If the answer is negative, because the legal text does not deal with that matter expressly or impliedly, then the adjudicator should consult the conflict of laws rules applicable to the situation in order to determine the proper law that governs the matter.[55]

With regard to the CISG, Article 4 sentence 1 outlines the matters that are governed by it: 'the formation of the contract of sale and the rights and obligations of the seller and the buyer arising from such a contract'. Article 4 sentence 2 CISG, on the other hand, enumerates the questions that are not dealt with by the Convention, unless expressly provided: (a) the validity of the contract or of any of its provisions or of any usage; (b) the effect which the contract may have on the property in the goods sold. Therefore, Article 4 CISG facilitates the first task of assessing whether one matter constitutes an internal gap or, rather, external one.

For instance, Article 78 CISG states that if a party fails to pay the price or any other sum that is in arrears, the other party is entitled to interest on it. However, the CISG does not provide for the interest rate to be applied in such a case. It is generally agreed that such state of affairs constitutes an internal gap; the interest rate applicable should result from the principles upon which the CISG is based.[56] On that matter, the CISG Advisory Council Opinion No. 14 has sustained that the general principle of full compensation anchored in Article 74 CISG, and the abstract calculation method provided in Article 76 CISG offer enough reference points to determine the applicable rate based on the CISG.[57] Accordingly, absent

[54] *Brands International Corporation v Reach Companies, LLC* [2023] U.S. Court of Appeals (8th Circuit) 23-2164, CISG-online 7006; *Frigera NV v DEC S.r.l.* [2024] Parket bij het Hof van Cassatie/ Parquet près la Cour de Cassation (Advocate General at the Belgian Supreme Court) C.23.0431.N, CISG-online 7066; Peter Schlechtreim, 'Interpretation, Gap-Filling and Further Development of the U.N. Sales Convention' (2004) 16 *Pace International Law Review* 292; Perales Viscasillas, 'Article 7' in Kröll, Mistelis, and Perales Viscasillas (eds) (n 1) para 56.

[55] *BURMS 3D Druck GmbH & Co KG v ROTEC S.a.r.l.* [2024] Cour d'appel de Rennes (Court of Appeal Rennes) 23/01565, CISG-online 7279; Schlechtreim (n 54) ; Ingeborg Schwenzer, 'Interpretation and Gap-Filling under the CISG' in Ingeborg Schwenzer, Petra Butler, and Yeşim M Atamer (eds), *Current Issues in the CISG and Arbitration* (Eleven International Publishing 2014) 114 ff, s 7.3.

[56] UNCITRAL, *Digest of Case Law on the United Nations Convention on the International Sale of Goods* (2016) 45, para 29 <https://uncitral.un.org/sites/uncitral.un.org/files/media-documents/uncitral/en/cisg_digest_2 016.pdf> accessed 21 November 2025. Also see *Italian-Swiss sales contracts case* [2023] Bezirksgericht Willisau (Court of First Instance Willisau) 1C4 23 84, CISG-online 7136; *Eurasiapatchwork S.p.r.l. v […]* [2023] Rechtbank Overijssel (District Court Overijssel) C/08/282110/HA ZA 22-201, CISG-online 6718; *Mastermedia Cioczek i Wójciak Sp J v MaKaDo Handelsbedrijf BV et al.* [2022] Rechtbank Den Haag (District Court The Hague) C/09/623157/HA ZA 22-23, CISG-online 6094; *Cozy Casa NV v Vidiled BV* [2022] Rechtbank Zeeland-West-Brabant (District Court Zeeland-West-Brabant) C/02/ 383574/HA ZA 21-149, CISG-online 5974; *Slovenian-Croatian sales contract (interest) case* [2022] Trgovački sud u Splitu (Commercial Court Split) 21. Povrv-607/2020-12, CISG-online 7312.

[57] CISG Advisory Council, 'CISG-AC Opinion No. 14, Interest under Article 78 CISG, Rapporteur: Professor Doctor Yeşim M. Atamer, Istanbul Bilgi University, Turkey. Adopted unanimously by the CISG Advisory Council following its 18th meeting, in Beijing, China on 21 and 22 October 2013' (2013) Black Letter Rule 1.

an agreement of the parties to that respect, the applicable interest rate is the one that the court at the creditor's place of business would grant in a similar contract of sale not governed by the CISG.[58]

Other CISG principles, which might be used to fill in internal gaps, are the principles of parties' autonomy (Article 6 CISG), freedom of form (Article 11 CISG), estoppel (Article 16(2)(b) and 29(2) CISG), right to withhold performance (Articles 58 and 71), reasonability of behaviours (Article 39 and 40), etc.[59]

As regards the PICC, their Preamble defines the scope of application and also the matters that are governed by them. The issue must thus concern an aspect of international commercial contracts. There are, however, certain matters expressly excluded by the PICC, such as those concerning legal capacity (Article 3.1.1), agency arising by operation of the law (Article 2.1.2(3)), and assignment of instruments governed by especial rules or the transfer of rights, contracts, and obligations in the course of transferring a business (Articles 9.1.2, 9.2.2, and 9.3.2).

The underlying PICC principles are to be read between the lines in their provisions. The principles of party autonomy and good faith are reflected in the black letter. Other principles might be drawn from the Official Comments to the PICC or the *travaux préparatoires*. Exercises of extensive interpretation of a given provision in light of the context of the PICC could also be used to subtract principles for matters of supplementation.[60]

In some particular instances, courts and scholars have proposed to apply the PICC as a reflection of the principles upon which the CISG is based in order to fill in what they considered internal gaps in the Convention.[61] This approach seems rather unconvincing from a systematic and dogmatic point of view.[62] Article 7(2) CISG requires filling in internal gaps in accordance with its own principles. Thus, all solutions developed must be based on the Convention itself and resorting to the

---

[58] Ibid Black Letter Rule 9.

[59] Hachem, 'Article 7 CISG: Interpretation of the Convention and Gap-Filling' in Schwenzer and Schroeter (eds) (n 1) para 6 ff.

[60] Vogenauer, 'Article 1.6' in Vogenauer (ed) (n 2) para 57.

[61] *Dutch-Italian sales contracts case* [2005] Nederlands Arbitrage Instituut (Netherlands Arbitration Institute) Interim Award, CISG-online 1621; *Scafom International BV v Lorraine Tubes SAS* [2009] Hof van Cassatie van België/Cour de cassation de Belgique (Belgian Supreme Court) C.07.0289.N, CISG-online 1963: in this decision exempting a party from its obligations to perform under the contract, the remedy granted was renegotiation of the price and the Court relied on the provisions on hardship in art 6.2.3 of the UNIDROIT PICC that reflected, in its view, the principles upon which the CISG is based according to Article 7(2) CISG; *SCEA GAEC Des Beauches Bernard Bruno v Teso Ten Elsen GmbH & Co KG* [1996] Cour d'appel de Grenoble (Court of Appeal Grenoble) 94/3859, CISG-online 305: in this decision, in an action for restitution of excess payments made to a seller, a general principle that payment is to be made at the creditor's domicile, a principle that is to be extended to other international trade contracts under art 6.1.6 of the UNIDROIT Principles, was applied; Peter Schlechtriem and Petra Butler, *UN Law on International Sales: The UN Convention on the International Sale of Goods* (Springer 2008) 50 ff.

[62] Michael G Bridge, *The International Sale of Goods* (4th edn, Oxford University Press 2017) 618, para 12.7; Franco Ferrari and Marco Torsello, *International Sales Law—CISG in a Nutshell* (2nd edn, West Academic Publishing 2018) 328–30.

PICC may violate the autonomy of the Convention.[63] The PICC provisions were drafted and published in 1994, after the CISG's entry into force.[64] Other provisions in the PICC were largely based on the CISG and, hence, they may express some of the CISG principles in more detail. However, the PICC include provisions on matters that were expressly or impliedly excluded from the Convention, for example validity, and that, in some instances, depart from the express provisions of the CISG, for example remedies in case of hardship under Article 79.

In the absence of general principles upon which the CISG or the PICC are based, matters must be solved in conformity with the law applicable by virtue of the rules of private international law. In other words, by the domestic rules determined by the conflict rules of the forum. Nevertheless, this interpretation should be the last resource,[65] pursuant to structure of Article 7 CISG and Article 1.6 PICC.

---

[63] Schwenzer and Muñoz (n 4) para 3.54.
[64] Ibid para 3.55.
[65] Hachem, 'Article 7 CISG: Interpretation of the Convention and Gap-Filling' in Schwenzer and Schroeter (eds) (n 1) para 42.

6

Formation and Interpretation of Contract

I. General: Mechanism

The CISG and the PICC follow the classic offer and acceptance mechanism for the formation of the contracts.[1] Broadly speaking, a contract is concluded when the offeror's offer is accepted by the offeree. This traditional mechanism might not be the most proper solution for present-day realities of trading; the content and number of communications leading to a final agreement make it difficult to

---

[1] See United Nations Convention on Contracts for the International Sale of Goods (CISG) 1980, arts 14–27; UNIDROIT Principles of International Commercial Contracts 2016 (PICC), arts 2.1.1–2.1.22.

identify them as offers, counter-offers, or acceptances.[2] The problems resulting in identifying the character of statements, that is, as offer, acceptance, or counter-offer, or the incorporation of standard terms are solved by systematic interpretation. Aware of this reality, the PICC drafters added Article 2.1.1 PICC to the classic offer and acceptance rules. Article 2.1.1 PICC acknowledges that the conduct of the parties may also suffice to demonstrate the existence of an agreement, and a contract may be concluded even if the exact moment of consent to X or Y obligation cannot be determined.[3]

II. Offer: Criteria, Public Offer, Effectiveness, Revocability, Termination

The CISG provisions governing the offer are found in Articles 14 to 17, while those in the PICC are in Articles 2.1.2 to 2.1.5. The PICC rules on the offer closely follow the CISG provisions. Article 14 CISG[4] and Article 2.1.2 PICC[5] provide two requirements for offers to be effective: first, the offer must be sufficiently definite, which can be done by specifying the *essentialia negotii* (essential features) of the intended transaction; second, the offer must express the intention of the offeror to be legally bound in case of acceptance.[6] These two conditions will be further discussed, in light of the applicable rules of interpretation (Article 8 CISG and Articles 4.1, 4.2, and 4.3 PICC).

1. The offer must be sufficiently definite

The first requirement for a valid offer is that the proposal must be sufficiently definite. The second sentence of Article 14(1) CISG states that a proposal meets this condition if it indicates the goods, and expressly or implicitly fixes or makes provision for determining the price and quantity.[7] The Official Comment on Article

---

[2] Ingeborg Schwenzer and Edgardo Muñoz, *Global Sales and Contract Law* (2nd edn, Oxford University Press 2022) para 10.74 ff.

[3] Luke Nottage, 'Article 2.1.1' in Stefan Vogenauer (ed), *Commentary on the UNIDROIT Principles of International Commercial Contracts (PICC)* (2nd edn, Oxford University Press 2015) para 5.

[4] *Concealed line gutters case* [2020] Gerechthof 's-Hertogenbosch (Court of Appeal 's-Hertogenbosch) 200.241.641/01, CISG-online 5331.

[5] *Aceros Asuncion SA v Compañia Integral De Construcciones SA* [2019] Tribunal de Apelación en lo Civil y Comercial de Asunción, Sexta Sala 63/2019.

[6] See Schwenzer and Muñoz (n 2) para 10.19; Ulrich Schroeter, 'Article 14 CISG: Offer (Including Incorporation of Standard Terms)' in Ingeborg Schwenzer and Ulrich G Schroeter (eds), *Schlechtriem & Schwenzer Commentary on the UN Convention on the International Sale of Goods (CISG)* (5th edn, Oxford University Press 2022) para 1 ff.

[7] *Magellan Int'l Corporation v Salzgitter Handel GmbH* (n 7) 22; *2P Commercial Agency s.r.o. v SRT USA, Inc* [2013] US District Court for the Middle District of Florida 2:11-cv-652-FtM-29SPC, CISG-online 2395; *Kolmar Petrochemicals Americas, Inc v Idesa Petroquímica SA de CV* [2005] Primer

2.1.2 PICC provides similar examples. An offer must, therefore, contain the *essentialia negotii* of the future transaction.

An offer does not fulfil the requirement of definiteness unless the goods have been sufficiently described, irrespective of whether they exist or not.[8] With regard to the quantity of the goods, it is enough if the parties provide a mechanism which makes the quantity of the goods determinable.[9] In addition, an offer must fix or make provision for determining the price of the goods under Article 14 CISG.[10] However, when the parties have performed the contract despite not having agreed on a fixed price, or have otherwise indicated their intention to proceed with the contract, the requirement of a sufficiently definite or determinable price in the offer, no longer applies. A valid contract has been concluded in such cases, and the price must be determined according to Article 55 CISG.[11] Pursuant to this Article, the price is generally the one charged at the time of the conclusion of the contract for such goods, sold under comparable circumstances in the relevant trade.

The apparent contradiction between Article 14(1) and Article 55 CISG—concerning the requirement of a price for contract formation—is examined in detail in Chapter 10. While Article 14(1) CISG sets a strict threshold by requiring the offer to indicate or make the price determinable,[12] Article 55 CISG allows for the formation of a contract even in the absence of a specified price,[13] relying instead on the price generally charged under comparable circumstances.[14] In Chapter 10, we explore this topic through various interpretative approaches that aim to reconcile the two provisions, particularly in light of commercial practices and the parties' intent to be bound by their contract.[15]

Tribunal Colegiado en Materia Civil del Primer Circuito (1st Panel of the Federal Court of Appeal for the 1st Circuit) 127/2005, CISG-online 1004.

[8] *Pig iron case I* [1998] China International Economic & Trade Arbitration Commission (CIETAC) CISG/1998/11, CISG-online 1135.

[9] See Schroeter, 'Article 14 CISG: Offer (Including Incorporation of Standard Terms)' in Schwenzer and Schroeter (eds) (n 6) para 3; Ulrich Schroeter, 'Introduction to Articles 14–24 CISG' in Schwenzer and Schroeter (eds) (n 6) para 99.

[10] *Fauba France FDIS GC Electronique v Fujitsu Mikroelektronik GmbH* [1995] Cour de Cassation (French Supreme Court) 92-16.993, CISG-online 138; Schroeter, 'Article 14 CISG: Offer (Including Incorporation of Standard Terms)' in Schwenzer and Schroeter (eds) (n 6) paras 8, 18.

[11] *Manufactured paint case* [2008] Nejvyšší soud České republiky (Supreme Court of the Czech Republic) 32 Odo 824/2007, CISG-online 1848.

[12] *Mixing equipment case* [2019] Court of Appeal of Warsaw VII AGa 1093/18, CISG-online 5298.

[13] Schroeter, 'Article 14 CISG: Offer (Including Incorporation of Standard Terms)' in Schwenzer and Schroeter (eds) (n 6) paras 17–18 considering that CISG art 55 concerning the purchase price is applicable only on the condition that the agreement has been validly concluded; Florian Mohs, 'Article 55 CISG: Price Determination in Case of Open Price Contracts' in Schwenzer and Schroeter (eds) (n 6) para 5.

[14] Schwenzer and Muñoz (n 2) 10.18.

[15] Schroeter, 'Article 14 CISG: Offer (Including Incorporation of Standard Terms)' in Schwenzer and Schroeter (eds) (n 6) para 23.

2. Intention to be bound in case of acceptance

An offer must indicate the offeror's intent to be bound in case of acceptance.[16] This can be ascertained by the language used by the offeror. If such language is not sufficiently clear, the provisions of Articles 8[17] and 9 CISG and Articles 4.1, 4.2, and 4.3 PICC must be considered, in order to determine whether the offeror had an intention to be bound.[18]

If a proposal is sufficiently definite under the first requirement (determination of price and goods), it can be understood that the sender has the intention to be bound. However, there might be instances in which the offeror does not have such intent until further transaction elements are agreed upon.[19] This might happen where the offer includes a clause excluding its binding nature. In the CISG case of Hanwha Corp. *v* Cedar Petrochemicals Inc., the Federal District Court of New York concluded that there was no intention to be bound, and therefore the proposal was not to be considered an effective offer, because 'the parties had created a practice between themselves of a two-step process of contract formation in which neither party was to perform until there was an agreement on the terms that were not included in the initial bids.'[20]

Furthermore, Article 14(2) CISG determines that a proposal which is not directed towards a particular person but towards the public is only to be considered as an invitation to make an offer, unless the contrary is clearly indicated by the person making the proposal. The Official Comment on Article 2.1.2 PICC approaches the issue similarly. The economic reason for such restriction is that if the person sending the invitation were to be bound by every addressee who accepted it, the person could end up with more contracts than could be reasonably handled.[21]

These offers are often considered an *invitatio ad offerendum*, an invitation to make offers. Generally, the purpose behind the party making these invitations is to outline the main content of a contract and propose its conclusion. However, an intention to be bound by such communication, in case of an acceptance by the

---

[16] Ibid para 23; Schwenzer and Muñoz (n 2) 10.19.

[17] *Italian steel coils (VAT) case* [2020] Tribunale d'appello Ticino (Court of Appeal Canton Ticino) 12.2018.110, CISG-online 5493.

[18] *Cobalt sulphate case* [1993] Landgericht Hamburg (District Court Hamburg) 404 O 175/92, CISG-online 215; Ingeborg Schwenzer and others, *International Sales Law: A Guide to the CISG* (3rd edn, Zed Books 2019) 104.

[19] Clayton P Gillette and Steven D Walt, *The UN Convention on Contracts for the International Sale of Goods: Theory and Practice* (2nd edn, Cambridge University Press 2016) 87.

[20] *Hanwha Corp v Cedar Petrochemicals, Inc* [2011] US District Court for the Southern District of New York 09 Civ. 10559 (AKH), CISG-online 2178.

[21] International Institute for the Unification of Private Law (ed), *UNIDROIT Principles of International Commercial Contracts* (UNIDROIT International Institute for the Unification of Private Law 2017) 36–7, art 2.1.2, off cmt 2.

other party, does not exist.[22] Some examples are price lists, circulars, advertise-ments in newspapers, radio, television, Internet, calls for tender, as well as shop displays.[23]

3. Effectiveness

Article 15(1) CISG and Article 2.1.3(1) PICC provide that an offer becomes ef-fective when it reaches the offeree. An offer reaches the offeree only if it has been sent with the consent of the offeror.[24] Article 24 CISG determines whether and when any communication in the context of contract formation reaches the ad-dressee. This takes place when it is made orally to him or *delivered* by any other means to him personally, to his place of business or mailing address, or, if he does not have a place of business or mailing address, to his habitual residence (Article 24 CISG).

In the context of electronic communications, CISG AC Revised Opinion No. 1 suggests that the term 'reaches' corresponds to the point in time when an electronic communication becomes capable of being retrieved by the addressee.[25] Article 10(2) of the United Nations Convention on the Use of Electronic Communication in International Contracts (CUECIC) follows a similar approach.[26] Under this provision, the time of receipt is the time when the communication becomes cap-able of being retrieved by the addressee, and this is presumed to take place when it reaches the addressee's electronic address.

The intention to be bound does not arise if the offeree has received or obtained the offer without the authorization of the offeror.[27] The offer cannot be accepted if it has not reached the offeree, even if the latter is aware of it in advance. The burden of proof to show the 'reaching' of the offer is on the party relying on the effective-ness of the offer, usually the offeree.[28]

---

[22] Reiner Schulze in Larry A DiMatteo and others (eds), *International Sales Law: A Handbook* (2nd edn, CH Beck 2021) 228.
[23] Schwenzer and Muñoz (n 2) para 10.23.
[24] *Jacques Olle de Cause v Miguel Arturo Vaccheta Boggino y Otros* [2020] Corte Suprema de Justicia—Sala Civil y Comercial 104.
[25] CISG Advisory Council, 'CISG-AC Opinion No. 1 (Revised), Electronic Communications under CISG, (14th October 2024). Rapporteur: Professor Christina Ramberg, Gothenburg, Sweden. Adopted Unanimously by the CISG Advisory Council during its 53th Meeting, in Pavia (Italy), 14–17 October 2024' (2024) comments 5.1–5.2.
[26] *Demex Pty Ltd v John Holland Pty Ltd* [2022] Supreme Court of Queensland QSC 259, CLOUT case 2148.
[27] Ulrich Schroeter, 'Article 15 CISG: Effectiveness and Withdrawability of Offer' in Schwenzer and Schroeter (eds) (n 6) para 2.
[28] *Pork case III* [2006] Oberlandesgericht Dresden (Court of Appeal Dresden) 9 U 0982/06, CISG-online 1625; Ulrich Schroeter, 'Article 24: Definition of "Reaches"' in Schwenzer and Schroeter (eds) (n 6) para 43 ff.

4. Withdrawal

The withdrawal of the offer before or at the same time it reaches the offeree, makes the offer ineffective (Article 15(2) CISG and Article 2.1.3(2) PICC). In practice, this rule is only relevant when the offeror uses a means of communication for the withdrawal that is faster than the means previously used to transmit the offer. The withdrawal must also reach the offeree.[29]

Following this approach and the strict wording of Article 15(2) CISG would mean that if an offer is sent by e-mail or other instantaneous means of communication, it may be virtually impossible for a withdrawal to bypass the offer. The original purpose of Article 15(2) CISG may have been to avoid evidentiary discussion about when the addressee became aware of the offer and to protect the latter's reliance on the same.[30] This sounds fair in times of the ordinary postal system or telegraph. However, nowadays traders can know when an e-mail, for example, has been opened and arguably read by the addressee.[31] As a scholar has pointed out, there is not much fairness in binding an offeror, whose offer sent by e-mail arrived at the addressee's server overnight and the latter took note of it at the same time as the withdrawal, which also arrived during non-business hours.[32] Moreover, new software technology allows recalling or deleting messages from the recipient's electronic inbox before they are even opened or read.[33] The assertion that the reason underlying Article 15(2) CISG is that if the addressee 'becomes aware of' the offer and its withdrawal at the same time, the offer will have been effectively withdrawn,[34] could not be more true today.

5. Revocation

Article 16(1) CISG and Article 2.1.4(1) PICC state that an offer may be revoked if the revocation reaches the offeree before it has dispatched the acceptance.[35] The

---

[29] Schroeter, 'Article 15 CISG: Effectiveness and Withdrawability of Offer' in Schwenzer and Schroeter (eds) (n 6) para 4.

[30] Ingeborg Schwenzer and Florian Mohs, 'Old Habits Die Hard: Traditional Contract Formation in a Modern World' (2006) 6 *Internationales Handelsrecht* 241–2.

[31] For example, Gmail allows you to integrate a read receipt in your e-mails, see Google, 'Request or Return a Read Receipt—Gmail Help' <https://support.google.com/mail/answer/9413651?hl=en> accessed 27 November 2025.

[32] Cesar Pereira and AJ Moniz de Aragão, 'Electronic Communications: Should the CISG Advisory Council Opinion No. 1 (2003) Be Updated?' in Schwenzer and others (eds) *The Electronic CISG: 7th MAA Schlechtriem CISG Conference* (Eleven International Publishing 2017).

[33] For example, Virtru and Zivver are secure e-mail add-ons for Gmail and Outlook that enhance e-mail privacy by adding encryption and advanced access controls. They allow users to revoke access to sent messages, set expiration dates, and disable forwarding—offering a more robust alternative to traditional e-mail recall.

[34] Schwenzer and Mohs (n 30) 242.

[35] *French prêt-à-porter clothing case* [2014] Tribunal de Première Instance de Genève (Court of First Instance Geneva) CISG-online 2714.

revocation of an offer under Article 16 CISG differs in timing and effect from the withdrawal of an offer under Article 15 CISG. Withdrawal occurs before the offer becomes effective, which is when it reaches the offeree; thus, a withdrawn offer never attains legal force. Revocation, on the other hand, applies after the offer has become effective but before it has been accepted, allowing the offeror to revoke unless it is irrevocable, as further discussed below.

The offeror makes its offer binding without the need for 'consideration' (promise of counter-performance from the other party) in the common law sense.[36] The revocation must reach the addressee to be effective under Article 24 CISG. In many instances, even a late withdrawal under Article 15 CISG and Article 2.1.3 PICC can be construed as a revocation if the offeree has not dispatched its acceptance.

The right to revoke the offer might be restricted even before the dispatch of the acceptance. Article 16(2)(a) CISG and Article 2.1.4(2)(a) PICC prevent the offeror from revoking the offer where there is a promise or indication that the offer will not be revoked. The same provisions also consider that fixing a period of time for acceptance might be an indication of the irrevocability of offers. This would be the solution where the parties or the offeree come from legal systems—often of civil law background—that regard an offer made subject to a time limit as binding. This is because Article 8(2) CISG and Article 4.2(2) PICC require that a statement be interpreted in accordance with the understanding of the recipient in the shoes of a reasonable person.[37] However, where the parties or the offeree are from legal systems—usually of common law background— that regard the fixing of a time for acceptance as an indication of the lapse of the offer after that period, such indication by itself might not mean that the offeror intended to be bound for that period; a clearer indication of revocability may be required.[38]

Moreover, pursuant to Article 16(2)(b) CISG and Article 2.1.4(2)(b) PICC, an offer cannot be revoked if it was reasonable for the offeree to rely on the offer as

---

[36] Schroeter, 'Introduction to Articles 14–24 CISG' in Schwenzer and Schroeter (eds) (n 6); Harry M Flechtner, *Honnold's Uniform Law for International Sales Under the 1980 United Nations Convention* (5th edn, Wolters Kluwer 2021) 273 ff.

[37] Ulrich Schroeter, 'Article 16: Revocability of Offer' in Schwenzer and Schroeter (eds) (n 6) para 9 ff. That was indeed the understanding of delegates from civil law jurisdictions during the Vienna Conference. However, delegates from common law jurisdictions, like the United Kingdom proposed an amendment to provide that the starting of a fixed time for acceptance would not of itself indicate that an offer was irrevocable. The UK proposal was never addressed. See United Nations (UN) Conference Official Records, 'Documents of the Conference and Summary Records of the Plenary Meetings and of the Meetings of the Main Committees' (1991) UN Doc A/CONF.97/C.1/SR.9 Consideration of Articles 1–82 of the Draft Convention on Contracts for the International Sale of Goods and of Draft Article 'Declarations Relating to Contracts in Writing' in the Draft Provisions Prepared by the Secretary-General Concerning Implementation, Declarations, Reservations and Other Final Clauses for the Draft Convention (agenda item 3)' (A/CONF.97/5) (continued) [1980].

[38] CISG, art 8(2) and art 16(2)(a).

being irrevocable and the offeree has acted in reliance on the offer.[39] For example, a buyer who receives a detailed and time-sensitive offer may begin arranging financing or securing regulatory approvals in the legitimate expectation that the offer will remain open. This rule finds support in both the common law and the civil law legal traditions. On the one hand, some civil law systems hold offers to be irrevocable for a reasonable period of time, which can give rise to a reliance on the offer as irrevocable in certain fact scenarios involving civil law parties.[40] On the other hand, common law systems, for example the US Restatement Second of Contracts Section 87, hold that reasonable reliance on the offer as irrevocable bars the revocation of offers.[41]

More important for the practice of international commercial contracts, Article 16(2)(b) CISG and Article 2.1.4(2)(b) PICC are an endorsement of the doctrine of estoppel (*venire contra factum proprium* in civil law terms) that has also been expressed in Article 1.8 PICC.[42] These provisions embody the rule that a person should not act in a contradictory manner, and bind a person to its original conduct where such conduct has induced reliance by the other party.

6. Termination

Article 17 CISG and Article 2.1.5 PICC provide that an offer terminates when a rejection by the offeree reaches the offeror. Article 17 CISG specifies that a rejection has such effect on the offer even if the latter was irrevocable.[43] The rejection can be declared expressly or impliedly. Article 8 CISG and Articles 4.1, 4.2, and 4.3 PICC are applied to uncover the intent of the offeree. A purported acceptance that contains additions, limitations or other modifications works as a rejection (Article 19(1) CISG). The rejection must reach the offeror. If the offeree changes its mind and intends to accept a terminated offer, it can make a similar offer to the original offeror. If no time is fixed for acceptance, the offer does not remain open indefinitely; it will be valid only for a reasonable time after reaching the offeree, after which it expires.

---

[39] Schroeter, 'Article 16: Revocability of Offer' in Schwenzer and Schroeter (eds) (n 37) para 36; Christoph Brunner, Stefanie Pfisterer, and Pascale Köster 'Article 16 (Revocability of Offer)' in Christoph Brunner and Benjamin Gottlieb (eds), *Commentary on the UN Sales Law (CISG)* (Kluwer Law International 2019) para 4; Nottage, 'Article 2.1.4' in Vogenauer (ed) (n 3) para 16.

[40] Schwenzer and Muñoz (n 2) para 10.29 ff.

[41] American Law Institute, *Restatement of the Law (2d) of Contracts* (American Law Institute) s 87(2).

[42] Nottage, 'Article 2.1.4' Vogenauer (ed) (n 39) para 16.

[43] *Coöperatieve Federatie van Edelpelsdierenhouders Nederasselt U.A. v Ceva Santé Animale S.A.* [2025] Netherlands Commercial Court, NCC C/13/736825, CISG-online 7354.

III. Acceptance

1. Criteria

Both the CISG and the PICC define an acceptance as the statement made by or other conduct of the offeree indicating assent to the offer.[44] Acceptance by a statement or by conduct must be interpreted under Article 8 CISG and Articles 4.1, 4.2, and 4.3 PICC. The offeree's assent to the offer, that is, an intention to be bound by it and its terms, does not require any specific wording, form, or language.[45] The addressee's indication of assent does not need to mention the word 'acceptance', it could simply assent using other terms.[46]

Examples of acceptance by conduct include the payment of the price,[47] the total or partial dispatch of the goods,[48] or the encashment of a cheque that was sent with the offer.[49] An assent expressed by conduct must reach the offeror to be effective.[50] However, when by virtue of the offer or the practice between the parties, the offeree is entitled to indicate its assent to the offer by performing an act without prior notice to the offeror, the acceptance takes place when the act is performed under Article 18(3) CISG and Article 2.1.6(3) PICC.[51] The conclusion of a contract without an acceptance reaching the offeror under these provisions, may occur only if the offeror has, or must be deemed to have, renounced to receive the acceptance of the offeree. This is because its offer is so provided or because this results from practices established between the parties or usages which are widely known and observed, and of which the offeror could not have been unaware (Article 9 CISG and Article 1.9 PICC).[52]

An acceptance must represent an expression of assent to all the terms proposed by the offeror and must not seek to introduce new terms or change the

---

[44] CISG, art 18; PICC 2016, arts 2.1.6 and 2.1.7; Schwenzer and Muñoz (n 2) para 10.49.

[45] Whether or not the statement or conduct indicates assent is subject to interpretation in accordance with the rules in CISG art 8(1)(2), see e.g. *Twisted yarn case* [2000] Oberlandesgericht Frankfurt am Main (Court of Appeal Frankfurt am Main) 9 U 13/00, CISG-online 594.

[46] Ulrich Schroeter, 'Article 18 CISG: Acceptance and Its Effectiveness' in Schwenzer and Schroeter (eds) (n 6) para 5.

[47] See e.g. *Interland Chemie BV v Tessenderlo Chemie BV* [2008] Rechtbank Breda (District Court Breda) 160136/HA ZA 06-826, CISG-online 2252: holding that an invoice that contained general terms and conditions was accepted when the buyer paid in accordance with art 18(1).

[48] *Paving stones case I* [2014] Cour de Cassation (French Supreme Court) 12-27188, CISG-online 2514: order of 761.60 square metres of paving stones followed by a delivery of 800 square metres of paving stones and partial payment.

[49] See e.g. *Italian marble steps case* [1996] Landgericht Kassel (District Court Kassel) 11 O 4185/95, CISG-online 191.

[50] Schroeter, 'Article 18 CISG: Acceptance and Its Effectiveness' (n 46) para 14.

[51] *Geneva Pharmaceuticals Tech v Barr Laboratories* [2002] US District Court, SD New York 201 F. Supp. 2d 236 (2002): 'industry custom' among US producers of pharmaceuticals and their suppliers; *Insulation material case* [2012] Oberster Gerichtshof (Austrian Supreme Court) 1 Ob 215/12t, CISG-online 2438.

[52] Schroeter, 'Article 18 CISG: Acceptance and its Effectiveness' in Schwenzer and Schroeter (eds) (n 46) para 33 ff; Flechtner, (n 36) 303.

ones in the offer, otherwise the purported acceptance will be treated as a rejection of the original offer, amounting to a counter-offer on the terms set out in the reply.

2. Effectiveness

The moment when the acceptance becomes effective, is very important. A contract is deemed to be concluded at that time under Article 23 CISG.[53] As a general rule, the declaration of acceptance must reach the offeror (Article 18(2) CISG and Article 2.1.6(2) PICC). Exceptionally, the acceptance is effective when the act that indicates acceptance is performed, provided that the requirements laid down in Article 18(3) CISG and Article 2.1.6(3) PICC are met.[54]

With regard to electronic communication the CISG Advisory Council Opinion No. 1 states that an acceptance becomes effective when an electronic indication of assent has entered the offeror's server, provided that the offeror has consented, expressly or impliedly, to receiving electronic communications of that type, in that format, and to that address.[55] Article 10(2) CUECIC follows a similar approach. Under this provision, the time of receipt occurs when the communication becomes capable of being retrieved by the addressee, and this is presumed to take place when it reaches the addressee's electronic address.

The acceptance must reach the offeror within the time or period stated in the offeror, if no time is fixed, within a reasonable time having regard to the circumstances (Article 18(2) CISG and Article 2.1.7 PICC).[56] The rapidity of the means of communication employed by the offeror is one circumstance to consider.

An oral offer must be accepted immediately unless the circumstances indicate otherwise.[57] The term 'oral' includes electronically transmitted sound in real-time.[58] An offer that is transmitted electronically in real-time communication must be accepted immediately unless the circumstances indicate that the addressee rejected, expressly or impliedly to receive communications of that type, in that format, and to that address.[59]

---

[53] *Fertilizantes Tocantins SA v TGO Agriculture (USA), Inc* [2024] US District Court for the Middle District of Florida 8:21-cv-2884-VMC-JSS, CISG-online 6878.

[54] Schroeter, 'Article 18 CISG: Acceptance and its Effectiveness' in Schwenzer and Schroeter (eds) (n 6) para 22.

[55] CISG Advisory Council, 'CISG-AC Opinion No. 1 (Revised)' (n 25) Black Letter Rule 2.

[56] Schwenzer and Muñoz (n 2) paras 10.49, 10.60.

[57] CISG, art 18(2); PICC 2016, art 2.1.7.

[58] CISG Advisory Council, 'CISG-AC Opinion No. 1 (Revised)' (n 25) Black Letter Rule 6.

[59] Ibid Black Letter Rule 2.

3. Silence and inactivity

Silence or inactivity in themselves do not amount to an acceptance for the purposes of the CISG or the PICC (Article 18(1) CISG and Article 2.1.6(1) PICC). Silence, in conjunction with other circumstances, however, could indicate acceptance, without a statement to that effect having reached the offeror.[60] If acceptance through silence or inactivity has become a valid practice or usage between the parties, it will lead to a binding agreement pursuant to Article 9 CISG and Article 1.9 PICC.[61] A possible example may be commercial letters of confirmation, which require rejection as a matter of usage in some industries or regions; otherwise, the contract is concluded under the terms offered therein.[62]

4. Mirror image rule

As a starting point, the CISG and the PICC follow the so-called 'mirror-image doctrine' as the main rule for contract formation in Article 19(1) CISG and Article 2.1.11(1) PICC. According to this rule, a contract is concluded if the acceptance completely matches the terms of the offer. This means that an acceptance must represent an expression of consent to all the terms proposed by the offeror and must not seek to change them or introduce new terms. If there is a divergence between the offer and the acceptance, the purported acceptance is considered a rejection of the original offer coupled with a new offer or a counter-offer, which needs to be accepted to conclude a contract.[63]

The exception to this rule is found in Article 19(2) CISG and Article 2.1.11(2) PICC. Herein, a reply to an offer that purports to be an acceptance but contains additional or different terms that do not materially alter the offer is considered as an acceptance, unless the offeror objects to it without undue delay, either orally or in writing. The distinction between material and immaterial terms is intended to counter the danger that, where merely minor differences exist between an offer and its acceptance, the mirror-image rule could be used to reject immaterial obligations by arguing that no contract had been formed.[64]

---

[60] *German health care products case II* [2008] Najvyšší súd Slovenskej republiky (Supreme Court of the Slovak Republic) 6 Obo 15/2008, CISG-online 1875.

[61] Schwenzer and others (n 18) 143; Andrea Fejős, 'Battle of the Forms under the Convention on Contracts for the International Sale of Goods (CISG): A Uniform Solution?' 11 *Vindobona Journal of International Commercial Law and Arbitration* 113, 115.

[62] Schroeter, 'Article 18 CISG: Acceptance and its Effectiveness' in Schwenzer and Schroeter (eds) (n 6) para 46.

[63] Schwenzer and Muñoz (n 2) 10.67; International Institute for the Unification of Private Law (n 21) 50, art 2.1.11, off cmt 2.

[64] Ulrich Schroeter, 'Article 19 CISG: Acceptance Modifying the Offer (Including "Battle of Forms")' in Schwenzer and Schroeter (eds) (n 6) para 6 ff.

Articles 19(3) CISG provides a non-exhaustive list of the terms that are deemed to operate as material changes: the price, payment, quality, and quantity of the goods, place and time of delivery, extent of one party's liability to the other or the settlement of disputes. The provision only sets up interpretative presumptions or guidelines for determining materiality. This means that, it may be possible to prove that a change in a term presumed to be material pursuant to Article 19(3) CISG is not material having regard to the facts of the individual case, the practices of the parties, preliminary negotiations, or a binding usage and vice versa.[65] There are additional modifications that are not listed in Article 19(3) CISG which may be regarded as material, depending on the circumstances of the individual case. These include a reference to a new set of standard terms;[66] a choice of law clause that would lead to the application of a law that would not be applicable absent that choice;[67] a proposed exclusion of the CISG's application by virtue of Article 6 CISG;[68] differences in respect of a contractual preclusion of set-offs have also been held to be material; the delivery date[69] and the limitation of the time for rejection of the goods to 30 days after the invoice date.[70] In the end, there will be hardly any deviation that is not deemed to be material under Article 19(3) CISG.

Article 2.1.11 PICC does not contain a similar provision. Its Official Comment acknowledges that what amounts to a material alteration cannot be determined in the abstract but will depend on the circumstances of the specific case. The Comment also provides a list of broad examples that mirror those listed in Article 19(3) CISG and advises considering whether the additional terms will come as a surprise in the relevant trade sector.[71] In the end, one might hardly think of a modification that is not material.

IV. Electronic Contracting

The use of electronic communications in the conclusion of international commercial contracts is no longer a novelty but a constant reality. The UNCITRAL Model

---

[65] Martin Schmidt-Kessel, 'Article 8 CISG: Interpretation of Parties' Statements or Conduct' in Schwenzer and Schroeter (eds) (n 6) para 31; Schroeter, 'Article 19 CISG: Acceptance Modifying the Offer (Including "Battle of Forms")' in Schwenzer and Schroeter (eds) (n 6) para 30.

[66] Schroeter, 'Article 19 CISG: Acceptance Modifying the Offer (Including 'Battle of Forms')' in Schwenzer and Schroeter (eds) (n 6) para 17.

[67] Franco Ferrari and Marco Torsello, *International Sales Law: CISG in a Nutshell* (2nd edn, West Academic Publishing 2018) 153.

[68] Schroeter, 'Article 19 CISG: Acceptance Modifying the Offer (Including "Battle of Forms")' in Schwenzer and Schroeter (eds) (n 6) para 17.

[69] *Ford Escort Cabrio case* [1999] 9 Zivilsenat (9th panel for civil matters) 9 U 146/98, CISG-online 512.

[70] *Wall tiles case* [1991] Landgericht Baden-Baden (District Court Baden-Baden) 4 O 113/90, CISG-online 24.

[71] International Institute for the Unification of Private Law (n 21) art 2.1.11, off cmt 2.

Law on Electronic Commerce 1996 (MLEC) (additions of 1998) and the United Nations Convention on the Use of Electronic Communications in International Contracts (ECC) of 2005 were prepared by UNCITRAL with the goal of assuring that the domestic and international contracts that were concluded, and other communications exchanged in the same context, were as valid and enforceable as their traditional paper-based equivalents. Both instruments are based upon three fundamental principles of electronic commerce legislation: non-discrimination, technological neutrality, and functional equivalence.

Article 8 ECC ensures non-discrimination, providing that communications are not to be denied legal validity solely on the grounds that they were made in electronic form.[72] Article 12 ECC guarantees the enforceability of contracts that are entered into by automated message systems, including situations when no natural person has reviewed the individual actions carried out by her. Article 8 ECC recognizes the equivalence between electronic communications and paper documents as well as between electronic authentication methods and handwritten signatures.

As commented above, the ECC defines the time and place of dispatch and receipt of electronic communications that are important in forming contracts, and in the context of other obligations requiring a party to communicate with the other party. In general terms, Article 10 ECC states that dispatch takes place when an electronic communication leaves an information system under the control of the originator, while receipt takes place when the addressee becomes capable of retrieving the electronic communication at a designated electronic address. An electronic communication is presumed to be capable of being retrieved when it reaches the addressee's electronic address. Article 10 ECC also states that an electronic communication is dispatched at the place where the originator has its place of business and is deemed to be received at the place where the addressee has its place of business.

Some have argued that the provisions of the ECC and the MLEC should influence the interpretation and be considered in the integration of other uniform law instruments like the CISG.[73] However, this approach should not be followed because it would violate the rule of autonomous interpretation in Article 7(1) CISG.[74] ECC and other rules on e-commerce may, of course, apply to questions outside the CISG's scope of application or questions not settled by it pursuant to Article 7(2) CISG.[75]

---

[72] *Tomich v Crosstown Holdings Pty Ltd* [2020] Supreme Court of Western Australia Case No. CIV 3054 of 2019, CLOUT case 1911: where the Court recognized formal validity to a communication via e-mail exercising the option to renew a lease agreement.

[73] See generally Pereira and Moniz de Aragão (n 32).

[74] Pascal Hachem, 'Article 7 CISG: Interpretation of the Convention and Gap-Filling' in Schwenzer and Schroeter (eds) (n 6) para 25 ff.

[75] Ibid para 27 ff.

The provisions of the CISG are applicable to and appropriate for the formation of contracts in the digital world. Notably, the CISG was drafted in the 1970s when trade actors could not have anticipated the commercial and technological innovations of the 1990s.[76] However, the drafters did not wish to impose restrictions to the conclusion of CISG contracts—for example, a writing requirement, which explains the primary rule under Article 11 CISG that the existence of the contract 'may be proven by any means'.[77] This has turned out to be a positive feature of incorporating newer means for contract formation. This can also be deducted from Article 13 CISG, which anticipates the principle of functional equivalence.[78]

The CISG Advisory Revised Opinion No. 1 has clarified some of the issues arising from the use of electronic communications. As commented above, the term 'reaches' corresponds to the point in time when an electronic communication becomes capable of being retrieved by the addressee.[79] An acceptance becomes effective when an electronic indication of assent has entered the offeror's server, provided that the offeror has consented, expressly or impliedly, to receiving electronic communications of that type, in that format, and to that address; the term 'oral' includes any electronic communication that is instantaneous and simultaneous when the parties are aware that they are simultaneously communicating and they have a possibility to respond immediately,[80] and so on.

The CISG provides for a complete regulation and pre-empts the concurrent provisions on domestic law, despite the fact that it reflects the provisions of the ECC and the MLEC.[81]

V. Inclusion of Standard Terms, Including Battle of Forms

The content of the CISG and the PICC contracts may not be set out only in the wording of the offer itself. Negotiating parties often refer to standard business terms, general conditions, technical norms, or other pre-established documents whose text is not printed in the offer or acceptance. The use of these standardized documents has increased due to electronic means of communication that facilitate their storage and dissemination.[82] Their practical importance is evident in today's

---

[76] See generally United Nations (UN) Conference Official Records, 'Documents of the Conference and Summary Records of the Plenary Meetings and of the Meetings of the Main Committees' (1991) UN Doc A/CONF.97/19.

[77] *Xiamen ITG Group Corp, Ltd v Peace Bird Trading Corp et al.* [2024] US District Court for the Eastern District of New York 19-CV-6524 (DLI) (ST), CISG-online 7182.

[78] Martin Schmidt-Kessel, 'Article 13 CISG: Definition of "Writing"' in Schwenzer and Schroeter (eds) (n 6) paras 8–9, 11.

[79] CISG Advisory Council, 'CISG-AC Opinion No. 1 (Revised)' (n 25) Black Letter Rule 5.

[80] Ibid Black Letter Rule 6.

[81] Schroeter, 'Introduction to Articles 14–24 CISG' in Schwenzer and Schroeter (eds) (n 6) para 74.

[82] Zachariasiewicz Maciej, 'Inclusion of Standard Terms in Electronic Form under the CISG' in Schwenzer and others (eds) (n 32) 96.

international trade, and thus, uniform law instruments have a role in determining when and how such terms become part of the contract.

1. Inclusion of standard terms

Article 2.1.19 PICC, as well as the CISG Advisory Council Opinion No. 13,[83] define standard terms as provisions prepared in advance for general and repeated use by one party and used without negotiation with the other party. Standard terms serve as a 'useful tool' in the bustling nature of international trade.[84] While the CISG does not have a specific provision on the incorporation of standard terms into the contract like the PICC does in Articles 2.1.19 to 2.1.22, it is commonly agreed that the CISG governs this matter in Articles 14 *et seq.* in conjunction with Articles 8 and 9.[85]

Standard terms must be made part of the offer or the counter-offer to be incorporated into the contract.[86] They can become part of the offer by reference (Articles 8(1) and 8(2) CISG), by practices between the parties, or by trade usage (Article 9 CISG and Article 1.9 PICC). Standard terms referred to after the formation of the contract are regarded as an offer to modify an already existing contract (under Article 29 CISG and Article 2.1.18 PICC).[87]

The offeror's intention to incorporate its standard terms must be apparent to the recipient. The offeror must express a discernible intent to do so, in a way that the other party under the given circumstances, knew or could not have been reasonably unaware of such intent.[88] A German Court of Appeals, dealing with a contract governed by the CISG, found that a reference made in a pre-contractual communication months before the conclusion of the contract, and not in the offer or acceptance itself, did not show a party's intent to incorporate its standard conditions pursuant to Article 8(2) and (3) CISG.[89]

---

[83] CISG Advisory Council, 'CISG-AC Opinion No. 13 Inclusion of Standard Terms under the CISG, Rapporteur: Professor Sieg Eiselen, College of Law, University of South Africa, Pretoria, South Africa, January 20 2013' (2013) comment 1.

[84] *DG Belgrano SA v Procter & Gamble Argentina SRL* [2013] Cámara Nacional de Apelaciones en lo Comercial.

[85] Michael G Bridge, *The International Sale of Goods* (4th edn, Oxford University Press 2017) 542–3.

[86] Schwenzer and Muñoz (n 2) para 12.06; Schroeter, 'Article 14 CISG: Offer (Including Incorporation of Standard Terms)' in Schwenzer and Schroeter (eds) (n 6) para 32 ff.

[87] Schroeter, 'Article 19 CISG: Acceptance Modifying the Offer (Including "Battle of Forms")' in Schwenzer and Schroeter (eds) (n 6) para 40; CISG Advisory Council, 'CISG-AC Opinion No. 13' (n 83) Black Letter Rule 4.

[88] CISG Advisory Council, 'CISG-AC Opinion No. 13' (n 83) Black Letter Rule 2.

[89] *MITEC Automotive AG v Ford Motor Company* [2010] Oberlandesgericht Jena (Court of Appeal Jena) 7 U 303/10, CISG-online 2216; Schroeter, 'Article 14 CISG: Offer (Including Incorporation of Standard Terms)' in Schwenzer and Schroeter (eds) (n 6) para 37.

The incorporation of standard terms could take place by reference in the offer.[90] Neither the CISG nor the PICC establish specific requirements as to the form or style of the reference to the standard terms themselves. However, Article 8(2) CISG and Article 4.2 PICC require that the reference be clear enough so that a reasonable person in the shoes of the recipient would understand its application.[91] Article 2.1.20 PICC stipulates that the language and presentation of standard terms could render them, or at least some of its individual terms, ineffective.[92] When the reference to the standard terms is made in a language that the other party does not understand or is different from the one in which the contract was drafted, the incorporation does not take place.[93]

Proper incorporation also requires that the addressee has a reasonable opportunity to take note of, and understand the standard terms.[94] A German District Court, in another CISG case, found that there had not been an effective inclusion of the standard terms because although the offeror had made a clear and understandable reference to its application, the transmission of the text of the terms was only to be effected upon request.[95]

If the offer is made by e-mail, it is enough that the text is contained in an attachment.[96] Moreover, the condition of 'making the standard terms' text otherwise available' is met if their text is available on the Internet when the contract was concluded through the same means.[97] Whether a link to a website containing the standard terms is enough for the purpose of incorporation must be decided on the facts and circumstances of each case.[98] The user should not be forced to conduct an extensive search for the terms by clicking through multiple pages, browsing through complicated lists of various terms, or having to decide which of the many

---

[90] *Propane gas case* [1996] Oberster Gerichtshof (Austrian Supreme Court) 10 Ob 518/95, CISG-online 224; Schroeter, 'Article 14 CISG: Offer (Including Incorporation of Standard Terms)' in Schwenzer and Schroeter (eds) (n 6) para 32; CISG Advisory Council, 'CISG-AC Opinion No. 13' (n 83) comment 2.7.

[91] Schroeter, 'Article 14 CISG: Offer (Including Incorporation of Standard Terms)' in Schwenzer and Schroeter (eds) (n 6) para 137.

[92] Tjakie Naudé, 'Article 2.1.20' in Vogenauer (ed) (n 3) para 14.

[93] *Car phones case* [2004] Oberlandesgericht Düsseldorf (Court of Appeal Düsseldorf) I-15 U 88/03, CISG-online 915.

[94] Ulrich Magnus, 'Incorporation of Standard Terms' in Larry A DiMatteo and others (eds), *International Sales Law: Contract, Principles & Practice* (CH Beck 2016) 248.

[95] *Material for metal covers case* [2008] Landgericht Landshut (District Court Landshut) 43 O 1748/07, CISG-online 1703.

[96] *Golden Valley Grape Juice and Wine, LLC v Centriys Corporation/Centriys Corporation v Separator Technology Solutions Pty Ltd* [2010] US District Court, Eastern District of California CV F 09-1424 LJO GSA; CISG Advisory Council, 'CISG-AC Opinion No. 13' (n 83) comment 2.11.

[97] Schroeter, 'Article 14 CISG: Offer (Including Incorporation of Standard Terms)' in Schwenzer and Schroeter (eds) (n 6) para 158 ff; CISG Advisory Council, 'CISG-AC Opinion No. 13' (n 83) comments 3.3–3.4.

[98] Schroeter, 'Article 14 CISG: Offer (Including Incorporation of Standard Terms)' in Schwenzer and Schroeter (eds) (n 6) para 158 ff; CISG Advisory Council, 'CISG-AC Opinion No. 13' (n 83) Black Letter Rule 3, comment 3.5.

terms the offeror has used to apply to the contract in question.[99] The burden of proof of the incorporation of such terms falls on the party who benefits from such incorporation.[100]

Prior practices between the parties might result in the incorporation of standard terms into an international contract.[101] In the CISG *Propane gas* case, the Austrian Supreme Court considered that unless there was evidence that the buyer had obtained, and was willing to enter into prior contracts on the basis of the sellers' standard terms, the latter could not be incorporated into the contract pursuant to Article 9(1) CISG.[102]

Moreover, Article 2.1.21 PICC provides that individually agreed-upon terms take precedence over standard terms since the former are more likely to reflect the parties' intentions than the latter.[103] CISG Advisory Council Opinion No. 13, endorses this rule.[104]

Whereas the incorporation of standard terms is covered by the CISG, validity issues fall outside the scope of the CISG.[105] Even the PICC do not contain specific provisions on the validity of standard terms.[106] Nonetheless, the PICC govern the validity of the content of the terms in specific cases. For instance, Article 7.1.6 PICC invalidates any clause which limits or excludes one party's liability for non-performance, or which permits one party to render performance substantially different from what the other party reasonably expected. In addition, Article 3.2.7 PICC allows a party to avoid the contract if any of the individual clauses gives one party an excessive advantage in an unjustifiable manner.

2. Battle of forms

The so-called battle of the forms is the situation in which the parties to an agreement try to incorporate their respective standard terms of business into their

---

[99] *Roser Technologies, Inc v Carl Schreiber GmbH* [2013] US District Court for the Western District of Pennsylvania 11cv302 ERIE, CISG-online 2490; Maciej (n 82); CISG Advisory Council, 'CISG-AC Opinion No. 13' (n 83) comment 3.4.

[100] *NF Smith & Associates, LP v Karl Kruse GmbH & Co KG* [2023] US District Court for the Southern District of Texas 4:22-CV-3877, CISG-online 6627.

[101] Schmidt-Kessel, 'Article 8 CISG: Interpretation of Parties' Statements or Conduct' in Schwenzer and Schroeter (eds) (n 6) para 56.

[102] *Propane gas case* (n 90).

[103] Naudé, 'Article 2.1.20' in Vogenauer (ed) (n 92).

[104] Schroeter, 'Article 14 CISG: Offer (Including Incorporation of Standard Terms)' in Schwenzer and Schroeter (eds) (n 6) para 158 ff; CISG Advisory Council, 'CISG-AC Opinion No. 13' (n 83) Black Letter Rule 8; see also Schmidt-Kessel, 'Article 8 CISG: Interpretation of Parties' Statements or Conduct' in Schwenzer and Schroeter (eds) (n 6) para 64; International Institute for the Unification of Private Law (n 21) 71–2, art 2.1.21.

[105] Franco Ferrari, 'Article 14' in Stefan M Kröll, Loukas A Mistelis, and Pilar Perales Viscasillas (eds), *UN Convention on Contracts for the International Sale of Goods (CISG): A Commentary* (2nd edn, CH Beck 2018) para 42.

[106] Naudé, 'Introduction to Arts 2.1.19–2.1.22' Vogenauer (ed) (n 3) para 1 ff.

declarations during the contract formation process.[107] The buyer's and the seller's standard terms typically differ considerably. Imagine that the buyer makes an offer through a purchase order that contains the contract's essential terms and refers to its standard conditions as well. In turn, the seller answers with an invoice or an agreement to sell, which also refers to its own standard conditions. Subsequently, the contract is performed without incident, until a dispute arises.

Was a contract formed? Which standard terms apply? The dispute regarding the formation of the contract and which of the two (or more) sets of standard conditions govern the contract in a 'battle of the forms' case has been addressed in different ways, which lead to diverse practical outcomes. This section will review the solutions proposed by the CISG and the PICC to this problem.

a.) Battle of forms under the CISG

A strict application of the mirror-image rule in Article 19 CISG would entail that if an acceptance includes a set of standard terms that are materially different from the standard terms previously incorporated into the offer, no contract is concluded, unless there are immaterial differences between the two sets, which rarely occurs.

In a battle of forms scenario, the strict application of Article 19 CISG should be rejected. The performance of the contract indicates that the offer was accepted, and therefore, the contract was concluded. Differences in the standard terms may only become relevant in the event of a dispute; parties are usually unaware of the contradictions between their general conditions and are more interested in the essential elements of their bargain.[108]

The battle of the forms must be solved according to the provisions and principles on which the CISG is based. One of the solutions might be found in Article 19 CISG, which endorses the so-called last-shot doctrine: the prevailing terms are those of the final communication used without being objected to and thus being accepted by the other party.[109] An important factual element advocating for this solution is that acceptance can occur, and often does occur, by conduct under Article 18 CISG; for example, by making delivery, paying the purchase price, or taking delivery of the goods.[110] If no performance of the contract is effected or an objection is raised, no contract is concluded.[111]

[107] Bruno Zeller, 'The CISG and the Battle of the Forms' in Larry A DiMatteo (ed), *International Sales Law: A Global Challenge* (Cambridge University Press 2014) 203 ff. See e.g. *New Excelsior, Inc v Amut Dolci Bielloni S.r.l* [2022] US District Court for the Western District of North Carolina 1:21-cv-193-MOC, CISG-online 6122; *Robert Weed Plywood Corp v Canusa Wood Products, Ltd* [2023] US District Court for the Northern District of Indiana 3:23-CV-30 RLM-MGG, CISG-online 6675.
[108] Schroeter, 'Article 19 CISG: Acceptance Modifying the Offer (Including "Battle of Forms")' in Schwenzer and Schroeter (eds) (n 6) para 73 ff.
[109] Schroeter, 'Article 19 CISG: Acceptance Modifying the Offer (Including "Battle of Forms")' in Schwenzer and Schroeter (eds) (n 6) para 84; Franco Ferrari, 'Article 19' in Kröll, Mistelis, and Viscasillas (eds) (n 105) para 15.
[110] Patrick Ostendorf, *International Sales Terms* (3rd edn, CH Beck 2018) 60.
[111] Schwenzer and Muñoz (n 2) para 12.28.

A US District Court has supported this solution, noting that the purported acceptance had materially altered the terms of the offer, and that therefore it was not an acceptance but a counter-offer, which was accepted by the offeror by executing the bills of sale. Accordingly, the prevailing terms were the ones proposed in the counter-offer.[112] Similarly, an Appellate Court in Germany found that the standard conditions sent last became a part of the sales contract since they had not been objected to and the other party had paid the invoice.[113]

An alternative solution is to apply the so-called knock-out rule. Under this solution, if there is an agreement on the essential terms of the contract and there is a mutual intention to be bound—demonstrated by the interpretation of the parties' statements or their conduct—it is assumed that the contract was formed without the colliding clauses, meaning that the inconsistent aspects of the seller's and buyer's standard terms cancel out each other.[114] In a CISG context, the knock-out rule was first applied by the French Supreme Court in 1998[115] and has since been followed by several courts.[116] Nowadays, there is a developing preference for the application of this solution.[117]

The knock-out rule results in the contract being formed by the terms on which there is an agreement, by the individually negotiated terms, the conditions of the standard forms that are common in substance, and the pertinent practices and trade usages.[118] The remaining gaps in the agreement are filled in by the provisions of the CISG.

The basis for this approach is the principle of party autonomy in Article 6 CISG, which is key in determining the content of the contract, and enables the parties to derogate from or vary the effect of any of the provisions of the CISG.[119] By virtue of this principle, one can assume that the parties have departed from the Convention's rules on contract formation, which are by nature dispositive, and in

---

[112] *Norfolk Southern Railway Co v Power Source Supply, Inc* [2008] US District Court for the Western District of Pennsylvania 07-140-JJf, CISG-online 1776.

[113] *Concrete slabs case* [2002] Oberlandesgericht Koblenz (Court of Appeal Koblenz) 8 U 1909/01, CISG-online 716.

[114] *Powdered milk case* [2002] Bundesgerichtshof (German Supreme Court) VIII ZR 304/00. CISG-online 651; Zeller, 'The CISG and the Battle of the Forms' in DiMatteo (ed) (n 107) 203 ff; CISG Advisory Council, 'CISG-AC Opinion No. 13 Inclusion of Standard Terms under the CISG' (n 83) comments 10.5–10.8.

[115] *Les Verreries de Saint Gobain SA v Martinswerk GmbH* [1998] Cour de Cassation (French Supreme Court) 96-11.984, CISG-online 344.

[116] Schroeter, 'Article 19 CISG: Acceptance Modifying the Offer (Including "Battle of Forms")' in Schwenzer and Schroeter (eds) (n 6) para 89. See e.g. *Powdered milk case* (n 114); *Rubber sealing members case* [2003] Oberlandesgericht Düsseldorf (Court of Appeal Düsseldorf) I-17 U 22/03, CISG-online 919; *Hanwha Corp. v Cedar Petrochemicals, Inc.* (n 21).

[117] Schwenzer and Muñoz (n 2) para 12.30; Naudé, 'Article 2.1.22' in Vogenauer (ed) (n 3); Schroeter, 'Article 19 CISG: Acceptance Modifying the Offer (Including 'Battle of Forms')' in Schwenzer and Schroeter (eds) (n 6) para 92.

[118] Schroeter, 'Article 19 CISG: Acceptance Modifying the Offer (Including 'Battle of Forms')' in Schwenzer and Schroeter (eds) (n 6) para 89; Ferrari, 'Article 19' in Kröll, Mistelis, and Viscasillas (eds) (n 105) para 15.

[119] Schroeter, 'Introduction to Articles 14–24 CISG' in Schwenzer and Schroeter (eds) (n 6) para 77.

particular, from Article 19 CISG which would require one of the parties' terms to apply. The approach assumes that if one of the parties wanted the application of its terms to be a condition *sine qua non* for the contract's conclusion, it would not have started performance of the contract.[120]

As put by the CISG Advisory Council in Opinion No. 13 'the knock-out rule has the advantage that it is in conformity with the intention of typical parties in international commercial relations and leads to acceptable results in cross-border trade situations. The rule avoids an arbitrary choice between the two sets of competing standard terms, instead using only those elements which are common to both sets. This accords with the actual intention of both parties.'[121] The leading CISG case endorsing this rule is the *Powdered milk case* decided by Germany's Supreme Court.[122]

b.) Battle of forms under the PICC

As previously mentioned, the rules on contract formation of the PICC take those in the CISG as a model.[123] However, unlike the latter, the PICC contain a specific provision regulating the battle of the forms in Article 2.1.22 PICC, which follows the knock-out doctrine: if the parties reach an agreement except on their standard conditions, the contract is concluded and is considered binding on them. In this case, the terms of the contract consist of the individually agreed terms and the standard terms that are common in substance.[124] In order to determine whether standard terms are 'common in substance', regard should be paid to the purpose and effect of a term, and not merely to its formulation.[125]

To fill in the gaps in the contract, the adjudicator must consider what the parties may have agreed to in framework agreements, established practices, or usages. In the absence of those criteria, the default rules of the PICC are applicable.[126]

The knock-out effect can be avoided if a party indicates, before the conclusion of the contract, that it does not intend to be bound unless its own standard terms apply.[127] What amounts to a 'clear' indication in that respect cannot be stated in absolute terms. The inclusion of such clause in the standard terms will not normally be sufficient, since a specific declaration in the offer or acceptance may be required.[128]

---

[120] Ibid.
[121] CISG Advisory Council, 'CISG-AC Opinion No. 13' (n 83) comment 10.6.
[122] *Powdered milk case* (n 114).
[123] María del Pilar Perales Viscasillas, '"Battle of the Forms" under the 1980 United Nations Convention on Contracts for the International Sale of Goods: A Comparison with Section 2-207 UCC and the UNIDROIT Principles' (1998) 10 *Pace International Law Review* 97, 131.
[124] International Institute for the Unification of Private Law (n 21) 73, off cmt 3.
[125] Naudé, 'Article 2.1.21' in Vogenauer (ed) (n 3) para 8.
[126] Ibid para 9.
[127] Ibid para 15.
[128] International Institute for the Unification of Private Law (n 21) 74, off cmt 3.

VI. Pre-contractual Duties

When parties commence the negotiation of a deal, they are neither strangers to each other any longer nor are they parties to the contract yet, which is required for the law to trigger all the rights and duties envisaged by a contractual relationship. Anything that happens during this grey area could be addressed either from the tort law perspective[129] or by means of specific provisions or principles imposing certain pre-contractual duties and liabilities. Some civil law systems, for example, have developed theories known as *culpa in contrahendo* (fault in negotiating), requiring the parties to negotiate in good faith, not to break off negotiations abruptly, to share relevant information, and to keep it confidential.[130] These principles have often turned into legislative rules in many civil law jurisdictions.[131] Some common law systems consider this issue in the context of rules and theories of misrepresentation.[132] In Australia[133] and the United States,[134] these questions may also be addressed by the notion of promissory or equitable estoppel.[135]

At the international level, the CISG does not contain any provision relating to pre-contractual duties and liabilities.[136] Pre-contractual relations are closely related to the CISG. While no express rules on this matter are contained in this treaty, a careful development of its provisions could be made to govern some questions that would otherwise be left to the realm of domestic law. The approach would ensure its uniform application under Article 7 CISG.[137]

However, it will not be possible to construct a comprehensive system of pre-contractual duties out of CISG principles. These matters are primarily governed by domestic law or other applicable international instruments.[138] That does not mean, however, that every pre-contractual duty of the underlying domestic law will apply to a CISG contract. The CISG may pre-empt the application of domestic *culpa in contrahendo* provisions in questions expressly or impliedly dealt with by the CISG.[139] For instance, some domestic rules on negligent misrepresentation about

---

[129] See e.g. French Code of Civil Procedure art 1382.

[130] Schwenzer and Muñoz (n 2) paras 23.01–23.10; Gerhard Dannemann, 'Choice of CESL and Conflict of Laws' in Gerhard Dannemann and Stefan Vogenauer (eds), *The Common European Sales Law in Context: Interactions with English and German Law* (Oxford University Press 2013) 47–9.

[131] Schwenzer and Muñoz (n 2) 23.01–23.10.

[132] Ibid.

[133] *Waltons Stores (Interstate) Ltd v Maher* [1988] High Court of Australia 164 CLR 387; *Thompson v Palmer* [1933] High Court of Australia [1933] HCA 61, 49 CLR 507.

[134] See e.g. *Prenger v Baumhoer* [1997] Missouri Court of Appeals, Western 939 S.W.2d 23; *Hoffman v Red Owl Stores, Inc* [1965] Supreme Court of Wisconsin 26 Wis. 2d 683, 133 NW 2d 267; American Law Institute (n 41) ss 205, 90.

[135] Schwenzer and Muñoz (n 2) 23.01–23.10.

[136] See generally United Nations Doc A/CONF.97/19 (n 76) 295; Schwenzer and Mohs (n 30). .

[137] See generally Lisa Spagnolo, 'Opening Pandora's Box: Good Faith and Precontractual Liability in the CISG' (2007) 21 *Temple International and Comparative Law Journal* 261.

[138] Pascal Hachem, 'Article 4 CISG: Substantive Scope of Convention' in Schwenzer and Schroeter (eds) (n 6) para 18.

[139] Schroeter, 'Introduction to Articles 14–24 CISG' in Schwenzer and Schroeter (eds) (n 6) para 124.

either the goods delivered or the solvency of a party cannot apply to a CISG contract because these matters are regulated by the Convention's provisions on conformity of the goods (Article 35 CISG) or anticipatory breach (Article 71 CISG).

Conversely, the PICC contain specific rules regarding negotiations in bath faith and the duty of confidentiality.[140]

1. Breaking off negotiations

The primary rule is that the parties are free to negotiate and are not liable for failure to reach an agreement. Article 2.1.15(1) PICC expresses this rule, which can also be inferred from the principle of freedom of contract in Article 6 CISG, as well as—more strongly still—from the general right to revoke an offer in Article 16(1) CISG.[141]

That being said, Article 2.1.15(2) PICC states that a party who negotiates or breaks off negotiations in bad faith is liable for the losses caused to the other party.[142] This PICC rule rests on the duty to act in good faith and fair dealing stated in Article 1.7 PICC and that is, perhaps, mainly a principle of the civil law tradition.[143] The PICC specify neither the type of liability that arises from the breach of this provision, that is, contractual or tortious liability, nor the type of indemnity, that is, reliance or expectation interest that the aggrieved party is entitled to. However, the Official Comment on this provision states that the aggrieved party may recover the expenses incurred in the negotiations and may also be compensated for the lost opportunity to conclude another contract with a third person (reliance interest, and *perte d'une chance*), but may generally not recover the profit which would have resulted on the conclusion of the original contract.[144] A significant distinction under the CISG is that it permits each party to terminate negotiations at its discretion without incurring any liability.

Because the application of the PICC requires that a contract first exist and that it be subjected to the PICC,[145] Article 2.1.15 PICC has limited application when compared with other pre-contractual duties and other liability provisions of domestic character. However, it could still apply to preliminary agreements, in the context of avoidance claims based on fraud, gross disparity, etc., and other similar events prior to the conclusion of the contract.[146]

---

[140] Ibid para 125 ff. By contrast, the PICC allow for damages in cases of bad faith, see International Institute for the Unification of Private Law (n 21) art 2.1.15 (2).

[141] Schroeter, 'Introduction to Articles 14–24 CISG' in Schwenzer and Schroeter (eds) (n 6) para 130.

[142] *Vš v AN, AN* [2006] Supreme Court of Lithuania 3K-P-382/2006.

[143] Zuloaga Rios, 'Article 2.1.15' in Vogenauer (ed) (n 3) paras 2–3. For the principle of freedom of contract, see Flechtner, (n 36) 132 ff.

[144] International Institute for the Unification of Private Law (n 21) art 2.1.15, off cmt 2; Rios, 'Article 2.1.15' in Vogenauer (ed) (n 3) 26 ff.

[145] PICC 2016, Preamble para 2.

[146] Ross G Anderson, 'Article 2.1.14' in Vogenauer (ed) (n 3) paras 30, 34.

The first situation that might trigger pre-contractual liability involves a party that enters into negotiations or continues to negotiate without any intention of concluding an agreement with the other party (Article 2.1.15(3) PICC). Other situations include a party that has revoked an irrevocable offer under the terms of the PICC[147] and a party that has deliberately or by negligence misled the other party as to the nature or terms of the proposed contract, either by actually misrepresenting facts or by not disclosing facts which, given the nature of the parties and/or the contract, should have been disclosed.[148] Ultimately, a bad faith break off will depend on the circumstances of the case.[149] It depends in particular on the extent to which the aggrieved party had reason to rely on the positive outcome of the negotiations as a result of the conduct of the breaking-off party,[150] and on the number of issues relating to the future contract on which the parties had already reached an agreement.[151]

2. Confidentiality

Article 2.1.16 PICC requires a party not to disclose confidential information obtained from the other party during the negotiations. Particularly, where information is given as confidential, parties should not disclose that information or use it improperly for their own purposes. The fact that the contract is finally concluded does not attenuate this rule. Again, this duty in the PICC is supported by the general duty of good faith in Article 1.7 PICC.[152] The CISG does not impose this duty.

This rule applies so long as a party declares that the information concerned is confidential.[153] In some industries, the conclusion of non-disclosure agreements that define confidential information and govern its use and treatment, during and after the negotiations, is standard practice. In that case, Article 2.1.16 PICC would usually take the second position after the non-disclosure or confidential agreement and it may only supplement the agreement, if necessary.[154]

Absent a confidentiality agreement or an express declaration that the information provided be treated as confidential, a duty of confidentiality may be implied from conduct and from the circumstances of the case under Articles 4.2 and 4.3 PICC.[155] Confidential information, in general terms, regards technical, strategic,

---

[147] Nottage, 'Article 2.1.4' in Vogenauer (ed) (n 3) 16.
[148] International Institute for the Unification of Private Law (n 21) art 2.1.15, off cmt 2.
[149] Hugh G Beale and others, *Cases, Materials and Text on Contract Law* (3rd edn, Hart Publishing 2018) 413–14.
[150] International Institute for the Unification of Private Law (n 21) art 1.8.
[151] Ibid art 2.1.15, off cmt 3.
[152] Ibid art 1.7, off cmt 1; ibid 2.1.16, Illustrations 1, 3.
[153] Ibid art 2.1.16, Illustrations 1, 3.
[154] Zuloaga Rios, 'Article 2.1.16' in Vogenauer (ed) (n 3) para 3.
[155] See International Institute for the Unification of Private Law (n 21) art 1.7, off cmt 1; ibid art 2.1.16, off cmt 1.

privileged, or secret information, which is too specific, private, or non-public, relating to know-how, business models, or commercial strategies. Lists of clients, due diligence reports, and balance sheets might also qualify for this category.[156]

A party might keep the confidential information it received but make use of it improperly. Examples of improper use include using the technology or business information received to create competing products or information used in breach of intellectual property rights. The second part of Article 2.1.16 PICC anticipates this scenario when it permits the adjudicator to calculate the damages caused to the aggrieved party based on the benefit received by the other party (disgorgement of profits, see Chapter 15).[157] Otherwise, the pre-contractual character of the duty of confidentiality requires placing the aggrieved party in the position it had, before the breach occurred (reliance interest), and in some circumstances, compensating for any lost business opportunity (*perte d'une chance*).[158]

Article 2.1.16 PICC is not specific about the period during which the other party is prohibited from disclosing confidential information. Where no time has been agreed by the parties, the duration must be reasonable, as established from the circumstances of the case.[159]

3. Information duties

Information duties primarily aim at protecting the economic interests of the parties. In this context, one party may be affected either because a contract does not come into existence or because the expectations in the concluded contract are disappointed due to the pre-contractual misconduct of the other party, particularly because of the lack of sufficient information about the object or the subject of the transaction. In determining the existence and scope of information duties, the nature and position of the parties involved must be considered.[160] In particular, where one party indicates that it needs counselling or guidance from the other party, or indicates that one specific point is of particular relevance, the latter is under a duty to inform about all circumstances relevant to achieving this need.[161]

Furthermore, it may become apparent to one party that the other party will incur expenses or indulge in other conduct demonstrating reliance on a statement of the former party. In such cases, there is a duty to inform the latter party of relevant circumstances that might influence this decision.[162] Pre-contractual

---

[156] Beale and others (n 149) 426.
[157] International Institute for the Unification of Private Law (n 21) art 2.1.16, off cmt 3.
[158] Ibid; Rios, 'Article 2.1.16' in Vogenauer (ed) (n 3)para 20.
[159] Rios, 'Article 2.1.16' in Vogenauer (ed) (n 3) paras 11–14.
[160] Schwenzer and Muñoz (n 2) para 24.05 ff.
[161] Thomas Neumann, *The Duty to Cooperate in International Sales: The Scope and Role of Article 80 CISG* (Sellier 2012) 110–11.
[162] Schwenzer and Muñoz (n 2) 24.05.

information duties may not only be relevant under the heading of *culpa in contrahendo* but also—especially in legal systems that do not know the principle of *culpa in contrahendo*—under headings such as misrepresentation, be it fraudulent or merely negligent.[163]

Last but not the least, it has to be noted that false or incomplete statements—especially concerning the features of the goods—that constitute a violation of pre-contractual information duties and thus give rise to a *culpa in contrahendo* claim, may well influence the very terms of the contract, and thus trigger remedies of a contractual nature for non-conformity.[164] In that case, the domestic *culpa in contrahendo* rules will be displaced by the applicable international contractual law such as Article 35 CISG, Article 7.1.1 PICC, and similar provisions.

VII. Modification of Contract and NOM Clauses

The modification or variation of the terms of a concluded contract is generally possible for international contracts. This possibility follows naturally from the general principle of party autonomy and freedom of contract. In addition, most international instruments contain specific provisions on the issue of modification of previously acquired obligations.[165] The clearest enactment is found in Article 29(1) CISG, according to which a CISG contract may be modified or terminated by the mere agreement of the parties.[166]

Under most international instruments, the rules on contract formation also apply to the agreement modifying the original contract.[167] The freedom of form also applies: the modification of the contract will not be subject to any requirement as to form.[168] In this regard, there is no uniform law requiring the written form for the conclusion of the contract that may be transposed to its modification, except for those CISG contracts involving parties from Contracting States that have made a declaration under Article 96 to apply Article 12 CISG.[169] According to this provision, a contract and its modification must be 'in writing', which includes means of

---

[163] *Oz Optics Ltd v Timbercon Inc* [2011] Court of Appeal (Ontario) 2011 ONCA 714 allowing a claim for damages caused by pre-contractual behaviour under the doctrine of negligent representation).

[164] Schwenzer and Muñoz (n 2) 24.07.

[165] For provisions dealing directly with the form of modification, see PICC 2016, art 2.1.18; Principles of European Contract Law (PECL) 2002, art 2:106. However, the OHADA AUDCG was and remains silent on this issue.

[166] *NF Smith & Associates, LP v Karl Kruse GmbH & Co KG* [2023] US District Court for the Southern District of Texas 4:22-CV-3877, CISG-online 6627.

[167] Schwenzer and Muñoz (n 2) 14.01.

[168] CISG, art 11; PICC 2016, art 1.2; Ulrich Schroeter, 'The Cross-Border Freedom of Form Principle Under Reservation: The Role of Articles 12 and 96 CISG in Theory and Practice' [2014] Journal of Law and Commerce, 81 ff.

[169] Schroeter, 'The Cross-Border Freedom of Form Principle Under Reservation: The Role of Articles 12 and 96 CISG in Theory and Practice' (n 168).

communication capable of leaving a written record, such as telex, telegrams, and other modes of more modern communication (Article 13 CISG).

Despite the fact that statutory form requirements for the modification of the contract are uncommon in uniform law instruments, in today's global commercial practice, parties regularly agree on no-oral modification clauses, also called NOM clauses. These clauses require any modification of the original contract to be in writing to be effective. In other words, an oral modification will lack any effect over the terms of the existing agreement.[170] The application of such a clause often creates problems. Courts and arbitral tribunals must interpret the parties' oral modification agreement to determine whether it is to be given effect or whether the parties' intentions regarding form requirements have not, in fact, changed.[171] It is clear that the existence of the original NOM clause is a factor to be considered in this interpretation process.

In addition, these international texts avoid harsh results by having recourse to doctrines of estoppel or waiver.[172] If a party has relied upon an oral modification and was entitled to do so by the other party's conduct, such reliance is protected. Reasonable reliance will typically be inferred where one party has performed the contract on the modified terms with the other party's knowledge.[173]

VIII.   Interpretation of Contract

Business people negotiate their contracts using terms and statements that may be sufficiently clear to the communicating party at that point, but once a dispute arises each party alleges that the contract must be interpreted in its favour. Accordingly, the importance of interpreting statements and conduct pertaining to the contract cannot be overstated. The outcome of disputes usually depends on determining precisely the obligations under a contract, as it is only after these have been determined that an assessment of compliance can be made.

Legal traditions have historically used different methods to interpret the statements of the contracting parties in a contract or about it. In the civil law tradition, the subjective method of interpreting contracts focuses on discerning the true intention of the parties involved. This approach prioritizes the actual will and agreement of the contracting parties, often considering their statements, actions, and the context in which the contract was formed. The goal is to honour the genuine intent behind the contract, even if it diverges from the literal wording.[174]

---

[170] See CISG art 29(2); Uniform Commercial Code (UCC) 2018 ss 2–209.

[171] See generally Schmidt-Kessel, 'Article 8 CISG: Interpretation of Parties' Statements or Conduct' Schwenzer and Schroeter (eds) (n 6) para 23.

[172] CISG art 29(2); Ulrich Schroeter, 'Article 29: Modifications of Contract: "No Oral Modification" Clauses' in Schwenzer and Schroeter (eds) (n 6) para 68.

[173] See also PICC 2016, art 1.8.

[174] Schwenzer and Muñoz (n 2) para 26.08.

Conversely, the common law tradition favours the objective method of contract interpretation, emphasizing on the importance of the text of the contract and the meaning that a reasonable person would derive from it.[175] This method relies on the plain language of the contract and on how it would be understood by an average person in the same circumstances, ensuring predictability and consistency in contract enforcement. The objective approach tends to limit the consideration of external factors such as the parties' subjective intentions, focusing instead on the written terms and the apparent intent they convey.[176] The CISG[177] and the PICC have rules on the interpretation of statements and contracts.[178] They have tried to strike a balance between a subjective and an objective method of interpreting the contract.

1. Subjective criterion—the parties' common intent

Under this criterion, which is retained by Article 8(1) CISG and Article 4.2(1) PICC, interpretation shall seek to unveil the true common intention of the parties. Therefore, statements made by and other conduct of a party are to be interpreted according to its intent if the other party knew or could not have been unaware of that intention.[179]

The problem with this subjective criterion is that when a dispute arises over the meaning of a contractual statement or conduct, the contending parties disagree on where their minds meet regarding the statement or conduct at stake. In addition, while the communicating party might be convinced of what its intent was when making the statement or when conducting itself in a given manner, it is often very difficult to prove that the other party shared such intent.[180]

---

[175] Bruno Zeller, 'Determining the Contractual Intent of Parties under the CISG and Common Law—a Comparative Analysis' (2002) 4 *European Journal of Law Reform* 629.

[176] Schwenzer and Muñoz (n 2) para 26.10.

[177] *Triage Matériel Professionnel S.a.r.l. v JGB-2 Sp z.o.o.* [2023] Cour d'appel de Paris (Court of Appeal Paris) 21/19946, CISG-online 6569.

[178] Both uniform law and projects contain provisions on interpretation. However, the reference points for these rules differ. While the PICC explicitly mentions both the interpretation of statements (see art 4.2 PICC) and the interpretation of contracts (see art 4.1 PICC), the CISG only mentions the interpretation of statements (art 8 CISG). Nevertheless, it is undisputed that art 8 CISG, despite its wording, does not only apply to the interpretation of statements but also to the interpretation of contracts. Schmidt-Kessel, 'Article 8 CISG: Interpretation of Parties' Statements or Conduct' in Schwenzer and Schroeter (eds) (n 6) para 3; Alberto L Zuppi, 'Article 8 CISG' in Kröll, Mistelis, and Viscasillas (eds) (n 105) para 7 ff: stating that despite the meaning of the word 'statement', art 8 is set forth to determine 'the intent of the parties'.

[179] *Caiato v Factor France SA* [1995] Cour d'appel de Grenoble (Court of Appeal Grenoble) 93/4126, CISG-online 157; *Gantry SA v Research Consulting Marketing* [1995] Tribunal de Commerce de Nivelles (Commercial Court Nivelles) 1707/93, CISG-online 366.

[180] See International Institute for the Unification of Private Law (n 21) 137, art 4.1, off cmt 1.

2. Objective method—the reasonable person

The inherent difficulty involved in adducing evidence of the parties' common subjective intent led international law instruments to adopt the objective criterion to interpret the parties' contractual statements and conduct.[181] Under this criterion, which is adopted by Article 8(2) CISG and Article 4.2(2) PICC, statements in a contract should be given the meaning that a reasonable person in the shoes of the concerned party would give to such words.[182] This rule is not about how an ordinary reasonable person would understand the statement at stake but about how a reasonable person in the position of the recipient would understand that statement or conduct.[183] So, if the parties are in a special trade, the interpretation must include the usages of the trade.[184]

3. Circumstances to be considered in the interpretation of contracts

While applying either subjective or objective interpretative criterion discussed above, the starting point must be the wording of the contract. However, adjudicators may also consider a range of supplementary elements to determine the meaning and content of statements and contracts. At the centre of interest lie the circumstances surrounding the pre-contractual relationship between the parties[185] and the conduct subsequent to the statement made or the contract concluded.[186] Both groups of factual materials belong to the more general group of extrinsic evidence and thus, their admissibility in the interpretation process is usually at stake in legal systems.[187]

---

[181] Stefan Vogenauer, 'Article 4.2' in Vogenauer (ed) (n 3) paras 6–7.

[182] Schmidt-Kessel, 'Article 8 CISG: Interpretation of Parties' Statements or Conduct' in Schwenzer and Schroeter (eds) (n 6) para 21; Larry A DiMatteo, *The Law of International Contracting* (2nd edn, Kluwer Law International 2009) 232; E Allan Farnsworth, *United States Contract Law* (Juris Publishing 1999) 80–1.

[183] *Italian fashion textiles case III* [1990] Landgericht Hamburg (District Court Hamburg) 5 O 543/88, CISG-online 21.

[184] DiMatteo (n 182) 232; *Italian socks case I* [1995] Oberlandesgericht Hamm (Court of Appeal Hamm) 11 U 206/93, CISG-online 141.

[185] See e.g. CISG, art 8(3); PICC 2016, art 4.3(a)(b); *ICC Case No 11849* [2003] ICC International Court of Arbitration Final Award; *Filling and packaging plant case* [2006] Zivilgericht Basel-Stadt (Court of First Instance Basel-Stadt) P 2004 152, CISG-online 1731; *Production line for the production of cellulose products case* [2018] Østre Landsret (Court of Appeal for the Eastern Circuit) B-424-17, CISG-online 4581.

[186] See e.g. CISG, art 8(3); PICC 2016, art 4.3; PECL, art 5:102(b).

[187] Schwenzer and Muñoz (n 2) para 26.31: traditionally, common law legal systems have been reluctant to allow adjudicators to make use of these factors when interpreting statements or contracts, although the main reason for concern seems to be having regard to subsequent behaviour. Civil law legal systems on the other hand have felt less constrained in allowing judges to make use of all available factual circumstances.

The CISG and the PICC explicitly provide that surrounding circumstances and subsequent conduct are to be used for the interpretation of statements or contracts. Article 8(3) CISG and 4.3 PICC follow the civil law approach to determine the parties' intent.[188] They provide that due consideration is to be given to all relevant circumstances of the case including the negotiations, any practices which the parties have established between themselves, usages, and any subsequent conduct of the parties. Article 4.3 PICC explicitly adds 'the nature and purpose of the contract' to the materials available in the task of interpretation.

The term 'surrounding circumstances' is a broad concept that includes the elements included in the above provisions, among others. Particularly relevant for interpretative purposes are circumstances that the parties themselves have created *before* the conclusion of the contract. This relates, first, to prior dealings between the parties that might help understand what was intended. Second, the communications between the parties in the negotiation phase may also assist the adjudicator in the interpretative task.[189] In some cases, parties get to create what could be referred to as a private dictionary—that is, they have attributed a certain meaning to certain terms and have always used the terms in the same way, although the term itself is open to several interpretations.

Other materials pertaining to the negotiation phase may include telephone conversations; minutes; private documents; messages; letters of intent; MOU; previous drafts, contracts, and negotiations; and company's acts or heads of agreement created by the parties.[190] In the drafting of the main contract, these points may have accidentally been left out or expressed in a different way. The meaning of the terms in the contract, the scope of rights and obligations, and contractual requirements regarding the quality of the goods or services contracted may be more easily clarified when having regard to these prior communications.[191]

As a material available for the interpretation of statements and contracts, subsequent conduct includes promises or performance relating to the contract.[192] For instance, in an international sale of goods, the contract may specify that the seller must 'ensure delivery in good condition', but it might be unclear whether this includes providing protective packaging for transit. If the seller subsequently provides such protective packaging for multiple shipments without charging extra or raising objections, this conduct strongly indicates that both parties understood the obligation to include the provision of protective packaging.

---

[188] Vogenauer, 'Article 4.3' in Vogenauer (ed) (n 3) paras 6–7.

[189] *Filling and packaging plant case* (n 185).

[190] See *Ioannis Kardassopoulos and Ron Fuchs v The Republic of Georgia* [2010] International Centre for Settlement of Investment Disputes ARB/05/18 and ARB/07/15.

[191] *Beijing Metals & Minerals Import/Export Corp v American Business Center, Inc* [1993] US Court of Appeals (5th Circuit) 92-2171, CISG-online 89; *Exclusive distribution contract case* [2018] Oberster Gerichtshof (Austrian Supreme Court) 8 Ob 149/18x, CISG-online 3912.

[192] *Alpha Prime Development Co v Holland Loader Co* [2010] US District Court for the District of Colorado 09-cv-01763-WYD-KMT, CISG-online 2111.

This broad opportunity to consider external material in the interpretation of statements and conduct, along with the possibility to modify the contract orally, is in contrast with the restrictions imposed by the plain meaning rule and the parol evidence rule in Anglo-American law.[193] The so-called plain meaning rule has been used to exclude all extrinsic evidence, that is, prior and subsequent, to interpret a contract when the writing is deemed unambiguous.[194] On the other hand, the parol evidence rule bars the admissibly of oral testimony that varies, adds to, or contradicts a written contract that the parties intended to be the final and complete expression of their agreement.[195]

However, the CISG and the PICC have been influenced by the less restrictive approach followed in civil law countries.[196] These instruments do not endorse the parol evidence rule[197] and allow the consideration of all extrinsic evidence in the interpretation of the sales contract. The wording of Article 8(3) CISG and Article 4.3 PICC, along with the freedom of form principle,[198] are incompatible with a rule that excludes the consideration of the surrounding events, usages, and practices or a rule that bars evidence of prior oral agreements.[199]

In international commercial practice, however, parties often limit the materials to be used by adjudicators when interpreting their contract, via a so-called merger or entire agreement clause. Such a clause is a term in a written contract, stating that the entire agreement between the parties has been expressed in the document and that any external evidence that is derived from representations made prior to the written agreement is excluded.[200]

At the international level, uniform law and uniform projects have struggled with the effects of merger clauses. The CISG does not contain specific rules on merger clauses, but on the grounds of Article 6 CISG, it allows for the modification of its rules of interpretation in Articles 8 and 9 CISG.[201] The validity of such

---

[193]   See e.g. Uniform Commercial Code ss 2–202.

[194]   DiMatteo (n 182) 231.

[195]   Ibid 212.

[196]   See generally Article 8(3) CISG at United Nations Doc A/CONF.97/19 (n 76).

[197]   DiMatteo (n 182) 233; CISG Advisory Council, 'CISG-AC Opinion No. 3, Parol Evidence Rule, Plain Meaning Rule, Contractual Merger Clause and the CISG, Rapporteur: Professor Richard Hyland, Rutgers Law School, Camden, NJ, USA, 23 October 2004.' Black Letter Rule 1. See e.g. Uniform Commercial Code ss 2–202.

[198]   For the freedom of form principle, see CISG, art 11; PICC 2016, art 1.2.

[199]   *MCC-Marble Ceramic Center, Inc v Ceramica Nuova D'Agostino S.pA* [1998] US Court of Appeals (11th Circuit) 97-4250, CISG-online 342; Schmidt-Kessel, 'Article 8 CISG: Interpretation of Parties' Statements or Conduct' in Schwenzer and Schroeter (eds) (n 6) para 35; CISG Advisory Council, 'CISG-AC Opinion No. 3' (n 197) comment 1.2.

[200]   CISG Advisory Council, 'CISG-AC Opinion No. 3' (n 197) comment 1.4; Schmidt-Kessel, 'Article 8 CISG: Interpretation of Parties' Statements or Conduct' in Schwenzer and Schroeter (eds) (n 6) para 35.

[201]   Schmidt-Kessel, 'Article 8 CISG: Interpretation of Parties' Statements or Conduct' in Schwenzer and Schroeter (eds) (n 6) para 35; Harry M Flechtner, 'The U.N. Sales Convention (CISG) and MCC-Marble Ceramic Center Inc. v. Ceramica Nuova D'Agostino, S.P.A.: The Eleventh Circuit Weighs in on Interpretation, Subjective Intent, Procedural Limits to the Convention's Scope, and the Parol Evidence Rule' 18 *Journal of Law and Commerce*.

clauses is subject to the applicable domestic law (Article 4, sentence 2(a) CISG). The effect of a merger clause in CISG contracts must be determined by the interpretation of the clause itself.[202] Where a subjective intention of the parties is established, which contradicts the objective meaning of the merger clause, the parties' subjective intent prevails. In practice, however, the usual result will be that a merger clause not only eliminates oral sub-agreements but also limits the circumstances to be considered when interpreting the contract. Where a merger clause is 'protected' by a 'no oral modification' clause, meaning that it can only be modified by a written agreement, Article 29 CISG also applies to the merger clause.[203]

Article 2.1.17 PICC explicitly addresses the effects of a merger clause and takes the same stance as the CISG: '[a] contract in writing which contains a clause indicating that the writing completely embodies the terms on which the parties have agreed, cannot be contradicted or supplemented by evidence of prior statements or agreements'. However, such statements or agreements may be used to interpret the writing.

Finally, the consideration of usages and practices between the parties under Article 8(3) CISG and Article 4.3 PICC highlights the importance of contextual and relational factors in contract interpretation. These provisions underscores the relevance of prior dealings and customary practices to ascertain the parties' intentions and the meaning of their terms. Commercial contracts are not isolated textual instruments but evolve within a specific transactional framework and community. However, reliance on usages and practices may also raise challenges, particularly in disputes involving international contracts with parties with divergent cultural or commercial standards. Thus, identifying the relevant practices and usages becomes crucial in the interpretative process, a determination guided by Article 9 CISG and Article 1.9 PICC, which are discussed in detail below.

4. Standard terms—*contra proferentem* rule

In the previous sections, the general approaches to the interpretation of statements and contracts have been laid out and the materials available for interpretative purposes have been outlined. However, in some instances, adjudicators may find themselves in a situation where doubt remains about ambiguous terms.

---

[202] CISG Advisory Council, 'CISG-AC Opinion No. 3' (n 197) comment 4.5; Schmidt-Kessel, 'Article 8 CISG: Interpretation of Parties' Statements or Conduct' in Schwenzer and Schroeter (eds) (n 6) para 35.

[203] Schroeter, 'Article 29: Modifications of Contract: "No Oral Modification" Clauses' in Schwenzer and Schroeter (eds) (n 6) para 17; Andrea A Björklund, 'Article 29 CISG' in Kröll, Mistelis, and Viscasillas (eds) (n 105) noting that the burden of proof might be higher.

International law instruments—like most domestic legal systems—have developed special rules of interpretation that provide guidance in these cases.

One of these special rules is known under the Latin name of *contra proferentem*. In essence, this principle states that any ambiguity in the terms is to be held against the party that has drafted the term.[204] Legal systems have regularly used this principle of interpretation primarily in consumer protection and often generally, where non-negotiated contracts were at issue.[205]

However, the principle of *contra proferentem* is no longer limited to business-to-consumer (B2C) transactions, its scope has been extended to encompass business-to-business (B2B) transactions. At the international level, the PICC explicitly establish this principle (Article 1.8 PICC)[206] and its application is virtually undisputed to CISG contracts through Article 8 CISG. It finds relevance in the context of international commercial contracts where standard terms are drafted and imposed by one of the parties, on the other,[207] and may also find application in similar scenarios.

IX. Contract Supplementation

Supplementation presupposes a gap in the contract concluded by the parties. Therefore, the initial requirement for supplementation to be applicable is that a contract must have been validly formed according to the rules governing contract formation. The second requirement is that one or more essential terms necessary for the performance of the contract have been omitted.[208] It is evident that parties almost never anticipate and provide for every legal issue that may arise during the performance of their contractual obligations. Generally, when the parties fail to address a legal question in their contract, and neither established practices nor trade usages offer a solution, the default rules of law apply. However, even with these mechanisms, the gap might remain unfilled. In such cases, the question arises whether adjudicators may intervene and fill the gap through contract supplementation. This effectively enables adjudicators to draft contract terms on behalf of the contracting parties.[209]

---

[204] *Bowling alleys case* [2014] Bundesgerichtshof (German Supreme Court) VIII ZR 410/12, CISG-online 2513: 'dispose of' does not only mean sale but also lease; Zuppi in Kröll, Mistelis, and Viscasillas (eds) (n 105) para 7 ff; International Institute for the Unification of Private Law (n 21) 146–7, art 4.6, off cmt.

[205] Schwenzer and Muñoz (n 2) para 26.61.

[206] Note by the Secretariat, 'Legal Guide to Uniform Legal Instruments in the Area of International Commercial Contracts (with a Focus on Sales)' (2020) Un Doc A/CN.9/1029: the PICC provide for the *contra proferentem* rule in the context of terms supply by one party.

[207] Schmidt-Kessel, 'Article 8 CISG: Interpretation of Parties' Statements or Conduct' in Schwenzer and Schroeter (eds) (n 6); Zuppi in Kröll, Mistelis, and Viscasillas (eds) (n 105) para 26.

[208] Schwenzer and Muñoz (n 2) 26.65.

[209] Ibid para 26.65.

1. Supplying of an omitted term by recourse to legal principles

The PICC acknowledge the authority of adjudicators to supplement contracts that display a gap (Article 4.8 PICC). In supplementing the contract, the PICC are rather vague and establish general factors to be considered, including the intention of the parties, the nature and purpose of the contract, good faith and fair dealing, and the general standard of reasonableness. The CISG is also familiar with supplementing agreements, which would first, have to be made by the parties, as shown by Article 35(2) CISG.[210]

2. Supplementing the contract through practices

Practices between the parties as well as usages in trade, are of great relevance for international commercial contracts. It has already been pointed out in the preceding section that practices and usages are among the most common factors to be considered when interpreting statements or contracts. However, their role is different when it comes to integrating the content of the contract. Here, practices and usages primarily supplement the possible gaps left by the parties in the contract.[211] The subject matter thus is not to clarify the real intent of the parties but to determine the rights, obligations, and the modalities of their performance under the contract.

The CISG and the PICC acknowledge the relevance of practices and usages for the purposes of establishing the content of the contract (Article 9 CISG and Article 1.9 PICC). From a conceptual standpoint, a practice is unique to the relationship between the two concerned parties. In that sense, a practice is the way in which two parties consistently conduct themselves in relation to each other and in the performance of the contract.[212] On the other hand, a usage as understood here is a more objective notion. It is not only the two concerned parties that determine it but rather all actors within the specific trade or industry. Usages of this kind are often published by peak industry bodies or institutions like the ICC, but not necessarily.[213]

Practices between the parties perform different functions depending on the stage that the contract has reached. They may be relevant to questions of contract

---

[210] Schmidt-Kessel, 'Article 8 CISG: Interpretation of Parties' Statements or Conduct' in Schwenzer and Schroeter (eds) (n 6) paras 26–27; *Sunprojuice DK A/S v San Sebastián SCA* [2007] Audiencia Provincial de Madrid (Court of Appeal Madrid) 92/2007, CISG-online 1637.

[211] Martin Schmidt-Kessel, 'Article 9 CISG: Usages and Practices' in Schwenzer and Schroeter (eds) (n 6) para 1.

[212] Ibid paras 9–10; Pilar Perales Viscasillas, 'Article 9' in Kröll, Mistelis, and Viscasillas (eds) (n 105) para 12.

[213] See e.g. where the parties use promissory notes or bills of exchange, the ICC Uniform Rules for Collections (URCC) 522 are treated as an international usage.

formation or may shape the rights and obligations of the parties.[214] For example, a practice established between the parties may alter the general rule that silence does not amount to acceptance of an offer to contract.[215] Also, where in previous dealings the buyer has borne the cost of licences for import and export, the buyer is obliged to do the same in future dealings also, although the contract may not have any provision in this regard. Accordingly, practices generally override the default rule in the CISG and the PICC, and may also vary or modify an initial (express) term of the contract.

Whether the parties have established a practice between themselves must be determined by the facts of each individual case. A practice can be established by reference to the frequency with which it is adopted, the duration over which it occurs, and the accuracy with which the parties adhere to the same conduct.[216] With regard to the CISG, as a very basic pattern, it can be said that merely repeating a certain conduct twice is generally not sufficient to establish a practice.[217] A practice may be ended by an express term of the contract, by conduct, or by a subsequent different practice established by the parties.

X. Usages of International Trade

Trade usages aim to facilitate business by relieving parties from the necessity of negotiating every detail of a transaction. Moreover, they allow the collective knowledge of the trade, especially regarding effective contractual mechanisms, to be shared and utilized.[218] As parties typically do not anticipate all potential issues that may arise during contract performance, trade usages offer a mechanism to clarify the distribution of risks, rights, and obligations.[219]

1. Agreed usages

The CISG and the PICC recognize the parties' freedom to make usages applicable by agreement (Article 9 CISG and 1.9 PICC). This agreement may be implicit, and there may even be a statutory presumption in this regard. In essence, this is no different from incorporating the content of the usage into the contract

---

[214] Perales Viscasillas, 'Article 9' in Kröll, Mistelis, and Viscasillas (eds) (n 105) (n 105) para 9.

[215] Schmidt-Kessel, 'Article 9 CISG: Usages and Practices' in Schwenzer and Schroeter (eds) (n 6) para 4.

[216] Christoph Brunner, Christoph Hurni, and Michael Kissling, 'Commentaries on Articles 8–9 CISG' in Brunner and Gottlieb (eds) (n 39) para 3; Schwenzer and Muñoz (n 2) para 27.12; Schmidt-Kessel, 'Article 9 CISG: Usages and Practices' in Schwenzer and Schroeter (eds) (n 6) para 10.

[217] Schmidt-Kessel, 'Article 9 CISG: Usages and Practices' (n 6) para 12.

[218] Ibid para 14.

[219] Ibid.

as an explicit contract term.[220] Express terms in a contract—be they negotiated or non-negotiated—override trade usages that would have otherwise applied.[221] Nevertheless, this may be different where, subsequent to the conclusion of the contract, the parties adhere to a trade usage which deviates from the terms of the contract.

2. International usages

In the absence of an express agreement, the CISG integrates the contract with international usages based on a presumed or implied intent of the parties. Article 9(2) CISG requires that the usage be widely known and regularly observed in 'international trade' in order to control a CISG contract. The reference to 'international trade' might be understood as limiting the relevant usages to only those that are observed worldwide. This would mean that usages in specific trade places would not apply to CISG contracts, but only such usages that are common to all trade places could be considered as usages of the general trade of the respective goods.[222] The CISG does not require a worldwide observance of the usage concerned.[223] This does not mean that local usages are applicable all the time; the transaction as a whole must be sufficiently linked to the relevant usage for it to apply. Factors to be considered include the location of the parties, the place of performance, the experience of the parties, and the international notoriety of the local usage.[224] It has been suggested that it is not sufficient for one party to simply have contact with the sphere of observance of the usage.[225]

The second requirement for the applicability of a usage is the relevant level of awareness of the usage by the parties. Article 9(2) CISG states that the parties are considered to have impliedly agreed to usages which they knew. This favours the binding nature of usages that the parties have implicitly agreed upon. The CISG, however, goes on to state that it is sufficient that the parties ought to have known of the usage concerned. This disconnects the application of the usage from the will of the parties and moves it to presumed will when the usage is notorious in the trade concerned.[226]

---

[220] Perales Viscasillas, 'Article 9' in Kröll, Mistelis, and Viscasillas (eds) (n 105) (n 105) para 14.

[221] Stefan Vogenauer, 'Article 1.9' in Vogenauer (ed) (n 3) para 21.

[222] Schmidt-Kessel, 'Article 9 CISG: Usages and Practices' in Schwenzer and Schroeter (eds) (n 6) para 22.

[223] *Austrian wood case* [1998] Oberster Gerichtshof (Austrian Supreme Court) 2 Ob 191/98x, CISG-online 380; Perales Viscasillas, 'Article 9' in Kröll, Mistelis, and Viscasillas (eds) (n 105) para 27.

[224] Schmidt-Kessel, 'Article 9 CISG: Usages and Practices' in Schwenzer and Schroeter (eds) (n6) para 19.

[225] *French chocolate products case* [1995] Oberlandesgericht Frankfurt am Main (Court of Appeal Frankfurt am Main) 9 U 81/94, CISG-online 258; Schmidt-Kessel, 'Article 9 CISG: Usages and Practices' in Schwenzer and Schroeter (eds) (n 6) para 19.

[226] *Transmar Commodity Group Ltd. v Cooperativa Agraria Industrial Naranjillo Ltda.* [2018] U.S. Court of Appeals for the Second Circuit, 16-3532-cv, CISG-online 3060; *Zodiac Seats US LLC v Synergy*

The PICC, on the other hand, state that a usage is applicable whenever it is widely known or is considered generally applicable by parties in the concerned trade or same situation (Article 1.9(2) PICC). In other words, even constructive knowledge is not necessary to trigger the application of the usage. Thus, where the necessary level of observance in the industry has been reached, the parties are presumed to have impliedly agreed on the application of the usage.[227] In practice, the approach taken by the PICC may ultimately differ only slightly from the position of the laws operating with the notion of constructive knowledge, such as the CISG. It is difficult to conceive of circumstances where the requirements under the PICC are met, yet constructive knowledge cannot be found.

The application of a usage is to be denied where such application is unreasonable (Article 1.9(2) PICC). The plain wording of the PICC would suggest that this does not cover situations where the usage itself is unreasonable but rather covers situations where its application in the particular circumstances of a case leads to an unreasonable result.[228] Were the phrase to cover situations where the usage itself is unreasonable, it would entitle the adjudicators to exercise control over the content of usage under the notion of reasonableness, which would become an issue of the validity of the usage that is to be assessed under the applicable provisions.[229]

Aerospace Corp. [2020] U.S. District Court for the Eastern District of Texas, 4:17-cv-00410, CISG-online 5172.

[227] Vogenauer, 'Article 1.9' in Vogenauer (n 3) paras 16–17.
[228] Ibid paras 19–20; International Institute for the Unification of Private Law (n 21) 26, art 1.9, off cmt 5.
[229] Vogenauer, 'Article 1.9' in Vogenauer (n 3) 20.

7

Validity of Contract

I. General

Society expects that contracts that infringe on the law and morality of the country be considered unenforceable.[1] Illegality and immorality are two terms that evoke a similar societal expectation. Society also expects its laws to reflect the prevailing moral standards or political choices, and thus, in theory, what is illegal might also be immoral and vice versa. The PICC contain some provisions dealing with this societal expectation. However, while they have adhered to the concept of 'illegal contracts', they did move away from the term 'immorality' and instead adopted notions such as 'contracts infringing mandatory rules'.[2]

Party autonomy in international commercial contracts also requires that the parties' intent be free of undue conduct.[3] Freedom of will is questioned in cases of mistake and misrepresentation, fraud, and duress, and excessive benefits and unfair advantages, although in different ways.[4] In the case of mistake, misrepresentation, and fraud (*error* and *dolus*) one party enters into the contract under a mistake induced by the other party. In the case of duress (or *violence*), the affected party entered into the contract about which it had no mistaken belief, however an

---

[1] Ingeborg Schwenzer and Edgardo Muñoz, *Global Sales and Contract Law* (2nd edn, Oxford University Press 2022) para 20.01.

[2] PICC 2016, art 3.3.1.

[3] Sebastian Lohsse, 'Validity' in Nils Jansen and Reinhard Zimmermann (eds), *Commentaries on European Contract Laws* (Oxford University Press 2018) 651.

[4] Ibid.

external conduct exercised pressure over the free process of contract formation.[5] The same holds for contracts resulting in an excessive benefit or unfair advantage to one of the parties. All these cases need a legal response if free consent is to be guaranteed. Such a response will most likely affect, however, the legitimate reliance of one of the parties, in particular when the consequence would be the rescission of the contract.[6]

CISG Article 4 sentence 2(a) excludes questions regarding the validity of contracts from the CISG's scope of application, except as otherwise provided within it.[7] There are different validity questions expressly covered by the CISG, such as the form requirements for the conclusion of the contract in Articles 11 and 12. In addition, other validity questions might be impliedly governed by the CISG.[8] In order to unveil those questions, however, the term validity has to be interpreted autonomously (Article 7(1) CISG).[9] Validity under Article 4 sentence 2(a) CISG includes the doctrines of mistake, fraud, misrepresentation, duress, duties of disclosure, initial impossibility, and lesion and illegality.[10] As a consequence, a party may not rely on the otherwise applicable law if the Convention provides for the matter covered by such doctrines, either expressly or by way of general principle in accordance with Article 7(2) CISG.[11] This happens when the CISG regulates the same factual situation as gives rise to a remedy under the otherwise applicable law, and the legal purpose of the regulation of the otherwise applicable law, and of the remedies provided by it, is the same as that of the CISG.[12]

Under this approach, cases of mistake and non-fraudulent misrepresentation, including the availability of any remedies, are usually governed exclusively by the CISG.[13] For example, a buyer cannot rely on otherwise applicable law if the mistake or non-fraudulent misrepresentation was as to any of the matters covered by

---

[5] Ibid.

[6] Ibid.

[7] Milena Djordjević, 'Article 4' in Stefan M Kröll, Loukas A Mistelis, and Pilar Perales Viscasillas (eds), *UN Convention on Contracts for the International Sale of Goods (CISG): A Commentary* (2nd edn, CH Beck 2018) para 12; Christoph Brunner, Thomas Murmann, and Marius Stucki, 'Article 4 (Issues Covered and Excluded; Validity and the Effect on Property Interest in the Goods Sold)' in Christoph Brunner and Benjamin Gottlieb (eds), *Commentary on the UN Sales Law (CISG)* (Kluwer Law International 2019) para 5 ff; Pascal Hachem, 'Article 4 CISG: Substantive Scope of Convention' in Ingeborg Schwenzer and Ulrich G Schroeter (eds), *Schlechtriem & Schwenzer Commentary on the UN Convention on the International Sale of Goods (CISG)* (5th edn, Oxford University Press 2022) para 4.

[8] Ulrich G Schroeter, 'Contract Validity and the CISG' (2017) 22 *Uniform Law Review* 47.

[9] See Chapter 5.II.1.

[10] Djordjević, 'Article 4' in Kröll, Mistelis, and Perales Viscasillas (eds) (n 7) para 21; Pascal Hachem, 'Article 7 CISG: Interpretation of the Convention and Gap-Filling' in Schwenzer and Schroeter (eds) (n 7) para 29 ff.

[11] Hachem, 'Article 7 CISG: Interpretation of the Convention and Gap-Filling' in Schwenzer and Schroeter (eds) (n 7) para 4.

[12] CISG Advisory Council, 'CISG-AC Opinion No. 23, Mistake, Fraud, Misrepresentation and Initial Impossibility in CISG Contracts, Rapporteur: Professor Hugh Beale, Universities of Warwick (Em.) and Oxford, United Kingdom. Adopted Unanimously by the CISG Advisory Council Following its 47th Meeting, in Kopaonik, Serbia, on December 12–14, 2023' (2023) comment 3.6.

[13] Ibid comment 3.6.

Articles 35, 41, and 42 CISG, including the substance or quality of the goods. When one or both parties have made a mistake in declaration, or when there is a mistake as to the identity of a party, the issue is to be decided according to the CISG rules on interpretation (Article 8 CISG) and formation (Articles 14 to 24 CISG) and a party may not rely on the otherwise applicable domestic law. Conversely, a party may rely on the otherwise applicable law if the mistake or non-fraudulent misrepresentation is as to a matter that is not provided for by the CISG.[14]

In all cases of fraud, the innocent party may rely on the rules on fraud of the otherwise applicable law, even if the party also has a remedy under the CISG.[15] Fraud means giving information, whether by words or conduct, that was incorrect, when the giver knew the information to be incorrect or knew that it did not know whether the information was correct or not, and the giver intended to deceive the other party, or knew that the other party might be deceived and gave the incorrect information nonetheless.[16] Fraud also includes deliberate non-disclosure of information that was known to be important to the other party's decision to contract.[17] In any event, a party which has been induced to enter the contract by the other party's fraud may resort to remedies under the otherwise applicable law even if it also has a remedy under the CISG; the affected party may choose the remedy it considers more favourable, or may combine remedies that are compatible.[18]

II. Illegality and Immorality

Whereas the CISG does not cover illegality and immorality and leaves these questions to be decided by the otherwise applicable domestic law, the PICC contain provisions regulating these matters.

The parties' freedom to contract is not unlimited. Legal systems control the content of the contract from terms regarded as illegally or morally offensive because they breach a legal or extra-legal norm. In such cases, a contract 'is of no effect' under the PICC, which means that the parties might not claim contractual remedies such as specific performance or damages for breach.[19] These contractual remedies are excluded independently of the will of the parties. In this regard, lack of enforceability or invalidity of illegal or immoral contracts can be regarded as a

---

[14] Ibid comment 5.1.

[15] Ibid Black Letter Rule 9; Djordjević, 'Article 4' in Kröll, Mistelis, and Perales Viscasillas (eds) (n 7) para 23; Brunner, Murmann, and Stucki, 'Article 4 (Issues Covered and Excluded; Validity and the Effect on Property Interest in the Goods Sold)' in Brunner and Gottlieb (eds) (n 7) para 10; Hachem, 'Article 4 CISG: Substantive Scope of Convention' in Schwenzer and Schroeter (eds) (n 7) para 37.

[16] CISG Advisory Council, 'CISG-AC Opinion No. 23' (n 12) Black Letter Rule 10; Schwenzer and Muñoz (n 1) para 18.03.

[17] CISG Advisory Council, 'CISG-AC Opinion No. 23' (n 12) para 10.8.

[18] Ibid Black Letter Rule 9.

[19] Sonja Meier, 'Illegality' in Jansen and Zimmermann (eds) (n 3) 1895.

sanction against the parties, and as an educational tool to remind society of the existence of untradeable values.

The PICC encompass rules on immoral and illegal contracts that can be traced back to notions of mandatory rules of law, public order, public policy, good custom, *boni mores*, etc.[20] However, the PICC avoid concepts such as illegality, *ordre public*, or *boni mores*.[21] They contain a provision on contracts infringing a mandatory rule.[22]

1. Immorality

It is generally accepted that a contract might be denied enforcement due to immorality even if the sanctioned behaviour is not expressly prohibited by a legal provision.[23] Immorality may be expressed by unwritten legal norms protecting the State, the general interest, or certain individual interests. However, the concept of immorality in contract law has become less relevant since most unwritten values and norms regarded as fundamental have been converted into legal norms, particularly by national constitutions containing catalogues of human rights.[24]

Usually, a contract will be of no effect to the extent that it is contrary to principles recognized as fundamental in the laws of the States. In determining whether a contract goes beyond the bounds of what is moral, courts often considered immoral contracts aiming at the commission or remuneration of a criminal act or a civil delict, unduly restricting a party's personal or economic autonomy, freedom of marriage or divorce, or contracts relating to a person's religious beliefs.[25] In the economic sphere, covenants not to compete made by former employees, former business partners, or sellers of a business, are held to be invalid if they appear excessive, taking into account their extent, their duration, and the counter-performance.[26] The same holds true for long-term contracts under which the operator of a petrol station or inn agrees to take all his fuel or beer from a particular oil company or

---

[20] Michael Joachim Bonell, 'The New Provisions on Illegality in the UNIDROIT Principles 2010' 16 *Uniform Law Review* 523 ff.

[21] Ibid.

[22] PICC 2016, art 3.3.1. See also Gilles Cuniberti, 'Article 3.3.1' in Stefan Vogenauer (ed), *Commentary on the UNIDROIT Principles of International Commercial Contracts (PICC)* (2nd edn, Oxford University Press 2015) para 1; International Institute for the Unification of Private Law (ed), *UNIDROIT Principles of International Commercial Contracts* (UNIDROIT International Institute for the Unification of Private Law 2017) 125, art 3.3.1, off cmt 1; Eckart Brödermann, *UNIDROIT Principles of International Commercial Contracts. An Article-by-Article Commentary* (2nd edn, Kluwer Law International 2023) ch 3, art 3.3.1, para 1a.

[23] Aurelia Colombi Ciacchi, 'Immortal Contracts in Europe: The First Common Core' in Aurelia Colombi Ciacchi, Chantal Mak, and Zeeshan Mansoor (eds), *Immoral Contracts in Europe* (Intersentia 2020) 3; Schwenzer and Muñoz (n 1) para 20.22 ff.

[24] Meier, 'Illegality' in Jansen and Zimmermann (eds) (n 3) 1889.

[25] Ibid 1891.

[26] Ibid 1892.

brewery, and contracts harming the interests of third parties in the economic sphere (e.g. contracts endangering other creditors).[27] Of special importance in international contracts are rules relating to bribery and money laundering.[28]

The PICC contain a rule on contracts infringing a mandatory rule of law.[29] This provision covers not only cases where the contract as such is prohibited by a statutory or a case law rule, but also cases where the purpose or formation of the contract involved unlawful conduct, and also which are traditionally dealt with under the heading of immoral contract (against *ordre public*, public policy, or *boni mores*).[30] The PICC do not have a rule on contracts violating extra-legal standards, since it is not easy to determine what these standards should be.[31] Accordingly, the PICC included, in Article 3.3.1, a conflict of laws solution that provides for the application of relevant extra-legal standards (see the section below).

2. Illegality

Domestic laws usually distinguish between two types of cases where contracts can be said to be illegal. On the one hand, the conclusion of the type of contract may be expressly or impliedly prohibited by statute or case law (e.g. illegality at common law). In these cases, the legal provision will often determine the effect of the infringement on the contract. Often, however, the statute, although imposing fines or other sanctions, is silent as to the effect of the infringement on the contract itself.[32] On the other hand, although not expressly or impliedly prohibited by statute or case law, the contract may involve an act or further an unlawful object. For example, equipment may be sold intended to be used for an illegal purpose, or the parties agree on a kind of illegal performance.[33]

The PICC do not refer to contracts prohibited by statute, case law, or related to unlawful aims or acts. What is required is merely a contract infringing a mandatory rule. This formulation encompasses both cases of illegal contracts addressed above. Of course, the mandatory rules include rules prohibiting the conclusion

---

[27] Ibid.

[28] Conventions addressing money laundering and bribery include the United Nations Convention Against Transnational Organized Crime (UNTOC) (2000), effective 29 September 2003, and the United Nations Convention Against Corruption (UNCAC) (2003), in force since 14 December 2005, which comprehensively tackle both issues. The OECD Convention on Combating Bribery of Foreign Public Officials in International Business Transactions (1997), effective 15 February 1999, specifically targets bribery in international commerce. Additionally, the Council of Europe Warsaw Convention (2005), effective 1 May 2008, strengthens measures against money laundering and terrorist financing.

[29] PICC 2016, art 3.3.1.

[30] International Institute for the Unification of Private Law (n 22) 126, art 3.3.1, off cmt 2; Brödermann (n 22) ch 3, art 3.3.1, para 2.

[31] Meier, 'Illegality' in Jansen and Zimmermann (eds) (n 3) 1893.

[32] Ibid 1900.

[33] Ibid 1901.

of certain contracts. Examples are legislation prohibiting court officials to engage in remunerated activities outside their employment, and statutes prohibiting the bribery of public officials or the employment of intermediaries in negotiating with governmental agencies.[34] However, the mandatory rules are not necessarily rules prohibiting the conclusion of contracts. In the international context, overriding mandatory provisions include all kinds of regulations that can be violated by certain kinds of performance or the aim pursued by the contract, like regulations concerning public health, safety, and environmental protection, which include regulations limiting the load a ship can carry, and safety regulations regarding the transport of dangerous goods or the building of chemical plants.[35]

Pursuant to Article 1.4 PICC, the relevant mandatory rules are those applicable in accordance with the relevant rules of private international law.[36] Article 9(3) Rome I Regulation, a rule of private international law, for instance, provides that effect may be given to the overriding mandatory provisions of the law of the country where the obligations arising out of the contract have to be, or have been performed, in so far as those overriding mandatory provisions render the performance of the contract unlawful. Mandatory rules, in this context, are rules that cannot be derogated from by parties in an international contract governed by the PICC.[37]

Under the PICC, where a contract infringes a 'mandatory rule of law' applicable by virtue of the rules of private international law,[38] the effects of that infringement upon the contract are the effects, if any, expressly prescribed by that mandatory rule. These effects could include voidness, unenforceability or nullity *ad initio* or by request of a party, or, conversely, that the infringement has no bearing on the validity of the contract.

In most cases, however, the mandatory rule, while providing criminal or administrative sanctions for infringements, is silent as to its effect on a contract that, in one way or another, infringes that rule. It is then for the law of contract to determine whether such a contract may be rendered invalid or unenforceable as a result of the infringement.[39] In such cases, the PICC state that the parties have the right to exercise such remedies under the contract as in the circumstances are reasonable and appropriate.[40] Relevant circumstances include the purpose of the infringed

---

[34] Ibid.

[35] Ibid.

[36] PICC 2016, art 1.4; Gilles Cuniberti, 'Article 1.4' in Vogenauer (ed) (n 22) paras 2–3; Cuniberti, 'Article 3.3.1' in Vogenauer (ed) (n 22) para 15; International Institute for the Unification of Private Law (n 22) 11, art 1.4, off cmt 2; Brödermann (n 22) ch 1, art 1.4, para 3.

[37] Meier, 'Illegality' in Jansen and Zimmermann (eds) (n 3) 1900.

[38] Bonell (n 20) 520 ff: The applicable mandatory rule is determined in accordance with the relevant rules of private international law.

[39] Meier, 'Illegality' in Jansen and Zimmermann (eds) (n 3) 1901.

[40] PICC 2016, art 3.3.1(2); Cuniberti, 'Article 3.3.1' in Vogenauer (n 22) para 14; International Institute for the Unification of Private Law (n 22) 128–9, art 3.3.1, off cmt 5; Brödermann (n 22) ch 3, art 3.3.1, para 3.

rule, the category of persons protected by the rule, any sanction imposed under the rule infringed, the seriousness of the infringement, whether one or both parties knew or ought to have known of the infringement, the closeness of the relationship between the infringement and the contract, and the parties' reasonable expectations.[41]

III. Mistake (and Misrepresentation)

As stated above, cases of mistake and non-fraudulent misrepresentation, including the availability of any remedies, are usually governed exclusively by the CISG over domestic law. If the PICC application is provided in a CISG contract as supplementing rules of law, the CISG will also displace the PICC rules on mistake and misrepresentation.[42] In this section, we review the provisions on mistake and misrepresentation applicable to PICC contracts.

The PICC refer to 'mistake' rather than using the continental terminology of error or even specific types of error.[43] This, at first sight, might seem to borrow the rather narrow English concept of mistake. However, the approach taken differs notably both from this concept and from most of the continental rules. The provisions on mistake allow rescission for unilateral mistakes irrespective of their quality and content and, thus, are not only broader than many civil law concepts, but also in contrast with English law they encompass both mistake and misrepresentation.[44]

Article 3.2.1 PICC defines mistake as 'an erroneous assumption relating to facts or law existing when the contract was concluded'.[45] Overall, the mistake must be of such importance that a reasonable person in the same situation as the party in error would only have concluded the contract on materially or fundamentally different terms or would not have concluded it at all if the true state of affairs had been known.[46] Accordingly, the mistake must be fundamental in nature.

In addition, the mistake must be caused by information given by the other party.[47] In other words, the party intending to rely on a mistake to rescind the contract should have been induced into such a mistake by information actively

---

[41] PICC 2016, art 3.3.1(3); Cuniberti, 'Article 3.3.1' in Vogenauer (ed) (n 22) paras 16–22; International Institute for the Unification of Private Law (n 22) 129–34, art 3.3.1, off cmt 6.

[42] Ulrich Schroeter, 'Introduction to Articles 14–24 CISG: General questions regarding the formation of the contract' in Schwenzer and Schroeter (eds) (n 7) para 145.

[43] Lohsse, 'Validity' in Jansen and Zimmermann (eds) (n 3) 658.

[44] Ibid.

[45] PICC 2016, art 3.2.1.

[46] PICC 2016, art 3.2.2(1); Peter Huber, 'Article 3.2.2' in Vogenauer (ed)(n 22) para 5; International Institute for the Unification of Private Law (n 22) 102, art 3.2.2, off cmt 1; Brödermann (n 22) ch 3, art 3.2.2, para 1.

[47] PICC 2016, art 3.2.2(1)(a); Huber, 'Article 3.2.2' in Vogenauer (ed) (n 22) para 13; International Institute for the Unification of Private Law (n 22) 102, art 3.2.2, off cmt 2; Brödermann (n 22) ch 3, art 3.2.2, para 2.

provided by the other party. That being said, free consent might also be affected by failure to disclose information which good faith and fair dealing require that party to disclose.[48] For a mistaken party to rely upon the breach of this information duty, however, the other party knew or ought to have known of the mistake; that is, this mistake must already have existed before the failure to inform.[49]

Other relevant circumstances in determining whether good faith and fair dealing require a party to disclose particular information might include whether that party had special expertise, the cost to the party of acquiring the relevant information, the ease with which the mistaken party could have acquired the information by other means, the nature of the information, the apparent importance of the information to the mistaken party, and good commercial practice in the situation concerned.[50]

Moreover, the PICC also contemplate the rescission of the contract where the other party made the same mistake, that is, if there is a mutual mistake of facts or law.[51]

The mistaken party will not be entitled to rescind the contract if, in the circumstances, its mistake was inexcusable. This may take place when, for instance, the non-mistaken party's misrepresentation is innocent rather than negligent, and the mistaken party has a good reason to find out the truth.[52] Moreover, even where the other party acted negligently in causing the mistake, gross negligence on the part of the mistaken party might serve as a barrier to rescission.[53]

The mistaken party will not be entitled to rescind the contract either if the risk of the mistake was assumed, or in the circumstances should be borne, by it. Typical examples include not only contracts with the purpose of distributing risk (speculative contracts), as well as explicit agreements between the parties, but also cases where one of the parties enters into the contract in conscious ignorance of a fact and thereby implicitly assumes the risk.[54]

---

[48] PICC 2016, art 3.2.2(1)(a).

[49] Huber, 'Article 3.2.2' in Vogenauer (ed) (n 22) para 19; International Institute for the Unification of Private Law (n 22) 103, art 3.2.2, off cmt 2; Lohsse, 'Validity' in Jansen and Zimmermann (eds) (n 3) 666.

[50] Lohsse, 'Validity' in Jansen and Zimmermann (eds) (n 3) 658.

[51] Huber, 'Article 3.2.2' in Vogenauer (ed) (n 22) para 10; PICC 2016, art 3.2.2(1)(a); Ole Lando and others (eds), *Principles of European Contract Law. Parts I–III. Prepared by The Commission on European Contract Law* (Kluwer Law International 2019) art 4:103(1)(a); Draft Common Frame of Reference (DCFR) art II. 7:201 (1)(b), as can be seen in Christian von Bar and others (eds), *Principles, Definitions and Model Rules of European Private Law: Draft Common Frame of Reference (DCFR)* (Sellier 2009) 198, II.-7:201: Mistake, s G.

[52] Lohsse, 'Validity' in Jansen and Zimmermann (eds) (n 3) 673.

[53] Ibid. He notes that, '[t]o ask for inexcusability of the mistake rather than provide a set scale of gross negligence as in PICC 3.5 (2)(a) could allow for such flexible balancing of the parties' interests. The solution provided for in the PECL and DCFR provisions should thus be given preference over PICC 3.5 (2)(a).'

[54] Ibid 671.

Finally, under the PICC, an error occurring in the expression or transmission of a statement is to be treated as a mistake of the person who made or sent the statement.[55] By defining errors in expression or in transmission as mistakes, these rules subject the rescission of the contract to the same prerequisites discussed above and applicable to mistakes on law and facts.[56]

IV. Fraud

Under the PICC, a party may rescind a contract when it has been led to conclude it by the other party's fraudulent representation.[57] Fraudulent misrepresentation may take the form of words or fraudulent non-disclosure of any information which in accordance with good faith and fair dealing one party should have disclosed to the other.[58]

The right to rescind the contract in case of fraud differs from the same right to rescind the contract for mistake in that only rescission for mistake requires the mistake to have been fundamental and in that the provisions on fraud—as opposed to those on mistake—also apply to non-communicative behaviour.[59]

V. Threats

Under Article 3.2.6 PICC, a party may rescind the contract if it was induced to conclude it by the other party's unjustified threat, which, considering the circumstances, was so imminent and serious that it left the first party with no reasonable alternative.[60] Specifically, a threat is deemed unjustified if the act or omission being threatened is inherently wrongful, or if it is wrongful to use such an act or omission to secure the conclusion of the contract.[61] Article 3.2.6 PICC emphasizes that threat may refer to harm inflicted by active behaviour and by omission.

---

[55] PICC 2016, art 3.2.3; Lando and others (n 51) art 4:107.

[56] Lohsse, 'Validity' in Jansen and Zimmermann (eds) (n 3) 677.

[57] PICC 2016, art 3.2.5; Jacques Du Plessis, 'Article 3.2.5' in Vogenauer (ed) (n 22) para 11; International Institute for the Unification of Private Law (n 22) 106, art 3.2.5, off cmt 1; Brödermann (n 22) ch 3, art 3.2.5, para 1.

[58] PICC 2016, art 3.2.5; Lando and others (n 51) art 4:107; Bar and others (n 51) 209–12, II.-7:205: Fraud.

[59] Du Plessis, 'Article 3.2.5' in Vogenauer (ed) (n 22) paras 3–5; International Institute for the Unification of Private Law (n 22) 107, art 3.2.5, off cmt 2; Lohsse, 'Validity' in Jansen and Zimmermann (eds) (n 3) 691; Brödermann (n 22) ch 3, art 3.2.5, para 1.

[60] PICC 2016, art 3.2.6 .

[61] PICC 2016, art 3.2.6; Jacques Du Plessis, 'Article 3.2.6' in Vogenauer (ed) (n 22) para 6; International Institute for the Unification of Private Law (n 22) 108, art 3.2.6, off cmt 2; Brödermann (n 22) ch 3, art 3.2.6, paras 1–2.

Provisions on threats in the PICC correspond to provisions that pertain to what in English law is known as duress (and, to a certain extent, undue influence) and to what in civil law jurisdictions is mainly referred to as threat, coercion, violence, or the like.[62]

Rescission for threat is based on illegitimate pressure exerted by one party over the threatened party. Accordingly, the most important question is what amounts to illegitimate pressure. The first answer is that of threats with harm to a person's physical integrity, property, reputation, etc. Some legal systems refer to a list of other protected interests. However, the PICC refrain from such an enumeration and merely provide for a general clause by requiring an act to be 'wrongful in itself'.[63] This reference is meant to clarify that the threat must relate not to a merely technically unlawful but to a socially unacceptable behaviour.[64] This includes cases where the other party threatened to do something lawful and pursued a legitimate objective, but where it was inappropriate to use an act of the sort actually used to achieve the objective pursued.

However, a threat is not regarded as having induced the contract if, in the circumstances, the harm was not so imminent and serious as to leave the threatened party no reasonable alternative.[65] This criterion intends to protect legal certainty by ensuring that rescission is not easily accessible. Article 3.2.6 PICC requires a serious and imminent threat. However, 'imminence' must relate to the harm, not the threat.[66] Under Article 3.2.6 PICC, the threat must be so imminent and serious that it leaves no reasonable alternative to the threatened party. However, the imminence and seriousness of the harm are to be judged from an objective standpoint.

VI. Excessive Benefits and Unfair Advantages

The PICC allow a party to rescind a contract or a term therein if, at the time of its conclusion, that party was dependent on the other party; was in economic distress or had urgent needs; was improvident, ignorant, or inexperienced; and the other party knew or could be expected to have known this and, in the light of the

---

[62] Lohsse, 'Validity' in Jansen and Zimmermann (eds) (n 3) 695.

[63] PICC, art 3.2.6; Du Plessis, 'Article 3.2.6' in Vogenauer (ed) (n 22) para 6; Lando and others (n 51), art 4.108(a); International Institute for the Unification of Private Law (n 22) 108, art 3.2.6, off cmt 2; Brödermann (n 22) ch 3, art 3.2.6, para 1.

[64] Lohsse, 'Validity' in Jansen and Zimmermann (eds) (n 3) 698; Brödermann (n 22) ch 3, art 3.2.6, para 1.

[65] PICC, art 3.2.6; Du Plessis, 'Article 3.2.6' in Vogenauer (ed) (n 22) para 6; Lando and others (n 51) art 4.108; Bar and others (n 51) 212, II.-7:206: Coercion or threats, s Introduction.

[66] Lohsse, 'Validity' in Jansen and Zimmermann (eds) (n 3) 699; International Institute for the Unification of Private Law (n 22) 107–8, art 3.2.6, off cmt 1.

circumstances and purpose of the contract, exploited the first party's situation by taking an excessive benefit or unfair advantage.[67]

The PICC thus integrate the requirements of disparity and exploitation of a position of weakness. Article 3.2.7 PICC, which is phrased openly, provides for an excessive advantage as a requirement.[68] Other uniform projects follow the model of undue influence in English law in acknowledging that a relationship of trust may result in a defect of consent.[69]

An unfair advantage is a defect in consent that leads to the rescission of the contract. Upon the request of the party entitled to rescission, a court may adapt the contract or term in order to make it accord with reasonable commercial standards of fair dealing. Moreover, a court may also adapt the contract or term upon the request of the party receiving notice of rescission, provided that that party informs the other party of its request promptly after receiving such notice and before the other party has reasonably acted in reliance on it.[70]

VII. Consequences of Mistake, Fraud, Threats, and Unfair Advantage

1. Rescission

A party entering into a contract due to defects in consent under the PICC may rescind the contract. Rescission means to invalidate a contract from the beginning, retrospectively. The contract and its terms are, in every respect, without effect; neither party can claim the performance owed under the contract, even if the performance was due before the rescission has become effective.[71] Where a ground of rescission affects only individual terms of the contract, the effect is limited to those terms unless, having regard to the circumstances, it is unreasonable to uphold the remaining contract.[72]

---

[67] PICC 2016, art 3.2.7; Du Plessis, 'Article 3.2.6' in Vogenauer (ed) (n 22) para 19; International Institute for the Unification of Private Law (n 22) 109–10, art 3.2.7, off cmt 1; Brödermann (n 22) ch 3, art 3.2.7, para 1.

[68] Jacques Du Plessis, 'Article 3.2.7' in Vogenauer (ed) (n 22) para 7; International Institute for the Unification of Private Law (n 22) 109–10, art 3.2.7, off cmt 1; Brödermann (n 22) ch 3, art 3.2.7, para 1.

[69] See for instance Lando and others (n 51) art 4:109; Bar and others (n 51) 215 ff, II.-7:207: Unfair exploitation.

[70] PICC 2016, art 3.2.7; Du Plessis, 'Article 3.2.7' in Vogenauer (ed) (n 22) para 21; International Institute for the Unification of Private Law (n 22) 111, art 3.2.7, off cmt 3; Brödermann (n 22) ch 3, art 3.2.7, para 3.

[71] Lohsse, 'Validity' in Jansen and Zimmermann (eds) (n 3) 725.

[72] PICC 2016, art 3.2.13; Peter Huber, 'Article 3.2.13' in Vogenauer (n 22) para 5; International Institute for the Unification of Private Law (n 22) 117, art 3.2.13, off cmt; Brödermann (n 22) ch 3, art 3.2.13, para 1.

Rescission has a retroactive effect on the contract. Upon rescission, either party may claim restitution of whatever it has supplied under the contract, or the part of it rescinded, provided that such party concurrently makes restitution of whatever it has received under the contract, or the part of it rescinded.[73] However, what has been received may have deteriorated or it may have been lost. Restitution in *natura* may be impossible due to the nature of what has been received. A recurrent example is services but also perishable products. If restitution in kind is not possible or appropriate, the monetary value has to be paid. As the purpose of rescission on grounds of defects of consent is to place the affected party in the position that it would have been if the contract had not been concluded, both parties will be required to return the performances at their current value and other benefits enjoyed during the life of the contract.

The recipient of the performance does not have to pay the monetary value if the impossibility to make restitution in kind is attributable to the other party.[74]

If a party who is entitled to rescind a contract on grounds of mistake, fraud, threats, and unfair advantage confirms the contract, expressly or impliedly, after the period of time for giving notice of rescission has begun to run, that party is no longer entitled to rescind the contract.[75] The right to rescission is excluded irrevocably by confirmation of the contract. This irrevocability follows from the perception that rescission after confirmation would be contrary to good faith.[76] Where the right to rescission is based on threat or certain cases of exploitation (urgent need, economic distress), confirmation depends on the party entitled to rescission having become capable of acting freely.

Rescission must be declared by notice to the other party indicating an intention to rescind the contract.[77] This is comparable to the exercise of remedies under the CISG where notice is also required. In requiring a notice, the PICC are based on the premise that defects in consent result in mere voidability rather than voidness of the contract.[78] If the rescission is justified, the effects of the remedies take place with no need for a court declaration.

---

[73] PICC 2016, art 3.2.15; Jacques Du Plessis, 'Article 3.2.15' in Vogenauer (ed) (n 22) para 1; International Institute for the Unification of Private Law (n 22) 118, art 3.2.15, off cmt 1; Brödermann (n 22) ch 3, art 3.2.15, para 1.

[74] PICC 2016, art 3.2.15; Du Plessis, 'Article 3.2.15' in Vogenauer (ed) (n 22) para 20; International Institute for the Unification of Private Law (n 22) 120, art 3.2.15, off cmt 3; Brödermann (n 22) ch 3, art 3.2.15, para 3.

[75] PICC 2016, art 3.2.9; Peter Huber, 'Article 3.2.9' in Vogenauer (ed) (n 22) para 9; International Institute for the Unification of Private Law (n 22) 112, art 3.2.9, off cmt; Brödermann (n 22) ch 3, art 3.2.9, para 1.

[76] Lohsse, 'Validity' in Jansen and Zimmermann (eds) (n 3) 721.

[77] PICC 2016, art 3.2.11; *Argentinean company v Chilean company* [1997] Ad hoc Arbitration, Buenos Aires Unknown: where the arbitral tribunal concluded that a communication sent by the buyer to the seller could not be considered a proper notice of avoidance according to the PICC as there was no indication of the intention to avoid the contract.

[78] Lohsse, 'Validity' in Jansen and Zimmermann (eds) (n 3) 714.

Notice of rescission must be given within a reasonable time, with due regard to the circumstances, after the rescinding party knew or ought to have known of the relevant facts or became capable of acting freely. However, a party may rescind an individual unfair term if it gives notice of rescission within a reasonable time after the other party has invoked the term.[79]

2. Adaptation

In a contract entered into under mistake, if the affected party is entitled to rescind the contract but the other party declares itself willing to perform, or actually does perform the contract as it was understood by the affected party, then the contract is deemed to be concluded as the mistaken party understood it.[80] However, the other party must declare that it will perform, or render such performance of the contract promptly after having been informed of the manner in which the affected party understood the contract and before that party acts in reliance on any notice of rescission.[81] After such a statement or performance, the right to rescind is lost and any earlier notice of rescission is ineffective.[82]

The basis for adaptation in case of mistake is the unexpected windfall that the mistaken party might experience, where the contract would not have been advantageous for itself even if it had been concluded as actually understood. Preserving the right to rescind the contract would, under the circumstances, permit the mistaken party to evade not only the contract as actually concluded but also to reconsider its original intentions.[83]

Adaptation is limited to cases of mistake; it does not apply to contracts concluded under fraud, threats, or excessive benefits. The rationale for this limitation is fairness. The fraudulent, abusive, or threatening party's willingness to agree to the affected party's true or free will should not work as an alternative to tying the victim to its abuser.

---

[79] PICC 2016, art 3.2.12; Du Plessis, 'Article 3.2.15' in Vogenauer (ed) (n 22) para 1; International Institute for the Unification of Private Law (n 22) 118, art 3.2.15, off cmt 1; Brödermann (n 22) ch 3, art 3.2.15, para 1.

[80] PICC 2016, art 3.2.10; Peter Huber, 'Article 3.2.10' in Vogenauer (ed) (n 22) para 4; International Institute for the Unification of Private Law (n 22) 114, art 3.2.10, off cmt 1; Brödermann (n 22) ch 3, art 3.2.10, para 2.

[81] PICC 2016, art 3.2.10; Huber, 'Article 3.2.10' in Vogenauer (ed) (n 22) para 5; International Institute for the Unification of Private Law (n 22) 114, art 3.2.10, off cmt 2; Brödermann (n 22) ch 3, art 3.2.10, para 3.

[82] PICC 2016, art 3.2.10; Huber, 'Article 3.2.10' in Vogenauer (ed) (n 22) para 10; International Institute for the Unification of Private Law (n 22) 114, art 3.2.10, off cmt 3.

[83] PICC 2016, art 3.2.10.

3. Damages

The function of damages for defects of consent is to redress the affected party's reliance on the conclusion of a valid contract. A party who rescinds a contract on grounds affecting its free contractual consent may recover damages from the other party to put the aggrieved party as nearly as possible into the same position as if it had not concluded the contract.[84]

If a party has the right to rescind a contract on grounds affecting its free contractual will, but does not exercise its right or has lost its right under the provisions discussed above, it may recover damages limited to the loss caused to it by the mistake, fraud, threat, or taking of excessive benefit or unfair advantage.

Whether the claim for damages is exercised along with the right to rescind the contract or not, the affected party will only succeed if the other party knew or ought to have known of the mistake, fraud, threat, or taking of excessive benefit or unfair advantage.[85]

---

[84] PICC 2016, art 3.2.16; Peter Huber, 'Article 3.2.16' in Vogenauer (n 22) para 6; International Institute for the Unification of Private Law (n 22) 123, art 3.2.16, off cmt 2; Brödermann (n 22) ch 3, art 3.2.16, para 1.
[85] PICC 2016, art 3.2.16; Huber, 'Article 3.2.16' in Vogenauer (ed) (n 22), para 10; International Institute for the Unification of Private Law (n 22) 123, art 3.2.16, off cmt 1.

8

Seller's Obligations Under the International Sales Contract

I. General: Hierarchy Of Legal Sources

This chapter focuses on the international contract for the sale of goods. Sales contracts impose obligations on sellers, which may be contractually agreed upon or subsidiarily stipulated in the applicable law. Article 30 CISG states that the seller must deliver the goods, transfer the property, and hand over any related documents.[1] However, the CISG is not the primary source of these obligations; it is the contract.[2] Other obligations of the seller may arise from the practices or the usages of international trade impliedly agreed upon by the parties (Article 9 CISG). The CISG provisions on the seller's obligation apply as default rules only if the contract, practices, or usages of trade do not provide differently.

The obligations to deliver goods and related documents in Article 30 CISG are further detailed in Articles 31 to 34 CISG. Article 30 mentions the obligation to transfer property, but the CISG does not govern the effects of a sales contract over the property of the goods (see Chapter 3). Article 31 CISG requires the seller to take measures to transfer property, but does not tell us how and when property

---

[1] CISG, art 30; *Protective masks case III* [2022] Landgericht Bonn (District Court Bonn) 1 O 188/21, CISG-online 6384; *Uhren Atelier Gehm GmbH v […]* [2024] Rechtbank Zeeland-West-Brabant (District Court ZeelandWest-Brabant) 10539076 CV EXPL 23-1326, CISG-online 7195.

[2] Corinne Widmer-Lüchinger, 'Delivery of Goods under the CISG' in Ingeborg H Schwenzer, Yeşim M Atamer, and Petra Butler (eds), *Current Issues in the CISG and Arbitration* (Eleven International Publishing 2014) 167–8.

passes from the seller to the buyer.[3] Still, parties can modify the provision to transfer property by contract and provide that the transfer of property might only occur when certain conditions are met, for instance, upon payment of a portion of or the full price.

In international sales contracts, parties often specify delivery terms, such as the ICC Incoterms, instead of relying on the CISG provisions. Trade terms outline the seller's delivery obligations and the delivery location, among various other matters that override the CISG provisions on the same questions.

II. Agreed Place of Delivery: ICC Incoterms® 2020

An agreement fixing matters like the place of delivery, passing of risk over the goods, etc., is often referred to as a trade term. The ICC has developed trade terms, and regard must be given to the particular ICC Incoterms in any contract. Furthermore, parties usually enjoy the freedom of amending an ICC Incoterms, which possess questions of contract interpretation. The ICC Incoterms® 2020 deal with the place of delivery in each respective A2 article. For this work, it is helpful to summarize their content. In the ICC Incoterms® 2020 Ex-works (EXW), the seller must place the goods at the buyer's disposal at a named place of delivery (like a factory or warehouse). That named place may or may not be the seller's premises. For delivery to occur, the seller does not need to load the goods on any collecting vehicle or clear the goods for export, where such clearance is applicable. If no specific point has been agreed upon within the named place and if several points are available, the seller may select the point at the place of delivery that best suits its purpose.[4]

Under the ICC Incoterms® 2020 Free Carrier (FCA), delivery occurs when the seller delivers the goods at the contractually named place and time. The term must provide further details as to the specific point in time and place at which delivery occurs, given that there are two potential scenarios concerning loading and unloading.[5] First, when the named place is the seller's premises, the goods are delivered after having been loaded on the buyer's means of transport. Secondly, when the named place is another place, the goods are delivered when the goods are placed at the disposal of the carrier or another person nominated by the buyer,

---

[3] CISG, art 31; *AGES Maut System GmbH & Co KG v Butler Nederland BV* [2023] Rechtbank Gelderland (District Court Gelderland) 10562327 CV EXPL 23-4193, CISG-online 6644; *Elettrocanali S.pA v AC Distribution S.a.r.l* [2023] Cour d'appel de Pau (Court of Appeal Pau) 22/00579, CISG-online 7063.

[4] Chambre de commerce internationale (ed), *Incoterms 2020: ICC Rules for the Use of Domestic and International Trade Terms* (International Chamber of Commerce 2019) 22.

[5] Hadleigh Reid, 'FCA (Free Carrier) Incoterm Explained' (*DCL Logistics*, 13 May 2022) <https://dclcorp.com/blog/shipping/fca-free-carrier-incoterm/> accessed 24 November 2025; Chambre de commerce internationale (n 4) 29.

with no obligation to unload the goods from the means of transport at that other place.[6]

Under the ICC Incoterms® 2020 Carriage Paid To (CPT) and Carriage and Insurance Paid To (CIP), the seller must deliver the goods to the carrier contracted by it or, if there are subsequent carriers, to the first carrier for transport to the agreed point at the named place. Thus, the location of delivery is where the goods are handed over, or by procuring the goods so delivered, to the first carrier.[7] The seller may hand over the goods by giving the carrier physical possession of the goods in the manner and at the place appropriate to the means of transport used. The reference to 'procure' here caters to multiple sales down a chain (string sales), particularly common in the commodity trades.[8] In these ICC Incoterms® 2020, two locations are important: the place or point (if any) at which the goods are delivered to the first carrier *and* the place or point agreed as the destination of the goods (as the point to which the seller promises to contract and pay for carriage, and in the case of CIF to also contract and pay for insurance).

In the ICC Incoterms® 2020 Free Alongside Ship (FAS), the goods must be placed alongside the vessel nominated by the buyer at the loading place named by the buyer at the named port of shipment or by procuring the goods so delivered. Under the ICC Incoterms® Free on Board 2020 (FOB), the delivery is complete when the goods are placed on board the buyer's nominated vessel at the named port of shipment or by procuring the goods so delivered. The reference to 'procure' in FAS and FOB caters to multiple sales down a chain (string sales), particularly common in the commodity trades.[9] Both the FAS and FOB terms entitle the seller to select a loading point that best suits its purpose within the named port of shipment if the buyer has indicated none.

In the ICC Incoterms® 2020 Cost and Freight (CFR) and Cost Insurance and Freight (CIF), goods are delivered 'on board' the vessel in the port of shipment or by procuring the goods so delivered, that is, the same place as under FOB.[10] In both CFR and CIF, two ports are important: the port where the goods are delivered on board the vessel and the port agreed as the destination of the goods. Thus, for instance, goods are placed on board a vessel in Shanghai (which is a port) for carriage to Southampton (also a port); delivery here happens when the goods are on board in Shanghai, with risk transferring to the buyer at that time, but the seller must make and pay for a contract of carriage from Shanghai to Southampton.[11]

---

[6] Chambre de commerce internationale (n 4) 29.

[7] Ibid 41; Margarida Lima Rego and Özlem Gürses, 'Chapter 12: Insurance Requirements in Incoterms® 2020' in Özlem Gürses (ed), *Research Handbook on Marine Insurance Law* (Elgar 2024) 245.

[8] Chambre de commerce internationale (n 4) 42.

[9] Ibid 94.

[10] See Cahit Ağaoğlu, 'Incoterms® 2020' (2020) 40 *Public and Private International Law Bulletin* 1141–43.

[11] Chambre de commerce internationale (n 4) 114.

Where carriage is effected through several carriers for different legs of sea transport, for example first by a carrier operating a feeder vessel from Hong Kong to Shanghai, and then onto an ocean vessel from Shanghai to Southampton, the question that arises here is where does delivery take place? The parties may well have agreed on this in the sales contract itself. Where there is no such agreement, the default position is that delivery occurs when placed on board of the first carrier, that is, in Hong Kong port, thus increasing the period during which the buyer incurs the risk of loss or damage.[12]

In ICC Incoterms® 2020 Delivery at Place (DAP), Delivery Duty Paid (DDP), and Delivery at Place Unloaded (DPU) delivery takes place when the goods are placed at the disposal of the buyer at a named place of destination or at the agreed point within that place, if any. In these ICC Incoterms® 2020 rules, the delivery and arrival at the destination are the same. DPU has superseded the former ICC Incoterms® 2010 DAT. The change emphasizes that the place of destination can be any place and not just a 'terminal', and underscores the sole difference—since under DAP the seller does not unload the goods, under DPU the seller does unload the goods.[13] Because delivery under DAP happens before unloading, ICC Incoterms® 2020 presents DPU after DAP. Similar to the 2010 edition, in the ICC Incoterms® 2020 all 'D' terms are suitable for all modes of transport. Except for the ICC Incoterms® DPU, the—still valid— general rule followed by all but one of the 'D' terms is that the goods need not be unloaded.[14]

Some legal systems have coined their trade terms and given them a specific meaning or definition. While the place of delivery may be easily obtained where the parties have specifically chosen the ICC Incoterms® 2020, the mere reference in a contract to a term such as FOB might give rise to the applicable default rule for interpretation of that term. In short, it must be determined whether the reference to a trade term is a reference to the ICC Incoterms or, instead, a reference to a domestic law definition. Where the CISG applies, it is recognized as an international trade usage under Article 9(2) CISG that mentioning a trade term is to be understood as a reference to the ICC Incoterms.[15]

[12] Ibid.

[13] Celal Samil Demirci, Kemal Burak Yalcin, and Mustaga Sait Okur, 'Incoterms 2020' 23 *GSI Articletter* 33.

[14] Sang Man Kim, 'Right Choice of DPU in Incoterms 2020' (2021) 16 *Global Trade and Customs Journal* 114.

[15] Corinne Widmer-Lüchinger, 'Article 30 CISG: General Obligations of the Seller' in Ingeborg Schwenzer and Ulrich G Schroeter (eds), *Schlechtriem & Schwenzer Commentary on the UN Convention on the International Sale of Goods (CISG)* (5th edn, Oxford University Press 2022) para 3; Christoph Brunner and Mariel Dimsey, 'Article 30 (Seller's Principal Obligations)' in Christoph Brunner and Benjamin Gottlieb (eds), *Commentary on the UN Sales Law (CISG)* (Wolters Kluwer Law International 2019) para 7.

III. Place of Delivery Under the CISG

When no agreement on an ICC Incoterms or other trade terms for delivery exists, the CISG default provisions apply. The CISG distinguishes between contracts of sales involving 'carriage' (Article 31(a) CISG) and those that do not (Article 31(b) (c) CISG). As per Article 31(a) CISG, it is understood that it is the responsibility of the seller to organize the transportation of goods for the buyer, thereby defining the phrase 'if the contract of sales involves carriage'.[16] The contract does not involve 'carriage' under Article 31(a) CISG if the buyer is responsible for transporting the goods after taking them over from the seller.[17] Transportation of this nature falls under Article 31(b)(c) CISG.

Against this background, the rule in Article 31(a) CISG is that the seller's obligation to deliver consists—if the contract of sale involves carriage of the goods—in handing over the goods to the first carrier for transmission to the buyer. A carrier within the meaning of Article 31(a) CISG is an independent company or natural person in the transportation business called to carry out all or part of the transportation of the goods for transmission to the buyer and to whom the goods can be handed over.[18] An independent carrier transports the goods on the basis of a contract of carriage. The seller himself is not a carrier under this provision. So, when the seller arranges for his employees to carry out part of the transportation, the goods are not handed over under Article 31(a) CISG until they leave the seller's control.[19] This is also important for the question of liability and passing of risk. The seller will be liable for breach of contract until it hands over the goods to the independent carrier. Once the independent carrier takes over the goods, the seller will no longer be liable for acts or omissions after that point.

When several independent carriers are involved in transporting the goods for transmission to the buyer, delivery occurs when the seller hands over the goods to the first independent carrier, regardless of whether the latter is responsible for all or only part of the transportation to the buyer. The seller may also instruct its own suppliers to deliver the goods to the buyer. In this case, however, suppliers are not considered independent carriers and delivery will only occur once they relinquish custody of the goods and hand them over to an independent transportation company.[20] Freight forwarders can be considered 'carriers' under Article 31 CISG if

---

[16] *Italian wooden products case* [2019] Okresný súd Dunajská Streda (District Court Dunajska Streda) 19Cb/67/2018/6118256517, CISG-online 5661; *Ghanaian gold case* [2023] Obergericht des Kantons Zürich (Court of Appeal Canton Zurich) LB210015-O/U, CISG-online 6759; Christoph Brunner and Mariel Dimsey, 'Article 31 (Place of Delivery)' in Brunner and Gottlieb (eds) (n 15) para 6.

[17] Harry M. Flechtner, *Honnold's Uniform Law for International Sales Under the 1980 United Nations Convention* (5th edn, Wolters Kluwer 2021) 417–18.

[18] Corinne Widmer-Lüchinger, 'Article 31 CISG: Place of Delivery' in Schwenzer, and Schroeter (eds), (n 15) para 11.

[19] Ibid para 18.

[20] Brunner and Dimsey, 'Article 31 (Place of Delivery)' in Brunner and Gottlieb (eds) (n 15) para 9; Burghard Piltz, 'Article 31' in Stefan M Kröll, Loukas A Mistelis, and Pilar Perales Viscasillas (eds), *UN*

they take possession or transport goods—beyond just organizing delivery—to the hired transportation company for delivery to the buyer.

The term 'handing over the goods' in Article 31 CISG means giving the carrier physical custody of the goods for transportation.[21] Merely preparing the goods for dispatch or handing over a document of title to the carrier is not enough. The carrier must take physical custody of the goods 'for transmission to the buyer'.[22] If the seller requests the carrier to take custody of the goods for storage until future notice, that conduct is insufficient for delivery under Article 31(a) CISG.

If the contract does not involve carriage of goods and the seller is not required to deliver elsewhere, Article 31(b) or (c) CISG govern the delivery obligation and place. Article 31(b) CISG provides that delivery takes place and the goods should be handed over to the buyer at the place where the parties know them to be situated or where the parties know they will be produced or manufactured.[23] This rule applies, in particular, to 1) contracts for the sale of goods located at a place known to both parties at the time of the conclusion of the contract; 2) contracts of sale for a specific quantity from a specific stock located at a place known to both parties at the time of the conclusion of the contract; 3) contracts for the sale of goods to be yet manufactured by the seller or a third party at a place known to both parties at the time of the conclusion of the contract; 4) contracts for the sale of (natural) goods that are yet to be produced, where both parties are aware upon the conclusion of the contract, where they are to be grown.[24]

According to Article 31(b) CISG, both parties must have known that the goods were at or to be produced at a particular place for it to be operative. If the buyer only learns of the location or production place afterwards, the provision does not apply. The fact that the buyer could not have been unaware of such a place will not suffice.

If the contract does not involve the carriage of goods (Article 31(a) CISG) and the parties have not agreed on a specific place of delivery, Article 31(c) CISG applies unless the requirements of Article 31(b) CISG are met. Under Article 31(c) CISG, the seller must deliver the goods by placing them at the buyer's disposal at the seller's place of business. If the seller has multiple places of business, the place of business with the closest connection to the contract under Article 10(a) of CISG

Convention on Contracts for the International Sale of Goods (CISG): A Commentary (2nd edn, CH Beck 2018) paras 21–26.

[21] Brunner and Dimsey, 'Article 31 (Place of Delivery) in Brunner and Gottlieb (eds) (n 15) para 7.
[22] Widmer-Lüchinger, 'Article 31 CISG: Place of Delivery' in Schwenzer and Schroeter (eds) (n 15) para 8.
[23] *Storage tanks of a fruit processing plant case* Oberster Gerichtshof [2017] Austrian Supreme Court) 8 Ob 12/17y, CISG-online 3043; *Glimm Screens BV v Elos Med SP* [2023] Gerechtshof Arnhem-Leeuwarden (Court of Appeal ArnhemLeeuwarden) 200.313.285/01, CISG-online 6449.
[24] Widmer-Lüchinger, 'Article 31 CISG: Place of Delivery' in Schwenzer and Schroeter (eds) (n 15).

is relevant.[25] In the absence of a place of business, the goods must be made available to the buyer at the seller's habitual residence (Article 10(b) CISG). The applicable place of business is determined at the time of contract conclusion.[26]

The goods are said to be placed at the buyer's disposal when the seller has taken all steps necessary to enable the buyer to collect the goods.[27] What this entails will depend on the circumstances of each case. Sometimes, the seller must prepare for the buyer's arrival by separating the goods from a more extensive stock and labelling them as the buyer's. The seller does not need to notify the buyer that the goods are available when the parties have agreed on a date for the buyer to collect them.[28] Only when the seller is to choose a date of delivery within a period will it be required to notify the buyer of the goods' availability.

In none of the situations specified in Article 31 CISG, the seller must load the goods onto the buyer's means of transport or a third-party carrier to fulfil its delivery obligation.

IV. Time for Delivery Under the CISG

It is up to the parties to agree upon the delivery time, as per the principle of freedom of contract that controls the CISG (Article 6 CISG). If the contract sets a specific date for the delivery of goods, whether explicitly or implicitly, that date will be considered binding according to Articles 6 and 33(a) CISG.[29] The seller may not deliver before this date without the buyer's consent (Article 52(1) CISG) and delivery *before* or *after* this date is a breach of contract (Article 45(1) CISG). The contract can establish a specific day for delivery or determinable date if it specifies how the date will be determined, such as by requiring delivery 'after the opening of a conforming letter of credit', 'against cash transfer', or 'within two weeks from the buyer's request'. However, if the contract only includes vague language like 'immediately' or 'as soon as possible', it will not be considered a fixed delivery date under Article 33(a) CISG.[30] In this situation, Article 33(c) CISG will be applied to determine a reasonable delivery time based on the circumstances. Whether delivery after business hours or on public holidays at the place of delivery is possible will be

---

[25] Brunner and Dimsey, 'Article 31 (Place of Delivery)' in Brunner and Gottlieb (eds) (n 15) para 12; Piltz, 'Article 31' in Kröll, Mistelis, and Perales Viscasillas (eds) (n 20) paras 36–40.

[26] Widmer-Lüchinger, 'Article 31 CISG: Place of Delivery' in Schwenzer and Schroeter (eds) (n 15) 46.

[27] Commentary on the Draft Convention on Contracts for the International Sale of Goods, prepared by the Secretariat A/CONF.97/5 Secretariat Commentary 1978 30, art 29, commentary 16.

[28] Widmer-Lüchinger, 'Article 31 CISG: Place of Delivery' in Schwenzer and Schroeter (eds) (n 15) 49.

[29] Burghard Piltz, 'Article 33' in Kröll, Mistelis, and Perales Viscasillas (eds) (n 20) para 4.

[30] Cf Widmer-Lüchinger, 'Article 33 CISG: Time of Delivery' in Schwenzer and Schroeter (eds) (n 15) para 7.

solved by the rules of contract interpretation in Article 8 CISG or any practice or usage applicable under Article 9 CISG.

If the parties do not specify a specific date for delivery under the contract, they may instead establish a period of time under Article 33(b) CISG. In this scenario, delivery should occur not earlier than the start of the specified period and no later than the end. A period of time is determinable from the contract if it provides that delivery shall be made, for instance, 'within one week from the opening of the letter of credit by the buyer' or 'at the latest within 15 days from agreeing on the sample of the goods'. The period may have the date of contract conclusion as its beginning for delivery or, it may provide that delivery must be made 'on or before June this year', 'during August', or 'first half of September'.[31] In some cases, it can be challenging to determine if the parties agreed upon a delivery date or upon a delivery period. For example, if they agreed on delivery '10 days after New Year's Eve', it may not be clear if the delivery should be made within 10 days after the event or exactly on the tenth day after the event. The conditions and terms used are particularly relevant. If they are not sufficiently precise, it could be understood that the parties did not fix a period of time.[32] The interpretation of the contract under Article 8 CISG will determine the appropriate course of action.

Once a delivery period has been established, the seller has the option to choose the specific delivery date within that time frame. However, the parties can deviate from this standard rule by explicitly or implicitly agreeing that the buyer can request the goods to be delivered on a date within the said period. If no agreement is in place, the buyer can still have the right to select the delivery date within a period according to Article 33(b) CISG based on certain circumstances.[33] This will regularly be the case with relation to 'just in time' contracts. These circumstances may also occur when the buyer is responsible for arranging transportation, mirroring what usually happens under ICC Incoterms® FCA, FAS, or FOB. In such a scenario, the buyer must inform the seller in advance of when the transportation means will be available at the agreed place to allow the seller to make the delivery. But typically, the seller decides the delivery date rather than the buyer. If the buyer wants to have control over the delivery date within a specific time frame, including this buyer's prerogative in the contract is recommended.

If the contract does not fix a date or period for delivery, then Article 33(c) CISG applies. Under this provision, the seller must deliver the goods 'within a reasonable

---

[31] *Steinbock-Bjonustan EHF v Duma NV* [2004] Rechtbank van Koophandel Kortrijk (Commercial Court Kortrijk) AR 2136/2003, CISG-online 945.

[32] *S&P Project Co Ltd v PVE Crane Rental BV* [2023] Rechtbank Zeeland-West-Brabant (District Court ZeelandWest-Brabant) C/02/399366/HA ZA 22-340, CISG-online 6553: where a Dutch court concluded that the terms used between the parties' statements were not sufficiently clear to conclude that a time period had been agreed upon.

[33] Christoph Brunner and Bernhard Lauterburg, 'Article 33 (Time for Delivery)' in Brunner and Gottlieb (eds) (n 15) para 3.

time' after the conclusion of the contract.[34] What is reasonable will depend on what is suitable and equitable in the circumstances. The analysis should consider the seller's and the buyer's interests equally. This may lead to periods for delivery of different durations depending on the particular case. However, specific circumstances pertaining to one of the parties that the other party did not know and could not have been aware of should not apply in determining what is reasonable under the case. The inherent principles of cooperation and information require that both seller and buyer communicate any circumstances that could affect the default rule pertaining to delivery time before the conclusion of the contract.[35]

One known or ought-to-know circumstance that may affect this matter is whether the contract relates to goods already in the seller's stock or whether the goods are yet to be manufactured, produced, or sourced by the seller from a third party.[36] If the goods are in stock, a shorter period for delivery should apply. The average production and manufacture time should be taken into account if the goods are to be produced or manufactured. The seller should not be allowed more time than is usually necessary.[37]

The seller may choose when to deliver the goods within the reasonable time allowed by Article 33(c) CISG. Although Article 33(c) CISG does not explicitly state this default rule, it can be inferred from Article 33(b) in accordance with Article 7(2) CISG.

V. Costs and Licences

If the parties have agreed upon an ICC Incoterms®, the matter of costs relating to delivery will usually be governed by rules A9 and B9 of the relevant trade term. If the parties have not agreed on this matter, the general principles of the CISG (Article 7(2) CISG) must be referred to since the CISG does not provide any explicit rules regarding the delivery costs. According to these principles, each party is responsible for paying the costs of its performance. This means that the seller bears the costs of delivery, while the buyer bears the costs of taking over the goods. If Article 31(a) CISG applies, the buyer must cover the cost of transportation from the point where the seller hands over the goods to the first carrier.[38] Under Article 32(2) CISG, even if the seller must arrange for carriage of the goods, the buyer also bears the costs of transportation. If the seller pays the carriage costs nonetheless, it

---

[34] *Facade panels for mountain lodge case* [2020] Tribunal Cantonal du Valais/Kantonsgericht Wallis (Court of Appeal Canton Valais) C1 19 260, CISG-online 5497.

[35] Widmer-Lüchinger, 'Article 33 CISG: Time of Delivery' in Schwenzer and Schroeter (eds) (n 15) paras 15–17.

[36] *Ribbon case* [2001] Rechtbank van Koophandel Kortrijk (Commercial Court Kortrijk) A.R. 3669/2000, CISG-online 757.

[37] Ibid.

[38] Brunner and Dimsey, 'Article 31 (Place of Delivery)' in Brunner and Gottlieb (eds) (n 15) para 13.

may claim reimbursement of those costs unless the parties have agreed otherwise, like under ICC Incoterms® CFR, CIF, CIP, or CP. If the seller is obliged to bring the goods to a particular place for delivery (like in ICC Incoterms® FOB and FAS), it must bear the costs of transport to that place.

As per Article 35(2)(d) CISG, the seller is responsible for the cost of packing the goods in a manner that protects and preserves them. If the purchase price is based on the size, number, or weight of the goods, or if this information is necessary for transportation, the seller is responsible for the cost of measuring, weighing, or counting the goods. The seller is also responsible for covering the costs of quality examinations that must be performed before delivery and any costs involved in making the goods ready for delivery.[39]

Customs duties and other charges incurred during the export or import of goods are not included in transportation costs. Therefore, if the contract involves carriage as per Article 31(a) CISG, the buyer must bear the transportation costs but not the export duties and charges.[40] On the other hand, if the seller bears the freight costs to destination, it does not necessarily mean that it will also bear the costs of importing the goods. The rule is that the seller bears the cost of exporting, while the buyer bears the cost of importing the goods. This is also the case under ICC Incoterms®, except for DDP, and they most likely reflect international trade usages under Article 9(2) CISG. However, if the contract requires the buyer to collect the goods, as per Article 31(b) or (c) CISG, the buyer will, in case of doubt, bear both the export and import charges. The ICC Incoterms® make more subtle distinctions; under EXW, the export and import costs and charges are borne by the buyer, while under FCA, FAS, and FOB, the export duties and charges are borne by the seller. If the seller must deliver the goods at destination it will also bear any import charges, as in the ICC Incoterms DDP, but not under DPU or DAP.

With regard to licences, the CISG general principles will require the seller to obtain an export licence and the buyer an import licence. However, there are some exceptions to this principle. For instance, when the buyer is required to collect the goods from the seller's premises, the buyer must also obtain an export licence. This approach is adopted under the ICC Incoterms® 2020 EXW, but not under ICC Incoterms® FCA or FAS. On the other hand, if the seller is required to deliver the goods at the destination, then the seller must generally obtain an import licence. This approach is adopted under the ICC Incoterms® DDP 2020, but not under DAP or DPU. If the party responsible for obtaining an export or import licence fails to do so, it may become liable under Article 45(1) CISG (for the seller) or

---

[39] Piltz, 'Article 31' in Kröll, Mistelis, and Perales Viscasillas (eds) (n 20) para 50.
[40] Brunner and Dimsey, 'Article 31 (Place of Delivery)' in Brunner and Gottlieb (eds) (n 15) para 13; Piltz, 'Article 31' in Kröll, Mistelis, and Perales Viscasillas (eds) (n 20) para 51.

Article 61(1) CISG (for the buyer). To avoid this risk, the contract should include an express provision that makes it clear who is responsible for obtaining any necessary licences.

VI. Documents

The parties may agree expressly or impliedly on the documents that the seller must hand over to the buyer.[41] In the absence of this agreement, the seller must provide any documents related to the goods under Articles 30 and 34 CISG.[42] Various documents are related to the goods, such as those controlling their disposition and other documents providing information about the goods. These documents include commercial invoices, insurance policies or certificates, survey reports, packing lists, certificates of origin, certificates of quality, and sanitary or phytosanitary certificates.[43]

In some instances, the parties might condition the buyer's payment to the seller's presentation of documents controlling the disposition of the goods (Article 58 CISG). The phrase 'documents controlling their disposition' as used in Article 58 CISG should be understood to include any document, be it electronic or paper-based, that authorizes the buyer to take possession of the goods or that verifies that the seller no longer has the right to control the disposition of the goods once they are in the buyer's possession.[44]

These documents typically include negotiable bills of lading, regardless of whether they are issued by an ocean carrier or an intermediary, such as a freight forwarder, multimodal transport operator (MTO), or non-vessel-operating common carrier (NVOCC). Also, included are non-negotiable bills of lading, the consignor's copy of an air waybill, the consignor's duplicate copy of a rail consignment note, the consignor's duplicate or first copy of a road consignment note, road and rail bills of lading in North America, warehouse receipts or warehouse warrants, and ship's delivery orders.[45]

---

[41] CISG Advisory Council, 'CISG-AC Opinion No. 11, Issues Raised by Documents under the CISG Focusing on the Buyer's Payment Duty, Rapporteur: Professor Martin Davies, Tulane University Law School, New Orleans, U.S. August 3, 2012' Black Letter Rule 2.

[42] Widmer-Lüchinger, 'Article 34 CISG: Handing over the Documents by the Seller' in Schwenzer and Schroeter (eds) (n 15) para 2.

[43] CISG Advisory Council (n 41) Black Letter Rule 1; Widmer-Lüchinger, 'Article 34 CISG: Handing over the Documents by the Seller' in Schwenzer and Schroeter (eds) (n 15) para 2.

[44] CISG Advisory Council, 'CISG-AC Opinion No. 11' (n 41) Black Letter Rule 5; Brunner and Lauterburg, 'Article 34 (Documents Relating to the Goods)' in Brunner and Gottlieb (eds) (n 15) para 1; Martin Davies, 'Documents That Satisfy the Requirements of CISG Art. 58' (2011) 59 *Belgrade Law Review* 63 ff.

[45] The CISG Advisory Council, 'CISG-AC Opinion No. 11' (n 41) Black Letter Rule 6.

Certain documents do not control the disposition of goods. These documents include sea waybills, dock receipts, quai receipts, or mate's receipts, commercial invoices, insurance policies or certificates, survey reports, certificates of origin, certificates of quality, and sanitary or phytosanitary certificates.[46]

VII. Transfer of Property

The development of consistent rules on the transfer of property title at the international level has been impeded by significant differences among domestic legal systems. Property law is heavily influenced by cultural notions and legal traditions, more so than contract law. Due to these differences, the drafters of the CISG could not reach a consensus, and they left out important matters related to property from the Convention's application (Article 4 sentence 2(b) CISG). Neither the PICC's drafters included rules on the effect of the contract on the transfer of property. This matter, which pertains to property law rather than contract law, is not governed by these international instruments. Other international instruments may address the transfer of title in specific scenarios. For instance, the 2001 UNIDROIT Convention on International Interests in Mobile Equipment, also known as the Cape Town Convention, permits the use of a retention of title clause and delineates its legal consequences.

That being said, Article 30 CISG requires the seller to take all necessary steps to ensure the transfer of property to the buyer. Whether the seller has fulfilled this obligation or not is determined by the law applicable in accordance with the rules of private international law (Article 7(2) CISG). This will usually be the *lex rei sitae*, that is the place where the goods are located. If the seller cannot transfer the property to the buyer due to a third party's property rights over the goods, the seller may be liable under Article 41 CISG.[47]

In addition, the CISG does not include any provisions on the possibility of retaining title. To determine the effectiveness of a retention of title clause, one must also refer to the law applicable by the proper private international law rule. However, no breach is committed in the case of the retention of title by the seller, where the property transfer is conditional on payment of the purchase price of the delivered goods. If payment can be made conditional for mere delivery (Article 58 CISG), then it can also be made conditional for the transfer of property.

---

[46] The CISG Advisory Council, 'CISG-AC Opinion No. 11' (n 41) Black Letter Rule 7; Davies (n 44).
[47] Brunner and Dimsey, 'Article 30 (Seller's Principal Obligations)' in Brunner and Gottlieb (eds) (n 15) para 14; Widmer-Lüchinger, 'Article 30 CISG: General Obligations of the Seller' (n 15) para 10.

VIII. Additional Obligations

The seller may have additional obligations that come from the contract, such as confidentiality or exclusivity agreements. These can also arise from practices that the parties have established between themselves or from trade usages under Article 9 CISG. Other obligations may arise from the principles upon which the CISG is based (Article 7(2) CISG).[48] If the contract falls within the Convention's scope, then these additional obligations will also be governed by the CISG's rules since they arise from the contract (Article 4, sentence 1). If the seller fails to perform these obligations, then Article 45 CISG *et seq* will apply.

The duty to cooperate is among the additional obligations binding upon the parties in international contracts,[49] although in the CISG it does not exist as a rule. This duty, as outlined in Article 5.1.3 PICC, comes from the principle of good faith and fair dealing, integral to performing contractual obligations. In the CISG it may be developed as a general principle in certain situations but does not originate from a rule of good faith. In the CISG context, Articles 32(3), 38, 39, 65(2), 77, and 79(4) CISG, to mention a few, reflect this duty on the parties.

The duty to cooperate dictates that a contract should not be viewed merely as an intersection of conflicting interests but as a collaborative project where each party must cooperate to ensure the contract's success. This perspective aligns with Article 1.7 PICC,[50] which underscores the importance of good faith in contract law, and Article 7.4.8 PICC, which mandates the obligation to mitigate harm in the event of non-performance. Article 5.1.3 PICC stipulates that parties must cooperate to the extent reasonably expected to fulfil their respective obligations.[51] Instances of such cooperation are specified throughout the PICC, either in explicit rules or implicit guidelines within the comments. The duty of cooperation must be bounded by reasonable expectations, ensuring that it does not disrupt the allocation of duties within the contract. Each party is obliged to avoid hindering the other's performance and may also need to take proactive steps to facilitate the others' obligations. For example, at least under the PICC, if one party is familiar with specific formalities required for the performance and the other is not, the knowledgeable party may be expected to provide assistance. This obligation to cooperate underscores the necessity for parties to engage actively in enabling each other's performance,

---

[48] Peter Schlechtriem, 'Interpretation, Gap-Filling and Further Development of the U.N. Sales Convention' (2004) 16 *Pace International Law Review* 279.

[49] CISG, art 80.

[50] *Georgian individual v Georgian joint-stock company* [2020] Supreme Court of Georgia AS-1548-2019, UNILEX Case 2234.

[51] *María José Ramírez de Aranda y otros v Hernán Darío Ramírez Almada* [2018] Corte Suprema de Paraguay—Sala Civil y Comercial 72/2018, UNILEX case 2171.

fostering a collaborative environment essential for the successful execution of the international commercial contract.[52]

In the context of long-term contracts, the duty of cooperation is particularly crucial. Such contracts often involve complex performances that require on-going collaboration between the parties. For instance, in construction projects, the employer must coordinate the work of various contractors to prevent disruptions, ensuring that each party can perform their tasks efficiently. Similarly, in distributorship or franchising agreements, the supplier or franchisor must avoid actions that could hinder the distributor or franchisee from meeting contractual expectations. The need for continuous cooperation in these contracts highlights the importance of maintaining reasonable expectations and ensuring that both parties work together to achieve the contract's objectives.

---

[52] International Institute for the Unification of Private Law (ed), *UNIDROIT Principles of International Commercial Contracts* (2016 edn, UNIDROIT International Institute for the Unification of Private Law 2017) art 5.1.3, off cmt 1-3.

9

Seller's Obligations II—Conformity of the Goods

I. General: Key Concept of CISG versus Domestic Approaches

In the CISG, conformity is broadly defined as the requirement for goods to meet the standards set out in the contract or the CISG itself.[1] If goods fail to meet these standards, it is considered non-conformity. This differs from domestic approaches, which may treat these issues separately.[2] Different to the civil law tradition, the CISG classifies the delivery of an *aliud* and a *peius* both as non-conformity and offers the same remedies to the buyer. Unlike common law jurisdictions, there are no distinctions between conditions or express and implied warranties at the international level.[3] Discrepancies in quantity, packaging defects and additional duties are also considered non-conformities under the CISG.[4] Finally, the CISG does not make a distinction between ordinary characteristics of goods and special purposes or between *vice apparent* and *vice caché* like it is the case under the civil law of contracts.[5]

The CISG only makes a distinction between two types of defects—those related to the goods themselves and those related to the title. This differentiation may not significantly impact the available remedies,[6] but it becomes crucial when assessing liability for non-conformity of which the buyer was aware. As per Article 35(3) CISG, a seller is not held responsible for non-conformity if the buyer could not have been unaware of it. In contrast, liability for title defects only ceases if the buyer has agreed to accept the goods subject to a third-party claim, as provided under Article 41 CISG. In addition, the two-year cut-off period to examine the goods under Article 39(2) CISG applies exclusively to non-conformity in the goods themselves, and not to title defects. While distinguishing between the two may not always be easy, non-conformity usually relates to specific features or packaging of the goods, while title defects often stem from rights or claims over the goods.[7]

---

[1] CISG, art 35(1); *Sunrise Foods Int'l, Inc v Ryan Hinton Inc* [2019] US District Court for the District of Idaho 1:17-CV-00457-CWD, CISG-online 4522.

[2] Ingeborg Schwenzer and Edgardo Muñoz, *Global Sales and Contract Law* (2nd edn, Oxford University Press 2022) para 31.38; *Carbomat NV v Pric Advies BV* [2020] Gerechtshof Arnhem-Leeuwarden (Court of Appeal ArnhemLeeuwarden) 200.258.522/01, CISG-online 5495.

[3] Schwenzer and Muñoz, *Global Sales and Contract Law* (n 2) para 31.34 ff.

[4] Ingeborg Schwenzer, 'Article 35 CISG: Conformity of Goods' in Ingeborg Schwenzer and Ulrich G Schroeter (eds), *Schlechtriem & Schwenzer Commentary on the UN Convention on the International Sale of Goods (CISG)* (5th edn, Oxford University Press 2022) para 4.

[5] See *French Code Civile* 1804, arts 1641, 1642; expressly so *TCE Diffusion S.a.r.l. v Elettrotecnica Ricci* [2000] Tribunal de Commerce de Montargis (Commercial Court Montargis) 2000/0788, CISG-online 577.

[6] Christoph Brunner and Benjamin Gottlieb, 'Article 35 (Conformity of the Goods)' in Christoph Brunner and Benjamin Gottlieb (eds), *Commentary on the UN Sales Law (CISG)* (Wolters Kluwer 2019) para 3; Schwenzer, 'Article 35 CISG: Conformity of Goods' in Schwenzer and Schroeter (eds) (n 4) para 6.

[7] Schwenzer, 'Article 35 CISG: Conformity of Goods' in Schwenzer and Schroeter (eds) (n 4) para 5.

II. Contractual Agreement (Article 35(1) CISG)

Primarily, conformity of the goods is assessed by considering the requirements stated in the contract. In particular, Article 35(1) CISG requires the seller to deliver goods which are of the quantity, quality, and description required by the contract and which are contained or packaged in the manner required by the contract.[8] Article 35 CISG uses the idea of a subjective defect,[9] which is also recognized in many domestic legal systems.

1. Quantity

The quantity of goods the seller delivers must align with the contractual requirements. However, discrepancies that are permissible in various trade sectors,[10] are not considered a lack of conformity.[11] In some industries, usages allow sellers to deliver a lesser or bigger quantity of goods than initially specified, typically due to the nature of the goods, industry standards, or logistical constraints. For agricultural commodities, a tolerance of ±5 per cent is commonly accepted for grains like wheat, corn, and barley, while fresh produce such as fruits and vegetables often allows for a tolerance of around ±3–10 per cent due to variations in size and weight.[12] In the metals and minerals trade sector, the ISO 16162 specifies thickness tolerances for hot-rolled steel sheets in coils, which can range from ±0.03 mm to ±0.19 mm, depending on the sheet's width and thickness.[13]

Otherwise, any discrepancy in quantity, whether more or less than the agreed-upon amount, constitutes a lack of conformity under Article 35(1) CISG.[14] This also applies if the discrepancy in quantity is already evident from the documents. In this case, there is a lack of conformity and not a partial failure to deliver.

---

[8] Ibid para 6.

[9] Brunner and Gottlieb, 'Article 35 (Conformity of the Goods)' in Brunner and Gottlieb (eds) (n 6) para 3; Schwenzer, 'Article 35 CISG: Conformity of Goods' in Schwenzer and Schroeter (eds) (n 4) para 6.

[10] Cf e.g. Schwenzer, 'Article 35 CISG: Conformity of Goods' in Schwenzer and Schroeter (eds) (n 4) para 8 note 34: according to Hunter, the German uniform conditions for trade in cereals permit a 5 per cent discrepancy in volume. The GAFTA 100 permit a discrepancy of 2 per cent.

[11] Brunner and Gottlieb, 'Article 35 (Conformity of the Goods)' in Brunner and Gottlieb (eds) (n 6) para 5; Schwenzer, 'Article 35 CISG: Conformity of Goods' in Schwenzer and Schroeter (eds) (n 4) para 8.

[12] See e.g. GAFTA Model Contract no. 41 for Grain in Bulk 2022, in which the seller is allowed to ship '2% more or less', with the option to ship 'a further 3% more or less on contract quantity'; nonetheless, excess or deficiency will be settled at the market price on the bill of lading. See Arbitration Grain and Free Trade (GAFTA), 'Grain and Feed Trade Contracts' <https://www.gafta.com/All-Contracts> accessed 24 November 2025.

[13] ISO, 'ISO 16162:2012—Cold-Rolled Steel Sheet Products—Dimensional and Shape Tolerances' (iTeh Standards) <https://standards.iteh.ai/catalog/standards/iso/74865495-fbc6-4003-ba69-e34e9 f158c34/iso-16162-2012> accessed 15 March 2025.

[14] Schwenzer, 'Article 35 CISG: Conformity of Goods' in Schwenzer and Schroeter (eds) (n 4) para 8.

2. Quality

Quality must be understood to encompass not only the physical condition of the goods,[15] but also all factual and legal circumstances pertaining to their production or harvest methods.[16] In this regard, the agreed origin of the goods, the adherence to certain manufacturing standards, particularly Good Manufacturing Practices (GMP or cGMP) and fundamental ethical principles,[17] as well as religious production requirements,[18] also form part of their quality characteristics. In specific cases, missing documents could also be considered a quality discrepancy if the document is indispensable to prove the agreed quality standards.[19]

For the purposes of determining the conformity of goods under Article 35(1) CISG, the extent of non-conformity is irrelevant. This consideration becomes relevant only when assessing whether a breach of contract is fundamental, thereby granting the right to avoid the contract, obtain substitute goods, or determine the buyer's loss for the purpose of calculating damages (see Chapter 14). Any discrepancy in quality—whether better or worse than stipulated in the contract—constitutes a lack of conformity.[20] However, in terms of quality, customary and permitted discrepancies within various trade sectors might not constitute a lack of conformity.[21]

Similarly, as discussed in section III.3, even mere suspicions of non-conformity may give rise to remedies under the CISG, regardless of their accuracy. Given the buyer's interest in receiving goods that conform to the contract, both the market's reaction to such suspicions and the timing considerations under

---

[15] Schwenzer, 'Article 35 CISG: Conformity of Goods' in Schwenzer and Schroeter (eds) (n 4) para 8; Brunner and Gottlieb, 'Article 35 (Conformity of the Goods)' in Brunner and Gottlieb (eds) (n 6) para 6.

[16] Schwenzer, 'Article 35 CISG: Conformity of Goods' in Schwenzer and Schroeter (eds) (n 4) para 8; *Organic rye case* [2023] Landgericht Halle (District Court Halle) 8 O 48/22, CISG-online 7197: where the seller delivered contaminated rye with insects, kernels, and high moisture content and not organic and pure rye as it had been agreed.

[17] Schwenzer, 'Article 35 CISG: Conformity of Goods' in Schwenzer and Schroeter (eds) (n 4) para 10; Brunner and Gottlieb, 'Article 35 (Conformity of the Goods)' in Brunner and Gottlieb (eds) (n 6) para 6.

[18] Ibid.

[19] Ingeborg Schwenzer and Edgardo Muñoz, 'Sustainability in Global Supply Chains Under the CISG' (2021) 23 *European Journal of Law Reform* 321; *Organic barley case* [2002] Oberlandesgericht München (Court of Appeal Munich) 27 U 346/02, CISG-online 786 NJW-RR 2003, 849, with the note by Hohloch, Jus 2003, 1134-35; *White crystal sugar case* [2008] Spoljnotrgovinska arbitraža pri Privrednoj komori Srbije (Foreign Trade Court of Arbitration of the Chamber of Commerce and Industry of Serbia) T-9/07, CISG-online 1946 certificate of origin, which would have exempted the buyer from any customs duty of the State of import.

[20] Schwenzer, 'Article 35 CISG: Conformity of Goods' in Schwenzer and Schroeter (eds) (n 4) para 9; Stefan Kröll, 'Article 39' in Stefan M Kröll, Loukas A Mistelis, and Pilar Perales Viscasillas (eds), *UN Convention on Contracts for the International Sale of Goods (CISG): A Commentary* (2nd edn, CH Beck 2018) para 19.

[21] Schwenzer, 'Article 35 CISG: Conformity of Goods' in Schwenzer and Schroeter (eds) (n 4) para 10; Brunner and Gottlieb, 'Article 35 (Conformity of the Goods)' in Brunner and Gottlieb (eds) (n 6) para 6.

Article 36(1) CISG must be taken into account when assessing conformity under Article 35(1) CISG.

3. Nature

Under the CISG, any difference in the agreed nature of the goods—however obvious—constitutes a breach of contract for the purposes of Article 35(1) CISG.[22] The distinction made in many civil legal systems between *peius* and *aliud* is irrelevant under the CISG.[23] If the seller agrees to sell olive oil and delivers water, it is a breach of contract, and the buyer must give notice of non-conformity under Article 39 CISG.[24] Although Article 35 CISG does not refer to the delivery of goods of a different kind, this does not remove such a delivery from the scope of the rules on lack of conformity as 'description' covers this case as well.[25] In other words, the delivery of *aliud*, different goods, does not mean lack of delivery under Article 30 CISG.[26] Treating the delivery of an *aliud* as a lack of conformity rather than a failure to deliver is also factually justified.[27] Due to Article 40 CISG (seller's awareness), the seller often cannot rely on the buyer's failure to give notice of non-conformity in cases where the goods delivered are obviously the wrong goods.[28] However, if the seller is acting in good faith, it should be protected. Particularly when manifestly the wrong goods are delivered, it should be easy for the buyer to recognize this and object to them.[29]

4. Packaging

If the parties have agreed on the type of packaging to be used for the goods, then the goods must comply with the agreed terms in order to conform to the contract.[30]

---

[22] *AXA France IARD SA v Actimeat SAS* [2024] Cour d'appel de Versailles (Court of Appeal Versailles) 23/04101, CISG-online 7027: where the seller delivered horse meat instead of beef; Schwenzer, 'Article 35 CISG: Conformity of Goods' in Schwenzer and Schroeter (eds) (n 4) para 11.

[23] Schwenzer and Muñoz, *Global Sales and Contract Law* (n 2) para 31.15; Schwenzer, 'Article 35 CISG: Conformity of Goods' in Schwenzer and Schroeter (eds) (n 4) para 11.

[24] Schwenzer, 'Article 35 CISG: Conformity of Goods' in Schwenzer and Schroeter (eds) (n 4) para 11.

[25] Ibid.

[26] United Nations (UN) Conference Official Records, 'Commentary on the Draft Convention on Contracts for the International Sale of Goods, prepared by the Secretariat' (1978) UN Doc A/CONF.97/5, art 29, para 3.

[27] Stefan Kröll, 'Article 35' in Kröll, Mistelis, and Perales Viscasillas (eds) (n 20) para 33.

[28] Schwenzer, 'Article 35 CISG: Conformity of Goods' in Schwenzer and Schroeter (eds) (n 4) para 11; Brunner and Gottlieb, 'Article 35 (Conformity of the Goods)' in Brunner and Gottlieb (eds) (n 6) para 8.

[29] Schwenzer, 'Article 35 CISG: Conformity of Goods' in Schwenzer and Schroeter (eds) (n 4) para 8.

[30] *Shenzen Synergy Digital Co., Ltd. v Mingtel, Inc.* [2023] U.S. Court of Appeals (5th Circuit) 22-40440, CISG-online 6392; Schwenzer, 'Article 35 CISG: Conformity of Goods' in Schwenzer and Schroeter (eds) (n 4) para 12.

This is different from many domestic legal systems, where a defect in the packaging of goods is not considered a breach of warranty but rather a breach of an ancillary duty.[31] While implied agreements regarding packaging are possible, it should not be assumed that goods will be packaged in a certain manner simply because previous deliveries were packaged in the same way.[32]

III. Objective Criteria to Determine Conformity (Article 35(2) CISG)

Article 35(2) CISG provides a set of objective criteria that should be used to determine if the goods conform to the contract,[33] as long as the contract does not contain sufficient details about the requirements to be met by the goods. Broadly speaking, Article 35(2) CISG calls for fitness for use. The particular purpose of the goods is especially relevant when applying these criteria.[34] This means that the goods that conform to the contract are those that reasonable parties would have agreed upon.[35] Accordingly, a buyer has the right to expect that the goods it receives are fit for their particular purpose made known to the seller (Article 35(2)(b) CISG). Alternatively, the buyer has also the right to expect that the goods are fit for the ordinary use of similar goods (Article 35(2)(a) CISG).[36] This is true for every characteristic of the goods not explicitly stated in the contract. The provisions of Article 35(2) CISG apply cumulatively unless there is a contradiction,[37] in which case a hierarchy between the obligations of Article 35(2)(a) to Article 35(2)(d) must be determined for each characteristic in question. The determination is based primarily on the parties' intention (Article 8 CISG) and any trade usage

---

[31] See e.g. *Linkafrica Holding BV v Rigo Trading SA* [2023] Rechtbank Amsterdam (District Court Amsterdam) C/13/722336 HA ZA 22-699. CISG-online 6387: where Linkafrica argued that the goods were non-conforming since the package did not contain the goldbear; Schwenzer and Muñoz, *Global Sales and Contract Law* (n 2) para 31.99; but see U.S. Uniform Commercial Code (UCC) § 2–314(2)(e), in which packaging is expressly referred to in the context of the warranty of merchantability.

[32] Schwenzer, 'Article 35 CISG: Conformity of Goods' in Schwenzer and Schroeter (eds) (n 4) para 12.

[33] Schwenzer, 'Article 35 CISG: Conformity of Goods' in Schwenzer and Schroeter (eds) (n 4) para 13; Brunner and Gottlieb, 'Article 35 (Conformity of the Goods)' in Brunner and Gottlieb (eds) (n 6) para 9.

[34] Schwenzer, 'Article 35 CISG: Conformity of Goods' in Schwenzer and Schroeter (eds) (n 4) para 13; Brunner and Gottlieb, 'Article 35 (Conformity of the Goods)' in Brunner and Gottlieb (eds) (n 6) para 9.

[35] Schwenzer, 'Article 35 CISG: Conformity of Goods' in Schwenzer and Schroeter (eds) (n 4) para 13.

[36] Schwenzer, 'Article 35 CISG: Conformity of Goods' in Schwenzer and Schroeter (eds) (n 4) para 13; Brunner and Gottlieb, 'Article 35 (Conformity of the Goods)' in Brunner and Gottlieb (eds) (n 6) para 10.

[37] Kröll, 'Article 35' in Kröll, Mistelis, and Perales Viscasillas (eds) (n 20) para 61; Harry Flechtner, 'Conformity of Goods: Inspection and Notice' in Larry A DiMatteo (ed), *International Sales Law: A Global Challenge* (Cambridge University Press 2014) 215, 218.

(Article 9 CISG).[38] If this does not provide a clear result, additional circumstances of the individual case must be assessed. Generally, Article 35(2)(c) takes priority over Article 35(2)(b),[39] which takes priority over Article 35(2)(a). Article 35(2)(d) applies consistently alongside Article 35(2)(a).[40] We address the default standards for conformity of the goods set forth in Article 35(2) CISG in more detail below.

1. Sale by sample or model, Article 35(2)(c) CISG

Under the CISG, the seller is obligated to ensure that the goods delivered have the same qualities as those presented previously in a sample or model. The mere act of presenting a sample or model creates an implied agreement on the goods' characteristics, and no further agreement is necessary.[41] If a sample or model has certain features, for good and for worse, these are the standards to assess conformity under Article 35(2)(c) CISG.[42] The sample is taken from the goods to be delivered, while the model is provided to the buyer for examination if the goods are unavailable. A model can represent any or all features of the goods, including colour.[43] If the seller provides a sample, it implies that the goods possess all the attributes of that sample. Regarding the model, the contract must be interpreted to determine which qualities of the goods are represented by the model and thus have been agreed upon in the contract.[44]

In some instances, discrepancies may arise between the sample or model of a product and its contractual description under Article 35(1) CISG.[45] If the contractual description does not conflict with the features of the sample or model, it can be assumed that the goods must possess both the contractually agreed features and the features of the sample or model. However, if there is a conflict between

---

[38] *PVC foil case* [2019] Oberlandesgericht Naumburg (Oberlandesgericht des Landes Sachsen-Anhalt) (Court of Appeal Naumburg) 12 U 152/18, CISG-online 2406; Martin Schmidt-Kessel, 'Article 9 CISG: Usages and Practices' in Schwenzer and Schroeter (eds) (n 4) para 14 ff.

[39] Schwenzer, 'Article 35 CISG: Conformity of Goods' in Schwenzer and Schroeter (eds) (n 4) para 27; Brunner and Gottlieb, 'Article 35 (Conformity of the Goods)' in Brunner and Gottlieb (eds) (n 6) para 22.

[40] Kröll, 'Article 35' in Kröll, Mistelis, and Perales Viscasillas (eds) (n 20) para 61.

[41] See *Italian shoes case XV* [1994] Landgericht Berlin (District Court Berlin) 52 S 247/94, CISG-online 399; *Realturf Systems, S.L. v Eurograss, Inc* [2019] 2014-CA-018348, CISG-online 6730.

[42] *Dcoop Sociedad Cooperativa Andaluza v Patano s.r.l.* [2023] Audiencia Provincial de Jaén (Court of Appeal Jaén) 1697/2021/1323/2023, CISG-online 6896; Schwenzer, 'Article 35 CISG: Conformity of Goods' in Schwenzer and Schroeter (eds) (n 4) para 16.

[43] Schwenzer, 'Article 35 CISG: Conformity of Goods' in Schwenzer and Schroeter (eds) (n 4) para 26.

[44] Schwenzer, 'Article 35 CISG: Conformity of Goods' in Schwenzer and Schroeter (eds) (n 4) para 26; Brunner and Gottlieb, 'Article 35 (Conformity of the Goods)' in Brunner and Gottlieb (eds) (n 6) para 22.

[45] Schwenzer, 'Article 35 CISG: Conformity of Goods' in Schwenzer and Schroeter (eds) (n 4) para 27; Brunner and Gottlieb, 'Article 35 (Conformity of the Goods)' in Brunner and Gottlieb (eds) (n 6) para 22.

the terms of the contract and the sample, the contract must be interpreted under Article 8 CISG to establish which qualities the parties intended to take priority.[46] There can also be inconsistencies with Article 35(2)(a) CISG (fitness for the ordinary purpose) if the sample does not meet the characteristics of similar goods or Article 35(2)(b) CISG (fitness for a particular purpose) if goods corresponding to the sample or model are not fit for the purpose intended by the buyer. In general, the characteristics of the goods reflected by the sample or model take priority since the spirit and purpose of a sale by sample or model is to give the buyer the possibility of examining the goods or using them in a trial run.[47] This means that in that respect, the buyer places no reliance on the seller's skill and judgment.

The seller is not held liable under Article 35(2)(c) CISG if the sample or model is provided 'without obligation'.[48] Although an explicit rule to that effect was not included in the CISG, the wording 'held out ... as a sample or model' suggests that the provision of such items on a non-obligatory basis does not fall under Article 35(2)(c).

Article 35(2)(c) CISG applies only when the seller has provided a sample or model, and not when the buyer has presented an 'order sample'. However, in the case of an 'order sample', the characteristics of the buyer's sample or model may be considered as having been implicitly agreed upon as part of the contract under Article 35(1) CISG.[49] Furthermore, Article 35(2)(c) CISG does not cover the scenario where the buyer initially orders a small quantity for a trial and then orders a larger quantity in a second contract, stipulating that the goods should be 'as previously delivered' or 'of equivalent quality'.[50] However, in such cases, an implicit agreement as to quality under Article 35(1) CISG may again be assumed.

2. Fitness for a particular purpose, Article 35(2)(b) CISG

Under Article 35(2)(b) CISG, the seller is only responsible for the fitness of the goods for a particular purpose if the seller was made aware of this purpose either explicitly or implicitly. Additionally, the buyer must have relied on the seller's expertise and judgment, and it must have been reasonable for it to do so. However, if

---

[46] In favour of a general priority of art 35(1): Kröll, 'Article 35' in Kröll, Mistelis, and Perales Viscasillas (eds) (n 20) para 133.

[47] Ibid para 135.

[48] *FBA Plants BV v Ovibell GmbH & Co KG* [2023] Rechtbank Gelderland (District Court Gelderland) C/05/401601/HA ZA 22-126, CISG-online 6360; Schwenzer, 'Article 35 CISG: Conformity of Goods' in Schwenzer and Schroeter (eds) (n 4) para 28.

[49] Schwenzer, 'Article 35 CISG: Conformity of Goods' in Schwenzer and Schroeter (eds) (n 4) para 27.

[50] Ibid para 29; Harry Flechtner, *Honnold's Uniform Law for International Sales Under the 1980 United Nations Convention* (5th edn, Wolters Kluwer 2021) 450.

the buyer uses the goods for a different purpose than what was intended, the seller will not be held liable.[51]

There can be different reasons for a particular purpose to exist. For instance, if someone is buying machines to use them in certain ground conditions or a wet environment,[52] that is the goods' particular purpose.[53] Additionally, if someone is operating in a market with a high emphasis on fair trade and ethical principles (that could come even out from the buyer's commercial name), that can also qualify as the goods' particular purpose.[54]

The seller must only be informed of the particular purpose for which the goods are being purchased. The phrase 'made known' is less restrictive than 'contractually agreed upon'. If the seller has been informed of the intended use of the goods, it is responsible for ensuring that the goods are fit for that purpose, including compliance with public laws and regulations, and any cultural, religious, or ideological practices.[55]

If the seller wants to avoid any liability, it can raise an objection to the buyer's informed particular purpose.[56] Even if the particular purpose is not communicated to the seller directly, but instead implicitly,[57] or through a third party or the seller's own sources,[58] the particular purpose exists under Article 35(2)(b) CISG. If the seller failed to recognize the particular purpose but should have, it will be liable. The wording of Article 35(2)(b) CISG, which focuses on the act of 'making known' the purpose to the seller, suggests that it should be sufficient if a reasonable seller could have recognized the particular purpose from the circumstances.[59] This interpretation makes sense for evidentiary reasons, as it is difficult to prove actual knowledge.

---

[51] Schwenzer, 'Article 35 CISG: Conformity of Goods' in Schwenzer and Schroeter (eds) (n 4) para 20.

[52] *Ölflex Solar XLSv cables case* [2021] Parket bij de Hoge Raad (Advocate General at the Dutch Supreme Court) 20/00933, CISG-online 5602: where the court analysed whether cables were suitable for laying in the ground and were resistant to long-term exposure to water and should be seen as an agreed special use; Brunner and Gottlieb, 'Article 35 (Conformity of the Goods)' in Brunner and Gottlieb (eds) (n 6) para 20.

[53] Brunner and Gottlieb, 'Article 35 [Conformity of the Goods]' in Brunner and Gottlieb (eds) (n 6) para 20; Schwenzer, 'Article 35 CISG: Conformity of Goods' in Schwenzer and Schroeter (eds) (n 4) paras 18–19.

[54] Schwenzer, 'Article 35 CISG: Conformity of Goods' in Schwenzer and Schroeter (eds) (n 4) para 10.

[55] Kröll, 'Article 35' in Kröll, Mistelis, and Perales Viscasillas (eds) (n 20) para 120.

[56] Schwenzer, 'Article 35 CISG: Conformity of Goods' in Schwenzer and Schroeter (eds) (n 4) para 23.

[57] Brunner and Gottlieb, 'Article 35 (Conformity of the Goods)' in Brunner and Gottlieb (eds) (n 6) para 18.

[58] Schwenzer, 'Article 35 CISG: Conformity of Goods' in Schwenzer and Schroeter (eds) (n 4) para 23.

[59] Brunner and Gottlieb, 'Article 35 (Conformity of the Goods)' in Brunner and Gottlieb (eds) (n 6) para 18; Kröll, 'Article 35' in Kröll, Mistelis, and Perales Viscasillas (eds) (n 20) para 111.

Article 35(2)(b) CISG requires that the buyer has relied on the seller's skill and judgment.[60] Typically, the buyer relies on the seller's expertise if the seller is a specialist in manufacturing or procuring goods for the intended purpose or if the seller represents itself as such.[61] The buyer's knowledge in the particular area does not nullify its reliance.[62] However, if the buyer has more experience than the seller, the situation may be different.[63] If the buyer selects the goods, influences the manufacturing process, provides precise specifications, or insists on a particular brand, there may not be reliance.[64] If the seller recognizes that the goods selected by the buyer are not fit for their intended purpose, the seller must inform the buyer.[65] If the buyer still insists on buying those goods, the seller is not liable under Article 35(2)(b) CISG.

Moreover, the buyer's reliance on the seller's skill and judgment may not be justified if the seller is an intermediary,[66] or refers the buyer to experts in the respective field.[67] The buyer can only reasonably rely on what can be expected from the skills and knowledge of the respective seller.[68]

3. Fitness for the purpose for which the goods would ordinarily be used, Article 35(2)(a) CISG

In the absence of contractual provision or a particular purpose, the goods are expected to be fit for their ordinary use. This is a common principle in various domestic legal systems.[69] The primary requirement for goods under Article 35(2)(a) CISG is that they must be fit for commercial purposes.[70] This means that they must

---

[60] Schwenzer, 'Article 35 CISG: Conformity of Goods' in Schwenzer and Schroeter (eds) (n 4) para 25.

[61] Cf ibid.

[62] Ibid.

[63] *Mitjavila SAS et al. v Copaco NV et al.* [2019] Hof van Beroep Gent (Court of Appeal Ghent) 2017/AR/853, CISG-online 6774: the buyer alleged that the goods were unsuitable. However, the buyer conducted tests with the samples of glass fabric provided by the seller. Therefore, the court held that the buyer could not have relied on the seller's skill and judgement; Schwenzer, 'Article 35 CISG: Conformity of Goods' in Schwenzer and Schroeter (eds) (n 4) para 25.

[64] Cf Schwenzer, 'Article 35 CISG: Conformity of Goods' in Schwenzer and Schroeter (eds) (n 4) para 25.

[65] Cf United Nations' Secretariat UN Doc A/CONF.97/5 (n 26) 32, art 33, para 9.

[66] Schwenzer, 'Article 35 CISG: Conformity of Goods' in Schwenzer and Schroeter (eds) (n 4) para 25.

[67] Ibid.

[68] Brunner and Gottlieb, 'Article 35 (Conformity of the Goods)' in Brunner and Gottlieb (eds) (n 6) para 18.

[69] Cf Germany: Bürgerliches Gesetzbuch (BGB) s 434(1); Switzerland: Schweizerisches Obligationenrecht of 30 March 1911 (OR) art 197(1); Austria: Allgemeines Bürgerliches Gesetzbuch of 1 June 1811 (ABGB) s 922; France: Civil Code art 1641; UK: Sale of Goods Act 1979, s 14(2B)(a); U.S.: UCC § 2–314(2).

[70] Schwenzer, 'Article 35 CISG: Conformity of Goods' in Schwenzer and Schroeter (eds) (n 4) para 14.

be resalable, especially if the buyer is in the resale business.[71] An official certification speaks in favour of the possibility of reselling the goods.[72] The fitness of the goods for other purposes for which they would ordinarily be used must be decided by a person in the concerned trade sector. For instance, ready-to-wear garments must correspond to the required measurements[73] or standards,[74] and food must be fit for consumption.[75] Machines intended for unmanned continuous serial production must be automated.[76] Ceramic baking dishes must be heat-resistant,[77] and visual deviations may impair the buyer's use of the goods.[78] Technical instructions regarding the operation and use of the product must be supplied, and any warnings required under product safety guidelines must be clearly stated. Incorrect assembly instructions can also constitute a lack of conformity under Article 35(2) (a) CISG.[79] Perishable goods must have a shelf life for a reasonable period after delivery. Even durable goods (machinery, manufactured goods, etc.) must remain fit for their ordinary purpose for a certain period.[80]

In the context of supply chain sustainable practices, the merchantability or use of the goods is not always related to the traditional tangible aspects of the quantity, quality, description, or packaging but also relates to standards concerning ethical, environmental, and health and safety considerations, and/or the process of designing, manufacturing, or producing the goods.[81] Standards defining the

---

[71] Schwenzer, 'Article 35 CISG: Conformity of Goods' in Schwenzer and Schroeter (eds) (n 4) para 15; *Shenzen Synergy Digital Co, Ltd v Mingtel, Inc* [2022] US District Court for the Eastern District of Texas 4:19-cv-00216, CISG-online 5845.

[72] Schwenzer, 'Article 35 CISG: Conformity of Goods' in Schwenzer and Schroeter (eds) (n 4) para 15.

[73] Ibid; *Clothes case IV* [2003] China International Economic & Trade Arbitration Commission (CIETAC) CISG/2003/01, CISG-online 1451; *Spanish clothes case* [2008] 서울중앙지방법원 (Central District Court Seoul) 2007GaHap19698, CISG-online 2510.

[74] *MaRa Medical-Technical-Aid GmbH v Ningbo Laida Automotive Technology Co. Ltd.* [2021] 浙江省宁波市中级人民法院 (Intermediate People's Court Ningbo, Zhejiang Province), (2021)浙 02 民初 824 号. CISG-online 6203; *4work SIA v DND Talis UAB* [2022] Rīgas pilsētas tiesa (District Court City of Riga) C-2279-22/72, CISG-online 6925.

[75] Schwenzer, 'Article 35 CISG: Conformity of Goods' in Schwenzer and Schroeter (eds) (n 4) para 15.

[76] *Okuma MA-400 machine case* [2024] Gerechthof 's-Hertogenbosch (Court of Appeal 's-Hertogenbosch) 200.311.762_01, CISG-online 7017: Machine that is intended for unmanned continuous serial production.

[77] *Musgrave Ltd. v Ceramique Culinaire de France SA.* [1995] Cour d'appel de Colmar (Court of Appeal Colmar), 1 B 9400488, CISG-online 226.

[78] United Nations Uniform Law on the International Sale of Goods 1964 (ULIS), art 33.

[79] Cf Council Directive (EC) 1999/44 on certain aspects of the sale of consumer goods and associated guarantees [1999] OJ L 171, art 2(5); last amended by Council Directive (EU) 2011/83 on the sale of consumer goods [2011] OJ L 304/64; BGB § 434(2), s 2.

[80] Cf also Schwenzer, 'Article 35 CISG: Conformity of Goods' (n 4) in Schwenzer and Schroeter (eds) para 15; Kröll, 'Article 35' in Kröll, Mistelis, and Perales Viscasillas (eds) (n 20) para 101 (several years for high-quality machines).

[81] Schwenzer and Muñoz, 'Sustainability' (n 19) 323–24; CISG Advisory Council, 'CISG-AC Opinion No. 19, Standards and Conformity of the Goods under Article 35 CISG, Rapporteur: Professor Djakhongir Saidov, King's College London, United Kingdom. Adopted by the CISG Advisory Council, 25 November 2018' (2018) comment 1.3.

ordinary use of similar goods under Article 35(2)(a) CISG may encompass uni-lateral statements or express self-commitments made by the seller. For example, if a supplier publicly commits to an individual or industry code of conduct for sustainable trade, advertises its membership in the UN Global Compact or similar initiatives, and displays such affiliations in its pre- and post-contractual communications, these statements may be relevant in defining the ordinary use of the goods under Article 35(2)(a) CISG—especially where other suppliers in the sector have similarly endorsed comparable sustainability standards.[82] Similar examples of pre-contractual statements or conduct pointing in favour of complying with sustainable standards will also become relevant in determining conformity under Article 35(2)(a) CISG, which may include the seller presenting itself as a supplier of sustainable products, which complies with applicable standards, or gives assurances that its products will be acceptable to the fair trade community.[83]

The buyer's reliance that the goods would comply with minimum ethical standards could also define what constitutes the ordinary use of the goods under Article 35(2)(a) CISG. For instance, even if previous contracts between the parties for the same goods did not expressly require compliance with sustainable standards, but the seller observed them in performing those contracts, that fact can still be relevant in determining ordinary use if the buyer relied on them by, for example, informing its clients that the goods will comply with such standards.[84] In addition, where the parties belong to the same industry, trade, organization, or association that has adopted or follows sustainable standards—reflected in industry codes of conduct or guidelines—that fact could indicate a common commercial context within which the parties operate and compliance with that can be part of the 'ordinary use' of the goods under Article 35(2)(a) CISG.[85]

Any suspicion affecting the market valuation and usability of goods should be treated as a non-conformity. Liability under Article 35(2)(a) CISG is not based on whether the suspicion is true, instead the buyer's interest in receiving usable goods should prevail. The importance of the market's reaction to suspicions and the temporal limitations of the seller's liability under Article 36(1) CISG must be considered in assessing conformity under Article 35(2)(a) CISG.[86] This allows allocating the risk of suspicions more effectively between the seller and the buyer. The seller should be liable for any suspicions affecting the usability of the goods at the time of passing of risk, while suspicions arising after this point fall

---

[82] Schwenzer and Muñoz, 'Sustainability' (n 19); CISG Advisory Council, 'CISG-AC Opinion No. 19' (n 81) comment 4.6.

[83] CISG Advisory Council, 'CISG-AC Opinion No. 19' (n 81) comment 3.3.

[84] Schwenzer and Muñoz, 'Sustainability' (n 19) 324; CISG Advisory Council, 'CISG-AC Opinion No. 19' (n 81) comment 4.16; Kröll, 'Article 35' in Kröll, Mistelis, and Perales Viscasillas (eds) (n 20) para 59.

[85] Schwenzer and Muñoz, 'Sustainability' (n 19) 324–25.

[86] Ingeborg Schwenzer and David Tebel 'Suspicions, Mere Suspicions: Non-conformity of the Goods?' (2014) 19(1) Uniform Law Review, 155.

within the buyer's sphere of risk. That being said, the seller has a duty to assist in dispelling suspicions after delivery, which includes issuing clearance certificates or making public statements to counter the suspicions, thereby restoring the goods' usability.[87]

The interpretation of 'fitness for the purposes for which goods would ordinarily be used' among legal scholars is disputed, particularly whether it means that generic goods should be of average quality.[88] This has led to differences in interpretation, with European and American courts considering that only goods of average quality can meet the requirements of Article 35(2)(a) CISG,[89] while English courts may consider goods of below-average quality acceptable as long as they can be resold.[90] However, an arbitral award rejected the notions of merchantability and average quality, finding them inconsistent with the CISG framework. Instead, it held that 'reasonable quality', derived from the general principles underlying the CISG, constitutes the appropriate standard for assessing the required quality of the goods under Article 35(2)(a) CISG, as it aligns with the buyer's reasonable expectations.[91]

Especially with regard to public law requirements, determining whose standard—buyer's or seller's State—is relevant to decide the characteristics that goods must possess to be fit for their ordinary purpose can be a matter of dispute. This issue is related to risk allocation between the seller and the buyer.[92] Some authors believe that the standard of the seller's State is relevant,[93] while others hold that the standards in the state of use or resale should control this issue.[94] However, the interpretation of the contract is the ultimate determinant of the relevant standard.[95] The primary concern is whether a 'particular purpose' exists as

---

[87] Ibid 161–2.

[88] Schwenzer, 'Article 35 CISG: Conformity of Goods' in Schwenzer and Schroeter (eds) (n 4) para 16; Brunner and Gottlieb, 'Article 35 (Conformity of the Goods)' in Brunner and Gottlieb (eds) (n 6) para 10.

[89] *Salzgitter Flachstahl GmbH v Riveco Generai Sider S.pA* [2022] Corte Suprema di Cassazione (Italian Supreme Court) 36144/2022, CISG-online 6009: the Court of Cassation found that the parties had not agreed on a minimum silicon content in the steel, and that the lower-than-average silicon percentage in the delivered steel rendered it unfit for further processing in accordance with its ordinary use.

[90] Cf *Cehave NV v Bremer Handelsgesellschaft mbH, The Hansa Nord* [1976] QB 44.

[91] *Rijn Blend oil case* [2002] Nederlands Arbitrage Instituut (Netherlands Arbitration Institute) 2319, CISG-online 740 note 71.

[92] Schwenzer, 'Article 35 CISG: Conformity of Goods' in Schwenzer and Schroeter (eds) (n 4) para 17; Brunner and Gottlieb, 'Article 35 (Conformity of the Goods)' in Brunner and Gottlieb (eds) (n 6) para 13.

[93] Cf *New Zealand mussels case*, Bundesgerichtshof (German Supreme Court) (1995)—VIII ZR 159/94, CISG-online 144; further information Schwenzer, 'Article 35 CISG: Conformity of Goods' in Schwenzer and Schroeter (eds) (n 4) para 17; Kröll, 'Article 35' in Kröll, Mistelis, and Perales Viscasillas (eds) (n 20) para 94.

[94] Schwenzer, 'Article 35 CISG: Conformity of Goods' in Schwenzer and Schroeter (eds) (n 4) para 17; Brunner and Gottlieb, 'Article 35 (Conformity of the Goods)' in Brunner and Gottlieb (eds) (n 6) para 13.

[95] CISG Advisory Council, 'CISG-AC Opinion No 19' (n 81) comments 5 ff; Kröll, 'Article 35' in Kröll, Mistelis, and Perales Viscasillas (eds) (n 20) para 39.

defined in Article 35(2)(b) CISG.[96] If there is a subsidiary reference to the ordinary purpose, then one can rely on the following considerations: if there is an international usage as to particular characteristics or manufacturing standards of the goods, those characteristics must be regarded as minimum quality requirements.[97] A standard applicable in both the buyer's and the seller's State should generally be observed, unless less stringent public standard applies in the State where the goods are to be used or resold, as determined by the contract or the specific circumstances of the case.[98]

According to the CISG Advisory Opinion No. 19, the seller may have an obligation to comply with any binding standard at the place of use or resale of the goods if, at the time of the conclusion of the contract, it knew or could not have been unaware of that place.[99] Yet the seller's standing must be taken into account. A small or medium-sized producer may not possess the same level of knowledge or access to information regarding the existence and content of public law standards applicable in a relevant country as an international trader typically would. Where the seller neither knew nor could not have been unaware of the place of use of the goods, it might still need to comply with any public law standards applicable at the buyer's place of business.[100] If the standards in the buyer's State are higher than those in the seller's State, the buyer must draw the seller's attention to that fact if the latter cannot be expected to know about it.[101] However, the buyer's standing must also be considered. A regular importer—such as a retailer or specialized buyer—is generally expected to be aware of and communicate the applicable public law standards to the seller. In contrast, occasional purchasers, such as a factory or hospital acquiring machinery or equipment for internal use, are subject to a lower duty in this regard.

In the case of supply chains and sustainable standards, however, the above default rules must be applied with caution. Sellers are usually part of a network of suppliers for different components where a single place of use or a single buyer's place of business is not discernible.[102] In addition, some suppliers of raw materials and components may lack the language skills and the resources to access information about foreign public sustainability standards. For that reason, additional factors should be considered in assessing whether a supplier has an obligation to comply with a local standard, for instance whether the supplier knew or could not have been unaware of the relevant standard at the place of intended use. It

---

[96] Schwenzer, 'Article 35 CISG: Conformity of Goods' in Schwenzer and Schroeter (eds) (n 4) para 17.

[97] Ibid; Kröll, 'Article 35' in Kröll, Mistelis, and Perales Viscasillas (eds) (n 20) para 75.

[98] Schwenzer, 'Article 35 CISG: Conformity of Goods' in Schwenzer and Schroeter (eds) (n 4) para 17.

[99] CISG Advisory Council, 'CISG-AC Opinion No. 19' (n 81) comment 5.1.

[100] Ibid comment 5.2.

[101] Ibid.

[102] Schwenzer and Muñoz, 'Sustainability' (n 19) 325.

might be unreasonable and unfair to expect the seller to comply with local standards if the standards are complex to understand, difficult to implement, or too different depending on the importing country's region.[103] On the other hand, if the seller's prior dealings at the place of intended use or at the relevant buyer's place of business, either because it has a branch or subsidiary in such places or has already exported or promoted its goods there, it is assumed to have actual or implied knowledge of the existence of local standards and therefore, an obligation to comply with them.[104] The same applies if the standard at the place of use or the relevant buyer's place of business also applies or is the same as the seller's place of business. As the same standard coincides in all relevant places (buyer's place, intended use and seller's place) it becomes the relevant context with reference to the 'ordinary use' under Article 35(2)(a) CISG.

The relevant standards are those existing at the time of the contract's conclusion.[105]

4. Usual or adequate packaging, Article 35(2)(d) CISG

The conformity of goods includes their packaging (Article 35(2)(d) CISG). Goods must generally be packaged in a manner usual for such goods, which may include packaging in containers.[106] The 'usualness' of the packaging is determined primarily by the trade industry's usages.[107] Local usages, such as the seller's or the buyer's, are irrelevant, unless they reflect established international trade usages for packaging the goods in question.[108] Thus, the focus should be on the packaging's purpose—ensuring the appropriate protection of goods during transport.[109] Markings and instructions, particularly those necessary for handling by carriers, may also be 'usual' for the packaging in question.

The obligation regarding the packaging of goods applies regardless of whether the goods are to be dispatched or merely placed at the buyer's disposal for

---

[103] Ibid.

[104] CISG Advisory Council, 'CISG-AC Opinion No. 19' (n 81) comment 5.5.

[105] Ibid Black Letter Rule 2; Schwenzer, 'Article 35 CISG: Conformity of Goods' in Schwenzer and Schroeter (eds) (n 4) para 19.

[106] Cf Schwenzer, 'Article 35 CISG: Conformity of Goods' in Schwenzer and Schroeter (eds) (n 4) para 31.

[107] Kröll, 'Article 35' in Kröll, Mistelis, and Perales Viscasillas (eds) (n 20) para 145; Brunner and Gottlieb, 'Article 35 (Conformity of the Goods)' in Brunner and Gottlieb (eds) (n 6) para 23; Schwenzer, 'Article 35 CISG: Conformity of Goods' in Schwenzer and Schroeter (eds) (n 4) para 31.

[108] Kröll, 'Article 35' in Kröll, Mistelis, and Perales Viscasillas (eds) (n 20) para 146; Schwenzer, 'Article 35 CISG: Conformity of Goods' in Schwenzer and Schroeter (eds) (n 4) para 31.

[109] *Coenegrachts Substraat NV v Shasta B.V.* [2020] Ondernemingsrechtbank Antwerpen (Commercial Court Antwerp) A/19/00853/2020/2972, CISG-online 6928: where the seller complied with its obligation by packing the goods in a manner they could be preserved; Schwenzer, 'Article 35 CISG: Conformity of Goods' in Schwenzer and Schroeter (eds) (n 4) para 31.

collection.[110] In the latter case, it may be inferred from the parties' agreement or commercial usage that the buyer is responsible for providing the necessary receptacles for transport, relieving the seller of the obligation to package the goods.[111]

If there are no established usages to determine the customary manner of packaging, adequate packaging is required. This is particularly true for goods that are new or specially manufactured for the buyer. In assessing whether packaging is adequate, factors such as the nature of the goods, the duration and type of transport, and climatic conditions must be considered.[112] Packaging must also offer sufficient protection against any diversion or onward carriage of the goods, which the seller was aware of at the time of contract conclusion.[113] If the packaging is damaged during transport without damaging the goods themselves, the seller is not liable if the packaging's sole purpose is to protect the goods during transport.[114] However, the seller is liable if the packaging forms part of the goods, such as the original packaging of branded goods or permanent packaging intended for resale (e.g. bottles or bags).[115] If the goods themselves are damaged during transport due to defective packaging, the seller is liable, even if the actual damage occurs after the passing of risk.[116]

Public law requirements concerning the packaging of goods at the place of resale, use, or the buyer's place of business may need to be observed, depending on the applicability of such standards as discussed in the preceding section.

5. Buyer's knowledge of lack of conformity under Article 35(3) CISG

Article 35(3) CISG provides that the seller is not liable for the lack of conformity of the goods under Article 35(2) CISG if the buyer knew or could not have been unaware of the lack of conformity at the time of contract conclusion. The buyer's knowledge must be of the specific defect claimed; knowing another defect does not exclude liability.[117] 'Could not have been unaware' implies more than gross

---

[110] Schwenzer, 'Article 35 CISG: Conformity of Goods' in Schwenzer and Schroeter (eds) (n 4) para 32.

[111] Ibid.

[112] Kröll, 'Article 35' in Kröll, Mistelis, and Perales Viscasillas (eds) (n 20) para 147; Brunner and Gottlieb, 'Article 35 (Conformity of the Goods)' in Brunner and Gottlieb (eds) (n 6) para 23; Schwenzer, 'Article 35 CISG: Conformity of Goods' in Schwenzer and Schroeter (eds) (n 4) para 33.

[113] Kröll, 'Article 35' in Kröll, Mistelis, and Perales Viscasillas (eds) (n 20) para 149; Schwenzer, 'Article 35 CISG: Conformity of Goods' in Schwenzer and Schroeter (eds) (n 4) para 33.

[114] Schwenzer, 'Article 35 CISG: Conformity of Goods' in Schwenzer and Schroeter (eds) (n 4) para 33; cf Kröll, 'Article 35' in Kröll, Mistelis, and Perales Viscasillas (eds) (n 20) para 144.

[115] Schwenzer, 'Article 35 CISG: Conformity of Goods' in Schwenzer and Schroeter (eds) (n 4) para 33.

[116] Kröll, 'Article 35' in Kröll, Mistelis, and Perales Viscasillas (eds) (n 20) para 151; Schwenzer, 'Article 35 CISG: Conformity of Goods' in Schwenzer and Schroeter (eds) (n 4) para 33.

[117] *Doscha B.V. v Walotex B.V. et al.* [2023] Gerechtshof Arnhem-Leeuwarden (Court of Appeal Arnhem-Leeuwarden) 200.317.640/01l, CISG-online 6639.

negligence[118] and excludes the seller's liability only for obvious defects, reducing the burden of proving actual knowledge.[119] This consideration involves the buyer's position rather than a purely objective standard and is especially relevant for specific goods like second-hand machines.[120]

Article 35(3) CISG does not cover situations where the seller guaranteed quality, specifically warranted a characteristic of the goods or fraudulently concealed a defect. Such cases fall under Article 35(1) CISG, making Article 35(3) CISG inapplicable.[121] In fraud cases, based on Article 40 and Article 7(1) CISG, the seller is liable even if the buyer could not have been unaware of the defect. A grossly negligent buyer deserves more protection than a deceptive seller.[122]

Article 35(3) CISG is not relevant for Article 35(2)(c) CISG, where goods must conform to a sample or model. Goods conform to the contract if they match the sample or model, even if defects were or should have been apparent to the buyer upon examination.[123]

IV. Time for Conformity

The goods must conform to the contract when the risk passes to the buyer (Article 36(1) CISG). The time at which the risk passes is determined by the parties' agreement—often through an ICC Incoterms®—or commercial usage or practices, or Articles 67 to 69 CISG. If the goods comply with the contract when the risk passes, the buyer usually has no rights if they deteriorate after that time due to external factors and no longer conform to the contract.

The seller is responsible for any lack of conformity that was already present when the risk passed, even if it was not noticeable at that time (such as hidden defects). Some examples of this are when the seller delivers a product that does not comply with a specific date of manufacture,[124] or when the goods

---

[118] Schwenzer, 'Article 35 CISG: Conformity of Goods' in Schwenzer and Schroeter (eds) (n 4) para 37.

[119] Kröll, 'Article 35' in Kröll, Mistelis, and Perales Viscasillas (eds) (n 20) para 155; Schwenzer, 'Article 35 CISG: Conformity of Goods' in Schwenzer and Schroeter (eds) (n 4) para 37.

[120] Brunner and Gottlieb, 'Article 35 (Conformity of the Goods)' in Brunner and Gottlieb (eds) (n 6) para 24; Schwenzer, 'Article 35 CISG: Conformity of Goods' in Schwenzer and Schroeter (eds) (n 4) para 37.

[121] Art 35(3) CISG only applies to lack of conformity under art 35(2) CISG, not to contractually agreed qualities under art 35(1) CISG, nor can it be applied by analogy.

[122] Schwenzer, 'Article 35 CISG: Conformity of Goods' in Schwenzer and Schroeter (eds) (n 4) para 40; Cf Kröll, 'Article 35' in Kröll, Mistelis, and Perales Viscasillas (eds) (n 20) para 162.

[123] Schwenzer, 'Article 35 CISG: Conformity of Goods' in Schwenzer and Schroeter (eds) (n 4) para 42.

[124] *Mest Prom 3 LLP v S. Avto OAO* [2007] судебная коллегия Высшего Арбитражного Суда Российской Федерации (Supreme Arbitrazh (Commercial) Court of the Russian Federation) ВАС-12842/2007, CISG-online 2525.

that are destined to shred aluminium, do not fulfil this function[125] required under the contract or the CISG. Similarly, if the goods are damaged during transport because of faulty packaging, they are considered non-conforming at the time of delivery, even if the effects of such non-conformity only appear later.[126]

Other breaches may have occurred before the passing of risk that led to non-conformity of the goods after that point in time. For instance, non-conformity could be due to the seller's choice of an unreliable carrier, an incorrect delivery route selection, or the provision of defective operating instructions.[127] The seller may also be held accountable for obligations breached after the risk has passed. For instance, if the seller damages the goods while collecting their container after the risk has passed, or if components are damaged after the risk has been passed to the buyer under a contract of sale with the seller's assembly obligations, then the seller can be held liable.[128]

The seller is also responsible for any lack of conformity that appears after the risk has passed to the buyer if such is a result of a breach of a guarantee which ensures that the goods will remain fit for their ordinary purpose or a particular purpose, or will retain specified qualities or characteristics (Article 36(2) CISG).[129] These guarantees are known as 'guarantees of durability'. It should be noted that, under Article 35 CISG, the seller is already responsible for ensuring that the goods remain usable for a certain period of time. If, after the risk has passed to the buyer, the goods are found not to satisfy a guarantee of durability given by the seller, it is generally assumed that the defects existed at the time when the risk passed to the buyer. As a result, the seller is liable for lack of conformity under Article 35 CISG in conjunction with Article 36(1) CISG. In this regard, Article 36(2) serves only to help the buyer in terms of easing the burden of proof.

Whether the guarantee of durability covers defects caused by the inappropriate use of the goods by the buyer, operating errors, or the use of the goods by third parties in a different way than intended or usual, is a matter of contract interpretation under Article 8 CISG. In some instances, the parties might have agreed that the seller guarantees the durability of their goods even in such scenarios. However,

---

[125] *Trinity Metals LLC v Shred-Tech North America et al.* [2022] U.S. District Court for the Southern District of Indiana, 1:21-cv-02876-RLY-DML, CISG-online 6258.

[126] *Hoogendik Import/Export B.V. et al. v Bluemarine Fish International, S.L.* [2014] Audiencia Provincial de Pontevedra (Court of Appeal Pontevedra) 251/2013/569/2014, CISG-online 2576; *Carlos Soto S.A. v Don Emiliano* [2015] Audiencia Provincial de Pontevedra (Court of Appeal Pontevedra) 681/2014/531/2015, CISG-online 2730.

[127] *[...] v Ed Fruit & Vegatables B.V.* [2009] Rechtbank Breda (District Court Breda) 197586/KG ZA 08-659, CISG-online 1789.

[128] *China North Chemical Industries Corp. v Beston Chemical Corp.* [2006] U.S. District Court for the Southern District of Texas, Civ. A. H-04-0912, CISG-online 1177.

[129] *4work SIA v DND Talis UAB* [2022] Rīgas pilsētas tiesa (District Court City of Riga), C-2279-22/72, CISG-online 6925.

such guarantees are highly unusual and should only be considered to exist if it is explicit that the seller intended to provide such a guarantee.

V. Burden and Standard of Proof

The CISG does not contain explicit provisions governing the burden or standard of proof. Nonetheless, this does not imply that such matters fall outside the scope of the Convention. On the contrary, questions of burden and standard of proof in the context of non-conformity must be settled in accordance with the general principles upon which the CISG is based,[130] as mandated by Article 7(2) CISG, since they are inherent in the operation and implied effects of several of its provisions.

By interpreting Articles 35, 38, and 39 CISG in a systematic and teleological manner, a coherent set of rules on the allocation of the burden of proof and the applicable standard emerges. First, with regard to burden of proof, the CISG reflects two interconnected principles: the 'rule and exception' approach and the principle of proximity to the evidence.[131] The party asserting the 'rule-based' position bears the burden to establish it; conversely, the party invoking an exception or deviation must prove the factual circumstances justifying that exception.

To succeed in a claim for non-conformity of the goods, the buyer must prove that the delivered goods failed to conform either to the specific contractual requirements (Article 35(1) CISG) or to the default conformity standards established in Article 35(2) CISG.[132]

Under Article 35(1) CISG, the buyer must prove the existence of agreed specifications or requirements that the goods failed to meet.[133] In the absence of express terms, under Article 35(2) CISG, the buyer must demonstrate that the goods were not fit for their ordinary purpose (subparagraph (a)), or for a particular purpose made known to the seller (subparagraph (b)).[134] In the latter case, the buyer must also prove that it was reasonable to rely on the seller's skill and judgment, unless the seller can show otherwise. In addition, when conformity is assessed against a sample or model (subparagraph (c)), the buyer must prove the qualities such goods were expected to exhibit.

---

[130] Schwenzer, 'Article 35 CISG: Conformity of Goods' in Schwenzer and Schroeter (eds) (n 4) para 52; Brunner and Gottlieb, 'Article 35 (Conformity of the Goods)' in Brunner and Gottlieb (eds) (n 6) para 27.

[131] Schwenzer, 'Article 35 CISG: Conformity of Goods' in Schwenzer and Schroeter (eds) (n 4) para 54; Brunner and Gottlieb, 'Article 35 (Conformity of the Goods)' in Brunner and Gottlieb (eds) (n 6) para 27; Kröll, 'Article 35' in Kröll, Mistelis, and Perales Viscasillas (eds) (n 20) para 178.

[132] Kröll, 'Article 35' in Kröll, Mistelis, and Perales Viscasillas (eds) (n 20) para 185.

[133] Ibid para 195.

[134] Schwenzer, 'Article 35 CISG: Conformity of Goods' in Schwenzer and Schroeter (eds) (n 4) para 56; Brunner and Gottlieb, 'Article 35 (Conformity of the Goods)' in Brunner and Gottlieb (eds) (n 6) para 31; Kröll, 'Article 35' in Kröll, Mistelis, and Perales Viscasillas (eds) (n 20) paras 198, 200.

In general, once the buyer has taken delivery, it bears the burden of proving that the goods were non-conforming at the time the risk passed.[135] However, this general rule is subject to exceptions. In certain circumstances, the burden may shift to the seller—particularly when the buyer rejects the goods or gives immediate notice of non-conformity upon taking delivery.[136] In such cases, it is reasonable to require the seller to prove that the goods complied with the contract or with Article 35 CISG at the relevant time. A similar shift in burden may occur where the seller, especially if it is the manufacturer or possesses superior knowledge of the goods, could reasonably have been aware of the defect before the buyer provided notice.[137]

If the seller invokes Article 35(3) CISG—claiming that the buyer knew or could not have been unaware of the non-conformity at the time of contract conclusion—it is the seller who must establish that knowledge or constructive awareness on the part of the buyer.[138]

As for the standard of proof, the Convention again remains silent, but recourse to Article 7(2) CISG allows the derivation of a uniform solution. Allowing national standards to govern this issue would undermine the international character of the CISG and fragment its application.[139] A general principle that has emerged from CISG jurisprudence and doctrine is that of reasonableness.[140] This standard, which permeates various provisions of the CISG, offers a suitable and autonomous benchmark for assessing proof. Accordingly, the party bearing the burden of proof must establish its claim—such as the non-conformity of the goods—with a reasonable degree of certainty, taking into account the circumstances of the case, the nature of the goods, and the roles and knowledge of the parties.

---

[135] Schwenzer, 'Article 35 CISG: Conformity of Goods' in Schwenzer and Schroeter (eds) (n 4) para 55; Kröll, 'Article 35' in Kröll, Mistelis, and Perales Viscasillas (eds) (n 20) para 189; *Used textile cleaning machine case*, Bundesgericht/Tribunal fédéral (Swiss Federal Supreme Court) (2003)—4C.198/2003, CISG-online 840; Florian Mohs, 'Anmerkung zu BGer, 13.11.2003—4C.198/2003' (2004) IHR 219.

[136] *Cables and wires case*, Bundesgericht/Tribunal fédéral (Swiss Federal Supreme Court) (2004) 4C.144/2004, CISG-online 848; *Kitchens case* VI Kreisgericht Wil (Court of First Instance Wil) (2016)—VV.2015.33-Wl2ZE-DWE, CISG-online 2936; Schwenzer, 'Article 35 CISG: Conformity of Goods' in Schwenzer and Schroeter (eds) (n 4) para 55; Kröll, 'Article 35' in Kröll, Mistelis, and Perales Viscasillas (eds) (n 20) paras 187, 188.

[137] Schwenzer, 'Article 35 CISG: Conformity of Goods' in Schwenzer and Schroeter (eds) (n 4) para 55; Brunner and Gottlieb, 'Article 35 (Conformity of the Goods)' in Brunner and Gottlieb (eds) (n 6) para 28.

[138] Schwenzer, 'Article 35 CISG: Conformity of Goods' in Schwenzer and Schroeter (eds) (n 4) para 57; Brunner and Gottlieb, 'Article 35 (Conformity of the Goods)' in Brunner and Gottlieb (eds) (n 6) para 31; Kröll, 'Article 35' in Kröll, Mistelis, and Perales Viscasillas (eds) (n 20) para 203.

[139] Brunner and Gottlieb, 'Article 35 (Conformity of the Goods)' in Brunner and Gottlieb (eds) (n 6) para 32.

[140] Schwenzer, 'Article 35 CISG: Conformity of Goods' in Schwenzer and Schroeter (eds) (n 4) para 58; Brunner and Gottlieb, 'Article 35 (Conformity of the Goods)' in Brunner and Gottlieb (eds) (n 6) para 33.

VI. Examination and Notice

1. Comparative background

The duty of a buyer to examine goods and notify the seller of any discovered defects is prevalent across many legal systems, though its purpose and operation vary significantly. In many civil law systems, particularly in commercial transactions, there is a strict notice requirement where the buyer must examine the goods and notify the seller of any defects to preserve remedies for breach of contract.[141] This requirement ensures legal certainty and facilitates quick transactions but is often criticized for overly protecting the seller at the buyer's expense. By contrast, common law systems, such as those following the English model, impose an indirect obligation on the buyer. Failure to notify the seller within a reasonable time results in the loss of the right to reject the goods but typically allows the buyer to retain the right to claim damages for non-conformity.[142]

In the United States, the notice requirement is twofold: the buyer loses the right to avoid the contract if it fails to notify the seller of non-conformities in a timely manner but can sometimes regain this right through revocation of acceptance. After accepting the goods, the buyer must notify the seller of any non-conformities within a reasonable period to retain the right to other remedies, especially damages.[143] Eastern European and Central Asian legal systems also require the buyer to examine the goods and notify the seller within a reasonable period. However, if the buyer fails to do so, the seller can refuse to cure if it proves that the failure has made curing impossible or disproportionately costly.[144] These systems are less explicit about the fate of other remedies, suggesting that the buyer might still retain rights like damages and avoidance.

Internationally, the CISG mandates the buyer to examine the goods (Article 38 CISG) and notify the seller of defects (Article 39). During the drafting of the CISG, concerns from developing countries led to a compromise in Article 44 CISG, which allows buyers to reduce the purchase price or claim damages, except for loss of profit, if they have a reasonable excuse for delayed notice.[145]

The obligation of examining goods and notifying defects is primarily intended to give the seller an opportunity to remedy the lack of conformity by delivering the missing or substitute goods, repairing the goods, or compensating the buyer

---

[141] Schwenzer and Muñoz, *Global Sales and Contract Law* (n 2) para 34.04. For example, Brazilian Civil Code arts 445, 446; Swiss Code of Obligations art 201; Chinese Civil Code arts 620, 621.

[142] Schwenzer and Muñoz, *Global Sales and Contract Law* (n 2) para 34.06. See in particular English Sale of Goods Act s 35(4).

[143] Schwenzer and Muñoz, *Global Sales and Contract Law* (n 2) para 34.07. See in particular Uniform Commercial Code ss 2-606, 2-607(2)(3), 2-608(3).

[144] Schwenzer and Muñoz, *Global Sales and Contract Law* (n 2) para 34.08. For example, Russian Civil Code art 483; Ukrainian Civil Code art 688; Lithuanian Civil Code art 6.348.

[145] Schwenzer and Muñoz, *Global Sales and Contract Law* (n 2) para 34.12.

in some other manner. The buyer's notification also allows the seller to prepare for any potential negotiation or dispute that may arise from the non-conformity, such as by obtaining supporting evidence. Additionally, the seller may need to prepare a claim against its supplier. Ultimately, the goal is to establish certainty for the seller regarding which accounts can be considered closed at any given time. If the buyer does not express any dissatisfaction with the goods and continues to process them, the seller may assume that the buyer has accepted the goods.

2. Examination

a.) Time

Article 38 CISG mandates that examination of the goods must be done 'within as short a period as is practicable in the circumstances'.[146] This flexible approach accounts for the diverse nature of goods in international trade, where a fixed time frame would not be appropriate for all scenarios. The duration of the examination period depends on the specific circumstances of the transaction and the reasonable opportunities available to the buyer to examine the goods, including factors such as their nature, delivery conditions, and the buyer's ability to perform the examination.

The nature of the goods plays a critical role in determining the examination period. Perishable goods, for example, demand immediate inspection, often within hours or days, to ensure their quality before they deteriorate.[147] For durable goods, buyers must promptly check the quantity, type, and any visible defects, though a more detailed examination may occur later. In the case of complex technical equipment or machinery, especially when unfamiliar to the buyer, a trial run or extended testing period may be necessary, potentially lasting weeks or months.[148] Similarly, when raw materials or components require further processing, defects might only become apparent after such steps.

The examination period typically begins when the goods are delivered or handed over to the buyer. If goods are delivered earlier than agreed, the buyer is not required to examine them until the agreed delivery date.[149] Conversely, late

---

[146] *Corian furniture for Geneva hair salon case* [2021] Tribunal de Première Instance de Genève (Court of First Instance Geneva) C/16258/2017/JTPI/9216/2021, CISG-online 5899.

[147] *Axarfruit S.L. v Organto Europe B.V.* [2024] Gerechthof 's-Hertogenbosch (Court of Appeal's-Hertogenbosch) 200.326.374_02, CISG-online 7060: where the court considered that the buyer had to examine the avocados in a rapid fashion since the goods were perishable.

[148] Stefan Kröll, 'Article 38' in Kröll, Mistelis, and Perales Viscasillas (eds) (n 20) para 92; Christoph Brunner and Flavio Peter, 'Article 38 (Time for Examining the Goods)' in Brunner and Gottlieb (eds) (n 6) para 7; Ingeborg Schwenzer, 'Article 38 CISG: Buyer's Examination of the Goods' in Schwenzer and Schroeter (eds) (n 4) para 15.

[149] Kröll, 'Article 38' in Kröll, Mistelis, and Perales Viscasillas (eds) (n 20) para 106; Brunner and Peter, 'Article 38 (Time for Examining the Goods)' in Brunner and Gottlieb (eds) (n 6) para 8; Schwenzer, 'Article 38 CISG: Buyer's Examination of the Goods' in Schwenzer and Schroeter (eds) (n 4) para 20.

delivery generally does not release the buyer from its obligation to inspect the goods, although the specific circumstances of the delay may influence the examination time frame.

When contracts involve carriage, Article 38(2) CISG specifies that the examination period does not commence until the goods arrive at their destination.[150] Buyers are not responsible for inspections conducted by carriers. If goods are redirected while in transit or re-dispatched to a new location, the examination period may be postponed until they reach the new destination, provided the seller was aware of this possibility at the time of the contract.[151]

In some circumstances, sellers are responsible for providing critical instructions, such as operating manuals, to enable proper examination, and delays in doing so can postpone the start of the examination period. Buyers must act promptly but are allowed reasonable time to inspect goods based on objective factors like technical facilities, business disruptions, and cultural practices.[152]

b.) Method

The method of examination is primarily the one agreed upon by the contracting parties. This agreement may specify details such as the number of test samples, chemical analyses, or procedures for examining machinery, including the type and duration of trial runs. If the parties have not agreed on a specific method, the examination should follow established commercial usage or practices relevant to the trade concerned under Article 9 CISG or the CISG underlying principle of reasonability.[153]

The parties may also agree on who should perform the examination. In some contracts, particularly those involving complex goods like machinery or plants, joint examinations by the buyer and seller are common. Alternatively, the parties may agree to involve a neutral third party, including government bodies and private enterprises. Without any agreement, the buyer, its employees, or third parties such as clients or experts typically perform the examination. If a third-party examination is defective, the buyer is usually responsible for the consequences unless the examination was conducted by a neutral third party agreed upon by both parties or insisted upon by the seller.[154]

---

[150] [...]xyz v A.N. International B.V. [2023] Rechtbank Zeeland-West-Brabant (District Court Zeeland-West-Brabant) C/02/390635/HA ZA 21-595 (E), CISG-online 6283.

[151] Jet'Sac S.A.S. v Lung Meng Machinery Co. Ltd. [2022] Cour d'appel de Douai (Court of Appeal Douai) 21/01679, CISG-online 6345.

[152] Kröll, 'Article 38' in Kröll, Mistelis, and Perales Viscasillas (eds) (n 20) para 86; Brunner and Peter, 'Article 38 (Time for Examining the Goods)' in Brunner and Gottlieb (eds) (n 6) para 6; Schwenzer, 'Article 38 CISG: Buyer's Examination of the Goods' in Schwenzer and Schroeter (eds) (n 4) para 18.

[153] Kröll, 'Article 38' in Kröll, Mistelis, and Perales Viscasillas (eds) (n 20) para 19; Brunner and Peter, 'Article 38 (Time for Examining the Goods)' in Brunner and Gottlieb (eds) (n 6) para 11; Schwenzer, 'Article 38 CISG: Buyer's Examination of the Goods' in Schwenzer and Schroeter (eds) (n 4) para 11.

[154] Kröll, 'Article 38' in Kröll, Mistelis, and Perales Viscasillas (eds) (n 20) para 19; Brunner and Peter, 'Article 38 (Time for Examining the Goods)' in Brunner and Gottlieb (eds) (n 6) para 11; Schwenzer, 'Article 38 CISG: Buyer's Examination of the Goods' in Schwenzer and Schroeter (eds) (n 4) para 11.

The purpose of the examination is to identify defects in the goods. Under the underlying principle of reasonability, the buyer must conduct the examination in a manner appropriate to the goods' nature, quantity, packaging, and other relevant factors. The method of examination may also account for subjective factors, such as the buyer's lack of experience or limited access to adequate facilities. An experienced buyer is expected to perform a thorough inspection, particularly if previous deliveries from the same seller had defects. If there is a risk of significant losses due to undetected defects, the examination must be more extensive, potentially requiring the engagement of experts. While the buyer bears the costs of the examination, the process should be reasonable and proportional to the circumstances, avoiding unnecessary or prohibited actions.[155]

For instance, when a large quantity of goods is delivered, the buyer is not required to examine every single item or the full mass. Instead, representative random sampling is often sufficient. This may involve visually inspecting the goods, weighing or measuring them, and, if necessary, using sensory tests such as smelling or tasting. The number of samples taken should be a small fraction of the total quantity unless initial inspections suggest that the goods are atypical. If goods must be destroyed—like unfreezing—the quantity to be inspected may be close to one per hundred or per thounsand depending on the unit value of the goods. For goods intended for further processing, sampling should ensure they meet the requirements of their intended use. For example, cloth materials should be tested for shrinkage, colour fastness, and dyeing consistency, but buyers are not expected to conduct tests that go beyond what is reasonable, such as washing every piece of clothing or testing for defects that only appear during wear.[156]

Complicated technical goods, such as machinery, processing equipment, or vehicles, require specific examination methods. The buyer needs to confirm that the equipment functions as intended, which may involve test runs or simulations under production-like conditions.[157] For machinery used in mass production, spot checks should simulate the production process under conditions similar to actual use.

Special considerations apply to perishable goods, which necessitate quick examinations to allow for timely notifications of defects.[158] For goods intended for

---

[155] Kröll, 'Article 38' in Kröll, Mistelis, and Perales Viscasillas (eds) (n 20) para 35; Brunner and Peter, 'Article 38 (Time for Examining the Goods)' in Brunner and Gottlieb (eds) (n 6) para 14; Schwenzer, 'Article 38 CISG: Buyer's Examination of the Goods' in Schwenzer and Schroeter (eds) (n 4) para 28.

[156] Kröll, 'Article 38' in Kröll, Mistelis, and Perales Viscasillas (eds) (n 20) paras 35–36, 55; Brunner and Peter, 'Article 38 (Time for Examining the Goods)' in Brunner and Gottlieb (eds) (n 6) paras 12–13; Schwenzer, 'Article 38 CISG: Buyer's examination of the Goods' in Schwenzer and Schroeter (eds) (n 4) para 14.

[157] Kröll, 'Article 38' in Kröll, Mistelis, and Perales Viscasillas (eds) (n 20) para 60; Schwenzer, 'Article 38 CISG: Buyer's Examination of the Goods' in Schwenzer and Schroeter (eds) (n 4) para 14.

[158] Kröll, 'Article 38' in Kröll, Mistelis, and Perales Viscasillas (eds) (n 20) para 91; Brunner and Peter, 'Article 38 (Time for Examining the Goods)' in Brunner and Gottlieb (eds) (n 6) paras 12–13; Schwenzer, 'Article 38 CISG: Buyer's Examination of the Goods' in Schwenzer and Schroeter (eds) (n 4) para 16.

human consumption, simple tests, such as viewing, smelling, or sampling, are typically sufficient. In the case of discrepancies in quantity, goods must be counted or weighed.[159] For high-value items such as artwork, the buyer should verify authenticity, especially if there is any concrete suspicion of issues.

3. Notice of non-conformity

a.) Content, form, method of transmission

Under Article 39(1) CISG, the buyer is required to notify any lack of conformity discovered during a proper examination or afterward. The content of the notification must be reasonable under the circumstances. Therefore, the notification must specify the nature of the non-conformity, enabling the seller to understand the issue and take appropriate action. While the notice must provide sufficient details about the non-conformity, it does not need to be excessively detailed.[160] A balanced objective-subjective standard is applied, taking into account factors such as the commercial positions of the parties, cultural differences, and the nature of the goods. Experts may be expected to provide more precise descriptions of non-conformity than non-experts, but general complaints or expressions of dissatisfaction are insufficient.[161] Similarly, simply placing an order for replacement goods does not qualify as a valid notice.[162] However, in the age of electronic communications, if the seller receives a vague or non-specific notice, it should make reasonable inquiries to clarify the issue. If the seller fails to do so, it may lose the ability to argue that the notice was inadequate.

The buyer must indicate any discrepancies, including whether the quantity is incorrect, whether there are quality issues, or whether the goods differ from the contractual agreement; each defect should be addressed separately.[163] In contracts involving multiple instalments, each instalment must be notified individually unless a defect affects all instalments due to a common manufacturing issue.

---

[159] Schwenzer, 'Article 38 CISG: Buyer's Examination of the Goods' in Schwenzer and Schroeter (eds) (n 4) para 14.

[160] *Frigera N.V. v D.E.C. S.r.l.* [2024] Parket bij het Hof van Cassatie/Parquet près la Cour de Cassation (Advocate General at the Belgian Supreme Court) C.23.0431.N, CISG-online 7066, and Hof van Cassatie van België/Cour de cassation de Belgique (Belgian Supreme Court), CISG-online 7068.

[161] Ingeborg Schwenzer, 'Article 39 CISG: Buyer's Notice of Non-conformity' in Schwenzer and Schroeter (eds) (n 4) para 7. See also, Kröll, 'Article 39' in Kröll, Mistelis, and Perales Viscasillas (eds) (n 20) para 31; Christoph Brunner and Flavio Peter, 'Article 39 (Notice of Lack of Conformity)' in Brunner and Gottlieb (eds) (n 6) para 4.

[162] Kröll, 'Article 39' in Kröll, Mistelis, and Perales Viscasillas (eds) (n 20) para 31; Schwenzer, 'Article 39 CISG: Buyer's Notice of Non-conformity' in Schwenzer and Schroeter (eds) (n 4) para 7.

[163] Brunner and Peter, 'Article 39 (Notice of Lack of Conformity)' in Brunner and Gottlieb (eds) (n 6) paras 8–9; Schwenzer, 'Article 39 CISG: Buyer's Notice of Non-conformity' in Schwenzer and Schroeter (eds) (n 4) para 10.

The level of detail required depends on the circumstances. If the effort to provide precise information would be unreasonable, such as when the goods are numerous or deteriorate quickly, only a general indication of the problem may be expected. For technical equipment or machinery, for instance, the buyer might only be required to describe symptoms generally, without needing to identify specific causes. Also, for durable goods, where the seller can more easily assess the extent of the issue, an approximate description from the buyer is usually sufficient.

The notice of lack of conformity does not need to follow a specific format. Under Articles 11 and 7(2) CISG, the buyer may use any form of communication, including phone, email, or other digital media. Article 27 CISG places the risk of communication on the seller, meaning that as long as the notice is dispatched appropriately, the seller bears the risk of any transmission failure.[164] Nowadays, postal services may only be considered reasonable for nearby regions with reliable service. Importantly, when notifying the seller of a lack of conformity, the buyer is not required to state its intention to assert its legal rights, only to provide information about the issue with the goods.[165]

b.) Notification within a reasonable time

Under the CISG, the time for giving notice of any non-conformity in goods may be freely agreed upon by the parties, as allowed under Article 6 CISG. In the absence of such an agreement, Article 39(1) CISG requires the buyer to notify the seller of any lack of conformity within a reasonable time after the buyer discovers or should have discovered it.[166] Two distinct periods are relevant here: the period for examining the goods under Article 38 CISG and the period for giving notice of the lack of conformity. These periods must not be combined.[167]

In the absence of agreement, the determination of what constitutes a 'reasonable time' for giving notice under Article 39 CISG depends on the specific circumstances of the case, including trade usages and any established practices between the parties. The nature of the goods is also crucial. For perishable goods, notice

---

[164] Kröll, 'Article 39' in Kröll, Mistelis, and Perales Viscasillas (eds) (n 20) para 52; Schwenzer, 'Article 39 CISG: Buyer's Notice of Non-conformity' in Schwenzer and Schroeter (eds) (n 4) para 11.

[165] Brunner and Peter, 'Article 39 (Notice of Lack of Conformity)' in Brunner and Gottlieb (eds) (n 6) para 10; Schwenzer, 'Article 39 CISG: Buyer's Notice of Non-conformity' in Schwenzer and Schroeter (eds) (n 4) para 13.

[166] *Shenzen Synergy Digital Co., Ltd. v Mingtel, Inc.* [2023] U.S. Court of Appeals (5th Circuit) 22-40440, CISG-online 6392.

[167] Kröll, 'Article 39' in Kröll, Mistelis, and Perales Viscasillas (eds) (n 20) para 58; Brunner and Peter, 'Article 39 (Notice of Lack of Conformity)' in Brunner and Gottlieb (eds) (n 6) paras 12–13; Schwenzer, 'Article 39 CISG: Buyer's Notice of Non-conformity' in Schwenzer and Schroeter (eds) (n 4) para 20; CISG-AC Opinion No 2, Examination of the Goods and Notice of Non-Conformity Articles 38 and 39, 7 June 2004. Rapporteur: Professor Eric E. Bergsten, Emeritus, Pace University School of Law, New York, Black Letter Rule 2, stating that the Convention requires these two periods to be distinguished and kept separate, even when the facts of the case would permit them to be combined into a single period for giving notice.

must be given quickly, often within hours or a few days.[168] Durable goods allow for a longer notice period, but goods that are seasonal, subject to price fluctuations, or require expert evaluation may necessitate a more rapid notice.[169] The buyer's intended remedy also impacts the time frame. If the buyer seeks to retain the goods while claiming damages or a price reduction, a more generous notice period may be allowed. However, if the buyer intends to reject the goods and avoid the contract or request substitute delivery, prompt notice is essential to give the seller an opportunity to remedy the defect and arrange for the goods' return.[170] Additionally, a longer notice period may be justified if the buyer requires time to await feedback from a subsequent buyer or analyse customer complaints. If there are no circumstances indicating a shorter period one may allow the buyer one month for giving notice.[171]

The time frame for giving notice begins when the buyer becomes aware or should have become aware of the lack of conformity for each delivery. If the buyer is already aware of the issue, the notice period starts immediately, regardless of whether the examination period has concluded. For instance, if a buyer notices a discrepancy in quantity upon delivery, they must report it even if they have not yet completed a quality inspection.[172] The determination of when the buyer 'should have discovered' a defect depends on the nature of the defect. For defects identifiable through proper examination, the notice period starts at the conclusion of the examination period, creating a sequential timeline. However, if the buyer delays the examination, they must compensate for the delay by promptly reporting any discovered defects.[173]

---

[168] Brunner and Peter, 'Article 39 (Notice of Lack of Conformity)' in Brunner and Gottlieb (eds) (n 6) para 13; Schwenzer, 'Article 39 CISG: Buyer's Notice of Non-conformity' in Schwenzer and Schroeter (eds) (n 4) para 16.

[169] *Portuguese clogs case* [2024] Rechtbank Overijssel (District Court Overijssel) C/08/309410/HA ZA 24-44, CISG-online 7206: where the buyer's notification had to be immediate.

[170] Brunner and Peter, 'Article 39 (Notice of Lack of Conformity)' in Brunner and Gottlieb (eds) (n 6) para 13; Schwenzer, 'Article 39 CISG: Buyer's Notice of Non-conformity' in Schwenzer and Schroeter (eds) (n 4) para 17.

[171] Schwenzer, 'Article 39 CISG: Buyer's Notice of Non-conformity' in Schwenzer and Schroeter (eds) (n 4) para 17; *Grinding set for hygienic tissues producing machine case*, Bundesgerichtshof (German Supreme Court), (1999)—VIII ZR 287/98, CISG-online 475 (treated one month as the 'regular' reasonable period for notice under CISG Article 39(1)); *Used textile cleaning machine case*, Bundesgericht/Tribunal fédéral (Swiss Federal Supreme Court) (2003)—4C.198/2003, CISG-online 840; *Denim 'New Elite Col' case*, Oberlandesgericht Düsseldorf (Court of Appeal Düsseldorf)(2015)— I-21 U 14/15, CISG-online 2731 (confirming that one month is a standard period); *Facade panels for mountain lodge case*, Tribunal Cantonal du Valais/Kantonsgericht Wallis (Court of Appeal Canton Valais)(2020)—C1 19 260, CISG-online 5497 (applying the usual Swiss approach of a 'rough average' of one month for non-perishable goods).

[172] Kröll, 'Article 39' in Kröll, Mistelis, and Perales Viscasillas (eds) (n 20) para 65; Schwenzer, 'Article 39 CISG: Buyer's Notice of Non-conformity' in Schwenzer and Schroeter (eds) (n 4) para 19.

[173] Kröll, 'Article 39' in Kröll, Mistelis, and Perales Viscasillas (eds) (n 20) para 68; Brunner and Peter, 'Article 39 (Notice of Lack of Conformity)' in Brunner and Gottlieb (eds) (n 6) para 14; Schwenzer, 'Article 39 CISG: Buyer's Notice of Non-conformity' in Schwenzer and Schroeter (eds) (n 4) para 20.

If defects are not apparent upon the initial examination, the buyer must notify the seller within a reasonable time after discovering them. Buyers are not obligated to conduct continuous examinations, such as operating machinery immediately to identify hidden defects. However, if symptoms of a defect emerge, the buyer must re-examine the goods and report any issues promptly. This ensures that buyers fulfil their duty to notify sellers of non-conformities while maintaining a practical approach that accommodates the varying circumstances of international trade.

c.) The two-year maximum period for giving notice

Under Article 39(2) CISG, a buyer must notify the seller of any lack of conformity at least within two years from the date the goods were handed over. This time limit applies when a lack of conformity was not visible or discoverable during a proper examination, could not reasonably have been detected later, or when the buyer had a reasonable excuse for failing to give notice under Article 39(1) CISG (as addressed in Article 44 CISG). Importantly, this two-year period is an absolute deadline and is not subject to suspension or interruption, nor can it be extended by courts.[174] However, the time limit is not mandatory under the CISG. Article 6 CISG allows parties to agree on shorter or longer periods, provided such agreements are valid under applicable national laws.[175]

It is crucial to differentiate this two-year period for giving notice of non-conformity from limitation periods for initiating legal proceedings, which are not governed by the CISG. Limitation periods are addressed under the Limitation Period Convention (LC) (see Chapter 17) or the otherwise applicable domestic law. According to Article 8 LC, the limitation period is four years from the date the goods are handed over. This creates no conflict with Article 39(2) CISG. However, issues may arise if an otherwise applicable national law provides shorter limitation periods for warranty claims. For example, Germany and EU Member States have resolved this by aligning their limitation periods with the two-year time frame under Article 39(2) CISG.[176] Switzerland implemented a similar adjustment in 2013, but discrepancies persist in other jurisdictions.[177] To mitigate these uncertainties, it is advisable for parties in countries with shorter limitation periods to expressly agree on a time frame aligned with Article 39(2) CISG. Such agreement may be included in their contract, provided the applicable domestic law permits modification of the statutory limitation period.

---

[174] Brunner and Peter, 'Article 39 (Notice of Lack of Conformity)' in Brunner and Gottlieb (eds) (n 6) para 16; Schwenzer, 'Article 39 CISG: Buyer's Notice of Non-conformity' in Schwenzer and Schroeter (eds) (n 4) para 24.

[175] Kröll, 'Article 39' in Kröll, Mistelis, and Perales Viscasillas (eds) (n 20) para 98; Brunner and Peter, 'Article 39 (Notice of Lack of Conformity)' in Brunner and Gottlieb (eds) (n 6) para 16.

[176] Schwenzer, 'Article 39 CISG: Buyer's Notice of Non-conformity' in Schwenzer and Schroeter (eds) (n 4) para 31.

[177] Ibid para 31.

The two-year notification period begins when the goods are physically handed over to the buyer, regardless of whether the risk of loss has passed or ownership has been transferred via documents. Physical transfer refers to the actual delivery of the goods. If goods are delivered directly to the buyer's customer, the relevant date is the handover to the customer. This applies even in cases where the goods are redirected under Article 38(3) CISG. However, if the goods are redispatched by the buyer to a customer after they have been handed over, the period begins at the initial handover. If the goods are destroyed, confiscated, or rejected, the start of the period is determined by the hypothetical handover date.[178]

Applying Article 39(2) CISG in international supply chains can be challenging as goods often pass through multiple parties before reaching the end-user. Defects may not be discovered within two years, potentially barring claims for non-conformity. One solution is for the parties in a supply chain to agree on specific events that trigger the start of the notification period and the maximum duration allowed for such notice. Alternatively, a good-faith interpretation of Article 39(2) under Article 7(2) CISG could allow the period to start when non-conformity is discovered or ought to have been discovered, thereby accommodating the complexities of supply chains.[179]

The two-year maximum period for giving notice of non-conformity under Article 39(2) CISG does not apply if there is a different contractual guarantee period agreed upon by the parties.[180] A guarantee can extend or shorten the two-year period depending on its wording. An extension may be found in a scenario where the seller guarantees that a machine will yield a certain output for five years. Conversely, a one-year guarantee for specific performance metrics (e.g. machine efficiency) does not conflict with the two-year period for reporting defects and thus Article 39(2) CISG applies.

d.) Consequence of failure to give notice

Article 39(1) CISG states that the buyer loses the right to claim lack of conformity if it fails to give proper notice. This results in the loss of all remedies under Article 45 CISG. The buyer must pay the agreed price even if fewer goods are delivered, the goods are of inferior quality, or they are a less valuable substitute. If the seller delivers more goods and the buyer does not give notice, the buyer must pay a higher price under Article 52(2) CISG. If more valuable goods are delivered, an analogy with Article 52(2) CISG may apply to avoid conflicts with non-uniform domestic remedies.[181] However, Article 40 CISG might prevent the seller from relying on

---

[178] Ibid para 25.
[179] Schwenzer and Muñoz, 'Sustainability' (n 19) 333–34.
[180] Schwenzer, 'Article 39 CISG: Buyer's Notice of Non-conformity' in Schwenzer and Schroeter (eds) (n 4) para 28.
[181] Kröll, 'Article 39' in Kröll, Mistelis, and Perales Viscasillas (eds) (n 20) para 101; Schwenzer, 'Article 39 CISG: Buyer's Notice of Non-conformity' in Schwenzer and Schroeter (eds) (n 4) para 32.

a failure to give notice in such a scenario, because it should have known the departure from the contract and, thus, the original price might be maintained. In successive delivery contracts, failure to give notice for one instalment only affects that instalment, not future ones under Article 73(2) CISG.

The exceptions to these rules are as follows: under Article 40 CISG, no notice is needed if the seller knew or should have known about the non-conformity and did not disclose it. The two-year limit in Article 39(2) CISG does not apply in this case. Article 44 CISG provides that if the buyer has a reasonable excuse for not giving notice, it can still claim a price reduction and damages, excluding loss of profit, though these claims are still subject to the two-year limit.[182] A buyer may have a reasonable excuse under Article 44 CISG if, in the specific circumstances of the case, considerations of equity warrant a certain degree of leniency and understanding.[183] Damages may be awarded for the diminution in the value of the goods as such—that is, the difference between the actual value of the non-conforming goods and the purchase price—which may, in some cases, amount to a total loss of value. In addition, the buyer may also recover other types of losses, including incidental and consequential (see Chapter 15), with the exception of lost profits. If the goods are entirely worthless a price reduction may lead to a reduction in the contract price to zero,[184] which practically amounts to an avoidance of the contract.

Finally, the seller can waive the objection to untimely or incorrect notice, especially if it acknowledges the defect, takes back goods, agrees to repairs, or accepts an expert examination. This waiver must be invoked in court. Forfeiture of the defence of late notification is limited to cases where the seller misleads the buyer into not taking other actions.

VII. Defects in Title and Intellectual Property Rights

1. General

In addition to ensuring conformity of the goods under Article 35 CISG, the seller is also obligated to deliver goods free from third-party rights or claims that could interfere with the buyer's use or disposal of the goods. These obligations are addressed in Articles 41 and 42 CISG, which distinguish between two categories of rights and claims. Article 41 CISG encompasses situations where the buyer's ownership or ability to freely use the goods is compromised by third-party property or

---

[182] Kröll, 'Article 39' in Kröll, Mistelis, and Perales Viscasillas (eds) (n 20) para 104; Schwenzer, 'Article 39 CISG: Buyer's Notice of Non-conformity' in Schwenzer and Schroeter (eds) (n 4) para 34.

[183] Ingeborg Schwenzer, 'Article 44 CISG: Buyer's Excuse for Not Giving Notice' in Schwenzer and Schroeter (eds) (n 4) para 5.

[184] *Coffee machines case*, Oberster Gerichtshof (Austrian Supreme Court) (2005) 3 Ob 193/04k, CISG-online 1041.

contractual rights or claims. Article 42 CISG, in contrast, specifically addresses infringements of intellectual property (IP) rights that may affect the buyer's ability to use or resell the goods in a particular jurisdiction. This separation reflects the CISG's recognition that IP claims require distinct considerations—particularly regarding the territorial scope and the seller's expected knowledge—given their technical and jurisdiction-specific nature. Unlike title defects, which are typically governed by the law of the place where the goods are located (*lex rei sitae*) and focus on ownership or possession, IP claims and rights require a nuanced analysis of registered and unregistered rights, licensing arrangements, and public notoriety within a particular market. The technical complexity and jurisdiction-specific application of IP law thus necessitate a separate legal framework under Article 42 CISG. The following sections examine the scope and application of each provision.

2. Legal title rights and claims

a.) Rights

Under Article 41 CISG, the seller is obligated to deliver goods free from any third-party rights or claims. This rule applies when the seller cannot transfer full ownership of the goods to the buyer. For instance, if the goods originate from a third party and the domestic law requirements for bona fide acquisition of title are not met, the buyer's ownership may be contested.[185] Even if the buyer is protected as a bona fide purchaser, the goods might still be subject to third-party claim. In such cases, the seller may be held liable under Article 41 CISG.[186]

The seller's responsibility covers both *rights in rem* and *rights in personam*, determined by the applicable law governing the goods' location (*lex rei sitae*). The critical factor is whether the third party's rights allow it to control, restrict, or limit the buyer's use, exploitation, or disposal of the goods.[187] For example, security interests held by the seller's creditors or warehouse owners may arise during delivery and should be evaluated under Article 30 CISG.[188] If these security interests

---

[185] Ingeborg Schwenzer, 'Article 41 CISG: Third Party Claims in General' in Schwenzer and Schroeter (eds) (n 4) para 3.

[186] *Stolen wheel loader case* [2023] Obergericht des Kantons Zug (Court of Appeal Canton Zug) Z1 2022 6, CISG-online 6313; Schwenzer, 'Article 41 CISG: Third Party Claims in General' in Schwenzer and Schroeter (eds) (n 4) para 13.

[187] *VW Crafter case* [2019] Oberlandesgericht Celle (Court of Appeal Celle) 7 U 158/18, CISG-online 5381; Stefan M Kröll, 'Article 41' in Kröll, Mistelis, and Perales Viscasillas (eds) (n 20) para 12; Schwenzer, 'Article 41 CISG: Third Party Claims in General' in Schwenzer and Schroeter (eds) (n 4) para 4.

[188] Kröll, 'Article 41' in Kröll, Mistelis, and Perales Viscasillas (eds) (n 20) para 13; David Tebel, 'Article 41 (Third-Party Claims to Goods)' in Brunner and Gottlieb (eds) (n 6) para 9; Schwenzer, 'Article 41 CISG: Third Party Claims in General' in Schwenzer and Schroeter (eds) (n 4) para 4.

persist after delivery, they can constitute a defect in title under Article 41 CISG.[189] However, contractual obligations binding only on the seller, such as prior agreements to sell the goods to a third party, do not automatically affect the buyer unless the title has already been transferred to the third party.[190] Nevertheless, the seller could still be liable under Article 41 if a third party brings a claim against the buyer based on such agreements.[191]

The relationship between public law encumbrances and defects in title under Article 41 CISG can be complex. Restrictions arising from public law, such as non-compliance with domestic rules for consumer, worker, or environmental protection, do not typically constitute defects in title. Instead, they may result in liability for quality defects under Article 35 CISG. Export or import prohibitions are usually tied to economic control measures and affect the obligations of the seller or buyer, depending on who is impacted.[192] For example, an export prohibition may impact the seller's duty to deliver (Article 30 CISG), while an import prohibition may affect the buyer's obligation to accept delivery (Article 53 CISG).[193]

Defects in title can also arise from official measures linked to the goods, such as seizure due to unpaid taxes or duties if the seller is responsible for them under the contract. Similarly, claims related to stolen goods or illegally removed cultural objects may restrict the buyer's right to possess and use the goods, constituting a defect in title under Article 41 CISG.[194] If such measures involve IP rights, such as the seizure of counterfeit goods, liability is, however, governed by Article 42 CISG rather than Article 41 CISG.[195] For cultural objects, measures taken to return them to their place of origin are considered defects in title under Article 41 CISG,[196] even if compensation is provided for their return.[197]

---

[189] Tebel, 'Article 41 (Third-Party Claims to Goods)' in Brunner and Gottlieb (eds) (n 6) para 10; Schwenzer, 'Article 41 CISG: Third Party Claims in General' in Schwenzer and Schroeter (eds) (n 4) para 4.

[190] Schwenzer, 'Article 41 CISG: Third Party Claims in General' in Schwenzer and Schroeter (eds) (n 4) para 4.

[191] Kröll, 'Article 41' in Kröll, Mistelis, and Perales Viscasillas (eds) (n 20) para 17; Tebel, 'Article 41 (Third-Party Claims to Goods)' in Brunner and Gottlieb (eds) (n 6) para 13; Schwenzer, 'Article 41 CISG: Third Party Claims in General' in Schwenzer and Schroeter (eds) (n 4) para 12.

[192] Kröll, 'Article 41' in Kröll, Mistelis, and Perales Viscasillas (eds) (n 20) para 28; Tebel, 'Article 41 (Third-Party Claims to Goods)' in Brunner and Gottlieb (eds) (n 6) para 15; Schwenzer, 'Article 41 CISG: Third Party Claims in General' in Schwenzer and Schroeter (eds) (n 4) para 6.

[193] Schwenzer, 'Article 41 CISG: Third Party Claims in General' in Schwenzer and Schroeter (eds) (n 4) para 6.

[194] Kröll, 'Article 41' in Kröll, Mistelis, and Perales Viscasillas (eds) (n 20) para 26; Tebel, 'Article 41 (Third-Party Claims to Goods)' in Brunner and Gottlieb (eds) (n 6) para 15; Schwenzer, 'Article 41 CISG: Third Party Claims in General' in Schwenzer and Schroeter (eds) (n 4) para 8.

[195] Schwenzer, 'Article 41 CISG: Third Party Claims in General' in Schwenzer and Schroeter (eds) (n 4) para 8.

[196] Kröll, 'Article 41' in Kröll, Mistelis, and Perales Viscasillas (eds) (n 20) para 26; Tebel, 'Article 41 [Third-Party Claims to Goods]' in Brunner and Gottlieb (eds) (n 6) para 15; Schwenzer, 'Article 41 CISG: Third Party Claims in General' in Schwenzer and Schroeter (eds) (n 4) para 8.

[197] Schwenzer, 'Article 41 CISG: Third Party Claims in General' in Schwenzer and Schroeter (eds) (n 4) para 8.

b.) Claims

Under Article 41 CISG, the seller is obligated to deliver goods free from any third-party claims, regardless of whether the third party's claim is valid.[198] This approach differs from many domestic legal systems,[199] where the seller's liability depends on the existence of an actual third-party right.[200] By imposing this obligation, the CISG aims to shield the buyer from the burden of dealing with third-party claims. Since third-party claims often arise due to the seller's previous conduct or events affecting the goods, it is more reasonable in international sales contracts to expect the seller to clarify any factual or legal uncertainties.[201]

The CISG does not distinguish between legitimate and frivolous claims. Even if the third party's claim is baseless, the seller remains liable under the first sentence of Article 41 CISG.[202] In the case of frivolous claims, the seller should be able to defeat them easily, avoiding a fundamental breach of contract and ensuring the buyer does not have grounds to avoid the contract.[203] If the buyer incurs costs because of a frivolous claim, the seller is liable to reimburse these costs as damages.[204] However, if the seller is unable to deliver goods free of third-party rights or claims due to an impediment that meets the requirements of Article 79(1) CISG, the seller may be exempt from liability for damages.[205] Additionally, Article 80 CISG precludes the buyer from relying on third-party claims if the buyer and the third party act in bad faith.[206]

---

[198] Kröll, 'Article 41' in Kröll, Mistelis, and Perales Viscasillas (eds) (n 20) para 15; Tebel, 'Article 41 (Third-Party Claims to Goods)' in Brunner and Gottlieb (eds) (n 6) para 11; Schwenzer, 'Article 41 CISG: Third Party Claims in General' in Schwenzer and Schroeter (eds) (n 4) para 10.

[199] Schwenzer and Muñoz, *Global Sales and Contract Law* (n 2) para 32.31, fn 86: some examples are Argentina, Civil and Commercial Code art 1044 (however, after its most recent reform, the Argentinian CCC does not expressly specify the need of a judicial ruling to declare an eviction); Armenia, Commercial Code art 476; Azerbaijan, Commercial Code art 572; Belarus, Commercial Code art 430; Guatemala, Commercial Code art 1548; Kaz Art 413 CC; Kyrgyzstan, Commercial Code art 423; Lithuania, Commercial Code art 6.321; Russian Federation, Commercial Code art 460; Tajikistan, Commercial Code art 496; Uzbekistan, Commercial Code art 393.

[200] Cf Schwenzer and Muñoz, *Global Sales and Contract Law* (n 2) para 32.31; Schwenzer, 'Article 41 CISG: Third Party Claims in General' in Schwenzer and Schroeter (eds) (n 4) para 10.

[201] Kröll, 'Article 41' in Kröll, Mistelis, and Perales Viscasillas (eds) (n 20) para 16; Tebel, 'Article 41 (Third-Party Claims to Goods)' in Brunner and Gottlieb (eds) (n 6) para 11; Schwenzer, 'Article 41 CISG: Third Party Claims in General' in Schwenzer and Schroeter (eds) (n 4) para 11.

[202] Kröll, 'Article 41' in Kröll, Mistelis, and Perales Viscasillas (eds) (n 20) para 19; Tebel, 'Article 41 (Third-Party Claims to Goods)' in Brunner and Gottlieb (eds) (n 6) para 11; Schwenzer, 'Article 41 CISG: Third Party Claims in General' in Schwenzer and Schroeter (eds) (n 4) para 11.

[203] Kröll, 'Article 41' in Kröll, Mistelis, and Perales Viscasillas (eds) (n 20) para 19; Schwenzer, 'Article 41 CISG: Third Party Claims in General' in Schwenzer and Schroeter (eds) (n 4) para 11.

[204] Kröll, 'Article 41' in Kröll, Mistelis, and Perales Viscasillas (eds) (n 20) para 40; Tebel, 'Article 41 (Third-Party Claims to Goods)' in Brunner and Gottlieb (eds) (n 6) para 32; Schwenzer, 'Article 41 CISG: Third Party Claims in General' in Schwenzer and Schroeter (eds) (n 4) para 11.

[205] Kröll, 'Article 41' in Kröll, Mistelis, and Perales Viscasillas (eds) (n 20) para 41; Tebel, 'Article 41 (Third-Party Claims to Goods)' in Brunner and Gottlieb (eds) (n 6) para 32; Schwenzer, 'Article 41 CISG: Third Party Claims in General' in Schwenzer and Schroeter (eds) (n 4) para 11.

[206] Tebel, 'Article 41 (Third-Party Claims to Goods)' in Brunner and Gottlieb (eds) (n 6) para 32; Schwenzer, 'Article 41 CISG: Third Party Claims in General' in Schwenzer and Schroeter (eds) (n 4) para 11.

A third party does not need to present their claim in a specific form or file legal action against the buyer for the seller's liability to arise. It is enough for the third party to indicate the existence of its claim in any manner.[207] And once this happens, the seller's liability is unaffected even if the buyer acquired the goods in good faith or free of encumbrances.[208] The broad wording of the first sentence of Article 41 CISG reflects the CISG's intention to protect the buyer from the risk of uncertainty and potential legal disputes over title. This ensures the buyer is not exposed to questions about whether the goods were acquired in good faith or free of any third-party rights.

c.) Time and geographical scope of rights and claims

Article 41 CISG establishes that 'goods must be delivered'. Delivery serves as the reference point for determining whether the seller has met their obligation to transfer the goods free of such claims.[209] However, this approach can lead to problematic outcomes in certain scenarios, particularly in contracts involving transportation or third-parties' claims. For example, when the contract includes carriage of goods, delivery occurs when the goods are handed over to the first carrier, as is often the case under ICC Incoterms® 2020 terms like EXW and FCA. If the seller's creditors seize the goods while they are in transit within the seller's State, the buyer's rights should not hinge on whether delivery was designated as 'ex-warehouse'[210] or 'at the border'.[211] Similarly, complications can arise if the seller has agreed to cover transportation costs but fails to pay them, as the carrier's right to security emerges simultaneously with delivery.[212]

The reliance on delivery as a key moment also creates challenges in cases involving third-party claims. Such claims typically surface after the goods have been delivered to the buyer. If the focus were solely on delivery, only legitimate third-party claims would be recognized, leaving buyers vulnerable to baseless claims.[213] Despite these challenges, the concept of delivery remains pivotal for

---

[207] Tebel, 'Article 41 (Third-Party Claims to Goods)' in Brunner and Gottlieb (eds) (n 6) para 13; Schwenzer, 'Article 41 CISG: Third Party Claims in General' in Schwenzer and Schroeter (eds) (n 4) para 12.

[208] Schwenzer, 'Article 41 CISG: Third Party Claims in General' in Schwenzer and Schroeter (eds) (n 4) para 13.

[209] Kröll, 'Article 41' in Kröll, Mistelis, and Perales Viscasillas (eds) (n 20) para 29; Tebel, 'Article 41 (Third-Party Claims to Goods)' in Brunner and Gottlieb (eds) (n 6) para 19; Schwenzer, 'Article 41 CISG: Third Party Claims in General' in Schwenzer and Schroeter (eds) (n 4) para 16.

[210] Kröll, 'Article 41' in Kröll, Mistelis, and Perales Viscasillas (eds) (n 20) para 30; Tebel, 'Article 41 (Third-Party Claims to Goods)' in Brunner and Gottlieb (eds) (n 6) para 19; Schwenzer, 'Article 41 CISG: Third Party Claims in General' in Schwenzer and Schroeter (eds) (n 4) para 16.

[211] Schwenzer, 'Article 41 CISG: Third Party Claims in General' in Schwenzer and Schroeter (eds) (n 4) para 16.

[212] By clauses such as 'CIF', 'C&F', and 'Carriage paid'; Schwenzer, 'Article 41 CISG: Third Party Claims in General' in Schwenzer and Schroeter (eds) (n 4) para 16.

[213] Kröll, 'Article 41' in Kröll, Mistelis, and Perales Viscasillas (eds) (n 20) para 29; Schwenzer, 'Article 41 CISG: Third Party Claims in General' in Schwenzer and Schroeter (eds) (n 4) para 16.

distinguishing the seller's and buyer's responsibilities. To address this, the critical test is whether the circumstances leading to a defect in title arose before or after delivery. In cases of third-party claims, it is particularly important to evaluate whether the alleged rights stem from events that occurred prior to delivery.[214]

Importantly, the formation of the contract does not impact the seller's general liability for defects in title.[215] The seller remains responsible for third-party claims that arise even after the contract is concluded. Additionally, Article 41 CISG does not impose any territorial limitations on the buyer's right to dispose of the goods. The buyer is entitled to assume that it has an unrestricted power to use or transfer the goods without any third-party interference.

d.) Buyer's consent

Under the CISG, it is possible for a buyer to consent to the purchase of goods subject to third-party title rights or claims at the time the contract is concluded. This consent may occur explicitly or implicitly, especially in cases where the contract specifies that the buyer will assume responsibility for outstanding storage costs of warehoused goods. When such an agreement is made, the purchase price is often reduced accordingly. However, mere knowledge that carriers or warehouse owners generally hold liens or security rights,[216] or that the seller owes a debt to a bank, is insufficient to infer the buyer's consent.[217] In such circumstances, the buyer is entitled to expect the seller to have properly discharged these obligations before transferring the goods.

There are instances where other factors may imply the buyer's consent to a third party's security interest over the goods. For example, if the seller explicitly informs the buyer about a third-party security interest and directs the buyer to pay the purchase price directly to the third-party creditor, the buyer's unconditional acceptance of the goods can indicate consent.[218] However, this consent must be clear and informed, as the seller's unilateral declarations or assurances alone are not enough to exclude liability under the CISG.[219] The buyer must be adequately informed and should have an opportunity to assess the implications of accepting goods encumbered by third-party claims.

---

[214] Kröll, 'Article 41' in Kröll, Mistelis, and Perales Viscasillas (eds) (n 20) para 29; Schwenzer, 'Article 41 CISG: Third Party Claims in General' in Schwenzer and Schroeter (eds) (n 4) para 15.

[215] Schwenzer, 'Article 41 CISG: Third Party Claims in General' in Schwenzer and Schroeter (eds) (n 4) para 17.

[216] Kröll, 'Article 41' in Kröll, Mistelis, and Perales Viscasillas (eds) (n 20) para 33; Schwenzer, 'Article 41 CISG: Third Party Claims in General' in Schwenzer and Schroeter (eds) (n 4) para 20.

[217] Kröll, 'Article 41' in Kröll, Mistelis, and Perales Viscasillas (eds) (n 20) para 33; Tebel, 'Article 41 (Third-Party Claims to Goods)' in Brunner and Gottlieb (eds) (n 6) para 23; Schwenzer, 'Article 41 CISG: Third Party Claims in General' in Schwenzer and Schroeter (eds) (n 4) para 20.

[218] Kröll, 'Article 41' in Kröll, Mistelis, and Perales Viscasillas (eds) (n 20) para 34; Schwenzer, 'Article 41 CISG: Third Party Claims in General' in Schwenzer and Schroeter (eds) (n 4) para 20.

[219] Schwenzer, 'Article 41 CISG: Third Party Claims in General' in Schwenzer and Schroeter (eds) (n 4) para 20.

3. Intellectual property rights and claims

The CISG governs the responsibility of the seller regarding the delivery of goods that may infringe on third-party IP rights, whether such infringement is real or alleged. However, the CISG does not cover the infringement of IP rights itself.[220]

a.) Scope and purpose of Article 42 CISG
The term IP should be interpreted autonomously (Article 7(1) CISG). According to Article 42 CISG, industrial property falls under the broader category of intellectual property. IP thus includes all rights that protect a commercial or intellectual achievement by attributing it to the right holder within a defined territory.[221] These rights include patents, utility models, designs, trademarks, semiconductor designs, plant breeder's rights, copyrights, and other similar rights and licence rights derived from them. IP rights, also under Article 42 CISG, include rights based on competition, tort, or unjust enrichment laws that protect commercial or intellectual achievements.[222]

Article 42 CISG applies to various situations involving IP rights. These situations include goods that are produced using a specific process protected by a process patent, goods used to apply a process that is also protected by a process patent, goods that are subject to personal name or personality rights, goods that are subject to measures taken by public authorities based on IP, and rights and claims that are based on the IP of the seller.[223]

Similar to Article 41 CISG, Article 42 CISG makes the seller liable if the goods sold are encumbered by third-party IP rights, even if no formal claim has been made. Likewise, the seller is liable for any third-party claims that the goods infringe an IP right, regardless of whether the right in question actually exists. As under Article 41 CISG, these claims may be frivolous or unfounded. Article 42 CISG works under the principle that buyers do not go to the market to face actual or threatened legal action.[224]

---

[220] CISG, art 42.

[221] Ingeborg Schwenzer, 'Article 42 CISG: Third Party Claims Based on Intellectual Property' in Schwenzer and Schroeter (eds) (n 4)) para 4; CISG Advisory Council, 'CISG-AC Opinion No. 22, The Seller's Liability for Goods Infringing Intellectual Property Rights under Article 42 CISG, Rapporteur: Dr. David Tebel, Rothorn Legal, Frankfurt Am Main, Germany, 7–9 August 2022' (2022) Black Letter Rule 2.

[222] CISG Advisory Council, 'CISG-AC Opinion No. 22' (n 221) Black Letter Rule 2.

[223] *Carbomat NV v Pric Advies BV* [2020] Gerechtshof Arnhem-Leeuwarden (Court of Appeal ArnhemLeeuwarden) 200.258.522/01, CISG-online 5495; *The North Face t-shirts case*, [2023] Rechtbank Noord-Holland (District Court Noord-Holland) C/15/331571/HA ZA 22-544, CISG-online 6736; CISG Advisory Council, 'CISG-AC Opinion No. 22' (n 221) Black Letter Rule 3.

[224] Stefan M Kröll, 'Article 42' in Kröll, Mistelis, and Perales Viscasillas (eds) (n 20) para 9; Schwenzer, 'Article 42 CISG: Third Party Claims Based on Intellectual Property' in Schwenzer and Schroeter (eds) (n 4) para 6; CISG Advisory Council, 'CISG-AC Opinion No. 22' (n 221) Black Letter Rules 4 and 5.

b.) Seller's liability and knowledge standard

The seller's liability under Article 42(1) CISG requires knowledge of the existence of the IP right or claim. Such knowledge exists when the seller cannot be unaware of the right or claim. Knowledge of whether an individual has the right to claim ownership of an intellectual property is based on certain circumstances.[225] These include whether the IP right has been published in official publications or databases, registered in official registers, or if it is well-known in the relevant sector (notoriety). Additionally, if an IP right can only be identified based on a deep understanding of the features and internal composition of goods or if there are other circumstances specific to the individual case, these will also be considered. Other factors that may be taken into account in determining knowledge of the seller of the IP rights include the nature and novelty of the goods, the seller's experience with the specific goods, experience with the specific market, size of business and sophistication, language skills, knowledge of the specific use intended by the buyer (in case of process patents), and any other relevant circumstances specific to the individual case.[226]

c.) Determining the relevant State of use or resale

Under Article 42(1)(a) CISG, the seller is only liable for IP rights and claims under the law of the State where the goods are to be resold or otherwise used. The State of resale or use may be determined in the contract or any agreement of the parties.[227] In the absence of an agreement, to establish the State of use as per Article 42(1)(a) CISG, the term 'use' is to be interpreted in a broad sense. It includes any action that the buyer intends to take or have taken regarding the goods. Use also covers the transit of the goods through a State other than their final destination.[228] The parties involved in a transaction only need to consider the use of the goods in a specific State if the seller can determine the buyer's intention to use the goods in that State based on the circumstances. A State of use is considered to have been contemplated if the buyer is active only in the market of that State and the seller is aware of this. Additionally, if transportation of the goods is intended to be through that State,[229]

---

[225] Kröll, 'Article 42' in Kröll, Mistelis, and Perales Viscasillas (eds) (n 20) para 25; David Tebel, 'Article 42 (Third-Party Claims Based on a Patent or Other Intellectual Property)' in Brunner and Gottlieb (eds) (n 6) para 10; Schwenzer, 'Article 42 CISG: Third Party Claims Based on Intellectual Property' in Schwenzer and Schroeter (eds) (n 4) para 15; CISG Advisory Council, 'CISG-AC Opinion No. 22' (n 221) Black Letter Rules 4 and 5.

[226] CISG Advisory Council, 'CISG-AC Opinion No. 22' (n 221) Black Letter Rule 6.

[227] Kröll, 'Article 42' in Kröll, Mistelis, and Perales Viscasillas (eds) (n 20) para 15; Tebel, 'Article 42 (Third-Party Claims Based on a Patent or Other Intellectual Property)' in Brunner and Gottlieb (eds) (n 6) para 14; Schwenzer, 'Article 42 CISG: Third Party Claims Based on Intellectual Property' in Schwenzer and Schroeter (eds) (n 4) para 10.

[228] Kröll, 'Article 42' in Kröll, Mistelis, and Perales Viscasillas (eds) (n 20) para 22; Schwenzer, 'Article 42 CISG: Third Party Claims Based on Intellectual Property' in Schwenzer and Schroeter (eds) (n 4) para 14; CISG Advisory Council, 'CISG-AC Opinion 22' (n 221) Black Letter Rule 7.

[229] Schwenzer, 'Article 42 CISG: Third Party Claims Based on Intellectual Property' in Schwenzer and Schroeter (eds) (n 4) para 11.

or if the instruction manuals or other documents accompanying the goods are to be in a specific language that is spoken only in that State,[230] or if the required design of the goods[231] points to that State, then it is also considered a state of use. Lastly, if mandatory or voluntary certificates are required only in that State, then it is also relevant to consider it as a State of use.[232]

d.) Timing of assessment

The seller's knowledge of the IP rights and the relevant State of use or resale are assessed at the time of contract conclusion. The assessment of whether the goods are encumbered with IP rights or claims under Article 42 CISG takes place at the passing of risk, based on the general principle outlined in Article 36 CISG.[233] If delivery takes place before the agreed date, the seller may cure any encumbrance until the agreed date, in line with the general principle stated in Article 37 CISG.[234] It may also cure the encumbrances afterwards subject to the buyer's remedy for breach of contract.

e.) Buyer's knowledge

The seller is not liable for the existence of IP rights or claims affecting the goods if, at the time of the conclusion of the contract, the buyer knew or could not have been unaware of the IP right or claim.[235] The buyer's awareness of any legal liabilities or claims associated with the goods, as stipulated in Article 42(2)(a) CISG, should be evaluated with the same legal standard as the seller's awareness requirement under Article 42(1) CISG. Similar factors should be taken into consideration, while considering any factual differences in the individual circumstances of both the buyer and the seller.[236]

f.) Buyer specifications and Article 42(2)(b) CISG defence

According to Article 42(2)(b) CISG, the seller is not responsible for any encumbrance if it is a necessary outcome of the agreement that requires the goods to meet the specifications provided by the buyer.[237] However, the seller cannot use

---

[230] Kröll, 'Article 42' in Kröll, Mistelis, and Perales Viscasillas (eds) (n 20) para 16; Tebel, 'Article 42 (Third-Party Claims Based on a Patent or Other Intellectual Property)' in Brunner and Gottlieb (eds) (n 6) para 14.

[231] Schwenzer, 'Article 42 CISG: Third Party Claims Based on Intellectual Property' in Schwenzer and Schroeter (eds) (n 4) para 11.

[232] CISG Advisory Council, 'CISG-AC Opinion 22' (n 221) Black Letter Rule 8.

[233] Ibid Black Letter Rule 10.

[234] Ibid.

[235] CISG, art 42(2)(a); Kröll, 'Article 42' in Kröll, Mistelis, and Perales Viscasillas (eds) (n 20) para 23; Tebel, 'Article 42 (Third-Party Claims Based on a Patent or Other Intellectual Property)' in Brunner and Gottlieb (eds) (n 6) para 18; Schwenzer, 'Article 42 CISG: Third Party Claims Based on Intellectual Property' in Schwenzer and Schroeter (eds) (n 4) para 8.

[236] CISG Advisory Council, 'CISG-AC Opinion 22' (n 221) Black Letter Rule 11.

[237] Kröll, 'Article 42' in Kröll, Mistelis, and Perales Viscasillas (eds) (n 20) para 41; Tebel, 'Article 42 (Third-Party Claims Based on a Patent or Other Intellectual Property)' in Brunner and Gottlieb

Article 42(2)(b) CISG as a defence if it was aware of any IP rights or claims under Article 42(1) CISG, and it knew or should have known that the buyer's specifications would lead to an encumbrance of the goods, but did not inform the buyer about it.[238]

g.) Remedies and burden of proof

If the seller is responsible for any third-party intellectual property rights or claims, then the buyer can use all the remedies listed in Article 45 CISG. This means that any provision that, by its wording, appears to apply exclusively to the delivery of non-conforming goods nevertheless extends to cases involving the delivery of goods encumbered by third-party IP rights or claims.[239]

Once the buyer has taken over the goods, it is responsible for proving that the seller is liable under Article 42 CISG.[240] This includes proving that the IP right or claim exists, that the goods are affected by the IP right or claim, that the seller knew about the encumbrance or could not have been unaware of it, and that the parties considered the State of use.[241]

On the other hand, the seller bears the burden of proof regarding the requirements of the defences pursuant to Article 42 CISG, including, in a case where the buyer relies on an encumbrance in the State in which it has its place of business, that only a different State of use was contemplated at the time of the conclusion of the contract.[242]

The seller must also prove that the contract required the goods to comply with the specifications provided by the buyer or that no infringement did occur, for example, due to the existence of licences.[243]

(eds) (n 6) para 22; Schwenzer, 'Article 42 CISG: Third Party Claims Based on Intellectual Property' in Schwenzer and Schroeter (eds) (n 4) para 20.

[238] Kröll, 'Article 42' in Kröll, Mistelis, and Perales Viscasillas (eds) (n 20) para 43; Tebel, 'Article 42 (Third-Party Claims Based on a Patent or Other Intellectual Property)' in Brunner and Gottlieb (eds) (n 6) para 23; Schwenzer, 'Article 42 CISG: Third Party Claims Based on Intellectual Property' in Schwenzer and Schroeter (eds) (n 4) para 22; CISG Advisory Council, 'CISG-AC Opinion 22' (n 221) Black Letter Rule 12.

[239] CISG Advisory Council, 'CISG-AC Opinion 22' (n 221) Black Letter Rule 13.

[240] Kröll, 'Article 42' in Kröll, Mistelis, and Perales Viscasillas (eds) (n 20) para 54; Tebel, 'Article 42 (Third-Party Claims Based on a Patent or Other Intellectual Property)' in Brunner and Gottlieb (eds) (n 6) para 28; Schwenzer, 'Article 42 CISG: Third Party Claims Based on Intellectual Property' in Schwenzer and Schroeter (eds) (n 4) para 31.

[241] CISG Advisory Council, 'CISG-AC Opinion 22' (n 221) Black Letter Rule 14.

[242] Kröll, 'Article 42' in Kröll, Mistelis, and Perales Viscasillas (eds) (n 20) para 55; Tebel, 'Article 42 (Third-Party Claims Based on a Patent or Other Intellectual Property)' in Brunner and Gottlieb (eds) (n 6) para 29; Schwenzer, 'Article 42 CISG: Third Party Claims Based on Intellectual Property' in Schwenzer and Schroeter (eds) (n 4) para 31.

[243] CISG Advisory Council, 'CISG-AC Opinion 22' (n 221) Black Letter Rule 15.

10
Buyer's Obligations

I. General

Buyers, just like sellers, have certain obligations that arise from their sales or service contracts. These obligations may be explicitly stated in the contract or may be based on applicable default rules. Some of the obligations of the seller and buyer are interdependent, meaning that they rely on each other to meet their respective obligations. For instance, it is logically impossible for the buyer to take delivery of the goods if the seller has not performed its delivery obligation.

Article 53 CISG sets out the buyer's two primary obligations. In particular, the buyer must pay the purchase price and take delivery of the goods.[1] The PICC contain several provisions relating to the performance of monetary obligations. These provisions regulate the means of payment (Articles 6.1.7 and 6.1.8 PIC), the currency of payment (Articles 6.1.9 and 6.1.10 PIC), and the right to request payment in money (Article 7.21 PICC).

---

[1] CISG, art 53; *Zhongshan Ruicheng Clothing Textile Co Ltd v AmeBalance BV* [2024] Rechtbank Den Haag (District Court The Hague) C/09/658069/HA ZA 23-1074, CISG-online 7185.

II. Purchase Price

1. Determination

In international commercial contracts, the parties usually agree on a fixed price or establish a way to determine the price.[2] The contract may specify that the price will be determined based on the prevailing market price at the time of delivery or some other agreed-upon date. Parties may also agree to tie the price to a specific index, such as a commodity price index or a currency exchange rate. These two methods are intended to protect both parties from fluctuations in market prices or currency exchange rates.[3] Sellers and service providers may also protect their interests using a cost-plus pricing method to determine the contract price, whereby a fixed profit percentage will be added to the total cost of production, including materials, labour, etc. This ensures that the seller and service providers cover all expenses and make a predetermined profit margin. Some international commercial contracts may incorporate escalation clauses allowing for adjustments to the price under certain circumstances, such as changes in production costs, inflation, or other economic factors.

In the case of open price contracts, that is, where the agreement does not stipulate a fixed price or way to determine the price, Article 55 CISG states that the market price will be applied. The price under Article 55 CISG should be similar to that charged in the relevant market under comparable circumstances at the time of the contract's conclusion.[4] This objective standard is intended to protect the buyer from excessively high prices, which a seller may try to charge unilaterally. However, this protection may work against the buyer in cases where the seller is willing to sell the goods at a lower price than the market rate.

The apparent contradiction between Articles 14(1) and 55 CISG reflects the tension between formal contract formation requirements and commercial practicality. While Article 14(1) CISG requires the price to be fixed or determinable for an offer to be valid, Article 55 CISG allows a contract to be formed without an agreed price, provided the parties intended to contract, and substitutes the price

---

[2] Petra Butler and Arjun Harindranath, 'Article 54' in Stefan Kröll, Loukas Mistelis, and Pilar Perales Viscasillas (eds), *UN Convention on Contracts for the International Sale of Goods (CISG). A Commentary* (2nd edn, CH Beck 2018) para 6; cf Ulrich G Schroeter, 'Article 14 CISG: Offer (Including Incorporation of Standard Terms' in Ingeborg Schwenzer and Ulrich Schroeter (eds), *Schlechtriem & Schwenzer: Commentary on the UN Convention on the International Sale of Goods* (5th edn, Oxford University Press 2022) para 8: for circumstances in which price can be fixed in other ways such as implicitly.

[3] Eckart Brödermann, *UNIDROIT Principles of International Commercial Contracts: An Article-by-Article Commentary* (2nd edn, Kluwer Law International 2023) ch 6, art 6.1.9, para 3: some Protection of the Obligee Against Currency Fluctuation for an analysis of the related provisions in the PICC.

[4] *Isola P EOOD v Nordmann, Rassmann Handelsgesellschaft mbH* [2021] Апелативен съд София (Court of Appeal Sofia) 2139/2020, CISG-online 5583.

generally charged under comparable circumstances.[5] To reconcile this conflict, several approaches can be adopted. One is an intent-based interpretation, focusing on the parties' clear intention to form a contract, allowing Article 55 CISG to fill the price gap.[6] Another approach is to rely on established trade practices and usages.[7]

Article 55 CISG is easier to apply when market prices exist. Article 76(2) CISG provides guidance on determining the relevant place for the current price, reflecting a general CISG principle.[8] According to this article, the current price at the place where the goods were supposed to be delivered is decisive. If there is no current price at that place, the price at another suitable place can be used as a reasonable substitute.[9] Transport costs must be considered, and the relevant market is that of the seller, not the buyer. Premiums and deductions in that market are also relevant. If no market price is available at the delivery or substitute place, the price may be inferred from common list prices.[10] However, this may not be a reasonable current price for goods manufactured or produced specifically for the buyer.[11] Sales under comparable circumstances require considering similar delivery and payment terms, including premiums, deductions,[12] and economic equivalents where terms differ.[13]

With regard to the time to fix the price under Article 55 CISG, the time of contract conclusion is relevant. The time of delivery is not decisive when determining the contract price under Article 55 CISG.[14] This particular provision serves to prevent both the seller (from a rise in price) and the buyer (from a fall in price) from

---

[5] Petra Butler and Arjun Harindranath, 'Article 55' in Kröll, Mistelis, and Perales Viscasillas (eds) (n 2) para 5; Florian Mohs, 'Article 55 CISG: Price Determination in Case of Open Price Contracts' in Schwenzer and Schroeter (eds) (n 2) para 3.

[6] Butler and Harindranath, 'Article 55' in Kröll, Mistelis, and Perales Viscasillas (eds) (n 2) paras 6, 7.

[7] Cf Franco Ferrari and Marco Torsello, *International Sales Law—CISG in a Nutshell* (3rd edn, West Academic Publishing 2022) 183: highlighting that some decisions have given precedence to Article 14 over Article 55.

[8] Christoph Brunner, Matthias Lerch, and Lukas Rusch, 'Article 55 (Determining the Purchase Price)' in Christoph Brunner and Benjamin Gottlieb (eds), *Commentary on the UN Sales Law (CISG)* (Kluwer Law International 2019) para 4; Harry M Flechtner, *Honnold's Uniform Law for International Sales under the 1980 United Nations Convention* (5th edn, Wolters Kluwer 2021) para 629.

[9] Butler and Harindranath, 'Article 55' in Kröll, Mistelis, and Perales Viscasillas (eds) (n 2) para 8; Brunner, Lerch, and Rusch, 'Article 55 (Determining the Purchase Price)' in Brunner and Gottlieb (eds) (n 8) para 4; Mohs, 'Article 55 CISG: Price Determination in Case of Open Price Contracts' in Schwenzer and Schroeter (eds) (n 2) para 15.

[10] Butler and Harindranath, 'Article 55' in Kröll, Mistelis, and Perales Viscasillas (eds) (n 2) para 9; Mohs, 'Article 55 CISG: Price Determination in Case of Open Price Contracts' in Schwenzer and Schroeter (eds) (n 2) para 10.

[11] Butler and Harindranath, 'Article 55' in Kröll, Mistelis, and Perales Viscasillas (eds) (n 2) para 9; Mohs, 'Article 55 CISG: Price Determination in Case of Open Price Contracts' in Schwenzer and Schroeter (eds) (n 2) para 15.

[12] Butler and Harindranath, 'Article 55' in Kröll, Mistelis, and Perales Viscasillas (eds) (n 2) para 7; *Isola P. EOOD v Nordmann, Rassmann Handelsgesellschaft mbH* [2021] Апелативен съд София (Court of Appeal Sofia) 2139/2020. CISG-online 5583; *Mixing equipment case* [2019] Sąd Apelacyjny w Warszawie (Court of Appeal Warsaw) VII AGa 1093/18, CISG-online 5298.

[13] Ingeborg Schwenzer, 'Article 76' in Schwenzer and Schroeter (eds) (n 2) para 4.

[14] Butler and Harindranath, 'Article 55' in Kröll, Mistelis, and Perales Viscasillas (eds) (n 2) para 7.

profiting from any potential changes in price.[15] Ultimately, the price must be reasonable, and where exact comparables are lacking, the reasonableness standard avoids recourse to domestic law that could undermine CISG uniformity.[16] This approach is also reflected in Article 5.1.7 PICC, which states that a reasonable price applies if it is impossible to determine the price generally charged for similar performance at the contract conclusion in comparable circumstances in the relevant trade.[17]

The purchase price generally covers all seller-incurred costs up to delivery, as defined by agreed trade terms (e.g. FCA, FOB, CIF). Taxes like value-added tax (VAT) are included when consistent with the parties' agreement, practice, or industry usage, and some courts consider it customary for the buyer to bear the VAT burden.[18]

Finally, if the price is fixed according to the weight of the goods, in case of doubt, it is to be determined by the net weight (Article 56 CISG).[19] In general, this rule applies only when the parties have neither explicitly nor implicitly agreed otherwise (Article 8 CISG) and are not obliged to follow any usages or practices (Article 9 CISG). For instance, if the price is mentioned as 'gross for net', this clause determines the price based on the weight of the goods, including their packaging. If the contract does not specify otherwise, the net weight refers to the weight of the goods without any packaging material.[20]

Neither the CISG nor the PICC has a concept of 'iustum pretium' (just price).[21] However, if extraordinary and fundamental changes in the economic circumstances occur, the buyer can rely on an exemption for performance or hardship (Article 79 CISG or Article 6.2.1 ff PICC).[22]

---

[15] Mohs, 'Article 55 CISG: Price Determination in Case of Open Price Contracts' in Schwenzer and Schroeter (eds) (n 2) para 16.

[16] Mohs, 'Article 55 CISG: Price Determination in Case of Open Price Contracts' in Schwenzer and Schroeter (eds) (n 2) para 17; cf Butler and Harindranath, 'Article 55' in Kröll, Mistelis, and Perales Viscasillas (eds) (n 2) para 9.

[17] Yesim M Atamer, 'Article 5.1.7' in Stefan Vogenauer (ed), *Commentary on the UNIDROIT Principles of International Commercial Contracts (PICC)* (2nd edn, Oxford University Press 2015) paras 8, 9.

[18] *Mixing equipment case* [2019] Sąd Apelacyjny w Warszawie (Court of Appeal Warsaw) VII AGa 1093/18, CISG-online 5298.

[19] Petra Butler and Arjun Harindranath, 'Article 56' in Kröll, Mistelis, and Perales Viscasillas (eds) (n 2) para 3; Florian Mohs, 'Article 56 CISG: Price Fixed by Weight' in Schwenzer and Schroeter (eds) (n 2) para 1 ff.

[20] United Nations (UN) Conference Official Records, 'Commentary on the Draft Convention on Contracts for the International Sale of Goods, prepared by the Secretariat' (1978) UN Doc A/CONF.97/5, 30, art 52, commentary 1; Mohs, 'Article 56 CISG: Price Fixed by Weight' in Schwenzer and Schroeter (eds) (n 2) para 3.

[21] Florian Mohs, 'Article 53 CISG: General Obligations of the Buyer' in Schwenzer and Schroeter (eds) (n 2) para 3.

[22] Ingeborg Schwenzer, 'Force Majeure and Hardship in International Sales Contracts' (2008) 39 *Victoria University of Wellington Law Review* 709, 713; Yesim M Atamer, 'Article 6.2.1' in Vogenauer (ed) (n 17) para 2 ff.

2. Currency

a.) Currency agreed

The parties can freely agree on the applicable currency for the purchase price payment, including crypto-currencies.[23] If parties do not agree on a currency, one needs to consider their practices or applicable trade usages (Article 9) to determine the currency implicitly.[24] In the commodity sector, for instance, the US dollar is the prevailing currency and thus will also be relevant usage to interpret (Article 8(3) CISG) or integrate (Article 9) the contract with regard to the applicable currency. The seller's intended currency can also be determined by the objective value of goods quoted at the offer or acceptance.[25]

b.) Absent an agreement on the currency

If the parties to a contract have not agreed on the currency for payment, the CISG provides a uniform solution.[26] Article 57(1) CISG can be used as a general principle to determine the currency applicable to a transaction (Article 7(2) CISG).[27] If payment is to be made against goods or documents, the applicable currency will be the currency at the place where the goods or documents are handed over to the buyer (Article 57(1)(b) CISG). In all other cases, the currency will be the currency at the seller's place of business (Article 57(1)(a) CISG). However, if the parties have agreed on a particular place of payment, that place determines the applicable currency. This is also the approach taken by Article 6.1.10 PICC, emphasizing the significance of the place of payment and its potential impact on the currency to be used.[28]

Article 6.1.9 PICC states that the buyer may pay the purchase price in the legal currency of the place of payment, even if the price is expressed in a different currency.[29] However, if the parties have agreed explicitly that the payment should be made in the currency in which the purchase price is expressed the buyer has no other option (Article 6.1.9(1)(b) PICC).[30] The CISG does not recognize this rule,

---

[23] See Andreea Bărnuț, 'Cryptocurrencies as a Payment Method in the Vienna Convention on International Sales of Goods' (2022) *Lawyers Week Juridice* <https://rlw.juridice.ro/21093/crypt ocurrencies-as-a-payment-method-in-the-vienna-convention-on-international-sales-of-goods. html> accessed 20 November 2025; Sebastian Omlor, 'The CISG and Libra: A Monetary Revolution for International Commercial Transactions?' (2020) *Stanford Journal of Blockchain Law and Policy* <https://stanford-jblp.pubpub.org/pub/cisg-and-libra/release/1> accessed 20 November 2025; Miklós Király, 'The Vienna Convention on International Sales of Goods and the Bitcoin' (2019) 16 *US-China Law Review* 181.

[24] Butler and Harindranath, 'Article 54' in Kröll, Mistelis, and Perales Viscasillas (eds) (n 2) para 8.

[25] Mohs, 'Article 53 CISG: General Obligations of the Buyer' in Schwenzer and Schroeter (eds) (n 2) para 4.

[26] Butler and Harindranath, 'Article 54' in Kröll, Mistelis, and Perales Viscasillas (eds) (n 2) para 10.

[27] See eg *Italian Wine Case IV* [1994] Kammergericht (Court of Appeal Berlin) 2 U 7418/92, CISG-online 130.

[28] See Brödermann (n 3) 288; Yesim M Atamer, 'Article 6.1.10' in Vogenauer (ed) (n 17) para 5.

[29] Yesim M Atamer, 'Article 6.1.9' in Vogenauer (ed) (n 17) para 3.

[30] Ibid.

and it cannot be founded on the general principles of the CISG as it would violate the principle of party autonomy under Article 6 CISG.[31] Domestic laws that secure payment in the legal currency of their respective countries are not applicable to an international sales contract under the CISG. Therefore, the buyer's right to pay in the currency of the place of payment cannot be derived from the law applicable under the rules of private international law in accordance with Article 7(2) CISG.[32] As noted above, absent agreement, payment is thus to be made in the currency of the place of delivery of goods or documents (Article 57(1)(b) CISG) or of the seller's place of business (Article 57(1)(a) CISG).

The seller does not have the right to demand payment in the currency of the place of payment unless it is impossible to pay in the agreed currency under Article 79 CISG. If the buyer has to pay in a different currency, it must be a reasonable substitute and payment must be made according to the prevailing exchange rate at the place of payment when payment is due. Article 6.1.9(3) PICC reflects the same rule. However, when payment is due but not made by the obligor, the obligee may demand payment based on the prevailing exchange rate at the due date or the actual payment date (Article 6.1.9(3) PICC).

Any conversion loss resulting from the exchange rate at the time of payment may be recoverable by the seller as damages under Article 74 CISG or Article 7.4.2 PICC.

3. Means of payment

Parties typically agree upon the buyer's payment method. This agreement is of the utmost importance and is recognized by Article 6 CISG.[33] If the buyer deviates from the agreed-upon payment method for one instalment, it does not necessarily mean that the contract is modified for future instalments.[34]

In case the parties to an international contract do not specify the payment method and an agreement cannot be implied, the CISG does not provide an express default rule.[35] Article 6.1.7.(1) PICC does: payment may be made in any form

---

[31] Mohs, 'Article 53 CISG: General Obligations of the Buyer' in Schwenzer and Schroeter (eds) (n 2) para 6.

[32] Butler and Harindranath, 'Article 54' in Kröll, Mistelis, and Perales Viscasillas (eds) (n 2) paras 12–14.

[33] Mohs, 'Article 53 CISG: General Obligations of the Buyer' in Schwenzer and Schroeter (eds) (n 2) para 10.

[34] See *Zhongshan Ruicheng Clothing Textile Co. Ltd v AmeBalance B.V.* [2024] Rechtbank Den Haag (District Court The Hague) C/09/658069/HA ZA 23-1074, CISG-online 7185.

[35] Mohs, 'Article 53 CISG: General Obligations of the Buyer' in Schwenzer and Schroeter (eds) (n 2) para 10; Petra Butler and Arjun Harindranath, 'Article 57' in Kröll, Mistelis, and Perales Viscasillas (eds) (n 2) para 20: 'the default rule is that the buyer has to pay in cash in the currency of the place of payment'.

used in the ordinary course of business at the place for payment.[36] A cheque or other promissory note is deemed to be accepted by the seller as a means of payment on condition that it will be honoured (Article 6.1.7(2) PICC).[37] However, CISG scholars advocate that, in the absence of an agreement, the buyer must make payment in cash, which includes bank transfers.[38] Below, we review some of the current methods of payment for international commercial contracts.

a.) Cash in advance (prepayment)

Cash in advance, also known as prepayment, requires the buyer to transfer funds to the seller before the goods are shipped or the services are provided. This means of payment provides the seller with immediate payment and reduces the risk of non-payment or default. It is often used when the seller has concerns about the buyer's creditworthiness or when dealing with new or unknown clients. On the other side, it may be less attractive to the buyer, as it bears the risk of non-delivery or dissatisfaction with the goods/services. It could also increase the financial burden on the buyer by requiring upfront payment.

Article 6.1.8(1) PICC provides that unless the obligee has indicated a particular account, payment may be made by a transfer to any of the financial institutions in which the obligee has made known it has an account. The payment obligation is fulfilled when the transfer to the obligee's financial institution becomes effective (Article 6.1.8(2) PICC).[39]

b.) Documentary credits (LCs)

A documentary credit or letter of credit is a financial instrument issued by a bank on behalf of the buyer, guaranteeing payment to the seller upon presentation of specified documents confirming the shipment of goods or the completion of services.[40] Given the importance of this means of payment in practice, we individually present it below in Section III.

c.) Documentary collections

Documentary collections involve the seller shipping the goods and presenting shipping documents to its bank, which forwards them to the buyer's bank. The buyer's bank releases the documents to the buyer upon payment of the price to the

---

[36] Yesim M Atamer, 'Article 6.1.7' in Vogenauer (ed) (n 17) para 2: for advantages of cash payments as default rule.

[37] Ibid para 10.

[38] Mohs, 'Article 53 CISG: General Obligations of the Buyer' in Schwenzer and Schroeter (eds) (n 2) para 10.

[39] Yesim M Atamer, 'Article 6.1.8' in Vogenauer (ed) (n 17) para 8.

[40] Mohs, 'Article 53 CISG: General Obligations of the Buyer' in Schwenzer and Schroeter (eds) (n 2). See also Ingeborg Schwenzer, 'The Danger of Domestic Pre-Conceived Views with Respect to the Uniform Interpretation of the CISG: The Question of Avoidance in the Case of Non-Conforming Goods and Documents' (2005) 36 *Victoria University of Wellington Law Review* 805.

bank, either by cash or acceptance of a bill of exchange. International sales contracts often use standard payment clauses such as D/A or D/P to refer to documentary collections as a means of payment. The ICC has published Uniform Rules for Collections, which can help determine the meaning of D/A and D/P as an international trade usage. D/P means 'documents against payment' and requires the buyer to pay in cash upon presentation of commercial papers. D/A means 'documents against acceptance' and allows the buyer to pay by bill of exchange upon presentation of the commercial documents.[41] The advantage of this method concerns the greater security that it provides when compared to open account transactions, as the buyer does not receive the shipping documents until payment or acceptance of the bill of exchange. It offers a compromise between cash in advance and open account terms. However, the seller retains legal possession of the goods until payment or acceptance, which may delay the buyer's ability to take possession.

d.) Open account

Open account terms involve the seller shipping the goods and invoicing the buyer with payment due at a specified future date, typically 30, 60, or 90 days after shipment. This means of payment provides convenience to the buyer, as it receives the goods before making payment. However, it carries a higher risk for the seller, as payment is dependent on the buyer's creditworthiness and trustworthiness. The seller may also incur costs associated with financing and managing credit risk.

e.) Bank guarantees

Bank guarantees are not actually a means of payment but a way to secure payment through financial instruments issued by banks to guarantee payment or performance obligations on behalf of their clients. They provide assurance to the beneficiary (seller or service provider) that they will receive payment if the buyer fails to fulfil its obligation to pay. Bank guarantees offer a high level of security for the seller or service provider as payment is guaranteed by the issuing bank.[42] It can also be used to secure performance obligations such as delivery of goods or completion of services. However, they are costly to obtain, as banks typically charge fees for issuing and administering guarantees.

f.) Payment platforms

Online payment platforms such as PayPal, Stripe, and TransferWise are now also used to facilitate the transfer of funds between contracting parties across borders.

---

[41] Petra Butler and Arjun Harindranath, 'Article 53' in Kröll, Mistelis, and Perales Viscasillas (eds) (n 2) para 21; Oxford Reference, 'Documents against Acceptance' (*Oxford Reference*) <https://www.oxfordreference.com/display/10.1093/oi/authority.20110803095724405> accessed 17 November 2025.
[42] Mohs, 'Article 53 CISG: General Obligations of the Buyer' in Schwenzer and Schroeter (eds) (n 2) para 32.

These platforms offer secure and convenient ways to transfer funds, often with lower fees compared to traditional banking methods.[43] Payment platforms may also provide additional services such as currency conversion and invoice management. However, some platforms may have limitations on transaction amounts or geographic coverage. There may also be concerns about security and fraud, although platforms typically employ advanced encryption and security measures.

4. Place of payment

a.) Agreement

Parties to a contract have the liberty to explicitly designate a place of payment (Article 57 CISG).[44] This designation is often evident when the contract specifies a particular bank account held by the seller, which may not necessarily be located in the seller's place of business but in another jurisdiction where the seller's bank is situated.[45] Similarly, an agreement between parties for payment via direct debit would establish the buyer's bank location as the place of payment.[46]

In cases where there is no explicit agreement between the parties, the place of payment may be implicitly determined. For instance, if the seller provides details of a specific bank account in its offer, acceptance, or invoices, the buyer's instruction to its bank to transfer funds to that account implicitly accepts this as the place of payment.[47] Conversely, if the seller introduces its bank account on an invoice for the first time and the buyer does not pay, no contractual place of payment exists, and Article 57(1)(a) CISG applies. Payment clauses such as 'net cash', 'cash against invoice', or 'cash before delivery' imply payment at the seller's place of business. On the other hand, clauses like 'documents against payment' or 'cash on delivery' imply the place of payment as the location where the documents or goods are handed over (same way as Article 57(1)(b) CISG).[48]

When parties agree on payment via a letter of credit, the sales contract may specify whether the letter of credit is payable at the issuing bank, often in the buyer's

---

[43] Ul Islam Khan and others, 'A Compendious Study of Online Payment Systems: Past Developments, Present Impact, and Future Considerations' (2017) 8 *International Journal of Advanced Computer Science and Applications* 266 ff.

[44] *Veal case I* [2017] Handelsgericht des Kantons Zürich (Commercial Court Canton Zurich) HG170107-O, CISG-online 3400; Butler and Harindranath, 'Article 57' in Kröll, Mistelis, and Perales Viscasillas (eds) (n 2) para 8; Florian Mohs, 'Article 57 CISG: Place of Payment' in Schwenzer and Schroeter (eds) (n 2) para 6.

[45] Mohs, 'Article 57 CISG: Place of Payment' in Schwenzer and Schroeter (eds) (n 2) para 6.

[46] *Telecommunication equipment case I* [2000] Landgericht Trier (District Court Trier) 7 HKO 155/00, CISG-online 595.

[47] Mohs, 'Article 57 CISG: Place of Payment' in Schwenzer and Schroeter (eds) (n 2) para 6. The opposing view see Christoph Brunner, Matthias Lerch, and Lukas Rusch, 'Article 57 (Place of Payment)' in Brunner and Gottlieb (eds) (n 8) para 6.

[48] *Omlat S.r.l. v Mecanumeric SA* [2023] Cour d'appel de Toulouse (Court of Appeal Toulouse) 18/03969, CISG-online 6647.

country, or any conforming bank, typically in the seller's country. This provision explicitly determines the place of payment.[49] In the absence of explicit or implicit determination of the place of payment, Article 9 CISG or Article 1.9 PICC may be invoked to consider parties' past practices and usages.[50] For instance, if past practice dictated that payment costs were always borne by the seller or service provider, then the place of payment might be the buyer's place of business. If the seller or service provider is granted direct debit authorization, the place of payment would be the buyer's bank location.[51]

b.) Payment against goods or documents

If the parties have not explicitly or implicitly determined the place of payment, Article 57(1)(b) CISG mandates that payment be made upon the transfer of goods or documents. In such instances, the buyer is obligated to remit the purchase price to the seller at the place of goods or document exchange.[52] Deciding whether payment correlates with the transfer of goods or documents is contingent upon contract interpretation or, in the absence of an explicit agreement, the application of Article 58 CISG.[53] If not specified otherwise, Article 58 CISG dictates that the buyer must fulfil the price payment obligation when the seller places the goods or documents controlling their disposition at the buyer's disposal as per the terms of the contract and the CISG.[54] Article 58(1) CISG establishes the overarching concept of simultaneous performance, wherein the buyer pays the purchase price concurrently with the seller's delivery of goods or documents, gradually and in tandem. Accordingly, Article 57(1)(b) CISG does not govern situations where one party is required to perform before the other. For instance, in mixed contracts involving the supply of goods and services (as per Article 3(2) CISG) with instalment payments, there is no simultaneous performance, neither in the overall transaction nor in each instalment, thus Article 57(1)(a) CISG is applicable: the buyer must pay at the seller's place of business. If payment is due within 30 days

---

[49] Butler and Harindranath, 'Article 57' in Kröll, Mistelis, and Perales Viscasillas (eds) (n 2) para 9; Brunner, Lerch, and Rusch, 'Article 57 (Place of Payment)' in Brunner and Gottlieb (eds) (n 8) para 5.

[50] *Rabobank Nederland v Teppich Fabrik Malans AG* [1994] Rechtbank 's-Hertogenbosch (District Court 's-Hertogenbosch Netherlands) 2548/43, CISG-Online 453: which held that previous place of payment was an established practice between the parties; but see for opposite view *AMC di Ariotti e Giacomini S.n.c. v Zimm & Söhne GmbH* [1998] Corte Suprema di Cassazione (Italian Supreme Court) 7759, CISG-online 538, 6: 'the practice may simply be the consequence of a mere tolerance by the seller and, as such, incapable of establishing a place of performance different from the legal one'.

[51] See *Telecommunication Equipment Case I* (n 46).

[52] Flechtner, (n 8) 639.

[53] See further, CISG Advisory Council, 'CISG-AC Opinion no 5, The buyer's right to avoid the contract in case of non-conforming goods or documents 7 May 2005, Badenweiler (Germany). Rapporteur: Professor Dr. Ingeborg Schwenzer, LL.M., Professor of Private Law, University of Basel' (2005) comment 8; CISG Advisory Council, 'CISG-AC Opinion No. 11, Issues Raised by Documents under the CISG Focusing on the Buyer's Payment Duty, Rapporteur Martin Davies, Tulane University Law School, New Orleans, U.S.A., 3 August 2012' (2012) comment 3.5.

[54] *Omlat S.r.l. v Mecanumeric SA* [2023] Cour d'appel de Toulouse (Court of Appeal Toulouse) 18/03969, CISG-online 6647.

upon presentation of documents, Article 57(1)(a) CISG similarly applies as there is no simultaneous performance occurring.[55]

If payment is tied to the transfer of goods or documents, the parties' agreement determines the location for handing over these items (Article 34 CISG). For instance, if 'cash against documents' or 'cash against delivery' (CAD) has been agreed upon, the seller must present the documents or goods at the buyer's place of business.[56] However, if the parties have arranged for document presentation at the buyer's chosen bank, then the bank's location becomes the place of payment.[57] In cases where documentary collection is agreed upon, where banks handle the documents until they reach the buyer, the payment place is the buyer's business location.[58] Regarding letters of credit, whether payment is to be made at the issuing or at the confirming bank depends on the contractual language and interpretation.[59]

Article 57(1)(b) CISG does not specify which documents it refers to, but it is linked with Article 58(1) CISG, where 'documents' holds the same meaning.[60] These documents include all relevant operational and commercial documents required by the sales contract and applicable laws and rules, including any Incoterms or documentary credit rules.[61] If the contract does not specify the documents, those controlling the goods' possession become relevant for Article 57(1)(b) CISG.

In contracts involving goods transportation, the seller usually acts first, delivering goods to the carrier per Article 31 CISG, while the buyer pays upon receiving either the goods or documents as per Article 58(1) CISG. However, if the seller arranges for delivery only upon payment, as per Article 58(2) CISG, then payment and delivery happen simultaneously, making Article 57(1)(b) applicable. This arrangement must be agreed upon if the seller organizes the carriage, such as under ICC Incoterms® CFR, CIF, CPT, and CIP. The same principles apply to goods in transit.[62]

For sales involving goods stored in a third-party warehouse, Article 57(1)(b) CISG applies if the warehouse keeper hands over the goods upon payment, either by agreement or by the seller's instruction under Article 58(2) CISG. If no such arrangement is made, Article 57(1)(a) CISG applies because simultaneous payment and delivery are not envisaged.

---

[55] Mohs, 'Article 57 CISG: Place of Payment' in Schwenzer and Schroeter (eds) (n 2) para 9.
[56] Butler and Harindranath, 'Article 57' in Kröll, Mistelis, and Perales Viscasillas (eds) (n 2) para 8; Brunner, Lerch, and Rusch, 'Article 57 (Place of Payment)' in Brunner and Gottlieb (eds) (n 8) para 5.
[57] Florian Mohs, 'Article 34' in Schwenzer and Schroeter (eds) (n 2) para 7.
[58] Mohs, 'Article 57 CISG: Place of Payment' in Schwenzer and Schroeter (eds) (n 2) para 10.
[59] Ibid.
[60] Butler and Harindranath, 'Article 57' in Kröll, Mistelis, and Perales Viscasillas (eds) (n 2) para 29; Mohs, 'Article 57 CISG: Place of Payment' in Schwenzer and Schroeter (eds) (n 2) para 11.
[61] See e.g. *Cobalt sulphate case* [1996] Bundesgerichtshof (German Supreme Court) VIII ZR 51/95, CISG-online 135.
[62] Butler and Harindranath, 'Article 57' in Kröll, Mistelis, and Perales Viscasillas (eds) (n 2) para 27.

c.) Seller's place of business

Seller's place of business is the place of payment under Article 57(1)(a) CISG only when there is no agreed place for payment and no simultaneous performance of the contract, which would trigger Article 57(1)(b) CISG. This means one party must perform before the other. For instance, if the seller ships goods with payment due 30 days later, the seller acts first, and the buyer pays at the seller's place of business according to Article 57(1)(a) CISG. This is also the case for open account payments when the seller delivers goods upfront, and the buyer settles the invoice later: the buyer will have to pay at the seller's place of business under Article 57(1)(a) CISG.[63] A 'net cash' or 'net cash after receipt of goods' clause in the contract signifies an open account agreement, in which the seller delivers the goods first and after that, the buyer makes the payment against an open invoice.[64]

The seller's place of business is also the place of payment in contracts involving goods transportation if the seller does not opt for payment terms where goods or documents are handed over only upon payment, as per Article 58(2) CISG. In such cases, the seller ships goods before payment, including goods in transit or stored in a third-party warehouse without specific payment terms.

Determining the seller's place of business, as per Article 10 CISG, is crucial for payment. If it changes, the buyer must pay at the new location, provided the seller informed the buyer of the change in a timely manner.[65] If not, payment can still occur at the original location (Article 80 CISG). The buyer might need to comply with new regulations or pay earlier due to the change, bearing the risk of transmission loss.[66] Any increase in payment-related expenses due to a change in the seller's place of business is the seller's responsibility, including interest or currency losses incurred by the buyer, as per Article 57(2) CISG.

5. Time of payment

a.) Parties agreement

Parties in international commercial contracts often establish payment terms, including time of payment, either explicitly or implicitly. The CISG and the PICC recognize such agreements.[67] Payment timing can be specified at a particular

---

[63] *Leather Goods Case* [1997] Oberlandesgericht München (Court of Appeal Munich) 7 U 2070/97 CISG-online 282: this means that the buyer is the one who bears the risks associated with payment.

[64] Brunner, Lerch, and Rusch, 'Article 57 (Place of Payment)' in Brunner and Gottlieb (eds) (n 8) para 12; Mohs, 'Article 57 CISG: Place of Payment' in Schwenzer and Schroeter (eds) (n 2) para 15.

[65] Florian Mohs, 'Article 58 CISG: Time of Payment; Principle of Payment Against Goods or Documents' in Schwenzer and Schroeter (eds) (n 2) para 12.

[66] Butler and Harindranath, 'Article 57' in Kröll, Mistelis, and Perales Viscasillas (eds) (n 2) para 16.

[67] CISG arts 6 and 58(1) and PICC 2016, art 6.1.1.(a); see further, *Mercedes, Porsche Cayennes and BMW's case* [2006] Oberlandesgericht München (Court of Appeal Munich) 23 U 2421/05, CISG-online 1394.

moment or within a defined period. It does not have to be exact but must be ascertainable. Any payment-related contract clause should be interpreted following the interpretation rules in the CISG (Articles 8 and 9) or the PICC (Articles 4.1 to 4.8).[68] Payment timing can also depend on certain acts by either party or even a third party, like issuing a notice of readiness, invoice, bill of lading, or buyer acceptance of an order confirmation. Often, payment time is inferred from payment clauses. For instance, 'cash against documents' or '40 days after receipt of invoice' are clear examples. Clauses like 'cash against invoice' set specific payment deadlines not tied to goods delivery but invoice issuance.[69]

In the absence of agreement, Article 6.1.1(c) PICC requires that performance, including the payment obligation, is made within a reasonable time after the conclusion of the contract.[70] Under the CISG, however, different default rules for payment time apply depending on whether the contract involves the transport of the goods or the payment against the goods or documents, as further explained below.

b.) Payment against goods

Pursuant to Article 58(1) CISG, the buyer's payment obligation arises when the seller has placed the goods or their representing documents at the buyer's disposal.[71] The specifics of this depend on the delivery terms agreed upon by the parties, either explicitly or implicitly through ICC Incoterms®, or inferred from Article 31 CISG.[72] When the seller places the goods at the buyer's disposal at its business premises or production/storage location, the buyer is typically required to pay upon such placement if it was aware that the goods were to be produced, stored, or harvested there (Article 31(b) CISG).

When the seller is required to deliver goods by placing them at the buyer's disposal, either at the buyer's place of business or some other location, it must make the goods available at that place.[73] If delivery is to take place at a specific place other than the buyer's place of business, the seller must inform the buyer accordingly. This applies to both F and D type ICC Incoterms®. For example, under the ICC Incoterms® 2020 DAP or DDP, the seller must place the goods at the buyer's disposal on any arriving means of transport that is ready for unloading at the designated place of destination.[74] Additionally, the seller must give the buyer any notice

---

[68] Mohs, 'Article 58 CISG: Time of Payment; Principle of Payment Against Goods or Documents' in Schwenzer and Schroeter (eds) (n 2) para 5.

[69] Ibid.

[70] Yesim M Atamer, 'Article 6.1.1' in Vogenauer (ed) (n 17) 717: the seller's obligations under PICC art 6.1.1 are modelled on CISG art 33 which also provides a default rule of reasonable time for delivery.

[71] *Congelados del Cibao v 3 Kids Corp. et al.* [2022] U.S. District Court for the Southern District of New York, 19-CV-7596 (LJL), CISG-online 6857.

[72] Mohs, 'Article 58 CISG: Time of Payment; Principle of Payment Against Goods or Documents' in Schwenzer and Schroeter (eds) (n 2) para 7.

[73] Ibid para 11.

[74] Chambre de Commerce Internationale (ed), Incoterms 2020: ICC Rules for the Use of Domestic and International Trade Terms (International Chamber of Commerce 2019) 66, 86, DAP or DDP,

required to enable it to take delivery of the goods. It is at the point in time when the seller makes the goods available or gives notice of availability that the buyer will need to pay the purchase price.[75]

c.) Goods to be transported

If the sales contract entails transporting the goods, under Article 31(a) CISG, the seller fulfils its obligation by handing the goods to the initial carrier for conveyance to the buyer.[76] Unless the seller has opted under Article 58(2) CISG to dispatch the goods with the condition that they will not be handed over until payment, the buyer is only required to pay after receiving the goods, as per Article 58(1) CISG.[77] The point of payment is not where the seller hands the goods to the first carrier but at the destination, where the buyer takes possession from that carrier.[78] The seller must notify the buyer upon arrival.[79] Depending on the payment method, the buyer will usually have ample time to make payment at the seller's place of business.[80] If the goods are lost or damaged during transit after the risk was vested in the buyer, Articles 67 and 66 CISG dictate that the buyer must still pay the price, at the anticipated arrival time to the destination. The same holds true for ICC Incoterms® 2020 C trade terms, where the seller arranges the transportation.[81] However, in practice, transactions involving goods transport are typically performed through letters of credit.

d.) Payment against documents

If payment against documents is specified in the contract, there are likely to be detailed provisions outlining how documents should be presented, specifying which documents must be presented to which bank and where. In this scenario, the purchase price only becomes payable when conforming documents are presented, meaning documents that meet the contractual requirements.[82] If requiring all contract documents for the purchase price to become payable contradicts the

---

respective comment A4; see generally Karibi Botoye, N Ejims Enwukwe, and Tamuno Bassey Amiesimaka, 'The Interplay between INCOTERMS and CISG on the International Sale of Goods' (2022) 2 *The Journal of Law and Policy* 102.

[75] Petra Butler and Arjun Harindranath, 'Article 58' in Kröll, Mistelis, and Perales Viscasillas (eds) (n 2) para 22.

[76] See CISG art 31(a) CISG.

[77] Butler and Harindranath, 'Article 58' in Kröll, Mistelis, and Perales Viscasillas (eds) (n 2) paras 24–25.

[78] Ibid para 23.

[79] Cf ICC Incoterms 2020, CIF.

[80] Butler and Harindranath, 'Article 58' in Kröll, Mistelis, and Perales Viscasillas (eds) (n 2) para 24.

[81] Cf ICC Incoterms 2020, CFR, CIF, CPT, CIP.

[82] CISG Advisory Council, 'CISG-AC Opinion No. 11, Issues Raised by Documents under the CISG Focusing on the Buyer's Payment Duty, Rapporteur: Professor Martin Davies, Tulane University Law School, New Orleans, U.S. August 3, 2012' (2012) comment 5.

narrow language of Article 58 CISG, which only mentions documents controlling goods disposition, it may be necessary to assume an implicit exception to Article 58 CISG.[83] The contract might explicitly or implicitly designate relevant documents, often referencing ICC Incoterms® 2020 in practice. Depending on the delivery mode and involvement of transportation/storage, the seller may need to provide traditional title documents like bills of lading and warehouse receipts. Most ICC Incoterms® typically require the seller to give the standard transport documents.[84] Title documents are crucial as they represent goods and act as their substitutes. Additional documents such as invoices, multi-modal/combined transport documents, insurance certificates, origin/quality certificates, and customs documents may be required by the contract. Including all necessary documents ensures strict compliance in a documentary transaction, failure of which may delay payment.[85] Usually, documents are made available to the buyer by presenting them to the buyer's bank (e.g. in 'cash against documents'), or at a confirming bank in the seller's country (e.g. with a letter of credit clause).[86]

If the contract stipulates payment against any given documents, the payment becomes due when the seller presents conforming documents.[87] But without further description of the documents to be handed over, Article 58 CISG states that the purchase price becomes payable when the seller provides documents controlling the disposition of goods.[88] This provision aims to ensure the purchase price does not become due solely with secondary documents. Whether the documents transfer goods' title or possession rights is irrelevant. The CISG Advisory Council Opinion No. 11 suggests that documents granting buyers exclusive disposition rights include various bills of lading, air waybill copies, road/rail consignment notes,[89] road/rail bills in North America, warehouse receipts, and ship delivery orders.[90] Documents not granting such rights include sea waybills, dock receipts,

---

[83]   Mohs, 'Article 58 CISG: Time of Payment; Principle of Payment Against Goods or Documents' in Schwenzer and Schroeter (eds) (n 2) para 15.

[84]   Chambre de commerce internationale (n 74) comment A6 for each INCOTERM.

[85]   Cf *Hummer Shoe Industry Co., Ltd. v Specialty Fashion Group Ltd.* [2018] 厦门市中级人民法院 (Intermediate People's Court Xiamen, Fujian Province) (2018) Min 02 Min Zhong No. 261, CISG-online 4803.

[86]   Mohs, 'Article 58 CISG: Time of Payment; Principle of Payment Against Goods or Documents' in Schwenzer and Schroeter (eds) (n 2) para 15.

[87]   Butler and Harindranath, 'Article 58' in Kröll, Mistelis, and Perales Viscasillas (eds) (n 2) para 28.

[88]   In the Vienna conference, it was agreed that 'documents controlling the disposition of the goods' did indeed mean only negotiable documents: see United Nations (UN) 'Report of the First Committee' (1980) UN Doc A/CONF.97/11 (1980) paras 13, 17; CISG Advisory Council 'CISG-AC Opinion No. 11, Issues Raised by Documents under the CISG Focusing on the Buyer's Payment Duty' (n 81) comment 4.5.

[89]   Ibid Black Letter Rule 6.4.

[90]   CISG Advisory Council, 'CISG-AC Opinion No. 11' (n 88) comments 6.2–6.7. See also Mohs, 'Article 58 CISG: Time of Payment; Principle of Payment Against Goods or Documents' in Schwenzer and Schroeter (eds) (n 2) para 16.

commercial invoices, survey reports, and insurance policies.[91] The potential necessity of non-disposing documents for customs clearance does not affect the purchase price's due date directly.[92]

6. Partial payments

In the absence of an agreement between the parties, the buyer is obligated to pay the full purchase price (Article 6.1.2 PICC).[93] Should the buyer fail to pay the entire sum and instead make only a partial payment, such partial performance constitutes a breach of the contract. The seller's right to refuse a partial payment is contingent upon the partial payment constituting a fundamental breach of contract under Article 25 CISG.[94] Instances of a fundamental breach involving the purchase price are rare and typically involve partial payments that are unreasonably inconvenient to the seller. Absent a fundamental breach, the seller is obligated to accept the partial payment, with any associated costs or losses being recoverable as damages against the buyer pursuant to Article 74 CISG.[95] The standard is slightly lower under the PICC, where the obligee may reject an offer to perform in part when the time performance is due, unless the obligee has no legitimate interest in so doing (Article 6.1.3 PICC).[96]

Additionally, the seller may retain the goods or documents pending full payment by the buyer.[97] Failure by the buyer to settle the full purchase price by the stipulated due date, as determined by Article 57 CISG, grants the seller the ability to pursue all available remedies under Article 61 ff (CISG).[98] This includes the option for the seller to set an additional period for payment under Article 63 CISG, failure of which permits the seller to avoid the contract under Article 64(1)(b) (CISG).

---

[91] CISG Advisory Council, 'CISG-AC Opinion No. 11' (n 88) Black Letter Rules 7.1–7.5.

[92] *Clothes case II* [1997] Kantonsgericht St. Gallen (Court of Appeal Canton St Gallen) 3 ZK 96-145, CISG-online 330; but *see* CISG Advisory Council 'CISG-AC Opinion No. 11' (n 88) Black Letter Rule 8.12.

[93] Yesim M Atamer, 'Article 6.1.2' in Vogenauer (ed) (n 17) para 1; for the CISG, see Butler and Harindranath, 'Article 53' in Kröll, Mistelis, and Perales Viscasillas (eds) (n 2) para 10.

[94] Mohs, 'Article 53 CISG: General Obligations of the Buyer' in Schwenzer and Schroeter (eds) (n 2) para 23: rejecting the majority view that breach of contract gives the seller the right to reject the partial payment.

[95] See ibid para 8.

[96] Yesim M Atamer, 'Article 6.1' in Vogenauer (ed) (n 17) paras 7–10: the right to accept or reject partial performance may also depend on the contract, and even implied in the contract.

[97] Butler and Harindranath, 'Article 58' in Kröll, Mistelis, and Perales Viscasillas (eds) (n 2) para 31.

[98] Mohs, 'Article 53 CISG: General Obligations of the Buyer' in Schwenzer and Schroeter (eds) (n 2) para 23.

7. Costs of payment

The parties involved in international commercial contracts may either explicitly or implicitly agree on who will bear the costs of payment. If no such agreement is made, Article 57(1)(a) CISG states that the buyer must pay the price at the seller's place of business, which usually means that the buyer will bear the costs of payment up to that place.[99] These costs include any commissions or charges due to banks for using the contractual means of payment. Therefore the buyer is responsible for the costs of transporting cash or any other necessary transaction until the money equivalent of the purchase price reaches the place of payment. For instance, if the buyer dispatches a cheque, it will bear the costs of transportation,[100] and if the cheque is dishonoured, the buyer will also bear the costs incurred by the seller's bank in trying to cash the cheque.[101] In the case of a documentary collection, the seller bears the costs of the collection, while the buyer must bear the costs of issuing the letter of credit in the case of a documentary credit arrangement.[102] This is consistent with Article 6.1.11 PICC, which states that each party must bear the costs of performing their obligations.[103]

III. Letters of Credit, in Particular ICC UCP 600

Letters of Credit are a common international trade practice. Their regulation has so far been based on uniform soft law rules. The most important source in this area is the Uniform Customs and Practice for Documentary Credits published by the ICC, the latest version of which was published by the ICC in 2007 (UCP 600). The UCP 600 are generally accepted and widely used. The first edition of the UCP goes back to 1933.[104] Certain commentators point out that the application of the UCP 600 is almost universal.[105] The UCP 600 play an important part in governing documentary credits since domestic law is not uniform in the various jurisdictions and, as is often the case, the same question of law may have a different answer, depending on the jurisdiction one has to consider.[106] Here we discuss the UCP 600

---

[99] Ibid para 22.

[100] *Italian Textiles Case II* [1996] Landgericht Duisburg (District Court Duisburg) 45 (19) O 80/94, CISG-online 186.

[101] *VW Passat and Golf case* [1998] Oberlandesgericht München (Court of Appeal Munich) 7 U 3771/97, CISG-online 339.

[102] Mohs, 'Article 53 CISG: General Obligations of the Buyer' in Schwenzer and Schroeter (eds) (n 2) para 22.

[103] See further Yesim M Atamer, 'Article 6.1.11' in Vogenauer (ed) (n 17) 777 ff.

[104] Roy Goode, 'Rule, Practice, and Pragmatism in Transnational Commercial Law' (2005) 54 *The International and Comparative Law Quarterly* 550.

[105] Jürgen Basedow, 'The State's Private Law and the Economy' (2008) 56 *The American Journal of Comparative Law* 709; Jan Ramberg, *International Commercial Transactions* (4th edn, International Chamber of Commerce) 142.

[106] In the United States, letters of credit are regulated in UCC art 5 (5-101 to 5-118).

as an example of a set of rules in this area of international trade law and their inter-actions with the CISG and the PICC.[107] However, it must be noted that the UCP 600 and similar rules regulate only the relationship between the parties and the bank, not the contractual relationship between the seller and the buyer.

Under a letter of credit, or in the UCP's language a documentary credit,[108] a bank[109] assumes an irrevocable, primary obligation to pay a credit against the pres-entation of documents by the beneficiary of the credit, usually the seller or the ser-vice provider.[110] The party instructing the bank is generally the buyer, also called the applicant, acting pursuant to the terms of a contract of sale, works, or services. The applicant's instruction to the bank is to the effect that the bank undertakes to honour a presentation of documents by the seller or the service provider in accord-ance with the terms of the credit.[111] The credit is, by its nature, a separate transac-tion from the sale contract on which it is based.[112]

The bank's undertaking to pay has two important aspects. On the one hand, it does not depend on default by the buyer, and in this sense, it is 'independent', giving rise to the guarantor's primary duty to pay the beneficiary irrespective of the applicant's default or breach of contract.[113] On the other hand, the bank is the seller's first port of call for payment. Therefore, the bank performs the payment obligation in lieu of the buyer but the bank is not liable under the sales contract for any delay or lack of payment, or other obligations of the buyer under that contract.

Neither the CISG nor the PICC explicitly require the buyer to open a letter of credit in order to pay the purchase price.[114] However, parties can agree on this payment method. Article 6 CISG and Article 6.1.7(1) PICC allow parties to cus-tomize their contract. The provisions of the CISG and the PICC governing an obli-gation to pay the price apply only insofar as the contract contains no other specific

---

[107] In addition to the UCP 600, one further important publication should be borne in mind which is the International Standard Banking Practice for the Examination of Documents under Documentary Credits (ISBP) (ICC Publication No. 681 (2007), which is a complement to the UCP 600.

[108] 'Documentary credit' is the term used by the UCP. Other synonyms are 'bankers' commercial credits', 'bankers' letters of credit', and 'documentary credits'.

[109] Identified as with the name of the issuing bank or confirming bank.

[110] UCP 600 defines 'credit' and the other words which are part of the definition of 'credit' as fol-lows: 'Credit means any arrangement, however named or described, that is irrevocable and thereby constitutes a definite undertaking of the issuing bank to honour a complying presentation. Honour means: a. to pay at sight if the credit is available by sight payment; b. to incur a deferred payment under-taking and pay at maturity if the credit is available by deferred payment. c. to accept a bill of exchange ("draft") drawn by the beneficiary and pay at maturity if the credit is available by acceptance. Issuing bank means the bank that issues a credit at the request of an applicant or on its own behalf.'

[111] Art 2 UCP 600 defines 'complying presentation' as 'a presentation that is in accordance with the terms and conditions of the credit, the applicable provisions of these rules and international standard banking practice'. Michael Bridge, *The International Sale of Goods* (3rd edn, Oxford University Press 2013) 276.

[112] Ibid 292.

[113] Goode (n 104) 550.

[114] Pursuant to CISG arts 53 and 54, the buyer's obligations include taking delivery of the goods, paying the price which also includes taking such steps and complying with such formalities as may be required under the contract or the law to enable payment.

provisions. As a result, the parties may agree upon the buyer's obligation to have a bank open a letter of credit for the seller's benefit.[115] In such a case, the contract of sale may determine the terms and characteristics of the letter of credit that the buyer is expected to open.[116] Where the contract as a whole falls within the scope of application of the CISG or the PICC, the obligation to open a letter of credit, but not the terms of the credit itself, will also be subject to their provisions since that would be an obligation arising from the underlying commercial contract.[117]

The parties to an international commercial contract may agree, for example, that a letter of credit be opened by the buyer and that the credit itself, that is, the relationship between the seller and the bank, be governed by the UCP 600. The UCP 600 will thus apply to the Letter of Credit by an indication in the underlying contract and in the credit itself. As the UCP 600 apply in this case by virtue of the parties' agreement, it follows that the application of their provisions may be amended or excluded by the express terms of the credit.[118] Absent an express choice by the parties, Article 8 and 9 CISG or Articles 1.9 PICC may enable a court or arbitration tribunal to find that the UCP 600 (or part of the provisions therein) apply to a letter of credit as part of the parties' practice or relevant trade usages.[119] The law of the credit, which may supplement the UCP 600, is different to the law governing the underlying sales or commercial contract. Accordingly, the law of the letter of credit will be determined by resorting to the conflict of laws rules applicable by the State court or arbitral tribunal under consideration.[120]

If both parties have agreed to make payment through a letter of credit, then the buyer needs to instruct its bank (i.e. the issuing bank, usually in its own country) to establish a documentary credit in favour of the seller.[121] In principle, the parties should stipulate in the underlying international commercial contract about what the terms of the credit should be.[122] If the letter of credit issued by the bank is not in

[115] Joseph Lookofsky, *Understanding the CISG* (4th edn, Wolters Kluwer 2012) 88–9.

[116] Ramberg (n 105) 47; Bridge (n 111) 292.

[117] Peter Schlechtriem, 'Interpretation, Gap-Filling and Further Developments of the U.N. Sales Convention' (2004) 16 *Pace International Law Review* 305.

[118] Bridge (n 111) 293.

[119] But see Goode (n 104) 550, 'the widely adopted Uniform Customs and Practice for Documentary Credits. These may be evidence of pre-existing usage but this will not be true of all the terms, since there will inevitably be some departures in order to improve current practice; indeed, some of the "rules" are merely precatory indications of desirable practice, such as the avoidance of excessive detail in a credit.'

[120] If one considers the question of the proper law of the credit in the context of proceedings pending or likely to be pending before a state court, then the applicable law will be determined by the conflicts rules applicable before such court. If, on the other hand, one considers the question of the proper law of the credit in the context of proceedings pending or likely to be pending before an arbitrator, then the applicable law will be determined by the conflict rules of the *lex arbitri*. In this regard, the law applicable to the letter of credit will be the law chosen by the Parties and in the absence of such choice the law where the issuing bank or the confirming back is located, since the issuing bank or the confirming bank is the party whose performance characterizes the letter of credit under, for example, the EC Rome Regulation on the applicable law to contracts, see Jonathan Hill, 'Choice of Law in Contract under the Rome Convention: The Approach of the UK Courts' (2004) 53 *The International and Comparative Law Quarterly* 334.

[121] Ramberg (n 105) 132.

[122] Lookofsky (n 115) 89, 90.

accordance with the terms of the underlying contract, the buyer may incur a breach of part of its obligation to pay the price. When the underlying contract is null and void or voidable for duress, undue influence, mistake, or any other legal grounds admissible under its applicable law, that contract's payment clause will most likely follow the same fate. However, the invalidity of the underlying commercial contract will not entail the nullity of the letter of credit since under the principle of independence, the letter of credit constitutes a separate agreement from the contract of sale or services. Therefore, the bank must honour a complying presentation of documents unless the seller's request to pay is fraudulent.

Since the principle of freedom of contract operates also at the level of the letter of credit (and not only at the level of the underlying contract), the parties are able to freely structure the type of letter of credit. In principle, letters of credit are irrevocable under the UCP 600, and the word 'irrevocable' need not be set out in the terms of the credit.[123] As the provisions in the UCP 600 may be modified,[124] the parties may agree that a credit is 'revocable'. Whether a credit is revocable will depend on the terms of the letter of credit itself.[125] In case of a revocable letter of credit, the issuing bank may cancel the credit without notice to the seller.

The underlying contract may also require the buyer to apply for a confirmed letter of credit.[126] In such a case the letter of credit will be issued by the issuing bank and then be confirmed by a further bank ('the confirming bank') upon the request or authorization of the issuing bank. By adding its confirmation to the credit issued by the issuing bank, the confirming bank assumes a definite undertaking to honour or negotiate a complying presentation of documents.[127] Such undertaking by the confirming bank is in addition to that of the issuing bank.[128] Moreover, the buyer may have an obligation to make payment available to the seller by sight payment,[129] deferred payment,[130] or negotiation,[131] and this characteristic will also depend on the payment terms of the underlying CISG contract which should eventually be reflected in the letter of credit.

A letter of credit has the advantage of providing security for both the buyer and the seller. The seller is assured of payment upon compliance with the terms of the

---

[123] UCP 600 art 3.

[124] UCP 600 art 1.

[125] Ramberg (n 105) 145.

[126] Lookofsky (n 115) 89–90.

[127] See UCP 600 art 2, Definitions of 'Confirmation' and 'Confirming bank' and UCP 600 art 8a.

[128] UCP 600 art 2.

[129] UCP 600 arts 2 and 6(b). A sight credit means that the letter of credit provides for payment against presentation of the documents. Payment is usually made by the advising bank. See Bridge (n 142) 287–8.

[130] Arts 2 and 6(b) UCP 600. A deferred payment credit means that payment takes place after the expiry of the designated period from shipment, from the bill of lading date or from presentation. The seller provides the documents to the buyer, before receiving payment. If the nominated bank pre-paid before maturity, the issuing bank must reimburse the nominated bank.

[131] UCP 600 arts 2 and 6(b).

letter of credit, while the buyer can ensure that payment is made only after the goods are shipped or the services are completed. However, a letter of credit can be complex and costly to set up, as banks typically charge fees for issuing and administering them. Disputes may arise if there are discrepancies between the documents and the terms of the letter of credit.

IV. Obligation to Take Delivery of the Goods, Including Incoterms© 2020

Taking delivery of the goods entails the buyer physically getting possession of them.[132] In simpler terms, taking over the goods is a factual action.[133] The location and time for taking over the goods do not necessarily coincide with the delivery location and time (as determined by Article 31 CISG for delivery location and Article 33 CISG for delivery time) or with the payment location and time (Article 57 CISG for payment location and Article 58 CISG for payment time). Nonetheless, in most instances, the place of taking delivery will align with the place where the seller must deliver the goods under the contract or Article 31 CISG.[134] If the goods are delivered at the buyer's or seller's place of business or any other designated location, the goods must be accepted at that location once they are made available to the buyer.[135] In contracts involving goods carriage or goods in transit, the place of taking over the goods is not where the seller transfers them to the initial carrier for transmission to the buyer (Article 31(a) CISG), but rather the destination. If the sold goods are stored in a third-party warehouse and the transaction does not involve handing over documents enabling the buyer to retrieve the goods from the warehouse, the buyer does not need to take any action equivalent to 'taking over the goods' because the seller arranges for the third-party warehouse keeper to hold the goods on the buyer's behalf and release them if necessary.[136]

Regarding the timing of the buyer's obligation to take over the goods or documents, Article 58(1) CISG applies.[137] Accordingly, the buyer must accept the goods or documents when they are made available to it. However, the buyer should be given a brief period to actually take over the goods or documents after receiving

---

[132] Petra Butler and Arjun Harindranath, 'Article 60' in Kröll, Mistelis, and Perales Viscasillas (eds) (n 2) para 2.

[133] Florian Mohs, 'Article 60' in Schwenzer and Schroeter (eds) (n 2) para 1.

[134] Christoph Brunner, Matthias Lerch, and Lukas Rusch, 'Article 60 (Buyer's Obligation to Take Delivery)' in Brunner and Gottlieb (eds) (n 8) para 2; Mohs, 'Article 60 CISG: Buyer's Obligations to Take Delivery' in Schwenzer and Schroeter (eds) (n 2) para 2.

[135] Mohs, 'Article 60 CISG: Buyer's Obligations to Take Delivery' in Schwenzer and Schroeter (eds) (n 2) para 2.

[136] Brunner, Lerch, and Rusch, 'Article 60 (Buyer's Obligation to Take Delivery)' in Brunner and Gottlieb (eds) (n 8) para 2; Mohs, 'Article 60 CISG: Buyer's Obligations to Take Delivery' in Schwenzer and Schroeter (eds) (n 2) para 3.

[137] See time of payment above.

notice from the seller that they are now at the buyer's disposal. The process of taking delivery is often determined in the contract or by utilizing specific trade terms.[138] Particularly, the question of which party is responsible for loading or unloading the goods becomes crucial. Rules A2 and A4 and B2 and B4 of all ICC Incoterms® delineate the obligation to take delivery and the loading and unloading obligations. For instance, under the EXW ICC Incoterms® 2020, the seller must not load the goods onto a collection vehicle; under FOB ICC Incoterms®, the seller must deliver the goods as per the customary manner at the port onboard the vessel; the same principle applies under CFR and CIF ICC Incoterms®; under DDP ICC Incoterms®, the seller must place the goods at the buyer's disposal on any arriving means of transport ready for unloading at the designated destination, but under DPU ICC Incoterms® the seller must in addition unload the goods.[139]

Although Article 60 CISG only mentions taking over the 'goods', the buyer holds the same obligation regarding any documents presented by the seller.

The actions expected of the buyer to facilitate the seller's delivery are typically outlined explicitly or implicitly in the contract.[140] The contract may require the buyer to inspect the goods before shipment.[141] The ICC Incoterms® delineate several additional buyer obligations ensuring the seller's ability to deliver the goods. For instance, under FOB ICC Incoterms®, the buyer must notify the seller regarding the vessel name, loading point, and, if needed, the agreed delivery time (B10 rule). Another example are call-off contracts where the buyer must request delivery of goods at its discretion. Depending on the specifics of the contract, the buyer's failure to request delivery of goods as per the contractual agreement may constitute a breach of its duty to accept delivery. If the contract mandates the buyer to specify the goods' characteristics, it must do so either on the agreed-upon day or within a reasonable time frame after receiving a request from the seller, as per Article 65 CISG. This specification obligation is part of the buyer's duty to accept delivery.[142] If the contract requires the buyer to provide plans or data for manufacturing goods, such preliminary obligations are indeed part of the buyer's duty to enable seller delivery.[143]

---

[138] Mohs, 'Article 60 CISG: Buyer's Obligations to Take Delivery' in Schwenzer and Schroeter (eds) (n 2) para 5.

[139] See ibid for an analysis with respect to ICC Incoterms® 2010; Brunner, Lerch, and Rusch, 'Article 60 (Buyer's Obligation to Take Delivery)' in Brunner and Gottlieb (eds) (n 8) para 2. Absent any agreement or usage, unloading and loading in own means of transportation is the buyer's obligation.

[140] Mohs, 'Article 60 CISG: Buyer's Obligations to Take Delivery' in Schwenzer and Schroeter (eds) (n 2) para 8.

[141] *Cushions case* [2000] China International Economic & Trade Arbitration Commission (CIETAC) CISG/2000/15, CISG-online 1592.

[142] Mohs, 'Article 60 CISG: Buyer's Obligations to Take Delivery' in Schwenzer and Schroeter (eds) (n 2) para 8. But see in favour of classification as a secondary obligation only, not an obligation to take delivery Butler and Harindranath, 'Article 60' in Kröll, Mistelis, and Perales Viscasillas (eds) (n 2) para 7.

[143] Butler and Harindranath, 'Article 60' in Kröll, Mistelis, and Perales Viscasillas (eds) (n 2) para 7.

Even in the absence of an express or implied contract term, the buyer is obligated to inform the seller of any specific circumstances in the buyer's country as part of the general duty to cooperate and inform.[144] The buyer may be required to complete customs procedures.[145] If delivery is set to occur at the buyer's business premises, it must prepare its site and facilities accordingly for taking over the goods. The buyer's duty to enable seller delivery also entails a negative obligation, meaning the buyer must not impede the seller's performance.

In some sales contracts, the parties may leave details for later determination. These contracts are still enforceable under the CISG if a specific procedure is outlined for later determination or if one party or a third party is empowered to make such determinations.[146] Particularly in cases where the buyer holds a call option for goods delivery, the buyer often retains the right to specify the time and place based on business needs. In such instances, the contract typically dictates the buyer's obligation to specify those elements according to a defined procedure.[147]

Even in the absence of direct mention of ICC Incoterms®, they might serve as interpretative tools for the parties' delivery terms if they reflect common practice in the specific trade concerned (Article 9(2) CISG) or because they constitute a relevant circumstance under Article 8(3) CISG.[148] Each ICC Incoterms® trade term delineates the buyer's obligations through rules B1 to B10. Depending on the chosen trade term, the buyer might need to perform different obligations to allow delivery, such as securing licenses, official authorizations, or handling customs procedures for the importation of goods, etc. Additionally, the buyer may have responsibilities regarding the transportation or insurance of the goods. Furthermore, the ICC Incoterms® specify cost-sharing arrangements between the seller and the buyer in rules A9 and B9, along with requiring the buyer to issue certain notifications to the seller in B10, such as vessel nomination, loading point, and stipulated delivery time under FOB terms. Through the incorporation of ICC Incoterms®, various cooperation duties are imposed on the buyer, including the obligation to acknowledge the seller's proof of delivery, transport documentation, and equivalent electronic communications. The exhaustive enumeration of

[144] Brunner, Lerch, and Rusch, 'Article 60 (Buyer's Obligation to Take Delivery)' in Brunner and Gottlieb (eds) (n 8) para 4; Mohs, 'Article 60 CISG: Buyer's Obligations to Take Delivery' in Schwenzer and Schroeter (eds) (n 2) para 9; cf Butler and Harindranath, 'Article 60' in Kröll, Mistelis, and Perales Viscasillas (eds) (n 2) para 7.

[145] Butler and Harindranath, 'Article 60' in Kröll, Mistelis, and Perales Viscasillas (eds) (n 2) para 6; Mohs, 'Article 60 CISG: Buyer's Obligations to Take Delivery' in Schwenzer and Schroeter (eds) (n 2) para 7.

[146] Mohs, 'Article 53 CISG: General Obligations of the Buyer' in Schwenzer and Schroeter (eds) (n 2) para 37.

[147] Ibid.

[148] Brunner, Lerch, and Rusch, 'Article 60 (Buyer's Obligation to Take Delivery)' in Brunner and Gottlieb (eds) (n 8) para 4.

duties and obligations stemming from ICC Incoterms® cannot be fully covered in this chapter.

In various scenarios, the buyer may withhold its cooperation with the seller's delivery. The buyer can refuse to take delivery if the seller delivers the goods before the agreed date.[149] This refusal also extends to any preliminary steps the buyer must take to facilitate seller delivery (Premature delivery, as per Article 52(1) CISG).[150] The buyer may also reject any surplus quantity if the seller delivers more goods than specified in the contract.[151] This right of rejection also encompasses any necessary actions the buyer must undertake to facilitate seller delivery (excess quantity, as per Article 52(2) CISG). On the other hand, the buyer must accept tardy delivery unless it has grounds to declare the contract avoided, as outlined in Article 49(1) and (2)(a) CISG.[152] If the seller eventually delivers the goods, the buyer can only avoid the contract if the seller's delayed delivery constitutes a fundamental breach or if delivery occurs after the additional period set by the buyer.[153] However, the buyer forfeits this right if it fails to exercise it within a reasonable timeframe after becoming aware of the delivery. In addition, the buyer cannot reject delivery of non-conforming goods unless the non-conformity constitutes a fundamental breach under Article 25 CISG.[154] In documentary sales, compliant document presentation is essential. Any document non-conformity entitles the buyer to reject them.[155] This rejection right is often assumed for CIF/CFR ICC Incoterms® or under UCP 600 for payment via documentary credit.[156] However, immediate avoidance rights might only be limited to specific situations, such as string trade scenarios where the buyer lacks interest in physical goods delivery.

---

[149] *Iron Ore Case*, CIETAC, 5 May 2005, CISG online 1685: the intent of the legislators is that the party may reject an earlier delivery, but may not reject the goods or avoid the contract.

[150] Mohs, 'Article 60 CISG: Buyer's Obligations to Take Delivery' in Schwenzer and Schroeter (eds) (n 2) para 12.

[151] Brunner, Lerch, and Rusch, 'Article 60 (Buyer's Obligation to Take Delivery)' in Brunner and Gottlieb (eds) (n 8) para 6; Mohs, 'Article 60 CISG: Buyer's Obligations to Take Delivery' in Schwenzer and Schroeter (eds) (n 2) para 12.

[152] See UNCITRAL, *Digest of Case Law on the United Nations Convention on the International Sale of Goods* (2016) art 60, para 9 <https://uncitral.un.org/sites/uncitral.un.org/files/media-documents/uncitral/en/cisg_digest_2016.pdf> accessed 24 November 2025.

[153] Brunner, Lerch, and Rusch, 'Article 60 (Buyer's Obligation to Take Delivery)' in Brunner and Gottlieb (eds) (n 8) para 6.

[154] Butler and Harindranath, 'Article 60' in Kröll, Mistelis, and Perales Viscasillas (eds) (n 2) para 8; Brunner, Lerch, and Rusch, 'Article 60 (Buyer's Obligation to Take Delivery)' in Brunner and Gottlieb (eds) (n 8) para 6; Mohs, 'Article 60 CISG: Buyer's Obligations to Take Delivery' in Schwenzer and Schroeter (eds) (n 2) para 15.

[155] Schlechtriem (n 116) 304; cf *St Paul Guardian Insurance Co and Travelers Insurance v Neuromed Medical Systems & Support GmbH et al.* (n 194), holding that the ICC Incoterms® can be used as a trade usage to interpret the term CIF even though the parties had not explicitly referred to the ICC Incoterms®.

[156] Schlechtriem (n 116) 305.

V. Other Obligations in the Sale of Goods and Services

In specific scenarios, the buyer might encounter additional duties beyond their typical obligations outlined in the CISG or the PICC, which primarily involve paying the purchase price and accepting delivery. These additional obligations could entail refraining from directly purchasing from the seller's suppliers, avoiding resale to certain countries,[157] or upholding confidentiality agreements. Such obligations typically stem from the contract itself, either through explicit agreement between the parties or from practices and usages.[158]

In addition, international agreements, especially long-duration contracts, often dictate communication exchanges between the parties to perform the contract properly. If a particular contract does not outline communication procedures or obligations, and there is no applicable practice or usage, the buyer is generally obligated to cooperate with the seller (Article 60(a) CISG in conjunction with Article 7(2) CISG). This cooperation duty encompasses the obligation to inform the seller about circumstances pertinent to contract performance.[159] While acknowledging this general cooperation duty is straightforward, its practical application to specific cases may pose significant challenges.[160]

Article 5.1.3 PICC expressly requires that each party cooperate with the other party when such cooperation may reasonably be expected for the performance of that party's obligations.[161] Especially in contracts involving long duration or complex performances, ongoing cooperation throughout the contract's duration is often vital for the transaction's success.[162] However, the parties' cooperation duty is subject to reasonable expectations. The obligation of cooperation must naturally be restricted within specific boundaries, meaning it exists only to the extent where cooperation can reasonably facilitate the other party's performance without disrupting the agreed allocation of responsibilities in the contract.[163] Within these boundaries, each party might have a duty not only to avoid obstructing the other party's obligations but also to proactively facilitate the other party's performance.

---

[157] Cf *Snowchains case* [2008] Kantonsgericht St. Gallen (Court of Appeal Canton St. Gallen) BZ.2007.55, CISG-online 1768.

[158] Mohs, 'Article 53 CISG: General Obligations of the Buyer' in Schwenzer and Schroeter (eds) (n 2) para 40.

[159] Ibid para 39.

[160] Ibid para 39.

[161] See generally Stefan Vogenauer, 'Article 5.1.3' in Vogenauer (ed) (n 17) 620–5; Butler and Harindranath, 'Article 60' in Kröll, Mistelis, and Perales Viscasillas (eds) (n 2) para 11: comparing the CISG and the PICC.

[162] Vogenauer, 'Article 5.1.3' in Vogenauer (ed) (n 17) para 1.

[163] International Institute for the Unification of Private Law (ed), *UNIDROIT Principles of International Commercial Contracts* (2016 edn, UNIDROIT International Institute for the Unification of Private Law 2017) 152–5, art 5.1.3.

11

Risk of Loss or Damages to the Goods in the International Sales Contract

I. General Extent and Notion of Risk of Loss, Exceptions

The concept of risk holds various interpretations within discussions concerning the sale of goods. For instance, a purchaser might assume the business risk of re-selling goods for profit or of getting the goods cleared for resale.[1] Alternatively, as detailed in this section, risk could pertain to what is commonly termed as 'price risk'. This refers to the possibility of bearing the expenses for damage to or loss of goods, with the buyer still being obligated to pay the purchase price, if the loss or damage occurs without fault of either party.[2]

The default rules of law governing the transfer of risk apply only when the parties do not have a specific agreement on the issue[3] and when neither party can be

---

[1] See generally Johan Erauw, 'Article 66' in Stefan M Kröll, Loukas A Mistelis, and Pilar Perales Viscasillas (eds), *UN Convention on Contracts for the International Sale of Goods (CISG): A Commentary* (2nd edn, CH Beck 2018); Pascal Hachem, 'Article 66 CISG: Loss after Risk Has Passed' in Ingeborg Schwenzer and Ulrich G Schroeter (eds), *Schlechtriem & Schwenzer Commentary on the UN Convention on the International Sale of Goods (CISG)* (5th edn, Oxford University Press 2022).

[2] Erauw, 'Article 66' in Kröll, Mistelis, and Perales Viscasillas (eds) (n 1) para 7.

[3] See generally Pascal Hachem, 'Article 6 CISG: Exclusion or Derogation by the Parties (Party Autonomy)' in Schwenzer and Schroeter (eds) (n 1); UNCITRAL, Digest of Case Law on the United

deemed responsible for the circumstances leading to it.[4] If the loss arises from a breach, the contractual liability regime applies.[5] Article 66 CISG explicitly states that after transfer of risk, the buyer remains obligated to pay the price even if the goods are lost or damaged, 'unless the loss or damage is due to an act or omission of the seller'.[6]

What price risk covers can be agreed upon by the Parties. Absent an agreement, price risk is understood to encompass situations where the integrity of goods is compromised[7]—such as damage, destruction, or theft.[8] However, whether situations involving governmental seizure or confiscation fall within the scope of risk contemplated by Article 66 CISG is less clear.[9] This risk is sometimes referred to as 'legal risk'.[10] The majority view is that governmental measures are encompassed in Article 66 CISG. This view argues that it should not matter how the goods are lost, but simply that they are lost.[11]

The transfer of risk has significant implications. It shifts the burden of loss from the seller to the buyer. If goods are damaged, destroyed, or lost before risk is transferred, the seller bears the loss. However, if the loss occurs after the risk has been transferred to the buyer, the buyer bears the loss despite having to pay the full purchase price.[12] Under Article 36 CISG, the transfer of risk also marks the time at which the conformity of the goods is assessed. 'Assessing' in this context refers to determining when the goods must have been non-conforming for a breach to occur.

Nations Convention on the International Sale of Goods (2016) art 66, 304 <https://uncitral.un.org/sites/uncitral.un.org/files/media-documents/uncitral/en/cisg_digest_2016.pdf> accessed 1 November 2025; CISG Advisory Council, 'CISG-AC Opinion No. 17, Limitation and Exclusion Clauses in CISG Contracts, Rapporteur: Prof. Lauro Gama Jr., Pontifical Catholic University of Rio de Janeiro, Brazil, 16 October 2015' (2015) comment 1.4.

[4]　See e.g. a notable exception, however, is the heading of US Uniform Commercial Code (UCC) 2018 ss 2–509, which reads 'Risk of Loss in the Absence of Breach'.

[5]　Ingeborg Schwenzer and Edgardo Muñoz, *Global Sales and Contract Law* (2nd edn, Oxford University Press 2022) 38.01–38.02.

[6]　*Metal lockers case* [2019] ВАРНЕНСКИ ОКРЪЖЕН СЪД (District Court Varna) 972/2016, CISG-online 5588.

[7]　Hachem, 'Article 66 CISG: Loss after Risk Has Passed' in Schwenzer and Schroeter (eds) (n 1) para 6; For the common law perspective, see M Bridge and Judah P Benjamin (eds), *Benjamin's Sale of Goods* (8th edn, Sweet Maxwell 2012) para 6-017.

[8]　Schwenzer and Muñoz (n 5) para 38.05.

[9]　Jonas Galer and Felix Luth, 'The Passing of Legal Risk Under the Vienna Sales Convention: Does Article 66 CISG Cover Acts of State?' (2012) 16 *Vindobona Journal* 19.

[10]　Schwenzer and Muñoz (n 5) para 38.04; Erauw 'Article 66' (n 1) para 34.

[11]　Hachem, 'Article 66 CISG: Loss after Risk Has Passed' in Schwenzer and Schroeter (eds) (n 1) para 9.

[12]　See also Ingeborg Schwenzer, 'Article 36 CISG: Relevant Time for Conformity of Goods' in Schwenzer and Schroeter (eds) (n 1) para 5 ff.

II. Contractual Allocation of Risk

In alignment with the overarching principle of contractual autonomy, it primarily falls upon the contracting parties to delineate the distribution of risk within their agreement. Particularly in the realm of international commerce, parties rarely overlook the inclusion of such contractual stipulations concerning risk transfer.[13] However, more often than not, the apportionment of risk does not stand independently within the contract but rather becomes integrated into the provisions governing delivery modalities, encompassing aspects such as transportation, expenses, price, and insurance. Typically, contracting parties resort to international trade terms. On a global scale, the ICC Incoterms® are of paramount importance as a comprehensive set of trade terms. These terms delineate the specific juncture at which risk transfer is to occur, defining the responsibilities and liabilities of the seller and the buyer in that and other matters.

Nevertheless, scenarios may arise where parties have not explicitly articulated a clause addressing risk transfer or utilized a trade term. In such instances, it may be plausible to infer an implicit agreement by scrutinizing other contractual clauses pertaining to performance. For instance, if the seller is mandated to insure the goods and it subsequently dispatches the insurance documentation to the buyer upon shipment, it could be construed that risk transfer was intended to happen at the moment of consignment to the carrier.[14]

Questions, however, may emerge in situations where parties have established provisions governing delivery modalities and have concurrently employed a trade term that contradicts other clauses within the contract. This dilemma might arise, for instance, if parties stipulate that the buyer is responsible for procuring insurance while simultaneously utilizing the CIF term in ICC Incoterms® 2020, which obligates the seller to obtain insurance. Here, the interpretation of delivery modality provisions under Article 8 CISG becomes pivotal in determining the precedence of terms, the applicability of trade term features, and the implications for risk transference.[15]

Conversely, when a clause explicitly addresses risk transfer, it could significantly impact the meaning of other clauses.[16] For instance, if the contract allocates the risk throughout the entire transportation phase to the seller but concurrently incorporates the ICC Incoterms® CIF, questions may arise regarding the classification of the contract as CIF and whether the obligations prescribed by the CIF term remain operative.

---

[13] CISG Advisory Council, 'CISG-AC Opinion No. 17' (n 3) comments 1.3–1.4, 1.9.
[14] Schwenzer and Muñoz (n 5) para 38.09.
[15] Ibid para 38.10.
[16] Bridge and Benjamin (n 7) 6-017.

III. Incoterms® 2020

As previously mentioned, in international trade, parties frequently rely on trade terms to delineate their contractual obligations and specify the moment when the risk of loss of or damage to the goods is transferred from the seller to the buyer. Notably, the ICC Incoterms® serve as a predominant framework for such specifications, particularly in associating the transfer of risk with the delivery of goods.[17] Consequently, the delivery obligations outlined within the respective ICC Incoterms® essentially dictate the timing of risk transfer.[18]

When parties employ a trade term, it becomes imperative to interpret the precise term chosen and its implications. The nuanced interpretation of shorthand trade terms may exhibit variations across jurisdictions, independent of any specific definition stipulated by the parties. But in cases where the CISG governs the contract, the insertion of a trade term into the CISG contract without further elaboration should be construed as a reference to the prevailing version of the ICC Incoterms®. Considering the universal influence of ICC Incoterms® in international trade since their inception in 1936, it could be argued that their versions represent a usage of which the parties knew or ought to have known and which in international trade is widely known to, and regularly observed by, parties to contracts of the type involved in the particular trade concerned, pursuant to Article 9 CISG.[19]

Accordingly, it seems pertinent to briefly delineate the implications for risk transfer across the various groups of terms in the ICC Incoterms® 2020 edition.

1. EXW

Under the ICC Incoterms® EXW (Ex Works), the seller's responsibility is minimal. It makes the goods available at its premises or another named place, that is, the factory, warehouse, depot, etc., which may not be the seller's premises. If the parties do not specify the precise delivery point, the seller can choose one that best serves its interests. However, this could mean the buyer bears the risk if the seller selects a point just before potential loss or damage occurs. To mitigate this risk, it is prudent for the buyer to pinpoint the exact delivery location within a designated place.

---

[17] Christoph Brunner, Désirée Klingler, and Marc André Mauerhofer, 'Introductory Remarks to Arts. 66–70' in Christoph Brunner and Benjamin Gottlieb (eds), *Commentary on the UN Sales Law (CISG)* (Wolters Kluwer Law International 2019) para 9.

[18] Ibid.

[19] *SMR Automotive Systems Spain, SAU v Bühler Motor GmbH* [2013] Juzgado de Primera Instancia e Instrucción No 2 de La Almunia de Dona Godina (Court of First Instance No 2 of La Almunia de Dona Godina) 107/2013, CISG-online 2532; *[…] v Edco Eindhoven BV* [2022] Rechtbank Oost-Brabant (District Court Oost-Brabant) C/01/364407/HA ZA 20-720, CISG-online 5906; *Fertilizantes Tocantins SA v TGO Agriculture (USA), Inc* [2024] US District Court for the Middle District of Florida 8:21-cv-2884-VMC-JSS, CISG-online 6878; JD Feltham, 'C.I.F. and F.O.B. Contracts and the Vienna Convention on Contracts for the International Sale of Goods' [1991] *Journal of Business Law* 416.

When goods are delivered under EXW, the transfer of risk occurs when the goods are placed, not loaded, at the buyer's disposal.[20] Despite this, if the seller handles the loading, the buyer could argue that the seller bears the risk during loading.[21] To address this uncertainty, the parties should agree beforehand on who bears the risk when the seller assists or takes care of the loading of the goods. Sellers often load goods at their premises due to logistical advantages or security concerns, exposing buyers to risks not under their control. In such cases, opting for the FCA rule (under the option that the goods are delivered at the seller's premises) may be prudent, as it obliges the seller to load the goods if delivery occurs at its premises, thus retaining the risk during loading.[22]

The seller must deliver the goods on the agreed date or within the agreed period. However, for delivery to take place and transfer of risk to happen, the goods must be clearly identified as the contract goods.[23] Unless a fixed time for delivery has been agreed, the seller must also give the buyer notice that the goods are ready for pick-up and provide any further notice necessary to enable the buyer to take delivery of the goods.[24] On the other hand, whenever it is agreed that the buyer is entitled to determine the time within an agreed period and/or the point of taking delivery within the named place, the buyer must give the seller sufficient notice.[25] If the buyer fails to give notice, then it bears all risks of loss of or damage to the goods from the agreed date or the end of the agreed period for delivery, provided that the goods have been clearly identified as the contract goods.[26]

2. FCA

Pursuant to the ICC Incoterms® FCA (Free Carrier), the seller must deliver the goods to the carrier or another person nominated by the buyer at the named point if any, at the named place, or it must procure goods so delivered. The seller must deliver the goods: first, on the agreed date, or second, at the time within the agreed period notified by the buyer, or third, if no such time is notified, then at the end of the agreed period. Delivery is completed: (a) if the named place is the seller's premises, when the goods have been loaded on the means of transport provided by the buyer; or (b) in any other case, when the goods are placed at the disposal of the carrier or another person nominated by the buyer on the seller's means of transport and are ready for unloading.[27] Whichever of the two is chosen as the

---

[20] Chambre de commerce internationale (ed), *Incoterms 2020: ICC Rules for the Use of Domestic and International Trade Terms* (International Chamber of Commerce 2019) 24–5, EXW, paras A3, B3.

[21] Ibid 32, FCA, para A2.

[22] Ibid 29, FCA, Explanatory Notes for Users.

[23] Ibid 25, EXW, para B3.

[24] Ibid 26 EXW, para A10.

[25] Ibid 27, EXW, para B10.

[26] Ibid 25, EXW, para B3.

[27] Ibid 32, FCA, para A2.

place of delivery, that place identifies where risk transfers to the buyer.[28] The parties are well advised to specify clearly the exact point of delivery within the designated location. This precision serves to establish a shared understanding of when delivery occurs, marking the pivotal moment when risk transfers to the buyer.[29] Failure to pinpoint this precise delivery point can lead to complications, primarily for the buyer. In such cases, the seller retains the right to select a delivery point that aligns with its interests. This chosen point becomes the official delivery point, initiating the transfer of risk to the buyer. However, this scenario exposes the buyer to the possibility that the seller may opt for a point perilously close to the potential for goods being lost or damaged. The term 'procure goods so delivered' accommodates situations where the seller may acquire goods for subsequent sale in a chain of transactions, commonly known as string sales.[30] This provision is particularly relevant in industries like commodity trading, although it may apply across various sectors.

For risk to be transferred under FCA, the seller must give the buyer sufficient notice,[31] either that the goods have been delivered as stated above or that the carrier or another person nominated by the buyer has failed to take the goods within the time agreed.[32] On the other hand, the buyer bears all risks of loss of or damage to the goods from the time they have been delivered, as stated above, if the buyer fails to nominate a carrier or another person to collect the goods at the place and time agreed by the parties or fails to give notice[33] of: (a) the name of the carrier or another person nominated within sufficient time as to enable the seller to deliver the goods; (b) the selected time, if any, within the period agreed for delivery when the carrier or person nominated will receive the goods; (c) the mode of transport to be used by the carrier or the person nominated including any transport-related security requirements; or (d) the point where the goods will be received within the named place of delivery.[34] The buyer bears the risk of loss of or damage to the goods as aforementioned, also in the case where the carrier or the person nominated by the buyer fails to take the goods into its charge, then the buyer bears all risks of loss of or damage to the goods: (i) from the agreed date; or in the absence of an agreed date, (ii) from the time selected by the buyer under (b) above; or, if no such time has been notified, (iii) from the end of any period agreed for delivery, provided that the goods have been clearly identified as the contract goods.[35]

---

28 Ibid 34, FCA, para A3.
29 Ibid 30, FCA, Explanatory Notes for Users, para 3.
30 Ibid 30, FCA, Explanatory Notes for Users, para 4.
31 Ibid 34, FCA, para A3.
32 Ibid 38, FCA, para A10.
33 Ibid 35, FCA, para B3.
34 Ibid 39, FCA, para B3.
35 Ibid 35, FCA, para B3.

3. CPT

In the ICC Incoterms® CPT (Carriage Paid To), the seller delivers the goods—and transfers the risk—to the buyer by handing over the goods to the carrier contracted by the seller or by procuring the goods so delivered.[36] The seller may do so by giving the carrier physical possession of the goods in the manner and at the place appropriate to the means of transport used. Thus, the risk associated with the goods transfers from the seller to the buyer when the goods are handed over to the carrier.[37] However, the seller is still responsible for arranging the carriage of the goods from the delivery point to the agreed destination.[38]

In CPT, two locations are important: the place or point (if any) at which the goods are delivered (for the transfer of risk) and the place or point agreed as the destination of the goods (as the point to which the seller promises to contract and pay for carriage). Regarding transfer of risk, the place or point of delivery must be identified with precision. This is important to cater for the common situation where several carriers are engaged, each for different legs of the transit from delivery to destination. Where this happens and the parties do not agree on a specific place or point of delivery, the default position is that risk transfers when the goods have been delivered to the first carrier at a point entirely of the seller's choosing and over which the buyer has no control. If the parties involved in a sale wish to transfer the risk of loss of or damage to the goods at a different point in the transportation process, they must clearly specify this in their contract.[39]

In addition, under the CPT rule, the buyer must, whenever it is agreed that the buyer is entitled to determine the time for dispatching the goods and/or the point of receiving the goods within the named place of destination, give the seller sufficient notice.[40] If the buyer fails to give such notice, then it bears all risks of loss of or damage to the goods from the agreed date or the end of the agreed period for delivery, provided that the goods have been clearly identified as the contract goods.[41]

4. CIP

The ICC Incoterms® CIP stands for 'Carriage and Insurance Paid To'. This rule is similar to CPT, but with the addition of insurance. The seller is responsible for arranging and paying for carriage to the named destination[42] and providing

---

[36] The reference to 'procure' here caters for multiple sales down a chain (string sales), particularly common in the commodity trades, see ibid 42, CPT, Explanatory Notes for Users, para 6.

[37] Ibid 41, CPT, Explanatory Notes for Users, para 1.

[38] Ibid 44 CPT, para A4.

[39] Ibid 42, CPT, Explanatory Notes for Users, para 4.

[40] Ibid 49, CPT, para B10.

[41] Ibid 45, CPT, para B3.

[42] Ibid 54, CIP, para A4.

insurance against the buyer's risk of loss or damage during carriage.[43] The seller delivers the goods—and transfers the risk—to the buyer by handing them over to the carrier contracted by the seller or by procuring the goods so delivered.[44] The seller may do so by giving the carrier physical possession of the goods in the manner and at the place appropriate to the means of transport used.[45] After the goods are delivered to the buyer, the seller is not responsible for ensuring that the goods reach their destination in good condition, in the right amount, or reach at all. This is because the risk passes from the seller to the buyer once the goods are handed over to the carrier.[46] However, the seller is still responsible for arranging the transportation of the goods and insuring them from the delivery point to the agreed destination.[47]

Similarly, and for the same reasons that apply to CPT, the parties agreeing on CIP are well advised to identify the point at the place of delivery as precisely as possible in the contract of sale. It is important to carefully consider the consequences of any such agreement in case the goods are lost or damaged.[48]

Under CIP, the buyer bears any loss of or damage to the goods from the moment they are delivered by the seller by handing them over to the carrier.[49] If the buyer has the right to decide when and where the goods will be delivered, it must inform the seller in advance.[50] Failure to do so will result in the buyer being responsible for any loss of or damage to the goods from the agreed date or the end of the agreed delivery period, provided that the goods have been clearly identified as the contract goods.[51]

5. DAP

Pursuant to ICC Incoterms® DAP (Delivered at Place), the seller delivers the goods when they are placed at the disposal of the buyer on the arriving means of transport, ready for unloading at the named place of destination or by procuring the goods so delivered.[52] The seller bears all risks and costs until the goods are delivered, that is, until the time they are ready for unloading at the agreed-upon destination.[53] In either case, the seller must deliver the goods on the agreed date or

---

[43] Ibid 56, CIP, para A5.

[44] See ibid 53, CIP, Explanatory Notes for Users, para 7. The reference to 'procure' here caters for multiple sales down a chain (string sales), particularly common in the commodity trades; ibid 54, CIP, para A2.

[45] Chambre de commerce internationale (n 20) 51, CIP, Explanatory Notes for Users, para 1.

[46] Ibid 54, CIP, para A3; ibid 51, CIP, Explanatory notes for users, para 1.

[47] Ibid 60, CIP, para A9.

[48] Ibid 52, CIP, Explanatory Notes for Users.

[49] Ibid 55, CIP, para B3.

[50] Ibid 61, CIP, para B10.

[51] Ibid 61, CIP, para B9(g); ibid 55, CIP, para B3.

[52] Ibid 66, DAP, para A2.

[53] Ibid 63, DAP, Explanatory Notes for Users, para 1.

within the agreed period. The seller must give the buyer any notice required to enable the buyer to receive the goods.[54] It is advisable for the parties to specify unambiguously the destination place or point, as the risk of loss or damage to the goods is transferred to the buyer at that juncture of delivery/destination.[55] The reference to 'procure' here caters for multiple sales down a chain (string sales), prevalent in the commodity trades.[56]

Therefore, in Incoterms® DAP, delivery and arrival at the destination are the same. This rule can be applied regardless of the mode of transport used, even if multiple modes are utilized. The buyer must, whenever it is agreed that the buyer is entitled to determine the time within an agreed period and/or the point of taking delivery within the named place of destination, give the seller sufficient notice.[57] If the buyer fails to give notice, then it bears all risks of loss of or damage to the goods from the agreed date or the end of the agreed period for delivery, provided that the goods have been clearly identified as the contract goods.[58]

6. DPU

In accordance with Incoterms® DPU (Delivered at Place Unloaded), delivery takes place when the goods are unloaded by the seller from the arriving means of transport and placed at the disposal of the buyer at the agreed point, if any, at the named place of destination or by procuring the goods so delivered. In either case, the seller must deliver the goods on the agreed date or within the agreed period.[59] In this Incoterms® rule, therefore, the delivery and arrival at the destination are the same.[60] The seller bears all risks involved in bringing the goods to and unloading them at the named place of destination.[61] . If the parties do not want the seller to bear the risk and cost of unloading, they should avoid using the DPU rule and instead use the DAP rule.[62]

Again, the parties should specify the destination point or place for the goods, as the risk of damage or loss of goods is transferred to the buyer at the point of delivery. The reference to 'procure' here caters for multiple sales down a chain (string sales), particularly common in commodity trades.[63]

[54] Ibid 70, DAP, para A10.
[55] Ibid 64, DAP, Explanatory Notes for Users, para 3.
[56] Ibid 64, DAP, Explanatory Notes for Users, para 4.
[57] Ibid 71, DAP, para B10.
[58] Ibid 67, DAP, para B3; see also ibid 69, DAP, para B9(e).
[59] Ibid 76, DPU, para A2.
[60] Ibid 73, DPU, Explanatory Notes for Users, para 1.
[61] Ibid 76, DPU, para A3.
[62] Ibid 72–73, DPU, Explanatory Notes for Users, para 3.
[63] Ibid 74, DPU, Explanatory Notes for Users, para 4.

The Incoterms® DPU can be applied regardless of the mode of transport used, even if multiple modes are utilized.[64]

If the buyer and the seller have agreed that the buyer can determine the time for delivery and the place of destination, the buyer must give the seller sufficient notice of such determination.[65] Failure to give notice means that the buyer will bear all risks of loss of or damage to the goods from the agreed date or the end of the agreed period for delivery. This applies only if the goods have been clearly identified as the contract goods.[66]

7. DDP

The Incoterms® DDP (Delivered Duty Paid) represents the maximum obligation for the seller.[67] Under this term, the seller delivers the goods to the buyer when the goods are placed at the disposal of the buyer, are cleared for import, on the arriving means of transport, ready for unloading at the named place of destination or at the agreed point within that place, if any such point is agreed. The seller bears all risks involved in bringing the goods to the named place of destination or to the agreed point within that place.[68] The seller also bears all the risks associated with customs clearance in the import of the goods through any intermediary and final country until delivery.[69] In this Incoterms® rule, therefore, delivery and arrival at destination are the same.[70]

Again, the parties should specify the destination point or place for the goods, as the risk of damage or loss of goods transfers to the buyer at the point of delivery.[71] The reference to 'procure' here caters for multiple sales down a chain (string sales), prevalent in commodity trades.[72]

If the buyer and the seller have agreed that the buyer can determine the time for delivery and the place of destination, the buyer must give the seller sufficient notice of such determination.[73] Failure to give notice means that the buyer will bear all risks of loss of or damage to the goods from the agreed date or the end of the agreed period for delivery. This applies only if the goods have been clearly identified as the contract goods.

---

[64] Ibid 73, DPU, Explanatory Notes for User, para 2.
[65] Ibid 81, DPU, para B10.
[66] Ibid 77, DPU, para B3; see also ibid 79, DPU, para B9.
[67] Chambre de commerce internationale (n 20) 84, DDP, Explanatory Notes for Users, para 3.
[68] Ibid 86, DDP, para A2.
[69] Ibid 88, DDP, para A7.
[70] Ibid 83, DDP, Explanatory Notes for Users, para 1.
[71] Ibid 84, DDP, Explanatory Notes for Users, para 4.
[72] Ibid 84, DDP, Explanatory Notes for Users, para 5.
[73] Ibid 89, DDP, para B10.

8. FAS

The Incoterms® FAS (Free Alongside Ship) means that the seller delivers the goods to the buyer when they are placed alongside the ship (e.g. on a quay or a barge) nominated by the buyer at the named port of shipment or when the seller procures goods already so delivered.[74] The risk of loss of or damage to the goods transfers when the goods are alongside the ship.[75]

Parties should clearly specify the loading point at the named port of shipment. The seller is responsible for the costs and risks up to that point. If the buyer has indicated no specific loading point, the seller may select the point within the named port of shipment that best suits its purpose.[76] 'Procure the goods' refers to multiple sales down a chain, common in commodity trades.[77]

In particular, the buyer must give the seller sufficient notice of any transport-related security requirements, the vessel name, loading point, and, if any, the selected delivery date within the agreed period.[78] The buyer bears all risks of loss of or damage to the goods from the time they have been delivered (as indicated above) if it fails to give the notice above referred to or the vessel nominated by the buyer: fails to arrive on time to enable the seller to comply with its delivery, fails to take the goods, or closes for cargo earlier than the time notified by the buyer. In that case, the buyer bears all risks of loss of or damage to the goods from the agreed date; in the absence of an agreed date, from the date selected by the buyer; or if no such date has been notified, from the end of any period agreed for delivery, provided that the goods have been clearly identified as the contract goods.[79]

9. FOB

The ICC Incoterms® FOB (Free on Board) requires the seller to deliver the goods on board the vessel nominated by the buyer at the named port of shipment or to procure the goods so delivered. Risk transfers from the seller to the buyer once the goods are on board,[80] meaning the seller is responsible for all costs and risks until this point.[81] If the buyer has not indicated a specific loading point, the seller may select the point within the named port of shipment that best suits its purpose.

The seller must deliver the goods on the agreed date or at a time within the agreed period notified by the buyer. If no such time is notified, then the goods must

---

[74] Ibid 96, FAS, para A2.
[75] Ibid 96, FAS, para A3.
[76] Ibid 96, FAS, para A2.
[77] Ibid 94, FAS, Explanatory Notes for Users, para 4.
[78] Ibid 101, FAS, para B10.
[79] Ibid 97, FAS, para B3.
[80] Ibid 106, FOB, para A1.
[81] Ibid 103 FOB, Explanatory Notes for Users, para 1; ibid 106, FOB, para A2.

be delivered at the end of the agreed period and in the manner customary at the port.[82]

The buyer must give the seller sufficient notice of any transport-related security requirements, the vessel name, loading point, and, if any, the selected delivery date within the agreed period.[83] The buyer bears all risks of loss of or damage to the goods from the time they have been delivered as required above if the buyer fails to give the referred notice; or the vessel nominated by the buyer fails to arrive on time to enable the seller to comply with the delivery, fails to take the goods, or closes for cargo earlier than the time notified. In that case, the buyer bears all risks of loss of or damage to the goods from the agreed date; in the absence of an agreed date, from the date selected by the buyer under the above notification; and if no such date has been notified, from the end of any agreed period for delivery, provided that the goods have been clearly identified as the contract goods.[84]

10. CFR

The Incoterms® CFR (Cost and Freight) is similar to FOB, but with the seller's add-itional obligation of arranging and paying the transportation from the delivery point to the named destination port.[85] The seller is responsible for delivering the goods on board the vessel or procuring them already so delivered such that the seller is taken to have performed its obligation to deliver the goods whether or not the goods actually arrive at their destination in sound condition, in the stated quantity, or, indeed, at all.[86]

Accordingly, two ports are important under this term: the port where the goods are delivered on board the vessel and the port agreed as the destination of the goods. Risk transfers from seller to buyer when the goods are delivered to the buyer by placing them on board the vessel at the shipment port or by procuring the goods already so delivered.[87] The reference to 'procure' here considers string sales.[88] However, the seller must contract for the carriage of the goods from delivery to the agreed destination. Thus, for example, goods are placed on board a vessel in Rotterdam (which is a port) for carriage to Singapore (also a port). Delivery here happens when the goods are on board in Rotterdam, with risk transferring to the buyer at that time, and the seller must make a contract of carriage from Rotterdam to Singapore.

---

[82] Ibid 96, FAS, para A2.
[83] Ibid 111, FOB, para B10.
[84] Ibid 107, FOB, para B3.
[85] See ibid 116, CFR, para A4.
[86] See ibid 116, CFR, para A2; ibid 117, CFR, para B3.
[87] Ibid 114, CFR, Explanatory Notes for Users, para 4.
[88] Ibid 114, CFR, Explanatory Notes for Users, para 3.

The contract usually indicates the CFR ICC Incoterms® followed by the destination port, but not the port of shipment. The risk transfer to the buyer occurs at the shipment port, which should be stated in the contract.[89] It is possible that goods can be transported by different carriers for different legs of sea transport. For example, a carrier may operate a feeder vessel from Hamburg to Rotterdam, and then an ocean vessel from Rotterdam to Singapore. The question that arises is when the risk of loss or damage transfers from the seller to the buyer: is it at Hamburg or at Rotterdam, where does delivery take place? The answer to this question may have been agreed upon in the sale contract. However, if there is no such agreement, the default position is that the risk transfers when the goods have been delivered to the first carrier, that is, Hamburg. This increases the period during which the buyer incurs the risk of loss or damage.[90] In light of it, the parties have an interest in identifying the shipment point as accurately as possible in the contract.

Again, the buyer must, whenever it is agreed that the buyer is entitled to determine the time for shipping the goods and/or the point of receiving the goods within the named port of destination, give the seller sufficient notice.[91] If the buyer fails to give such notice, then it bears all risks of loss of or damage to the goods from the agreed date or the end of the agreed period for shipment, provided that the goods have been clearly identified as the contract goods.

11. CIF

The Incoterms® CIF (Cost, Insurance, and Freight) is similar to CFR, but the seller also has to procure marine insurance against the buyer's risk of loss or damage during carriage.[92] The seller bears all risks and costs until the goods are on board the vessel at the port of shipment.[93]

IV. Subsidiary Rules in the CISG

The transfer of risk rules in the CISG have limited relevance due to the widespread use of trade terms, especially the ICC Incoterms®. The CISG and ICC Incoterms® are compatible with each other.[94] There is a significant overlap between both sets of rules. They never conflict with each other. Under Article

---

[89] Ibid 114, CFR, Explanatory Notes for Users, para 5.
[90] Ibid 114, CFR, Explanatory Notes for Users, para 7.
[91] Ibid 133, CFR, para B10.
[92] Ibid 128, CIF, para A5.
[93] Ibid 126, CIF, para A3.
[94] Johan Erauw, 'Article 67' in Kröll, Mistelis, and Perales Viscasillas (eds) (n 1) para 33; Brunner, Klingler, and Mauerhofer, 'Introductory Remarks to Arts. 66–70' in Brunner and Gottlieb (eds) (n 17) para 9.

6 CISG, any term agreed upon by the parties takes precedence over the default rules of the CISG. Therefore, if the parties agree to a specific trade term covering a particular subject matter, the default CISG rules on that same matter stand aside. Using a trade term does not mean that CISG is entirely excluded. The scope of each term and its priority over the default CISG rules is ultimately a matter of interpretation under Articles 8 and 9 CISG. This is particularly true when determining whether a contract clause is meant solely to allocate costs or also includes provisions for the transfer of risk, as often is the intention of the parties in practice.

1. Principles on risk transfer in the CISG

The CISG deals with the passing of risk in Articles 66 to 70, using the handing-over approach as the starting point[95] rather than the delivery approach of the ICC Incoterms®,[96] although in practice there is often a coincidence between the handing over of the goods of risk transfer and the delivery point in the CISG.[97] The CISG also applies special rules for goods sold in transit.[98] Therefore, the passing of risk is not linked to the conclusion of the contract or the transfer of title. The allocation of costs for transportation and insurance is irrelevant in determining which party bears the risk of loss or damage.

The use of the handing-over approach is appropriate, especially in distance selling, which is typical in international trade. Domestic laws that link the transfer of risk to the passing of title or the conclusion of the contract would create many uncertainties, particularly for buyers. The rules on the passing of risk in the CISG are exhaustive and pre-empt domestic provisions.[99]

The CISG requires the identification of goods for the transfer of risk. Although this requirement is mentioned only in two places, it is a general requirement.[100] Depending on the circumstances of the case, different acts of identification may be necessary. A safe option for the seller is to attach markings to the goods that clearly identify the buyer as the recipient. Transport documents and packing lists can also

---

[95] Pascal Hachem, 'Article 67 CISG: Passing of Risk When Sale Involves Carriage' in Schwenzer and Schroeter (eds) (n 1) para 17; Schwenzer and Muñoz (n 5) para 38.41; UNCITRAL (n 3) 303, para 2. For handing-over of goods, see CISG, pt III: Delivery of the goods and handing over of documents.

[96] Chambre de commerce internationale (n 20) 2, para 5.

[97] Christoph Brunner, Désirée Klingler, and Marc André Mauerhofer, 'Article 66 (Loss or Damage After Passing of Risk to Buyer)' in Brunner and Gottlieb (eds) (n 17) para 1.

[98] Erauw, 'Article 67' in Kröll, Mistelis, and Perales Viscasillas (eds) (n 1) para 29.

[99] Pascal Hachem, 'Introduction to Articles 66–70: General Questions Regarding the Passing of Risk' in Schwenzer and Schroeter (eds) (n 1) para 19.

[100] Harry M Flechtner, *Honnold's Uniform Law for International Sales under the 1980 United Nations Convention* (5th edn, Wolters Kluwer 2021) 693; Erauw, 'Article 67' in Kröll, Mistelis, and Perales Viscasillas (eds) (n 1) para 19.

help allocate the goods to the contract. These questions mainly arise in the context of contracts involving the carriage of goods and goods sold during transit, especially when dealing with bulk shipments.

Article 66 CISG requires that the loss of or damage to the goods not be attributable to the seller for risk transfer. Article 36 CISG embodies the same principle.[101] This provision links the relevant point in time for conformity of the goods to the passing of risk (Article 36(1) CISG). This general rule, however, does not apply where non-conformity materializes after the passing of risk but is attributable to a breach of contract by the seller. Under Article 66 CISG, the seller is under a continued obligation not to endanger the objective of the contract.

2. Passing of risk in sales involving carriage

Pursuant to Article 67(1) CISG, if the sale contract involves the carriage of goods and the seller is not obligated to deliver the goods at a specific place, the risk of loss of or damage to the goods passes to the buyer when the goods are handed over to the first carrier for transmission to the buyer per the terms of the sale contract.[102] The contract will provide for the carriage of the goods where a carrier or multiple carriers, rather than the seller or the buyer itself, are in charge of transporting the goods to the destination. The dependence or independence of the carriage from the parties is thus decisive in determining whether the transporter chosen is a 'carrier'.[103] The ICC Incoterms® 2020 also share this understanding. Freight forwarders[104] are considered 'carriers' for this purpose. What counts is that the seller gives control to a third party involved in the transport of the goods. Thus, carriage by the seller's own personnel does not qualify as an independent carrier for the purposes of Article 67(1) CISG.[105]

Also, under Article 67(1) CISG, if the seller is bound to hand the goods over to a carrier at a particular place, the risk does not pass to the buyer when they are

---

[101] *CLOUT case 253* [1998] Repubblica e Cantone del Ticino, La seconda Camera civile del Tribunale d'appello 12.97.00193, Issue 25 CLOUT Case 253.

[102] *AGES Maut System GmbH & Co KG v Butler Nederland BV* [2023] Rechtbank Gelderland (District Court Gelderland) 10562327CV EXPL 23-4193, CISG-online 6644; *Jaxtal Imports Pty Ltd v Shanghai Xinlian Textile Import & Export Co, Ltd* [2018] People's Court Shanghai Changning District (2017) Hu 0105 Min Chu No. 19401, CISG-online 4118; Flechtner (n 100) 691; Christoph Brunner, Désirée Klingler, and Marc André Mauerhofer, 'Article 67 (Risk When the Contract Involves Carriage)' in Brunner and Gottlieb (eds) (n 17) paras 3–5.

[103] The term 'carrier' in CISG, art 67(1) corresponds to the use of the term in CISG art 31(a), see *Pizza boxes case* [2000] Amtsgericht Duisburg (Local Court Duisburg) 49 C 502/00, CISG-online 659.

[104] The entity or person who coordinates and organizes the movement of shipments on behalf of a shipper (party that arranges an item for shipment) by liaising with carriers (party that transports goods).

[105] See Erauw, 'Article 66' in Kröll, Mistelis, and Perales Viscasillas (eds) (n 1) 211.

handed over to the first carrier, but until the goods are handed over to the carrier at the place agreed. The carrier may be the first or a subsequent carrier. The agreed location could be a railway station, a port, an airport, etc. But this provision does not apply when the place agreed is the seller's premises or the place where the goods are located at the time of the conclusion of the contract. In those cases, it may be interpreted that the buyer is obligated to collect the goods and thus, no carriage is involved.[106]

Handing over the goods under Article 67(1) CISG means that the seller gives control over the goods.[107] It is not enough that the seller places the goods at the carrier's disposal, be it the first or the agreed place. The carrier needs to take custody of the goods so that they are handed over and risk passes under this provision. This usually happens when the relevant carrier (including freight forwarders) acknowledges the reception of the goods through the relevant receipts, depending on the means of transport to be used.[108]

The fact that the seller withholds the documents controlling the disposition of the goods does not prevent the passing of risk under Article 67(1) CISG. This is consistent with the CISG principle that the passing of risk is independent of the transfer of property title or the delivery of conforming goods or documents.[109] If the seller eventually decides to take the goods back on the basis of the withheld documents that represent the title, the risk falls back to it at that moment. For instance, if the seller sells the goods, which by then are already in transit, for a second time, and redirects the goods to the new buyer, then in accordance with Article 68 CISG the seller bears the risk for the time before the conclusion of the contract with the second buyer. The risk is not borne by the original buyer who would otherwise have borne it from the time of handing over of the goods to the carrier.

When the goods are handed over to the carrier in question, they must be clearly identified to the contract, whether by markings on the goods, shipping documents, notice given to the buyer, or otherwise. Failure to identify the goods clearly will stop the passing of risk to the buyer, and the seller will be liable for any loss or damage to them until clear identification.[110]

---

[106] Hachem, 'Article 67 CISG: Passing of Risk When Sale Involves Carriage' in Schwenzer and Schroeter (eds) (n 1) para 2; Brunner, Klingler, and Mauerhofer, 'Article 67 (Risk When the Contract Involves Carriage)' in Brunner and Gottlieb (eds) (n 17) para 4.

[107] Hachem, 'Article 67 CISG: Passing of Risk When Sale Involves Carriage' in Schwenzer and Schroeter (eds) (n 1) para 17.

[108] Ibid para 18.

[109] Joseph Lookofsky, 'The 1980 United Nations Convention on Contracts for the International Sale of Goods' in J Herbots and Roger Blanplain (eds), *International Encyclopaedia of Laws: Contracts* (4th edn, Kluwer Law International 2016) 143; Flechtner (n 100) 692.

[110] CISG, art 67(2).

3. Passing of risk when the goods are sold in transit

For goods sold in transit, the first sentence of Article 68 CISG states that the buyer bears the risk of loss of or damage to the goods from the time of the conclusion of the contract. To apply this rule of passing of risk, the goods must be sold 'in transit'. In order to fulfil this requirement, the goods should be under the custody of the carrier. It is not necessary that the goods are being loaded or are in transit with the carrier. Since the goods are already in transit when the contract is concluded, it might not always be possible to ascertain if the goods were lost or damaged during the transit period.[111] The buyer's duty to examine the goods until after the goods have arrived at their destination (Article 38(2) CISG) may not help in establishing the state of the goods at the time of contract conclusion.

The second sentence of Article 68 CISG provides that the passing of risk for goods sold in transit will exceptionally take place at the time when the goods are handed to the carrier who issued the documents embodying the contract of carriage, 'if the circumstances so indicate'. When do the circumstances indicate that exceptional rule? This is not clear from the text of the CISG itself. Some scholars argue that the necessary 'circumstances' exist if goods are insured from delivery to contract conclusion.[112] This also applies if insurance becomes available to the buyer by way of assignment. However, this circumstance triggers the exceptional rule only if the buyer can turn to the insurer for the very event that caused the loss of or damage to the goods.

Pursuant to the second sentence of Article 68 CISG, the carrier who issued the documents of transport becomes the place and point in time for the passing of risk. The documents must evidence the existence of a contract of carriage, and would include a bill of lading, waybill, or transport receipt. If several carriers are involved in a chain of transportation, such as in multimodal transportation, the first carrier is considered the relevant carrier under this provision. The document or its equivalent may be issued in hardcopy paper or electronic form.[113]

If goods are sold in transit and the seller knew or should have known that the goods were lost or damaged at the time of the conclusion of the contract but did not disclose this to the buyer, then the non-disclosed loss or damage is at the risk of the seller (Article 68, third sentence). This rule of estoppel applies only to prevent the application of the second sentence of Article 68, that is, when 'circumstances so indicate' that the buyer had assumed the risk from the time of handing over the goods to the relevant carrier.

---

[111] Pascal Hachem, 'Article 68' in Schwenzer and Schroeter (eds) (n 1) para 1; Christoph Brunner, Désirée Klingler, and Marc Mauerhofer, 'Article 68 (Sale of Goods During Transit)' in Brunner and Gottlieb (eds) (n 17) para 1.

[112] Hachem, 'Article 68' in Schwenzer and Schroeter (eds) (n 1) para 10; Flechtner (n 100) 698 ff.

[113] Brunner, Klingler, and Mauerhofer, 'Article 68 (Sale of Goods During Transit)' in Brunner and Gottlieb (eds) (n 17) para 3.

4. Passing of risk in other cases

Article 69 CISG provides specific rules for risk transfer in cases that do not qualify as contracts involving the carriage of goods or contracts for goods sold in transit.[114]

Article 69(1) CISG addresses sales where the parties are in the same place. The first alternative under this provision addresses the primary case where the buyer takes over the goods at the seller's place: the risk passes to the buyer when the buyer, its staff, or the instructed carrier, take over the goods. The taking over of the goods starts once the loading process begins, during which the buyer bears the risk.[115] Even if the buyer takes over the goods before the date of delivery, the risk passes to it. This rule is similar to EXW ICC Incoterms® 2020.[116]

According to the same provision, if a buyer delays taking over the goods, it cannot prevent the passing of risk to it. In other words, the seller cannot be burdened continuously with the risk of loss of or damage to the goods. If the buyer does not take over the goods on time, even though they have been made available to it by adequately placing them at its disposal, the risk passes to the buyer. The seller does not need to notify the buyer of its delay or grant an additional period to take over the goods for the risk of passing them to the buyer after the delivery date.[117]

Article 69(2) CISG governs sales where the seller must bring the goods to the buyer's premises or to any other agreed-upon place.[118] In this scenario, the risk passes when delivery is due and the buyer is aware that the goods are placed at its disposal at that place. The time of passing of risk is thus linked to the time at which delivery is due (Article 33 CISG).[119] However, two conditions must be met for risk transfer to occur at that moment: the placing of goods at the buyer's disposal and the latter's *knowledge* of it. As to the first of them, goods are placed at the buyer's disposal for the purposes of Article 69(2) CISG once it can claim possession over the goods. This is the case where, for example, the buyer may be in possession of a negotiable instrument embodying the claim for the goods against the warehouse keeper and the latter acknowledges the seller's instruction to hand over the goods to the buyer or the buyer's right to possession over the goods. As to the second condition, the buyer must have actual knowledge that the goods have been placed at

---

[114] *Okuma MA-400 machine case* [2024] Gerechthof 's-Hertogenbosch (Court of Appeal 's-Hertogenbosch) 200.311.762_01, CISG-online 7017.

[115] Christoph Brunner, Désirée Klingler, and Marc Mauerhofer, 'Article 69 (General Residual Rules on Risk)' in Brunner and Gottlieb (eds) (n 17) para 1.

[116] Pascal Hachem, 'Article 69 CISG: Passing of Risk in Other Cases' in Schwenzer and Schroeter (eds) (n 1) para 7: points out that under EXW placing the goods at the disposal is sufficient; Chambre de commerce internationale (n 20) 21–2, EXW, Explanatory Notes for Users 1, 5.

[117] Flechtner (n 100) 706.

[118] See eg *Pizza Boxes Case* (n 103); *Business cards case* [2006] Cour de Justice de Genève (Court of Appeal Canton Geneva) ACJC/47/2006, CISG-online 1504.

[119] Brunner, Klingler, and Mauerhofer, , 'Article 69 (General Residual Rules on Risk)' in Brunner and Gottlieb (eds) (n 17) para 3.

its disposal.[120] Unawareness due to negligence or even gross negligence does not stop transfer of risk. Notification by the seller will typically be necessary to make the buyer aware that the goods have been placed at its disposal. In some scenarios, the buyer may become aware that the goods are at its disposal without notification from the seller.

According to Article 69(3) CISG, accurately identifying the goods to the contract is necessary. When read in conjunction with Article 67(2) CISG, this provision establishes a general principle under Article 7(2) CISG, which dictates that the transfer of risk can only occur when the goods have been adequately identified.[121]

V. Transfer of Risk and Fundamental Breach

Article 70 CISG governs the relationship between the passing of risk and the buyer's remedies when the seller commits a fundamental breach of contract. The language of Article 70 is ambiguous and can lead to misunderstandings. This provision states that 'if the seller has committed a fundamental breach of contract, articles 67, 68 and 69 do not impair the remedies available to the buyer on account of the breach'. However, it does not address cases where the seller's fundamental breach causes the loss of or damage to the goods. In such situations, per Article 66 CISG, the passing of risk is irrelevant, with the focus instead being on the goods' conformity. Article 70 CISG addresses scenarios where there is no link between the fundamental breach and subsequent loss of or damage to the goods, ensuring the buyer retains remedies despite the coincidental loss.[122]

Article 70 CISG preserves the buyer's remedies in case of a fundamental breach, including delivery of substitute goods, repair, avoidance of contract, price reduction, and damages.[123] The drafters are likely to have focused on avoidance and substitute delivery, as these align best with the buyer's interests.[124] If goods are lost coincidentally, repair or price reduction is less useful, making avoidance or substitute delivery preferable. The provision should also cover cases where the buyer avoids the contract due to delayed delivery under Article 49(1)(b) CISG.[125]

---

[120] Ibid para 7.

[121] See Hachem, 'Article 69 CISG: Passing of Risk in Other Cases' in Schwenzer and Schroeter (eds) (n 1) para 25; Johan Erauw, 'Article 69' in Kröll, Mistelis, and Perales Viscasillas (eds) (n 1) para 7.

[122] Pascal Hachem, 'Article 70 CISG: Effect of Fundamental Breach on Passing' in Schwenzer and Schroeter (eds) (n 1) para 1 ff; Johan Erauw, 'Article 70' in Kröll, Mistelis, and Perales Viscasillas (eds) (n 1) paras 1–3.

[123] Erauw, 'Article 70' in Kröll, Mistelis, and Perales Viscasillas (eds) (n 1) para 2; Hachem, 'Article 70 CISG: Effect of Fundamental Breach on Passing' in Schwenzer and Schroeter (eds) (n 1) para 6; Christoph Brunner, Désirée Klingler, and Marc Mauerhofer, 'Article 70 (Risk When Seller is in Breach)' in Brunner and Gottlieb (eds) (n 17) para 6.

[124] Erauw, 'Article 70' in Kröll, Mistelis, and Perales Viscasillas (eds) (n 1) para 7; Hachem, 'Article 70 CISG: Effect of Fundamental Breach on Passing' in Schwenzer and Schroeter (eds) (n 1) paras 3–4.

[125] Hachem, 'Article 70 CISG: Effect of Fundamental Breach on Passing' in Schwenzer and Schroeter (eds) (n 1) para 8.

Consider a buyer who orders 500 laptops from a seller, with the contract speci-fying that the laptops must meet certain technical specifications that are 'essential'. Upon delivery, the buyer discovers that the laptops do not meet these specifica-tions, which constitutes a fundamental breach of contract. The buyer notifies the seller of the non-conformity and requests delivery of substitute laptops. While the defective laptops are still in the buyer's warehouse, a fire occurs due to a lightning strike, destroying the laptops. According to Article 70 CISG, the buyer retains the right to remedies for the fundamental breach, despite the accidental destruction of the goods.[126] The passing of risk to the buyer is irrelevant here because the seller's breach occurred before the loss.[127] The buyer can still demand substitute laptops or avoid the contract entirely.

This ensures that the seller cannot claim the purchase price for the destroyed laptops, as the risk falls back on the seller due to its initial fundamental breach. The loss caused by the fire does not negate the seller's responsibility to provide goods that conform to the contract. Thus, the buyer is protected and can seek appropriate remedies even though the laptops were destroyed by an unforeseen event.

Article 70 CISG is silent on breaches below the threshold of Article 25 CISG, but this does not mean such breaches eliminate the buyer's remedies. The buyer still bears the risk but can exercise standard remedies for breach, excluding avoid-ance or substitute delivery.[128] Price reduction or damages claims are available if the goods are damaged coincidentally.[129]

---

[126] Joseph M Lookofsky, *Understanding the CISG: A Compact Guide to the 1980 United Nations Convention on Contracts for the International Sale of Goods* (6th edn, Kluwer Law International 2022) 105.

[127] Ibid.

[128] Hachem, 'Article 70 CISG: Effect of Fundamental Breach on Passing' in Schwenzer and Schroeter (eds) (n 1) para 9.

[129] Ibid para 10; Brunner, Klingler, and Mauerhofer, 'Article 70 (Risk When Seller is in Breach) in Brunner and Gottlieb (eds) (n 17) para 4.

12
Remedies I—General

I. Structure of Remedies, Unified Approach

The CISG is a notable proponent of a modern approach to remedies for breach of contract that has departed from domestic laws on this matter.[1] This modern approach has been influential on international instruments like the PICC. In addition, some domestic laws have structured their entire contract law and general remedial system in accordance with the CISG, including China, Japan, Romania, and Hungary, to mention a few (see Chapter 1). Others have adopted the structure of the Convention for their sales legislation specifically. Finally, some systems—especially those in the EU—have included the CISG structure only in their consumer protection legislation, as the EC Consumer Sales Directive heavily drew on the CISG.[2]

The modern approach of the CISG and PICC has largely adopted the breach-of-contract approach, which has already been discussed in Chapter 9 on conformity. The practice of equal treatment of breaches means that distinctions drawn in domestic systems based on the cause of the breach are no longer necessary. Examples of such distinctions include the traditional differences between impossibility, delayed delivery or lack of delivery, and non-conformity. As discussed in Chapter 9

---

[1] Ingeborg Schwenzer and Edgardo Muñoz, *Global Sales and Contract Law* (2nd edn, Oxford University Press 2022) para 41.45.
[2] Ibid para 41.46.

and in the chapters that follow, the CISG applies the same rules to both initial and subsequent impossibility, unlike many domestic laws that treat them separately. Similarly, the CISG subjects delayed delivery and non-delivery to the same remedies. Furthermore, the distinction in some domestic laws between remedies for non-conformity (redhibitory defects) and non-performance (failure to deliver) is rejected by the CISG.

While the CISG and PICC primarily follow the breach-of-contract approach, they have also been influenced by the cause-oriented approach. Unlike some traditional breach-of-contract approach jurisdictions, the CISG and PICC do not generally disfavour specific performance as a remedy. Additionally, their approach actively supports a reduction-of-price remedy, which is a key feature of the cause-oriented approach. Finally, the *Nachfrist* principle of German origin has been integrated into the system of avoidance in situations where non-performance does not amount to a fundamental breach.

Generally speaking, the remedy of specific performance is available both to the seller and to the buyer under the CISG. The former may sue the latter for payment of the purchase price and taking delivery of the goods. The buyer may claim delivery of the goods and in case of non-conformity repair or, if the breach is fundamental, replacement. The PICC, which do not contain specific sales law provisions, refer to the performance of monetary and non-monetary obligations. However, the CISG,[3] as well as the PICC,[4] have attempted to accommodate concerns from common law legal systems by establishing certain exceptions to the availability of specific performance which are discussed in the next chapter.

A traditional solution, derived from Roman law,[5] which is common in cause-oriented legal systems, is the reduction of price included in the CISG in case of non-conformity.[6] The concept of the reduction of price has not been used in the breach-of-contract approach, but it has proven its usefulness and has been included in the CISG but not in the PICC.

The CISG and the PICC have incorporated the *Nachfrist* rule, with some particularities.[7] *Nachfrist* is a term used in German law which refers to an additional period of time granted to the obligor for proper performance. It belongs to the cause-oriented approach and offers a second chance to the obligor to perform once it is delayed. During the additional period, the obligee cannot take any additional

---

[3] CISG, art 28; *Solea International BVBA v Bassett & Walker International Inc* [2019] Court of Appeal of Ontario C66182/2019 ONCA 617, CISG-online 4505: where the court held that art 28 CISG is a compromise position between the common law's preference for money damages in the event of a breach of contract and the civil law's preference for performance.

[4] PICC 2016, art 7.2.2(a).

[5] Schwenzer and Muñoz (n 1) para 48.02.

[6] CISG, art 50; PICC, art 7.4.6; *Protective masks case IV* [2025] Oberlandesgericht Köln (Court of Appeal Cologne) U 46/23. CISG-online 7261; *Facade panels for mountain lodge case* [2020] Tribunal Cantonal du Valais/Kantonsgericht Wallis (Court of Appeal Canton Valais) C1 19 260, CISG-online 5497.

[7] Schwenzer and Muñoz (n 1) para 41.52.

legal action against the obligor for the same breach of contract. This principle emphasizes the traditional priority of specific performance. The modernized German law of obligations has maintained this original function of the *Nachfrist* principle amongst more recent codifications.

Although the *Nachfrist* term itself has been integrated into the legal terminology of many legal systems, its function has changed to some extent. The CISG and the PICC have not adopted the priority of specific performance. As a general proposition, the obligee is therefore not bound to fix a *Nachfrist* but rather simply is given the option to do so. However, it may be bound to do so where it intends to avoid the contract.[8] As discussed further in Chapter 14, avoidance of the contract has developed into a remedy of last resort. Hence, under the CISG and the PICC, avoidance of the contract is possible only in case of a fundamental breach.[9] Where non-delivery or non-payment do not amount to a fundamental breach, for example because time is not of the essence, the aggrieved party may only avoid the contract if it has fixed an additional period of time and the other party fails to perform within that period. The PICC has also adopted this approach in Article 7.1.5.[10]

II. Concurrent Domestic Remedies

The interaction between the CISG and concurrent domestic remedies might be more clearly understood by looking into some common scenarios. Imagine, for instance, that a buyer is mistaken about the value of the goods. Under Article 35 CISG, the seller is not liable as all features agreed upon are present. May the buyer still rely on the invalidity remedy of mistake under domestic law? Now consider that due to an error in its declaration, the seller offers the goods to the buyer for $4,000 instead of $5,000. May the seller resort to the invalidity remedy of mistake under domestic law? What if the goods negotiated no longer existed when the contract was concluded? May the buyer rely on the initial impossibility to recover the purchase price, although the CISG remedy would fail? Last but not least, could the buyer rely on a domestic tort remedy if the defective packaging of the goods spoils them?

The starting point to address these questions is Article 4 CISG.[11] This provision clarifies the scope of the Convention. It states that the CISG applies only to the formation of the contract of sale and the rights and obligations of the seller and

---

[8] Ibid para 41.53.
[9] Ibid.
[10] Harriet Schelhaas, 'Article 7.1.5' in Stefan Vogenauer (ed), *Commentary on the UNIDROIT Principles of International Commercial Contracts (PICC)* (2nd edn, Oxford University Press 2015) paras 3–4.
[11] See Pascal Hachem, 'Article 4 CISG: Substantive Scope of Convention' in Ingeborg Schwenzer and Ulrich G Schroeter (eds), *Schlechtriem & Schwenzer Commentary on the UN Convention on the International Sale of Goods (CISG)* (5th edn, Oxford University Press 2022) para 19.

the buyer resulting from such a contract. Specifically, Article 4 CISG states that the Convention does not deal with the following matters unless they are expressly addressed in the Convention:[12] (a) the validity of the contract, any of its provisions, or any usage (under Article 9 CISG); and (b) the effect the contract may have on the property in the goods sold, such as whether the title of the goods is transferred or when the title transfer occurs.

In other words, the CISG governs the rights and obligations arising from the contract, the conclusion, modification, and termination of such contract, the rules to interpret it, as well as the unwinding of the contract. In principle, the convention does not cover validity issues, tort remedies, and procedural questions. An exception to this principle is in case it is 'otherwise expressly provided' through its text or principles.[13] This is sometimes called the counter-exception in Article 4 CISG.

The question then becomes how we define the areas of validity, tort, or procedural law that fall outside of the CISG. The starting point is, therefore, to figure out what amounts to validity, tort, or procedural issues. Not surprisingly, the answer would be different depending on each domestic law consulted. The answer thus should lie in Article 7(1) CISG. This provision requires that in interpreting the CISG, regard is to be had to its international character and the need to promote uniformity in its application and the observance of good faith in international trade. As a consequence, what Article 4 CISG means with 'validity of the contract', for instance, should be interpreted autonomously, that is, through the rules of methods of interpretation in Article 7 CISG that we discussed in Chapter 5.

It also means that the phrase 'otherwise expressly provided', in the counter-exception, should be understood in light of Article 7(2) CISG. This provision infers that a situation can either be expressly settled in the Convention's text or can be determined by relying on the general principles of the CISG. Based on this legal framework, the CISG Advisory Council Opinion No. 23 states that the Convention applies exclusively when the same factual situation is addressed by both the Convention and the otherwise applicable rules, and the purpose of the otherwise applicable rules is broadly the same as that of the Convention.[14]

Under these circumstances, the CISG pre-empts domestic law remedies based on, for instance, mistake, misrepresentation, and initial impossibility in CISG

[12] Ibid para 29 ff; Milena Djordjević, 'Article 4' in Stefan M Kröll, Loukas A Mistelis, and Pilar Perales Viscasillas (eds), *UN Convention on Contracts for the International Sale of Goods (CISG): A Commentary* (2nd edn, CH Beck 2018) para 12.
[13] CISG, art 7; Djordjević, 'Article 4' in Kröll, Mistelis, and Perales Viscasillas (eds) (n 12) para 12; Hachem, 'Article 4 CISG: Substantive Scope of Convention' in Schwenzer and Schroeter (eds) (n 11) para 29.
[14] CISG Advisory Council, 'CISG-AC Opinion No. 23, Mistake, Fraud, Misrepresentation and Initial Impossibility in CISG Contracts, Rapporteur: Professor Hugh Beale, Universities of Warwick (Em.) and Oxford, United Kingdom. Adopted Unanimously by the CISG Advisory Council Following Its 47th Meeting, in Kopaonik, Serbia, on December 12-14, 2023' (2023) Black Letter Rule 3; *Co-owners [...] v Angevine de Construction Bois (ABC) S.a.r.l. et al.* [2021] Cour d'appel de Rennes (Court of Appeal Rennes) 18/03460 CISG-online 5598.

contracts. It also prevails over tort law and procedural law in some instances.[15] These situations are not only differently defined among domestic laws but also have different effects on the contract. Leaving the answer to these situations, which are covered by the CISG, to the otherwise applicable domestic law would undermine the goal and mandate of uniform application in Article 7 CISG.

1. Concurrent remedies on mistake or negligent misrepresentation

Let us explore situations where domestic laws would be excluded in case of mistake or negligent misrepresentation as defined by the CISG itself. For instance, if either party was induced to enter into the contract by a mistake or non-fraudulent misrepresentation as to any of the matters covered by Articles 35, 41, and 42, the situation will be governed by the CISG instead of by the otherwise applicable domestic law.[16] The same will hold if either party was induced to enter into the contract by a mistake or non-fraudulent misrepresentation as to the value of the goods; if either party was induced to enter into the contract by a mistake or non-fraudulent misrepresentation as to a matter covered by Articles 71 to 73 CISG; in cases of initial impossibility; or if the parties have entered into the contract under a shared mistake as to any matter covered by the Convention.[17]

Conversely, if the mistake or non-fraudulent misrepresentation was as to a matter that is not governed by the Convention, the otherwise applicable rules of law apply.[18] For instance, a buyer is ready to purchase a fleet of electric vehicles for $500,000 from the seller, provided that the vehicles qualify for a government rebate of $50,000. The seller genuinely believes this rebate is available but should have known that the government recently terminated the rebate programme. The buyer agrees to the purchase, assuming it will receive the rebate. There is no reference to the rebate in the contract documents. The buyer may be able to invoke the domestic law on mistake or misrepresentation, as this scenario is not covered by the contract or the Convention. As in this example, the matter is not governed by the Convention, the buyer's only remedy in this case, if there is one, will be under the otherwise applicable rules of law.

---

[15] CISG Advisory Council, 'CISG-AC Opinion No. 23, Mistake, Fraud, Misrepresentation and Initial Impossibility in CISG Contracts' (n 14) Black Letter Rule 1, comment 1.5.

[16] Ibid Black Letter Rule 4(a).

[17] Ibid Black Letter Rule 4(c)–(e); Ingeborg Schwenzer, 'Article 35 CISG: Conformity of Goods' in Schwenzer and Schroeter (eds) (n 11) paras 48–51.

[18] *Vintage Porsche 911 S Targa case* [2023] Oberlandesgericht München (Court of Appeal Munich) U 1224/21. CISG-online 6641; CISG Advisory Council, 'CISG-AC Opinion No. 23, Mistake, Fraud, Misrepresentation and Initial Impossibility in CISG Contracts' (n 14) Black Letter Rule 5.

2. Concurrent remedies for mistake in declaration

Regarding any errors in declarations, including those that are unilateral or common in relation to the content or meaning of a declaration, statement, or other conduct, or the identity of a party, the rules on interpretation (Article 8 CISG) and formation of the contract (Articles 14–24 CISG) of the Convention apply.[19] These rules should be followed instead of the otherwise applicable rules of law.

3. Concurrent remedies based on fraud

As stated above, remedies covered by the validity exception in Article 4 sentence 2(a) CISG, including fraud, must be defined independently. The CISG Advisory Council considers that fraud under the CISG includes giving incorrect information, whether by words or conduct, when:

1. the giver knew the information to be incorrect or was aware that it did not know whether the information was correct or not; and
2. the giver intended to deceive the other party or was aware that the other party might be deceived and gave the incorrect information nonetheless.[20]

Now, if a party is induced to enter into the contract by the other party's fraud, the aggrieved party may resort to remedies under the otherwise applicable rules of law even if it also has a remedy under the Convention.[21] The aggrieved party may choose the remedy it considers more favourable or combine compatible remedies.[22]

---

[19] *Protective masks case VII* [2025] Oberlandesgericht Köln (Court of Appeal Cologne) 8 U 38/23, CISG-Online 7282: holding that the rules of interpretation of Art 8 CISG apply to all provisions of a contract subject to the CISG. *EPS granules case* [2025] Oberlandesgericht Linz (Court of Appeal Linz) 2 R 14/25d, CISG-online 7288: applying Art 14 CISG; CISG Advisory Council, 'CISG-AC Opinion No. 23, Mistake, Fraud, Misrepresentation and Initial Impossibility in CISG Contracts' (n 14) Black Letter Rule 7; Martin Schmidt-Kessel, 'Article 8 CISG: Interpretation of Parties' Statements or Conduct' in Schwenzer and Schroeter (eds) (n 11) para 7; Alberto L Zuppi, 'Article 8 CISG' in Kröll, Mistelis, and Perales Viscasillas (eds) (n 12) para 15 ff.

[20] CISG Advisory Council, 'CISG-AC Opinion No. 23, Mistake, Fraud, Misrepresentation and Initial Impossibility in CISG Contracts' (n 14) Black Letter Rule 10.

[21] Ibid Black Letter Rule 9; Schwenzer and Muñoz (n 1) para 49.32; Christoph Brunner, Diana Akikol, and Lucien Bürki, 'Article 45 (Remedies Available to Buyer)' in Christoph Brunner and Benjamin Gottlieb (eds), *Commentary on the UN Sales Law (CISG)* (Wolters Kluwer 2019) para 32.

[22] *Gramercy Holdings I, LLC v Matec S.r.l. et al.* [2023] US District Court for the Southern District of New York 20 Civ. 3937 (JPC), 20 Civ. 4136 (JPC), CISG-online 6477: 'CISG art. 4. Courts in this District have therefore commonly applied New York tort law, not the CISG, when analyzing fraudulent inducement and negligent misrepresentation claims brought in cases involving contracts governed by the CISG.... However, [j]ust because a party labels a cause of action a 'tort' does not mean that it is automatically not preempted by the CISG. A tort that is in actuality a contract claim, or that bridges the gap between contract and tort law may very well be preempted.... Thus, a party cannot avoid the CISG simply by calling its breach of contract claim a claim for fraud—say, by claiming the defendant committed fraud by making contractual promises it intended to violate.'

4. Concurrent remedies for initial impossibility

Under some domestic rules, a contract might be unenforceable, void, or invalidated for initial impossibility. The terminology and effect also vary if the subject matter, for instance the goods, do not exist at the time of the conclusion of the contract. However, this is an issue governed with by the CISG as shown in Article 68 CISG.[23] Whether the seller will be excused from liability for non-delivery depends on whether the seller can invoke Article 79 CISG, which seems unlikely. More broadly, Article 30 CISG imposes an obligation on the seller to deliver the goods. If the goods were specific and no longer exist, or ceased to exist either before or after the contract was concluded, the seller will be unable to fulfil this obligation. The seller's liability in such cases is again governed by Article 79 CISG.[24]

The CISG would also pre-empt domestic provisions stipulating the unenforceability or nullity of the contract when the subject matter belongs to a third party at the time of contract conclusion.[25] For this situation, the buyer will have to rely on Article 41 CISG. This provision addresses the problem with requirements to assess the lack of conformity based on the property title and the remedies derived thereof.

5. Concurrent tort remedies

Some domestic legal systems provide for concurrent sale and tort law remedies in case of damage to the chattel itself, or where damage is caused to property which is attached to the goods, or with which the goods are combined or blended, or which are processed by the goods, in the ordinary course of business or the course of regular use.

The CISG covers situations of property damage as a natural consequence of non-conformity of the purchased goods, for instance compensation for consequential

---

[23] Article 68 CISG, which addresses goods sold in transit, specifically deals with the scenario where the goods have been lost or damaged at the time the contract was formed. It stipulates that if the seller knew or should have known of the loss or damage but did not disclose this to the buyer, the seller would bear the risk, see Pascal Hachem, 'Article 68 CISG: Passing of Risk When Goods Are Sold in Transit' in Schwenzer and Schroeter (eds) (n 11) para 15 ff.

[24] *[.] v Luka Food d.o.o.* [2021] Vrhovni kasacioni sud/Врховни касациони суд (Serbian Supreme Court) 135/2021, CISG-online 6859; CISG Advisory Council, 'CISG-AC Opinion No. 23' (n 14) Black Letter Rule 4.

[25] *Perkins Manufacturing Comp v Haul-All Equipment Ltd* [2020] US District Court for the Northern District of Illinois 19 cv 03769, CISG-online 5233: holding that Federal Courts throughout the United States agree that the CISG pre-empts state contract law; CISG Advisory Council, 'CISG-AC Opinion No. 23' (n 14) Black Letter Rule 4, comment 4.27.

or incidental losses under Article 74 CISG. In those cases, concurrent domestic tort remedies will be pre-empted in favour of the CISG provisions.[26]

In case of damage to property that does not necessarily come in close contact with the goods, the remedies of the otherwise applicable domestic tort law will apply alongside the CISG.

6. Concurrent procedural rules

Some procedural matters under domestic law may also be covered by the CISG. For instance, a few legal systems treat post-judgment interest as a procedural question. However, Article 78 CISG does not make any distinction between the right to interest and the interest rate applicable pre- and post-judgment. Accordingly, domestic procedural rules on interest or other procedural matters, such as the burden of proof of different questions, would also be pre-empted by the CISG. All other procedural matters that the CISG does not regulate will need to be governed by the otherwise applicable procedural rules.

III. Right to Withhold Performance

Contracts are premised on the synallagmatic obligations of the parties: each undertakes to perform in the expectation that the other will likewise perform. Naturally, there is always a risk of non-performance. A party therefore has a legitimate interest in performing only when confident that the other party will reciprocate. This concern may arise in two common scenarios: first, when the other party has already breached its reciprocal obligations; and second, when circumstances give rise to a reasonable belief that the other party will commit a breach in the future. In either situation, the non-breaching party faces a dilemma: performing despite doubts may expose it to significant losses, while refusing to perform may itself constitute a breach. To resolve this tension, legal systems generally allow a party to withhold or suspend its own performance without adverse consequences as an exception to liability and a means to mitigate loss. The right to *withhold* typically responds to an existing breach, whereas the right to *suspend* may be invoked in anticipation of future non-performance. Both remedies serve to protect the balance inherent in synallagmatic contracts and ensure that performance is not demanded without adequate assurance of reciprocity.

---

[26] CISG Advisory Council, 'CISG-AC Opinion No. 23' (n 14) Black Letter Rule 4, comment 4.27; Ingeborg Schwenzer, 'Article 74 CISG: Calculation of Damages in General' in Schwenzer and Schroeter (eds) (n 11) para 5 ff.

This section addresses the right to withhold performance. The right to suspend performance, by contrast, is examined in Chapter 14.

The CISG does not expressly establish a general right to withhold performance. The PICC, on the other hand, provide such a right in Article 7.1.3.[27] That being said, the CISG impliedly states that the right to withhold performance depends on the contract terms. First, a party may make the payment of the buyer a condition for the handing over of the goods or documents or rendering services. Second, the seller may dispatch the goods for carriage on terms whereby the goods and documents controlling their disposition will be handed over to the buyer only against payment. The same can be agreed upon for the benefit of a service or labour provider.[28] The buyer may withhold payment of the price until the seller has placed the goods or documents at the disposal of the buyer or/and the buyer has had a chance to examine them under Article 58(3) CISG.[29]

Besides those contractual stipulations of the right to withhold performance, it has also become generally accepted that the CISG contains a general right to withhold performance. This is commonly based on Articles 58, 71, and 80, as well as the second sentences of Articles 81(2), 85, and 86(1), which are considered to embody a general principle under Article 7(2) CISG.[30]

IV. Cure by Non-performing Party

Pursuant to Article 48 CISG, the seller has the right to cure any problems with the goods even after the agreed-upon delivery date. This cure must be carried out promptly and at the seller's own cost, without causing the buyer unreasonable inconvenience or uncertainty about being reimbursed for any expenses incurred.[31] However, the buyer can still claim damages according to the contract or

---

[27] Harriet Schelhaas, 'Article 7.1.3' in Vogenauer (ed) (n 10) para 1.

[28] PICC 2016, art 7.1.3(2).

[29] Christiana Fountoulakis, 'Article 71 CISG: Suspension of Performance' in Schwenzer and Schroeter (eds) (n 11) para 14.

[30] *Búfalo SA v Alberto Mazzilli* [2020] Tribunal de Apelaciones en lo Civil de Segundo Turno 431-622/2018/33/2020, CISG-online 5416; *Triage Matériel Professionnel S.a.r.l v JGB-2 Sp z.o.o.* [2023] Cour d'appel de Paris (Court of Appeal Paris) 21/19946, CISG-online 6569; *Wiesenhof International GmbH v Estonian Meat House OÜ* [2023] Tartu Maakohus (County Court Tartu) 2-22-11320, CISG-online 6648; *Protective masks case VII* [2025] Oberlandesgericht Köln (Court of Appeal Cologne) 8 U 38/23, CISG-online 7282; *Protective masks case IV* (n 5); CISG Advisory Council, 'CISG-AC Opinion No. 5, The Buyer's Right to Avoid the Contract in Case of Non-Conforming Goods or Documents, Rapporteur: Professor Dr. Ingeborg Schwenzer, LL.M., Professor of Private Law, University of Basel, 7 May 2005' (2005) comments 4.18–4.21. See e.g. Various courts recognizing a general right of retention under arts 58, 71, 80, and 81 CISG.

[31] Peter Huber, 'Article 48' in Kröll, Mistelis, and Perales Viscasillas (eds) (n 12) para 1; Markus Müller-Chen, 'Article 48 CISG: Seller's Right to Cure after Date for Delivery' in Schwenzer and Schroeter (eds) (n 11) para 1.

the Convention (Article 48(1) CISG). A similar rule and requirements for the right to cure by the breaching party are stated in Article 7.1.4 PICC.[32]

Under Article 48 CISG, the seller has a right to cure 'subject to article 49'.[33] In other words, the seller's right to cure is excluded in case of a fundamental breach of contract. The CISG Advisory Council has commented that a fundamental breach would occur if there is non-usability and non-curability of the goods in time.[34] Unless time is of the essence, there is no reason to limit the seller's right to cure in Article 48 CISG. Therefore, the friction between the seller's right to cure and the buyer's right to avoid the contract under Article 49(1)(a) CISG mainly depends on the definition of a fundamental breach. If a fundamental breach is denied in cases where cure is possible, and the seller is willing to cure within the limits of Article 48(1) CISG, at least in practice, the controversy of the relation of Articles 48 and 49 CISG proves to be fruitless.[35] In the end, the buyer may only avoid the contract if the non-conformity amounts to a fundamental breach, that is, goods being unusable and non-conformity not being curable in time.

The PICC condition that 'the aggrieved party has no legitimate interest in refusing cure' in Article 7.1.4 could be understood similarly.[36] If the performance is still curable within a reasonable time because performance on the initially agreed date was not of the essence, then it would be appropriate in the circumstances, and the non-breaching party would have no legitimate interest in refusing the cure that also complies with the additional requirements in Article 7.1.4 PICC.

Article 48(1) CISG limits the seller's right to cure to cases where it 'can do so without unreasonable delay and without causing the buyer unreasonable inconvenience or uncertainty of reimbursement by the seller of expenses advanced by the buyer'. First, 'without unreasonable delay' may be found where, after a specific date, the buyer can no longer be expected to accept performance by the seller.[37] Thus, the question is whether the buyer would be substantially

---

[32] Harriet Schelhaas, 'Article 7.1.4' in Vogenauer (ed) (n 10) para 1.

[33] Huber, in Kröll, Mistelis, and Perales Viscasillas (eds) (n 12) para 16; Müller-Chen, 'Article 48 CISG: Seller's Right to Cure after Date for Delivery' in Schwenzer and Schroeter (eds) (n 11) para 14; Christoph Brunner, Diana Akikol, and Lucien Bürki, 'Article 48 (Cure After Date for Delivery; Requests for Clarification)' in Brunner and Gottlieb (eds) (n 21) para 8.

[34] *Dominion Denmark A/S v Polytex Composite s.r.o.* [2023] Sø- og Handelsretten (Maritime and Commercial Court) BS-48358/2019-SHR, CISG-online 6331: holding that the seller's refusal to replace GPR lining amounted to a waiver of its right to repair under art 48 CISG. CISG Advisory Council, 'CISG-AC Opinion No. 21, Delivery of Substitute Goods and Repair under the CISG, Rapporteurs: Professor (Em.) Dr. Ingeborg Schwenzer, LL.M., University of Basel, Switzerland, and Dr. Ilka H. Beimel, Germany, 3 and 4 February 2020' (2020) Black Letter Rule 11.

[35] *Hama GmbH & Co KG v Yongkang Kangteng Film Equipment Co, Ltd* [2018] Intermediate People's Court Jinhua, Zhejiang Province (2018) Zhejiang 07 Minzhong No. 361, CISG-online 4782; CISG Advisory Council, 'CISG-AC Opinion No. 21' (n 34) comments 3.57–3.59.

[36] Schelhaas, 'Article 7.1.4' in Vogenauer (ed) (n 10) para 16.

[37] Müller-Chen, 'Article 48 CISG: Seller's Right to Cure after Date for Delivery' in Schwenzer and Schroeter (eds) (n 11) para 9; Brunner, Akikol, and Bürki, 'Article 48 (Cure After Date for Delivery; Requests for Clarification)' in Brunner and Gottlieb (eds) (n 21) para 5.

deprived of what it can expect under the contract at the time the cure was executed by the seller or not. The case's individual circumstances must be taken into account; there is no definite time from which the delay should be calculated. Article 7.1.4 PICC requires that 'cure is effected promptly', but the rationale is similar to the requirement in Article 48(1) CISG. The PICC's Official Commentary on this provision confirms that time is of the essence in the exercise of the right to cure.[38] The non-performing party cannot delay cure by locking the aggrieved party into an extended waiting period, even if the aggrieved party is not inconvenienced.

Further, the seller is not allowed to cure if this implies any other unreasonable inconvenience to the buyer.[39] In general, the term 'unreasonable inconvenience' is to be understood in the same manner as in Article 37 CISG. Cases of 'unreasonable inconvenience' occur where cure causes suspension or disruption of the buyer's production, the buyer's customers are threatening actions for damages, or obviously unprofessional actions by the seller lead to several attempts of subsequent performance.[40] Unreasonable inconvenience can arise when the buyer loses trust in the seller's ability or willingness to remedy the situation. However, this loss of trust must be reasonable in itself. Otherwise, it would be possible to bypass the requirement of reasonableness set out in Article 48 CISG.

The PICC, on the other hand, require that the 'cure is appropriate in the circumstances' in Article 7.1.4(1)(b).[41] However, whether the cure is appropriate in the circumstances depends on whether it is reasonable from the perspective of a third party. Accordingly, the same reasonableness analysis for Article 48(1) CISG can be useful here.

Finally, under Article 48(1) CISG, the seller may not cure the non-conformity if it causes uncertainty of reimbursement of expenses advanced by the buyer. It is important to note that if a seller fails to fulfil their obligations, they must bear the costs of fixing the problem.[42] In cases where the buyer incurs additional costs, such as disruptions to production or increased manpower, the seller must also cover these foreseeable expenses.

---

[38] International Institute for the Unification of Private Law (ed), *UNIDROIT Principles of International Commercial Contracts* (UNIDROIT International Institute for the Unification of Private Law 2017) 231–2, art 7.1.4, off cmt 5; Schelhaas, 'Article 7.1.4' in Vogenauer (ed) (n 10) para 11 ff.

[39] Brunner, Akikol, and Bürki, 'Article 48 (Cure After Date for Delivery; Requests for Clarification)' in Brunner and Gottlieb (eds) (n 21) para 6.

[40] Ingeborg Schwenzer, 'Article 37 CISG: Seller's Right to Cure Prior to Date of Delivery' in Schwenzer and Schroeter (eds) (n 11) para 12 ff.

[41] Schelhaas, 'Article 7.1.4' in Vogenauer (ed) (n 10) para 11.

[42] Huber, in Kröll, Mistelis, and Perales Viscasillas (eds) (n 12) para 19; Brunner, Akikol, and Bürki, 'Article 48 (Cure After Date for Delivery; Requests for Clarification)' in Brunner and Gottlieb (eds) (n 21) para 7; Müller-Chen, 'Article 48 CISG: Seller's Right to Cure after Date for Delivery' in Schwenzer and Schroeter (eds) (n 11) para 8.

If the seller then asks the buyer to confirm whether it will accept the remedial actions and the buyer does not respond within a reasonable time, the seller can go ahead and perform the remedial actions within the time frame specified in its request.[43] During this period, the buyer cannot take any action that would interfere with the seller's efforts to cure (Article 48(2) CISG). Article 7.1.4(1) and (3) PICC provide similarly. The breaching party must, without undue delay, give notice indicating the proposed manner and timing of the cure.[44] Upon receipt of such a notice, the aggrieved party's rights that are inconsistent with the non-performing party's performance are suspended until the cure period expires. However, under the PICC, the right to withhold performance is not precluded pending cure (Article 7.1.4 (4) PICC).

In practice, conflicts may arise between the two parties setting different periods of time: The buyer may first set a period under Article 47(1) CISG or Article 7.1.5 PICC, which must be reasonable. What is reasonable must be determined on a case-by-case basis.[45] Relevant criteria are *inter alia* the nature of the obligation to be performed or cured, the goods, the initial length of the period to deliver, and the location of both parties and the goods (especially whether the shipment is necessary or not). Concerning non-conformity, the additional period of time must give the seller a realistic opportunity to deliver substitute goods or repair the defective goods. If the period is too short according to all these circumstances, it causes a reasonable period to commence. Even if the seller does not react to the buyer setting this *Nachfrist* period, the buyer is bound to its declaration during this period or—if it is too short—during a period of reasonable length. However, if the seller simply rejects the buyer's request for performance of cure (under Article 47(1) CISG or Article 7.1.5 PICC) without offering cure during an alternative period of time (under Article 48(2) CISG), the buyer is no longer bound and may immediately resort to the remedies being otherwise available.

Article 48(2) CISG (or Article 7.1.4 PICC) also governs cases where the buyer did not set any additional period of time under Article 47(1) CISG (or Article 7.1.5 PICC). If the buyer, in that situation, does not comply with the seller's request within a reasonable time, the seller may perform within the time indicated in its request. If the buyer, however, objects, the seller may still perform within the time that is deemed to be reasonable under Article 48(1) CISG (or Article 7.1.4 PICC).

---

[43] Huber, in Kröll, Mistelis, and Perales Viscasillas (eds) (n 12) para 30; Brunner, Akikol, and Bürki, 'Article 48 (Cure After Date for Delivery; Requests for Clarification)' in Brunner and Gottlieb (eds) (n 21) para 16; Müller-Chen, 'Article 48 CISG: Seller's Right to Cure after Date for Delivery' in Schwenzer and Schroeter (eds) (n 11) para 24 ff.

[44] Schelhaas, 'Article 7.1.4' in Vogenauer (ed) (n 10) paras 9–10.

[45] Müller-Chen, 'Article 48 CISG: Seller's Right to Cure after Date for Delivery' in Schwenzer and Schroeter (eds) (n 11) para 9.

V. Contractual Modification of Remedies

The principle of freedom of contract, embodied in Article 6 CISG and Article 1.5 PICC, permits the parties both to expand and limit the remedies provided by law through their contractual agreement.[46] This means that they can modify or extend the default remedies for breach of contract. On the other hand, parties can contractually exclude or limit default remedies in the CISG and the PICC. In most cases, parties try to exclude the application of a default remedy entirely or try to restrict the scope of the remedy in question.

There are two common ways for parties involved in a contract to change the default remedies. First, they may choose to exclude specific remedies. The effectiveness of such exclusion is subject to the applicable law governing their validity under Article 4 sentence 2(a) CISG.[47] A common example of a remedy that a party may try to exclude is the right to avoid the contract. Instead, that party may prefer to offer repair or replacement of the product in order to prevent financial issues associated with returning the purchase price and losing any profit from the contract. The parties may agree that, in the event of non-performance, the aggrieved party shall only be entitled to claim damages, thereby avoiding the complexities and potential delays associated with compelling specific performance of contractual obligations.

In certain situations, instead of completely excluding a remedy, the scope of the remedy may be limited or its prerequisites may be modified.[48] This is a common approach taken by contract drafters to comply with laws that prevent the complete exclusion of a remedy. This approach is especially relevant in the case of damages. For instance, it is usual for the obligors to make their liability for damages conditional on a certain degree of fault. Typical limitation-of-liability clauses exclude the obligor's liability unless they have acted with at least gross negligence.

Parties in a contract may restrict their liability for certain types of losses. For instance, a seller may exclude its liability for consequential losses or loss of profit. Another way is to limit liability to a certain amount. This can be done by capping the amount recoverable at a specific sum. However, in some cases, parties may not refer to a particular sum but instead make a general statement that liability will be limited to the maximum extent allowed by law. This is an attempt to ensure that the limitation clause remains valid even if there are regulations regarding

---

[46] See Chapter 4.

[47] *Transportes Peñón Blanco SAPI de CV et al. v Volvo Group North America, LLC et al.* [2024] US District Court for the Middle District of North Carolina 1:23CV176, CISG-online 6909; CISG Advisory Council, 'CISG-AC Opinion No. 17, Limitation and Exclusion Clauses in CISG Contracts, Rapporteur: Prof. Lauro Gama Jr., Pontifical Catholic University of Rio de Janeiro, Brazil, 16 October 2015' (2015) Black Letter Rule 1.

[48] CISG-AC Opinion No. 17 (n 47) comment 1.5; Pascal Hachem, 'Article 6 CISG: Exclusion or Derogation by the Parties (Party Autonomy)' in Schwenzer and Schroeter (eds) (n 11) paras 28–29; Loukas A Mistelis, 'Article 6' in Kröll, Mistelis, and Perales Viscasillas (eds) (n 12) para 25.

reasonableness or minimum standards of protection. Again, the effectiveness of such clauses will be determined by the applicable law.[49]

The freedom of the parties to modify the default remedies regime naturally has limits. Broadly speaking, legal systems typically do not accept that a party is left without any protection. Article 1.5 PICC provides that some of its provisions may not be derogated and, with regard to remedies, Article 7.4.13(2) PICC prohibits derogation on the reduction of excessive penalties for breach, Article 7.1.6 PICC on the test of gross unfairness for exemption clauses, and Article 10.3(2) PICC on restriction over limitation periods.[50] At a domestic level, Section 2-719 UCC, Official Comment 1, states that '[i]t is of the very essence of a sales contract that at least minimum adequate remedies be available. If the parties intend to conclude a contract for sale within this Article they must accept the legal consequence that there be at least a fair quantum of remedy for breach of the obligations or duties outlined in the contract. Thus any clause purporting to modify or limit the remedial provisions of this article in an unconscionable manner is subject to deletion ....'[51]

On this point, the CISG Advisory Council has stated that the Convention governs the incorporation and interpretation of clauses providing for the limitation and exclusion of liability of the obligor for failure to perform ('limitation and exclusion clauses').[52] However, the CISG does not pre-empt provisions for the protection of the obligee under the applicable law or rules of law, relying on notions such as intentional or wilful breach, gross negligence, breach of an essential term, gross unfairness, unreasonableness, or unconscionability.[53]

Concerning clauses providing for the payment of agreed sums for failure to perform the contract ('agreed sums'), the CISG Advisory Council has also stated that the Convention does not exclude provisions on the protection of the obligor of the otherwise applicable law or rules of law, except for form requirements.[54]

In both cases, limitation/exclusion clauses and agreed sums, the provisions on the protection of the obligor of the otherwise applicable law or rules of law relying on notions such as reasonableness, excessiveness, or proportionality must be applied in accordance with an international standard. This standard must be developed from the underlying principles of the CISG.[55]

---

[49] CISG Advisory Council, 'CISG-AC Opinion No. 10, Agreed Sums Payable upon Breach of an Obligation in CISG Contracts, Rapporteur: Dr. Pascal Hachem, Bär & Karrer AG, Zurich, Switzerland, 3 August 2012' (2012) Black Letter Rules 3, 4.
[50] Gilles Cuniberti, 'Article 1.5' in Vogenauer (ed) (n 10) para 12.
[51] United States Uniform Commercial Code (UCC) 1952.
[52] CISG Advisory Council, 'CISG-AC Opinion No. 17 (n 42) Black Letter Rule 1.
[53] Ibid Black Letter Rule 4(a).
[54] CISG-AC Opinion No. 10 (n 49) Black Letter Rule 3.
[55] Ibid Black Letter Rule 4(a).

13

Remedies II—Specific Performance

I. General: Domestic and Uniform Approaches

The claim for specific performance is a complex issue from a comparative law perspective. Legal systems have different approaches to this matter, which are rooted in centuries-long legal traditions.[1] In general, the central question is whether the obligee should have the right to claim specific performance, and if so, to what extent. Legal systems disagree on whether specific performance should be available as a default remedy or only be available in specific circumstances.

1. Civil law tradition

Civil law legal systems are known for their favourable approach to claims for specific performance, which is considered to be one of their distinguishing characteristics. In general, all civil law legal systems, including the Nordic systems, provide for the claim for specific performance as part of the default system.[2] It has been said that specific performance is the backbone of the obligation.

---

[1] Ingeborg Schwenzer and Edgardo Muñoz, *Global Sales and Contract Law* (2nd edn, Oxford University Press 2022) para 43.10.

[2] Ibid para 43.12; *Solea International BVBA v Bassett & Walker International Inc* [2019] Court of Appeal of Ontario C66182/2019 ONCA 617, CISG-online 4505: holding that art 62 CISG adopts in principle the position of the civil law tradition as to the availability of specific performance as of right for any breach of any obligation of the buyer.

The right to specific performance in these systems is based on the general principle of *pacta sunt servanda*, which means that contracts should be kept. This approach argues that when two parties willingly enter into a contract, they also agree to perform it as required by their agreement.[3] The primary focus is on the promise of performance, and it is emphasized that promises must not be broken.

In recent times, the protection of trust in the performance of the contract has become increasingly justified on economic grounds, too. Ensuring that the performance owed under the contract is delivered, minimizes the number of breaches, reduces transaction costs, and eliminates the need to take costly measures to avoid damages.[4] Breach of contracts can also threaten healthy business relationships, which are necessary to encourage market activities. If the law endorses distrust, it will hardly be an incentive to invest in a market.

In addition, in traditional civil law legal systems, there is a question as to whether non-conforming goods delivered should be classified as a completely different product (*aliud*) or as the same type of product owed but not conforming to the contract (*peius*).[5] This distinction is practically relevant for the claim for specific performance. If the non-conforming goods are classified as *peius*, the remedies for non-conformity apply, which usually include only damages and price reduction, but ultimately depend on the applicable law.[6] However, if the non-conforming goods delivered are considered to be an *aliud*, meaning that they are considered a different product altogether, this is considered a case of total non-delivery where specific performance, consisting in the delivery of the proper goods might be granted.[7]

The distinction between *aliud* and *peius* has been abandoned in modern civil law legal systems. This means that if the delivered goods do not match the contractual requirements in terms of quantity or quality, it is considered a case of non-conformity.[8] In such cases, it needs to be determined whether the buyer can

---

[3] Ibid para 43.06; Michael G Bridge, *The International Sale of Goods* (4th edn, Oxford University Press 2017) para 12.47; Markus Müller-Chen, 'Article 28 CISG: Judgement for Specific Performance' in Ingeborg Schwenzer and Ulrich G Schroeter (eds), *Schlechtriem & Schwenzer Commentary on the UN Convention on the International Sale of Goods (CISG)* (5th edn, Oxford University Press 2022) para 1; Andrea A Björklund, 'Article 28' in Stefan M Kröll, Loukas A Mistelis, and Pilar Perales Viscasillas (eds), *UN Convention on Contracts for the International Sale of Goods (CISG): A Commentary* (2nd edn, CH Beck 2018) para 5; *Consorcio ALYR Berlín SAS v Impala Terminals Barrancabermeja SA* [2019] Centro de Arbitraje y Conciliación Mercantil de la Cámara de Comercio de Bogotá (Center of Arbitration and Conciliation of the Chamber of Commerce Bogota) 5332, CISG-online 6700: referring to the importance of the *pacta sunt servanda* principle.

[4] Bridge (n 3) para 12.47; Björklund, 'Article 28' in Kröll, Mistelis, and Perales Viscasillas (eds) (n 3) para 3; Schwenzer and Muñoz (n 1) para 43.06; *Zodiac Seats US LLC v Synergy Aerospace Corp* [2020] US District Court for the Eastern District of Texas 4:17-cv-00410, CISG-online 5172: holding the right to request repair by the seller to avoid further losses.

[5] For more explanation on the distinction, see *Pallets case I* [2002] Amtsgericht Viechtach (Local Court Viechtach) C 419/01, CISG-online 755; Schwenzer and Muñoz (n 1) para 43.13.

[6] Schwenzer and Muñoz (n 1) para 31.15.

[7] Ibid.

[8] Ibid para 43.14.

demand a cure for the non-conformity as a type of specific performance. In Roman sales law, the buyer did not have the right to seek a cure for non-conformity.[9] This means that the buyer could only reduce the purchase price, avoid the contract, or claim damages in the case of fraud or breach of an express warranty by the seller. Legal systems that follow Roman law in this regard generally do not allow the buyer to demand a cure. However, the CISG and the PICC have departed from this old approach.[10]

2. Common law legal tradition

Under the common law tradition, when a contract is breached, the primary remedy is damages. Specific performance is considered an equitable remedy, which can only be used when common law damages are insufficient.[11] This differs from civil law legal systems. Even after the English Supreme Court of Judicature Acts 1873–1875 merged common law and equity, the traditional view remains in England and most common law legal systems.[12]

The concept of specific performance as an equitable remedy was initially acknowledged in the United States, with the same basic principle that it will only be granted when damages are not sufficient.[13] While this principle remains unchanged, some bodies of law, like the UCC, contain an express provision on specific performance that outlines the requirements for the claim's availability.[14]

Today, common law jurisdictions are generally opposed to the standard availability of the claim for specific performance, based on three main economic arguments.[15] The first is based on the doctrine of efficient breach of contract, which rejects the concept of specific performance on the grounds that it poses a deterrent to efficient breach of contract.[16] Related to this is the fear that even if damages fully compensate the aggrieved party, the availability of specific performance may

---

[9] Raphael Dessemontet, 'The Non-Conformities, Limitation Periods and Duties of the Buyer in the International Sales of Goods: A Comparison of the CISG, the UNIDROIT Principles, the UCC, and the Swiss, French, and German Laws' (2011) 6 *International Business Law Journal* 603.

[10] Ingeborg Schwenzer, 'Article 37 CISG: Seller's Right to Cure Prior to Date of Delivery' in Schwenzer and Schroeter (eds) (n 3) para 2; Schwenzer and Muñoz (n 1) para 43.52.

[11] Andrew Burrows, 'We Do This At Common Law But That In Equity' (2022) 22 *Oxford Journal of Legal Studies* 1, 3; Müller-Chen, 'Article 28 CISG: Judgement for Specific Performance' in Schwenzer and Schroeter (eds) (n 3) para 2; Bridge (n 3) 12.47; Björklund, 'Article 28' in Kröll, Mistelis, and Perales Viscasillas (eds) (n 3) para 9.

[12] Michael Lobban, 'What Did the Makers of the Judicature Acts Understand by "Fusion"?' in John CP Goldberg, Henry E Smith, and PG Turner (eds), *Equity and Law: Fusion and Fission* (Cambridge University Press 2019) 70–95.

[13] Andrew Burrows, *Remedies for Torts, Breach of Contract and Equitable Wrongs* (Oxford University Press 2019) 406 ff.

[14] U.S. Uniform Commercial Code (UCC) Section 2-716(1).

[15] Schwenzer and Muñoz (n 1) para 43.27.

[16] Dawinder S Sidhu, 'The Immorality and Inefficiency of an Efficient Breach' (2006) 8 *The Tennessee Journal Of Business Law* 61, 65.

still result in the exploitation of the breaching party by the aggrieved party. The second argument is that specific performance is not economically favourable to contracting parties, and that it would have to be supervised by courts, thus creating social costs.[17] The third argument is that the standard availability of the claim for specific performance would discourage parties from complying with their duty to mitigate losses.[18]

The statement that specific performance is only available when damages are not sufficient is naturally ambiguous and allows different factors to be prioritized, depending on the individual circumstances of the case. There is also general uncertainty as to whether the requirement of inadequacy of damages should be interpreted restrictively or liberally. Under English law, damages are unlikely to ever be considered inadequate.[19]

II. The Modern Approach under CISG and PICC

The differences in legal systems, particularly between common law and civil law, have been considered while developing modern approaches to claims for specific performance. These approaches aim to provide more flexibility regarding the availability of the claim for specific performance. The strict priority given to the claim for specific performance in civil law legal systems ensures legal certainty by guaranteeing the aggrieved party the ability to enforce the expected contract terms. However, this approach may not adequately consider the interests of market actors trading in generic goods, where damages may be the preferred remedy. The common law approach, while better suited for the generic goods market, places the risk of not obtaining performance as expected under the contract on the obligee, creating uncertainty.

1. The CISG

The CISG drafters had extensive discussions on whether the claim for specific performance should be included in the Convention.[20] More than 40 years after the

---

[17] Theodore Eisenberg and Geoffrey P Miller, 'Damages Versus Specific Performance: Lessons from Commercial Contracts' (2015) 12 *Journal of Empirical Legal Studies* 38. The US restatement further adds that specific performance will be refused if such relief 'would cause unreasonable hardship or loss to the party in breach or to third persons'.

[18] Ibid.

[19] Burrows (n 11) 1.

[20] United Nations (UN) Conference Official Records, 'Documents of the Conference and Summary Records of the Plenary Meetings and of the Meetings of the Main Committees' (1991) UN Doc A/CONF.97/19, 305, para 41 ff; Björklund, 'Article 28' in Kröll, Mistelis, and Perales Viscasillas (eds) (n 3) para 1.

CISG was finalized and roughly 35 years after it came into force, experience shows that the issue has not caused any practical difficulties. To begin with, the CISG provides for the default availability of the claim for specific performance for both the buyer and the seller. According to Article 46(1) CISG, the buyer has a claim for the delivery of the goods,[21] while under Article 62 CISG, the seller has a claim for the payment of the purchase price.[22] The claim for specific performance of the delivery obligation is clearly of civil law descent, but the claim for the purchase price on the side of the seller also maintains the traditional common law claim for the price.[23]

The CISG does not aim to balance civil law's and common law's different approaches. Instead, it seeks to keep both approaches alive in full.[24] This means that while the CISG generally establishes the default availability of the claim for specific performance, it does not guarantee the obligee's success in bringing the claim. The contract will serve as the primary basis for determining whether the parties are entitled to seek the remedy of specific performance.[25] In addition, according to Article 28 CISG, a court is not obligated to enter a judgment for specific performance unless it would do so under its own law, which refers to the law of the forum excluding conflict-of-laws rules.[26] In the case of an arbitral tribunal, the situation is less clear. It is undisputed among commentators that Article 28 CISG applies to arbitrations as well as cases litigated before state courts.[27] However, an arbitral tribunal does not have its own law. It has been suggested that the matter should be resolved by the *lex arbitri*.[28]

There is an ongoing debate about whether Article 28 CISG applies to a claim for specific performance under Article 62 CISG, which refers to the claim for the

---

[21] *Jura BV v Willemen Infra NV* [2020] Gerechthof 's-Hertogenbosch (Court of Appeal's-Hertogenbosch) 200.241.641_01, CISG-online 5331.

[22] *Albrecht & Dill Trading GmbH v ERST Finance AS et al.* [2023] Tallinna Ringkonnakohus (Court of Appeal Tallinn) 2-21-10111, CISG-online 6841; *Boxmark Leather GmbH & Co KG v Sals Leather Services S.r.l.* [2024] Tribunal de Apelaciones en lo Civil de Segundo Turno (Court of Appeal for the Second Circuit) 171/2024/2-19258/2022, CISG-online 7035; Müller-Chen, 'Article 28 CISG: Judgement for Specific Performance' in Schwenzer and Schroeter (eds) (n 3) para 6; Björklund, 'Article 28' in Kröll, Mistelis, and Perales Viscasillas (eds) (n 3) para 13.

[23] Lobban (n 12).

[24] Müller-Chen, 'Article 28 CISG: Judgement for Specific Performance' in Schwenzer and Schroeter (eds) (n 3) para 1.

[25] See e.g. *Prime electrolytic tinplate case* [2019] ICC International Court of Arbitration ICC Case No. 23605/DDA/TO (Final Award), CISG-online 5966: holding that specific performance under Art 46 CISG in that particular case was not available as a remedy under the contract.

[26] Christoph Brunner and Rouven Bodenheimer, 'Article 28 (Specific Performance and Rules of the Forum)' in Christoph Brunner and Benjamin Gottlieb (eds), *Commentary on the UN Sales Law (CISG)* (Wolters Kluwer 2019) para 1; Björklund, 'Article 28' in Kröll, Mistelis, and Perales Viscasillas (eds) (n 3) para 15.

[27] Müller-Chen, 'Article 28 CISG: Judgement for Specific Performance' in Schwenzer and Schroeter (eds) (n 3) para 8; Joseph M Lookofsky, *Understanding the CISG: A Compact Guide to the 1980 United Nations Convention on Contracts for the International Sale of Goods* (Kluwer Law International BV 2017) 112; Harry M Flechtner, *Honnold's Uniform Law for International Sales Under the 1980 United Nations Convention* (5th edn, Wolters Kluwer 2021) 395.

[28] Müller-Chen, 'Article 28 CISG: Judgement for Specific Performance' in Schwenzer and Schroeter (eds) (n 3) para 9.

purchase price. Some believe that Article 28 CISG should be applicable to both subsequent provisions that enable claims for specific performance, relying on the drafting history and the systematic position of Article 28 CISG, which is included in the general provisions of the Convention. In our opinion, the issue may be of less significance as most domestic legal systems, including those from the common law tradition, allow a claim for specific performance in the form of payment of the purchase price.[29]

In some cases, limiting the seller's claim for the purchase price may be necessary as per Article 62 CISG.[30] This limit is probably based on the underlying duty to mitigate damages under Article 77 CISG (see Chapter 15), rather than only under domestic law of the forum.[31] Such a limit is applicable mainly in contracts for goods that require manufacturing. For instance, if a buyer orders a machine that takes three years to produce and cancels the order shortly after the contract is concluded, the seller might not have even started production. In such a scenario, technically, the seller can continue with the production, compel the buyer to receive the machine, and pay the purchase price. However, holding the seller's claim for specific performance would seem unfair, despite the buyer's breach. As a result, the seller cannot insist on specific performance by the buyer but can only claim damages, albeit with different justifications.[32]

When it comes to scenarios of delivery of non-conforming goods, the claim is one for cure, either by repair or by substitute goods. It is worth noting that a claim for cure under the CISG is not considered to be part of the remedy of specific performance under Article 28 CISG. As stated by the CISG Advisory Council, the general remedy of requiring specific performance under Article 46(1) CISG is subject to Article 28 CISG.[33] Article 46(2) and 46(3) CISG are *leges speciales*, 'qualifying the general provision of Article 28 CISG'.[34] Furthermore, applying Article 28 CISG to Article 46(2) and 46(3) CISG disregards the interplay between these provisions and the seller's right to cure under Article 48 CISG, which is not constrained by Article 28 CISG.[35] This could result in some sellers being privileged by a buyer

---

[29] Björklund, 'Article 28' in Kröll, Mistelis, and Perales Viscasillas (eds) (n 3) para 10; Bridge (n 3) para 12.48.

[30] For more on the limitation of the seller's claim, see Schwenzer and Muñoz (n 1) para 43.31.

[31] Florian Mohs, 'Article 62 CISG: Seller's Right to Require Performance' in Schwenzer and Schroeter (eds) (n 3) para 16.

[32] Garry F Bell, 'Article 62' in Kröll, Mistelis, and Perales Viscasillas (eds) (n 3) para 8.

[33] CISG Advisory Council, 'CISG-AC Opinion No. 21, Delivery of Substitute Goods and Repair under the CISG, Rapporteurs: Professor (Em.) Dr. Ingeborg Schwenzer, LL.M., University of Basel, Switzerland, and Dr. Ilka H. Beimel, Germany, 3 and 4 February 2020' (2020) Black Letter Rule 1, comments 3.1–3.2.

[34] See *X-ray tubes case* [2015] VIII Zivilsenat (8th panel for civil matters), Bundesgerichtshof (German Supreme Court) VIII ZR 352/13, CISG-online 2596; and *Punching line case* [2023] Bezirksgericht Willisau (Court of First Instance Willisau) 1A4 18 9, CISG-online 7179.

[35] *Dominion Denmark A/S v Polytex Composite s.r.o.* [2023] Sø- og Handelsretten (Maritime and Commercial Court) BS-48358/2019-SHR, CISG-online 6331.

who has no rights under Article 46(2) and 46(3) CISG, disrupting the balance of interests established by Article 46(2) and 46(3) and Article 48 CISG.[36]

Even though Article 46(2)(3) CISG seems to limit the right to require delivery of substitute goods or repair to cases of non-conformity under Article 35 CISG, these remedies also apply to third-party rights or claims (Article 41 CISG) and third-party rights or claims based on industrial or intellectual property (Article 42 CISG) (see section III below).

Opportunely, the CISG did not adopt traditional civil law distinctions of generic versus specific goods and *aliud* versus *peius*, defects of title or legal encumbrances. Rather, the drafters of the Convention have established the claim for specific performance and cure in all its forms in Article 46 CISG.[37] Consequently, the buyer may claim repair of the goods as provided for in Article 46(3) CISG, unless it is unreasonable.[38] The CISG Advisory Council has recently provided a list of non-exclusive factors that may be considered in determining whether repair by the seller is unreasonable.[39] The specificities of the claim for repair are addressed in the next section. One important restriction to that right is that repair must be requested either with the notification of the non-conformity under Article 39(1) CISG or within a reasonable time thereafter on a case-by-case basis.[40]

The buyer is also generally entitled to claim replacement of the non-conforming goods as provided for in Article 46(2) CISG. However, substituting the goods is always costly as new goods must be delivered, and the goods originally delivered typically have to be taken back by the seller. In international contracts, this often requires transportation over long distances. To prevent economically unfavourable developments in this regard, the buyer may require the replacement of the non-conforming goods only if the non-conformity amounts to a fundamental breach of contract as defined in Article 25 CISG.[41] Under Article 46(2) CISG, a fundamental breach of contract can only be found if the non-conforming goods cannot be used as intended and if it is reasonable for the buyer to refuse repair. In addition, the buyer's right to require delivery of substitute goods is excluded if it

---

[36] CISG Advisory Council, 'CISG-AC Opinion No. 21' (n 33) Black Letter Rule 1, comments 3.1–3.2; *Hungarian injection moulding tools case* [2014] VIII Zivilsenat (8th panel for civil matters) Bundesgerichtshof (German Supreme Court) VIII ZR 394/12, CISG-online 2545.

[37] *Lamborghini Countach 112 case* [2021] Handelsgericht des Kantons Aargau (Commercial Court Canton Aargau) HSU.2021.4, CISG-online 5824.

[38] Markus Müller-Chen, 'Article 46 CISG: Buyer's Right to Require Performance, Delivery of Substitute Goods or Repair' in Schwenzer and Schroeter (eds) (n 3) para 39; Peter Huber, 'Article 46' in Kröll, Mistelis, and Perales Viscasillas (eds) (n 3) para 46.

[39] CISG Advisory Council, 'CISG-AC Opinion No. 21' (n 33) Black Letter Rule 6.

[40] *AWB v General Company for Silos and Storage* [2020] Court of Cassation (Egyptian Supreme Court) 2490 of Judicial Year 81, CISG-online 5708.

[41] Bridge (n 3) para 12.08; Müller-Chen, 'Article 46 CISG: Buyer's Right to Require Performance, Delivery of Substitute Goods or Repair' in Schwenzer and Schroeter (eds) (n 3) para 23; Christoph Brunner, Diana Akikol, and Lucien Bürki, 'Article 46 (Buyer's Right to Compel Performance)' in Brunner and Gottlieb (eds) (n 26), para 21.

is disproportionate having regard to all the circumstances.[42] The specifics of the claim for substitute goods are addressed in the next section. Again, the request for replacement must be placed with the seller either upon notification of the non-conformity or within a reasonable time thereafter.

Unlike the civil law tradition, the buyer is not required to first resort to the claims established in Article 46 CISG, which are for delivery, repair, or replacement. Instead, the buyer may immediately resort to damages, avoid the contract in case of fundamental breach, or reduce the purchase price.[43]

2. The PICC

The PICC also aim to achieve greater flexibility in the availability of the claim for specific performance. Similar to the CISG, the starting point is that both parties can request specific performance of monetary and non-monetary obligations (Articles 7.2.1 and 7.2.2 PICC).

Regarding monetary obligations, the PICC briefly state that a party may require payment of a sum owed (Article 7.2.1 PICC).[44] The restrictions to that claim are the general restrictions to the claim for specific performance, namely hardship and *force majeure* or duty to mitigate damages, which might play a role in these cases.

Regarding non-monetary obligations, the claim for specific performance is generally available, but it is subject to certain restrictions.[45] However, instead of offering an escape route such as Article 28 CISG, the PICC establish the relevant restrictions to the claim for specific performance of non-monetary obligations directly within the provisions establishing the claim for specific performance (Article 7.2.2 PICC). The key limitation—which aligns the PICC more closely with the common law tradition—is that specific performance is denied when the obligee could reasonably have obtained performance from another source (Article 7.2.2(c) PICC).[46] Other restrictions include impossibility and hardship (Article 7.2.2(a) (b) PICC).[47] Additionally, specific performance is only available if the performance sought is not of a personal nature (Article 7.2.2(d) PICC), which is seldom an issue in commercial contracts.[48] This is important to note from a common law

---

[42] *Lori s.r.l. v Parandian GmbH* [1994] Oberlandesgericht Frankfurt am Main (Court of Appeal Frankfurt am Main) 5 U 15/93, CISG-online 123.

[43] Müller-Chen, 'Article 46 CISG: Buyer's Right to Require Performance, Delivery of Substitute Goods or Repair' in Schwenzer and Schroeter (eds) (n 3) para 1.

[44] Harriet Schelhaas, 'Article 7.2.1' in Stefan Vogenauer (ed), *Commentary on the UNIDROIT Principles of International Commercial Contracts (PICC)* (2nd edn, Oxford University Press 2015) para 1.

[45] Harriet Schelhaas, 'Article 7.2.2' in Vogenauer (ed) (n 44) paras 6–7; Ingeborg Schwenzer, 'Specific Performance and Damages According to the 1994 UNIDROIT Principles of International Commercial Contracts' (1998) 1 *European Journal of Reforms* 289.

[46] Schelhaas, 'Article 7.2.2' in Vogenauer (ed) (n 44) para 34 ff.

[47] Ibid para 18 ff.

[48] Ibid para 42 ff.

perspective, in particular when a specific performance consists of requesting performance of the original obligation or a second performance, like the delivery of replacement services, works, or goods.[49] Finally, specific performance can only be requested within a reasonable period of time after the obligee becomes aware of the non-performance (Article 7.2.2(e) PICC).

The approach adopted by the PICC aims to balance the different approaches taken by traditional common law and civil law jurisdictions.[50] In comparison to civil law legal systems, the claim for specific performance is granted with more flexibility and greater protection against abuse. However, the obligee is granted more protection for its expectation of performance under the contract than in common law legal systems.

III. Replacement and Repair in Particular

Article 46(1) CISG sets out the buyer's general right to require specific performance of the seller's obligations. When the goods do not conform to the contract, Article 46(2) and 46(3) CISG provide more specific remedies: the buyer may request the seller to repair the goods or, if the non-conformity amounts to a fundamental breach under Article 25 CISG, to deliver substitute goods.[51] The buyer's request must be made within a reasonable time after giving notice of the lack of conformity or simultaneously with such notice (Article 39 CISG). It is debated, however, whether the remedies in Article 46(2) and 46(3) CISG constitute specific forms of performance under Article 46(1), or whether they are distinct remedies tailored to cases of non-conformity.

1. Replacement

As stated before, the buyer is entitled to request the delivery of substitute goods if the non-conformity of the goods amounts to a fundamental breach. Parties can agree on what is fundamental or essential to the contract. Absent an agreement, a breach is fundamental under Article 25 CISG if it substantially deprives the buyer of what they expect from the contract.[52] The CISG Advisory Council has explained that under Article 46(2) CISG, a fundamental breach of contract can only be found

---

[49] Olivier Moréteau, 'Remedies for Breach of Contract: A Theoretical and Practical Approach to Specific Performance in International Commercial Law' [2017] *International Business Law Journal* 639.
[50] Ibid.
[51] Müller-Chen, 'Article 46 CISG: Buyer's Right to Require Performance, Delivery of Substitute Goods or Repair' in Schwenzer and Schroeter (eds) (n 3) para 23; Huber, 'Article 46' in Kröll, Mistelis, and Perales Viscasillas (eds) (n 3) para 31.
[52] *Protective masks case VII* [2025] Oberlandesgericht Köln (Court of Appeal Cologne) 8 U 38/23, CISG-online 7282.

if the non-conforming goods cannot be used as intended and if it is reasonable for the buyer to refuse repair.[53] A buyer's intended use is decisive. If the intended use is unclear, the purpose of the sale matters. Resale value matters if the buyer is in the resale business. Balancing the interests of the parties is necessary in determining if a fundamental breach has occurred. The fundamental breach requirement is consistent with the purpose of the CISG, which aims to prevent costly returns of goods and restricts the buyer's right to end the contract.

In non-conformity cases where goods can be repaired, the buyer can either require repair or claim damages and a purchase price reduction. Repair may make a breach non-fundamental, but in exceptional circumstances, the breach is fundamental if the buyer reasonably refuses repair.[54] For instance, if timely delivery of conforming goods is critical, the buyer may refuse repair.[55] If time is of the essence, the buyer may choose another remedy instead of requesting substitute goods under Article 46(2) CISG.[56]

If the goods are usable by the buyer, it generally means that there is no serious breach of the contract. In such a case, the buyer is entitled to other remedies, including repair (Article 46(3) CISG), claim for damages (Article 74 CISG), or reduction of the purchase price (Article 50 CISG). However, even if repair of the goods is not possible, but the buyer can still use them, it does not necessarily indicate a fundamental breach of the contract.[57]

In Germanic legal systems, delivery of substitute goods is only possible in cases of defects in quality and where goods of a different kind have been delivered, usually with generic goods.[58] However, no differentiation between generic and identified goods should be made under the CISG;[59] the parties' interests and the substitutability of the goods should guide the application of Article 46(2) CISG. The differentiation between generic and identified goods is not mentioned in the

---

[53] *Capsule filling machine case* [2019] İstanbul 9 Asliye Ticaret Mahkemesi (9th Commercial Court Istanbul) 2014/402/2019/566, CISG-online 5144; CISG Advisory Council, 'CISG-AC Opinion No. 21' (n 33) Black Letter Rule 3; Müller-Chen, 'Article 46 CISG: Buyer's Right to Require Performance, Delivery of Substitute Goods or Repair' in Schwenzer and Schroeter (eds) (n 3) para 24; Brunner, Akikol, and Bürki, 'Article 46 (Buyer's Right to Compel Performance)' in Brunner and Gottlieb (eds) (n 26) para 21.

[54] Ulrich Schroeter, 'Article 25 CISG: Fundamental Breach of Contract' in Schwenzer and Schroeter (eds) (n 3) para 44.

[55] Ibid para 33; Müller-Chen 'Article 46 CISG: Buyer's Right to Require Performance, Delivery of Substitute Goods or Repair' in Schwenzer and Schroeter (eds) (n 3) para 41; Brunner, Akikol, and Bürki, 'Article 46 (Buyer's Right to Compel Performance)' in Brunner and Gottlieb (eds) (n 26) para 26.

[56] Ingeborg Schwenzer and Beimel Ilka, 'Replacement and Repair of Non-Conforming Goods under the CISG' (2017) 17 *Internationales Handelsrecht* 185.

[57] Schroeter, 'Article 25 CISG: Fundamental Breach of Contract' in Schwenzer and Schroeter (eds) (n 3) para 207; Andrea A Björklund, 'Article 25' in Kröll, Mistelis, and Perales Viscasillas (eds) (n 3) para 37; Christoph Brunner and Benjamin Leisinger, 'Article 25 (Definition of "Fundamental Breach")' in Brunner and Gottlieb (eds) (n 26) para 15.

[58] CISG Advisory Council, 'CISG-AC Opinion No. 21' (n 33) comment 3.23.

[59] Müller-Chen, 'Article 46 CISG: Buyer's Right to Require Performance, Delivery of Substitute Goods or Repair' in Schwenzer and Schroeter (eds) (n 3) para 20.

CISG, and the omission was intentional.[60] A practical approach is to rely on an interpretation of the contract and determine the substitutability of the goods, guided by the parties' intentions and interests.

As further discussed in the next section, a buyer requiring delivery of substitute goods is subject to Article 82 CISG.[61]

In addition, the buyer's right to require delivery of substitute goods is also excluded if it is disproportionate in regard to all the circumstances.[62] Article 46(3) CISG requires a reasonable balancing of both parties' interests, but Article 46(2) CISG does not. Proportionality is a principle underlying the CISG, which should also apply to the substitution of goods as a remedy for specific performance. Cases of unreasonable replacement may include unavailability, high costs, or an upgrade of the goods. Examining proportionality in Article 46(2), CISG may consider the seller's position and ability to substitute, costs, the nature of goods, and the parties' interests. The outcome depends on contract interpretation, including whether a cap on damages applies to substitute delivery.

The PICC also contemplate a right to request replacement or substitution of defective performances in Article 7.2.3 PICC. However, this provision only establishes the general restriction that replacement will only be granted 'in appropriate cases'.[63] The more specific limits to this remedy come from the application of Article 7.2.2. PICC to which Article 7.2.3 PICC makes a cross-reference. In this regard, relevant restrictions to the claim of substitute performance include impossibility and hardship (Article 7.2.2(a)(b) PICC), unavailability of substitute performance of obligations of a personal nature (Article 7.2.2(d) PICC), which is seldom an issue in commercial contracts, or where the obligee could have reasonably obtained performance from another source (Article 7.2.2(c) PICC). Finally, substitute performance can only be requested within a reasonable period of time after the obligee becomes aware of the non-performance (Article 7.2.2(e) PICC).[64]

2. Repair

Article 46(3) CISG states that if the goods do not conform to the contract, the buyer may require the seller to repair the lack of conformity. However, this request must be reasonable considering all the circumstances.[65] The buyer must make this

---

[60] CISG Advisory Council, 'CISG-AC Opinion No. 21' (n 33) comment 3.23.

[61] Ibid Black Letter Rule 4.

[62] CISG Advisory Council, 'CISG-AC Opinion No. 21' (n 33) Black Letter Rule 5; Müller-Chen, 'Article 46 CISG: Buyer's Right to Require Performance, Delivery of Substitute Goods or Repair' in Schwenzer and Schroeter (eds) (n 3) para 17.

[63] Harriet Schelhaas, 'Article 7.2.3' in Vogenauer (ed) (n 44) para 4.

[64] Harriet Schelhaas, 'Article 7.2.2' in Vogenauer (ed) (n 44) para 47.

[65] Müller-Chen, 'Article 46 CISG: Buyer's Right to Require Performance, Delivery of Substitute Goods or Repair' in Schwenzer and Schroeter (eds) (n 3) para 39; Huber, 'Article 46' in Kröll, Mistelis,

request for repair either at the same time as notifying the seller of the issues with the goods (under Article 39 CISG) or within a reasonable period afterwards.[66]

In determining whether a seller's repair is unreasonable, the following factors may be considered: a. whether the buyer is better placed to arrange for repair of the goods; b. whether the seller offers to advance the costs for repair by the buyer or a third party; c. whether repair imposes costs on the seller that are disproportionate to the actual or prospective loss of or benefit to the buyer.[67] Under a. above, repair may not be reasonable if the buyer is in a better position to arrange for the repair itself. This could be the case if the problem can be easily fixed by the buyer or a third party.[68] For example, if the seller is just a retailer and not the manufacturer of the goods, or if the repair is too complex for the seller to fix. In addition, if the cost of repair by the buyer or a third party is less expensive than the cost of repair by the seller, then the buyer may be better placed to repair the goods itself. Under b. above, if the seller offers to pay for the repair by the buyer or a third party, this may make the repair by the seller unreasonable. This is because the buyer may have all the necessary funds to repair the goods itself. Letter c. above also considers the cost of repair imposed on the seller and the actual or potential loss or benefit to the buyer. When determining the buyer's loss, the general principles of calculating damages should be considered. Therefore, Article 77 CISG should be applied by analogy when defining reasonableness in the sense of Article 46(3) CISG.[69] If the buyer hires a third party to repair the goods and then claims the cost incurred as damages, it must be determined whether the buyer has properly mitigated its loss. In the end, the reasonableness of repair remains an issue that must be decided on a case-by-case basis. If repair is impossible, it is clearly unreasonable.[70]

The PICC provide a right to seek a repair or other cure for defective perform-ances under Article 7.2.3 PICC.[71] However, this right is subject to a general limi-tation as it can only be granted 'in appropriate cases'. Specific boundaries to this

---

and Perales Viscasillas (eds) (n 3) para 46; Brunner, Akikol, and Bürki, 'Article 46 (Buyer's Right to Compel Performance)' in Brunner and Gottlieb (eds) (n 26) para 30.

[66] *Pelliculest S.a.r.l. et al. v Morton International GmbH et al.* [2000] Cour d'appel de Colmar (Court of Appeal Colmar) 200002525, CISG-online 578: where the court considered a period of two years between the notification of defects and the request for repair to be reasonable due to meantime negoti-ations; *Realturf Systems, SL v Eurograss, Inc* [2019] Circuit Court of the 11th Judicial Circuit (Miami-Dade County) of the State of Florida 2014-CA-018348, CISG-online 6730: holding that the buyer lost its right to rely on a lack on conformity because it did not give notice to the seller specifying the nature of the non-conformity.

[67] CISG Advisory Council, 'CISG-AC Opinion No. 21' (n 33) Black Letter Rule 6.

[68] Müller-Chen, 'Article 46 CISG: Buyer's Right to Require Performance, Delivery of Substitute Goods or Repair' in Schwenzer and Schroeter (eds) (n 3) para 40; Huber, 'Article 46' in Kröll, Mistelis, and Perales Viscasillas (eds) (n 3) para 48; Brunner, Akikol, and Bürki, 'Article 46 (Buyer's Right to Compel Performance)' in Brunner and Gottlieb (eds) (n 26) para 30 .

[69] Müller-Chen, 'Article 46 CISG: Buyer's Right to Require Performance, Delivery of Substitute Goods or Repair' in Schwenzer and Schroeter (eds) (n 3) para 46.

[70] Huber, 'Article 46' in Kröll, Mistelis, and Perales Viscasillas (eds) (n 3) para 45.

[71] Harriet Schelhaas, 'Article 7.2.3' in Vogenauer (ed) (n 44) para 1.

remedy come from Article 7.2.2. PICC, which is cross-referenced in Article 7.2.3 PICC. The limitations to claiming a repair or other cure for performance include impossibility and hardship (Article 7.2.2(a)(b) PICC), unavailability of a repair or other cure for obligations of a personal nature (Article 7.2.2(d) PICC), which is rarely an issue in commercial contracts, or where the obligee could have reasonably obtained a repair or other cure from another source (Article 7.2.2(c) PICC). Finally, the obligee can request a repair or other remedy of performance only within a reasonable period after becoming aware of the non-performance (Article 7.2.2(e) PICC).

3. Consequences

Several important questions arise when a buyer requests a replacement delivery or repair for non-conforming goods. These include the costs associated with the request, the need for retrofitting, specific details regarding restitution of the goods, like what happens with its benefits or betterment, the application of Articles 38, 39, and 43 CISG on examination and notice of non-conformity, the location where substitute delivery and repair will take place, and the right to withhold performance.

On the first question, if the goods have been combined with other goods or installed, the costs of retrofitting may be recovered as damages by the buyer but in general are *not* borne by the seller as part of the remedy of delivery of substitute goods or repair.[72] However, if in a mixed contract, the seller has also assumed the obligation of combining or installing the goods, the costs of retrofitting are borne by the seller as part of the remedy of delivery of substitute goods or repair.[73] The terms retrofitting and installation refer to any necessary actions to put goods in place so they are ready to be used.[74] The definition of retrofitting and installation in this context is broad. According to the principle of strict liability under the CISG, the seller of the goods is responsible for any non-conformity, even if the non-conformity is due to its supplier or the manufacturer of the goods. The claim for damages covering the costs of retrofitting and installation may be included under the full compensation principle of Articles 74 CISG *et seq*. To make this claim for damages, it must be foreseeable that the costs for retrofitting and installation would be a possible consequence of the breach.[75] The critical question is what a

---

[72] CISG Advisory Council, 'CISG-AC Opinion No. 21' (n 33) Black Letter Rule 7.
[73] Ibid.
[74] Ibid comment 3.7.
[75] Ingeborg Schwenzer, 'Article 74 CISG: Calculation of Damages in General' in Schwenzer and Schroeter (eds) (n 3) para 47; Milena Djordjević, 'Article 74' in Kröll, Mistelis, and Perales Viscasillas (eds) (n 3) para 26; Christoph Brunner, Nils Schmidt-Ahrendts, and Mark Czarnecki, 'Article 74 (General Rule for Measuring Damages)' in Brunner and Gottlieb (eds) (n 26).

reasonable person in the shoes of the promisor, who is aware of the circumstances at the time of the contract's conclusion, ought to have foreseen.[76] In other words, the seller must have foreseen the need for retrofitting and installation. For instance, in a sale of pipes that can be used in various ways, it is doubtful whether the seller foresaw or should have foreseen that the pipes would be used on a construction site underwater. In such a case, without providing additional information, the seller is unlikely to be held responsible for the costs required to reach the pipes underwater.

With regard to the restitution question in cases of delivery of substitute goods or repair of the goods by delivery of substitute parts, the buyer must make restitution to the seller of the goods or parts first delivered pursuant to Article 82(1) CISG. Article 82 CISG is based on the idea that restitution is the 'natural consequence' of the delivery of substitute goods.[77] The wording does not require restitution of the goods in the same condition. Only if the change in the condition of the goods is of such importance that it would no longer be proper to require the seller to take the goods back as the equivalent of what it had delivered to the buyer, the buyer fails to fulfil its obligation. When goods perish between the buyer's request for replacement and the delivery of substitute goods, the buyer's claim for substitute goods is not excluded, but the buyer may be liable for damages.

The costs of restitution must be borne by the seller.[78] In other words, the delivery of substitute goods or repair of goods by delivery of substitute parts winds up the initial delivery, which is not addressed by Article 46 CISG but by Articles 81 to 84 CISG. The principles of Section V CISG (see Chapter 16) apply to these goods or parts substituted under Article 46 CISG.

On the other hand, the buyer is *not* bound to make restitution of benefits derived from the substituted non-conforming goods or parts first delivered. Neither is the buyer is bound to account for any betterment caused by the delivery of substitute goods or repair of the goods by delivery of substitute parts.[79] In other words, benefits, in other words advantages derived from substituted non-conforming goods or parts first delivered, are excluded from restitution. The buyer's right to benefit from the goods remains justified even when requesting delivery of substitute goods. Therefore, the seller's claims for restitution of benefits must be rejected in cases of delivery of substitute goods or parts. The buyer is not required to account for any betterment caused by the delivery of substitute goods or repair of the goods by delivery of substitute parts. Betterment refers to all sorts of improvements made to the delivered goods and other goods or values. In light of the performance principle and the seller's general warranty for the conformity of the goods

---

[76] *Vaccum cleaners case* [1998] Oberlandesgericht Celle (Court of Appeal Celle) 3 U 246/97, CISG-online 506.

[77] Christiana Fountoulakis, 'Article 82 CISG: Buyer's Loss of Rights Where Restitution of Goods Is Impossible' in Schwenzer and Schroeter (eds) (n 3) para 2.

[78] CISG Advisory Council, 'CISG-AC Opinion No. 21' (n 33) Black Letter Rule 8.

[79] Ibid Black Letter Rule 9.

under the CISG, it is most convincing to discharge the buyer from any accounting of betterments.

Finally, regarding the buyer's examination and notice obligations in Articles 38, 39, and 43 CISG, the buyer has to comply with such obligations after substitution or repair. And, in case of non-conformity of the goods, the two-year cut-off period (Article 39(2) CISG) starts to run with the actual handing over of the substitute goods or repair.[80] If the goods are still not in conformity after the first substitution, the buyer may use Articles 45 CISG *et seq.* again.[81] The additional examination costs can be claimed as damages. Furthermore, the two-year cut-off period under Article 39(2) CISG applies again. It generally starts to run with the actual handing over of the goods, that is, the physical handing over to the buyer. The purpose of Article 39(2) CISG is to balance the interests of both parties and protect buyers in cases where the defects are not immediately apparent, as well as to protect sellers against claims which arise long after the goods have been delivered. In cases of Article 46(2) and 46(3) CISG, these interests need to be protected regarding substituted or repaired goods. The physical handing over occurs again in these cases.[82]

If the substituted goods come from the same source as the goods first delivered, it is questionable whether the seller is aware of any new lack of conformity or could not have been unaware of it, according to Article 40 CISG. For example, in the case of non-conforming stones due to cracks in the stones that hinder processing, this question arises if the delivery of substituted stones comes from the same rock as the stones first delivered. However, Article 40 CISG should be restricted to 'special circumstances', as it will usually require more than the mere fact of the goods originating from the same source.

IV. Judicial Penalty (PICC)

All legal systems empower courts to impose penalties on parties who fail to comply with court orders. In both common law and civil law jurisdictions, however, such fines are generally payable to the state. Uniquely, French law provides that the penalty, called *astreinte*,[83] is payable to the obligee.[84]

The PICC adapted a version of the French model of *astreinte* in Article 7.2.4 PICC, despite the fact that the concept of *astreinte* cannot be considered a general principle of law.[85] The PICC expressly allow a court or an arbitral tribunal to

---

[80] Ibid Black Letter Rule 10.

[81] *Ingredients for ice cream production case* [2013] Oberlandesgericht Koblenz (Court of Appeal Koblenz) 2 U 50/12, CISG-online 2469; 'Article 46 CISG: Buyer's Right to Require Performance, Delivery of Substitute Goods or Repair' in Schwenzer and Schroeter (eds) (n 3) para 37.

[82] Schwenzer and Ilka (n 56) 185.

[83] *Code des procédures civiles d'exécution* art L131-1.

[84] Ibid.

[85] Schwenzer and Muñoz (n 1) 43.67.

order a breaching party to pay a penalty if they do not comply with the order to perform.[86] Like the French model, the aggrieved party is the beneficiary of the payment, and claims for damages are not excluded (Article 7.2.4 PICC).

The judicial penalty established by the PICC is only of limited practical relevance and is expected to be imposed only in exceptional circumstances. However, the general language in which Article 7.2.4 PICC is written has been criticized for giving too much discretion, as it provides little guidance on when such a judicial penalty is appropriate, how to calculate it, or what the maximum amount should be. The Official Commentary on Article 7.2.4 PICC states that a judicial penalty may be imposed in the form of a lump sum payment or of a payment by instalments.[87] The procedure relating to the imposition of a judicial penalty is governed by the *lex fori*.

Although, according to Article 1.11 PICC, 'court' includes an arbitral tribunal, whether arbitrators might also be allowed to impose a penalty is doubtful. According to Article 7.2.4 PICC Official Commentary, most legal systems do not grant arbitrators the power to impose penalties.[88] However, some modern legislation and recent court practice have recognized this power. As the execution of a penalty imposed by arbitrators can only be carried out by a court or with their assistance, there is adequate supervision to prevent any potential abuse of power by the arbitrators.

---

[86]   Harriet Schelhaas, 'Article 7.2.4' in Vogenauer (ed) (n 44) para 7.

[87]   International Institute for the Unification of Private Law (ed), *UNIDROIT Principles of International Commercial Contracts* (UNIDROIT International Institute for the Unification of Private Law 2017) 250, art 7.2.4, off cmt 5.

[88]   Ibid 250, art 7.2.4, off cmt 6.

14

Remedies III—Avoidance: Price Reduction

I. General: Terminology, Restricting Avoidance

Avoidance is a serious remedy that goes against the principle of *pacta sunt servanda*, which means that agreements must be kept. It interferes with the contractual relationship between parties, which can be complicated to unwind, making it a last-resort remedy.[1] This is especially true for international contracts governed by the CISG and the PICC, where the requirements for avoidance are high.[2] However, before we explore the requirements of this remedy under the CISG and the PICC, we need to clarify some conceptual and terminology issues.

---

[1] Peter Huber, 'Article 7.3.1' in Stefan Vogenauer (ed), *Commentary on the UNIDROIT Principles of International Commercial Contracts (PICC)* (2nd edn, 2015) para 6; Peter Huber, 'Comparative Sales Law' in Mathias Reimann and Reinhard Zimmermann (eds), Peter Huber, *The Oxford Handbook of Comparative Law* (Oxford University Press 2019) 961.

[2] Peter Huber, 'Introduction to Section 7.3 of the PICC' in Vogenauer (ed) (n 1) para 1.

1. Concept and terminology

This chapter presents the concept of contract avoidance as a reaction to a disturbance in the performance of the contract. In dealing with this concept of avoidance, this work follows the CISG. Hence, avoidance, as understood here, covers termination under the PICC.

The concept of avoidance, which is the basis of this chapter, needs to be differentiated from other related concepts. First, the nature of avoidance should not be confused with the ideas of 'withdrawal' or 'revocation' mentioned in Chapter 6 on contract formation.[3] The latter concepts refer to determining the time when a declaration has taken effect and whether a contract has been established. Second, it is important to note that 'avoidance' and 'rescission' and similar concepts are not the same thing. 'Rescission', 'invalidity', 'voidability', and similar concepts regularly refer to the ability under domestic laws to set aside a contract due to mistakes, fraud, duress, or other cases of illegality or invalidity. On the other hand, 'termination' or 'rescission' under domestic laws is often used in the same way as 'avoidance' in this chapter.

Third, ambiguities also may arise regarding the terminology used, particularly at the international level. While the CISG uses 'avoidance', as explained above, the PICC use this term for situations involving mistake, fraud, duress, and similar concepts.[4] The term used by PICC to describe the remedy for breach of contract is 'termination'.[5] Therefore, for the purpose of this chapter, 'termination' as used by the PICC is referred to here as 'avoidance', and 'rescission' is used here to refer to what is termed 'avoidance' in the PICC.

Finally, contracts can end for various reasons under domestic contract law, aside from avoidance due to breach of contract. Some of these reasons overlap with the grounds for avoidance under the CISG. Certain cases fall under domestic categories like validity, which is the case with the initial impossibility of performance in civil law systems. In some legal systems, subsequent impossibility automatically avoids the contract. In common law jurisdictions, sales contracts that cannot be performed due to goods that have already perished at the time of contracting are considered void.[6] Frustration can also bring a contract to an end after its conclusion.[7] Moreover, contracts may be dissolved in situations of hardship in many jurisdictions. These situations, called by different terminology in domestic laws, are covered by the concept of avoidance in the CISG and this chapter. In addition,

---

[3] See Chapter 6.
[4] PICC 2016, arts 3.2.1–3.2.17.
[5] PICC 2016, arts 7.3.1–7.3.7.
[6]   England Sale of Goods Act 1979, s 6; Hong Kong Sale of Goods Ordinance 1924, s 8; New Zealand Sale of Goods Act 1908, s 8; Scotland Sale of Goods Act 1979, s 6; Singapore Sale of Goods Act 1979, s 6.
[7] Ingeborg Schwenzer and Edgardo Muñoz, *Global Sales and Contract Law* (2nd edn, Oxford University Press 2022) para 47.33.

parties can agree on the termination of the contract mutually. This shared agreement to terminate can arise from various circumstances, such as a change in circumstances, the realization that the contract is no longer beneficial to either party or simply by common consent.

2. Restricting avoidance

The CISG and the PICC follow a modern approach that establishes a central requirement for avoidance. This requirement is independent of the reason why the contract's performance created problems. In simpler words, if there is a problem with the contract's performance, it is considered non-performance, which covers issues like late performance, defective performance, for instance, the delivery of non-conforming goods (including defects in title, IP rights and so on) or services, and impossibility.[8] However, the only thing that needs to be determined is whether non-performance justifies the avoidance of the contract. This approach has given rise to two sub-approaches. One sub-approach, which is more prominent, focuses on the seriousness of the breach, that is, the occurrence of a fundamental breach. The second sub-approach focuses on the concept of fixing an additional period of time for (proper) performance (*Nachfrist*). However, this second approach only works for lack of payment or non-delivery of the goods, since *Nachfrist* cannot be used to raise a breach based on defective performance, like non-conformity of the goods, to a fundamental breach.

The next sections will review these sub-approaches of the central approach to avoidance in the CISG and the PICC.

II. Fundamental Breach

Parties can only terminate a contract if the counterparty's breach is fundamental, as per Articles 49(1)(a),[9] 64(1)(a) CISG,[10] and Article 7.3.1(1) PICC.[11] The concept of fundamental breach is designed to limit the use of extreme measures in cases where the breach is egregious. Unwinding a contract can be complicated and expensive, especially in international transactions that involve long distances and where goods that have been delivered must be transported back usually through

---

[8] Ingeborg Schwenzer, 'Avoidance of the Contract in Case of Non-Conforming Goods (Article 49(1)(a) CISG)' (2005) 25 *Journal of Law and Commerce* 437.

[9] *Frese Biogas GmbH & Co KG v Circular Values BV et al.* [2024] Rechtbank Zeeland-West-Brabant (District Court Zeeland West-Brabant) C/02/367340/HA ZA 20-1, CISG-online 7014.

[10] *Brands International Corporation v Reach Companies, LLC* [2023] US District Court for the District of Minnesota 0:2021cv01026, CISG-online 6279.

[11] *Gente Oil Ecuador Pte Ltd v Republic of Ecuador* [2022] Permanent Court of Arbitration Case No. 2018-12.

countries' borders and customs. Accordingly, the contract should not be avoided for an unqualified or minor breach.

1. Notion

The term 'fundamental breach' is quite broad and, as a result, it can be defined in several ways. Parties themselves are the primary source for a definition. In any given contract, the parties can stipulate which breaches they consider fundamental.[12] Under the CISG, there are no objections to defining 'fundamental breach' in their contract, including in standard clauses, as their validity is subject to applicable domestic law.[13] For instance, making the time of the essence is a prime example of a contractual stipulation of what is fundamental.[14] The negotiation process may also be important, especially if one party has repeatedly drawn attention to the importance of a particular clause.[15] In addition, trade usages and practices may indicate that a breach is fundamental. For instance, in documentary sales, the presentation of clean documents is essential, and a breach of such a requirement would typically be considered fundamental.[16]

Without any definitions provided by the parties, it is necessary to rely on the definitions provided by the PICC or the CISG. Article 25 CISG states that a breach of contract is fundamental 'if it results in such detriment to the other party as substantially to deprive him of what he is entitled to expect under the contract, unless the party in breach did not foresee and a reasonable person of the same kind in the same circumstances would not have foreseen such a result'. These requirements are also one of the criteria established by PICC Article 7.3.1(2) to determine whether a failure to perform is a fundamental breach.[17]

The PICC provide additional criteria to determine whether the breach is fundamental. They provide that where the breaching party has acted intentionally or

---

[12] Ulrich Schroeter, 'Article 25 CISG: Fundamental Breach of Contract' in Ingeborg Schwenzer and Ulrich G Schroeter (eds), *Schlechtriem & Schwenzer Commentary on the UN Convention on the International Sale of Goods (CISG)* (5th edn, Oxford University Press 2022) para 21 ff; Andrea A Björklund, 'Article 25' in Stefan M Kröll, Loukas A Mistelis, and Pilar Perales Viscasillas (eds), *UN Convention on Contracts for the International Sale of Goods (CISG): A Commentary* (2nd edn, CH Beck 2018) para 17.

[13] Schroeter, 'Article 25 CISG: Fundamental Breach of Contract' in Schwenzer and Schroeter (eds) (n 12) para 25 ff.

[14] Ibid para 24 ff.

[15] Ibid.

[16] CISG Advisory Council, 'CISG-AC Opinion No. 5, The Buyer's Right to Avoid the Contract in Case of Non-Conforming Goods or Documents, Rapporteur: Professor Dr. Ingeborg Schwenzer, LL.M., Professor of Private Law, University of Basel, 7 May 2005' (2005) comments 4.13 and 4.14; Schroeter, 'Article 25 CISG: Fundamental Breach of Contract' in Schwenzer and Schroeter (eds) (n 12) para 25 ff.

[17] PICC 2016, art 7.3.1(2).

recklessly, this should be relevant (Article PICC 7.3.1(2)(c)). However, intention or recklessness does not automatically render the breach fundamental. The CISG rightly does not refer to such fault-based behaviour.

2. Foreseeability

The gravity of the breach is, however, not the only requirement for the avoidance. The substantial detriment caused by the breach must have been foreseeable for the breaching party. A promisee can only rely on something as a 'substantial' expectation 'under the contract' (Article 25 CISG) if their contracting partner knew, or a reasonable person in the same circumstances would have known, that such a particular expectation would arise by entering into the contract. Anything unknown and unforeseeable cannot be rightfully expected and, therefore, cannot cause a breach of the contract to be 'fundamental'.

The PICC consider not only the effects of the breach on the aggrieved party but also the effects that the avoidance of the contract would have on the breaching party. The PICC state that in determining whether a breach is fundamental, it must also be considered whether the breaching party would suffer disproportionate losses in case the avoidance of the contract is allowed (Article 7.3.1 PICC).

3. Breach due to non-performance of an obligation

As stated earlier, for the CISG and the PICC it does not matter what breach is committed, the only question is whether the breach amounts to a fundamental breach of contract. Concerning non-performance in general, this means that non-delivery by the seller and non-payment and the failure to take delivery by the buyer must also meet this requirement.

While at first glance, it would seem appealing to say that delivery and payment are the defining obligations of a sales contract and that, therefore, any failure of these obligations amounts to a fundamental breach, this is not the position taken by legal systems operating with the concept of fundamental breach, like the CISG and the PICC. It is only when the delay in delivery or the delayed payment substantially deprives the aggrieved party of what it was entitled to expect under the contract that avoidance is justified. The CISG indicates that a delay in delivery or payment does not necessarily amount to a fundamental breach triggering the right to avoid the contract under Articles 49(1)(a) and 64(1)(b) CISG. Rather, Articles 49(1)(b) and 64(1)(b) CISG contemplate that the individual situation of the delay in and of itself does not amount to a fundamental breach as both buyer and seller are equipped with the opportunity to fix an additional period of time and to avoid the contract after upon its expiration. The same position is taken by Article 7.3.1(3) PICC.[18]

Situations where the seller is unable to deliver the goods due to an impediment under Article 79 CISG are different and may amount to a fundamental breach, depending on the duration of the impediment.[19] In addition, if the seller sells and delivers the goods to a third party before the delivery date agreed upon with the buyer, it is considered a fundamental breach of contract where the goods are not ready and replaceable in the seller's stock.[20] A definite refusal to perform or a threat to not perform unless a requested modification is accepted also amounts to a fundamental breach.

Delays in performance may not always be considered a fundamental breach of a contract unless timely performance is an essential aspect of the agreement. The concept of fundamental breach sets a high threshold, and determining whether the contract should stand or fall due to timely performance depends on the parties' intent and the language used in the agreement. In the case of the CISG, phrases such as 'at the latest' have been deemed to make time of the essence,[21] but whether the phrase 'as soon as possible' satisfies this test is still a point of contention.[22]

The use of ICC Incoterms® can determine whether time is of the essence or not. Traditionally, the terms CIF and FOB are considered to establish strict time requirements for delivery-related obligations.[23] Under the CISG, a differentiated approach is suggested based on the interplay of the rules on contract interpretation and ICC Incoterms®. The terms CIF and FOB generally indicate that time is of the essence under the rules on contract interpretation in Articles 8 and 9 CISG. However, according to Article 8(1) CISG, the intention of the parties prevails over the general understanding of the ICC Incoterms®. Therefore, if other circumstances indicate that the parties did not intend time to be of the essence, the delay does not amount to a fundamental breach despite the use of the ICC Incoterms®.[24]

If the parties fail to agree on the significance of timely performance, the particular case must be considered. The initial factors to be considered include the

---

[18] See Huber, 'Article 7.3.1' in Vogenauer (ed) (n 1) para 65.

[19] *German goods case* [1999] ICC International Court of Arbitration 9978 (Final Award), CISG-online 708; Schroeter, 'Article 25 CISG: Fundamental Breach of Contract' in Schwenzer and Schroeter (eds) (n 12) para 37.

[20] See *Used printing machines case I* [1995] Oberlandesgericht Celle (Court of Appeal Celle) 20 U 76/94, CISG-online 152; concurring Schroeter, 'Article 25 CISG: Fundamental Breach of Contract' in Schwenzer and Schroeter (eds) (n 12) para 37.

[21] See for the CISG, *Memory modules case* [2001] Oberlandesgericht Hamm (Court of Appeal Hamm) 13 U 102/01, CISG-online 1430.

[22] *Car phones case* [2004] Oberlandesgericht Düsseldorf (Court of Appeal Düsseldorf) I-15 U 88/03, CISG-online 915; cf *Memory modules case* (n 21).

[23] See generally and for the PICC Huber, 'Article 7.3.1' in Vogenauer (ed) (n 1) para 67. For the CISG, *Iron molybdenum case* [1997] Oberlandesgericht Hamburg (Court of Appeal Hamburg) 1 U 167/95, CISG-online 261.

[24] Huber, 'Article 7.3.1' in Vogenauer (ed) (n 1) para 67. For the CISG, *Iron molybdenum case* (n 23).

communication between the parties. For instance, the buyer may have notified the seller about a specific deadline that must be met for the sake of its customers.[25] It may also be appropriate to consider the nature of the goods, particularly if they are seasonal, timely delivery is of the essence and failure to do so can amount to a fundamental breach.[26] If the buyer, as a frequent dealer in the goods, has the possibility of using them despite the delay, time may not be of the essence, and thus, reasonable delay will not amount to a fundamental breach.[27]

When time is not a crucial factor, the delay in performance does not necessarily mean a fundamental breach of contract. However, the party who has suffered from the delay can still exercise the right to avoid the contract by setting an additional period of time for the other party to perform (as specified in Articles 49(1)(b), 64(1)(b), and 47 CISG and Articles 7.3.1(3) and 7.1.5 PICC).[28] If the other party fails to perform within this additional time period, the aggrieved party can declare the contract avoided. In this regard, the *Nachfrist* rule can be applied to convert the breach of untimely performance into a fundamental breach, as will be further reviewed below.

4. Breach due to non-conformity of performance (goods and documents)

a.) Goods

The CISG establishes a high threshold for avoidance to prevent expensive re-transfers of goods worldwide. Therefore, the question is: under what circumstances can the non-conformity of goods amount to a fundamental breach of contract? As a starting point, we must admit that it is impossible to provide a comprehensive list of cases in which the delivery of non-conforming goods amounts to a fundamental breach of contract due to the wide range of goods and contractual agreements encompassed by the CISG, as well as the necessary broadness of Article 25 CISG.

---

[25] See for the CISG, *FCF SA v Adriafil Commerciale S.r.l.* (Egyptian cotton case II) [2000] Bundesgericht/Tribunal fédéral (Swiss Federal Supreme Court) 4C.105/2000, CISG-online 770 25; *Diversitel Communications, Inc v Glacier Bay Inc* [2003] Superior Court of Justice of Ontario 03-CV-23776 SR, CISG-online 1436; Schroeter, 'Article 25 CISG: Fundamental Breach of Contract' in Schwenzer and Schroeter (eds) (n 12) para 39.

[26] See for the CISG, Schroeter, 'Article 25 CISG: Fundamental Breach of Contract' in Schwenzer and Schroeter (eds) para 39; Björklund, 'Article 25' in Kröll, Mistelis, and Perales Viscasillas (eds) (n 12) para 34; *FCF S.A. v Adriafil Commerciale S.r.l.* (Egyptian cotton case II) (n 25); *Italdecor s.a.s. v Yiu's Industries (HK) Limited* [1998] Corte di Appello di Milano (Court of Appeal Milan) 790, CISG-online 348; *Calzaturificio Piceno di Roberto Catinari & Uvaldo Raccosta v Vivace Mode GmbH* [1997] Oberlandesgericht Düsseldorf (Court of Appeal Düsseldorf) 6 U 87/96, CISG-online 385. For the PICC Huber, 'Article 7.3.1' in Vogenauer (ed) (n 1) para 68.

[27] Schroeter, 'Article 25 CISG: Fundamental Breach of Contract' in Schwenzer and Schroeter (eds) (n 12) para 40; Packages for animal food case [1997] Turun hovioikeus (Court of Appeal Turku) S 95/1023, CISG-online 1297.

[28] See CISG arts 49(1)(b), 64(1)(b), 47; PICC 2016, arts 7.3.1(3), 7.1.5.

Nevertheless, the CISG Advisory Council has developed guidelines to resolve individual cases.

First, in assessing fundamental breach, the contract terms should be given the utmost importance as they define the interests that the parties intend to pursue under the transaction regarding the goods' characteristics.[29] For instance, if the contract specifies *exact* measurements or quality requirements for the goods, stating that there is no room for deviation, then any failure to meet those requirements may be considered a fundamental breach.[30]

If there are no specifications in the contract regarding the goods, then the intended use becomes relevant in assessing the possibility of a fundamental breach.[31] If the buyer is unable to use the goods at all, then, as a matter of principle, it is considered that the seller committed a fundamental breach of the contract. However, if the buyer could have used the goods reasonably but differently, that should not be enough to reach the fundamental breach standard. Only in cases where the buyer cannot use the goods at all in the buyer's course of business, the contract can be avoided on fundamental breach grounds.[32]

If the buyer is a reseller, it is considered a fundamental breach of contract by the seller if the buyer is unable to resell the goods. This is particularly applicable in circumstances where the goods are in breach of public health regulations. It likewise extends to other situations in which the goods are rendered entirely unsellable, such as the absence of the requisite European Union CE marking, the affixation of counterfeit trademarks, the failure to comply with mandatory product safety standards—such as flammability or electrical safety requirements—or the use of prohibited materials under environmental or consumer protection laws.[33] In addition, if the goods have lost their reputation to such an extent that they cannot be sold even at low prices, it is also deemed that a fundamental breach of contract took place.[34] However, in all other cases, the buyer is expected to resell the goods at even lower prices. This is different when the buyer risks damaging its reputation.

The right to avoid the contract may be impacted by the possibility of curing non-conformity under the CISG (Articles 48(1) and 49(1)(a) CISG). Article 48(1) CISG states that the seller may cure the non-conformity at its expense, provided it does not cause unreasonable inconvenience to the buyer, subject to Article 49 (see

---

[29] CISG Advisory Council, 'CISG-AC Opinion No. 5 (16) comment 4.2; Schroeter, 'Article 25 CISG: Fundamental Breach of Contract' in Schwenzer and Schroeter (eds) (n 12) para 44.

[30] *Protective masks case IV* [2025] Oberlandesgericht Köln (Court of Appeal Cologne) 8 U 46/23, CISG-online 7261; *Protective masks case VII* [2025] Oberlandesgericht Köln (Court of Appeal Cologne) 8 U 38/23, CISG-online 7282.

[31] CISG Advisory Council, 'CISG-AC Opinion No. 5' (n 16) comment 4.3.

[32] Ibid.

[33] Schroeter, 'Article 25 CISG: Fundamental Breach of Contract' in Schwenzer and Schroeter (eds) (n 12) para 51.

[34] CISG Advisory Council, 'CISG-AC Opinion No. 5' (n 16) comment 4.3.

Chapter 12).[35] The debate revolves around the words 'subject to Article 49'. The question being asked is whether non-conformities that can be cured by the seller or a third party without causing the buyer unreasonable inconvenience can ever amount to a fundamental breach.[36] Those in the minority, support the view that the expressed priority of Article 49 CISG over the seller's right to cure indicates that there may be a fundamental breach of contract that excludes the seller's right to cure.[37] In contrast, the CISG Advisory Council, which adheres to the majority view, considers that if cure is possible, non-conformity of the goods will not meet the high threshold of a fundamental breach of contract.[38]

As long as the non-conformity of the goods does not amount to a fundamental breach, the buyer may not avoid the contract but is restricted to a claim for damages or the remedy of price reduction. The seller may avail itself of the right to cure, if this does not cause unreasonable inconvenience to the buyer. If that is the case, the buyer cannot refuse cure by the seller before resorting to damages. While this procedure may at first glance resemble the *Nachfrist* approach outlined below, the crucial difference is that if the non-conformity does not amount to a fundamental breach of contract, the buyer cannot avoid the contract, even if it has allowed the seller an additional period of time for cure and even if cure has failed.[39]

b.) Documents

An obligation to deliver documents along with the goods can arise either from the sale of goods contract, including from an ICC Incoterms®, from practices established between the parties or usages (Article 9 CISG),[40] a particular default rule in the CISG like Articles 30 and 34 CISG or, in some cases, from the underlying principle of cooperation in the CISG. Whether failure to deliver a particular document or set of documents constitutes a fundamental breach in the sense of Article 25 CISG may also depend on the kind of document concerned but will primarily be determined by the documentary obligation's role within the framework of the particular contract.

---

[35] Markus Müller-Chen, 'Article 48 CISG: Seller's Right to Cure after Date for Delivery' in Schwenzer and Schroeter (eds) (n 12) para 14.

[36] Schroeter, 'Article 25 CISG: Fundamental Breach of Contract' in Schwenzer and Schroeter (eds) (n 12) paras 47–48; Miquel dels Sants and Mirambell Fargas (eds), *The Seller's Right to Cure under Article 48 CISG* (Eleven International Publishing 2018) 186, s 4.2.4.

[37] Müller-Chen, 'Article 48 CISG: Seller's Right to Cure after Date for Delivery' in Schwenzer and Schroeter (eds) (n 12) para 17.

[38] CISG Advisory Council, 'CISG-AC Opinion No. 5' (n 16) Black Letter Rule 11; Müller-Chen, 'Article 48 CISG: Seller's Right to Cure after Date for Delivery' in Schwenzer and Schroeter (eds) (n 12) para 17; dels Sants and Fargas (n 36) 229, s 5.2.6.

[39] Müller-Chen, 'Article 48 CISG: Seller's Right to Cure after Date for Delivery' in Schwenzer and Schroeter (eds) (n 12) para 23; Peter Huber, 'Article 48' in Kröll, Mistelis, and Perales Viscasillas (eds) (n 12) para 16.

[40] See *BP Oil International, Ltd v Empresa Estatal Petroleos de Ecuador (PetroEcuador)* [2003] US Court of Appeals (5th Circuit) 02-20166, CISG-online 730.

A contract of sale may require the seller to deliver the goods and provide certain documents related to the goods to the buyer or a third party. This duty, usually contemplated in trade terms like the ICC Incoterms®, might include handing over negotiable documents like bills of lading or warehouse warrants, duplicate consignment notes, delivery notes, quay receipts, certificates of origin, certificates of analysis or examination, insurance policies, commercial invoices, customs documents, instruction manuals, or handbooks.[41] These obligations are common in commercial practice.

The CISG Advisory Council has pointed out that whether the breach of an obligation to hand over accompanying documents constitutes a 'fundamental breach of contract' under Article 25 CISG depends on the same rules developed with respect to the seller's obligation to deliver conforming goods.[42] Suppose the seller fails to provide the necessary documents as per the contract. In that case, it can be considered a fundamental breach if it hinders the buyer from utilizing the goods as intended. For instance, if the goods cannot be exported or imported without a certificate of origin, or if the quality certificate and insurance policy are missing, which leads to the goods not being processed by the customs authority and the buyer being unable to receive them, the seller might have committed a fundamental breach.[43] The same applies when hardware, machines, or software cannot be used without the necessary user documentation. Moreover, suppose the seller does not provide an invoice required for tax purposes. In that case, it can be considered a fundamental breach, if the buyer is unable to import or resell the goods as intended. Of course, again the breach of an obligation to provide accompanying documents can only be considered as 'fundamental' if it cannot be reasonably remedied by the seller without unreasonable inconvenience for the buyer.[44]

In some sales contracts, the seller's main obligation is to provide specific documents, which is given equal importance as their obligation to deliver the goods or even replace them. This is frequently seen in the sale of commodities. Such sales are known as documentary sales and are common when the trade term CIF is included in the sales contract or when payment is to be made through documentary credit or collection. The contract clauses state that the seller must provide specified documents at a specific time.[45]

Documentary sales require strict compliance with contractual specifications.[46] This principle applies to CISG contracts and is incorporated into documentary

---

[41] Schroeter, 'Article 25 CISG: Fundamental Breach of Contract' in Schwenzer and Schroeter (eds) (n 12) para 48.

[42] CISG Advisory Council, 'CISG-AC Opinion No. 5' (n 16) Black Letter Rule 5.

[43] Markus Müller-Chen, 'Article 46 CISG: Buyer's Right to Require Performance, Delivery of Substitute Goods or Repair' in Schwenzer and Schroeter (eds) (n 12) para 26.

[44] Markus Müller-Chen, 'Article 49 CISG: Buyer's Right to Avoid Contract' in Schwenzer and Schroeter (eds) (n 12) para 11.

[45] Carlos Eduardo Fujita, *The CISG and Commodity Sales* (International Commerce and Arbitration Series, Eleven International Publishing 2022) 146.

[46] Ibid 147.

sales contracts by Article 9(2) CISG. The principle mandates that the documents submitted must conform precisely to the contract, be complete, and be free from contradictions. The smallest non-conformity of the documents tendered entitles the buyer to reject them because timely delivery by handling over clean documents is always of the essence of the contract.[47]

Suppose the CISG contract clauses suggest that the seller must provide strictly compliant documents as fundamentally important. In that case, the buyer might be entitled to avoid the contract, even if the seller's failure to provide the correct documents has not resulted in financial loss for the buyer (such as due to rising market prices). In cases where a seller provides non-conforming documents, the buyer's bank can immediately reject them and the buyer might declare the contract avoided under Article 49(1)(a) CISG in conjunction with Article 25 CISG, particularly in commodity transactions. A fundamental breach of contract could also occur when a seller requests a modification of the contractual documentary requirements before fulfilling its obligations. However, the CISG Advisory Council has suggested that there is no fundamental breach in documentary sales if the seller can remedy the non-conformity of the documents consistently with the weight accorded to the time of performance.[48]

The importance of the contractual time for tendering documents in documentary sales contracts depends on the terms of the contract as interpreted under Article 8(2) and (3) CISG and applicable practices or usages under Article 9 CISG.[49]

5. Defects in the goods title and IP rights

Article 41 CISG requires the seller to deliver goods free from any right or claim of a third party.[50] This provision does not specifically deal with the buyer's remedies in respect of defects in title; instead, those remedies follow from Article 45 CISG and the other provisions referred to therein. Accordingly, the buyer may claim avoidance of the contract if the defect in title amounts to a fundamental breach of contract (Article 49(1)(a) CISG). But not every defect in title may amount to a fundamental breach. A fundamental breach occurs when a third party has the right to take the goods immediately or stop the buyer from using the goods as intended.[51]

---

[47]   CISG Advisory Council, 'CISG-AC Opinion No. 5' (n 16) comment 4.17.
[48]   Ibid Black Letter Rule 6.
[49]   Ibid Black Letter Rule 7.
[50]   *Stolen wheel loader case* [2023] Obergericht des Kantons Zug (Court of Appeal Canton Zug) Z1 2022 6, CISG-online 6313.
[51]   Stefan M Kröll, 'Article 41' in Kröll, Mistelis, and Perales Viscasillas (eds) (n 12) para 43; David Tebel, 'Article 41 (Third-Party Claims to Goods)' in Christoph Brunner and Benjamin Gottlieb (eds), *Commentary on the UN Sales Law (CISG)* (Kluwer Law International 2019) para 27; Ingeborg Schwenzer, 'Article 41 CISG: Third Party Claims in General' in Schwenzer and Schroeter (eds) (n 12) para 24.

If it is impossible to remove the third party's right, or if it is unreasonable to do so, then that is a fundamental breach, too. However, if the third party's right does not directly affect the buyer's use of the goods, and it can be removed within a reasonable amount of time, then it is not considered a fundamental breach. The simplified avoidance of the contract by fixing an additional period of time according to Article 49(1)(b) CISG is not possible for a defect in title, as it is not a case of non-delivery.[52]

The available remedies in case the goods are burdened by third-party intellectual property rights under Article 42 CISG are similar to those available for general defects in title in Article 41 CISG. However, in some circumstances, the fact that the goods are subject to third-party intellectual property rights may not affect the buyer's interest in utilizing the goods in any way. For instance, when the goods are subject to a third-party right under the law of the State where the buyer has its place of business but not under the law of the State where the buyer uses the goods. In such cases, it is essential to focus on the severity of the breach to strike a reasonable balance between the interests of the parties involved, including the right to avoid the contract.[53] The state of use is decisive.

6. Lack of payment

The parties can agree that the seller can avoid the contract immediately if the buyer fails to pay the price on time or fails to take such steps and comply with such formalities as may be required under the contract to enable payment on time, such as timely opening a letter of credit (Article 6 CISG).

In the absence of an agreement, if the buyer finally fails to pay the price, it will be considered a fundamental breach of the contract. However, it is not easy to determine whether or not the buyer will pay the purchase price. In practice, non-payment will only be deemed to exist if the buyer informs the seller that it will not perform the contract. If the buyer informs the seller before the due date, the seller may declare the contract avoided for the anticipatory breach of contract as per Article 72(1) CISG.

Late payment by a buyer does not automatically lead to a fundamental breach of contract, allowing the seller to avoid the contract. The seller's interest in timely payment is usually covered by the buyer's obligation to pay interest on the purchase price (Article 78 CISG). Therefore, the seller can give the buyer an additional

---

[52] Schwenzer, 'Article 41 CISG: Third Party Claims in General' in Schwenzer and Schroeter (eds) (n 12) para 24; Kröll, 'Article 41' in Kröll, Mistelis, and Perales Viscasillas (eds) (n 12) para 43; Tebel, 'Article 41 (Third-Party Claims to Goods)' in Brunner and Gottlieb (eds) (n 51) para 27.

[53] David Tebel, 'Article 42 (Third-Party Claims to Goods)' in Brunner and Gottlieb (eds) (n 51) para 26; Ingeborg Schwenzer, 'Article 42 CISG: Third Party Claims Based on Intellectual Property' in Schwenzer and Schroeter (eds) (n 12) para 27.

period of time to pay (Article 63(1) CISG), and only avoid the contract if the buyer still fails to pay (Article 64(1)(b)). However, suppose the buyer intentionally delays payment for an unreasonable time or has a significant amount of money in default for an extended period.[54] In that case, the seller may avoid the contract for fundamental breach without setting an additional period of time.

Late payment can lead to a fundamental breach of contract if payment on time is of the essence. Whether payment on time is of the essence depends on the contract interpretation and usages under Articles 8 and 9 CISG. Payment on time is of the essence when goods have a limited lifespan, or when the contractual currency is subject to significant fluctuations in the currency markets, or when goods are subject to strong price fluctuations in volatile markets.[55]

When parties agree on payment through a letter of credit, the buyer must open a fully workable letter of credit within the terms of the contract within a set deadline. If the buyer fails to open the letter of credit on time, the seller can withhold its obligations but cannot avoid the contract immediately. If the opening of the letter of credit is linked to loading the goods, the seller might avoid the contract immediately if the letter of credit is not opened on time.[56]

Failure to comply with the formalities to enable payment in accordance with Article 54 CISG may constitute a fundamental breach of contract. For example, failing to provide a bank guarantee may entitle the seller to suspend performance or avoid the contract. If the buyer fails to take the necessary steps, the seller may set an additional period of time to do so. If the buyer still fails to comply, the seller can avoid the contract without showing a fundamental breach of contract under Article 64(1)(b) CISG.

Suppose the buyer opens a letter of credit but the terms must be altered because they depart from the parties' agreement. In that case, the seller may request the buyer to amend the letter of credit within a specified additional time frame. If the buyer fails to comply, the seller can declare the contract avoided under Article 64(1)(b) CISG.

7. Failure to take delivery

The buyer that permanently fails to take delivery of the goods commits a fundamental breach of contract.[57] A buyer may give notice that it will not take delivery,

---

[54] Gary F Bell, 'Article 64' in Kröll, Mistelis, and Perales Viscasillas (eds) (n 12) para 43; Christoph Brunner and Benjamin Leisinger, 'Article 64 (Seller's Right to Avoid the Contract)' in Brunner and Gottlieb (eds) (n 51) para 4; Florian Mohs, 'Article 64 CISG: Seller's Right to Avoid Contract' in Schwenzer and Schroeter (eds) (n 12) para 7.

[55] Mohs, 'Article 64 CISG: Seller's Right to Avoid Contract' in Schwenzer and Schroeter (eds) (n 12) para 7.

[56] Ibid paras 9–10.

[57] *Bloom Lake General Partner Ltd et al. v Worldlink Resources Ltd* [2014] ICC International Court of Arbitration 18209/VRO/AGF/ZF (c. 18251/VRO/AGF) (Final award), CISG-online 5277 para

and this will make it pretty clear that the seller might proceed with the avoidance of the contract. But before it is definitely clear that the buyer will fail to take delivery, it may be difficult to determine whether there is a fundamental breach, except in cases where the buyer rejects or returns the goods or documents with no reason.

If the buyer fails to take delivery of goods at the agreed time, it does not necessarily mean that it has fundamentally breached the contract.[58] A fundamental breach would only exist if the seller has a specific interest in the buyer's timely performance of its obligation to take over the goods. This is the case when perishable goods are to be delivered. Additionally, a fundamental breach occurs if the seller needs the timely clearance of its storage rooms or unloading its carrier at the delivery point.[59] The same applies when bulk commodities have been delivered and the carrier requires the buyer to unload them before leaving.

In the case of documentary sales, if the buyer refuses to accept clean documents, it may not necessarily be considered a fundamental breach of contract. Instead, the buyer may be given a chance to remedy the situation during an additional period of time fixed by the seller. However, if the transfer of documents is a crucial part of the contract's performance and the seller is unable to ship due to the buyer's refusal to accept them, it will be considered a fundamental breach of contract. In such cases, the seller is entitled to avoid the contract immediately.[60]

If there is a requirement contract in place, where the buyer is obligated to call for delivery of the next instalment by the seller, or where the buyer is required to specify the goods under Article 65 CISG, the buyer's failure to do so will not usually be considered a fundamental breach of contract.[61] However, in such cases, the seller will need to set an additional period of time for the buyer to fulfil this obligation. Whether the seller can make the necessary specifications will depend on the contract terms and the circumstances. In case the seller is entitled to do so, the

---

106: 'actions or conduct of a party clearly demonstrating such party's determination to reject the [contract] or not to perform or continue performing its obligations thereunder' constitutes fundamental breach; Schroeter, 'Article 25 CISG: Fundamental Breach of Contract' in Schwenzer and Schroeter (eds) (n 12) para 257.

[58] *Bloom Lake General Partner Ltd. et al. v Worldlink Resources Ltd.* (n 57) paras 114, 118, 122: the repeated refusal to take delivery in the circumstances of the case was not considered fundamental breach; *Valero Marketing & Supply Co v Greeni Oy* [2007] US Court of Appeals (3rd Circuit) 06-3390, 06-3525, CISG-online 1510; Schroeter, 'Article 25 CISG: Fundamental Breach of Contract' in Schwenzer and Schroeter (eds) (n 12) para 258.
[59] *Italian shoes case XXV* [2004] Oberlandesgericht Düsseldorf (Court of Appeal Düsseldorf) I-6 U 210/03, CISG-online 916; Schroeter, 'Article 25 CISG: Fundamental Breach of Contract' in Schwenzer and Schroeter (eds) (n 12) para 258.
[60] Mohs, 'Article 64 CISG: Seller's Right to Avoid Contract' in Schwenzer and Schroeter (eds) (n 12) para 15.
[61] Florian Mohs, 'Article 65 CISG: Seller's Right to Specify Features of Goods' in Schwenzer and Schroeter (eds) (n 12) para 5 ff.

buyer is still required to take delivery of the goods according to the contract or the Convention.[62]

In a long-term contract that calls for the delivery of a certain quantity over a certain time period, if the buyer fails to take enough goods in one year, the seller may only be entitled to declare the contract avoided under Article 73(2) CISG if it has good grounds to conclude that a fundamental breach of contract will occur with respect to future instalments, provided that it does so within a reasonable time.[63] This shortage in quantity does not automatically constitute a fundamental breach of contract in relation to the entire contract. But if, for example, it becomes clear during the year of delivery that the buyer will not be able to take delivery of the required quantity for that year, it may be considered an anticipatory breach of contract. In such cases, the seller may avoid the contract under Article 73(2) CISG.[64] The buyer's inability to take delivery of the full quantity shortly before the end of the year may be due to various reasons, such as vessel availability and availability of the goods.

8. Other breaches

The classification as a 'main' or 'ancillary' obligation is irrelevant to the importance of the promise's corresponding interest in its performance. A fundamental breach of contract occurs when a party is substantially deprived of what it is entitled to expect under the contract by the other party's breach.[65] Therefore, a fundamental breach of contract may occur when minor or details of main obligations are violated. Sometimes, multiple minor breaches of a contract by a party can accumulate and lead to a major breach, or the initial minor breach can worsen over time and become a fundamental breach.[66] The aggrieved party's interest in the fulfilment of the contract should be evaluated based on individual circumstances and on a case-by-case basis.[67]

---

[62] *Hearing implants case* [1993] Landgericht Aachen (District Court Aachen) 43 O 136/92, CISG-online 86: the seller had the right to avoid the contract after an unsuccessful lapse of additional period to accept the goods.

[63] Christiana Fountoulakis, 'Article 73 CISG: Avoidance of Instalment Contracts' in Schwenzer and Schroeter (eds) (n 12) para 24 ff; Christoph Brunner, Beat Schläpfer, and Christopher Boog, 'Article 73 (Avoidance in Installment Contracts)' in Brunner and Gottlieb (eds) (n 51) para 9.

[64] *Austrian insulation material (distribution agreement) case* [2023] Oberlandesgericht Graz (Court of Appeal Graz) 5 R 73/23d-23, CISG-online 6628.

[65] CISG art 25.

[66] *Chinese wire rod case II* [2015] Bundesgericht/Tribunal fédéral (Swiss Federal Supreme Court) 4A_614/2014, CISG-online 2592; Schroeter, 'Article 25 CISG: Fundamental Breach of Contract' in Schwenzer and Schroeter (eds) (n 12) para 70; Christoph Brunner and Benjamin Leisinger, 'Article 25 (Definition of "Fundamental Breach")' in Brunner and Gottlieb (eds) (n 51) para 7.

[67] Schroeter, 'Article 25 CISG: Fundamental Breach of Contract' in Schwenzer and Schroeter (eds) (n 12) paras 88–94.

Examples of such breaches include the buyer's obligation to order certain quantities of goods from the seller or agree on a delivery plan and the seller's obligation to package goods adequately for preservation and protection or arrange for appropriate transportation. Furthermore, a fundamental breach of contract may also consist of the violation of an obligation that arises only once a remedy under the CISG has been exercised by the non-breaching party, such as the seller's obligation to return the goods to the buyer after they have been repaired under Article 46(3) CISG.[68]

While deciding whether to grant or deny the avoidance of the contract for the breach of secondary obligations, it could be important to consider whether the remedy of damages (Articles 74–77 CISG) is sufficient to compensate the injured party.[69] This may be the case, for instance, where the contract prohibits the buyer from reimporting the goods into the seller's country, and the buyer fails to comply with this obligation, thereby undermining the seller's legitimate interests in a way that damages alone may not adequately address.

III. *Nachfrist* Principle

The CISG also allows the buyer (Article 49(1)(b)) or the seller (Article 64(1)(b)) to avoid the contract after fixing an additional period of time (*Nachfrist*)[70] in cases of non-delivery, non-payment, or failure to take delivery. This so-called *Nachfrist* procedure provides an additional but independent option to avoid the contract. It does not affect the parties' right to rely on a fundamental breach of contract under Articles 49(1)(a) or 64(1)(a) CISG, should such a breach have occurred. This right is not excluded in cases where a party could have or has fixed an additional period of time for performance.

The CISG intentionally restricts the possibility of fixing an additional period of time to cases of non-delivery, non-payment, or failure to take delivery. Where non-conforming goods have been delivered or some other breach of contract has occurred, the contract may be avoided only if the defect constitutes a fundamental breach of contract within the meaning of Article 25 CISG.[71] In contrast, the lapse of an additional period of time for curing the non-conformity (Article 46 or 48 CISG) does not allow for avoiding the contract in these cases; there must be a fundamental breach under Article 25 CISG again.[72] The *Nachfrist* procedure is

---

[68] Müller-Chen, 'Article 46 CISG: Buyer's Right to Require Performance, Delivery of Substitute Goods or Repair' in Schwenzer and Schroeter (eds) (n 12) paras 26, 36 ff.

[69] Ingeborg H Schwenzer, 'Article 74 CISG: Calculation of Damages in General' in Schwenzer and Schroeter (eds) (n 12) para 3.

[70] *Nachfrist* is a German term which essentially means 'additional period'.

[71] Schroeter, 'Article 25 CISG: Fundamental Breach of Contract' in Schwenzer and Schroeter (eds) (n 12) para 88; Brunner and Leisinger, 'Article 25 (Definition of "Fundamental Breach")' in Brunner and Gottlieb (eds) (n 51) para 1.

[72] dels Sants Mirambell Fargas (n 36) 227, s 5.2.5.

particularly useful for a party suffering from a breach whenever the importance of such a disturbance under Article 25 CISG is doubtful, but in the specific scenarios stated, that is, non-delivery, non-payment, or failure to take delivery.

Article 7.3.1(3) PICC allows the aggrieved party to avoid the contract if the other party fails to perform *any* obligation within the reasonable period of time set by the aggrieved party under Article 7.1.5(3) PICC. In other words, Article 7.3.1(3) of the PICC permits the avoidance of the contract after the expiration of a *Nachfrist* period, irrespective of the type of obligation breached—that is, it is not limited to the specific scenarios of non-delivery, non-payment, or failure to take delivery as it is the case under the CISG.[73]

When a *Nachfrist* is granted, the party who grants the extension cannot avoid the contract during the extension period. The outcome of an extension period depends on whether the late performance (or defective performance under the PICC as well) was fundamental at the time the extension was granted. If the late performance was already fundamental and the contract is not completely fulfilled during the extension, the right to avoid the contract for fundamental non-performance will be reinstated as soon as the extension period expires.[74] However, if the late performance was not yet fundamental, the avoidance of the contract would only be possible at the end of the extension period if the extension was of reasonable length.[75]

IV. Restrictions in Case of Delivery and Payment

According to Article 49(2) and Article 64(2) CISG, parties lose the right to avoid the contract regardless of its fundamental nature in certain cases if they do not declare its avoidance within a reasonable period. The time limit aims to clarify the fate of the contract and the obligations of the parties. One of these cases takes place when the seller has already delivered the goods under Article 49(2) CISG. In such a case, the buyer must declare the contract avoided within a *reasonable* time. The reasonable period starts when the buyer becomes aware of the delivery. The buyer must dispatch its declaration of avoidance within that period.[76]

---

[73] International Institute for the Unification of Private Law (ed), UNIDROIT Principles of International Commercial Contracts (UNIDROIT International Institute for the Unification of Private Law 2016) 236, art 7.1.5, off cmt 2; Huber (n 1) para 69.

[74] Ivo Bach, 'Article 49' in Kröll, Mistelis, and Perales Viscasillas (eds) (n 12) para 63; Christoph Brunner and Benjamin Leisinger, 'Article 49 (Buyer's Right to Avoid the Contract)' in Brunner and Gottlieb (eds) (n 51) para 6; Müller-Chen, 'Article 49 CISG: Buyer's Right to Avoid Contract' in Schwenzer and Schroeter (eds) (n 12) para 16.

[75] Brunner and Leisinger, 'Article 49 (Buyer's Right to Avoid the Contract)' in Brunner and Gottlieb (eds) (n 51) para 6; Bach, 'Article 49' in Kröll, Mistelis, and Perales Viscasillas (eds) (n 12) para 63.

[76] [...] Sà.r.l. v Emerito SL [2024] Cour d'appel de Montpellier (Court of Appeal Montpellier) 22/01909, CISG-online 6846.

What is a reasonable period for declaring avoidance once the goods have already been delivered depends on the specific circumstances. In case of rejected delivery, the seller has a considerable interest in being informed promptly to dispose of the goods otherwise. A reasonable time under Article 49(2)(a) CISG should be set shorter rather than longer. If the buyer fails to declare the contract avoided within that time, it loses the right to do so for late delivery and must pay the price.[77] It retains the right to declare the contract avoided for other breaches of contract.

When the buyer fails to take delivery, the seller must declare the contract avoided within a reasonable time, too, as per Article 64(2)(b) CISG. What constitutes a reasonable time frame depends on the particular circumstances of each case, including the amount of time a reasonable third party would require to make a decision and fulfil the obligation at hand. The reasonable period is determined by two approaches: from the point when the seller knew or ought to have known of the breach (Article 64(2)(b)(i) CISG) or from the expiration of the additional period of time fixed by the seller under Article 63(1) CISG or the buyer's declaration of non-performance (Article 64(2)(b)(ii) CISG).[78]

The PICC applies the same rule to all cases of breach. Under Article 7.3.2(2) PICC, an aggrieved party who intends to terminate the contract must give notice to the other party within a reasonable time after it becomes or ought to have become aware of the non-performance. The PICC Official Commentary suggests the need for immediate notice of avoidance in situations where the aggrieved party can easily obtain a substitute performance and speculate on price fluctuations.[79]

V. Avoidance by Declaration

The mechanism for avoiding a contract and its legal consequences depend on the individual approach taken by a legal system. They might include approaches like avoidance *ipso facto*, that is, when the breach occurs, avoidance by court decision and avoidance by party declaration. This mechanism determines when avoidance takes effect and whether it eliminates the contract for the future only or works retroactively. The legal regime for unwinding international commercial contracts is addressed in Chapter 16.

---

[77] Brunner and Leisinger, 'Article 49 (Buyer's Right to Avoid the Contract)' in Brunner and Gottlieb (eds) (n 51) para 15; Bach, 'Article 49' in Kröll, Mistelis, and Perales Viscasillas (eds) (n 12) para 70; Müller-Chen, 'Article 49 CISG: Buyer's Right to Avoid Contract' in Schwenzer and Schroeter (eds) (n 12) para 29.

[78] Bell, 'Article 64' in Kröll, Mistelis, and Perales Viscasillas (eds) (n 12) para 21; Brunner and Leisinger, 'Article 64 (Seller's Right to Avoid the Contract)' in Brunner and Gottlieb (eds) (n 51) para 11; Mohs, 'Article 64 CISG: Seller's Right to Avoid Contract' in Schwenzer and Schroeter (eds) (n 12) para 30.

[79] International Institute for the Unification of Private Law (n 73) 258, art 7.3.2(2), off cmt 3.

At the international level, the CISG and the PICC require the aggrieved party to declare the avoidance of the contract (Article 26 CISG and Article 7.3.2.(1) PICC).[80] The approach entails more than the *ipso facto* avoidance and less than avoidance by court order. A notice given by the aggrieved party is sufficient—but also necessary.

The declaration does not need to follow a particular form requirement; it may be in writing, including through electronic communications, but also orally or impliedly communicated (Article 26 CISG and Article 7.3.2(1) PICC).

The parties are entitled to change the mechanism for avoidance under both the CISG and the PICC.[81] They could, for example, agree that avoidance takes place *ipso facto* upon a breach with no need to declare the contract avoided. For instance, when the buyer becomes insolvent before paying the purchase price, it is considered a fundamental breach of the contract. However, sometimes, the seller may not know about the buyer's financial difficulties until the buyer files for bankruptcy. To avoid this situation, many international contracts contain clauses that automatically avoid the contract if one of the parties files for bankruptcy. These clauses are known as material adverse change clauses. The CISG recognizes such clauses under Article 6 CISG

Conversely, that no avoidance effect might take place but upon court declaration.[82] Similarly, the parties could agree to impose a form requirement on the declaration of avoidance (Article 6 CISG and Article 1.5 PICC).

The CISG and the PICC are silent on the exact content the declaration of avoidance must have. Generally speaking, whether a statement amounts to a declaration of avoidance is a matter of interpretation under Article 8 CISG or Articles 4.1 to 4.8 PICC. Although it may seem like a good idea to demand complete clarity in situations where avoiding a contract could have serious consequences, courts are typically willing to accept any indication from the party that they no longer wish to be bound by the contract, such as sending back the goods.[83]

The question at which point in time the declaration of avoidance takes effect can be of significance. This is even more true when the notice is lost on the way to the addressee. The CISG has different approaches to different types of declarations. While in the contract formation process a declaration must reach the other party to take effect,[84] this is not the case concerning the declaration of avoidance.

---

[80] *Dcoop Sociedad Cooperativa Andaluza v Patano S.r.l* [2023] Audiencia Provincial de Jaén (Court of Appeal Jaén) 1697/2021/1323/2023, CISG-online 6896.

[81] Müller-Chen, 'Article 49 CISG: Buyer's Right to Avoid Contract' in Schwenzer and Schroeter (eds) (n 12) para 49.

[82] Ibid para 23: according to the CISG even if the breach is fundamental it would never lead *ipso facto* to avoidance of the contract.

[83] Ibid para 24; Brunner and Leisinger, 'Article 49 (Buyer's Right to Avoid the Contract)' in Brunner and Gottlieb (eds) (n 51) para 7; Bach, 'Article 49' in Kröll, Mistelis, and Perales Viscasillas (eds) (n 12) para 65.

[84] See CISG art 24.

Regarding the latter, Article 27 CISG clarifies that the notice travels at the recipient's risk.[85] The drafters of the PICC chose to simplify matters and opted for a strict application of the receipt approach without exceptions about the declaration's goal. Therefore, for a declaration of avoidance to be effective under the PICC, it must reach the breaching party (Article 1.10(2) PICC).

VI. Partial Avoidance

In some cases, a breach may affect only a portion of the contract. This could occur when a seller delivers only part of the goods or when a portion of the goods does not meet the agreed-upon specifications. On the other hand, if a buyer only pays part of the purchase price and it becomes apparent that it is unable to pay the remaining balance, the seller may choose to keep the amount paid and take back the portion of the goods for which payment is still due.[86] This would allow the seller to sell the goods to someone else.

This partial avoidance of the contract is generally possible under the CISG and the PICC. The usual rules on remedies for the breach of obligations apply, including those that regulate the right to avoid the contract. However, the CISG specifically contemplates the case where a seller delivers only part of the goods, or where only part of the goods conform to the contract or the convention. Where this occurs, the buyer is able to rely on all its remedies under the CISG as far as they apply to the defective or non-delivered part, including the right to avoid the contract in case the partial performance amounts to a fundamental breach of the whole contract (Article 51(1) CISG). However, the buyer may also avoid the contract partially, that is, the part missing or in non-conformity if there has been a fundamental breach under Article 51(2) CISG.

VII. Right to Suspend Performance and Stoppage in Transit

Article 71 CISG allows either party to suspend the performance of its obligations, providing an important self-help remedy that prevents further damage and costs for the aggrieved party.[87] Article 71(1) CISG sets out five requirements that must be met in order to exercise the right to suspend performance. The requirements

---

[85] See Christiana Fountoulakis, 'Article 26 CISG: Notice of Avoidance' in Schwenzer and Schroeter (eds) (n 12) para 10.

[86] Schwenzer and Muñoz (n 7) para 47.1.

[87] *R&R Manufacturing SAS v Everestt International Industries Ltd* [2023] Cour d'appel de Besançon (Court of Appeal Besançon) 21/01330, CISG-online 6643; *Triage Matériel Professionnel S.a.r.l. v JGB-2 Sp z. o.o.* [2023] Cour d'appel de Paris (Court of Appeal Paris) 21/19946, CISG-online 6569; *Q-railing glass partition for swimming pool case* [2022] Rechtbank Gelderland (District Court Gelderland) C/05/393151/HA ZA 21-468, CISG-online 5954.

may be formulated as follows: if after the contract is concluded, it becomes apparent (1), that a substantial portion of the debtor's contractual obligations (2), will not be fulfilled (3), due to the reasons mentioned in Article 71(1)(a) and (b) CISG (4), the creditor may suspend performance of its own obligations (5).[88]

Concerning the first element, the impending breach must become apparent after the contract is concluded, and the right of suspension is unavailable if it could have been identified earlier. Whether and when the breach became apparent must be determined objectively, and the creditor is expected to have common knowledge and information. Impediments that existed before the contract can be considered under Article 71(1) CISG, if they became apparent afterwards. Domestic law on mistake or misrepresentation cannot be used if Article 71 CISG covers such facts, but fraud or fraudulent misrepresentation can be applied in addition to Article 71 CISG.[89]

As to the second element, the right to suspend performance hinges on the threat of a breach of a significant portion of the other party's obligations. This requirement should not be confused with a fundamental breach of contract as outlined in Article 25 CISG; the standard in Article 71 CISG is lower.[90] This distinction arises because the remedy of suspending performance is provisional in nature. Otherwise, Article 72 CISG, which permits contract avoidance in cases of fundamental anticipatory breach, would serve no purpose. Determining what constitutes a 'substantial part' must be based on the contract as a whole. The key factor is whether the creditor had a legitimate expectation of full performance of those obligations. Consequently, the debtor must know or should have known that the creditor had a specific interest in the other party fulfilling the obligation.

To prevent a creditor from relying too quickly on Article 71 CISG and breaching the contract, the third element requires a high degree of probability to assert the remedy of suspension immediately. The objective view of a reasonable person is necessary to determine the probability of a future breach of contract. Unilateral modifications of the contract may indicate the likelihood of a breach of contract, but it is not necessarily the case. In case law, a breach of contract was held to be probable where the buyer refused to make the agreed advance payment,[91] open

---

[88] Djakhongir Saidov, 'Article 71' in Kröll, Mistelis, and Perales Viscasillas (eds) (n 12) para 4 ff; Christoph Brunner and Christoph Berchtold, 'Article 71 (Suspension of Performance)' in Brunner and Gottlieb (eds) (n 51) para 2; Christiana Fountoulakis, 'Article 71 CISG: Suspension of Performance' in Schwenzer and Schroeter (eds) (n 12) para 18.

[89] CISG Advisory Council, 'CISG-AC Opinion No. 23, Mistake, Fraud, Misrepresentation and Initial Impossibility in CISG Contracts, Rapporteur: Professor Hugh Beale, Universities of Warwick (Em.) and Oxford, United Kingdom, December 12–14, 2023' (2023) Black Letter Rule 1.

[90] Cf *Italian shoes case XV* [1994] Landgericht Berlin (District Court Berlin) 52 S 247/94, CISG-online 399; Saidov, 'Article 71' in Kröll, Mistelis, and Perales Viscasillas (eds) (n 12) para 4.

[91] *Thai-made emulsion case* [1989] China International Economic & Trade Arbitration Commission (CIETAC) CISG-online 1230.

or renew a letter of credit,[92] or provide a bank guarantee.[93] The contract was also likely to be breached by the seller where the seller disputed that the delivered goods were defective and intended to deliver more of the same,[94] where the seller refused to provide proof that the goods were free from third-party rights,[95] or where the goods had been stolen, and the seller was unable to retrieve them.[96]

The fourth element encompasses the reasons mentioned in Article 71(1)(a) and (b) CISG. Article 71(1)(a) CISG lists situations that may cause an impending breach of contract, including factual impediments, such as a strike or loss of production facilities by fire or other natural phenomena, and legal impediments.[97] Serious creditworthiness deficiency is treated similarly, and tardiness in payment may be insufficient. Serious deficiency in creditworthiness[98] can, for example, be caused by insolvency and similar events or by cessation of payment.[99] However, not paying a sum relating to another contract does not fall under Article 71(1) (a) CISG.

Article 71(1)(b) CISG also allows suspension where the debtor's conduct in preparing to perform or in performing the contract raises doubts about whether it can perform a substantial part of its obligations. Time is a crucial factor for this element. If the debtor refuses to perform without justification, the buyer can always suspend payment of the price. However, mere rumours about the debtor's inability to perform its contractual obligations are not sufficient grounds for suspension. Neither is the fact that the debtor failed to perform some contracts with

---

[92] *Mansonville Plastics (BC) Ltd v Kurtz GmbH et al.* [2003] Supreme Court of British Columbia C993594, CISG-online 1017; *Lentils case* [1996] China International Economic & Trade Arbitration Commission (CIETAC) CISG/1996/56, CISG-online 2281.

[93] *Hungarian mushrooms case* [1995] Arbitration Court attached to the Hungarian Chamber of Commerce and Industry VB/94124, CISG-online 250.

[94] *Italian shoes case XV* (n 90).

[95] *OIL Otto International Leasing AG v Zernopererabatyvayuschy kombinat Barnaulskaya melnitsa* [2002] Federal Arbitrazh Court for the Western Siberia Circuit F04/2712-494/A03-2002, CISG-online 2282.

[96] *Hungarian furniture case* [1998] Oberlandesgericht Hamm (Court of Appeal Hamm) 19 U 127/ 97, CISG-online 434.

[97] Outbreak of war, export embargo, strike, and fire are mentioned in literature, cf United Nations (UN) Conference Official Records, 'Documents of the Conference and Summary Records of the Plenary Meetings and of the Meetings of the Main Committees' (1991) UN Doc A/CONF.97/19, 52, art 62, para 4; art 71(1)(a) has, for example, been applied to affirm the buyer's right to suspend payment where the seller was obviously incapable of delivering goods because it no longer possessed them, cf *Hungarian furniture case* (n 96). Saidov, 'Article 71' in Kröll, Mistelis, and Perales Viscasillas (eds) (n 12) para 10; Brunner and Berchtold, 'Article 71 (Suspension of Performance)' in Brunner and Gottlieb (eds) (n 51) paras 20–24; Fountoulakis, 'Article 71 CISG: Suspension of Performance' in Schwenzer and Schroeter (eds) (n 12) paras 22–26.

[98] Saidov, 'Article 71' in Kröll, Mistelis, and Perales Viscasillas (eds) (n 12) para 11; Brunner and Berchtold, 'Article 71 (Suspension of Performance)' in Brunner and Gottlieb (eds) (n 51) para 22; Fountoulakis, 'Article 71 CISG: Suspension of Performance' in Schwenzer and Schroeter (eds) (n 12) para 23.

[99] Fountoulakis, 'Article 71 CISG: Suspension of Performance' in Schwenzer and Schroeter (eds) (n 12) para 24.

other partners or delivered late once without causing further inconveniences.[100] Distinguishing Article 71(1)(a) from (b) CISG may be difficult,[101] but it is not essential since the legal consequences are the same.[102]

Distinctive of the CISG and some domestic laws (English, United States, and Scandinavian),[103] the seller also has a right to prevent the delivery of goods from the time they are dispatched until they are handed over to the buyer (right of stoppage in transit in Article 71(2) CISG). Its practical significance is confined to cases where the buyer's diminishing ability to perform becomes apparent after the goods have been dispatched. In other situations, the seller will already prevent the dispatch of the goods under Article 71(1) CISG.[104] The right of stoppage amounts to a 'suspension of performance after performance': it nullifies the effects of the seller's performance, treating the seller as if it had never performed. This metaphor of 'suspension of performance after performance' typically applies when the seller fulfils its obligation by handing the goods over to the first carrier, as stated in Article 31(a) CISG. When the goods must be delivered to the buyer's place of business or another specified destination, as with contracts containing a D-clause under the ICC Incoterms® 2020,[105] the place of performance is that specified location. Under those trade terms, the critical factor for the decision to apply Article 71(1) or 71(2) CISG is when the seller becomes aware of the impending breach of contract. Article 71(2) CISG applies exclusively to the seller. The requirements for the right of stoppage are identical to those for the right of suspension[106] reviewed above in this section. However, this provision does not extend to the relationship with the independent carrier of the goods. The carrier is typically a third party engaged in transporting the goods and is not directly involved in the contractual obligations between the buyer and seller under the CISG.

Finally, a party suspending performance, before or after dispatch of the goods, must immediately notify the other party and continue with performance if the other party provides adequate assurance of its performance (Article 71(3) CISG).

---

[100] *Auto-Moto Styl S.r.o. v Pedro Boat BV* [2005] Gerechtshof Leeuwarden (Court of Appeal Leeuwarden) 0400549, CISG-online 1100 note 2.6.4.1: no right to suspend partial payment on the ground that the seller had performed the preceding step of contract performance with a substantial delay, if this did not cause any loss to the buyer.

[101] Cf e.g. *Ketchup bottles case* [2003] Oberlandesgericht Rostock (Court of Appeal Rostock) 3 U 19/03, CISG-online 920 note II.3.

[102] Fountoulakis, 'Article 71 CISG: Suspension of Performance' in Schwenzer and Schroeter (eds) (n 12) para 24.

[103] English Sale of Goods Act 1979, ss 44-46; as well as Joseph Chitty, *Chitty on Contracts* (35th edn, Sweet & Maxwell 2023) II, para 43.357 ff; U.S. Uniform Commercial Code (UCC) 2003, s 2-609, 2-705; as well as Swedish Sales Law s 39; Schwenzer and Muñoz (n 7) para 36.62.

[104] Fountoulakis, 'Article 71 CISG: Suspension of Performance' in Schwenzer and Schroeter (eds) (n 12) para 18 ff; Brunner and Berchtold, 'Article 71 (Suspension of Performance)' in Brunner and Gottlieb (eds) (n 51) para 2.

[105] Cf the clauses DAT, DAP, and DDP.

[106] Fountoulakis, 'Article 71 CISG: Suspension of Performance' in Schwenzer and Schroeter (eds) (n 12) para 41.

Notice of suspension is required since it can help improve communication and cooperation between the parties, potentially saving the contract and increasing the chances of its performance. Additionally, it may serve as a way to pressure the debtor.

The right to suspend performance ends if the conditions to exercise such right also cease or if the debtor gives adequate assurance that it will perform.[107] Adequate assurance of due performance can take various forms, based on the contract's context and concerns. Typical forms include advance payment, letters of credit, bank or corporate guarantees, performance bonds, collateral, regular progress reports or milestones, audited financial statements, third-party verification, and detailed written assurances.[108] The appropriate form depends on the specific circumstances, should be clearly communicated, and should be sufficient from a reasonable third-person perspective to address performance doubts effectively.

VIII. Anticipatory Breach

According to Article 72 CISG, if it becomes apparent before the date of performance that the other party will commit a fundamental breach of the contract, the innocent party can declare avoidance of the contract before the due date. The same provision exists under Article 7.3.3 PICC. This means that the innocent party does not have to wait for the actual fundamental breach to occur and can act early to avoid any potential losses.[109] The possibility of anticipatory avoidance of contract is designed to ensure efficiency by allowing an early response to potential breaches, while also balancing the interests of both parties.[110] This approach respects the creditor's need to swiftly regain its freedom of disposition while also giving the debtor a chance to demonstrate its readiness to perform.[111]

A question may arise as to whether there is a duty under Article 77 CISG to make use of Article 72 CISG as a reasonable measure to mitigate losses. If it is evident that a fundamental breach is imminent and avoiding the contract would

---

[107] Saidov, 'Article 71' in Kröll, Mistelis, and Perales Viscasillas (eds) (n 12) para 50; Brunner and Berchtold, 'Article 71 (Suspension of Performance)' in Brunner and Gottlieb (eds) (n 51) para 30; Fountoulakis, 'Article 71 CISG: Suspension of Performance' in Schwenzer and Schroeter (eds) (n 12) para 52.

[108] Saidov, 'Article 71' in Kröll, Mistelis, and Perales Viscasillas (eds) (n 12) para 53; Brunner and Berchtold, 'Article 71 (Suspension of Performance)' in Brunner and Gottlieb (eds) (n 51) para 30; Fountoulakis, 'Article 71 CISG: Suspension of Performance' in Schwenzer and Schroeter (eds) (n 12) para 54.

[109] Peter Huber, 'Article 7.3.3' in Vogenauer (ed) (n 1) para 1.

[110] Djakhongir Saidov, 'Article 72' in Kröll, Mistelis, and Perales Viscasillas (eds) (n 12) para 3; Christiana Fountoulakis, 'Article 72 CISG: Avoidance in Case of Anticipatory Breach of Contract' in Schwenzer and Schroeter (eds) (n 12) para 4.

[111] Fountoulakis, 'Article 72 CISG: Avoidance in Case of Anticipatory Breach of Contract' in Schwenzer and Schroeter (eds) (n 12) para 4.

prevent significant further losses, then it could be argued that a party has a duty under Article 77 CISG to use Article 72 CISG to declare the contract avoided. This would align with the principle of mitigating losses by taking reasonable steps to prevent further damage.[112] However, avoiding a contract under Article 72 CISG also involves considering the specific circumstances and potential consequences of avoidance. If avoidance would lead to additional complications or costs that outweigh the benefits of mitigating the initial loss, it may not be deemed a reasonable measure under Article 77 CISG.

Whether the creditor can prematurely avoid the contract under Article 72(1) CISG or Article 7.3.3 PICC depends on the probability that the anticipated interference will occur or persist at the performance date. Comparatively, Article 72(1) CISG and Article 7.3.3 PICC demand the highest level of probability, exceeding the prognosis requirements in Articles 71(1) and 73(2) CISG. Whether this high probability is met must be determined according to the objective standard of a reasonable person, as outlined in Article 8(2) CISG and Article 4.1(2) PICC.

The creditor may also declare the contract avoided if the debtor unequivocally states it will not perform its obligations, leading to a fundamental breach of contract (Article 72(3) CISG). The determination depends on whether a reasonable person in the creditor's position would understand it as a refusal (Article 8(2) CISG and Article 4.1(2) PICC). The 'clearness' requirement in Article 72(1) CISG guides the seriousness of the refusal of the debtor to perform.

Notice of intention to avoid the contract under Article 72(2) CISG is essential for effective contract avoidance. The notice requirement in Article 72(2) CISG must comply with Articles 26 and 27 CISG, using appropriate means of communication under the circumstances, with the debtor bearing the transmission risk. Declaring avoidance without notice when time allows is ineffective; the contract remains intact unless the other party accepts termination or avoids the contract itself.[113] The debtor can accept an unjustified declaration, resulting in a mutual agreement to avoid the contract. The duty to give notice under Article 72(2) CISG is crucial for giving the debtor a chance to keep the contract alive by giving adequate assurances that it will perform.

The assurance provided by the debtor must be 'adequate' (Article 72(2) CISG and also in Article 7.3.4 PICC). It can include alternatives to traditional bank securities, as long as it guarantees contract performance or compensates for a fundamental breach. For example, a third party's confirmation to fulfil obligations or

---

[112] See for instance a similar reasoning under US domestic law UCC § 2-610(a): the creditor who does not terminate the contract after a 'commercially reasonable time' cannot claim compensation of the loss that could have been avoided by terminating the contract on time.

[113] Saidov, 'Article 72' in Kröll, Mistelis, and Perales Viscasillas (eds) (n 12) para 19; Christoph Brunner and Markus Altenkirch, 'Article 72 (Avoidance Prior to Date for Performance)' in Brunner and Gottlieb (eds) (n 51) para 7; Fountoulakis, 'Article 72 CISG: Avoidance in Case of Anticipatory Breach of Contract' in Schwenzer and Schroeter (eds) (n 12) para 40.

proof of a reliable supply source can be adequate.[114] If the debtor's assurance is adequate, as determined objectively (Article 8(2) CISG and Article 4.1(2) PICC), the creditor must accept it and loses the right to avoid the contract.[115] If the debtor refuses or fails to provide adequate assurance within a reasonable time, the right of avoidance may be exercised without delay under Article 72(2) CISG and Article 7.3.4 PICC.[116] If the debtor provides inadequate assurance or fails to provide it timely, its efforts should not be ignored. They should have a chance to provide adequate assurance subsequently, without unreasonable delay or inconvenience to the creditor (Article 48(1) CISG).[117] The debtor must provide assurance within a reasonable time to prevent contract avoidance in any case under Article 7.3.4 PICC.[118] The assurance declaration becomes effective upon receipt by the creditor (Article 1.10 PICC), not governed by Article 27 CISG.[119] Article 72(2) CISG requires the debtor to bear the risk of loss or delay, making the declaration effective only upon receipt.

Finally, suppose the requirements of Article 72(1) CISG are met and the debtor has not provided adequate assurance or refuses to perform (Article 72(3) CISG). In that case, the creditor may avoid the contract by declaring avoidance under Article 26 CISG and Article 7.3.4 PICC, separate from the notice of intention to avoid under Article 72(2) CISG.[120] The declaration should be made promptly to avoid indefinite suspension, as prolonged suspension can lead to speculation and cannot be fully compensated by damages. The breaching party also has an interest in ending the suspension.[121] After a reasonable period, avoidance is blocked until the obligation becomes due, then general rules (Articles 49 and 64 CISG) apply. The creditor is entitled to damages for losses caused by the debtor's anticipatory breach, calculated under Article 74 *et seq.*

---

[114] Fountoulakis, 'Article 72 CISG: Avoidance in Case of Anticipatory Breach of Contract' in Schwenzer and Schroeter (eds) (n 12) para 31.

[115] Michael Bridge, 'The CISG from the Common Lawyer's Point of View' in Peter Mankowski and Wolfgang Wurmnest (eds), *Festschrift für Ulrich Magnus zum 70. Geburtstag* (De Gruyter 2014) 172.

[116] Fountoulakis, 'Article 72 CISG: Avoidance in Case of Anticipatory Breach of Contract' in Schwenzer and Schroeter (eds) (n 12) paras 18–19; Fountoulakis, 'Article 71 CISG: Suspension of Performance' in Schwenzer and Schroeter (eds) (n 12) para 37.

[117] Fountoulakis, 'Article 72 CISG: Avoidance in Case of Anticipatory Breach of Contract' in Schwenzer and Schroeter (eds) (n 12) para 33; Saidov, 'Article 72' in Kröll, Mistelis, and Perales Viscasillas (eds) (n 12) para 25.

[118] International Institute for the Unification of Private Law (n 73) 289, art 7.4.13, off cmt 2; Stefan Vogenauer, 'Article 7.4.13' in Vogenauer (ed) (n 1) para 3.

[119] Ulrich Schroeter, 'Article 27 CISG: Dispatch Principle' in Schwenzer and Schroeter (eds) (n 12) para 9 ff.

[120] Saidov, 'Article 72' in Kröll, Mistelis, and Perales Viscasillas (eds) (n 12) para 19; *Metal concentrate case* [1996] ICC International Court of Arbitration 8574 (Final Award), CISG-online 1293; *Downs Invest P/L v Perwaja Steel SDN BHD* [2000] Supreme Court of Queensland [2000] QSC 421/SC No 10680 of 1996, CISG-online 587 859, note 80.

[121] Saidov, 'Article 72' in Kröll, Mistelis, and Perales Viscasillas (eds) (n 12) para 22; Fountoulakis, 'Article 72 CISG: Avoidance in Case of Anticipatory Breach of Contract' in Schwenzer and Schroeter (eds) (n 12) para 27.

IX. Long-term Contracts

'Long-term contract' might refer to a contract that is to be performed over a period of time. It normally involves varying degrees of complexity in the transaction and an ongoing relationship between the parties (Article 1.11 PICC). The PICC considers some special needs of long-term contracts in Articles 1.11, 2.1.14, 5.1.7, 5.1.8, and 7.3.7 PICC. Regarding the avoidance of the contract, Article 5.1.8 PICC suggests that either party may avoid a contract for an indefinite period subject to the same requirements to avoid other contracts. The effects of avoidance in general, as well as restitution, are dealt with in Articles 7.3.5 and 7.3.7 PICC and will also be reviewed in Chapter 16 of this work.

On the other hand, Article 73 CISG can also be applied to long-term contracts. Article 73 CISG addresses issues in instalment contracts, distinguishing three scenarios. First, if one instalment involves the occurrence of a fundamental breach, the creditor can avoid the contract for that instalment alone, aligning with the CISG principle of contract preservation (Article 73(1) CISG). Second, if a breach in one instalment indicates a future fundamental breach with respect to future instalments, the creditor can avoid the contract for the future (Article 73(1) CISG). Third, a breach in one delivery can lead to avoidance of the entire contract if it affects its entirety due to interdependence between past or future deliveries. These remedies apply to both parties except for Article 73(3) CISG, which is exclusive to the buyer. The defective performance might be related to lack of payment or defective payment (e.g. agreed currency, modes or place, etc.), non-delivery, late delivery, or non-conforming goods, etc. We will briefly deal with the three scenarios here.

Article 73(1) CISG deals with contracts for goods delivered in instalments, requiring at least two successive deliveries with a time gap between them.[122] Remedies for these contracts hinge on each delivery being separable,[123] not necessarily affecting the entire contract, following general CISG rules, and avoiding the contract only in case of fundamental breaches.[124] Determining an instalment contract depends on evaluating the transaction as a whole. Independent deliveries may form part of a single instalment contract if logically linked, like continuous deliveries or unified payment terms. Supply agreements exemplify instalment contracts, where the buyer places orders and the seller delivers single lots as required under the contract. Similarly, a distribution agreement may qualify as an

---

[122] Cf *Czech cheese case* [1998] Schiedsgericht der Hamburger freundschaftlichen Arbitrage (Hamburg Friendly Arbitration) CISG-online 638; *Macedonian lambskin coats case* [1998] Handelsgericht des Kantons Zürich (Commercial Court Canton Zurich) HG 930634, CISG-online 415.

[123] United Nations (UN) Conference Official Records, UN Doc A/CONF.97/19 (n 97) 54, art 64, para 1.

[124] Christiana Fountoulakis, 'Article 73 CISG: Avoidance of Instalment Contracts' in Schwenzer and Schroeter (eds) (n 12) para 18.

instalment contract if buyer and seller obligations are clear, even if they involve different products as long as they are related. Instalment contracts often entail payment in instalments, though lump-sum payments or non-coincident instalment terms can also be agreed upon in this kind of contract. Conversely, paying in instalments alone does not define an instalment contract.

Article 73(1) CISG requires a fundamental breach on an instalment, and it is irrelevant what was its position or value.[125] Assessing fundamental breach in this scenario might be difficult if the instalment is part of a whole. The critical question is whether the breach affects the entire contract, as it determines its fundamentality, as illustrated in Article 73(3) CISG. For instance, the non-delivery of assembly tools needed for equipment fitting may not endanger the entire contract if alternatives are available. Thus, there may be no fundamental breach concerning the single instalment.[126]

Article 73(2) CISG allows the creditor to avoid an instalment contract for the future (*ex nunc*) if an instalment is not performed correctly, leading to good grounds for assuming a future fundamental breach, provided avoidance is declared within a reasonable time. Avoidance under Article 73(2) requires only a failure to perform any obligation in an instalment, unlike Article 73(1), which needs a fundamental breach.[127] Examples include repetitive delays, non-conforming goods,[128] or unauthorized instalments. Sporadic delays can indicate a future fundamental breach if they become frequent. The creditor can set a deadline for performance; if missed, it establishes grounds for future avoidance. The current breach must indicate a risk of a future fundamental breach.[129] Multiple minor breaches might collectively indicate this risk. The standard is that of a reasonable person in the creditor's position (Article 8(2) CISG).[130] The breach must provide 'good grounds' for predicting a future fundamental breach, judged by Article 25 CISG.[131] In this

[125] Djakhongir Saidov, 'Article 73' in Kröll, Mistelis, and Perales Viscasillas (eds) (n 12) para 8; Brunner, Schläpfer, and Boog, 'Article 73 (Avoidance in Installment Contracts)' in Brunner and Gottlieb (eds) (n 51) para 5; Fountoulakis, 'Article 73 CISG: Avoidance of Instalment Contracts' in Schwenzer and Schroeter (eds) (n 12) para 6.

[126] Fountoulakis, 'Article 73 CISG: Avoidance of Instalment Contracts' in Schwenzer and Schroeter (eds) (n 12) paras 12–14.

[127] Saidov, 'Article 73' in Kröll, Mistelis, and Perales Viscasillas (eds) (n 12) para 16; Brunner, Schläpfer, and Boog, 'Article 73 (Avoidance in Installment Contracts)' in Brunner and Gottlieb (eds) (n 51) para 9; Fountoulakis, 'Article 73 CISG: Avoidance of Instalment Contracts' in Schwenzer and Schroeter (eds) (n 12) para 27.

[128] *Spanish orange juice case* [2010] Oberlandesgericht Düsseldorf (Court of Appeal Düsseldorf) I-17 U 132/08, CISG-online 2171 note 89 ff.

[129] Saidov, 'Article 73' in Kröll, Mistelis, and Perales Viscasillas (eds) (n 12) para 18; Brunner and others, 'Article 73 (Avoidance in Installment Contracts)' in Brunner and Gottlieb (eds) (n 51) para 9; Fountoulakis, 'Article 73 CISG: Avoidance of Instalment Contracts' in Schwenzer and Schroeter (eds) (n 12) para 23.

[130] Fountoulakis, 'Article 73 CISG: Avoidance of Instalment Contracts' in Schwenzer and Schroeter (eds) (n 12) para 22.

[131] Cf *Skin care products case* [1998] Helsingin hovioikeus (Court of Appeal Helsinki) S 96/1215, CISG-online 1304.

regard, the prediction threshold is lower than the one set in Article 72 CISG, which requires a 'clear' indication of future fundamental breach. The severity must be proportionate to the remaining contract. Good grounds for future fundamental breaches include the seller's inability to deliver after payment,[132] failure to provide substitutes,[133] consistently defective goods,[134] or buyer's refusal to honour exclusivity clauses.[135] The focus is on whether future performance is in serious doubt due to substantial non-delivery or persistent defects.[136] For payment obligations, Article 73(2) CISG applies if the expected breach's severity is significant relative to the remaining contract.[137]

Unlike the typical avoidance case, the right to avoid the contract under Article 73(2) CISG is limited to future instalments. Preparations for delivering an instalment already made by one party do not prevent the avoidance of that or other instalments due to the divisibility and relative independence of each instalment.[138] There is no explicit duty to give notice of the intended avoidance to allow the other party to provide performance assurance. Despite the close and often long-standing relationships in instalment contracts, such a duty would be appropriate but is not implied in Article 73(2) CISG.[139] However, abruptly declaring avoidance without contacting the contractual partner may breach the duty to mitigate loss under Article 77 CISG.

As mentioned above, Article 73(3) CISG applies exclusively to the buyer, allowing avoidance of the entire contract or parts of it[140] if the seller commits a fundamental breach in a single instalment (Article 73(1)) and this breach, along with the interdependence of the instalments, impairs the contract as a whole or

---

[132] *Italian sunflower oil case* [1997] Handelsgericht des Kantons Zürich (Commercial Court Canton Zurich) HG 950347, CISG-online 327.

[133] *Paprika powder case I* [1995] Landgericht Ellwangen (District Court Ellwangen) 1 KfH O 32/95, CISG-online 279.

[134] *Spanish orange juice case* (n 128); *Shanghai Anlili International Trading Co. Ltd. v J & P Golden Wings Corp.* [2008] 上海市第一中级人民法院 (Intermediate People's Court Shanghai No. 1) IPC/34, CISG-online 2059; *Dingxi Longhai Dairy, Ltd v Becwood Technology Group LLC* [2011] US Court of Appeals (8th Circuit) 10-2612, CISG-online 2256: goods delivered in prior instalments were wrapped in mouldy packaging.

[135] Cf *BRI Production 'Bonaventure' S.a.r.l. v Pan African Export* [1995] Cour d'appel de Grenoble (Court of Appeal Grenoble) 93/3275, CISG-online 151.

[136] *Shanghai Anlili International Trading Co. Ltd. v J & P Golden Wings Corp.* (n 134).

[137] Saidov, 'Article 73' in Kröll, Mistelis, and Perales Viscasillas (eds) (n 12) para 18; Brunner, Schläpfer, and Boog, 'Article 73 (Avoidance in Installment Contracts)' in Brunner and Gottlieb (eds) (n 51) para 9; Fountoulakis, 'Article 73 CISG: Avoidance of Instalment Contracts' in Schwenzer and Schroeter (eds) (n 12) para 26.

[138] *Dingxi Longhai Dairy, Ltd v Becwood Technology Group, LLC* [2008] US District Court for the District of Minnesota 08-762 DSD/SRN, CISG-online 1774.

[139] Michael Bridge, 'Issues Arising Under Articles 64, 72 and 73 of the United Nations Convention on Contracts for the International Sale of Goods' (2005) 25 *Journal of Law & Commerce* 405, who suggests granting the buyer the possibility to prevent avoidance by providing assurance (arts 71[3], 72[2]) also under art 73(2) by means of art 7(2). Of the same view as it is held here see Saidov, 'Article 73' in Kröll, Mistelis, and Perales Viscasillas (eds) (n 12) para 26.

[140] Fountoulakis, 'Article 73 CISG: Avoidance of Instalment Contracts' in Schwenzer and Schroeter (eds) (n 12) para 32.

significantly. The timing of avoidance for the single instalment is relevant for the rest of the contract. Article 73(3) CISG extends the buyer's response to a single in-stalment breach Article 73(3) requires the buyer to have a right of avoidance due to a fundamental breach in an instalment (Article 73(1) CISG).

X. Price Reduction

The buyer's remedy of price reduction for non-conforming goods[141] is a distinct and crucial mechanism for fairness within the framework of international sales law. It allows the buyer to adjust the agreed price for conforming goods to reflect the actual value of the goods delivered. This remedy is distinct from a claim for damages. Even in situations where the debtor is exempt from liability for damages due to an impediment to performance under Article 79 CISG, the creditor may nevertheless be entitled to invoke the remedy of price reduction (see Chapter 15). This remedy specifically addresses the discrepancy between what was contractu-ally agreed and what was actually delivered.

Under Article 50 CISG, when non-conforming goods are delivered and the buyer does not avoid the contract, the buyer has the right to reduce the price.[142] This right is subject to the seller's opportunity to remedy the non-conformity (Article 46 CISG). Article 50 CISG is limited to addressing non-conforming goods (including physical, non-physical and legal defects under Articles 41 and 42)[143] and cannot be invoked for other breaches by the seller, such as failure to deliver, delays in delivery, or breaches of other contractual obligations. In such instances, the buyer must resort to other remedies the CISG provides, such as specific per-formance, claiming damages, or avoiding the contract.

It is important to note that the seller's exemption from liability in damages under Article 79 CISG does not affect the buyer's right to reduce the price.[144] Thus, if the seller is prevented by an impediment from delivering conforming goods, nothing

---

[141] Comparing laws, cf Schwenzer and Muñoz (n 7) para 48.6 ff.

[142] *China Railway No 10 Engineering Group Co Ltd v Triorient LLC* [2020] American Arbitration Association—International Centre for Dispute Resolution (AAA/ICDR) 01-19-0003-0137, CISG-online 5639; Schwenzer and Muñoz (n 7) para 48.6 ff; Markus Müller-Chen, 'Article 50 CISG: Buyer's Right to Reduce Price' in Schwenzer and Schroeter (eds) (n 12) para 1; Christoph Brunner and Markus Altenkirch, 'Article 50 (Remedy of Reduction of Price)' in Brunner and Gottlieb (eds) (n 51) para 3; Ivo Bach, 'Article 50' in Kröll, Mistelis, and Perales Viscasillas (eds) (n 12) para 9.

[143] In other words, the remedy applies to non-conformity under Article 35 CISG as well as in cases involving third-party rights or claims under CISG art 41, and third-party rights or claims based on in-dustrial or intellectual property under CISG art 42, see CISG Advisory Council, 'CISG-AC Opinion No. 22, The Seller's Liability for Goods Infringing Intellectual Property Rights under Article 42 CISG, Rapporteur: Dr. David Tebel, Rothorn Legal, Frankfurt Am Main, Germany, 7–9 August 2022' (2022) comment 13.11.

[144] Ingeborg Schwenzer, 'Article 79 CISG: Exemption from Liability for Damages' in Schwenzer and Schroeter (eds) (n 12) para 56.

stops the buyer from reducing the purchase price under the mechanism in Article 50 CISG.

However, the buyer cannot exercise this remedy during the reasonable period given to the seller under Article 47 CISG to perform its obligations, or while the seller is attempting to cure the non-conformity under Article 37 CISG or Article 48 CISG.[145] Additionally, the price reduction is not available if the contract has been avoided (Article 49 CISG).

The buyer may exercise the right to reduce the price by notifying the seller or through other conduct interpreted under Article 8 CISG. Once the buyer notifies the seller of a price reduction, it cannot subsequently declare avoidance of the contract for non-conformity of the goods under Article 49 CISG.[146] However, if the buyer declares avoidance wrongly, it will not be precluded from price reduction thereafter. If the buyer has already paid the contract price, the difference between the contract price and the reduced price may be recovered from the seller.[147] If payment has not yet been made, the buyer may fulfil its payment obligation by paying the reduced price. If the seller challenges the reduction of the price claimed by the buyer, the proper price reduction under Article 50 CISG, as well as the effect on other remedies claimed by the Parties, will then be decided by the competent court or arbitral tribunal.

The price reduction under Article 50 CISG is calculated based on the ratio of the actual value of the non-conforming goods at the time of delivery to the value that conforming goods would have had at that time.[148] Under Article 50 CISG, the buyer is not entitled to the difference between the value that conforming goods would have had at the time of delivery and the actual value of the non-conforming goods, as would be appropriate in a damages action where the contract price is not considered.[149] Price reduction is not intended to fulfil the buyer's expected interest.

Let us understand the price reduction mechanism in Article 50 CISG with the following examples. The contract price of goods is $54,000. On a rising

---

[145] Brunner and Altenkirch, 'Article 50 (Remedy of Reduction of Price)' in Brunner and Gottlieb (eds) (n 51) para 13; Bach, 'Article 50' in Kröll, Mistelis, and Perales Viscasillas (eds) (n 12) para 6; Müller-Chen, 'Article 50 CISG: Buyer's Right to Reduce Price' in Schwenzer and Schroeter (eds) (n 12) para 7.

[146] Brunner and Altenkirch, 'Article 50 (Remedy of Reduction of Price)' in Brunner and Gottlieb (eds) (n 51) para 63; Bach, 'Article 50' in Kröll, Mistelis, and Perales Viscasillas (eds) (n 12) para 12; Müller-Chen, 'Article 50 CISG: Buyer's Right to Reduce Price' in Schwenzer and Schroeter (eds) (n 12) para 17.

[147] Brunner and Altenkirch, 'Article 50 (Remedy of Reduction of Price)' in Brunner and Gottlieb (eds) (n 51) para 11; Bach, 'Article 50' in Kröll, Mistelis, and Perales Viscasillas (eds) (n 12) para 51; Müller-Chen, 'Article 50 CISG: Buyer's Right to Reduce Price' in Schwenzer and Schroeter (eds) (n 12) para 16.

[148] Brunner and Altenkirch, 'Article 50 (Remedy of Reduction of Price)' in Brunner and Gottlieb (eds) (n 51) para 7; Bach, 'Article 50' in Kröll, Mistelis, and Perales Viscasillas (eds) (n 12) para 36; Müller-Chen, 'Article 50 CISG: Buyer's Right to Reduce Price' in Schwenzer and Schroeter (eds) (n 12) para 8.

[149] Bach, 'Article 50' in Kröll, Mistelis, and Perales Viscasillas (eds) (n 12) para 36; Müller-Chen, 'Article 50 CISG: Buyer's Right to Reduce Price' in Schwenzer and Schroeter (eds) (n 12) para 8.

market, conforming goods would have been worth $60,000 at delivery. In their non-conforming state, they are worth $48,000. The adjusted price is eight-tenths of $54,000 = $43,200. Now, if the contract price of goods is $55,000, on a falling market, conforming goods would have been worth $50,000 at delivery. In their non-conforming state, they are worth $45,000. The adjusted price is nine-tenths of $55,000 = $49,500.

A damages action would benefit the buyer in a rising market and disadvantage them in a falling market. In Example 1, a damages action would yield the buyer $12,000 ($60,000 – $48,000), while Article 50 CISG would provide $10,800 ($54,000 – $43,200). In Example 2, a damages action would give the buyer $5,000 ($50,000 – $45,000), whereas Article 50 would result in $5,500 ($55,000 – $49,500).

The price reduction formula under Article 50 CISG distributes the risk of post-contractual market fluctuations between the seller and buyer according to the contract, whereas a damages action places the risk solely on the buyer if the contract is not avoided. This formula maintains the original equivalence ratio between the goods' objective value and the reduced price.[150]

Under Article 51 CISG, the price may also be reduced using the formula in Article 50 CISG when only some of the goods delivered conform to the contract or when the quantity of conforming goods is less than what was contracted. The value of the goods is determined at the time and place of delivery and, where goods are traded in market conditions, by reference to the market.

For goods not traded in market conditions, the presumed difference in value between non-conforming and conforming goods is the repair cost. The price may be reduced to zero under Article 50 CISG if the goods are entirely valueless due to their non-conformity.[151] The buyer bears the burden of proving the loss of value and its extent under this provision.

Furthermore, the reduced value attributed to non-conformity may be treated as a loss under Article 74 CISG, allowing the buyer to claim damages for that loss instead of reducing the price. In addition to a price reduction under Article 50 CISG, the buyer may claim damages for further loss, subject to Article 74 CISG.[152]

---

[150] Brunner and Altenkirch, 'Article 50 (Remedy of Reduction of Price)' in Brunner and Gottlieb (eds) (n 51) para 2; Bach, 'Article 50' in Kröll, Mistelis, and Perales Viscasillas (eds) (n 12) para 37; Müller-Chen, 'Article 50 CISG: Buyer's Right to Reduce Price' in Schwenzer and Schroeter (eds) (n 12) para 8.

[151] Brunner and Altenkirch, 'Article 50 (Remedy of Reduction of Price)' in Brunner and Gottlieb (eds) (n 51) para 11; Bach, 'Article 50' in Kröll, Mistelis, and Perales Viscasillas (eds) (n 12) para 48; Müller-Chen, 'Article 50 CISG: Buyer's Right to Reduce Price' in Schwenzer and Schroeter (eds) (n 12) para 13.

[152] Brunner and Altenkirch, 'Article 50 (Remedy of Reduction of Price)' in Brunner and Gottlieb (eds) (n 51) para 12; Bach, 'Article 50' in Kröll, Mistelis, and Perales Viscasillas (eds) (n 12) para 64; Müller-Chen, 'Article 50 CISG: Buyer's Right to Reduce Price' in Schwenzer and Schroeter (eds) (n 12) para 18.

Sums paid by the buyer and recoverable from the seller under Article 50 CISG bear interest at the rate appropriate for restitution under Article 84 CISG, not the rate for sums payable in arrears under Article 78 CISG.[153] This nuanced approach ensures the buyer is compensated fairly while maintaining the contractual balance.

[153] Brunner and Altenkirch, 'Article 50 (Remedy of Reduction of Price)' in Brunner and Gottlieb (eds) (n 51) para 11; Bach, 'Article 50' in Kröll, Mistelis, and Perales Viscasillas (eds) (n 12) para 57 ff.

15

Remedies IV—Damages, Exemption, and Interest

I. General: Prerequisites, Strict Liability, Exemptions

This chapter addresses the remedy of damages and interest for breach of contract under the principle of strict liability in the CISG and the PICC. It also explores the limits of the promisor's liability, considering exemptions such as *force majeure* and hardship. Article 74 CISG and Article 7.4.2 PICC stipulate that the aggrieved party has the right to be fully compensated for all disadvantages suffered as a result of the breach of contract. In the case of the CISG, Article 74 CISG requires the existence of a claim for damages on the part of the buyer pursuant to Article 45(1)(b) CISG or on the part of the seller pursuant to Article 61(1)(b) CISG, both of which in turn require the breach of a contractual or statutory obligation.[1] As a general provision, Article 74 CISG is supplemented by Articles 75 CISG and 76 CISG, which, in case of contract avoidance, base the calculation of damages for non-performance on an actual or hypothetical cover transaction.[2] The PICC stipulate similar alternative methods in Articles 7.4.5 and 7.4.6. In addition, the promisor's liability is limited by Article 77 CISG and Article 7.4.8 PICC according to which the promisee is obliged to mitigate its losses.[3]

Following the system of strict liability, both the CISG and the PICC make the promisor liable for all losses arising from non-performance, irrespective of fault,[4] unless it is exempted in accordance with Articles 79 (impediments and hardship) and 80 (aggrieved party's conduct) CISG or Articles 7.1.7 (impediments), 6.2.1 (hardship), and 7.1.2 PICC (aggrieved party's conduct), respectively.[5] However, Article 5.1.4(2) PICC expressly allows for departing from the strict liability principle if an obligation only requires a party to make a reasonable person's best efforts to fulfil it.[6]

II. *Force Majeure* and Hardship

In all legal systems, the principle of *pacta sunt servanda*, or sanctity of contract, places the burden of changes in the original contracting conditions upon the obligor.[7] However, the law often provides a valid exemption from performance in case of impossibility, *force majeure*, hardship, and similar impediments.[8] The

---

[1] Christoph Brunner, Nils Schmidt-Ahrendts, and Mark Czarnecki, 'Article 74' in Christoph Brunner and Benjamin Gottlieb (eds), *Commentary on the UN Sales Law (CISG)* (3rd edn, Kluwer Law International 2019) para 1; Milena Djordjević, 'Article 74' in Stefan Kröll, Loukas Mistelis, and Pilar Perales Viscasillas (eds), *UN Convention on Contracts for the International Sale of Goods (CISG). A Commentary* (2nd edn, CH Beck 2018) para 2.

[2] Brunner, Schmidt-Ahrendts, and Mark Czarnecki, 'Article 74' in Brunner and Gottlieb (eds) (n 1) para 1.

[3] See generally Ingeborg Schwenzer, 'Article 77 CISG: Mitigation of Damages' in Ingeborg Schwenzer and Ulrich Schroeter (eds), *Schlechtriem & Schwenzer: Commentary on the UN Convention on the International Sale of Goods* (5th edn, Oxford University Press 2022); Ewan McKendrick, 'Article 7.4.8' in Stefan Vogenauer (ed), *Commentary on the UNIDROIT Principles of International Commercial Contracts (PICC)* (2nd edn, Oxford University Press 2015); UNCITRAL, Digest of Case Law on the United Nations Convention on the International Sale of Goods (2016) 334, art 74, para 11; International Institute for the Unification of Private Law (ed), *UNIDROIT Principles of International Commercial Contracts* (UNIDROIT International Institute for the Unification of Private Law 2017) 282, art 7.4.5, off cmt 1.

[4] Christoph Brunner, *Force Majeure and Hardship under General Contract Principles: Exemption for Non-Performance in International Arbitration* (Wolters Kluwer 2008) 61; *Indian glass mosaic tiles case* [2013] Oberster Gerichtshof (Austrian Supreme Court) 4 Ob 208/12k, CISG-online 2398, note 4.

[5] Ingeborg Schwenzer, 'Article 74 CISG: Calculation of Damages in General' in Schwenzer and Schroeter (eds) (n 3) para 3; Harriet Schelhaas, 'Article 7.1.1' in Vogenauer (ed) (n 3) paras 1, 10.

[6] Stefan Vogenauer, 'Article 5.1.4' in Vogenauer (ed) (n 3) para 5.

[7] Ingeborg Schwenzer, 'Force Majeure and Hardship in International Sales Contracts' (2008) 39 *Victoria University of Wellington Law Review* 709, 709.

[8] Ibid 710.

CISG contains a provision governing the consequences of certain events that obstruct agreed performance, without specific reference to domestic law theories such as acts of God, *force majeure*, or hardship. Article 79 CISG pertinently relieves a party from paying damages only if the breach was due to an unforeseeable and unavoidable impediment beyond its control. Conversely, the PICC has two distinctive provisions to address *force majeure* (Article 7.1.7 PICC) and hardship (Articles 6.2.1–6.2.3 PICC) separately. In this chapter, we regroup both impediments, often categorized in domestic laws as *fait du prince*, hardship, impracticability, and *force majeure*, etc., into the general concepts of *force majeure* (making performance impossible or nearly so) and hardship (making performance excessively onerous).

1. The contract

The contract terms should be the starting point to determine whether *force majeure* or hardship exists and its consequences. The CISG and the PICC endorse the principle of freedom of contract, enabling parties to handle unforeseen impediments and changing circumstances as they see fit.[9] However, generally, parties must fulfil the contract according to its original terms.

Concerning CISG contracts, the primary question is which party in the sales contract is affected by *force majeure* or hardship. The chosen trade term (e.g. EXW, FOB, CIF, DPU) determines the delivery point and allocates the risk for transport, export/import control, tariffs, and delivery documents.[10] Depending on the agreed term and timing of the *force majeure* or hardship, either the seller or the buyer bears the impediment's consequences.

Despite the risk allocation in ICC Incoterms® 2020, a *force majeure* or hardship clause may exempt a party liable for breach. Parties can specify events and thresholds for exemptions.[11] Model clauses like the ICC Force Majeure and Hardship Clauses (1985, 2003, 2020) are often used in international commercial contracts.[12]

---

[9] Harry M Flechtner, *Honnold's Uniform Law for International Sales under the 1980 United Nations Convention* (5th edn, Wolters Kluwer 2021) 804.

[10] *Suministros industriales diversos, S. A. v Hunan Pulaili Pipe Co., Ltd. (Welded Carbon Steel Pipe Case)* [2019] Hunan Changsha Tianxin District People's Court, (2018) Xiang 0103 Min Chu No. 3578, CISG-online 5504: considering the FOB Incoterm to allocate the risk of loss on the buyer for damaged goods during transport hired by buyer. See for a detailed analysis Johan Erauw, 'Article 67' in Kröll, Mistelis, and Perales Viscasillas (eds) (n 1) para 23 ff; see also Florian Mohs, 'Introduction to Articles 66–70' in Schwenzer and Schroeter (eds) (n 3) para 8 ff.

[11] Brunner, 'Force Majeure and Hardship under General Contract Principles: Exemption for Non-Performance in International Arbitration' (n 4) 117–18.

[12] International Chamber of Commerce (ICC) Force Majeure Clause 1985 ICC publication 421; ICC Force Majeure Clause 2003, ICC publication 650; ICC Force Majeure Clause 2020; Ingeborg Schwenzer, 'Article 79 CISG: Exemption from Liability for Damages' in Schwenzer and Schroeter (eds) (n 3) para 58. See Flechtner (n 9) 816 ff; Clayton P Gillette and Steven D Walt, *The UN Convention on Contracts for the International Sale of Goods: Theory and Practice* (2nd edn, Cambridge University Press 2016) 336–7: on reconciling the contractual provision with art 79.

Parties use them to define impediments or clarify the measures warranting exemptions. A *force majeure* clause might lower or raise the threshold for invocation.[13] Contracts may specify the necessary performance cost increase or value decrease for hardship exemptions.

2. Requirements under the CISG and the PICC

The CISG and the PICC contain default rules balancing the principle of *pacta sunt servanda* with performance impediments, considering both sellers' and buyers' interests. Article 79 CISG covers all impediments to performance and is widely accepted to include hardship.[14] The CISG addresses hardship using principles of reasonableness and loyalty found in Articles 39, 46, 48, and 54 CISG.[15] On the other hand, Article 7.1.7 PICC mirrors the general principles in Article 79 CISG under the title of *force majeure*.[16] In addition, the PICC govern the specific change of circumstances resulting in hardship and its remedies in Articles 6.2.1 to 6.2.3 PICC.

a.) Definitions of impediment and hardship

Article 79(1)(5) CISG and Article 7.1.7(1)(4) PICC (*force majeure*) exempt a party from liability for damages if the failure to perform is due to an impediment. The CISG does not expressly define 'impediment'. However, based on the Convention's rules of interpretation (Article 7(1)) and the wording of Article 79, an impediment may be understood as an objective circumstance that prevents performance, is external to the promisor,[17] and is beyond its control—one that could not reasonably have been anticipated at the time of the contract's conclusion and could not have been avoided or overcome.

Under the CISG, hardship is considered under the general impediment provision in Article 79 CISG, with the clarification that merely increased onerousness

---

[13] Yesim M Atamer, 'Article 79' in Kröll, Mistelis, and Perales Viscasillas (eds) (n 1) para 89; Martin Davies and David Snyder, *International Transactions in Goods: Global Sales in Comparative Context* (Oxford University Press 2014) 326.

[14] See ICC Hardship Clause 2020, para. (2)(b); CISG Advisory Council, 'CISG-AC Opinion No. 20, Hardship under the CISG, Rapporteur: Prof. Dr. Edgardo Muñoz, Universidad Panamericana, Guadalajara, Mexico. Adopted by the CISG Advisory Council following its 27th meeting, in Puerto Vallarta, Mexico on 2–5 February 2020' (2020) comment 1.8; CISG Advisory Council, 'CISG-AC Opinion No. 7, Exemption of Liability for Damages under Article 79 of the CISG, Rapporteur: Professor Alejandro M. Garro, Columbia University School of Law, New York, N.Y. 12 October 2007' (2007) Black Letter Rule 3.1; Schwenzer, 'Article 79 CISG: Exemption from Liability for Damages' in Schwenzer and Schroeter (eds) (n 3) para 4.

[15] CISG Advisory Council, 'CISG-AC Opinion No. 20' (n 14) Black Letter Rule 2.2.

[16] Pascal Pichonnaz, 'Article 7.1.7' in Vogenauer (ed) (n 3) para 1, note 184: The genesis of art 7.1.7 explains why this contribution makes many references to literature on the CISG as a source of inspiration

[17] Schwenzer, 'Article 79 CISG: Exemption from Liability for Damages' in Schwenzer and Schroeter (eds) (n 3) para 11.

does not exempt performance. Hardship exists when performance becomes excessively onerous, the utility of performance significantly decreases, or the contract's equilibrium is fundamentally altered. This approach aligns with the CISG Advisory Council opinion No. 20,[18] and the hardship provisions in Articles 6.2.1 and 6.2.2 PICC.

b.) Outside one party's control and sphere of risk

The allocation of risks, practices, and international usages under Article 9 CISG and Article 1.9 PICC is crucial for defining the sphere of risk in each contract. Unless otherwise agreed, the promisor is liable for internal circumstances. Unforeseeable illness or death may not be an impediment beyond control since such events are part of an organization's risk.[19] Only events outside the promisor's control can lead to an exemption under *force majeure* or hardship in both the CISG and the PICC.[20] These might include earthquakes, floods, storms, droughts, fires, and epidemics if these impede performance. State interventions like quotas, bans, and rationing typically fall outside the parties' control. The promisor is liable for impediments originating from its sphere, including personal issues, operational failures, and proper contract preparation.[21] It is also responsible for personnel who are not considered third parties under Article 79(2) CISG.[22] Exemption may be available when third parties, that have a material inference in the performance of the contract, affect the promisor ability to perform.[23] Exemption for labour strikes depends on whether the dispute is beyond the promisor's control.[24] Internal strikes are typically the promisor's risk, while general strikes may exempt it, considering foreseeability and mitigation efforts.[25] The promisor's financial capacity, including procuring foreign currency,[26] is its responsibility.[27] Exemption is not granted for

---

[18] CISG Advisory Council, 'CISG-AC Opinion No. 20' (n 14) Black Letter Rule 4.

[19] Atamer, 'Article 79' in Kröll, Mistelis, and Perales Viscasillas (eds) (n 1) para 47: any endogenous impediment, such as death or severe illness, will not suffice for exoneration even if they were unforeseeable or uncontrollable. See also Schwenzer, 'Article 79 CISG: Exemption from Liability for Damages' in Schwenzer and Schroeter (eds) (n 3) para 12; Brunner, *Force Majeure and Hardship under General Contract Principles* (n 4) 168–9.

[20] See UNCITRAL (n 3) 375, art 79, para 6.

[21] Atamer, 'Article 79' in Kröll, Mistelis, and Perales Viscasillas (eds) (n 1) para 47 ff.

[22] Schwenzer, 'Article 79 CISG: Exemption from Liability for Damages' in Schwenzer and Schroeter (eds) (n 3) para 35.

[23] *Urangesellschaft GmbH v Nynco Trading Ltd.* [2021] ICC International Court of Arbitration, ICC Case 23069/GR (Final Award), CISG-online 6665.

[24] Atamer, 'Article 79' in Kröll, Mistelis, and Perales Viscasillas (eds) (n 1) para 47; Christoph Brunner, 'Article 79 (Impediment Excusing a Party from Damages)' in Brunner and Gottlieb (eds) (n 1) para 10; Schwenzer, 'Article 79 CISG: Exemption from Liability for Damages' in Schwenzer and Schroeter (eds) (n 3) para 22.

[25] Brunner, *Force Majeure and Hardship under General Contract Principles* (n 4) 169.

[26] See *Automatic diffractometer case* [1995] Международный коммерческий арбитражный суд при Торгово–промышленной палате Российской Федерации (Tribunal of International Commercial Arbitration at the Russian Federation Chamber of Commerce and Industry (MKAC)) 123/1992, CISG-online 207.

[27] United Nations (UN) Conference Official Records, 'Commentary on the Draft Convention on Contracts for the International Sale of Goods, prepared by the Secretariat' (1978) UN Doc A/CONF.97/

unreliable intermediaries failing to transfer payments.[28] Exemptions may apply if state measures prohibit performance.[29] For generic goods with a ready market, the seller bears the procurement risk and must seek substitutes if necessary. No exemption shall be granted unless the parties agree on a specific source for generic goods, such as a certain steel mill, and in this case if that certain mill is shut down by a fire or so on, exemption may be granted.[30] Hacking attacks do not constitute a *force majeure* event to exempt liability.[31]

For specific goods, the seller is exempt if delivery is prevented by the impediment. *Force majeure* and hardship rules can apply if the seller fails to provide conforming goods[32] or goods free of third-party claims due to the impediment.[33] This is rare, particularly for manufacturers who are strictly liable for defects.[34] Intermediaries are also liable for hidden defects from reliable suppliers.[35] The exemption also applies if a party cannot be expected to perform the contract for ethical reasons.[36] This is particularly relevant for 'dual-use goods', which can be misused to produce chemical, biological, or nuclear weapons.[37] If the seller

5, art 65, para 10: regarding the buyer's payment obligation; Brunner, 'Article 79 (Impediment Excusing a Party from Damages)' in Brunner and Gottlieb (eds) (n 1) para 11; Atamer, 'Article 79' in Kröll, Mistelis, and Perales Viscasillas (eds) (n 1) para 47.

[28] *Italian tiles case III* [1995] Amtsgericht Alsfeld (Local Court Alsfeld) 31 C 534/94, CISG-online 170.
[29] Schwenzer, 'Article 79 CISG: Exemption from Liability for Damages' in Schwenzer and Schroeter (eds) (n 3) para 26.
[30] Brunner, 'Article 79 (Impediment Excusing a Party from Damages)' in Brunner and Gottlieb (eds) (n 1) para 12; cf e.g. *Audiencia Provincial de Valladolid, Dry Top N.V. v Sociedad Cooperativa Piñón-Sol* [2015] Audiencia Provincial de Valladolid (Court of Appeal Valladolid) 69/2015, CISG-online 2619: the Court considered the volatility in the pine kernel market and deemed that a reduction in production was not unexpected, the seller might have protected itself from such market-inherent risks. See also *Bulbs for four-leaf clover case* [2019] Oberlandesgericht Düsseldorf (Court of Appeal Düsseldorf). I-6 U 2/19, CISG-online 4614: holding that the seller was exempt from paying damages under art 79(1) CISG, holding that the entirety of the flower bulbs destroyed by a fire in the seller's supplier's refrigerated warehouse constitutes an obstacle which would be beyond the seller's control.
[31] *[...] v Luka Food d.o.o.* [2021] Vrhovni kasacioni sud/Врховни касациони суд (Serbian Supreme Court) 135/2021, CISG-online 6859: holding that the generation of a false message from the seller's address at the time of contract conclusion cannot be accepted as valid to exempt the buyer's liability.
[32] For prevailing view on question of conformity of goods within CISG art 79 see CISG Advisory Council, 'CISG-AC Opinion No. 7' (n 14) comments 7, 10; Brunner, *Force Majeure and Hardship under General Contract Principles* (n 4) 189 ff; Schwenzer, 'Article 79 CISG: Exemption from Liability for Damages' in Schwenzer and Schroeter (eds) (n 3) para 7.
[33] Schwenzer, 'Article 79 CISG: Exemption from Liability for Damages' in Schwenzer and Schroeter (eds) (n 3) para 29.
[34] Atamer, 'Article 79' in Kröll, Mistelis, and Perales Viscasillas (eds) (n 1) para 75; Brunner, 'Article 79 (Impediment Excusing a Party from Damages)' in Brunner and Gottlieb (eds) (n 1) para 24.
[35] *Vine wax case* [1999] Bundesgerichtshof (German Supreme Court) VIII ZR 121/98, CISG-online 396; Atamer, 'Article 79' in Kröll, Mistelis, and Perales Viscasillas (eds) (n 1) para 76; Brunner, 'Article 79 (Impediment Excusing a Party from Damages)' in Brunner and Gottlieb (eds) (n 1) paras 15, 25; Schwenzer, 'Article 79 CISG: Exemption from Liability for Damages' in Schwenzer and Schroeter (eds) (n 3) para 30.
[36] Cf discussion in Ingeborg Schwenzer and B Leisinger, 'Ethical Values and International Sales Contracts' in Ross Cranston, Jan Ramberg, and Jacob Ziegler (eds), *Commercial Law Challenges in the 21st Century—Jan Hellner in Memoriam* (Stockholm Centre for Commercial Law 2007) 272 ff.
[37] Brunner, 'Article 79 (Impediment Excusing a Party from Damages)' in Brunner and Gottlieb (eds) (n 1) para 23.

realizes that the buyer intends to misuse the goods or that the buyer's country will confiscate them for such purposes, the seller is exempted from performing.[38] Additionally, there might be grounds to grant the seller the right to avoid the contract in such situations.[39]

c.) Non-foreseeable events

To exempt the disadvantaged party from liability, obstacles (*force majeure*) and changed circumstances (hardship) must be unforeseeable. Foreseeability is measured based on the objective or reasonable person standard under Article 8(2) CISG. Furthermore, the special circumstances of the case must also be given attention to. It is assumed, for example, that a seller who is delivering to or from a region prone to frequent labour strikes or transportation blockades has assumed the risk of delivery delays if no specific disclaimer is included in the contract.[40] If foreseeable, the risk is assumed unless contractually allocated otherwise.[41] Past, existing, and future obstacles may not be foreseeable at contract conclusion. Foreseeability does not imply that every conceivable impediment—such as earthquakes, pandemics, or volcanic eruptions—must automatically be accounted for by the obligor. The likelihood of the specific impediment occurring must reach a certain threshold, so that the obligor can reasonably be expected to take timely precautions, such as arranging alternative suppliers or routes.[42] Difficult cases involve new government measures based on known or ought-to-know events.[43]

For the particular case of hardship, the CISG Advisory Council Opinion No. 20 recommends considering some non-exclusive factors, in particular whether either party assumed the risk of a change in circumstances, whether the contract is speculative, the extent of previous market fluctuations, and the contract duration.[44]

Contract interpretation through Article 8 CISG and Article 1.4 PICC and risk allocation in standard trade terms can show accepted risks and thus foreseeability too. Highly speculative contracts imply assumed risks.[45] Courts may not exempt

---

[38] Ibid para 23; Schwenzer, 'Article 79 CISG: Exemption from Liability for Damages' in Schwenzer and Schroeter (eds) (n 3) para 33.

[39] Schwenzer, 'Article 79 CISG: Exemption from Liability for Damages' in Schwenzer and Schroeter (eds) (n 3) para 33.

[40] Atamer, 'Article 79' in Kröll, Mistelis, and Perales Viscasillas (eds) (n 1) para 50.

[41] Brunner, *Force Majeure and Hardship under General Contract Principles* (n 4) 156–7; Atamer, 'Article 79' in Kröll, Mistelis, and Perales Viscasillas (eds) (n 1) para 50; Brunner, 'Article 79 (Impediment Excusing a Party from Damages)' in Brunner and Gottlieb (eds) (n 1) para 39.

[42] Atamer, 'Article 79' in Kröll, Mistelis, and Perales Viscasillas (eds) (n 1) para 51.

[43] See *Macromex Srl v Globex International Inc* [2007] American Arbitration Association – International Centre for Dispute Resolution (AAA/ICDR) 50181T 0036406 (Interim Award), CISG-online 1645: the measures of the Romanian government considered 'unexpected', hence the exemption; cf ICC Case 4462 of 1985 and 1987, *Yb.Com.Arb. 1991* 54 Collection of ICC Arbitral Awards III 3.

[44] CISG Advisory Council, 'CISG-AC Opinion No. 20' (n 14).

[45] CISG Advisory Council, 'CISG-AC Opinion No. 20' (n 14) comment 7.7; Brunner, *Force Majeure and Hardship under General Contract Principles* (n 4) 220; Ewan McKendrick, 'Article 6.2.2' in Vogenauer (ed) (n 3) para 8: the threshold is likely to be higher where the parties have entered into a highly speculative contract or the contract has been concluded in a market that is highly volatile.

a party even if market prices triple in this scenario.[46] Typical price fluctuations in commodity trade generally do not qualify for hardship. For example, a 70 per cent price increase might not be considered hardship, as seen in a Belgian court case applying PICC to fill in the gaps in Article 79 CISG.[47] In a more recent case, a Danish court held that fluctuations in prices due to the Russia–Ukraine conflict and COVID-19 were not sufficient to establish hardship since in the specific case they were expected.[48] Long-term contracts might have a lower threshold for alteration if the disadvantaged party faces imminent financial ruin.[49] The timing of hardship events is crucial in calculating performance values.[50]

d.) Not possible to overcome

The impediment must be one that cannot be reasonably avoided or overcome.[51] Whether the obligor can overcome an impediment depends on the contractual or legal threshold. As a general rule, the obligor would be required to incur excess costs or even losses to overcome the impediment and perform the contract.[52]

For what may be called *force majeure* impediments, once the occurrence of an unforeseen event becomes sufficiently concrete, the obligor must do everything within its capacity to prevent timely performance from being affected. To mitigate the effects of such an event, the obligor generally needs to act before it materializes.[53] He cannot merely stand by as a passive observer. The impact on contractual performance of a hurricane, forecast several days in advance, or of an imminent labour strike, or of new regulations announced for imminent enactment, can often be mitigated if appropriate measures are taken in due time.[54]

To assess whether an event can be overcome, one should consider the alternative means of performance that are available and adequate to satisfy the obligee. If,

---

[46]   *Steel bars case I* Steel bars case I [1989] ICC International Court of Arbitration 6281 (Final Award), CISG-online 8: a price increase of 13.16 per cent is not enough; *Iritecna S.pA v Marc Rich & Co AG* [1993] Tribunale di Genova (District Court Genova) 1912, CISG-online 540: a price increase of 43.71 per cent is not enough, but applying Italian domestic law, Code of Commerce art 1467.

[47]   *Scafom International BV v Lorraine Tubes SAS* [2009] Hof van Cassatie van België/Cour de cassation de Belgique (Belgian Supreme Court) C.07.0289.N, CISG-online 1963.

[48]   See *Gasum Oy, v Gazprom Export LLC* [2022] Ad hoc Arbitral Tribunal, CISG-online 7151: where the arbitral tribunal, despite affirming that the Russia–Ukraine conflict was unforeseeable, held that price fluctuations where 'to be expected'; see also *Attianese S.p.A. v P. S. Import ApS* [2024] Sø- og Handelsretten (Maritime and Commercial Court) BS-40411/2023-SHR, CISG-online 7177.

[49]   Brunner, *Force Majeure and Hardship under General Contract Principles* (n 4) 438, 439; CISG Advisory Council, 'CISG-AC Opinion No. 20' (n 14) comment 7.12.

[50]   Brunner, *Force Majeure and Hardship under General Contract Principles* (n 4) 462–3; CISG Advisory Council, 'CISG-AC Opinion No. 20' (n 14) comment 7.13.

[51]   Atamer, 'Article 79' in Kröll, Mistelis, and Perales Viscasillas (eds) (n 1) paras 54–55; Schwenzer, 'Article 79 CISG: Exemption from Liability for Damages' in Schwenzer and Schroeter (eds) (n 3) para 15.

[52]   Brunner, 'Article 79 (Impediment Excusing a Party from Damages)' in Brunner and Gottlieb (eds) (n 1) para 34; Schwenzer, 'Article 79 CISG: Exemption from Liability for Damages' in Schwenzer and Schroeter (eds) (n 3) para 34.

[53]   Atamer, 'Article 79' in Kröll, Mistelis, and Perales Viscasillas (eds) (n 1) para 54.

[54]   Ibid.

for example, the impediment destroys or damages the goods, the seller must procure substitutes if the risk is still his and the goods are generic.[55] If the buyer cannot pay due to sudden banking sanctions, it may be expected to use funds from accounts abroad. Accessory obligations, such as transport or packaging, may also be affected. For instance, if the usual shipping route is blocked, the seller must seek alternatives.[56] Regarding the extent of the additional or alternative measures the obligor is expected to take to overcome the impediment, the CISG Advisory Council Opinion No. 7 suggests exceeding the 'limit of sacrifice' to meet this threshold.[57] This means that measures falling below this threshold do not amount to an exempting impediment under Article 79 CISG.

For hardship, there is no fixed threshold under Article 79 CISG or Article 6.2.2 PICC.[58] The PICC 1994 edition once suggested a 50 per cent alteration as 'fundamental', but later editions refrain from specifying exact figures.[59] A threshold of at least 100 per cent has been suggested as a general rule,[60] but in some cases, it has been concluded that even a 100 per cent price change might not suffice for hardship.[61]

Excessive value changes in performance may not make the contract economically impossible. For instance, if the buyer's final product price increases proportionally with input costs already covered in stock, the hardship event might not substantially alter the contract's equilibrium.[62] The 'reasonable expectation test' applies to determine hardship.[63] A party may be exempt if performance, though possible, requires excessive and disproportionate costs.[64] The financial loss must be significantly greater than the risk a reasonable person would assume at contract formation.[65] Primary consideration should be given to individual case circumstances.[66]

---

[55] Ibid para 55.

[56] Ibid para 55.

[57] CISG Advisory Council, 'CISG-AC Opinion No. 7' (n 14) comment 43.

[58] See McKendrick, 'Article 6.2.2' in Vogenauer (n 3) paras 8–9.

[59] International Institute for the Unification of Private Law (n 3) 182–3, art 6.2.2, off cmt 2; McKendrick, 'Article 6.2.2' in Vogenauer (ed) (n 3) para 8, footnote 42.

[60] Brunner, 'Article 79 (Impediment Excusing a Party from Damages)' in Brunner and Gottlieb (eds) (n 1) para 29; Brunner, *Force Majeure and Hardship under General Contract Principles* (n 4) 428 ff;

[61] Cf *Behr France S.a.r.l. v Romay AG* [2004] Cour de Cassation (French Supreme Court) Y 01-15.964, CISG-online 870; Schwenzer, 'Force Majeure and Hardship in International Sales Contracts' (n 7) 716–17. But different *Scafom International BV v Lorraine Tubes S.A.S.* (n 47): price increase of 70 per cent already sufficient.

[62] See CISG Advisory Council, 'CISG-AC Opinion No. 20' (n 14) comment 4.6: suggesting the Eisenberg Formula; Melvin Eisenberg, 'Impossibility, Impracticability, and Frustration' (2009) 1 *Journal of Legal Analysis* 207, 245.

[63] CISG Advisory Council, 'CISG-AC Opinion No. 20' (n 14) comments 4.6, 7.4, 12.5; see further Yasutoshi Ishida, 'CISG Article 79: Exemption of Performance, and Adaptation of Contract through Interpretation of Reasonableness—Full of Sound and Fury, but Signifying Something' (2018) 30 *Pace International Law Review* 331, 374, 377.

[64] Flechtner, *Honnold's Uniform Law* (n 9) 820–21.

[65] See further Schwenzer, 'Force Majeure and Hardship in International Sales Contracts' (n 7) 717–19: for time factor for impediments.

[66] CISG Advisory Council, 'CISG-AC Opinion No. 20' (n 14) comment 7.5.

Finally, if the seller secured goods before the hardship event, they might not withhold delivery for resale at a higher profit.[67] Each factor helps to determine whether a party can claim *force majeure* or hardship, focusing on the specific circumstances and contract terms.

3. Scope of obligations covered

Force majeure and hardship under the CISG and the PICC might be invoked whenever a party to the contract fails to perform or improperly performs any of their contractual duties.[68] The various forms of non-performance—whether due to impossibility, delay, or defective performance—are treated uniformly.[69] The broad concept of non-performance in the CISG and the PICC aligns with *force majeure* and hardship rules. Therefore, the provisions on *force majeure* and hardship address breaches of obligations that incur liability, like lack of performance, partial performance, or non-conformity, but they also cover breaches of ancillary obligations or obligations arising from the contract winding up.[70] While sellers rarely rely on *force majeure* or hardship in cases of non-conformity of goods because they are typically strictly liable for ensuring conformity, regardless of their awareness of supplier errors, it does not mean that sellers might not be entitled to invoke these exemption rules in different situations.

4. Time of *force majeure* or hardship events

Under the CISG, hardship and *force majeure* can arise from events occurring before or after the contract's conclusion if the parties were unaware and could not have known about these events.[71] For instance, if the contracted goods were destroyed before the contract's conclusion, but the seller was unaware and could not have prevented this, the seller may be exempted under Article 79(1) CISG.[72] Similarly, for hardship under the PICC, Article 6.2.2(a) states that hardship can be

---

[67] Ibid comment 7.14.

[68] Ibid Black Letter Rule 1.

[69] See Flechtner (n 9) 807.

[70] Atamer, 'Article 79' in Kröll, Mistelis, and Perales Viscasillas (eds) (n 1) para 8; Schwenzer, 'Article 79 CISG: Exemption from Liability for Damages' in Schwenzer and Schroeter (eds) (n 3) para 7.

[71] CISG Advisory Council, 'CISG-AC Opinion No. 7' (n 14) Black Letter Rule 1, comment 8; Atamer, 'Article 79' in Kröll, Mistelis, and Perales Viscasillas (eds) (n 1) para 48; Ingeborg Schwenzer and Edgardo Muñoz, 'Duty to Renegotiate and Contract Adaptation in Case of Hardship' (2019) 24 *Uniform Law Review* 149, 158; Schwenzer, 'Article 79 CISG: Exemption from Liability for Damages' in Schwenzer and Schroeter (eds) (n 3) para 13.

[72] CISG Advisory Council, 'CISG-AC Opinion No. 7' (n 14) Black Letter Rule 1, comment 8; Schwenzer, 'Force Majeure and Hardship in International Sales Contracts' (n 7) 717.

found if the events causing the imbalance occur or become known to the disadvantaged party after the contract's conclusion.[73]

An initial impediment or a gross imbalance arising from unknown and unavoidable circumstances is governed by the CISG in order to preserve the uniformity rules for international trade, which would otherwise be undermined by the application of divergent domestic laws.[74] Under the PICC, an initial gross disparity (Article 3.2.7 PICC) or initial impossibility (Article 3.1.3 PICC) in the parties' performances typically leads to remedies for mistakes.[75] These remedies may coexist within a single legal system like the PICC but pose challenges in CISG sales contracts. Since the CISG lacks specific provisions on mistake,[76] some may argue that these issues must be resolved using applicable domestic law,[77] leading to unpredictable results.[78] For example, it might be unclear when production costs rose—before or after the contract's conclusion.[79] Applying domestic law on mistake or impossibility to this question could jeopardize uniformity in sales law. The same reasoning that treats initial and subsequent impediments equally in *force majeure* cases should apply to hardship.[80] The CISG's notion of hardship or economic impediment should be broadly interpreted to include changes in circumstances after the contract's conclusion and gross disparities existing at the time of conclusion.[81]

5. Liability for third persons

The primary rule under Article 79(1) CISG is that the obligor is responsible for the acts and conduct of its own personnel, as they are deemed to be within its control. This also applies to independent entrepreneurs who, organizationally, are subject to the promisor while providing their services (e.g. providing a crane and operator to load goods).[82] Similarly, under Article 79(2) CISG, the promisor is liable for the conduct of third persons engaged to perform the whole or part of the

---

[73] See McKendrick, 'Article 6.2.2' in Vogenauer (ed) (n 3) para 10.

[74] CISG Advisory Council, 'CISG-AC Opinion No. 20' (n 14) comments 6.2, 6.3.

[75] McKendrick, 'Article 7.4.8' in Vogenauer (ed) (n 3) para 11.

[76] Atamer, 'Article 79' in Kröll, Mistelis, and Perales Viscasillas (eds) (n 1) para 48.

[77] See the position in most domestic systems in Ingeborg Schwenzer and Edgardo Muñoz, *Global Sales and Contract Law* (2nd edn, Oxford University Press 2022) paras 17.43, 49.15 ff.

[78] CISG Advisory Council, 'CISG-AC Opinion No. 20' (n 14) comment 6.4.

[79] See for an example *Amalgamated Investment & Property Co Ltd v John Walker & Sons Ltd* [1977] 1 WLR 164, CA: a case where it was difficult to determine the timing of the impediment arising; CISG Advisory Council, 'CISG-AC Opinion No. 20' (n 14) comment 6.4.

[80] Schwenzer, 'Article 79 CISG: Exemption from Liability for Damages' in Schwenzer and Schroeter (eds) (n 3) para 13.

[81] CISG Advisory Council, 'CISG-AC Opinion No. 20' (n 14) comment 6.4; Schwenzer and Muñoz, *Global Sales and Contract Law* (n 77) paras 45.14, 45.98.

[82] Cf *Art books case* [1999] Handelsgericht des Kantons Zürich (Commercial Court Canton Zurich) HG 970238.1, CISG-online 488; see also Final award in ICC Case No. 9466, *Yearbook of Commercial Arbitration* (2002) 170–80; Schwenzer, 'Article 79 CISG: Exemption from Liability for Damages' in Schwenzer and Schroeter (eds) (n 3) para 35.

contract.[83] This provision covers individuals acting independently and outside the promisor's organizational sphere but under its responsibility.[84] Engaging a carrier for transport, when it is part of the promisor's contractual obligations, is generally considered a partial undertaking of performance by a third person and falls under Article 79(2) CISG.[85]

Distinguishing between personnel assisting in performance (liable under Article 79(1) CISG) and independent third persons (liable under Article 79(2) CISG) can be challenging, but often has little practical impact. Engagement under Article 79(2) CISG assumes the third person was brought in after the contract's conclusion to aid in performance. This includes banks and freight carriers if their performance is part of the promisor's obligations. The promisee's personnel can also be third persons under Article 79(2) CISG.[86] Upstream suppliers are generally not considered third persons under Article 79(2) CISG as they create preconditions or assist in preparation but are not entrusted with performance.[87] Their impediments are treated under Article 79(1) CISG, making the promisor liable for procurement risks. Consequently, the seller is typically not exempt if the supplier fails to deliver or provides defective goods, even if unforeseeable to the seller.[88]

Under Article 79(2) CISG, the promisor can only be exempted from liability if it proves two cumulative elements. First, that the impediment meets the requirements reviewed above for exemption. Second, that the third person engaged to perform—if it were itself the promisor—would also qualify for exemption under Article 79(1) CISG. Since these requirements are cumulative, Article 79(2) effectively imposes a strict liability:[89] the obligor cannot excuse itself merely by showing that it exercised due diligence in selecting, instructing, or supervising the third person, as liability under the CISG is not fault-based.[90]

For example, if a carrier entrusted with the goods is prevented from delivering them on time because of an unexpected government-imposed port closure due to a natural disaster—a circumstance beyond the control of both the obligor and the carrier—both could be exempted under Article 79. Conversely, if the carrier delays

---

[83]   Atamer, 'Article 79' in Kröll, Mistelis, and Perales Viscasillas (eds) (n 1) para 60; Brunner, 'Article 79 (Impediment Excusing a Party from Damages)' in Brunner and Gottlieb (eds) (n 1) para 14; Schwenzer, 'Article 79 CISG: Exemption from Liability for Damages' in Schwenzer and Schroeter (eds) (n 3) para 35; Brunner, *Force Majeure and Hardship under General Contract Principles* (n 4) 185 ff.

[84]   Brunner, 'Article 79 (Impediment Excusing a Party from Damages)' in Brunner and Gottlieb (eds) (n 1) para 14; Schwenzer, 'Article 79 CISG: Exemption from Liability for Damages' in Schwenzer and Schroeter (eds) (n 3) para 35.

[85]   Cf *Art books case* (n 82).

[86]   *Italian tiles case III* (n 28).

[87]   CISG Advisory Council, 'CISG-AC Opinion No. 7' (n 14) Black Letter Rule 2.3, comment 18.

[88]   Atamer, 'Article 79' in Kröll, Mistelis, and Perales Viscasillas (eds) (n 1) para 64; Brunner, 'Article 79 (Impediment Excusing a Party from Damages)' in Brunner and Gottlieb (eds) (n 1) para 15; Schwenzer, 'Article 79 CISG: Exemption from Liability for Damages' in Schwenzer and Schroeter (eds) (n 3) para 38.

[89]   Ibid para 40.

[90]   Atamer, 'Article 79' in Kröll, Mistelis, and Perales Viscasillas (eds) (n 1) para 60.

delivery due to its own internal strike, the obligor would not be exempted, because the carrier's failure would not satisfy the stringent conditions of Article 79 CISG.

The PICC do not have a similar provision to Article 79(2) CISG regarding the liability of the promisor for third parties' conduct in the performance of the contract. However, similar rules might be extracted from the PICC underlying general principles pursuant to Article 1.6(2) PICC.[91]

6. Passing impediment

The exemption is effective for the duration of the *force majeure* or hardship period (see Article 79 CISG and Article 7.1.7(2) PICC).

7. Duty to give notice

Pursuant to Article 79(4) CISG and Article 7.1.7(3) PICC, a party failing to perform must provide timely notice of the impediment and its effect on its ability to perform. This notice requirement applies to *force majeure* and hardship situations.[92] The notice must be given within a reasonable time after the affected party knew or should have known of the *force majeure* or hardship (Article 79(4) CISG and Article 7.1.7(3) PICC).[93] To fulfil its purpose, the notice must describe the *force majeure* event or changes in economic circumstances and their severity, nature, and probable duration in sufficient detail.[94] Whether notice is given within a reasonable time depends on the circumstances and the parties' agreement, such as the available means or possibility to transmit the notice and whether timely performance was of the essence.[95] The notice is not subject to any form requirements.[96] Unlike Article 27 CISG, under Article 79(4) CISG, the risk that the notice fails to reach the addressee within a reasonable time is placed on the party affected by *force majeure* or hardship. The same approach is taken under Article 7.1.7(3) PICC.[97] However, a teleological reading of these provisions may exempt

---

[91] Pichonnaz, 'Article 7.1.7' in Vogenauer (ed) (n 3) para 22.

[92] See Schwenzer and Muñoz, *Global Sales and Contract Law* (n 77) para 45.108.

[93] Schwenzer, 'Article 79 CISG: Exemption from Liability for Damages' in Schwenzer and Schroeter (eds) (n 3) para 45; Atamer, 'Article 79' in Kröll, Mistelis, and Perales Viscasillas (eds) (n 1) para 95; Pichonnaz (n 16) para 37.

[94] Pichonnaz (n 16) para 40; Atamer, 'Article 79' in Kröll, Mistelis, and Perales Viscasillas (eds) (n 1) para 96; Schwenzer, 'Article 79 CISG: Exemption from Liability for Damages' in Schwenzer and Schroeter (eds) (n 3) para 45.

[95] Brunner, *Force Majeure and Hardship under General Contract Principles* (n 4) 343.

[96] Atamer, 'Article 79' in Kröll, Mistelis, and Perales Viscasillas (eds) (n 1) para 96; Schwenzer, 'Article 79 CISG: Exemption from Liability for Damages' in Schwenzer and Schroeter (eds) (n 3) para 46.

[97] Brunner, *Force Majeure and Hardship under General Contract Principles* (n 4) 343.

the aggrieved party from the obligation to give notice if the other party was aware of the relevant circumstances.[98]

A party's failure to give notice does not preclude it from invoking the exemption.[99] The general exemption from damages remains unaffected.[100] The consequence of failing to give proper and timely notice of the impediment is liability for damages.[101] For example, if the buyer could have arranged for an alternative supplier to mitigate its losses had they been informed promptly of the impediment faced by the seller, the seller might be liable for the additional costs the buyer incurred due to not receiving timely notice.[102] This liability for consequential damages due to lack of notice is expressly stated by the second sentence of Article 79(4) CISG, and reflected in Article 7.1.7(3) PICC.

8. Consequences

According to Article 79(5) CISG, in case of exoneration under Article 79 CISG or Article 7.1.7 PICC, nothing prevents either party from exercising any right other than to claim damages. In other words, the obligor is not liable for damages for as long as the impediment persists.

Similarly, a claim for specific performance under the contract's original terms is not enforceable as long as the impediment or substantial disequilibrium in the parties' performances persists. Under the CISG, neither the obligation to deliver substitute goods nor the obligation to cure any non-conformity of the goods by repair can be enforced against the disadvantaged party during the period of *force majeure* or hardship.[103]

In cases of hardship—for example, where the seller's costs double—the seller may propose a modification of the contract by demanding a higher price and may refuse to deliver at the original price. The buyer may reject this unilateral modification, avoid the contract, procure substitute goods (cover purchase), and claim damages for the difference between the contract price and the cover price. It is for

---

[98] Pichonnaz (n 16) para 41; Atamer, 'Article 79' in Kröll, Mistelis, and Perales Viscasillas (eds) (n 1) para 96.

[99] CISG Advisory Council, 'CISG-AC Opinion No. 20' (n 14) comment 8.4; Brunner, 'Article 79 (Impediment Excusing a Party from Damages)' in Brunner and Gottlieb (eds) (n 1) para 43; Brunner, *Force Majeure and Hardship under General Contract Principles* (n 4) 343–5.

[100] CISG Advisory Council, 'CISG-AC Opinion No. 20' (n 14) comment 8.4; Atamer, 'Article 79' in Kröll, Mistelis, and Perales Viscasillas (eds) (n 1) para 97.

[101] CISG Advisory Council, 'CISG-AC Opinion No. 20' (n 14) comment 8.4; Atamer, 'Article 79' in Kröll, Mistelis, and Perales Viscasillas (eds) (n 1) para 97.

[102] CISG Advisory Council, 'CISG-AC Opinion No. 20' (n 14) comment 8.4; Atamer, 'Article 79' in Kröll, Mistelis, and Perales Viscasillas (eds) (n 1) para 97.

[103] Atamer, 'Article 79' in Kröll, Mistelis, and Perales Viscasillas (eds) (n 1) paras 87–88; Schwenzer, 'Article 79 CISG: Exemption from Liability for Damages' in Schwenzer and Schroeter (eds) (n 3) paras 42–43.

the court or arbitral tribunal to determine whether the seller's hardship exempts it from liability;[104] if hardship is established, the seller will not be held liable for the resulting damages.

The same would be true for similar obligations under the PICC contracts.

9. Other remedies

Parties may agree on consequences or remedies in case of impediments to perform, in particular for hardship. For instance, the ICC Hardship Clause 2020 requires the parties to negotiate alternative terms within a reasonable time.[105] Option 3B allows contract adaptation or termination by a judge or arbitrator if adaptation is impossible. Additional remedies include termination rights under options 3A and 3C.[106] The scope and consequences of these clauses are determined by contract interpretation under Article 8 CISG and Article 4.1 PICC, respectively. The next paragraphs explore the default remedies still available under the CISG and the PICC.

a.) *Force majeure*
Rights not affected by an exemption under Article 79 CISG include the other party's right to withhold performance (Article 71 CISG), reduce the price (Article 50 CISG), avoid the contract (Articles 48(1), 64(1) CISG), claim interest (Article 78 CISG), or expenses for preserving goods (Articles 85, 86 CISG).[107] The PICC are also clear that nothing in Article 7.1.7 PICC prevents a party from exercising a right to avoid the contract or withhold performance, or request interest on money due.[108]

A party may suspend performance if it becomes clear that the other party will not perform a substantial part of its obligations.[109] The right to withhold performance under the CISG and the PICC does not expressly mention impediments, but it may be included under 'serious deficiency in ability to perform.'[110] Proper notice of the impediment allows the other party to withhold performance and avoid further losses. Article 50 CISG allows the buyer to reduce the price of non-conforming goods.[111] *Force majeure* and hardship rarely affect already delivered

---

[104] CISG Advisory Council, 'CISG-AC Opinion No. 20' (n 14) comment 9.9.

[105] See ICC Hardship Clause 2020, para (2)(b).

[106] See ICC Hardship Clause 2020, para 3A, 3B and 3C.

[107] CISG Advisory Council, 'CISG-AC Opinion No. 20' (n 14) comment 9.10; Schwenzer, 'Article 79 CISG: Exemption from Liability for Damages' in Schwenzer and Schroeter (eds) (n 3) para 57; Atamer, 'Article 79' in Kröll, Mistelis, and Perales Viscasillas (eds) (n 1) para 40 ff.

[108] Brunner, *Force Majeure and Hardship under General Contract Principles* (n 4) paras 366–81.

[109] CISG Advisory Council, 'CISG-AC Opinion No. 20' (n 14) comment 9.5; Flechtner, (n 9) 723; Brunner, *Force Majeure and Hardship under General Contract Principles* (n 4) 366–7; see also Schwenzer, 'Force Majeure and Hardship in International Sales Contracts' (n 7) 721.

[110] CISG Advisory Council, 'CISG-AC Opinion No. 20' (n 14) comment 9.5.

[111] Atamer, 'Article 79' in Kröll, Mistelis, and Perales Viscasillas (eds) (n 1) para 41.

non-conforming goods, but a buyer may claim a deduction for missing parts the seller cannot deliver due to an impediment. The right to avoid the contract under the CISG and the PICC requires a fundamental breach.[112] Finally, a buyer delaying payment due to *force majeure* or hardship must pay interest from the agreed date.[113] This applies to any monetary obligation delayed due to *force majeure* or hardship unless caused by the other party.[114]

b.) Hardship

Pursuant to Article 6.2.3 PICC, when a party faces hardship, it is entitled to request contract renegotiations.[115] This request must be made promptly and clearly outline the reasons for the request.[116] It is important to note that simply requesting renegotiation does not give the disadvantaged party the right to withhold their performance under the contract (Article 6.2.3(1) PICC). Both parties are still expected to fulfil their contractual obligations unless they are legitimately entitled to do so under the contract or the law.[117] If the parties cannot reach an agreement within a reasonable timeframe, either party has the right to take the matter to court (or arbitration when such a right exists). The court, upon finding that hardship exists, has the authority to either avoid the contract or adapt it in a way that restores its balance (Article 6.2.3(3) PICC).[118] The court's decision to avoid or adapt the contract will depend on what is deemed reasonable under the circumstances.

Under the CISG, the parties may, if they agree, renegotiate their contract in case of hardship.[119] As stated above, contract clauses may provide for such a procedure.[120] This is often the most rational and practical solution. Voluntary renegotiation allows parties to address market or value distortions quickly and efficiently.[121] CISG case law shows that parties typically attempt to resolve issues amicably before seeking remedies under the Convention.[122] That being said,

---

[112] See CISG arts 25, 45(1)(a), 64(1)(a); PICC 2016, art 7.3.1(1), (2).

[113] CISG Advisory Council, 'CISG-AC Opinion No. 7' (n 14), comments 3.47 and 3.48.

[114] CISG art 80; CISG Advisory Council, 'CISG-AC Opinion No. 7' (n 14) comment 3.47.

[115] Ewan McKendrick, 'Article 6.2.3' in Vogenauer (ed) (n 3) para 1: renegotiation is based on the principle of good faith and duty to cooperate; Schwenzer and Muñoz, 'Duty to Renegotiate and Contract Adaptation in Case of Hardship' (n 71) 160.

[116] McKendrick, 'Article 6.2.3' in Vogenauer (ed) (n 3) paras 2–3.

[117] McKendrick, 'Article 6.2.3' in Vogenauer (ed) (n 3) para 4; International Institute for the Unification of Private (n 3) 225, art 6.2.3, Illustration 4.

[118] Brunner, *Force Majeure and Hardship under General Contract Principles* (n 4) 490 ff; McKendrick, 'Article 6.2.3' in Vogenauer (ed) (n 3) paras 6–10.

[119] Schwenzer and Muñoz, 'Duty to Renegotiate and Contract Adaptation in Case of Hardship' (n 71) 16; but see CISG Advisory Council, 'CISG AC Opinion No. 7' (n 14) comment 40; ICC Award [1999] No 5953 Clunet 1990, 1056: the duty to renegotiate may be traced to the principle of good faith.

[120] See ICC Hardship Clause 2003 para (2)(b).

[121] Schwenzer and Muñoz, 'Duty to Renegotiate and Contract Adaptation in Case of Hardship' (n 71) 161: stating that imposing a duty is neither desirable nor necessary.

[122] *Hannaford v Australian Farmlink Pty Ltd* [2008] Federal Court of Australia [2008] FCA 1591/ ACN 087 011 541, CISG-online 1782; *Fashion products case* [2003] ICC International Court of Arbitration 11849, CISG-Online 1421; *Suspension of delivery case* [2010] 대구지방법원 (District Court Daegu) 2007GaHap11525, CISG-Online 2505.

renegotiation, like negotiation, relies on willingness and trust. It cannot be imposed by coercion. Therefore, under the CISG the parties have no duty to renegotiate the contract in case of hardship. Imposing a renegotiation duty under the CISG would be impractical under Article 79 CISG, which releases the breaching party from damages but does not require renegotiation.[123] Hardship cases often involve complex factual situations, making it difficult to determine bad faith in negotiations.[124] Imposing renegotiation is unsuitable for international transactions that require promptness and legal certainty.

Under the CISG, a court or arbitral tribunal may not adapt the contract in case of hardship.[125] Article 79 CISG does not allow contract adaptation by a court or tribunal, reflecting a rejection of this remedy. Creating a separate remedy for economic impediments is unnecessary and contradicts the parties' autonomy.[126] Arguments suggesting that Article 50 CISG on price reduction implies a general principle for adjusting contracts to changed circumstances, are flawed.[127] Price reduction stems from breach of contract, whereas contract adaptation in hardship affects the party not responsible for the change of circumstances.[128] Proposals to use Article 6.2.3(4) PICC as an underlying CISG principle or international usage for contract adaptation under CISG are not possible.[129] There is no gap in the CISG regarding hardship remedies, and the adaptation remedy is not universally accepted.

Under the CISG, a court or arbitral tribunal is not permitted to avoid the contract in cases of hardship.[130] The CISG requires avoidance by party declaration, ensuring certainty and speed, especially in international transactions (see Chapter 14).

III. Failure to Perform Caused by the Other Party

Under Article 80 CISG and Article 7.1.2 PICC, a party cannot rely on the nonperformance of the other party if the non-performance was caused by the first party's actions or omissions.[131] The promisee's fault is irrelevant,[132] and it cannot

---

[123] Schwenzer and Muñoz, 'Duty to Renegotiate and Contract Adaptation in Case of Hardship' (n 71) 162.

[124] Ibid.

[125] Joseph Lookofsky, *Understanding the CISG* (6th edn, Kluwer Law International 2022) 167; CISG Advisory Council, 'CISG-AC Opinion No. 20' (n 14) Black Letter Rule 12.

[126] Schwenzer and Muñoz, 'Duty to Renegotiate and Contract Adaptation in Case of Hardship' (n 71) 167.

[127] CISG Advisory Council, 'CISG-AC Opinion No. 20' (n 14) comment 12.4.

[128] Ibid comments 12.4 and 12.5.

[129] Ibid comment 12.7; see Schwenzer and Muñoz, 'Duty to Renegotiate and Contract Adaptation in Case of Hardship' (n 71) 168 ff, for an in-detail analysis on efficiency issues and so on.

[130] CISG Advisory Council, 'CISG-AC Opinion No. 20' (n 14) Black Letter Rule 13.

[131] Harriet Schelhaas, 'Article 7.1.2' in Vogenauer (ed) (n 3) para 3.

[132] Christoph Brunner, Christopher Boog, and Beat Schläpfer, 'Article 80' in Brunner and Gottlieb (eds) (n 1) para 7.

claim an exemption under Article 79 CISG or Article 7.1.7 PICC.[133] Acts of the promisee under Article 80 CISG and Article 7.1.2 PICC include providing incorrect or incomplete instructions, or tendering defective drawings or supplies for packaging tests,[134] and not following an instruction manual.[135] This also covers incorrect or incomplete transportation instructions[136], failed payment,[137] failure in obtaining a price guarantee,[138]or attempts to bypass the seller to have goods delivered directly from the manufacturer at the buyer's expense.[139] An omission is equivalent to an act if an action in the promisee's interest was necessary and objectively suited to enable performance.[140] This typically involves cases where the promisee refuses necessary cooperation, such as not acquiring the required import license or not informing the seller of the delivery address[141] or schedule.[142] Other examples include failing to specify goods, refusing to accept substitute deliveries,[143] or not allowing the seller to remedy non-conformities.[144] An act or omission by a person whose conduct falls within the promisee's sphere of risk or for whom it is responsible under Article 79(2) CISG is treated as the promisee's own act or omission, expressed in Article 7.1.2 PICC.[145]

---

[133] Schelhaas, 'Article 7.1.2' in Vogenauer (ed) (n 3) para 4; Thomas Neumann, *The Duty to Cooperate in International Sales: The Scope and Role of Article 80 CISG* (Sellier European Law Publishers 2012) 144–5.

[134] *Inmed v Etablissements JR Maruani* [2019] Cour de Cassation (French Supreme Court) 18-10969, CISG-online 4631: holding the exemption of liability of the seller under art 80 CISG due to the poor quality of the rolls supplied by the buyer that led to unsatisfactory results of the tests for the packaging machine ordered by the buyer.

[135] Yesim M Atamer, 'Article 80' in Kröll, Mistelis, and Perales Viscasillas (eds) (n 1) para 4; Ingeborg Schwenzer, 'Article 80 CISG: Breach Caused by Creditor' in Schwenzer and Schroeter (eds) (n 3) para 3.

[136] *Glimm Screens B.V. v Elos Med S.P.* [2023] Gerechtshof Arnhem-Leeuwarden (Court of Appeal ArnhemLeeuwarden) 200.313.285/01, CISG-online 6449: analysing whether the failure in the transportation was attributable to the seller or the buyer under art 80 CISG.

[137] *ICC Case No. 17768* [2013] ICC International Court of Arbitration 17768: holding that under art 7.1.2 PICC a contractual party may not avail itself of its breach of a contractual term (such as failed payments) to claim any other contractual remedy.

[138] *VSL Middle East LLC v Trenzas y Cables de Acero PSC SL* [2013] Audiencia Provincial de Cantabria (Court of Appeal Cantabria) 400/2013, CISG-online 2487.

[139] Cf the facts of the case in [1995] *Key press case* [1995] Bundesgerichtshof (German Supreme Court) VIII ZR 18/94, CISG-online 149 (previous instances [1992] Landgericht Düsseldorf (District Court Düsseldorf) 31 O 223/91.

[140] *Clay case* [2011] Oberlandesgericht Koblenz (Court of Appeal Koblenz) 6 U 555/07, CISG-online 2301: obligation or non-actionable duty to act; Atamer, 'Article 80' in Kröll, Mistelis, and Perales Viscasillas (eds) (n 1) para 6 ('duty to act or cooperate').

[141] Cf *Propane gas case* [1996] Oberster Gerichtshof (Austrian Supreme Court) 10 Ob 518/95, CISG-online 224.

[142] *Artem v Gray Fox Logistics* [2020] Arbitration Institute of the Stockholm Chamber of Commerce (SCC) V 2019/066, CISG-online 5548.

[143] *Hiking guidebooks case* [2013] Oberlandesgericht Köln (Court of Appeal Cologne) 16 U 106/12, CISG-online 2480.

[144] Atamer, 'Article 80' in Kröll, Mistelis, and Perales Viscasillas (eds) (n 1) para 5; Schwenzer, 'Article 80 CISG: Breach Caused by Creditor' in Schwenzer and Schroeter (eds) (n 3) para 3.

[145] For the CISG see Neumann (n 133) 169 ff. A clarification to art 80 was not made at the Vienna Conference only because such an interpretation was generally agreed upon; for the PICC, see Schelhaas, 'Article 7.1.2' in Vogenauer (ed) (n 3) para 7.

The promisee's act or omission must have caused the promisor's failure to perform both logically and objectively, preventing performance wholly or partially.[146] Indirect causation suffices if a risk materialized from the promisee's conduct within its sphere of risk.[147]

Article 80 CISG and Article 7.1.2 PICC will prevent the promisee from relying on the promisor's failure to perform, thus losing all remedies for non-performance, including claims for damages, specific performance, contract avoidance, and in CISG contracts also price reduction. The right to claim interest is also lost. However, the exemption only covers non-performance aspects caused by the promisee's conduct. For instance, if the seller ships goods late to an incorrectly specified address, the promisee can claim rights from the late shipment but not from the delay caused by the wrong delivery address.

If non-performance is caused by both parties, the legal consequences must be judged based on each party's contribution to causation.[148] Monetary claims should be reduced proportionately.[149] The degree of probability of each party's conduct leading to the loss, degree of fault, and severity of the breach should be considered.[150] Courts and tribunals have great discretion here. Non-monetary rights such as contract avoidance or performance in principle cannot be apportioned.[151] However, the promisee should decide whether to require specific performance or contract avoidance, provided it compensates the promisor proportionally for the breach.[152] For example, suppose the buyer delivers defective material, and the contributions to causation are two-thirds (buyer) and one-third (seller). In that case, the buyer retains the right to specific performance if willing to pay two-thirds of additional production costs. This solution is economically reasonable and consistent with Article 77 CISG principles.[153] Excluding non-financial remedies under Article 80 CISG and Article 7.1.2 PICC is only reasonable if the promisor's contribution is practically insignificant.

---

[146] Cf Atamer, 'Article 80' in Kröll, Mistelis, and Perales Viscasillas (eds) (n 1) para 8; Brunner, Boog, and Schläpfer, 'Article 80' in Brunner and Gottlieb (eds) (n 1) para 6.

[147] See e.g. *Solarpower GmbH v Servis FVE a. s. et al.* [2018] Nejvyšší soud České republiky (Supreme Court of the Czech Republic) 32 Cdo 2978/2016, CISG-online 4197: holding that compensation for indirect damages was also available under the CISG subject to their foreseeability; Neumann (n 133) 158.

[148] Brunner, *Force Majeure and Hardship under General Contract Principles* (n 4) 114.

[149] See *Beer case I* [2013] Oberlandesgericht Brandenburg (Court of Appeal Brandenburg) 6 U 5/12, CISG-online 2400, note 4.4.

[150] Atamer, 'Article 80' in Kröll, Mistelis, and Perales Viscasillas (eds) (n 1) para 18; Brunner, Boog, and Schläpfer, 'Article 80' in Brunner and Gottlieb (eds) (n 1) para 11; Schwenzer, 'Article 80 CISG: Breach Caused by Creditor' in Schwenzer and Schroeter (eds) (n 3) para 10.

[151] See further *Clay case* [2012] Bundesgerichtshof (German Supreme Court) VIII ZR 100/11, CISG-Online 2348.

[152] See Thomas Neumann, 'Shared Responsibility under Article 80 CISG' (2009) *Nordic Journal of Commercial Law* 1, 11 ff.

[153] Atamer, 'Article 80' in Kröll, Mistelis, and Perales Viscasillas (eds) (n 1) para 20; Brunner, Boog, and Schläpfer, 'Article 80 (Failure of Performance Caused by Other Party)' in Brunner and Gottlieb (eds) (n 1) para 11; Schwenzer, 'Article 80 CISG: Breach Caused by Creditor' in Schwenzer and Schroeter (eds) (n 3) para 10.

IV. Damages Claims

Pursuant to Article 7.4.1 PICC, any non-performance gives the aggrieved party a right to damages either exclusively or in conjunction with any other remedies except where the non-performance is excused. Articles 45(1)(b) and 61(1)(b) CISG also entitle the buyer and seller, respectively, to claim damages in case of breach of any of the obligations under the contract or the convention.

1. Full compensation

The CISG and the PICC provide for the principle of full compensation (Article 74 CISG and 7.4.2 PICC).[154] Under this principle, the promisee has the right to be fully compensated for all disadvantages suffered due to the breach of contract.[155] Following the system of strict liability, the promisor is liable for all losses arising from non-performance, irrespective of fault, unless exempted by *force majeure*, hardship or by the other party's conduct (Articles 79 and 80 CISG or Articles 7.1.7, 6.2.1 to 6.2.3, or 7.1.2. PICC).[156]

Compensation must satisfy not only the promisee's expectation interest (i.e. obtaining the benefits from performance)[157] but also the indemnity interest (i.e. avoiding damage to other interests as a result of non-performance).[158] Additionally, Articles 74 CISG and 7.4.2 PICC protect the reliance interest (i.e. expenditures made in reliance on the contract's existence).[159] The express reference to lost profit merely clarifies its recoverability.[160]

Compensation must be made in money; the CISG does not grant the right to restitution in kind.[161] The wording of Article 74 CISG ('[d]amages … consist of a sum equal to the loss') leaves no room for doubt.

---

[154] CISG Advisory Council, 'CISG-AC Opinion No. 6, Calculation of Damages under CISG Article 74, Rapporteur: Professor John Y. Gotanda, Villanova University School of Law, Villanova, Pennsylvania, USA, 2006'(2006) Black Letter Rule 1; Schwenzer, 'Article 74 CISG: Calculation of Damages in General' in Schwenzer and Schroeter (eds)(n 3) para 5; Ingeborg Schwenzer and Pascal Hachem, 'The Scope of the CISG Provisions on Damages' in Djakhongir Saidov and Ralph Cunnington (eds), *Contract Damages: Domestic and International Perspectives* (Bloomsbury Publishing 2008) 92.

[155] See *Cooling machine case* [2002] Oberster Gerichtshof (Austrian Supreme Court) 7 Ob 301/01t, CISG-online 643.

[156] Brunner, *Force Majeure and Hardship under General Contract Principles* (n 4) 61; *Indian glass mosaic tiles case* (Oberster Gerichtshof (Austrian Supreme Court)) (n 4) note 4; Schwenzer, 'Article 74 CISG: Calculation of Damages in General' in Schwenzer and Schroeter (eds) (n 3) para 3; Schelhaas, 'Article 7.1.1' in Vogenauer (ed) (n 3) paras 1, 10.

[157] CISG Advisory Council, 'CISG-AC Opinion No. 6' (n 154) comment 3.1.

[158] Ibid comment 3.1; Schwenzer, 'Article 74 CISG: Calculation of Damages in General' in Schwenzer and Schroeter (eds) (n 3) para 21.

[159] Schwenzer and Hachem, 'The Scope of the CISG Provisions on Damages' in Saidov and Cunnington (eds) (n 154) 92.

[160] United Nations, 'UN Doc A/CONF.97/5' (n 27) 59, art 70, para 3.

[161] Djordjević, 'Article 74' in Kröll, Mistelis, and Perales Viscasillas (eds) (n 1) para 21.

Liability for damages under PICC and the CISG arises when either party fails to fulfil any obligations under the contract or the PICC or the CISG, as the case might be.[162] In other words, there must be causation; the losses must be a consequence of the breach.[163] The breach does not need to be 'fundamental'. A mere breach of any contractual obligation is sufficient to trigger liability. It is enough that, when due, an obligation is either completely unfulfilled or inadequately performed; the promisor does not need to be at fault or formally declared in default, such as through a warning or an additional period (*Nachfrist*).[164] Additionally, failing to meet the obligation to make restitution of performances when the contract is avoided results in liability under the PICC or the CISG (see Chapter 16).

2. Category of losses

The CISG and the PICC compensate for financial losses arising from a breach of contract, including loss of profit. However, they do not specify in detail which losses are recoverable. Therefore, recoverability must be determined in accordance with the overall objective of achieving full compensation, considering the specific purpose of the contract.[165]

a.) Non-performance loss
Non-performance damages consist of the promisee's primary or direct loss.[166] They refer, for instance, to the buyer not receiving an adequate counterpart for the purchase price. If the contract is avoided, non-performance loss might be calculated under Articles 75 and 76 CISG or Articles 7.4.5 and 7.4.6 PICC based on cover transaction costs or market value. If the contract is not avoided, non-performance damages can be calculated under Article 74 CISG or Article 7.4.5 PICC based on substitute transaction costs, with the defective goods' value deducted from the cover transaction costs.[167]

---

[162] *Greenyard Fresh France v Banaland, LLC* [2021] Cour d'appel de Paris (Court of Appeal Paris) 19/21002, CISG-online 5795; Flechtner (n 9) 755; Djordjević, 'Article 74' in Kröll, Mistelis, and Perales Viscasillas (eds) (n 1) para 30; Schwenzer, 'Article 74 CISG: Calculation of Damages in General' in Schwenzer and Schroeter (eds) (n 3) para 11.

[163] See *THI Medical, SAC v Filmore Management Trading, LLC et al.* [2023] US District Court for the Southern District of Florida 21-21632-Civ-GAYLES/TORRES, CISG-online 6489; *Protective masks case IV* [2025] Oberlandesgericht Köln (Court of Appeal Cologne) 8 U 46/23, CISG-online 7261.

[164] Djordjević, 'Article 74' in Kröll, Mistelis, and Perales Viscasillas (eds) (n 1) para 9; Schwenzer, 'Article 74 CISG: Calculation of Damages in General' in Schwenzer and Schroeter (eds) (n 3) para 12.

[165] Schwenzer, 'Article 74 CISG: Calculation of Damages in General' in Schwenzer and Schroeter (eds) (n 3) para 21; Ewan McKendrick, 'Article 7.4.3' in Vogenauer (ed) (n 3) para 3 ff.

[166] *Minh Dung Aluminum Company, Ltd v Aluminum Alloys MFG LLC* [2021] U.S. District Court for the Middle District of Pennsylvania, 1:20-cv-01764, CISG-online 5633.

[167] For the PICC see Ewan McKendrick, 'Article 7.4.5' in Vogenauer (ed) (n 3) paras 1–2. For the CISG, CISG Advisory Council, 'CISG-AC, Opinion No. 6' (n 154) comment 8.1; Flechtner (n 9) 773.

For defective goods, non-performance damages are the difference between the defective goods' objective value and their value if they conformed with the contract. This difference can be claimed regardless of resale.[168] In difficult market value assessments, saved manufacturing costs can serve as a minimum for non-performance damages.[169] If the goods' non-conformity is curable, non-performance loss includes the costs of repair, as well as necessary expenses for replacing installed objects.[170] Non-performance damages can be based on abstract repair costs even without actual repairs.[171]

Delays in contract performance entitle the promisor to compensation of non-performance losses.[172] If the seller delivers late, the buyer can recover costs for measures taken to bridge the gap and avoid consequential loss, including rental costs for a replacement object.[173] Additional cover purchase costs due to late delivery are also recoverable.[174] For late payment, the seller can recover bridging loan costs[175] or lost profit due to missed investment opportunities.[176] Proof of such loss is required, but courts usually apply a generous standard.[177] Abstract calculation based on average market rental or refinancing costs is also possible.[178]

---

[168] Schwenzer and Hachem, 'The Scope of the CISG Provisions on Damages' in Saidov and Cunnington (eds) (n 154) 94.

[169] Cf ibid 99, 100; Nils Schmidt-Ahrendts, 'Disgorgement of Profits under the CISG' in Ingeborg Schwenzer and Lisa Spagnolo (eds), *State of Play: The 3rd Annual MAA Schlechtriem CISG Conference* (Eleven International Publishing 2010) 101.

[170] *South Korean stainless wire case* [1997] Bundesgerichtshof (German Supreme Court) VIII ZR 300/96, CISG-online 277; *Delchi Carrier, SpA v Rotorex Corp* [1995] US Court of Appeals (2nd Circuit) 95-7182, 95-7186, CISG-online 140; see also *Tex-Isle Supply, Inc. v Tecnotubi S.p.A. et al.* [2023] American Arbitration Association—International Centre for Dispute Resolution (AAA/ICDR), 01-20-0015-5404 (Final Award), CISG-online 6682.

[171] Schwenzer, 'Article 74 CISG: Calculation of Damages in General' in Schwenzer and Schroeter (eds) (n 3) para 25.

[172] CISG Advisory Council, 'CISG-AC Opinion No. 6' (n 154) comment 3.2; Djordjević, 'Article 74' in Kröll, Mistelis, and Perales Viscasillas (eds) (n 1) para 44; Schwenzer, 'Article 74 CISG: Calculation of Damages in General' in Schwenzer and Schroeter (eds)(n 3) para 26.

[173] Schwenzer and Hachem, 'The Scope of the CISG Provisions on Damages' in Saidov and Cunnington (eds) (n 154) 96.

[174] Schwenzer, 'Article 74 CISG: Calculation of Damages in General' in Schwenzer and Schroeter (eds) (n 3) para 26.

[175] *Butter case* [1997] Helsingin hovioikeus (Court of Appeal Helsinki) S 96/605, CISG-online 782.

[176] *Italian shoes case III* [1989] Landgericht Stuttgart (District Court Stuttgart) 3 KfH O 97/89, CISG-online 11; *Italian fashion textiles case II* [1990] Amtsgericht Oldenburg in Holstein (Local Court Oldenburg in Holstein) 5 C 73/89, CISG-online 20.

[177] *Italian fashion textiles case III* [1990] Landgericht Hamburg (District Court Hamburg) 5 O 543/88, CISG-online 21; *Failure to open letter of credit and penalty clause case* [1992] ICC International Court of Arbitration 7197, CISG-online 36; *Goodman Food Products, Inc. v Sunrise Foods Int'l Inc.* [2022] U.S. District Court for the Central District of California, 2:21-cv-06518-SB-ADS, CISG-online 6047; *Cold-rolled metal sheets case I* [1994] Vienna International Arbitral Centre of the Austrian Federal Economic Chamber (VIAC) SCH-4318, CISG-online 120: bank interest common in the seller's country.

[178] Schwenzer, 'Article 74 CISG: Calculation of Damages in General' in Schwenzer and Schroeter (eds) (n 3) para 26.

Late payment can cause loss due to exchange rate changes or currency devaluation. Abstract calculation of these losses is recognized, especially when the contract currency is foreign to the promisee.[179] If the contract currency is the promisee's domestic currency, inflation-related value loss is generally not compensable.[180]

b.) Incidental loss

Incidental losses are expenses incurred to avoid additional disadvantages, not directly related to expectation interest.[181] Although not explicitly mentioned in Article 74 CISG or Article 7.4.4 PICC, they are recoverable under the principle of full compensation. Examples include extra costs from unjustified refusal to perform,[182] seller's expenses for tendering or storing goods,[183] and buyer's additional transport costs due to late or defective delivery.[184] Reasonable inspection expenses are also recoverable.[185]

Recovering costs for pursuing rights against the breaching party, like litigation or arbitration, or extra-judicial expenses, should be arranged in the contract or through a forum selection clause. Litigation costs are not recoverable under Article 74 CISG or Article 7.4.4 PICC and are governed by domestic law or arbitration rules.[186] The recovery of these costs is governed by the applicable domestic law or arbitration rules on the allocation of costs. The main reason is that allowing the recovery of litigation costs under Article 74 CISG would result in only the successful plaintiff being entitled to recover such costs, while a successful defendant

---

[179] See recently *Ponte Vecchio Beheer BV v DST Global Solutions (Realty) Limited* [2024] Parket bij de Hoge Raad (Advocate General at the Dutch Supreme Court) 23/02925, CISG-online 7028: applying CISG principles to the recoverability of losses resulting from declining currency exchange rates under Dutch domestic law; Schwenzer, 'Article 74 CISG: Calculation of Damages in General' in Schwenzer and Schroeter (eds) (n 3) para 27.

[180] *Italian shoes case XIII* [1994] Oberlandesgericht Düsseldorf (Court of Appeal Düsseldorf) 17 U 146/93, CISG-online 119.

[181] Schwenzer, 'Article 74 CISG: Calculation of Damages in General' in Schwenzer and Schroeter (eds) (n 3) para 28.

[182] See ibid para 28 with further references.

[183] *Production line for foamed boards case* [1992] ICC International Court of Arbitration 7585, CISG-online 105.

[184] Cf *Hungarian wheat case* [2006] Oberlandesgericht Karlsruhe (Court of Appeal Karlsruhe) 7 U 1001/04, CISG-online 1328.

[185] *Lamborghini hauler case* [2013] Oberlandesgericht Koblenz (Court of Appeal Koblenz) 3 U 223/13, CISG-online 2472 note II.1.b]cc).

[186] *Medical-Technical-Aid GmbH v Ningbo Automotive Technology Co. Ltd.* [2021] 浙江省宁波市中级人民法院 (Intermediate People's Court Ningbo, Zhejiang Province) (2021)浙 02 民初 824 号, CISG-online 6203: dismissing litigation fees claimed under Art. 74 CISG citing CISG-AC Opinion No. 6; see also *Hefei Ziking Steel Pipe Co., Ltd. v Meever & Meever* et al. [2021] U.S. District Court for the Southern District of Texas, 4:20-CV-00425, CISG-online 5685: holding that attorney's fees are governed by the law of the forum state; and, *Goodman Food Products, Inc. v Sunrise Foods Int'l Inc.* [2022] U.S. District Court for the Central District of California, 2:21-cv-06518-SB-ADS, CISG-online 6047: holding that art 74 CISG does not itself provide for an award of attorney's fees; see also CISG Advisory Council, 'CISG-AC Opinion No. 6' (n 154) Black Letter Rule 5, comment 5.4;

could not, as it would be unable to establish a breach of contract by the plaintiff as a basis for damages.[187] This would undermine the principle of equality of the parties under the CISG.[188]

Extra-judicial costs are controversial; some support their recovery under the CISG,[189] but they should generally follow procedural rules to avoid favouring successful plaintiffs.[190] Suppose a buyer in Mexico contracts to purchase electronic components from a seller in the United States. The components delivered are defective, leading the buyer to incur costs in addressing the breach. Before initiating formal litigation or arbitration, the buyer engages in several extra-judicial actions to resolve the issue. These actions include consulting with a legal advisor to draft a formal demand letter to the seller, meetings, and lawyers' intervention to settle the matter and even pre-trial work.[191] These costs are considered extra-judicial expenses. If the buyer's contract includes provisions for recovering such costs, or if a forum selection clause addresses these expenses, the buyer may be able to claim these costs from the seller. However, if the contract is silent on this matter, the recovery of these extra-judicial costs could be controversial and dependent on procedural rules, as they are not explicitly covered under Article 74 CISG or Article 7.4.4 PICC.[192]

---

[187] See Schwenzer, 'Article 74 CISG: Calculation of Damages in General' in Schwenzer and Schroeter (eds) (n 3) para 30; *Brands International Corporation v Reach Companies, LLC*, No 23-2164 (8th Cir, 30 May 2024): stating that: although a prevailing plaintiff would always be entitled to an award of attorney's fees, a prevailing defendant could never recover them, since there would be no breach of contract and thus art 74 would not apply. See 313 F.3d at 388–9. Such an interpretation would do violence to the CISG's principle of equality between contractual counterparties.

[188] Ibid.

[189] For instance, a Dutch court has recently supported the recoverability of extra-judicial expenses under Art. 74 CISG. See also *Portuguese clogs case* [2024] Rechtbank Overijssel (District Court Overijssel) C/08/309410/HA ZA 24-44, CISG-online 7206; *Sofas case* [2024] Rechtbank Zeeland-West-Brabant (District Court ZeelandWest-Brabant) 10251115\CV EXPL 22-3954 (E), CISG-online 7254; *Zhongshan Ruicheng Clothing Textile Co. Ltd v AmeBalance B.V.* [2024] Rechtbank Den Haag (District Court The Hague) C/09/658069/HA ZA 23-1074, CISG-online 7185; *IBS Engineering GmbH v Holland Filter B.V.* [2024] Gerechthof 's-Hertogenbosch (Court of Appeal's-Hertogenbosch) 200.332.839/01, CISG-online 7158; *Berrycare Group d.o.o. v ABB Growers B.V.* [2024] Gerechthof 's-Hertogenbosch (Court of Appeal's-Hertogenbosch) 200.318.359_01, CISG-online 6881.

[190] *Zapata Hermanos Sucesores, SA v Hearthside Baking Comp* [2002] US Court of Appeals (7th Circuit) 01-3402, 02-1867, 02-1915 CISG-online 684; and more recently *Brands International Corporation v Reach Companies, LLC* [2024] US Court of Appeals (8th Circuit) 23-2164, CISG-online 7006: 'Holding that loss in article 74 including attorney's fees would require us to ignore this carefully constructed equality, creating a conflicting interpretation of the relationship between contractual counterparties in the event of a breach.'

[191] A court granting their recovery: *Chinese graphite electrodes case* [2024] Oberlandesgericht Stuttgart (Court of Appeal Stuttgart) 5 U 65/23, CISG-online 6942: holding that the plaintiff's pre-trial legal fees payment falls within the scope of art 74 CISG.

[192] See Schwenzer and Hachem, 'The Scope of the CISG Provisions on Damages' in Saidov and Cunnington (eds) (n 154) 104. See also Djordjević, 'Article 74' in Kröll, Mistelis, and Perales Viscasillas (eds) (n 1) para 90; Brunner, Schmidt-Ahrendts, and Mark Czarnecki , 'Article 74 (General Rule for Measuring Damages)' in Brunner and Gottlieb (eds) (n 1) para 31; Schwenzer, 'Article 74 CISG: Calculation of Damages in General' in Schwenzer and Schroeter (eds) (n 3) para 31.

c.) Consequential loss

Consequential damages include additional losses beyond non-performance itself, the promisee's liability to third parties, including costs of warning and recall, due to the breach. If the buyer has resold goods or the object of the contract, it may be liable to its customers for non- or defective performance caused by the other party. Contractual penalties or liquidated damages in subsequent contracts are also recoverable under this category, if foreseeable.[193] Even though the seller's liability for death or personal injury caused by the goods to any person is not governed by the CISG under Article 5,[194] damages arising from the buyer's liability for third-party death or personal injury caused by defective products, as determined under the otherwise applicable law, are considered part of the buyer's financial damage and thus recoverable as consequential damages.[195]

Consequential losses on the part of the seller may occur if the buyer refuses to take delivery, such as causing the seller to terminate supplier contracts.[196] Efforts to rectify defects involve significant time and costs. However, only additional personnel costs and workload caused by the breach are recoverable under this category.[197]

Legal costs incurred by the promisee in disputes with third parties can also be recovered from the promisor as consequential damages. Consequential loss also includes the buyer breaching contracts with its customers, damaging its reputation (loss of reputation, loss of goodwill).[198] These damages are generally recoverable as far as their value quantum is proven. Loss of reputation is distinct from loss of profit, but the latter can indicate the former.[199]

d.) Loss of profit

While the term 'loss' within the meaning of Article 74 CISG refers to the detriment to existing assets at the time of contract conclusion,[200] loss of profit covers

---

[193] Djordjević, 'Article 74' in Kröll, Mistelis, and Perales Viscasillas (eds) (n 1) para 40 ff; Brunner, Schmidt-Ahrendts, and Mark Czarnecki, 'Article 74 (General Rule for Measuring Damages)' in Brunner and Gottlieb (eds) (n 1) para 33 ff; Schwenzer, 'Article 74 CISG: Calculation of Damages in General' in Schwenzer and Schroeter (eds) (n 3) paras 33, 58.

[194] Ibid para 33.

[195] See CISG Advisory Council, 'CISG-AC, Opinion No. 12, Liability of the Seller for Damages Arising Out of Personal Injuries and Property Damage Caused by Goods and Services under the CISG, Rapporteur: Professor Hiroo Sono, School of Law, Hokkaido University, Sapporo, Japan, 20 January 2013' (2013) Black Letter Rule 2.3, comment 2.3.1 ff; Pascal Hachem, 'Article 5 CISG: Liability for Death or Personal Injury' in Schwenzer and Schroeter (eds) (n 3) para 10; Michael Bridge, *The International Sale of Goods* (3rd edn, Oxford University Press 2013) para 11.21.

[196] *Hearing implants case* [1993] Landgericht Aachen (District Court Aachen) 43 O 136/92, CISG-online 86.

[197] *Castel Electronics Pty Ltd v Toshiba Singapore Pte Ltd* [2010] Federal Court of Australia [2010] FCA 1028, CISG-online 2158.

[198] Ewan McKendrick, 'Article 7.4.2' in Vogenauer (ed) (n 3) para 19. Cf CISG Advisory Council, 'CISG-AC Opinion No. 6' (n 154) comment 7.1.

[199] Ibid 36.

[200] *Krane-Maschinen-Service GmbH & Co Handels-KG v Grúas Andaluza, SA* [2010] Audiencia Provincial de Murcia (Court of Appeal Murcia) 408/2010, CISG-online 2130: damages for loss of profit

any increase in assets prevented by the breach or, in the words of Article 7.4.2(1) PICC: 'any gain of which it was deprived'.[201] Generally, both types of loss are treated equally. However, if the buyer fails to give notice of non-conformity under Article 39 CISG—even with a reasonable excuse—it cannot claim loss of profit pursuant to Article 44 CISG.

Loss of profit includes the profit the buyer could have realised from resale or lease, loss due to the seller's breach, and loss from the inability to keep the business running because of the breach.[202] According to the principle of full compensation, recoverable profits include both those lost up to the court or arbitral decision and predictably achievable and calculable future profits. Loss of profit includes net profit and fixed costs (general expenses) on a pro-rata basis,[203] reduced by expenses that would have been incurred in realizing this profit.[204]

The loss of a chance of winning is generally recognized as recoverable under Article 74 CISG,[205] acknowledging its economic value.[206] Article 7.4.3(2) PICC also supports reimbursement for loss of chances.[207]

Instead of claiming lost profit, the promisee can claim recovery of frustrated expenses.[208] For instance, if the buyer builds a warehouse for ordered goods that are not delivered, it can claim these costs as damages. In commercial trade, it is assumed that expected profit will at least cover expenses related to the contract.[209] Therefore, frustrated expenses represent the minimum loss incurred, which is crucial for the buyer when a higher loss of profit cannot be proven.

---

were set at the difference between the amount of resale and the price of the goods acquired by the buyer, in addition to the buyer's costs.

[201] McKendrick, 'Article 7.4.2' in Vogenauer (ed) (n 3) para 11; loss of profit may also take the form of 'loss of chance' under 7.4.3, see International Institute for the Unification of Private Law (n 3) 272, art 7.4.2, off cmt 2; see also McKendrick, 'Article 7.4.3' in Vogenauer (ed) (n 3) para 9.
[202] Schwenzer, 'Article 74 CISG: Calculation of Damages in General' in Schwenzer and Schroeter (eds) (n 3) para 38.
[203] *Shamo jeans case* [1999] Oberlandesgericht Hamburg (Court of Appeal Hamburg) 1 U 31/99, CISG-online 515; Schwenzer, 'Article 74 CISG: Calculation of Damages in General' in Schwenzer and Schroeter (eds) (n 3) para 38.
[204] Cf *Ski wear and sportswear case* [2010] Handelsgericht des Kantons Zürich (Commercial Court Canton Zurich) HG070223/U/dz, CISG-online 2160.
[205] CISG Advisory Council, 'CISG-AC Opinion No. 6' (n 154) Comment 3.15; Djakhongir Saidov, 'Damages: The Need for Uniformity' (2005) 25 Journal of Law and Commerce 393, 403; Schwenzer and Hachem, 'The Scope of the CISG Provisions on Damages' in Saidov and Cunnington (eds) (n 154) 91, 98.
[206] See Schwenzer and Hachem, 'The Scope of the CISG Provisions on Damages' in Saidov and Cunnington (eds) (n 154) 98.
[207] See McKendrick, 'Article 7.4.3' in Vogenauer (ed) (n 3) paras 3–4.
[208] Schwenzer, 'Article 74 CISG: Calculation of Damages in General' in Schwenzer and Schroeter (eds) (n 3) para 40.
[209] Ibid para 40.

e.) Non-financial loss

Article 7.4.2 PICC provides for the compensation of non-pecuniary losses, including physical suffering or emotional distress.[210] The CISG does not expressly exclude liability for non-pecuniary loss. Thus, purely non-pecuniary damages may be recoverable if the intangible purpose of performance becomes part of the contract, making the loss a typical consequence of non-performance.[211] However, if one adopts the preferable view that damages like loss of reputation or loss of chance are pecuniary, it is difficult to imagine any non-pecuniary losses that commercial contracts aim to protect against.[212] Specifically, damages for pain and suffering, mental distress, and loss of amenities are difficult to claim by companies, traders or corporations in this context.[213]

V. Calculation of Loss

1. General

The promisee's loss resulting from a breach of contract must generally be calculated concretely (Articles 74 and 75 CISG and Articles 7.4.2 and 7.4.5 PICC). However, with respect to actual non-performance loss, Article 76 CISG and Article 7.4.6 PICC stipulate an abstract calculation of damages when the contract has been avoided. This is achieved by calculating the difference between the contract price and the market price of the goods or contracts' object, precluding the promisor from arguing that no substitute transaction was carried out to calculate the loss concretely.[214]

Article 74 CISG and Article 7.4.2 PICC might also be used to calculate the compensation for non-performance losses abstractly with no requirement of contract avoidance. The principle of full compensation inherently demands the admissibility of abstract calculation under the CISG and the PICC. It is unjustifiable that a machinery supplier must compensate a construction company for the costs of rented equipment in case of non-delivery, while the same breach of contract has no consequences when the buyer is a humanitarian organization intending to use the machinery to build shelters in disaster-stricken areas and cannot rent substitute

---

[210] See McKendrick, 'Article 7.4.2' in Vogenauer (ed) (n 3) paras 15–20.

[211] See generally Djordjević, 'Article 74' in Kröll, Mistelis, and Perales Viscasillas (eds) (n 1) para 24.

[212] Schwenzer, 'Article 74 CISG: Calculation of Damages in General' in Schwenzer and Schroeter (eds) (n 3) para 41.

[213] Djordjević, 'Article 74' in Kröll, Mistelis, and Perales Viscasillas (eds) (n 1) para 24; Schwenzer, 'Article 74 CISG: Calculation of Damages in General' in Schwenzer and Schroeter (eds) (n 3) para 41.

[214] Ibid para 43; Ewan McKendrick, 'Article 7.4.6' in Vogenauer (ed) (n 3) paras 1–2.

equipment where needed.[215] Abstract damages from loss of use can be easily calculated due to the existence of rental markets for virtually every type of goods.

2. Concrete calculation

Article 75 CISG and Article 7.4.5 PICC govern the concrete calculation of non-performance loss when a contract has been avoided. The promisee can determine its expectation interest through a substitute transaction entered into after contract avoidance.[216] For instance, a buyer entitled to damages can claim the difference between the contract price and the higher substitute purchase price, while a seller can claim the difference between the contract price and the lower substitute sale price.[217] This simplifies the promisee's calculation and proof of loss, with additional damages claimable under Article 74 CISG and Article 7.4.2 PICC.

Article 75 CISG and Article 7.4.5 PICC apply only if the promisee has entered into a substitute transaction, not merely if it considered it. The transaction need not be completed but must be linked to the contract at stake and intended to fulfil the promisee's expectation interest.[218] Disposing of spoiled goods,[219] or renting substitute goods is not a substitute transaction under these provisions but may be claimed under other rules (Article 74 CISG and Article 7.4.2 PICC).[220] A buyer can use existing goods to meet client contracts and charge the seller for acquisition costs.[221] If the buyer has not returned goods upon contract avoidance, it may deliver similar goods to clients.[222] These provisions also apply if a buyer manufactures the contract's object or goods in-house, with production costs treated as substitute transaction costs.

---

[215] Schwenzer, 'Article 74 CISG: Calculation of Damages in General' in Schwenzer and Schroeter (eds) (n 3) para 43; see for details Schwenzer and Hachem, 'The Scope of the CISG Provisions on Damages' in Saidov and Cunnington (eds) (n 154) 94–5.

[216] Ingeborg Schwenzer, 'Article 75 CISG: Calculation of Damages in Case of Avoidance and Substitute Transaction' in Schwenzer and Schroeter (eds) (n 3) para 1; Milena Djordjević, 'Article 75' in Kröll, Mistelis, and Perales Viscasillas (eds) (n 1) para 1.

[217] CISG Advisory Council, 'CISG-AC Opinion No. 8 Calculation of Damages under CISG Articles 75 and 76. Rapporteur: Professor John Y. Gotanda, Villanova University School of Law, Villanova, Pennsylvania, USA. Adopted by the CISG-AC following its 12th meeting in Tokyo, Japan, on 15 November 2008' (2008) Black Letter Rule 2.1; Schwenzer, 'Article 75 CISG: Calculation of Damages in Case of Avoidance and Substitute Transaction' in Schwenzer and Schroeter (eds) (n 3) para 1.

[218] Djordjević, 'Article 75' in Kröll, Mistelis, and Perales Viscasillas (eds) (n 1) para 11; for the PICC see McKendrick, 'Article 7.4.5' in Vogenauer (ed) (n 3) para 6.

[219] *Bacon case I* [1992] Oberlandesgericht Hamm (Court of Appeal Hamm) 19 U 97/91, CISG-online 57.

[220] Schwenzer, 'Article 75 CISG: Calculation of Damages in Case of Avoidance and Substitute Transaction' in Schwenzer and Schroeter (eds) (n 3) para 2.

[221] Ibid; Christoph Brunner, Nils Schmidt-Ahrendts, and Mark Czarnecki, 'Article 75 (Calculation of Loss in the Case of Avoidance of the Contract and Substitute Transaction)' in Brunner and Gottlieb (eds) (n 1) para 4.

[222] Schwenzer, 'Article 75 CISG: Calculation of Damages in Case of Avoidance and Substitute Transaction' in Schwenzer and Schroeter (eds) (n 3) para 2.

Challenges arise in identifying a substitute transaction when the promisee deals continuously in such goods. The first post-avoidance transaction is not necessarily the substitute transaction.[223] The promisee should prove which transaction was intended, with issues resolved using the duty to mitigate damages (Article 77 CISG and Article 7.4.8 PICC).[224] Notifying the promisor of the substitute transaction avoids proof problems.[225]

Substitute transactions under Article 75 CISG and Article 7.4.5 PICC must occur after contract avoidance.[226] In some cases, advance damage claims or notifications of substitute transactions in advance are sufficient.[227] Exceptions exist if it is certain that the promisor will not perform, particularly with definitive refusal, preventing the promisor from claiming a lack of avoidance notification.[228] Calculation of non-performance can proceed without avoidance under Article 74 CISG and Article 7.4.2 PICC, too.

Costs and the content of the substitute transaction must be reasonable in time and terms, under Article 75 CISG and Article 7.4.5 PICC, aligning with the original contract's terms and quality, though deviations are permissible based on the circumstances of the case.[229] Premature substitute transactions are generally excluded from Article 75 CISG and Article 7.4.5 PICC calculations, but non-performance loss claims can still proceed under Article 74 CISG or Article 7.4.2 PICC based on such transactions, subject to the duty to mitigate damages.

Compensation for a disadvantageous price in a substitute transaction often does not fully restore the promisee's economic position. The CISG and the PICC principle of full compensation will allow for 'further damages' under Article 74 CISG and Article 7.4.2 PICC general rules, but are subject to the foreseeability rule.[230] These can include losses from delayed payments,[231] rental costs until the substitute

---

[223] Ibid para 13. See for a minority view suggesting that the first contract after avoidance is to be identified as the substitute Flechtner (n 9) 771.

[224] Schwenzer, 'Article 75 CISG: Calculation of Damages in Case of Avoidance and Substitute Transaction' in Schwenzer and Schroeter (eds) (n 3) para 3; Djordjević, 'Article 75' in Kröll, Mistelis, and Perales Viscasillas (eds) (n 1) para 13; cf CISG Advisory Council, 'CISG-AC Opinion No. 8' (n 217) comment 2.3.4.

[225] CISG Advisory Council, 'CISG-AC Opinion No. 8' (n 217) comment 2.3.4; Flechtner (n 9) 771.

[226] CISG Advisory Council, 'CISG-AC Opinion No. 8' (n 217) comment 2.3.3; Schwenzer, 'Article 75 CISG: Calculation of Damages in Case of Avoidance and Substitute Transaction' in Schwenzer and Schroeter (eds) (n 3) para 5; Djordjević, 'Article 75' in Kröll, Mistelis, and Perales Viscasillas (eds) (n 1) para 6.

[227] Cf Italian shoes case XXV [2004] Oberlandesgericht Düsseldorf (Court of Appeal Düsseldorf) I-6 U 210/03, CISG-online 916.

[228] Djordjević, 'Article 75' in Kröll, Mistelis, and Perales Viscasillas (eds) (n 1) para 10; CISG Advisory Council, 'CISG-AC Opinion No. 8' (n 217) comment 2.3.3.

[229] Schwenzer, 'Article 75 CISG: Calculation of Damages in Case of Avoidance and Substitute Transaction' in Schwenzer and Schroeter (eds) (n 3) para 6; CISG Advisory Council, 'CISG-AC Opinion No. 8' (n 217) comment 2.3.4.

[230] Schwenzer, 'Article 75 CISG: Calculation of Damages in Case of Avoidance and Substitute Transaction' in Schwenzer and Schroeter (eds) (n 3) para 11; Djordjević, 'Article 75' in Kröll, Mistelis, and Perales Viscasillas (eds) (n 1) para 29.

[231] Italian shoes case XIII (n 176); CISG Advisory Council, 'CISG-AC Opinion No. 8' (n 217) comment 3.1.

transaction is completed,[232] futile tender or temporary storage costs, and useless delivery expenses.[233]

Loss of profit is generally not recoverable as 'further damages' because the substitute transaction is meant to preserve the promisee's profit opportunity.[234] However, if the promisee loses profit from missing an additional transaction due to the need for a substitute transaction (the 'lost volume' problem), it could claim lost profit under Article 74 CISG and Article 7.4.2 PICC. Article 75 CISG and Article 7.4.5 PICC aim to strengthen the promisee's position, not limit other compensation rights.[235] Similarly, a buyer who has not received goods can claim lost profit from resale and temporary storage costs if foreseeable.[236]

3. Abstract calculation

Article 76 CISG and Article 7.4.6 PICC entitle a party who has avoided the contract to calculate non-performance loss abstractly as the difference between the contract price and the market price without concrete proof of a substitute transaction.[237] This is based on the notion that the promisee has the right to make a substitute transaction at the market price. The promisor should not benefit if the promisee chooses a different course of action instead. Under these provisions, the breaching party cannot argue that the other party does not need the contract's object or is not held liable by third parties.[238] If Article 76 CISG and Article 7.4.6

---

[232] CISG Advisory Council, 'CISG-AC Opinion No. 8' (n 217) comment 3.1.

[233] Djordjević, 'Article 75' in Kröll, Mistelis, and Perales Viscasillas (eds) (n 1) para 29; Schwenzer, 'Article 75 CISG: Calculation of Damages in Case of Avoidance and Substitute Transaction' in Schwenzer and Schroeter (eds) (n 3) para 11.

[234] See e.g. *Sunrise Foods Int'l, Inc. v Ryan Hinton Inc.* [2019] U.S. District Court for the District of Idaho, 1:17-CV-00457-CWD, CISG-online 4522: holding under Arts. 74 and 75 CISG that further damages cannot put the injured party in a better position than it would have enjoyed if the contract had been properly performed; see also *Shenzen Synergy Digital Co., Ltd. v Mingtel, Inc.* [2022] U.S. District Court for the Eastern District of Texas, 4:19-cv-00216, CISG-online 5845.

[235] Schwenzer, 'Article 75 CISG: Calculation of Damages in Case of Avoidance and Substitute Transaction' in Schwenzer and Schroeter (eds) (n 3) para 12; see also Djordjević, 'Article 75' in Kröll, Mistelis, and Perales Viscasillas (eds) (n 1) paras 37–38.

[236] Djordjević, 'Article 75' in Kröll, Mistelis, and Perales Viscasillas (eds) (n 1) paras 37–38; Brunner, Schmidt-Ahrendts, and Czarnecki, 'Article 75 (Calculation of Loss in the Case of Avoidance of the Contract and Substitute Transaction)' in Brunner and Gottlieb (eds) (n 1) para 8; Schwenzer 'Article 75 CISG: Calculation of Damages in Case of Avoidance and Substitute Transaction' in Schwenzer and Schroeter (eds) (n 3) para 12.

[237] McKendrick, 'Article 7.4.6' in Vogenauer (ed) (n 3) para 1; Ingeborg Schwenzer, 'Article 76 CISG: Calculation of Damages in Case of Avoidance Without Substitute Transaction' in Schwenzer and Schroeter (eds) (n 3) para 1; Milena Djordjević, 'Article 76' in Kröll, Mistelis, and Perales Viscasillas (eds) (n 1) para 1.

[238] Schwenzer, 'Article 76 CISG: Calculation of Damages in Case of Avoidance Without Substitute Transaction' in Schwenzer and Schroeter (eds) (n 3) para 1; Djordjević, 'Article 76' in Kröll, Mistelis, and Perales Viscasillas (eds) (n 1 para 2.

PICC are not applicable, the promisee can still calculate damages using the market price rule under Article 74 CISG and Article 7.4.2 PICC.[239]

Article 76 CISG and Article 7.4.6 PICC only apply if no substitute transaction has been made.[240] Using one's own stocks is generally not considered a substitute transaction.[241] If a substitute transaction has occurred, concrete calculation of damages under Article 75 and Article 7.4.5 PICC takes precedence.[242] However, the abstract calculation may still apply if the promisee permanently deals in the market and cannot prove a specific substitute transaction.[243]

Abstract calculation is possible only if the goods have a market price, understood as the average price for goods of the same kind, traded regularly at a particular location. The market price depends on the intended delivery time and must be adjusted for differing contract conditions.[244] The relevant market price is the wholesale price, not the retail price, which includes the retailer's margin. An official or unofficial market price listing is helpful but not necessary.[245] Claims must be made under Article 74 CISG and Article 7.4.2 PICC's framework if no market price exists.[246]

When the requirements of Article 76 CISG and Article 7.4.6 PICC are met, the party entitled to damages can claim the difference between the market price and the contract price as the actual non-performance loss.[247] The relevant market price is that at the place of delivery when the contract is avoided.[248] Further losses can

---

[239] Schwenzer, 'Article 74 CISG: Calculation of Damages in General' in Schwenzer and Schroeter (eds) (n 3) para 43; see also CISG Advisory Council, 'CISG-AC Opinion No. 8' (n 217) comment 5; according to the opposing majority view, art 74 only allows concrete calculation.

[240] Djordjević, 'Article 76' in Kröll, Mistelis, and Perales Viscasillas (eds) (n 1) para 13; Schwenzer, 'Article 76 CISG: Calculation of Damages in Case of Avoidance Without Substitute Transaction' in Schwenzer and Schroeter (eds) (n 3) para 2; Flechtner (n 9) 774.

[241] Schwenzer, 'Article 76 CISG: Calculation of Damages in Case of Avoidance Without Substitute Transaction' in Schwenzer and Schroeter (eds) (n 3) para 2.

[242] See *Bacon case I* (n 219); Djordjević, 'Article 76' in Kröll, Mistelis, and Perales Viscasillas (eds) (n 1) para 13.

[243] CISG Advisory Council, 'CISG-AC Opinion No. 8' (n 217) comment 4.1.5; Djordjević, 'Article 76' in Kröll, Mistelis, and Perales Viscasillas (eds) (n 1) para 15.

[244] CISG Advisory Council, 'CISG-AC Opinion No. 8' (n 217) comment 4.3.1; Mark Czarnecki, Christoph Brunner, and Nils Schmidt-Ahrendts, 'Article 76 (Calculation of Loss in Case of Goods with Market Prices)' in Brunner and Gottlieb (eds) (n 1) para 5; Djordjević, 'Article 76' in Kröll, Mistelis, and Perales Viscasillas (eds) (n 1) para 9.

[245] CISG Advisory Council, 'CISG-AC Opinion No. 8' (n 217) comment 4.3.1; for the PICC, see International Institute for the Unification of Private Law (n 3) 274, art 7.4.6, off cmt 2: professional organizations, chambers of commerce, etc.

[246] Brunner, Schmidt-Ahrendts, and Mark Czarnecki, 'Article 76 (Calculation of Loss in Case of Goods with Market Prices)' in Brunner and Gottlieb (eds) (n 1) para 5; Djordjević, 'Article 76' in Kröll, Mistelis, and Perales Viscasillas (eds) (n 1) para 11.

[247] Cf Schwenzer, 'Article 76 CISG: Calculation of Damages in Case of Avoidance Without Substitute Transaction' in Schwenzer and Schroeter (eds) (n 3) para 5; Djordjević, 'Article 76' in Kröll, Mistelis, and Perales Viscasillas (eds) (n 1) para 16.

[248] See for the PICC McKendrick, 'Article 7.4.6' in Vogenauer (ed) (n 3) para 3; see for the CISG Flechtner (n 9) 777.

be claimed under the full compensation principle in Article 74 CISG and Article 7.4.2 PICC.

The decisive market price is the one at the place where the goods should have been delivered or the services rendered, *i.e.* the place of performance of the most characteristic obligation.[249] If there is no market price at the place of performance, Article 76(2) CISG and Article 7.4.6(2) PICC suggest using the market price at a reasonable substitute location.[250] A place is a reasonable substitute if it offers comparable conditions and is least disadvantageous for the liable party, considering transportation costs.[251] If multiple reasonable substitutes exist, the nearest one is chosen.[252] An international market price can be considered with case-specific modifications.

Under Article 76(2) CISG and Article 7.4.6(2) PICC, the market price at the time of contract avoidance is used. To prevent speculation, the duty to mitigate damages under Article 77 CISG and Article 7.4.8 PICC applies, potentially making the earliest possible avoidance time decisive.[253] Later market changes do not affect the calculation, even if they result in a 'windfall profit' for the promisee.[254]

In CISG contracts, however, if the promisee avoids the contract after taking over the goods, the market price at the time of takeover is relevant (Article 76(1) CISG). This applies to the buyer,[255] even if the grounds for avoidance were unknown at the time of takeover (e.g. non-conforming goods).[256] Using the takeover time prevents speculation but may be inappropriate if the market price rises significantly before avoidance.[257] The buyer may calculate additional losses under Article 74 CISG in such cases.

---

[249] *Bacon case I* (n 208); cf Djordjević, 'Article 76' in Kröll, Mistelis, and Perales Viscasillas (eds) (n 1) para 22.

[250] See United Nations, 'UN Doc A/CONF.97/5' (n 27) 61, art 72 (now art 76 CISG), para 7; Flechtner (n 9) 777; Djordjević, 'Article 76' in Kröll, Mistelis, and Perales Viscasillas (eds) (n 1) para 22; Schwenzer, 'Article 76 CISG: Calculation of Damages in Case of Avoidance Without Substitute Transaction' in Schwenzer and Schroeter (eds) (n 3) para 9.

[251] CISG Advisory Council, 'CISG-AC Opinion No. 8' (n 217) comment 4.5.2; Djordjević, 'Article 76' in Kröll, Mistelis, and Perales Viscasillas (eds) (n 1) para 22; Schwenzer, 'Article 76 CISG: Calculation of Damages in Case of Avoidance Without Substitute Transaction' in Schwenzer and Schroeter (eds) (n 3) para 9.

[252] CISG Advisory Council, 'CISG-AC Opinion No. 8' (n 217) comment 4.5.2: regards the nearest place as 'typically' being the reasonable substitute place.

[253] See Djordjević, 'Article 76' in Kröll, Mistelis, and Perales Viscasillas (eds) (n 1) para 19; Schwenzer, 'Article 76 CISG: Calculation of Damages in Case of Avoidance and Without Substitute Transaction' in Schwenzer and Schroeter (eds) (n 3) para 10.

[254] Schwenzer, 'Article 76 CISG: Calculation of Damages in Case of Avoidance Without Substitute Transaction' in Schwenzer and Schroeter (eds) (n 3) para 10.

[255] See Flechtner (n 9) 776, para 544: the special time for measuring damages provided by art 76(1) second sentence will seldom apply to avoiding sellers.

[256] CISG Advisory Council, 'CISG-AC Opinion No. 8' (n 217) comment 4.4.2.

[257] Ibid comment 4.4.2.

Further losses recoverable in addition to the price difference under Article 76 CISG and Article 7.4.6 PICC include those recoverable as non-performance losses under the principle of full compensation.[258] In addition, Article 76 CISG and Article 7.4.6 PICC do not preclude recovering lost profit, adhering to the principle of full compensation. However, it must be evaluated if the promisee could have avoided the loss of profit by a timely substitute transaction.[259] 'Lost volume' damages, such as increased production costs from reduced workload, may also be claimed.[260] Frustrated expenses may be recoverable if not already included in the abstractly calculated difference.[261]

4. Betterment

If the promisee obtains benefits from the breach of contract or from the damages received, it is questionable whether these should be deducted.[262] Article 7.4.2 PICC expressly takes the view that the aggrieved party must not be enriched by damages for non-performance, stipulating that any gain resulting from the non-performance must be considered in damages compensation.[263] This gain could take the form of expenses not incurred (e.g. not having to pay for a warehouse for materials never delivered) or a loss avoided (e.g. non-performance of what would have been a losing bargain).[264] A narrower view must be advocated under the CISG. A deduction of benefits under the CISG is permissible only if it does not contradict the performance principle and does not jeopardize the promisee's full compensation.[265]

---

[258] McKendrick, 'Article 7.4.6' in Vogenauer (ed) (n 3) para 6; Djordjević, 'Article 76' in Kröll, Mistelis, and Perales Viscasillas (eds) (n 1) para 25; Schwenzer, 'Article 76 CISG: Calculation of Damages in Case of Avoidance Without Substitute Transaction' in Schwenzer and Schroeter (eds) (n 3) para 13.

[259] Flechtner (n 9) 782; Schwenzer, 'Article 76 CISG: Calculation of Damages in Case of Avoidance Without Substitute Transaction' in Schwenzer and Schroeter (eds) (n 3) para 13.

[260] CISG Advisory Council, 'CISG-AC Opinion No. 8' (n 217) comments 4.1.4 and 6.4.

[261] See Schwenzer, 'Article 75 CISG: Calculation of Damages in Case of Avoidance and Substitute Transaction' in Schwenzer and Schroeter (eds) (n 3) para 12.

[262] See Schwenzer, 'Article 74 CISG: Calculation of Damages in General' in Schwenzer and Schroeter (eds) (n 3) para 44; see generally Mareike Schmidt, 'Profiting from Substitute Transactions? Offsetting Losses and Benefits under the CISG' in Andrea Buechler and Markus Müller-Chen (eds), *Private Law, National—Global—Comparative: Festschrift für Ingeborg Schwenzer zum 60. Geburtstag* (Stämpfli 2011) 1499 ff; see for the PICC—no enrichment principle McKendrick, 'Article 7.4.2' in Vogenauer (ed) (n 3) para 12.

[263] PICC 2016 art 7.4.2.

[264] McKendrick, 'Article 7.4.2' in Vogenauer (ed) (n 3) para 12.

[265] Schwenzer, 'Article 74 CISG: Calculation of Damages in General' in Schwenzer and Schroeter (eds) (n 3) para 44.

5. Disgorgement of profits

The indemnity based on the defendant's profits is often referred to as 'disgorgement of profits'. It involves compelling a party who has wrongfully profited at the expense of another to surrender those profits.[266] In contract law, disgorgement may be ordered when a party breaches a contract and profits from that breach.[267] The remedy aims to strip the breaching party of any economic gain derived from failing to uphold its contractual obligations.[268] This is particularly relevant in cases involving fiduciary duties or where specific performance of a contract term is unenforceable.

Disgorgement of profits as a private law remedy has been mainly developed in the common law tradition. In English law, the legal basis for disgorgement of profits as a contract law remedy lies in the principles of equity and restitution.[269] Equity seeks to achieve fairness and justice in situations where the strict application of the law may lead to an unjust outcome. Disgorgement can be seen as an equitable remedy in contract law where compensatory damages are inadequate to address the breach. English case law examples most notably include *Attorney General v Blake* (2001).[270] In this case, the House of Lords held that a spy who breached a confidentiality clause of his employment contract by publishing a memoir without permission could be required to disgorge the book's profits, as compensatory damages were totally inadequate to address the breach. More recently, in *FHR European Ventures LLP v Cedar Capital Partners LLC* (2014), the United Kingdom Supreme Court clarified the availability of disgorgement as a remedy for breaches of fiduciary duty in the context of a breach of contract, further establishing the principle that disgorgement may be available in cases where compensatory damages are insufficient.[271]

Regarding the CISG, the paramount performance principle, the idea that a breach of contract must not be profitable, would also allow the disgorgement of profits.[272] Targeting the promisor's profits is necessary and feasible in certain situations. For instance, when the seller resells the goods at a higher profit than the

---

[266] Djordjević, 'Article 74' in Kröll, Mistelis, and Perales Viscasillas (eds) (n 1) para 60.

[267] See for the US domestic law Flechtner (n 9) 756.

[268] Ewoud Hondius and André Janssen, 'Chapter 26: Disgorgement of Profits: Gain-Based Remedies throughout the World' in Ewoud Hondius and André Janssen (eds), *Disgorgement of Profits: Gain-Based Remedies throughout the World* (Springer 2015) 471 ff.

[269] See generally Stephen Watterson, 'Gain-Based Remedies for Civil Wrongs in England and Wales' in ibid 29 ff.

[270] *Attorney General v Blake* [2001] 1 AC 268 (HL).

[271] *FHR European Ventures LLP v Cedar Capital Partners LLC* [2014] UKSC 45.

[272] Edgardo Muñoz and David Obey Ament-Guemez, 'Calculation of Damages on the Basis of the Breaching Party's Profits under the CISG' (2017) 8 *The George Mason Journal of International Commercial Law* 201, 202 ff; Schwenzer, 'Article 74 CISG: Calculation of Damages in General' in Schwenzer and Schroeter (eds) (n 3) para 45; Schwenzer and Hachem, 'The Scope of the CISG Provisions on Damages' in Saidov and Cunnington (eds) (n 154) 101–2.

original contract;[273] the seller reduces production costs by violating contractual obligations to maintain humane and environmentally friendly conditions, thereby increasing profit,[274] or, when the buyer, against contract terms, supplies a market with the purchased goods and earns profits.[275] This was the particular case decided by the Court of Appeals of Grenoble in 1995. In this CISG case, a French jeans manufacturer agreed to deliver goods to a buyer in the United States, with the stipulation that they be sold only in South America and Africa to avoid parallel imports, particularly to Spain. Despite this, the buyer shipped the jeans to Spain. The Court ordered the buyer to pay 10,000 French francs for abusing the procedure and causing inconvenience to the seller.[276] The profits made by the buyer from reselling in Spain reflected the seller's lost profits, supporting their disgorgement.[277]

In a different CISG case under Stockholm Chamber of Commerce arbitration rules, a Brazilian seller agreed to sell high-quality pressure sensors to a Chinese buyer, who would integrate them into new products for sale in Asia.[278] The contract included a confidentiality clause as the seller would share confidential information. The buyer claimed damages for the seller's breach of delivery obligations, while the seller counter-claimed for breach of the confidentiality clause. The seller argued that the buyer entered into the agreement only to access the seller's proprietary technology, which the buyer then used to develop competing products. Tests showed that the buyer's sensors had signal responses identical to the seller's, indicating the buyer incorporated the seller's proprietary technology. The seller also claimed that the buyer shared this technology with a third-party manufacturer. The tribunal agreed that the similarities were too great to be coincidental and concluded the buyer copied the seller's confidential information, breaching the agreement. The tribunal awarded damages equal to the buyer's profits over the 24-month period the buyer used the seller's technology, considering all case facts without citing a specific CISG provision.[279] In these cases, the performance principle mandates disgorging the promisor's profits gained from the breach.

---

[273] Ibid; but see Schmidt-Ahrendts (n 169) 98, 99: for a reduced standard of proof. This is known as 'efficient breach of contract' as the second sale after breach is more profitable as the proceeds exceed the damages to be paid to the buyer under the original contract.

[274] Schwenzer, 'Article 74 CISG: Calculation of Damages in General' in Schwenzer and Schroeter (eds) (n 3) para 45.

[275] Schwenzer, 'Article 74 CISG: Calculation of Damages in General' in Schwenzer and Schroeter (eds) (n 5) para 45; but see Schmidt-Ahrendts (n 169) 99.

[276] *BRI Production 'Bonaventure' S.a.r.l. v Pan African Export* [1995] Cour d'appel de Grenoble (Court of Appeal Grenoble) 93/3275, CISG-online 151; for analysis see Schwenzer and Hachem, 'The Scope of the CISG Provisions on Damages' in Saidov and Cunnington (eds) (n 154) 101.

[277] Djakhongir Saidov, *The Law of Damages in International Sales: The CISG and Other International Instruments* (Bloomsbury Academic 2008) 35.

[278] *Pressure sensors case* [2007] Arbitration Institute of the Stockholm Chamber of Commerce (SCC) CISG-online 1521.

[279] See for analysis Muñoz and Ament-Guemez (n 272) 210–11. The award does not mention the concept of disgorgement of profits explicitly but has taken the profits of the breaching party to arrive at a fair outcome.

Disgorgement can also serve to calculate the promisee's damages when they are otherwise difficult or impossible to prove.[280] Article 7(1) CISG emphasizes the importance of good faith in interpreting the convention. When other methods of calculating damages fail, Article 74 CISG may be expanded to include calculations based on the profits of the breaching party.[281] For instance, if the seller decides to breach the contract and resell the same goods to a second buyer, the seller deprives the first buyer of the opportunity to resell the goods at the higher market price. That lost opportunity is the expectation interest existing at the time of the conclusion of the contract, and it is just, fair, and reasonable (good faith as required by Article 7 CISG) that the profits made by the breaching party are taken as the baseline to calculate the indemnity for the damages, where there are no other elements to prove them.[282] This might be the case where, for example, the buyer who suffers a breach consisting of the non-delivery of the goods is unable to calculate its loss because, at the time of the breach, it had neither pre-orders from its own customers nor had it ever in the past traded with the unique type of goods at stake in that transaction, or when it deals in a new business sector that has no record of sales to compare prices with, making it impossible for the aggrieved buyer to prove an assumed loss from its own books or market data.[283]

VI. Foreseeability Rule

The promisor's strict liability for contractual obligations is moderated by CISG's and PICC's limitation of compensation to foreseeable loss (Article 74 CISG and Article 7.4.4 PICC).[284] The foreseeability rule restricts the promisor's liability and the extent of damages to risks foreseeable at the time of contract conclusion, considering the circumstances and purpose of the contract. This rule concerns the consequences of liability, not the liability itself, and applies even to intentional breaches.

Pursuant to Article 74 CISG and Article 7.4.4 PICC, foreseeability is determined from the perspective of the party in breach at the time of contract conclusion.[285] The promisor's awareness of additional risks after this point is irrelevant.[286] Article 74 CISG requires only that the party in breach foresaw or ought to have foreseen

---

[280] Ibid 209.
[281] Ibid 205 ff.
[282] Ibid 209.
[283] Ibid 210.
[284] Djordjević, 'Article 74' in Kröll, Mistelis, and Perales Viscasillas (eds) (n 1) para 26; Schwenzer, 'Article 74 CISG: Calculation of Damages in General' in Schwenzer and Schroeter (eds) (n 3) para 47; Ewan McKendrick, 'Article 7.4.4' in Vogenauer (ed) (n 3) para 1 ff.
[285] Cf Djordjević, 'Article 74' in Kröll, Mistelis, and Perales Viscasillas (eds) (n 1) paras 29, 31.
[286] Ibid 29; Schwenzer, 'Article 74 CISG: Calculation of Damages in General' in Schwenzer and Schroeter (eds) (n 3) para 49.

the damage as a 'possible consequence' of the breach at the time of contract conclusion. However, Article 7.4.4 PICC requires the party in breach to foresee or ought to have foreseen the damage as the 'likely result', thus favouring the party in breach.[287] Foreseeability must consider case-specific circumstances, providing a normative limitation.[288]

Foreseeability is generally determined using an objective standard, considering what a reasonable person in the promisor's position would have foreseen at the time of contract conclusion.[289] Factors such as risk allocation, contract purpose, and intended protection must be considered.[290] Foreseeability can also be extended if the promisee informs the promisor of special, unforeseeable circumstances.[291] Only the loss incurred must have been foreseeable, not the breach itself.[292] The key question is whether the possibility and nature of the damage were foreseeable to the promisor at the time of contract conclusion, assuming a breach. While the precise amount of the loss need not be foreseen, the general extent must be.

Let us provide some examples. Non-performance loss is generally foreseeable, including reduction in value due to non-conformity and costs to place the promisee in the position it would have been in had the contract been properly performed, such as repair or rental costs.[293] Loan costs from late payments and exchange rate losses are also foreseeable.[294] Incidental loss is also generally foreseeable, though measures by the promisee that were unforeseeable may violate the duty to mitigate losses in the CISG and the PICC.[295] The foreseeability rule is particularly relevant in the context of consequential losses, which are regularly influenced by the promisee's specific circumstances, arrangements made, or the economic environment.[296]

---

[287] See McKendrick, 'Article 7.4.4' in Vogenauer (ed) (n 3) para 2; *Printed circuit boards case* [2019] Cour d'appel de Paris (Court of Appeal Paris) 18/04137, CISG-online 5765.

[288] Schwenzer, 'Article 74 CISG: Calculation of Damages in General' in Schwenzer and Schroeter (eds) (n 3) para 50.

[289] Brunner, Schmidt-Ahrendts, and Czarnecki, 'Article 74' in Brunner and Gottlieb (eds) (n 1) para 12.

[290] Schwenzer, 'Article 74 CISG: Calculation of Damages in General' in Schwenzer and Schroeter (eds) (n 3) para 51.

[291] This is part of the subjective test: Schwenzer, 'Article 74 CISG: Calculation of Damages in General' in Schwenzer and Schroeter (eds) (n 3) para 51; Djordjević, 'Article 74' in Kröll, Mistelis, and Perales Viscasillas (eds) (n 1) para 28: the application of the subjective test sometimes yields more favourable results.

[292] Schwenzer, 'Article 74 CISG: Calculation of Damages in General' in Schwenzer and Schroeter (eds) (n 3) para 52; Brunner, Schmidt-Ahrendts, and Czarnecki, 'Article 74' in Christoph Brunner and Benjamin Gottlieb (eds) (n 1) para 12.

[293] *Coöperatieve Federatie van Edelpelsdierenhouders Nederasselt U.A. v Ceva Santé Animale S.A.* [2025] Netherlands Commercial Court, NCC C/13/736825, CISG-online 7354; *Xiamen Suncare Medical Device Ltd. v Bunnik Creations B.V.* [2025] Rechtbank Rotterdam (District Court Rotterdam) C/10/631379/HA ZA 22-2, CISG-online 7332.

[294] Schwenzer, 'Article 74 CISG: Calculation of Damages in General' in Schwenzer and Schroeter (eds) (n 3) para 54.

[295] Ibid para 55.

[296] Ibid para 56.

Profits from the resale of goods are regularly foreseeable when sold to commercial traders, but the foreseeability of business process interruptions depends on the specific circumstances.[297] If the buyer refuses to take delivery, common trading margins are foreseeable profits. Frustrated expenses are foreseeable up to the expected profit. In special cases involving defective goods, sellers must anticipate liability to buyers' customers,[298] or the costs of taking back goods.[299] Recall campaigns in certain markets, such as the car industry,[300] and reasonable contractual penalties aligned with trade practices are foreseeable.[301] Fines to the buyer in countries with supply chain legislation making local companies liable for sustainability violations by suppliers in third countries might be foreseeable. Loss of goodwill is foreseeable if the contract supports or preserves the buyer's reputation, especially in sensitive markets. Consequential damages to the buyer's other property are generally foreseeable unless caused by improper use of the goods.[302]

VII. Burden and Standard of Proof

Though not explicitly stated, the CISG and the PICC govern the allocation of the burden of proof. The promisee bears the burden of proof for the extent of its loss and causation by the breach of contract,[303] with a distinction in the CISG for the delivery of non-conforming goods. The burden of proof regarding the foreseeability of the loss is on the promisor.[304] This allocation does not exclude alleviating the burden of proof by establishing certain case types, particularly in actual non-performance loss.

Regarding the standard of proof, many consider this question to be a matter of procedural law, governed by the *lex fori*.[305] However, simply categorizing rules

---

[297] *Propane gas case* (n 141).

[298] *Natural stones case III* [2010] Oberster Gerichtshof (Austrian Supreme Court) 8 Ob 30/10k, CISG-online 2296.

[299] *Propane gas case* (n 141); *Frozen meat case for Egypt case I* [1998] Bundesgericht/Tribunal fédéral (Swiss Federal Supreme Court) 4C.179/1998, CISG-online 413.

[300] Schwenzer, 'Article 74 CISG: Calculation of Damages in General' in Schwenzer and Schroeter (eds) (n 3) para 58.

[301] *Indian-Russian sales contract case I* [2004] MKAC 97/2004, CISG-online 1188.

[302] See *Vine wax case* (n 35); *KRAPE S.A. v LIK Supply, Corp.* [2022] U.S. District Court for the Eastern District of New York, 21-CV-03742-AMD-JRC, CISG-online 6024; *THI Medical, S.A.C. v Filmore Management Trading, LLC* et al. [2023] U.S. District Court for the Southern District of Florida, 21-21632-Civ-GAYLES/TORRES, CISG-online 6489; Schwenzer, 'Article 74 CISG: Calculation of Damages in General' in Schwenzer and Schroeter (eds) (n 3) para 59.

[303] McKendrick, 'Article 7.4.2' in Vogenauer (ed) (n 3) para 23; Djordjević, 'Article 74' in Kröll, Mistelis, and Perales Viscasillas (eds) (n 1) para 15; Schwenzer, 'Article 74 CISG: Calculation of Damages in General' in Schwenzer and Schroeter (eds) (n 3) para 66.

[304] It is disputed but this is the correct view: Schwenzer, 'Article 74 CISG: Calculation of Damages in General' in Schwenzer and Schroeter (eds) (n 3) para 66. *Dye for clothes case* [1997] Audiencia Provincial de Barcelona (Court of Appeal Barcelona) 755/95-C, CISG-online 338.

[305] See UNCITRAL (n 3) 337, art 74, para 37; *Ski wear and sportswear case* (n 204); Djordjević, 'Article 74' in Kröll, Mistelis, and Perales Viscasillas (eds) (n 1) para 18 with further references of applying the standard of the *lex fori*.

of proof as procedural or substantive is not appropriate.[306] Allowing different domestic rules on the standard of proof would undermine the uniform interpretation and application of the CISG and the principle of full compensation. The CISG, as part of the *lex fori*, therefore governs the standard of proof.[307] The suggested standard is the 'reasonable certainty' that the damage claimed occurred and is the consequence of the breach.[308] The CISG frequently uses the standard of a 'reasonable person'. Thus, the promisee must prove its damage and loss of profit with a reasonable degree of certainty. In cases of intentional breach of contract, the necessary standard of proof might be reduced, especially concerning loss of profit, loss of reputation, and loss of a chance. The principle of 'reasonableness' implies that the amount of non-quantifiable damages must be based on a reasonable assessment by the court,[309] making recourse to domestic law of evidence unnecessary and impermissible. This coincides with the standard of reasonable degree of certainty for damages in Article 7.4.3(1) PICC.[310]

VIII. Contractual Stipulations on Liability: Agreed Sums, Limitation of Liability

The CISG and the PICC allow the parties to contractually regulate the scope of their liability through Article 6 CISG and Article 1.5 PICC, respectively. Based on freedom of contract, parties may stipulate agreed sums payable upon breach or set limitations of liability. Suppose such clauses are included in standard terms and conditions of sale. In that case, their incorporation is governed by the rules on contract formation and interpreted according to Article 8 CISG and Article 7.4 PICC.[311] The effectiveness of these agreements relies on the applicable PICC or CISG validity rules and principles and subsidiarily on the otherwise applicable domestic law (*lex causae*).

---

[306] Cf in particular CISG Advisory Council, 'CISG-AC Opinion No. 6' (n 154) comment 2.3; Schwenzer, 'Article 74 CISG: Calculation of Damages in General' in Schwenzer and Schroeter (eds) (n 3) para 67; Schwenzer and Hachem, 'The Scope of the CISG Provisions on Damages' in Saidov and Cunnington (eds) (n 154) 99.

[307] Schwenzer, 'Article 74 CISG: Calculation of Damages in General' in Schwenzer and Schroeter (eds) (n 3) para 67.

[308] CISG Advisory Council, 'CISG-AC Opinion No. 6' (n 154) comments 2.3–2.5; Djordjević, 'Article 74' in Kröll, Mistelis, and Perales Viscasillas (eds) (n 1) para 18; Schwenzer and Muñoz, *Global Sales and Contract Law* (n 77) para 44.331.

[309] CISG Advisory Council, 'CISG-AC Opinion No. 6' (n 154) comment 2.9; Cf also the corresponding solution in PICC art 7.4.3 (III).

[310] McKendrick, 'Article 7.4.3' in Vogenauer (ed) (n 3) para 2; Institute for the Unification of Private Law (n 3) 270, art 7.4.3, off cmt 1, also uses the term 'sufficiently certain'.

[311] CISG Advisory Council, 'CISG-AC Opinion No. 13 Inclusion of Standard Terms under the CISG, Rapporteur: Professor Sieg Eiselen, College of Law, University of South Africa, Pretoria, South Africa, January 20 2013' (2013) comment 1.1 ff; Ulrich Schroeter, 'Article 14 CISG: Offer (Including Incorporation of Standard Terms)' in Schwenzer and Schroeter (eds) (n 3) para 40 ff.

1. Agreed sums

Traditionally, a distinction is made between liquidated damages clauses and contractual penalties. This is significant in common law countries, where contractual penalties are unenforceable,[312] while in civil law countries, both are generally enforceable but may be reduced by the court if requested by the burdened party.[313] The modern view reflected in Article 7.4.13 PICC tends to discard this distinction, considering agreed sums payable upon breach generally permissible. If the agreed sum is grossly disproportionate to the actual loss, courts or arbitral tribunals may reduce it, as it is the solution in Article 7.4.13(2) PICC.[314] These rules should also apply to contractual clauses modifying the damages provisions in the CISG by stipulating an agreed sum.[315] Interpreting the respective agreement determines whether an agreed sum is exhaustive regarding other remedies.[316]

The CISG Advisory Council has addressed additional aspects of agreed sums in case of breach of CISG contracts in Opinion No. 10. The CISG Advisory Council has asserted that parties may derogate from Articles 74 to 79 CISG by including such clauses.[317] It has also stated that provisions protecting the obligor based on notions such as reasonableness, excessiveness, or proportionality must be applied according to an international standard derived from the underlying principles of the CISG.[318] Agreed sums do not fail solely because they compel the obligor to perform, as in some common law systems. The question of whether an impediment exempts the obligor from payment of the agreed sum is primarily a matter of contract interpretation under Articles 8 and 9 CISG; unless otherwise agreed, Article 79(1) CISG exempts the obligor from the obligation to pay an agreed sum.[319] The CISG Advisory Council also asserted that if the obligee has contributed to the obligor's failure that triggers the agreed sum, Article 80 CISG bars the obligee from relying

---

[312] See Jack Graves, 'Penalty Clauses as Remedies: Exploring Comparative Approaches to Enforceability' (2013) 29 *Touro Law Review* 681–94. Cf for England the leading case *Dunlop Pneumatic Tyre Co. Ltd v New Garage and Motor Co, Ltd* [1915] AC 79.

[313] Cf e.g. Germany BGB s 343(1); Switzerland Schweizerisches Obligationenrecht 1911 (OR) art 160(3); French Civil Code art 1150; for a comparative overview see Graves (n 301) 166; Bruno Zeller, 'Penalty Clauses: Are They Governed by the CISG' (2011) 23 *Pace International Law Review* 1, 3 ff, 39 ff.

[314] International Institute for the Unification of Private Law (n 3) 285, art 7.4.13, off cmt 3: to prevent possibility of abuse (identical provision in 9:509 PECL); Ewan McKendrick, 'Article 7.4.13' in Vogenauer (ed) (n 3) para 16; see also CISG Advisory Council, 'CISG-AC Opinion No. 10, Agreed Sums Payable upon Breach of an Obligation in CISG Contracts, Rapporteur: Dr. Pascal Hachem, Bär & Karrer AG, Zurich, Switzerland, 3 August 2012' (2012) comments 3.4–3.6.

[315] Cf CISG Advisory Council, 'CISG-AC, Opinion No. 10' (n 314) Black Letter Rule 1; Zeller (n 313) 5 ff; criticism by Michael Bridge, 'The CISG and the UNIDROIT Principles of International Commercial Contracts' (2014) 19 *Uniform Law Review* 623, 637.

[316] *Production line for foamed boards case* (n 183) JDI 1995, 1015, 1019; CISG Advisory Council, 'CISG-AC, Opinion No. 10' (n 314) comment 8; Zeller (n 313) 12.

[317] CISG Advisory Council, 'CISG-AC, Opinion No. 10' (n 314) Black Letter Rule 2.

[318] Ibid Black Letter Rule 4a, comments 4.2.1 ff.

[319] Ibid Black Letter Rule 5.

on agreed sums to the extent it caused the breach.[320] However, a failure to take reasonable measures to mitigate the loss (Article 77 CISG) does not affect the amount recoverable as an agreed sum.[321] Finally, the CISG Advisory Council has reflected that, unless otherwise agreed, the following rules apply: specific performance may be claimed in addition to the agreed sum only if the agreed sum is not intended to replace performance of the contract, avoidance of the contract does not affect an agreed sum (Article 81(1) CISG), and no further damages may be claimed beyond the agreed sum.[322]

2. Limitation of liability

Parties may limit liability to specific amounts, types of losses, breaches, or conduct, and may even exclude damages altogether (Article 6 CISG, Article 7.1.6 PICC). Under Article 4 sentence 2(a) CISG, the question of validity is left to the otherwise applicable domestic law. With regard to the CISG, its principles, particularly the principle of full compensation, must be considered alongside domestic validity tests.[323] Comparative law reveals consistent parameters, such as the promisee retaining at least a minimum adequate remedy,[324] and the invalidity of advance waivers for gross negligence and intentional acts.[325] When determining the validity of such clauses under the PICC, Article 7.1.6 PICC and other validity provisions must be considered.[326]

The CISG Advisory Council has addressed additional aspects of limitation of liability clauses CISG contracts in Opinion No. 17.[327] The CISG Advisory Council has asserted that the CISG governs the incorporation and interpretation of clauses that limit or exclude the liability of the obligor for failure to perform.[328] According to the principle of freedom of contract laid down in Article 6 CISG, parties are allowed to derogate from the provisions of the CISG by including such clauses.[329]

---

[320] Ibid comments 6.1 ff.

[321] Ibid Black Letter Rule 7, comments 7.1, 7.2.

[322] Ibid Black Letter Rules 8a, 8b.

[323] Schwenzer, 'Article 74 CISG: Calculation of Damages in General' in Schwenzer and Schroeter (eds) (n 3) para 62; see also Bridge (n 315) 637; Pascal Hachem, 'Article 4 CISG: Substantive Scope of Convention' in Schwenzer and Schroeter (eds) (n 3) para 38.

[324] Cf Schwenzer and Muñoz, *Global Sales and Contract Law* (n 77) para 44.310; Ingeborg Schwenzer and Pascal Hachem, 'The CISG—Successes and Pitfalls' (2009) 57 *American Journal of Comparative Law* 457, 474.

[325] Schwenzer and Muñoz, *Global Sales and Contract Law* (n 77) para 44.311; Schwenzer and Hachem, 'The CISG—Successes and Pitfalls' (n 324) 473, 474 with references to domestic provisions.

[326] See further International Institute for the Unification of Private Law (n 3) 233–5, art 7.1.6, off cmts 1, 5.

[327] CISG Advisory Council, 'CISG-AC Opinion No. 17, Limitation and Exclusion Clauses in CISG Contracts, Rapporteur: Prof. Lauro Gama Jr., Pontifical Catholic University of Rio de Janeiro, Brazil, 16 October 2015.' (2015).

[328] CISG Advisory Council, 'CISG-AC Opinion No. 7' (n 14) Black Letter Rule 1; Djordjević, 'Article 74' in Kröll, Mistelis, and Perales Viscasillas (eds) (n 1) para 38.

[329] CISG Advisory Council, 'CISG-AC Opinion No. 7' (n 14) Black Letter Rule 2.

Article 11 CISG pre-empts the application of any form requirements for limitation and exclusion clauses that might be provided by otherwise applicable laws or rules of law. But while the CISG pre-empts form requirements, it does not override provisions aimed at protecting the obligee under applicable laws or rules of law, including those based on notions such as intentional or wilful breach, gross negligence, breach of an essential term, gross unfairness, unreasonableness, or unconscionability.[330] The CISG Advisory Council has stated that when applying these protective provisions, it is essential to observe the international character of the contract and the general principles underlying the CISG.[331]

IX. Duty to Mitigate

A party who suffers a breach of contract must mitigate losses arising from such breach (Article 77 CISG and Article 7.4.8 PICC). The rationale behind this duty is that the aggrieved party should not be compensated for avoidable loss.[332] Loss resulting from a breach of contract, including loss of profit, is not compensable to the extent it could have been reduced by reasonable steps or measures.[333] A loss that could have been entirely prevented by such measures cannot be recovered.[334] However, the duty to mitigate losses applies only when the promisee has positive knowledge of the impending breach.

The duty to mitigate damages is not an enforceable contractual obligation but a non-actionable duty taken in the aggrieved party's own interest.[335] Failure to comply does not result in liability for damages but precludes recovery of any avoidable loss (Article 77, second sentence CISG and Article 7.4.8(2) PICC). It is irrelevant whether the aggrieved party was at fault for failing to mitigate damages.[336] Generally, the aggrieved party may not claim exemption from this duty under *force majeure* provisions (Article 79 CISG or Article 7.1.7 PICC).[337] If an impediment exists, reasonable measures to prevent loss are unlikely to be possible.[338] A duty

---

[330] Ibid Black Letter Rule 4a.

[331] Ibid Black Letter Rule 4b.

[332] BGH, 26 September 2012, CISG-online 2348; McKendrick, 'Article 7.4.8' in Vogenauer (ed) (n 3) para 1; Schwenzer, 'Article 77 CISG: Mitigation of Damages' in Schwenzer and Schroeter (eds) (n 3) para 1; Milena Djordjević, 'Article 77' in Kröll, Mistelis, and Perales Viscasillas (eds) (n 1) para 1; Christoph Brunner and Friederike Schäfer, 'Article 77 (Mitigation of Damages)' in Brunner and Gottlieb (eds) (n 1) para 1.

[333] Schwenzer, 'Article 77 CISG: Mitigation of Damages' in Schwenzer and Schroeter (eds) (n 3) para 1.

[334] Ibid para 1.

[335] Djordjević, 'Article 77' in Kröll, Mistelis, and Perales Viscasillas (eds) (n 1) para 5; Schwenzer, 'Article 77 CISG: Mitigation of Damages' in Schwenzer and Schroeter (eds) (n 3) para 2; Brunner and Schäfer, 'Article 77 (Mitigation of Damages)' in Brunner and Gottlieb (eds) (n 1) para 1.

[336] Schwenzer, 'Article 77 CISG: Mitigation of Damages' in Schwenzer and Schroeter (eds) (n 3) para 2.

[337] Ibid.

[338] Ibid.

to mitigate damages arises even before a breach happens, such as in anticipatory breaches under Article 72(1) CISG or Article 7.3.3 PICC.[339] If there is a risk of a very high loss, the promisee must alert the promisor.[340]

The duty to mitigate damages influences other remedies; for instance, speculative delays in contract avoidance reduce any damages claims. In the case of mitigable loss by contract avoidance, a claim for specific performance by the buyer is problematic, especially for contracts involving goods to be manufactured.[341] The duty to mitigate may directly apply to specific performance claims, or reduce such claims by unnecessary production costs.

There is a distinction between 'contributory/comparative negligence' and 'mitigation of damages'. Article 80 CISG and Article 7.4.7 PICC address the promisee's contribution to the promisor's non-performance, excluding all remedies.[342] In contrast, Article 77 CISG and Article 7.4.8 PICC deal with the promisee's failure to mitigate loss caused solely by the promisor.[343]

The duty to mitigate damages in the CISG and the PICC requires reasonable measures to mitigate loss based on the relevant circumstances, considering the parties' practices and international trade usages (Article 9 CISG and Article 1.9 PICC). The standard is the conduct of a reasonable person in similar circumstances.[344] Therefore, the promisee is not obliged to undertake measures involving extraordinary, disproportionately high costs.[345] Measures may include preserving goods or performances, selling perishable items,[346] or legal actions against governmental acts impeding contract performance.[347] For non-conforming goods or defective performance, buyers may need to remedy defects to prevent further loss, or replace defective items essential for production.[348] Buyers must sometimes stop using defective goods unless continued use is induced by the seller.[349] Granting

---

[339] Djordjević, 'Article 77' in Kröll, Mistelis, and Perales Viscasillas (eds) (n 1) para 6.
[340] Schwenzer, 'Article 77 CISG: Mitigation of Damages' in Schwenzer and Schroeter (eds) (n 3) para 3.
[341] Ibid para 5.
[342] Ibid para 6; Eckart J Brödermann, *UNIDROIT Principles of International Commercial Contracts: An Article-by-Article Commentary* (2nd edn, Kluwer Law International 2023) Article 7.4.7. para 3.
[343] Schwenzer, 'Article 77 CISG: Mitigation of Damages' in Schwenzer and Schroeter (eds) (n 3) para 6; cf Djordjević, 'Article 77' in Kröll, Mistelis, and Perales Viscasillas (eds) (n 1) para 10; Brunner and Schäfer, 'Article 77 (Mitigation of Damages)' in Brunner and Gottlieb (eds) (n 1) para 3.
[344] *Diammonium phosphate case* [2023] Cairo Regional Centre for International Commercial Arbitration (CRCICA), 1527/2021 (Final Award), CISG-online 6272.
[345] Brunner and Schäfer, 'Article 77 (Mitigation of Damages)' in Brunner and Gottlieb (eds) (n 1) paras 8, 9; Schwenzer, 'Article 77 CISG: Mitigation of Damages' in Schwenzer and Schroeter (eds) (n 3) para 7.
[346] *Failure to open letter of credit and penalty clause case* (n 177).
[347] Schwenzer, 'Article 77 CISG: Mitigation of Damages' in Schwenzer and Schroeter (eds) (n 3) para 8.
[348] *Prakasa Indústria e Comércio de Utilidades do Lar Ltda v Mercomáquinas Indústria Comércio e Representações Ltda* [2009] Tribunal de Justiça do Estado do Rio Grande do Sul (Court of Appeal of the State of Rio Grande do Sul) 70025609579, CISG-online 2368.
[349] Cf *Vine wax case* (n 35); Schwenzer, 'Article 77 CISG: Mitigation of Damages' in Schwenzer and Schroeter (eds) (n 3) para 8.

customers a price reduction for non-conforming goods or performance may also be required to prevent further loss.[350] The duty to mitigate damages might also oblige negotiations with the promisor in breach,[351] such as accepting part of the goods or performance at a lower price if it mitigates loss more effectively than a substitute transaction.[352]

Generally, the duty might also require entering into substitute transactions to prevent or mitigate loss, distinguishing between various situations.[353] If compatible with the contract's performance, substitute transactions must be made to avoid loss.[354] After contract avoidance, the duty to mitigate loss may require a substitute transaction if it results in a lower loss than the market price rule of Article 76 CISG or Article 7.4.6 PICC.[355] Whether the promisee must avoid the contract or may wait for specific performance in case of an anticipatory breach depends on the circumstances, especially regarding goods or performances with fluctuating prices.[356] Substitute transactions must be timely; otherwise, damages are based on a hypothetical transaction at a reasonable avoidance time.[357] This typically applies with regard to the market price rule of Article 76 CISG or Article 7.4.6 PICC.[358]

Expenses necessary to prevent or mitigate losses can be claimed as damages under Article 74 CISG and directly under Article 7.4.8(2) PICC.[359] Recovery is limited to objectively necessary expenses, excluding entirely useless measures (Article 7.4.8(2) PICC).[360] However, any forecast risk should be borne by the breaching party.

---

[350] Cf *Hungarian T-shirts case* [2006] Oberlandesgericht Koblenz (Court of Appeal Koblenz) 6 U 113/06, CISG-online 1407.

[351] Cf *Pharmaceutical glycerin case* [2017], Oberlandesgericht Wien (Court of Appeal Vienna) Austria, CISG-online 2814; *Brassiere cups case* [2008], Cour d'appel de Rennes (Court of Appeal Rennes) R.G. 07/03098, CISG-online 1746.

[352] Schwenzer, 'Article 75 CISG: Calculation of Damages in Case of Avoidance and Substitute Transaction' in Schwenzer and Schroeter (eds) (n 3) para 6. See also Djordjević, 'Article 77' in Kröll, Mistelis, and Perales Viscasillas (eds) (n 1) para 20.

[353] *Cold-rolled metal sheets case I* [1994] Vienna International Arbitral Centre of the Austrian Federal Economic Chamber (VIAC) SCH-4318, CISG-online 120.

[354] Schwenzer, 'Article 77 CISG: Mitigation of Damages' in Schwenzer and Schroeter (eds) (n 3) para 10.

[355] *Bacon case I* (n 216); Schwenzer, 'Article 77 CISG: Mitigation of Damages' in Schwenzer and Schroeter (eds) (n 3) para 10.

[356] Schwenzer, 'Article 77 CISG: Mitigation of Damages' in Schwenzer and Schroeter (eds) (n 3) para 10 footnote 45: the prevailing view generally follows the latter approach, but makes an exception where the avoidance of the contract is delayed for speculative reasons or damages are the only remedy available. Cf *Italian shoes case XIII* (n 171).

[357] Schwenzer, 'Article 76 CISG: Calculation of Damages in Case of Avoidance Without Substitute Transaction' in Schwenzer and Schroeter (eds) (n 3) para 10; Djordjević, 'Article 76' in Kröll, Mistelis, and Perales Viscasillas (eds) (n 1) para 19.

[358] Schwenzer, 'Article 77 CISG: Mitigation of Damages' in Schwenzer and Schroeter (eds) (n 3) para 10.

[359] See ibid para 11; McKendrick, 'Article 7.4.8' in Vogenauer (ed) (n 3) para 7.

[360] See for unreasonable expenses *Lagden v O'Connor* [2003] UKHL 64, [2004] 1 AC 1067; Cf *Lamborghini hauler case* (n 185) note II.2.b); *South Korean stainless wire case* (n 170).

According to Article 77 CISG and Article 7.4.8 PICC, failure to prevent avoidable loss reduces the claim for damages by the avoidable amount. The specific circumstances may also lead to the complete exclusion of compensation. The burden of proof that the aggrieved party violated its duty to mitigate damages rests on the party in breach.[361] Conversely, the promisee bears the burden of proof for claiming damages under Article 74 CISG and Article 7.4.2 PICC for measures taken to avoid or mitigate loss.[362]

X. Interest

The CISG and the PICC establish a straightforward entitlement to interest for late payment, emphasizing the importance of prompt payment in international commercial contracts and the need to compensate the aggrieved party for the use of its money (Article 78 CISG and Article 7.4.9 PICC). These provisions apply to contractual obligations, whether they are primary claims to performance or secondary claims to damages, and whether they are explicitly mentioned in the contract or derived from the law or norms of the law applicable.[363] Interest is payable even if the precise amount of the claim is uncertain.[364] They also cover both failures to pay the price and any other sums in arrears.[365] These other sums may include expenses incurred on behalf of the other party (e.g. transport costs advanced by a party which are the responsibility of the other), part of the price already paid after reduction pursuant to Article 50 CISG, and expenses from depositing the goods according to Article 87 CISG.[366]

Regarding the preconditions for interest, under Article 78 CISG or Article 7.4.9 PICC, interest is owed only if the sum is due.[367] The time of payment of the price

---

[361] *Hewlett-Packard France v Matrox Graphics Inc.* [2020] Cour supérieure du Québec/Superior Court of Québec, 2020 QCCS 78/500-05-070786-023, CISG-online 4876; Schwenzer, 'Article 77 CISG: Mitigation of Damages' in Schwenzer and Schroeter (eds) (n 3) para 13; Djordjević, 'Article 77' in Kröll, Mistelis, and Perales Viscasillas (eds) (n 1) para 33.

[362] Schwenzer, 'Article 77 CISG: Mitigation of Damages' in Schwenzer and Schroeter (eds) (n 3) para 13.

[363] *Jiangsu Taiping Rubber Co., Ltd. v Kumwoo Investment Co., Ltd.* [2018] Intermediate People's Court Zhenjiang, Jiangsu Province (2016) Su 11 Min Chu No. 337, CISG-online 4120; *REC Solar Grade Silicon Co., Ltd. v Hairun Photovoltaic Technology Co., Ltd* [2018] Intermediate People's Court Wuxi, Jiangsu Province (2018) Su 02 Min Chu No. 131, CISG-online 4107; Klaus Bacher, 'Article 78 CISG: Obligation to Pay Interest' in Schwenzer and Schroeter (eds) (n 3) para 5.

[364] Yesim Atamer, 'Article 78' in Kröll, Mistelis, and Perales Viscasillas (eds) (n 1) para 9; cf Christoph Brunner and Michael Feit, 'Article 78 (Interest on Sums in Arrears)' in Brunner and Gottlieb (eds) (n 1) para 3.

[365] Bacher, 'Article 78 CISG: Obligation to Pay Interest' in Schwenzer and Schroeter (eds) (n 3) para 6.

[366] Ibid; CISG Advisory Council, 'CISG-AC Opinion No. 14, Interest under Article 78 CISG, Rapporteur: Professor Doctor Yeşim M. Atamer, Istanbul Bilgi University, Turkey. Adopted unanimously by the CISG Advisory Council following its 18th meeting, in Beijing, China on 21 and 22 October 2013' (2013) comments 3.17–3.18.

[367] Ewan McKendrick, 'Article 7.4.9' in Vogenauer (ed) (n 3) paras 6–7; Bacher, 'Article 78 CISG: Obligation to Pay Interest' in Schwenzer and Schroeter (eds) (n 3), para 8.

330 GLOBAL COMMERCIAL CONTRACTS

is determined by the parties' agreement or, in the absence of agreement, by the default rules on the time of payment under the CISG or the PICC.[368] For other claims that do not specify the due date, it must be assumed that payment is due immediately when the claim arises.[369] Interest is payable even for periods when the claim has arisen but is not yet certain.[370] For damages claims, interest starts accruing when the loss occurs.[371] Changes in the value of the loss over time may affect the calculation date for damages but not the obligation to pay interest, which begins on the relevant calculation date.[372]

If the debtor is prevented from paying because it does not know the amount of the claim, interest should still be paid if the uncertainty results from the debtor's breach.[373] Even without a breach, such as when the price depends on the quantity of delivered goods, the creditor is entitled to interest from the time of actual expenditure, but this might tempt the creditor to delay the claim.[374] Therefore, payment may be postponed until the creditor names the claim amount, for example by providing an invoice.[375]

In the event of a price reduction, the buyer should be entitled to interest on the repaid amount from the time the price was paid.[376] Interest on damages claims is payable from the time the loss occurred, regardless of whether the claim amount has been established.[377]

Interest accrues solely based on whether a payment is due and unpaid by the agreed date, without needing the creditor to suffer a loss or issue a warning. No additional requirements, such as a request for payment, demand, or any compliance with formalities, are necessary for interest to start accruing.[378] The debtor cannot claim exemption from paying interest due to *force majeure* and must pay interest even if it is unable due to external factors, such as a ban on acquiring foreign currency.[379]

---

[368] See CISG art 58; cf McKendrick, 'Article 7.4.9' in Vogenauer (ed) (n 3) para 9.

[369] Atamer, 'Article 78' in Kröll, Mistelis, and Perales Viscasillas (eds) (n 1) para 18.

[370] CISG Advisory Council, 'CISG-AC Opinion No. 14' (n 366) comment 3.10; Ewan McKendrick, 'Article 7.4.10' in Vogenauer (ed) (n 3) para 3; International Institute for the Unification of Private Law (n 3) 286, art 7.4.10.

[371] Bacher, 'Article 78 CISG: Obligation to Pay Interest' in Schwenzer and Schroeter (eds) (n 3) para 17.

[372] Brunner and Feit, 'Article 78 (Interest on Sums in Arrears)' in Brunner and Gottlieb (eds) (n 1) para 3; Bacher, 'Article 78 CISG: Obligation to Pay Interest' in Schwenzer and Schroeter (eds) (n 3) para 17.

[373] CISG Advisory Council, 'CISG-AC Opinion No. 14' (n 366) comment 3.10.

[374] Bacher, 'Article 78 CISG: Obligation to Pay Interest' in Schwenzer and Schroeter (eds) (n 3) para 14.

[375] Ibid.

[376] Cf Markus Müller-Chen, 'Article 50' in Schwenzer and Schroeter (eds) (n 3) para 16.

[377] Bacher, 'Article 78 CISG: Obligation to Pay Interest' in Schwenzer and Schroeter (eds) (n 3) para 16.

[378] CISG Advisory Council, 'CISG-AC Opinion No. 14' (n 366) comment 3.19.

[379] Atamer, 'Article 78' in Kröll, Mistelis, and Perales Viscasillas (eds) (n 1) para 12.

Interest stops accruing when the principal obligation is paid in full or is extinguished.[380] If the debtor pays only the principal without accrued interest, the creditor should retain the right to claim the interest separately.[381] If the debtor has a counterclaim, the obligation to pay interest ceases from the moment the counterclaim exists, irrespective of set-off or suspension.[382] In some cases, interest claims may cease for other reasons, such as voiding an existing interest claim.[383]

The PICC provides a detailed mechanism for determining the interest rate in Article 7.4.9(2) PICC.[384] Absent an agreement on the interest rate, the PICC prioritize the average bank short-term lending rate to prime borrowers at the place of payment.[385] If such a rate does not exist, it defaults to the rate in the State of the currency of payment,[386] or as last resort the appropriate rate fixed by that State's law.[387] This aims to provide a fair and consistent method for calculating interest, reducing uncertainty.

The CISG does not *expressly* provide the rate of interest in Article 78 CISG.[388] However, all aspects of interest are governed by the Convention and its underlying general principles.[389] The rate of interest may be determined by the agreement of the parties, even implicitly.[390] In the absence of such an agreement, the CISG Advisory Council has asserted that the applicable rate is the one that the court at the creditor's place of business would grant in a similar contract of sale not governed by the CISG.[391] Compound interest may be payable if agreed upon by the parties or if the court at the creditor's place of business would allow it in a similar contract not governed by the CISG.[392]

---

[380] CISG Advisory Council, 'CISG-AC Opinion No. 14' (n 366) comment 3.49.

[381] Ibid.

[382] Ibid.

[383] Ibid.

[384] McKendrick, 'Article 7.4.9' in Vogenauer (ed) (n 3) paras 1, 11 ff: also the reason for its popularity, and it being used to supplement Article 78 CISG.

[385] Ibid 12.

[386] Ibid 13.

[387] Brödermann, (n 342) Art. 7.4.9., para 4.

[388] Bacher, 'Article 78 CISG: Obligation to Pay Interest' in Schwenzer and Schroeter (eds) (n 3) para 33.

[389] *VÚB a.s. v LITOZ s.r.o.* [2019] Nejvyšší soud České republiky (Supreme Court of the Czech Republic) 23 Cdo 427/2017-336, CISG-online 4867; *Realturf Systems, S.L. v Eurograss, Inc.* [2019] Circuit Court of the 11th Judicial Circuit (Miami-Dade County) of the State of Florida, 2014-CA-018348, CISG-online 6730; *China Railway No. 10 Engineering Group Co. Ltd. v Triorient LLC* [2020] American Arbitration Association – International Centre for Dispute Resolution (AAA/ICDR) 01-19-0003-0137, CISG-online 5639; CISG Advisory Council, 'CISG-AC Opinion No. 14' (n 366) Black Letter Rule 1; Flechtner (n 9) 795 ff; Atamer, 'Article 78' in Kröll, Mistelis, and Perales Viscasillas (eds) (n 1) para 24

[390] See e.g. *Solea International BVBA v Bassett & Walker International Inc.* [2018] Superior Court of Justice of Ontario, CV-15-527848/2018 ONSC 4261, CISG-online 4194: awarding interest to the plaintiff at EURIBOR rate (8%) applying Art. 78 CISG by conceding the argument of an implicit determination of the rate by the parties; Atamer, 'Article 78' in Kröll, Mistelis, and Perales Viscasillas (eds) (n 1) para 20.

[391] CISG Advisory Council, 'CISG-AC Opinion No. 14' (n 366) Black Letter Rule 9.

[392] CISG Advisory Council, 'CISG-AC Opinion No. 14' (n 366) Black Letter Rule 10; but see Bacher, 'Article 78 CISG: Obligation to Pay Interest' in Schwenzer and Schroeter (eds) (n 3) paras 51–53.

Interest should be paid in the same currency and at the same place, complying with the same payment formalities, as the principal sum.[393] Any loss suffered by the creditor that is not recoverable as interest under Article 78 CISG may be recovered as damages in accordance with Article 74 CISG.[394] This is also the express solution provided by Article 7.4.9(3) PICC.

---

[393] CISG Advisory Council, 'CISG-AC Opinion No. 14' (n 366) Black Letter Rule 11.
[394] *Fundiciones Balaguer, S.A. v Ferrell-Ross Roll Mfg.* [2024] U.S. District Court for the Southern District of Texas, 4:23-cv-4437, CISG-online 7229; CISG Advisory Council, 'CISG-AC Opinion No. 14' (n 366) Black Letter Rules 11 and 12.

16
Unwinding of Contract

I. General

The unwinding of contracts is a complex legal process that involves reversing or upholding contractual obligations and returning parties, to the extent possible, to their pre-contractual or pre-breach positions.[1] This chapter explores the unwinding of the international commercial contract due to cases of invalidity and avoidance, and the relevant legal regimes governing these processes under the CISG and the PICC.

1. Cases: Invalidity—avoidance

The unwinding of contracts primarily hinges on issues of validity and grounds for avoidance. The issue of validity concerns whether the contract was legally formed and whether it meets the necessary legal criteria to be enforceable. On the other hand, the question of avoidance involves the unwinding of the contract due to breach.[2]

Cases concerning the validity of a contract often address whether the essential elements of a contract—free intent, legality, capacity, possibility, etc.—are present. If these elements are lacking or are tainted by factors such as misrepresentation, fraud, mistake, gross disparity, coercion, etc., the contract may be deemed invalid.[3]

---

[1] Ingeborg Schwenzer and Edgardo Muñoz, *Global Sales and Contract Law* (2nd edn, Oxford University Press 2022) para 50.01 ff.

[2] Ibid para 50.15 ff.

[3] Schwenzer and Muñoz (n 1) para 50.02.

As explained in Chapter 12, the CISG pre-empts domestic law with respect to some of the aforementioned factors; consequently, the unwinding of the contract in relation to those covered matters is governed exclusively by the CISG.

Avoidance comes into play when a valid contract is in place but subsequent issues warrant its end. These could include fundamental breaches, agreed-upon termination, or other factors that justify the termination of the contract.[4] The process of avoidance seeks to release the parties from their contractual obligations[5] and, ideally, to restore them to their original or pre-breach positions.[6]

2. Legal regimes

Under the CISG, matters of contract validity are generally left to the domestic law applicable by virtue of the conflict of law rules of the forum. As commented in Chapter 12, Article 4 CISG excludes issues of contract validity and property effects, unless expressly covered by the CISG. The issues of validity are defined autonomously under Article 7(1) CISG. However, the counter-exception in Article 4 CISG allows some matters of validity to be governed by the CISG if expressly provided in its text or principles. The CISG Advisory Council Opinion No. 23 confirms the Convention's exclusive application when its provisions overlap with domestic rules aiming at similar purposes.[7] Thus, the CISG pre-empts domestic law remedies in cases of mistake or misrepresentation. For all other matters of validity, the unwinding of contracts due to invalidity is governed by domestic laws.[8]

Articles 81 CISG and subsequent provisions outline the consequences and duties after contract avoidance. Article 81(1) CISG states that avoidance releases the parties from their obligations under the contract, subject to any damages that may be due.[9] Furthermore, restitution must be made for any performance that has already been rendered.[10] The details of these conditions and consequences are addressed below.

The PICC provide specific provisions regarding the unwinding of the contract due to invalidity. Article 3.2.15 PICC addresses the case of restitution following a contract's rescission, ensuring that parties return any benefits received under the contract. Article 3.3.2 PICC deals with the restitution of performance in case of

---

[4] Ibid para 47.01 ff.
[5] CISG art 81(1); PICC 2016, art 7.3.5. See also Schwenzer and Muñoz (n 1) para 50.15.
[6] Ibid paras 50.22–50.26; see also [1995] Landgericht Düsseldorf 2 O 506/94, Unilex.
[7] CISG Advisory Council, 'CISG-AC Opinion No. 23, Mistake, Fraud, Misrepresentation and Initial Impossibility in CISG Contracts, Rapporteur: Professor Hugh Beale, Universities of Warwick (Em.) and Oxford, United Kingdom, December 12–14, 2023' (2023) Black Letter Rules 1, 4.
[8] See Chapter 7.
[9] *Dimur Fruits SL v Fairtrasa Holland BV* [2021] Rechtbank Den Haag (District Court The Hague) C/09/592683/HA ZA 20-472, CISG-online 5564.
[10] CISG, art 81(2); see *Solmed Supplies SL v Dieha Capital BV* [2023] Rechtbank Zeeland-West-Brabant (District Court Zeeland-WestBrabant) C/02/383910/HA ZA 21-168 (E), CISG-online 6434.

invalid contracts due to illegality, emphasizing the need for restitution on reasonable terms.

In case of avoidance due to contractual breach, Articles 7.3.5 to 7.3.7 PICC detail the process of unwinding. Under Article 7.3.5 PICC, avoidance releases both parties from future obligations but does not prevent claims for damages due to past non-performance. Additionally, avoidance under both the PICC and the CISG does not affect provisions for dispute settlement or other terms meant to remain in effect post termination.[11] This ensures that critical clauses, like those for confidentiality or indemnity, continue to be enforceable. Article 7.3.6 PICC states that upon avoidance of a one-time performance contract, either party can claim restitution for whatever it has provided, given that it also returns what it has received. If restitution for the actual performance is not possible, reasonable monetary compensation must be made. Article 7.3.7 PICC provides that upon avoidance of a long-term contract, restitution can only be claimed for the period following the avoidance, provided the contract is divisible. Any restitution required must adhere to the provisions of Article 7.3.6 PICC.

II. Unwinding of Invalid Contract

The unwinding of invalid contracts is a critical aspect of contract law. It aims to reverse the effects of a contract that has been declared invalid. This process aims to ensure that the parties are restored to their pre-contractual positions as much as possible. The approach to unwinding invalid contracts varies from domestic legal regimes to international frameworks such as the PICC.[12]

In domestic legal systems, the unwinding of invalid contracts is typically addressed through principles of unjust enrichment and property law. Unjust enrichment involves the return of any benefits unjustly received under an invalid contract. For example, if one party delivered goods but did not receive payment because the contract was invalid, it could claim the return of the goods or their value. Property law principles may also come into play, particularly in determining the ownership and return of goods or property exchanged under the invalid contract.[13]

The PICC provide a structured approach to the unwinding of invalid contracts. Article 3.2.15 PICC addresses the issue of restitution when a contract is rescinded on grounds of invalidity. Upon rescission, either party may claim restitution for

---

[11]   CISG Advisory Council, 'CISG-AC Opinion No. 9, Consequences of Avoidance of the Contract, Rapporteur: Professor Michael Bridge, London School of Economics, London, United Kingdom, 15 November 2008' (2008) comment 3.3. See also, *Chinese goods case* [1996] Schiedsgericht der Handelskammer Hamburg (Court of Arbitration of the Hamburg Chamber of Commerce) Partial Award (on the merits) CISG-online 187.

[12]   Schwenzer and Muñoz (n 1) para 50.01.

[13]   CISG Advisory Council, 'CISG-AC Opinion No. 23' (n 7) comment 2.5.

what it has supplied, as long as it concurrently returns what it has received.[14] This creates a balanced approach, ensuring that no party benefits unjustly from an invalid contract. For example, if a buyer returns the goods received, the seller must refund the purchase price.

Restitution is typically in kind, but there are instances where this is not possible or appropriate.[15] In such cases, a monetary restitution must be made, reflecting the value of the received performance (Article 3.2.15(2) PICC).[16] This is especially relevant when returning the actual performance is impractical or excessively costly.[17] For instance, monetary compensation is the reasonable alternative if goods have been consumed or altered.

The allocation of risk is a critical component of restitution. If restitution in kind is impossible due to circumstances attributable to the other party, no monetary allowance is required to be made (Article 3.2.15(3) PICC). Conversely, if the recipient of the performance is unable to restitute in kind due to its fault, it must compensate the other party. This principle ensures that risk lies with the party in control of the performance, promoting fairness in the process of restitution.[18]

The practical application of these rules is illustrated through various scenarios. For instance, if a painting is destroyed due to one party's negligence, the other party can reclaim the purchase price without compensating for the painting's value. However, if a hurricane destroys equipment after its sale, the buyer must compensate for the equipment's value despite rescinding the contract.

Parties may also claim compensation for reasonable expenses incurred to preserve or maintain the performance received (Article 3.2.15(4) PICC). This rule acknowledges that maintaining the received goods or the object of the contract might involve costs, which should be recoverable upon contract avoidance. For example, if a buyer incurs costs to care for a horse received, which is later returned, it can claim these costs as compensation.

On the other hand, Article 3.3.2 PICC addresses the issue of restitution when a contract is rescinded on grounds of illegality. When a contract violates a mandatory rule, parties are generally denied remedies under the contract.[19] However, Article 3.3.2 PICC allows restitution if it is deemed reasonable under the circumstances. This modern approach is in contrast with traditional views where parties

---

[14] PICC 2016, art 3.2.15(1); Reinhard Zimmermann, 'The Unwinding of Failed Contracts in the UNIDROIT Principles 2010' (2011) 25 *Uniform Law Review* 570.

[15] International Institute for the Unification of Private Law (ed), *UNIDROIT Principles of International Commercial Contracts* (UNIDROIT International Institute for the Unification of Private Law 2017) 119, art 3.2.15, off cmt 2, Illustration 2; 229–30, art 7.3.6, off cmt 2.

[16] PICC 2016, art 7.3.6(2).

[17] International Institute for the Unification of Private Law (n 15) 119, art 3.2.15, off cmt 2.

[18] Ibid 120, art 3.2.15, off cmt 3.

[19] Gilles Cuniberti, 'Article 3.3.1' in Stefan Vogenauer (ed), *Commentary on the UNIDROIT Principles of International Commercial Contracts (PICC)* (2nd edn, Oxford University Press 2015) paras 5, 8.

aware of the infringement of the rule could not recover benefits.[20] Instead, Article 3.3.2 PICC balances whether it is more appropriate for the recipient to retain the benefits or for the performer to reclaim them. The criteria for determining the reasonableness of restitution under Article 3.3.2 PICC align with those for determining the contractual remedies under Article 3.3.1(3) PICC.[21] These criteria help evaluate whether restitution should be granted based on the specifics of each case, even though the outcomes for contractual and restitutionary remedies might differ. For instance, if a contractor almost completes a power plant but the government later claims that the contract is invalid due to corruption, it would be unfair for the government to retain the plant without full payment. The contractor may receive monetary compensation for the value of the work done.

If restitution is granted under Article 3.3.2 PICC, the rules under Article 3.2.15 PICC apply, with necessary adaptations.[22] This means that restitution should be aligned with the principles of rescinding contracts, considering the contract's ineffectiveness due to the infringement of mandatory rules. This ensures consistency and fairness in the application of the principles of restitution. For instance, a contractor who pays a commission to secure a project may still be entitled to compensation for the completed work if a new government invalidates the contract due to the commission's illegality. On the other hand, in cases where a service provider transports dangerous goods without meeting safety requirements, restitution may be denied to prevent incentivizing such violations.

III. Unwinding Upon Avoidance of Contract

1. Under the CISG

The CISG provides a comprehensive framework for contract avoidance, the subsequent unwinding of obligations, and restitution between the parties involved. Article 81(1) CISG stipulates that upon avoidance of a contract, the parties are released from their obligations under the contract. This means that neither party is required to fulfil any further contractual duties.[23] However, any provision of

---

[20] Stefan Vogenauer, 'The UNIDROIT Principles of International Commercial Contracts at Twenty: Experiences to Date, the 2010 Edition, and Future Prospects' (2014) 19(4) *Uniform Law Review* 496; for the PICC's approach, see Michael Joachim Bonell, 'The New Provisions on Illegality in the UNIDROIT Principles 2010' (2011) *Uniform Law Review* 517, 531, 532; for the approach of the domestic law, see e.g. American Law Institute, *Restatement of the Law (2d) of Contracts* (American Law Institute) s 198; for comparative studies, see Michael Storme, 'Harmonisation of the Law on (Substantive) Validity of Contracts (Illegality and Immorality)' in Jürgen Basedow, Klaus J Hopt, and Hein Kötz (eds) *Festschrift für Ulrich Drobnig zum siebzigsten Geburtstag* (Mohr Siebeck 2024) 198.

[21] Gilles Cuniberti, 'Article 3.3.2' in Vogenauer (ed) (n 19) paras 1–2, 5.

[22] PICC 2016, art 3.3.2(3); International Institute for the Unification of Private Law (n 15) 136, art 3.3.2, off cmt 3, 136; Bonell (n 20) 535.

[23] Ulrich Magnus, 'The Remedy of Avoidance of Contract Under CISG—General Remarks and Special Cases' (2005) 25 *Journal of Law & Commerce* 423–36.

the contract for the settlement of disputes or any other provision governing the rights and obligations of the parties, consequent upon the avoidance of the contract, remains unaffected by the avoidance.[24] This ensures that clauses relating to dispute resolution mechanisms—most importantly arbitration clauses—choice of law, limitation of liability, confidentiality, non-competition, return of materials, intellectual property rights, agreed sums, etc., are be enforceable as initially agreed upon.[25]

Article 81(2) CISG requires the restitution of what has been performed under the contract. This means that any goods, services, or payments exchanged must be returned concurrently. The goal is to restore the parties to their original positions, to the extent possible.[26]

Where restitution of the goods is impossible in substantially the condition in which the buyer received them, avoidance of the contract and substitute delivery may be barred (Article 81(1) CISG). However, this rule is considered antiquated, with damages being a more practical and fairer solution in modern contexts.[27] This loss of right does not apply if the inability to make restitution is not due to the buyer's actions or omissions, or if the goods have deteriorated due to the necessary examination under Article 38 CISG, or if the goods have been sold, consumed, or transformed in the normal course of business before the buyer discovered the non-conformity (Article 82(2) CISG). This provision ensures that buyers are not unfairly penalized for actions beyond their control.

The nature of restitution claims raises questions about the effects of avoidance on property. Article 4 sentence 2(b) CISG clarifies that the CISG does not govern the effect of contract avoidance on the property of the goods. However, property rights are affected by the rules on restitution to a certain extent.[28] Articles 81 to 84 CISG provide a comprehensive set of rules on restitution under the Convention. The contract continues to exist during the time of contract liquidation, meaning the legal basis for acquiring property—the contract—remains in effect until the contract is fully unwound. As long as this process is ongoing, the application of domestic restitution law, which may provide for actions *in rem*, is excluded. Only

---

[24] CISG Advisory Council, 'CISG-AC Opinion No. 9' (n 11) comment 3.3.

[25] *Filanto, S.pA v Chilewich International Corp* [1992] US [Federal] District Court for the Southern District of New York 91 Civ. 3253 (CLB), CISG-online 45; *German goods case* [1999] ICC International Court of Arbitration 9978 (Final Award), CISG-online 708.

[26] *Mercedes Maybach case* [2019] Oberster Gerichtshof (Austrian Supreme Court) 4 Ob 110/ 19h, CISG-online 4509; Michael Bridge, 'Article 81' in Stefan M Kröll, Loukas A Mistelis, and Pilar Perales Viscasillas (eds), *UN Convention on Contracts for the International Sale of Goods (CISG): A Commentary* (2nd edn, CH Beck 2018) para 19; Christiana Fountoulakis, 'Article 81 CISG: Parties' Release from Obligations; Restriction' in Ingeborg Schwenzer and Ulrich Schroeter, *Schlechtriem & Schwenzer: Commentary on the UN Convention on the International Sale of Goods* (5th edn, Oxford University Press 2022) para 9. See also CISG Advisory Council, 'CISG-AC Opinion No. 9' (n 11) comments 3.7 ff.

[27] See generally Schwenzer and Muñoz (n 1) para 44.01 ff; CISG Advisory Council, 'CISG-AC Opinion No. 9' (n 11) comment 3.8.

[28] CISG Advisory Council, 'CISG-AC Opinion No. 9' (n 11) comment 3.6.

after the liquidation of the contract is complete will domestic laws become relevant for determining whether the cancellation of the contract directly affects the parties' property rights over the goods.[29]

If goods are damaged *after* the contract is avoided, Article 74 CISG provides for damages.[30] This ensures that the party receiving the damaged goods is compensated appropriately, maintaining fairness in the restitution process.

Article 84(1) CISG addresses the issue of interest on the purchase price that must be restituted. If the seller is required to refund the purchase price, it must also pay interest on this amount from the date the price was initially paid, regardless of whether interest was actually earned.[31] The seller's duty to pay interest under Article 84(1) rests on an irrebuttable presumption that the seller benefited from the price paid, thereby avoiding any inquiry into its actual use or tracing it through the seller's activities. Given this presumption and the restitutionary nature of Article 84 CISG, the commercial investment rate at the seller's place of business should generally apply.[32]

The interest rate under Article 84 CISG may differ from that applicable under Article 78 CISG. As addressed in Chapter 15, in the absence of an agreement, the rate under Article 78 CISG is the one that the court at the creditor's place of business would grant in a similar contract of sale not governed by the CISG. Since Article 78 CISG aims at fully compensating the creditor's loss from late payment, and the creditor is deprived of the money at their place of business, the economic loss is naturally tied to the conditions at that location. If this logic were applied under Article 84, the interest rate at the buyer's place of business—rather than the seller's—would apply. However, as noted above, Article 84 has a restitutionary character and embodies the idea of disgorgement of benefits. Thus, the seller must return the price together with interest at a rate that reflects the irrebuttable presumption of benefit at its own place of business. Article 84(2) CISG extends this to benefits derived from the goods, including surrogates, fruits, and use, without relying on abstract calculations.[33] Article 84(2) CISG stipulates that the buyer must account for any benefits derived from the goods if it is required to make restitution.[34] This requirement applies in two scenarios: first, when the buyer must return the goods; second, when the buyer declares the contract avoided or requests substitute goods but is unable to return the goods in substantially the same

---

[29] Ibid comment 1.4.

[30] Ingeborg Schwenzer, 'Article 74 CISG: Calculation of Damages in General' in Schwenzer and Schroeter (eds) (n 26) para 9.

[31] CISG Advisory Council, 'CISG-AC Opinion No. 9n 11) comments 3.24 and 3.25.

[32] CISG Advisory Council, 'CISG-AC Opinion No. 14, Interest under Article 78 CISG, Rapporteur: Professor Doctor Yeşim M. Atamer, Istanbul Bilgi University, Turkey. Adopted unanimously by the CISG Advisory Council following its 18th meeting, in Beijing, China on 21 and 22 October 2013' (2013) comments 3.30.

[33] See PICC 2016, art 3.2.15; see also, Schwenzer and Muñoz (n 1) para 19.27.

[34] *DSM Dyneema B.V. v Electromichaniki Kimis EPE* [2009] Polimeles Protodikio Athinon (Multimember Court of First Instance Athens) 4505/2009, CISG-online 2228.

condition as received. By obliging the buyer to account for the benefits, the CISG ensures that the seller is not disadvantaged by the buyer's use or partial consumption of the goods.

2. Under the PICC

The PICC also provide a comprehensive framework for the unwinding of contracts in case of avoidance due to breach or agreed termination. The PICC ensure that parties are restored to their pre-breach or pre-contract positions in a fair and equitable manner when a contract is avoided. Articles 7.3.5, 7.3.6, and 7.3.7 PICC outline the key provisions for this process, drawing parallels with the CISG while addressing unique aspects of contract unwinding.

Article 7.3.5 PICC is akin to Article 81(1) CISG.[35] It outlines the effects of contract termination, emphasizing that avoidance releases both parties from their obligations to perform future duties under the contract. However, this release does not preclude the right to claim damages for non-performance.[36] For instance, if machinery sold turns out to be defective and the contract is avoided, the buyer can still seek damages for the losses incurred due to the defect. As stated above in section I.2, avoidance does not affect provisions in the contract that are intended to operate even after avoidance. This continuity ensures that sensitive information and critical post-termination obligations are safeguarded.[37]

Article 7.3.6 PICC addresses the process of restitution when a contract to be performed at one time is terminated. Both parties can reclaim what they have given under the contract, provided they return what they received.[38] For instance, in a contract for the sale of machinery, if the buyer terminates the contract due to defects, the seller must return the purchase price while the buyer must return the machinery. When restitution in kind is not possible or appropriate, an allowance in money must be made. This might occur if the goods have been consumed, transformed, or deteriorated.[39] For example, if a company hires another to develop software and the software does not function as intended, the contract can be avoided, and the buyer can reclaim the payment while providing a reasonable monetary allowance for the service or benefit received. This ensures that even when physical

---

[35] Florian Mohs, 'Effects of Avoidance and Restitution of the Goods: Remarks on the Manner in Which Articles 7.3.5 and 7.3.6 of the UNIDROIT Principles Compare with Articles 81 and 82 of the CISG' in John Felemegas (ed), *An International Approach to the Interpretation of the United Nations Convention on Contracts for the International Sale of Goods (1980) as Uniform Sales Law* (Cambridge University Press 2007).

[36] International Institute for the Unification of Private Law (n 15) 257, art 7.3.5 off cmt 2; Peter Huber, 'Article 7.3.5' in Vogenauer (ed) (n 19) para 4.

[37] Huber, 'Article 7.3.5' in Vogenauer (ed) (n 19) paras 5–6.

[38] Peter Huber, 'Article 7.3.6' in Vogenauer (ed) (n 19) para 6.

[39] For examples where restitution in kind is not possible or appropriate, see International Institute for the Unification of Private Law (n 15) 264–5, art 7.3.6 off cmt 3.

restitution is impractical, the party giving the benefit is compensated fairly, the software developer in this case, reflecting the value of the received performance by the buyer.

Additionally, Article 7.3.6 PICC addresses the allocation of risk and compensation for preservation expenses. The party unable to make restitution in kind due to reasons attributable to the other party is not required to provide monetary allowance. Moreover, if expenses are incurred to preserve the received performance, reasonable compensation can be claimed.[40] For instance, if a horse sold under a misrepresented pedigree is returned, the buyer can claim expenses for feeding and caring for the horse.

IV. Long-term Contracts

The PICC have specific provisions for the unwinding of long-term contracts. Article 7.3.7 PICC introduces a critical distinction between contracts to be performed at one time and long-term contracts. This distinction acknowledges the different complexities involved in unwinding these types of contracts. The unwinding process is typically straightforward for contracts performed at one time, involving the return of goods or payments. However, the process is more complex for long-term contracts, requiring careful consideration of the period after the contract is avoided. Article 7.3.7 PICC provides that when a long-term contract is avoided, restitution can only be claimed for the period after termination has taken effect, provided the contract is divisible.[41] This distinction recognizes the impracticality of unravelling performance that may have been rendered over an extended period before avoidance. For instance, if a service contract is avoided midway, the party paying for future services can reclaim payments made for those services, but not for services already rendered.

If the long-term contract is indivisible, restitution for past performance is required.[42] In cases where the contract's purpose cannot be fulfilled without complete performance, restitution may be necessary. For example, if an artist is commissioned to create a series of paintings as a unified project and fails to complete it, the buyer can reclaim the advance payments, provided it returns the partial work. This ensures that the incomplete performance does not leave one party at a disadvantage. Additionally, Article 7.3.7 PICC aligns with Article 7.3.6 PICC in governing the mechanics of restitution, ensuring consistency in the application of these principles across different types of contracts.[43]

---

[40] International Institute for the Unification of Private Law (n 15) 264-267, art 7.3.6, off cmt 3, 5; Vogenauer (n 20) 481.
[41] Peter Huber, 'Article 7.3.7' in Vogenauer (ed) (n 19) paras 5–6.
[42] Ibid para 7.
[43] Ibid para 6.

V. Preservation of Goods

In international trade, the breach of contracts can create significant challenges, particularly concerning the fate of goods. Also, when the contract is avoided, determining the appropriate course of action for the goods can be complex. The CISG addresses this issue comprehensively through Articles 85 to 88 CISG. These provisions outline the obligations and rights of parties in preserving goods. They ensure that the goods are maintained in proper condition and that losses are minimized.[44] The PICC, however, do not have equivalent provisions.

When a buyer fails to take delivery or fails to pay the price when payment and delivery are to be made concurrently, the seller must take reasonable steps to preserve the goods (Article 85 CISG). This obligation exists as long as the seller is in possession of the goods or is in a position to control their disposition. The seller is entitled to retain the goods until it is reimbursed for the reasonable expenses incurred in preserving them. This provision ensures that goods are not left unattended or exposed to damage or deterioration. It protects both parties' interests by maintaining the value of the goods.

If a buyer receives goods and intends to exercise the right to reject them, Article 86(1) CISG requires the buyer to take reasonable steps to preserve the goods.[45] The buyer can retain the goods until the seller reimburses the reasonable expenses incurred in preserving them. Additionally, Article 86(2) CISG mandates that if goods dispatched to the buyer have been placed at its disposal at their destination and the buyer rejects them, the buyer must take possession of the goods, provided it does not involve unreasonable inconvenience or expense. This duty arises even if the buyer does not accept the goods. It reflects the principle that parties must co-operate to mitigate losses and must responsibly manage goods.[46]

The nature of the goods dictates the specific measures required to preserve them. The CISG provides guidelines on these measures to ensure that appropriate actions are taken based on the type and condition of the goods. Article 87 CISG allows a party bound to preserve goods to deposit them in a third-party warehouse at the other party's expense, provided the expenses incurred are not unreasonable. This provision is particularly relevant when goods require specific conditions for storage to prevent damage or deterioration.

The CISG outlines provisions for the self-help sale of goods, which might be important to mitigate losses in certain situations. Article 88(1) CISG permits a party to sell the goods if the other party unreasonably delays taking possession, taking

---

[44] Klaus Bacher, 'Introduction to Articles 85–88 CISG: General Questions Regarding the Preservation of the Goods' in Schwenzer and Schroeter (eds) (n 26) 1 ff; Harry M Flechtner, *Honnold's Uniform Law for International Sales Under the 1980 United Nations Convention* (5th edn, Wolters Kluwer 2021) 519.

[45] *Solmed Supplies S.L. v Dieha Capital B.V.* (n 10).

[46] See Hiroo Sono, 'Article 86 CISG' in Kröll, Mistelis, and Perales Viscasillas (eds) (n 26) para 6.

them back, or paying the price or the cost of preservation. Reasonable notice of the intention to resell must be given to the other party, allowing it a final opportunity to fulfil its obligations before the goods are sold.[47] This measure prevents unnecessary losses as it enables the selling party to recoup costs and mitigate damages.

In cases where the goods are subject to rapid deterioration or where their preservation would involve unreasonable expense, Article 88(2) CISG mandates an emergency sale.[48] The party must take reasonable measures to sell the goods and, to the extent possible, give notice to the other party of the intention to sell.[49] This provision allows for quick action to prevent significant losses due to the perishable nature of the goods.

Proceeds from any self-help or emergency sale must be handled appropriately. According to Article 88(3) CISG, the party conducting the resale can retain an amount equal to the reasonable expenses of preserving and selling the goods. Any remaining balance must be accounted for and returned to the other party.[50] This ensures transparency and fairness in handling the proceeds and covering expenses related to the preservation and sale of the goods.

The CISG's detailed provisions on the preservation of goods in Articles 85 to 88 are critical for managing contract breaches. These articles provide a structured approach to preserving goods, highlighting the responsibilities of both buyers and sellers in various scenarios. By mandating reasonable measures based on the nature of the goods, the CISG ensures that goods are protected and losses are minimized. This comprehensive framework underscores the importance of cooperation and responsible action in international trade, promoting fair and efficient unwinding of the contract.

---

[47] *Gimex, SA v Basque Imagen Grafica y Textil, SL* [2003] Audiencia Provincial de Navarra (Court of Appeal Navarra) 73/2002, CISG-online 811.

[48] See *Venison case* [1999] Oberlandesgericht Braunschweig (Court of Appeal Braunschweig) 2 U 27/99, CISG-online 510.

[49] Hiroo Sono, 'Article 88 CISG' in Kröll, Mistelis, and Perales Viscasillas (eds) (n 26) para 15; Klaus Bacher, 'Article 88 CISG: Self-help and Emergency Sale of Preserved Goods' in Schwenzer and Schroeter (eds) (n 26) para 14.

[50] *Shamo jeans case* [1999] Oberlandesgericht Hamburg (Court of Appeal Hamburg) 1 U 31/99, CISG-online 515.

17

Limitation of Actions

I. General: Domestic Approaches, Uniform Law

The limitation of actions in international contracts is a critical aspect that governs the time frame within which parties must bring legal claims. Various legal frameworks address this issue, each offering distinct approaches to managing limitation periods.

A comparative analysis of different legal systems reveals significant variations in the treatment of limitation periods. These differences can influence the strategies and expectations of parties involved in international contracts. For instance, under the traditional civil law approach, general limitation periods are typically long, ranging from 10 to 30 years, but they come with numerous exceptions. Some legal systems differentiate between business-to-business (B2B) and other contracts, while others have special regimes for consumer-to-consumer (C2C) transactions or consumer-to-business (C2B) claims.[1] Historically, Germany had a 30-year limitation period, but this was reduced to three years under the new law of obligations introduced in 2002.[2] A notable exception in these systems involves contracts for the sale of goods, where extremely short limitation periods apply for non-conforming goods. This has led courts to often rely on the distinction between *aliud* (something entirely different) and *peius* (inferior goods), with shorter periods applying

---

[1] Ingeborg Schwenzer and Edgardo Muñoz, *Global Sales and Contract Law* (2nd edn, Oxford University Press 2022), para 51.34.

[2] See Germany Bürgerliches Gesetzbuch (BGB) s 477 (old version) and s 438(1) No 3 (current version); Ingeborg Schwenzer, 'Article 39 CISG: Buyer's Notice of Non-conformity' in Ingeborg Schwenzer and Ulrich G Schroeter (eds), *Schlechtriem & Schwenzer Commentary on the UN Convention on the International Sale of Goods (CISG)* (5th edn, Oxford University Press 2022) para 31.

only to *peius*.[3] These systems may also allow for concurrent remedies such as rescission for mistake or tort liability for damage to the goods themselves.

In contrast, the common law approach to limitation periods is generally simpler. There is usually one limitation period for all contractual claims, which typically varies between four and six years and starts running when the breach occurs. For cases of non-conformity of goods, this period usually begins upon delivery. The UN Convention on the Limitation Period in the International Sale of Goods, 1974 (LC) has also adopted this straightforward approach. However, countries like India and Pakistan have developed more complex systems, listing over 100 different types of actions with varying limitation periods ranging from one to 60 years, reflecting a more intricate legal landscape for limitation periods in contract law.[4]

The CISG does not explicitly address limitation periods. However, Article 39(2) CISG introduces a cut-off period for notifying the non-conformity of goods, indirectly influencing the action limitation. In legal systems where the limitation period for non-conformity of goods is less than two years, significant coordination issues arise when these countries are parties to the CISG. According to Article 39(2) CISG, a buyer is allowed up to two years from the date the goods are handed over to notify the seller of hidden defects.[5] Therefore, any domestic limitation period shorter than this two-year cut-off creates a direct conflict. Given that the public international obligations of CISG member states take precedence over domestic law, it is now widely accepted that shorter limitation periods must be adjusted to comply with Article 39(2) CISG, by simply extending the shorter limitation period to two years, with its commencement starting from the delivery of the goods. An alternative solution would be to apply the general limitation period for the breach of obligations, which under most legal systems, usually exceeds two years. A third solution will be to apply the short limitation period in domestic law but starting from the notification of non-conformity under Article 39 CISG.[6]

At an international level, the LC—a sister convention to the CISG—provides a more explicit framework for limitation periods. This convention establishes uniform rules for the limitation period applicable to international sales contracts. It aims to harmonize the disparate limitation rules across different jurisdictions. The

---

[3] *Hubstaplerfall* [2005] Bundesgericht (Swiss Federal Supreme Court) 121 III 453; Ingeborg Schwenzer and Pascal Hachem, 'The CISG—Successes and Pitfalls' (2009) 57 *American Journal of Comparative Law* 457, 465.

[4] Schwenzer and Muñoz (n 1) para 51.34.

[5] *Park Plus Inc. v Sotefin SA* [2023] Swiss Arbitration Centre, 500146-2022 (Final Award), CISG-online 7020; *MMA IARD SA et al. v Inter Mutuelles Entreprises SA et al.* [2024] Cour d'appel de Toulouse (Court of Appeal Toulouse) 18/05127, CISG-online 6920; *OKWIND v TGB Group Technologies, S.L.* [2024] Audiencia Provincial de Barcelona (Court of Appeal Barcelona), 749/2022/981/2024, CISG-online 7300; *Corsetti S.r.l. v Préfac Béton Environnement S.A.S.* [2025] Cour d'appel de Riom (Court of Appeal Riom), 23/00524, CISG-online 7367.

[6] Schwenzer, 'Article 39 CISG: Buyer's Notice of Non-conformity' in Schwenzer and Schroeter (eds) (n 2) para 31.

LC shares a similar sphere of application with the CISG. The LC applies exclusively under two specific conditions: first, if at the time the contract is concluded, the parties' places of business are located in Contracting States; or second, if the rules of private international law designate the law of a Contracting State as applicable to the contract of sale.[7] However, there are notable differences. One key distinction is outlined in Article 3(2) LC, which states that opting out of its provisions must be explicit. In addition, while in the CISG most provisions may be derogated, the LC does not permit variations in the limitation period as specified in Article 22(1) LC.

The next section reviews the limitation periods to bring claims under this convention. The LC has seen varying levels of adoption over the years. In its 1974 version, the convention had 30 Member States.[8] A Protocol amending the Convention in 1980, was ratified by 23 Member States.[9] The United States has adopted the convention, while the People's Republic of China has not. This disparity in adoption reflects differing national priorities and legal traditions regarding the limitation of actions in international sales.

The PICC also address the issue of limitation periods through Articles 10.1–10.11 PICC. These provisions offer comprehensive guidelines on the commencement, duration, suspension, and renewal of limitation periods. The PICC's approach is characterized by its flexibility and adaptability. They expressly allow parties to tailor limitation rules to their specific needs and circumstances, whereas the LC does not allow for party autonomy.[10]

II. Limitation Periods

1. The LC

Under Article 8 LC, the standard limitation period is set at four years.

Under the LC, the commencement of this period is governed by several provisions. Article 9(1) LC establishes that the limitation period begins on the date the claim accrues, with certain exceptions provided in Articles 10, 11, and 12 LC. Furthermore, Article 9(2) LC clarifies that the start of the limitation period cannot be delayed by specific procedural requirements. These include the need for a notice as described in Article 1(2) LC or a clause in an arbitration agreement stipulating

---

[7] Convention on the Limitation Period in the International Sale of Goods 1974, art 3.

[8] UNCITRAL, 'Status—Convention on the Limitation Period in the International Sale of Goods (New York, 1974)' <https://uncitral.un.org/en/texts/salegoods/conventions/limitation_period_inte rnational_sale_of_goods/status> accessed 23 November 2025.

[9] Ibid.

[10] Convention on the Limitation Period in the International Sale of Goods 1974, art 22(1). However, under art 22(2) LC, it may be extended by a written declaration of the debtor made while the period is still running.

that no rights arise until an arbitration award is made. This provision ensures that the limitation period is strictly observed.

Article 10 LC provides additional guidance. This provision delineates the specific points at which claims related to breaches of contract accrued. According to Article 10(1) LC, a claim for breach of contract begins on the date the breach occurs. For claims related to defects or non-conformity, Article 10(2) LC specifies that the limitation period starts when the goods are actually delivered or when taking delivery is refused by the buyer. Additionally, Article 10(3) LC addresses claims based on fraud, stipulating that the limitation period commences when the fraud is discovered or could reasonably have been discovered.

Article 11 LC addresses situations where the seller provides an express undertaking or warranty regarding the conformity of the goods, effective for a specified period. In such cases, the limitation period for claims arising from this undertaking begins when the buyer notifies the seller of the relevant issue. However, this period cannot extend beyond the expiration date of the undertaking itself. This provision ensures that buyers have a clear timeframe to report issues covered by the seller's guarantee while protecting sellers from indefinite liability.

2. The PICC

The PICC leave the parties to agree upon and modify the limitation periods applicable to their contracts (PICC Article 10.3). This provision recognizes that business persons, typically experienced and knowledgeable, do not require the same protections as consumers, and thus can negotiate terms suited to their specific needs. However, the article also acknowledges that mandatory rules of other applicable laws may impose restrictions on such modifications, that is, the LC. Despite this flexibility, certain boundaries are set to prevent potential abuse. The general limitation period cannot be shortened to less than one year from when the party gains actual or constructive knowledge of the claim,[11] and the maximum limitation period cannot be reduced to less than four years.[12] Additionally, the maximum period can be extended up to a limit of 15 years but no further.[13] These limitations

---

[11] PICC 2016, art 10.3(2)(a); Robert Wintgen, 'Article 10.3' in Stefan Vogenauer (ed), *Commentary on the UNIDROIT Principles of International Commercial Contracts (PICC)* (2nd edn, Oxford University Press 2015) para 8; International Institute for the Unification of Private Law (ed), *UNIDROIT Principles of International Commercial Contracts* (UNIDROIT International Institute for the Unification of Private Law 2017) 357, art 10.3, off cmt 2; Eckart Brödermann, *UNIDROIT Principles of International Commercial Contracts. An Article-by-Article Commentary* (2nd edn, Kluwer Law International 2023) ch 10, art 10.3, para 4.

[12] PICC 2016, art 10.3(2)(b); Wintgen, 'Article 10.3' in Vogenauer (ed) (n 11) para 11; International Institute for the Unification of Private Law (n 11) 357, art 10.3, off cmt 2; Brödermann (n 11) ch 10, art 10.3, para 5.

[13] PICC 2016, art 10.3(2)(c); Wintgen, 'Article 10.3' Stefan Vogenauer (ed) (n 11) para 12; International Institute for the Unification of Private Law (n 11) 357, art 10.3, off cmt 2; Brödermann (n 11) ch 10, art 10.3, para 5.

ensure that parties cannot unduly disadvantage one another by excessively short-ening or lengthening the time frames within which claims must be brought. This protection is particularly important in scenarios where one party might have su-perior bargaining power or more information than the other. For instance, while parties can agree to a maximum limitation period of 15 years for claims based on hidden defects, extending this period to 25 years would be invalid.

Unlike the LC, which has a single four-year period, the PICC adopted a two-tier system. According to Article 10.2(1) PICC, the general limitation period is three years, commencing the day after the obligee knows or should have known the facts that give rise to the claim. This approach ensures that the obligee has a reasonable amount of time to pursue its claim once it is aware of its right. Moreover, Article 10.2(2) PICC sets a maximum limitation period of 10 years from the day the right can be exercised, ensuring that claims are not indefinitely delayed and providing a definitive end to potential legal disputes.

For instance, if a construction error leads to a bridge collapse years later, the limitation period starts when the damage occurs and becomes apparent, not at the initial construction date. However, if too much time has passed, exceeding the maximum 10-year period, claims would be barred, providing finality and legal certainty. Combining flexibility with a definitive long-stop period, this solution aims to protect both parties' interests in international commercial contracts.

However, the length of the limitation period is not the sole determinant of when rights can no longer be exercised. The starting point of the period and circum-stances that may affect its running, such as agreements between parties or specific prerequisites for initiating the period, also play crucial roles.

III. Renewal and Extension

Under Article 10.4 PICC, the obligor's acknowledgement of a right before the gen-eral limitation period expires triggers a new general limitation period. This new period begins the day after the acknowledgement is made. The same applies under Article 20(1) LC; however, in this case, the acknowledgment must be made in writing. These rules ensure that if the obligor recognizes the obligee's claim, the ob-ligee has additional time to pursue the claim effectively. Under the PICC, however, Article 10.4 PICC does not reset the maximum limitation period. While the gen-eral limitation period can start anew, the total duration allowed for pursuing the claim can extend beyond the original maximum limitation period by up to three years, provided that the acknowledgement occurs before the maximum period ex-pires. This mechanism helps maintain fairness by allowing the obligee more time without indefinitely extending the liability of the obligor.

Article 10.4 PICC clarifies that such acknowledgement does not create a new obligation but merely affects the limitation period. A simple acknowledgement will not revive the claim if the limitation period has already expired. However, parties can agree to create a new obligation or waive the defence of expiration through mechanisms like novation.

Modifications to the limitation periods can be agreed upon at any time, either before or after the commencement of the limitation period (Article 10.3 PICC). However, an agreement made after the expiration of the limitation period cannot be modified, but it might still have legal consequences, such as constituting a waiver of the defence that the period has expired or forming a new promise by the obligor.

Bibliography

Chapter 1

Bantekas, Ilias, and others, *UNCITRAL Model Law on International Commercial Arbitration: A Commentary* (Cambridge University Press 2020).

Born, Gary, *International Arbitration and Forum Selection Agreements: Drafting and Enforcing* (6th edn, Kluwer Law International BV 2021).

Born, Gary, *International Arbitration: Law and Practice* (3rd edn, Kluwer Law International 2021).

Born, Gary, *International Commercial Arbitration* (3rd edn, Kluwer Law International 2022).

Brunner, Christoph, 'Introduction' in Christoph Brunner and Benjamin Gottlieb (eds), *Commentary on the UN Sales Law (CISG)* (Kluwer Law International BV 2019).

Chen, Jihong, and others, 'Identifying Factors Influencing Total-Loss Marine Accidents in the World: Analysis and Evaluation Based on Ship Types and Sea Regions' (2019) 191 *Ocean Engineering* <https://www.sciencedirect.com/science/article/pii/S0029801819306377> accessed 23 September 2024.

Davis, Jean, 'LibGuides: International Commercial Arbitration & International Commercial Law Research: Databases: Int'l. Commercial Law' <https://guides.brooklaw.edu/commercial/commercial_law_databases> accessed 24 April 2024;

David, Jean, 'CISG Database' (*Institute of International Commercial Law*, 9 May 2015) <https://iicl.law.pace.edu/cisg/cisg> accessed 24 April 2024.

De Meulemeester, Dirk, and Lefebvre, Paul, 'The New York Convention: An Autopsy of Its Structure and Modus Operandi' (2018) 35 *Journal of International Arbitration* 413.

Emery, Cyril, 'International Commercial Contracts' (*GlobaLex | Foreign and International Law Research*) para 2.2 <https://www.nyulawglobal.org/globalex> accessed 23 September 2024.

Garcimartín, Francisco, and Saumier, Geneviève, *Explanatory Report on the Convention of 2 July 2019 on the Recognition and Enforcement of Foreign Judgments in Civil or Commercial Matters: HCCH 2019 Judgments Convention* (HCCH 2020).

Greineder, Daniel, 'Arbitrators Don't Speak Esperanto: The Difficulties and Dominance of English as a Procedural Language in Arbitration' (*Kluwer Arbitration Blog*, 7 November 2021) <https://arbitrationblog.kluwerarbitration.com/2021/11/07/arbitrators-dont-speak-esperanto-the-difficulties-and-dominance-of-english-as-a-procedural-language-in-arbitration/> accessed 27 September 2024.

Gustavo Meira Moser, Luiz, 'Inside Contracting Parties' Minds: The Decision Making Processes in Cross-Border Sales' (2017) 8 *Journal of International Dispute Settlement* 250.

Hague Conference on Private International Law (HCCH), 'Status Table—Convention of 30 June 2005 on Choice of Court Agreements' <https://www.hcch.net/en/instruments/conventions/status-table/?cid=98> accessed 24 April 2024.

ICC, '2017 ICC Dispute Resolution Statistics' (2018) 2 *ICC Dispute Resolution Bulletin*.

ICC Commission Reports, 'Issues for Arbitrators to Consider Regarding Experts (2021 Update)' (2021) 2 *ICC Dispute Resolution Bulletin*.

Kischel, Uwe, 'The Basic Context of Civil Law' in Andrew Hammel (tr), *Comparative Law* (Oxford University Press 2019).

König, Michał, 'Non-State Law in International Commercial Arbitration' (2015) 35 *Polish Yearbook of International Law* 278.

Nationen, Vereinte, and Nationen, Vereinte (eds), *UNCITRAL Secretariat Guide on the Convention on the Recognition and Enforcement of Foreign Arbitral Awards (New York, 1958)* (2016 edn, United Nations 2016).

Reyes, Anselmo (ed), *Recognition and Enforcement of Judgments in Civil and Commercial Matters* (Hart 2019).

Schulz, Andreas, 'The Hague Convention of 30 June 2005 on Choice of Court Agreements' in *Yearbook of Private International Law* (Sellier de Gruyter 2009) <https://www.degruyter.com/document/doi/10.1515/9783866537187.1.1/html> accessed 23 September 2024.

Schwenzer, Ingeborg, 'Introduction' in Ingeborg Schwenzer and Ulrich G Schroeter (eds), *Schlechtriem & Schwenzer Commentary on the UN Convention on the International Sale of Goods (CISG)* (5th edn, Oxford University Press 2022).

Schwenzer, Ingeborg, and Muñoz, Edgardo, *Global Sales and Contract Law* (2nd edn, Oxford University Press 2022).

Schwenzer, Ingeborg, and Schroeter, Ulrich G (eds), *Schlechtriem & Schwenzer: Commentary on the UN Convention on the International Sale of Goods* (5th edn, Oxford University Press 2022).

Slomp Aguiar, Anelize, 'The Law Applicable to International Trade Transactions with Brazilian Parties: A Comparative Study of the Brazilian Law, the CISG, and the American Law About Contract Formation' (2012) *IX Revista Brasileira de Arbitragem* 33.

Stringer, Dana, 'Choice of Law and Choice of Forum in Brazilian International Commercial Contracts: Party Autonomy, International Jurisdiction, and the Emerging Third Way' (2006) 44 *Columbia Journal of Transnational Law* 959.

White Case, '2021 International Arbitration Survey: Adapting Arbitration to a Changing World | White & Case LLP' (6 May 2021) <https://www.whitecase.com/publications/insight/2021-international-arbitration-survey> accessed 23 September 2024.

UNCITRAL, 'Arbitration Centres That Follow UNCITRAL Arbitration Rules' <https://uncitral.un.org/en/texts/arbitration/contractualtexts/arbitration/centres> accessed 20 January 2025.

UNCITRAL, 'CLOUT Network (Contributors to the CLOUT System) | United Nations Commission on International Trade Law' <https://uncitral.un.org/en/cloutnetwork> accessed 24 April 2024.

UNCITRAL, 'Status: Convention on the Recognition and Enforcement of Foreign Arbitral Awards (New York, 1958) (the 'New York Convention') | United Nations Commission on International Trade Law' <https://uncitral.un.org/en/texts/arbitration/conventions/foreign_arbitral_awards/status2> accessed 25 September 2024.

UNCITRAL, 'Status: United Nations Convention on International Settlement Agreements Resulting from Mediation | United Nations Commission on International Trade Law' <https://uncitral.un.org/en/texts/mediation/conventions/international_settlement_agreements/status> accessed 27 June 2025.

UNIDROIT, 'UNIDTROIT Principles 2016, Official Languages' <https://www.unidroit.org/instruments/commercial-contracts/unidroit-principles-2016/> accessed 6 May 2025.

UNILEX, 'UNILEX Case Database' <https://www.unilex.info/instrument/principles> accessed 5 February 2025.

Weltbank and World Trade Organization (eds), *Trade in Services for Development: Fostering Sustainable Growth and Economic Diversification* (World Trade Organization 2023) 14 <https://www.wto.org/english/res_e/booksp_e/trade_in_services_and_development_e.pdf> accessed 7 June 2024.

World Trade Organization, 'Evolution of Trade under the WTO: Handy Statistics' <https://www.wto.org/english/res_e/statis_e/trade_evolution_e/evolution_trade_wto_e.htm#fnt-1> accessed 23 November 2025.

World Trade Organization (ed), *World Trade Report 2024: Trade and Inclusiveness* (WTO 2024) <https://www.wto.org/english/res_e/booksp_e/wtr24_e/wtr24_e.pdf> accessed 24 November 2025.

World Trade Organization, *World Trade Statistical Review 2024* ([Erscheinungsort nicht ermittelbar] WTO 2023) < https://www.wto.org/english/res_e/statis_e/world_trade_statistics_e.htm> accessed 23 November 2025.

Zeynalova, Yuliya, 'The Law on Recognition and Enforcement of Foreign Judgments: Is It Broken and How Do We Fix It?' (2013) 31 *Berkeley Journal of International Law* 150.

Case law

M v H [1995] BGer BGE 121 III 453.

Schill, Stephan W, (ed), 'ICC 2023-3. Partial Award in Case No. ICC-PA-2023-052', *ICC AWARDS SERIES*, vol I (ICCA & Kluwer Law International 2023).

Legislative instruments

Brazilian Arbitration Act 1996.

Brazilian Code of Civil Procedure ('BCCP') in Portuguese, *LEI Nº 13.105, DE 16 DE MARÇO DE 2015 Código de Processo Civil* 2015.

Cairo Regional Centre for International Commercial Arbitration (CRCICA) Rules 2011.

Convention on the Law Applicable to Contracts for the International Sale of Goods 1955.

DIS Rules 2018.

English Arbitration Act 2025.

French Code of Civil Procedure.

German Arbitration Institute (DIS) Rules 1998.

Inter-american Convention on the Law Applicable to International Contracts 1994.

Law of the Russian Federation on International Commercial Arbitration 1993.

Regulation (EC) No 593/2008 of the European Parliament and of the Council of 17 June 2008 on the law applicable to contractual obligations (Rome I) [2008] OJ L 177/6.

Regulation (EU) No 1215/2012 of the European Parliament and of the Council of 12 December 2012 on jurisdiction and the recognition and enforcement of judgments in civil and commercial matters (recast) [2012] OJ L 351.

Swiss Arbitration Rules.

Switzerland's Federal Act on International Private Law.

Chapter 2

Andres Momberg Uribe, Rodrigo, 'The Process of Harmonisation of Private Law in Latin America: An Overview' in Rodrigo Momberg and Stefan Vogenauer (eds), *The Future of Contract Law in Latin America: The Principles of Latin American Contract Law* (Hart Publishing 2020).

Bantekas, Ilias, and others, *UNCITRAL Model Law on International Commercial Arbitration: A Commentary* (Cambridge University Press 2020).

Bonell, Michael Joachim, 'The Law Governing International Commercial Contracts and the Actual Role of the UNIDROIT Principles' (2018) 23 *Uniform Law Review* 15.

Bonnell, Michael Joachim, 'The New Provisions on Illegality in the UNIDROIT Principles 2010' (2011) 16 *Uniform Law Review* 517.

Bridge, Michael G, *The International Sale of Goods* (4th edn, Oxford University Press 2017).

Brödermann, Eckart, *UNIDROIT Principles of International Commercial Contracts: An Article-by-Article Commentary* (2nd edn, Nomos 2023).

Brunner, Christoph, 'Introduction' in Christoph Brunner and Benjamin Gottlieb (eds), *Commentary on the UN Sales Law (CISG)* (Kluwer Law International BV 2019).

Ciurtin, Horia, 'A Quest for Deterritorialisation: The "New" Lex Mercatoria in International Arbitration' (2019) 85 *Arbitration: The International Journal of Arbitration, Mediation and Dispute Management* 123.

CISG, 'CISG Contracting and Non-Contracting States by Foreign Trade Volume | CISG-Online. Org' <https://cisg-online.org/cisg-contracting-states/contracting-states-by-foreign-trade-volume> accessed 24 November 2025.

Connerty, Anthony, 'Lex Mercatoria: Reflections from an English Lawyer' (2014) 30 *Arbitration International* 701.

Cordero-Moss, Giuditta, 'UNIDROIT' in Petra Butler (ed), *International Commercial Contracts: Law and Practice* (2013).

Han, Shiyuan, 'Principles of Asian Contract Law: An Endeavor of Regional Harmonization of Contract Law in East Asia' (2014) 58 *Villanova Law Review*.

HCCH, 'Status Table of the Convention of 30 June 2005 on Choice of Court Agreements' <https://www.hcch.net/en/instruments/conventions/status-table/?cid=98> accessed 19 November 2025.

HCCH, 'Status Table—Principles on Choice of Law in International Commercial Contracts' <https://www.hcch.net/en/instruments/conventions/publications1/?dtid=41&cid=135> accessed 24 November 2025.

ICC, *ICC Uniform Customs and Practice for Documentary Credits: 2007 Revision (UCP 600)* (International Chamber of Commerce 2007).

ICC, 'Incoterms® Rules History' (*International Chamber of Commerce*) <https://iccwbo.org/business-solutions/incoterms-rules/incoterms-rules-history/> accessed 25 November 2025.

International Bar Association, *Perspectives in Practice of the UNIDROIT Principles 2016* (2019) <https://www.ibanet.org/MediaHandler?id=D266F2AF-3E0B-4DC0-AFCE-662E5D49BB7E> accessed 24 November 2025.

Lake, Sarah, 'An Empirical Study of the UNIDROIT Principles—International and British Responses' (2011) 16 *Uniform Law Review* 669.

Mustill, Michael, 'The New Lex Mercatoria: The First Twenty-Five Years' (2017) *XIV Revista Brasileira de Arbitragem* 205.

OHADA, 'State Members—OHADA' <https://www.ohada.org/en/state-members/> accessed 6 February 2025.

Ramberg, Christina C, 'Principles of Latin American Contract Law: Conference Notes' (2016) 21 *Uniform Law Review—Revue de droit uniforme* 129.

Schwenzer, Ingeborg, 'Introduction' in Ingeborg Schwenzer and Ulrich G Schroeter (eds), *Schlechtriem & Schwenzer Commentary on the UN Convention on the International Sale of Goods (CISG)* (5th edn, Oxford University Press 2022).

Schwenzer, Ingeborg, 'The CISG Advisory Council' in MG Bridge, Ulrich G Schroeter, and Ingeborg Schwenzer (eds), *The CISG Advisory Council opinions* (2nd edn, Eleven International Publishing 2021).

Schwenzer, Ingeborg, and Muñoz, Edgardo, *Global Sales and Contract Law* (2nd edn, Oxford University Press 2022).

Schwenzer, Ingeborg, and Spagnolo, Lisa, (eds), *Globalization versus Regionalization: 4. Annual MAA Schlechtriem CISG Conference, 18 March 2012, Hong Kong* (Eleven Publishing 2013).

UNCITRAL, 'Frequently Asked Questions—Mandate and History | United Nations Commission on International Trade Law' (*Origin, Mandate and Composition of UNCITRAL*) <https://uncitral.un.org/en/about/faq/mandate_composition/history> accessed 24 November 2025.

UNCITRAL, 'Legal Guide to Uniform Legal Instruments in the Area of International Commercial Contracts (with a focus on sales)' (53rd session, 2020) UN Doc A/CN.9/1029 V.20-01178.

UNCITRAL, Secretariat of the General Assembly, 'Proposal by Switzerland on possible future work by UNCITRAL in the Area of International Contract Law' (2012) UN Doc A/CN.9/758.

UNICITRAL, 'Status: United Nations Convention on Contracts for the International Sale of Goods (Vienna, 1980) (CISG) | United Nations Commission on International Trade Law' <https://uncitral.un.org/en/texts/salegoods/conventions/sale_of_goods/cisg/status> accessed 24 November 2025.

UNIDROIT, 'States Parties' <https://www.unidroit.org/instruments/cultural-property/1995-convention/status/> accessed 27 June 2025.

UNIDROIT, 'Status of the Convention' <https://www.unidroit.org/instruments/factoring/convention/status/> accessed 27 June 2025.

UNIDROIT, 'Status of the Convention' <https://www.unidroit.org/instruments/leasing/convention/status/> accessed 27 June 2025.

UNIDROIT, 'Member States 'States Parties Cape Town Convention' <https://www.unidroit.org/instruments/securityinterests/cape-town-convention/states-parties/> accessed 27 June 2025.

Van Gool, Elias, and Michel, Anaïs, 'The New Consumer Sales Directive 2019/771 and Sustainable Consumption: A Critical Analysis' (2021) 10 *Journal of European Consumer and Market Law* 136.

Vogenauer, Stefan (ed), Commentary on the UNIDROIT Principles of International Commercial Contracts (PICC) (2nd edn, Oxford University Press 2015).

Zeller, Bruno, 'Regional Harmonisation of Contract Law—Is It Feasible?' (2016) 3 *Journal of Law, Society and Development* 85.

Zimmermann, Reinhard, 'The Unwinding of Failed Contracts in the UNIDROIT Principles 2010' (2011) 16 *Uniform Law Review* 563.

Case law

Busrel Inc v Dotton et al [2022] US District Court for the Western District of New York 1:20-cv-01767, CISG-online 6111.

Chilean Sea Bass Inc v Kendell Seafood Imports, Inc [2024] US District Court for the District of Rhode Island 21-cv-337-JJM-LDA, CISG-online 6990.

Genfoot Inc v SCHENKERocean Ltd [2019] Noregs Høgsterett (Norwegian Supreme Court) HR-2019-231-A (sak nr. 18-051892SIV-HRET), CISG-online 4318.

Legislative instruments

Acte Uniforme Portant sur le Droit Commercial Général 2010.

'Convention of 2 July 2019 on the Recognition and Enforcement of Foreign Judgments in Civil or Commercial Matters' <https://www.hcch.net/en/instruments/conventions/specialised-secti ons/judgments> accessed 24 April 2024.

Council Directive 2011/7/EU of the European Parliament and of the Council of 16 February 2011 on Combating Late Payment in Commercial Transactions (Recast) [2011] OJ L 48/1.

Council Directive 2011/83/EU of the European Parliament and of the Council of 25 October 2011 on Consumer Rights [2011] OJ L 304/64.

Council Directive 2019/770/EU of the European Parliament and of the Council of 20 May 2019 on Certain Aspects Concerning Contracts for the Supply of Digital Content and Digital Services [2019] L136/1.

Council Directive 2019/771/EU of the European Parliament and of the Council of 20 May 2019 on Certain Aspects Concerning Contracts for the Sale of Goods [2019] OJ L 136/28.

Council Regulation (EC) No 593/2008 of the European Parliament and of the Council of 17 June 2008 on the Law Applicable to Contractual Obligations (Rome I) [2008] OJ L 177/6.

Council Regulation (EU) No 1215/2012 of the European Parliament and of the Council of 12 December 2012 on Jurisdiction and the Recognition and Enforcement of Judgments in Civil and Commercial Matters (Recast) [2012] OJ L 351/1.

Hague Conference on Private International Law Principles on Choice of Law in International Commercial Contracts (HCCH Principles).

PICC 2016

Statute of the Hague Conference on Private International Law 1955.

Treaty on the Functioning of the European Union 1957.

Chapter 3

Basedow, Jurgen, 'The State's Private Law and the Economy: Commercial Law as an Amalgam of Public and Private Rule-Making' (2008) 56 *The American Journal of Comparative Law*.

Brödermann, Eckart, *UNIDROIT Principles of International Commercial Contracts: An Article-by-Article Commentary* (2nd edn, Kluwer Law International BV 2023).

Brunner, Brunner, Meier, Fabian, and Stacher, Marco, 'Article 2 (Exclusions from the Convention)' in Christoph Brunner and Benjamin Gottlieb (eds), *Commentary on the UN Sales Law (CISG)* (Wolters Kluwer 2019).

CISG Advisory Council, 'CISG-AC Opinion No 4, Contracts for the Sale of Goods to Be Manufactured or Produced and Mixed Contracts (Article 3 CISG), 24 October 2004, Rapporteur: Professor Pilar Perales Viscasillas, Universidad Carlos III de Madrid [2004]' (2004).

CISG, 'CISG by Jurisdiction Hong Kong SAR (China)' <https://cisg-online.org/CISG-by-juris diction?command=detail&detail=100> accessed 26 November 2025.

Cronican, William Patrick, 'Buyer Beware: Electronic Letters of Credit and the Need for Default Rules' (2013) 45 *McGeorge Law Review* 383.

Filip De, Ly, 'The UN Convention on Independent Guaranteed and Stand-by Letters of Credit' 33 *The International Lawyer*.

Goode, Roy, 'Rule, Practice, and Pragmatism in Transnational Commercial Law' (2005) 54 *International and Comparative Law Quarterly*.

Hachem, Pascal, 'Article 1 CISG: Sphere of Application' in Ingeborg Schwenzer and Ulrich G Schroeter (eds), *Schlechtriem & Schwenzer Commentary on the UN Convention on the International Sale of Goods (CISG)* (5th edn, Oxford University Press 2022).

Hachem, Pascal, 'Article 7 CISG: Interpretation of the Convention and Gap-Filling' in Ingeborg Schwenzer and Ulrich G Schroeter (eds), *Schlechtriem & Schwenzer Commentary on the UN Convention on the International Sale of Goods (CISG)* (5th edn, Oxford University Press 2022).

Flechtner, Harry M., *Honnold's Uniform Law for International Sales the 1980 United Nations Convention* (5th edn, Wolters Kluwer 2021).

ICC (ed), *Incoterms 2020: ICC Rules for the Use of Domestic and International Trade Terms* (International Chamber of Commerce 2019).

International Institute for the Unification of Private Law (ed), *UNIDROIT Principles of International Commercial Contracts* (UNIDROIT International Institute for the Unification of Private Law 2017).

Manner, Simon, and Schmitt, Moritz, 'Article 6 [The Contract and the Convention (Primacy of the Contract)]' in Christoph Brunner and Benjamin Gottlieb (eds), *Commentary on the UN sales law (CISG)* (Wolters Kluwer 2019).

Michaels, Ralf, 'Preamble I: Purposes, Legal Nature, and Scope of the PICC; Applicability by Courts; Use of the PICC for the Purpose of Interpretation and Supplementation and as a Model' in Stefan Vogenauer (ed), *Commentary on the UNIDROIT Principles of International Commercial Contracts (PICC)* (2nd edn, Oxford University Press 2015).

Mohs, Florian, 'Article 53 CISG: General Obligations of the Buyer' in Ingeborg Schwenzer and Ulrich G Schroeter (eds), *Schlechtriem & Schwenzer Commentary on the UN Convention on the International Sale of Goods (CISG)* (5th edn, Oxford University Press 2022).

Perales Viscasillas, Pilar, '7. Extending the Scope of the 1980 Vienna Convention on the International Sale of Goods to Framework Distribution Contracts' in Ingeborg Schwenzer (ed), *35 years CISG and beyond*, vol 19 (Eleven International Publishing 2016).

Ramberg, Jan (ed), *International Commercial Transactions* (4th edn, ICC 2011).

Saidov, Djakhongir, 'Cases on CISG Decided in the Russian Federation' (2003) 7(1) *Vindobona Journal of International Commercial Law and Arbitration*.

Santacruz, Federico, and Oria, Jorge, 'Documentary Credits' (2008) 27 *International Financial Law Review* 64.

Scherer, Matthias, 'Preamble II: The Use of the PICC in Arbitration' in Stefan Vogenauer (ed), *Commentary on the UNIDROIT Principles of International Commercial Contracts (PICC)* (2nd edn, Oxford University Press 2015).

Schroeter, Ulrich G, 'Article 93 CISG: Multi-Territorial States' in Ingeborg Schwenzer and Ulrich G Schroeter (eds), *Schlechtriem & Schwenzer Commentary on the UN Convention on the International Sale of Goods (CISG)* (5th edn, Oxford University Press 2022).

Schwenzer, Ingeborg, and Muñoz, Edgardo, *Global Sales and Contract Law* (2nd edn, Oxford University Press 2022).

Seppala, Christopher R, 'The ICC Uniform Rules for Demand Guarantees ("URDG") in Practice: A Decade of Experience' *A Contractor's View of the URDG* (2001).

UN, Report of the Secretary-General, 'Uniform Customs and Practice for Documentary Credits' (1994) UN Doc A/CN.9/395.

UNCITRAL, 'Status: Convention on the Limitation Period in the International Sale of Goods (UNCITRAL 1974)' <https://uncitral.un.org/en/texts/salegoods/conventions/limitation_period_international_sale_of_goods/status> accessed 27 June 2025.

UNCITRAL, 'Status: United Nations Convention on Contracts for the International Sale of Goods (Vienna, 1980) (CISG) | United Nations Commission On International Trade Law'

<https://uncitral.un.org/en/texts/salegoods/conventions/sale_of_goods/cisg/status> accessed 26 November 2025.

Case law

[...] v Tarkett Sports BV [2024] Rechtbank Oost-Brabant (District Court Oost-Brabant) C/01/388535 / HA ZA 22-678, CISG-online 7150.

AM PNEU s.r.o v N[.] [2019] Okresný súd Malacky (District Court Malacky) 10Cb/161/2017, CISG-online 6144.

Arbitral Award, 10 December 1997, Ad-Hoc Arbitration, seat Buenos Aires, abstract available at <http://www.unilex.info/principles/case/646> accessed 22 April 2025.

Arbitral Award, November 1996, ICC International Court of Arbitration, seat Paris, Case No. 8502, published in the *ICC International Court of Arbitration Bulletin* (1999) 10(2) 7, abstract available at <http://www.unilex.info/principles/case/655> accessed 22 April 2025.

Artificial fish (violation of intellectual property) case [2018] Cour d'appel de Paris (Court of Appeal Paris) 16/21302, CISG-online 5622.

Bruno Rimini (Furniture) Ltd v Connor Marketing, Inc [2015] US District Court for the Eastern District of California 1:14-01906 WBS SAB, CISG-online 2662.

Cast v Festilight Cour d'appel de Reims (Court of Appeal Reims) 11/01950, CISG-online 2479.

Dodge Grand Caravan case [2020] Landgericht Landshut (District Court Landshut) 73 O 3793/19, CISG-online 5282.

Garage Door Systems, LLC v Blue Giant Equipment Corp [2024] US District Court for the Southern District of Indiana 1:23-cv-02223-JMS-KMB, CISG-online 7026.

ICC Award Case No. 9029 in *ICC International Court of Arbitration Bulletin*, (1999) 10(2), 88–96.

INTRAVAL SL v ECOM Industries GmbH [2020] Tribunal Supremo (Spanish Supreme Court) 3133/2017 / 398/2020, CISG-online 5370.

LS v JS [2020] Viši privredni sud u Banjaluci (High Commercial Court Banja Luka) 57 0 Ps 123777 19 Pž, CISG-online 5724.

NoriDane Foods A/S v Anexo Comercial Ltda [2017] Tribunal de Justiça do Estado do Rio Grande do Sul (Court of Appeal of the State of Rio Grande do Sul) 70072362940, CISG-online 2818.

Park Plus Inc v Sotefin SA [2023] Swiss Arbitration Centre 500146-2022 (Final Award), CISG-online 7020.

Potato chips plant case [2017] Bundesgerichtshof (German Supreme Court) VII ZR 101/14, CISG-online 2961.

Prada S.pA v Caporicci USA Corp [2019] Camera Arbitrale Milano (CAM) (Milan Chamber of Arbitration) ARB/17/00120 (Final Award), CISG-online 5573.

Pulse Electronics, Inc v UD Electronic Corp [2021] US District Court for the Southern District of California 18-cv-00373-BEN-MSB, CISG-online 5547.

Punching line case [2023] Bezirksgericht Willisau (Court of First Instance Willisau) 1A4 18 9, CISG-online 7179.

R&R Manufacturing SAS v Everestt International Industries Ltd [2023] Cour d'appel de Besançon (Court of Appeal Besançon) 21/01330, CISG-online 6643.

Reecon North America, LLC v Du-Hope Int'l Group et al [2019] US District Court for the Western District of Pennsylvania 2:18-CV-00234-JFC, 2:18-CV-00631-JFC, CISG-online 4425.

RGB LED neon signs case [2020] Visoki trgovački sud Republike Hrvatske (High Commercial Court of the Republic of Croatia) 57 Pž-59/2019-2, CISG-online 7296.

Stephan W Schill (ed), 'Distributor (Xanadu) v Supplier (Utopia) (Final Award) [2022] SCC No. 2023-5' 1 ICCA Awards Series 1.

Stolen wheel loader case [2023] Obergericht des Kantons Zug (Court of Appeal Canton Zug) Z1 2022 6, CISG-online 6313.

Target Corp v JJS Developments Ltd [2018] US District Court for the District of Minnesota 16-cv-1184 (JNE/TNL), CISG-online 3046.

Transportes Peñón Blanco SAPI de CV et al v Volvo Group North America, LLC et al [2024] US District Court for the Middle District of North Carolina 1:23CV176, CISG-online 6909.

Triage Matériel Professionnel S.a.r.l v JGB-2 Sp z o.o [2023] Cour d'appel de Paris (Court of Appeal Paris) 21/19946, CISG-online 6569.

Used car case II [2009] Oberlandesgericht Hamm (Court of Appeal Hamm) 28 U 107/08, CISG-online 1978.

Used car case III [2017] Oberlandesgericht Köln (Court of Appeal Cologne) 19 U 101/16, CISG-online 2946.

Zodiac Seats US LLC v Synergy Aerospace Corp [2019] US District Court for the Eastern District of Texas 4:17-cv-00410-ALM-KPJ, CISG-online 4234.

Legislative instruments

Convention on the Use of Electronic Communications in International Contracts 2005.

Council Regulation (EC) No 593/2008 of the European Parliament and of the Council of 17 June 2008 on the law applicable to contractual obligations (Rome I) [2008] OJ L 177/6.

French Civil Code.

ICC Rules of Arbitration.

ICC Rules of Arbitration 2021 (ICC Rules).

ICC Uniform Rules for Demand Guarantees 2010 (URDG 758).

Mexico Credit Institutions Act (Ley de Instituciones de Crédito) 2008.

Swiss Private International Law Act 1987.

UN Convention on the Assignment of Receivables in International Trade 2001.

UN Convention on Independent Guarantees and Stand-By Letters of Credit (1995).

UN Convention on Electronic Communications 2005.

UNCITRAL Model Law on Commercial Conciliation 2002, art 2(2); UNCITRAL Model Law on Electronic Signatures 2001.

UNCITRAL Model Law on International Commercial Arbitration 1985 and 2006 (MAL 2006).

UNIDROIT Convention on Agency in the International Sale of Goods (Geneva) 1983.

UNIDROIT Convention on International Factoring (Ottawa) 1988.

UNIDROIT Convention on International Financial Leasing (Ottawa) 1988.

UNIDROIT Convention on International Interests in Mobile Equipment 2001.

UNIDROIT, 'UPICC Model Clauses - UNIDROIT' (19 June 2021) <https://www.unidroit.org/instruments/commercial-contracts/upicc-model-clauses/> accessed 27 November 2025.

United States of America (USA), Uniform Commercial Code (UCC).

Chapter 4

Bonell, Michael Joachim, 'The Law Governing International Commercial Contracts and the Actual Role of the Unidroit Principles' (2018) 23 *Uniform Law Review* 15.

Bridge, Michael G, *The International Sale of Goods* (4th ed, Oxford University Press 2017).

Chitty, Joseph, *Chitty on Contracts* (35th edn, Sweet & Maxwell 2023).

CISG Advisory Council, 'CISG-AC Opinion No. 1 (Revised), Electronic Communications under CISG (14 October 2024). Rapporteur: Professor Christina Ramberg, Gothenburg, Sweden. Adopted unanimously by the CISG Advisory Council during its 53th meeting, in Pavia (Italy), 14–17 October 2024' (2024).

CISG Advisory Council, 'CISG-AC Opinion No. 16, Exclusion of the CISG under Article 6, Rapporteur: Doctor Lisa Spagnolo, Monash University, Australia. Adopted by the CISG Advisory Council Following its 19th Meeting, in Pretoria, South Africa on 30 May 2014' (2014).

CISG Advisory Council, 'CISG-AC Opinion No. 23, Mistake, Fraud, Misrepresentation and Initial Impossibility in CISG Contracts, Rapporteur: Professor Hugh Beale, Universities of Warwick (Em.) and Oxford, United Kingdom. Adopted Unanimously by the CISG Advisory Council Following its 47th Meeting, in Kopaonik, Serbia, on December 12–14, 2023' (2023).

Cuniberti, Gilles, and Vogenauer, Stefan, 'Article 1.5' in Stefan Vogenauer (ed), *Commentary on the UNIDROIT Principles of International Commercial Contracts (PICC)* (2nd edn, 2015).

DiMatteo, Larry A, *International Contracting: Law and Practice* (3rd edn, Wolters Kluwer, Law & Business 2013).

Ferrari, Franco, and Torsello, Marco, *International Sales Law--CISG in a Nutshell* (2nd edn, West Academic Publishing 2018).

Gillette, Clayton P, and Walt, Steven D, 'Judicial Refusal to Apply Treaty Law: Domestic Law Limitations on the CISG's Application' (2017) 22 *Uniform Law Review* 452.

Hachem, Pascal, 'Article 1 CISG: Sphere of Application' in Ingeborg Schwenzer and Ulrich G Schroeter (eds), *Schlechtriem & Schwenzer Commentary on the UN Convention on the International Sale of Goods (CISG)* (5th edn, Oxford University Press 2022).

Hachem, Pascal, 'Article 7 CISG: Interpretation of the Convention and Gap-Filling' in Ingeborg Schwenzer and Ulrich G Schroeter (eds), *Schlechtriem & Schwenzer Commentary on the UN Convention on the International Sale of Goods (CISG)* (5th edn, Oxford University Press 2022).

Flechtner, Harry M., *Honnold's Uniform Law for International Sales under the 1980 United Nations Convention* (5th edn, Wolters Kluwer 2021).

ICC (ed), *Incoterms 2020: ICC Rules for the Use of Domestic and International Trade Terms* (International Chamber of Commerce 2019).

International Institute for the Unification of Private Law (ed), *UNIDROIT Principles of International Commercial Contracts* (UNIDROIT International Institute for the Unification of Private Law 2016).

Manner, Simon, and Schmitt, Moritz, 'Article 6 [The Contract and the Convention (Primacy of the Contract)]' in Christoph Brunner and Benjamin Gottlieb (eds), *Commentary on the UN sales law (CISG)* (Wolters Kluwer 2019).

Marshall, Brooke, 'The Hague Choice of Law Principles, CISG, and PICC: A Hard Look at a Choice of Soft Law' (2018) 66 *The American Journal of Comparative Law*.

Mistelis, Loukas A, 'Article 6' in Stefan M Kröll, Loukas A Mistelis, and Pilar Perales Viscasillas (eds), *UN Convention on Contracts for the International Sale of Goods (CISG): A Commentary* (2nd edn, CH Beck 2018).

Muñoz, Edgardo, *Modern Law of Contracts and Sales in Latin-America, Spain and Portugal* (Eleven International Publishing 2011).

Perales Viscasillas, Pilar, 'Article 11' in Stefan M Kröll, Loukas A Mistelis, and Pilar Perales Viscasillas (eds), *UN Convention on Contracts for the International Sale of Goods (CISG): A Commentary* (2nd edn, CH Beck 2018).

Perales Viscasillas, Pilar, 'Comments on the Draft Digest Relating to Articles 14–24 and 66–70' in Franco Ferrari and others (eds), *The Draft UNCITRAL Digest and Beyond: Cases, Analysis and Unresolved Issues in the U.N. Sales Convention: Papers of the Pittsburgh Conference Organized by the Center for International Legal Education (CILE)* (Sweet & Maxwell 2004).

Schmidt-Kessel, Martin, 'Article 11 CISG: Freedom of Form' in Ingeborg Schwenzer and Ulrich G Schroeter (eds), *Schlechtriem & Schwenzer Commentary on the UN Convention on the International Sale of Goods (CISG)* (5th edn, Oxford University Press 2022).

Schroeter, Ulrich G, 'Contract Validity and the CISG' (2017) 22 *Uniform Law Review* 47.

Schroeter, Ulrich, 'Article 29 CISG: Modification of Contract: "No Oral Modifications" Clauses' in Ingeborg Schwenzer and Ulrich G Schroeter (eds), *Schlechtriem & Schwenzer Commentary on the UN Convention on the International Sale of Goods (CISG)* (5th edn, Oxford University Press 2022).

Schwenzer, Ingeborg, and Muñoz, Edgardo, *Global Sales and Contract Law* (2nd edn, Oxford University Press 2022).

Case law

4work SIA v DND Talis UAB [2022] Rīgas pilsētas tiesa (District Court City of Riga) C-2279-22/72, CISG-online 6925.

Boxmark Leather GmbH & Co KG v Sals Leather Services S.r.l [2024] Tribunal de Apelaciones en lo Civil de Segundo Turno (Court of Appeal for the Second Circuit) 171/2024 / 2-19258/2022, CISG-online 7035.

Bunker Partner OU et al v Golden Arrow Olieproducten Amsterdam BV [2024] Rechtbank Rotterdam (District Court Rotterdam) C/10/656674 / HA ZA 23-392, CISG-online 7118.

CeDe Group AB v KAN Sp z o.o [2020] Högsta domstolen (Swedish Supreme Court) T 6032-16, CISG-online 5500.

Chilean Sea Bass Inc v Kendell Seafood Imports, Inc [2024] US District Court for the District of Rhode Island 21-cv-337-JJM-LDA, CISG-online 6990.

Citroen Type C 5 case [2006] Oberlandesgericht Linz (Court of Appeal Linz) 6 R 160/05z, CISG-online 1377.

Coffee roasters case [2023] Rechtbank Gelderland (District Court Gelderland) C/05/413314 / HZ ZA 23-2, CISG-online 6394.

Construction materials case IV [2004] Tribunal Cantonal du Jura (Court of Appeal Canton Jura) Ap 91/04, CISG-online 965.

Cybernetix SA v CD Systems de Columbia SA [2011] Cour de Cassation (French Supreme Court) 09-70305, CISG-online 2311.

Czech Insurer v Russian Buyer [2020] ICC International Court of Arbitration ICC Case No. FA-2020-225, CISG-online 5553.

Diammonium phosphate case [2023] Cairo Regional Centre for International Commercial Arbitration (CRCICA) 1527/2021 (Final Award), CISG-online 6272.

Dongguan Jianqun Shoes Company, Ltd v Consolidated Shoe Company, Inc et al. [2022] US District Court for the Western District of Virginia 6:21-cv-00048, CISG-online 6092.

Electronic electricity meters case [2018] Appellationsgericht Basel-Stadt (Court of Appeal Canton Basel-Stadt) ZB.2017.20 (AG.2018.557), CISG-online 3906.

Ersanlar Tarim SMS v F.lli Rinaldi s.n.c. [2021] Tribunale di Foggia (District Court Foggia) 5410/2014, CISG-online 5787.

German equipment case [2000] Tribunal of International Commercial Arbitration at the Russian Federation Chamber of Commerce and Industry (MKAC) 356/1999, CISG-online 1077.

Ground mace case [2020] Bundesgerichtshof (German Supreme Court) I ZR 245/19, CISG-online 5488.

Horse case VII [2024] Rechtbank Noord-Nederland (District Court Northern Netherlands) C/18/231001 / KG ZA 24-7, CISG-online 6902.

Magna Automotive (CZ) s.r.o. v Faurecia Sièges d'Automobile SAS [2022] Cour d'appel de Versailles (Court of Appeal Versailles) 21/03438, CISG-online 6160.

Niederreiter GmbH v DEVON Medical Inc [2016] ICC International Court of Arbitration ICC Case 21196/FS, CISG-online 5988.

NoriDane Foods A/S v Anexo Comercial Ltda [2017] (Tribunal de Justiça do Estado do Rio Grande do Sul (Court of Appeal of the State of Rio Grande do Sul)) 70072362940, CISG-online 2818.

Pharmaceutical products case IV [2021] Oberlandesgericht Hamburg (Court of Appeal Hamburg) 6 Sch 3/21, CISG-online 5767.

Pomeranian puppies case [2022] Rechtbank Limburg (District Court Limburg) C/03/293528 / HA ZA 21-320, CISG-online 5920.

Raw sugar case [2017] Sąd Apelacyjny w Białymstoku (Court of Appeal Bialystok) I ACa 715/16, CISG-online 4415.

Salzgitter Flachstahl GmbH v Riveco Generai Sider S.pA [2022] Corte Suprema di Cassazione (Italian Supreme Court) 36144/2022, CISG-online 6009.

Stolen wheel loader case [2023] Obergericht des Kantons Zug (Court of Appeal Canton Zug) Z1 2022 6, CISG-online 6313.

United Auto Enterprises BVBA v OC Group BV [2023] Gerechtshof Den Haag (Court of Appeal The Hague) 200.308.899/01, CISG-online 6429.

Winches case [2019] Landgericht Koblenz (District Court Koblenz) 1 O 38/19, CISG-online 4529.

ZEVETA Bojkovice, a.s v FAGOR ARRASATE S COOP [2019] Nejvyšší soud České republiky (Supreme Court of the Czech Republic) 23 Cdo 3439/2018, CISG-online 5670.

Legislative instruments

Brazilian Civil Code 1942, Decree-Law 4.657.

Council Regulation (EC) No 593/2008 of the European Parliament and of the Council of 17 June 2008 on the law applicable to contractual obligations (Rome I) [2008] OJ L 177/6.

England Sale of Goods Act.

German Civil Code (BGB).

Hong Kong International Arbitration C Administered Arbitration Rules 2024.

Inter-American Convention on the Law Applicable to International Contracts 1994.

Permanent Court of Arbitration Rules.

Russian Federation Civil Code.

Sales of Goods Act 1895.

Singapore International Arbitration Centre Rules 2016.

Switzerland Federal Act on the Amendment of the Swiss Civil Code 1911

United Arab Emirates, Federal Decree by Law No. (35) of 2022 Promulgating the Law of Evidence in Civil and Commercial Transactions.

UPICC Model Clauses—UNIDROIT (19 June 2021) <https://www.unidroit.org/instruments/commercial-contracts/upicc-model-clauses/> accessed 24 November 2025.

Chapter 5

Allan Farnsworth, E, *Contracts* (4th edn, Aspen Publishers 2004).

Ammann, Odile, *Domestic Courts and the Interpretation of International Law: Methods and Reasoning Based on the Swiss Example* (Brill 2020).

Bazinas, Spiros V, 'Uniformity in the Interpretation and the Application of the CISG: The Role of CLOUT and the Digest' in *Celebrating Success: 25 Years United Nations Convention on Contracts for the International Sale of Goods' Collation of Papers at UNCITRAL SIAC Conference 22–23 September 2005, Singapore, Singapore International Arbitration Centre 18.*

Bridge, Michael G, *The International Sale of Goods* (4th edn, Oxford University Press 2017).

Brunner, Christoph, and Wagner, Philipp K, 'Article 7 (Interpretation of the Convention and Gap-Filling)' in Christoph Brunner and Benjamin Gottlieb (eds), *Commentary on the UN Sales Law (CISG)* (Wolters Kluwer Law International 2019).

Brunner, Christoph, 'Article 29 (Modification of Contract; Writing Requirement)' in Christoph Brunner and Benjamin Gottlieb (eds), *Commentary on the un Sales Law (CISG)* (Wolters Kluwer Law International 2019).

Chianale, Angelo, 'The "CISG" as a Model Law: A Comparative Law Approach' [2016] *Singapore Journal of Legal Studies* 29.

CISG, 'CISG-Online | CISG-Online.Org' <https://cisg-online.org/home> accessed 22 October 2024.

CISG Advisory Council, <https://cisgac.com/> accessed 22 October 2024.

CISG Advisory Council, 'CISG-AC Opinion No. 14, Interest under Article78 CISG, Rapporteur: Professor Doctor Yeşim M. Atamer, Istanbul Bilgi University, Turkey. Adopted unanimously by the CISG Advisory Council following its 18th meeting, in Beijing, China on 21 and 22 October 2013' (2013).

De Cruz, Peter, *Comparative Law in a Changing World* (3rd edn, Routledge-Cavendish 2007).

DiMatteo, Larry A, *International Contracting: Law and Practice* (3rd edn, Wolters Kluwer, Law & Business 2013).

DiMatteo, Larry A, and Janssen, Andre, 'Interpretive Methodologies in the Interpretation of the CISG' in Larry A DiMatteo (ed), *International Sales Law: A Global Challenge* (Cambridge University Press 2014).

Ferrari, Franco, and Torsello, Marco, *International Sales Law—CISG in a Nutshell* (2nd edn, West Academic Publishing 2018).

Ferrari, Franco, 'Homeward Trend: What, Why and Why Not' in André U Janssen and Olaf Meyer (eds), *CISG Methodology* (Sellier 2009).

Hachem, Pascal, 'Article 7 CISG: Interpretation of the Convention and Gap-Filling' in Ingeborg Schwenzer and Ulrich G Schroeter (eds), *Schlechtriem & Schwenzer Commentary on the UN Convention on the International Sale of Goods (CISG)* (5th edn, Oxford University Press 2022).

Hachem, Pascal, 'Introduction to Articles 1-6 CISG: General Questions Regarding the Sphere of Application' in Ingeborg Schwenzer and Ulrich G Schroeter (eds), *Schlechtriem & Schwenzer Commentary on the UN Convention on the International Sale of Goods (CISG)* (5th edn, Oxford University Press 2022).

Kornet, Nicole, *Contract Interpretation and Gap Filling: Comparative and Theoretical Perspectives* (Intersentia 2006).

Magnus, Ulrich, 'Tracing Methodology in the CISG: Dogmatic Foundations' in André Janssen and Olaf Meyer (eds), *ISG Methodology* (European Law Publishers 2009).

Manner, Simon Cornelius, and Schmitt, Moritz, 'Article 1 [Basic Rules of Application; Relation to Contracting State]' in Christoph Brunner and Benjamin Gottlieb (eds), *Commentary on the un Sales Law (CISG)* (Wolters Kluwer Law International 2019).

Mazzotta, Francesco G, 'Good Faith Principle: Vexata Quaestio' in Larry A DiMatteo (ed), *International Sales Law: A Global Challenge* (Cambridge University Press 2014).

Michaels, Ralf, 'Preamble I: Purposes, Legal Nature, and Scope of the PICC; Applicability by Courts; Use of the PICC for the Purpose of Interpretation and Supplementation and as a Model' in Stefan Vogenauer (ed), *Commentary on the UNIDROIT Principles of International Commercial Contracts (PICC)* (2nd edn, Oxford University Press 2015).

Nedzel, Nadia, 'A Comparative Study of Good Faith, Fair Dealing, and Precontractual Liability' 12 *Tulane European and Civil Law Forum* 97.

Nicholas, Barry, 'Fault and Breach of Contract' in J Beatson and Daniel Friedmann (eds), *Good Faith and Fault in Contract Law* (Clarendon 1997).

Perales Viscasillas, Pilar, 'Article 7' in Stefan M Kröll, Loukas A Mistelis, and Pilar Perales Viscasillas (eds), *UN Convention on Contracts for the International Sale of Goods (CISG): A Commentary* (2nd edn, CH Beck 2018).

Posner, Richard, 'Let Us Never Blame a Contract Breaker' in Omri Ben-Shahar and Ariel Porat (eds), *Fault in American Contract Law* (Cambridge University Press 2010).

Schlechtreim, Peter, 'Interpretation, Gap-Filling and Further Development of the U.N. Sales Convention' (2004) 16 *Pace International Law Review* 292.

Schlechtriem, Peter, and Butler, Petra, *UN Law on International Sales: The UN Convention on the International Sale of Goods* (Springer 2008).

Schroeter, Ulrich G, 'Article 29 CISG: Modification of Contract; "no Oral Modifications" Clauses"' in Ingeborg Schwenzer and Ulrich G Schroeter (eds), *Schlechtriem & Schwenzer Commentary on the UN Convention on the International Sale of Goods (CISG)* (5th edn, Oxford University Press 2022).

Schwenzer, Ingeborg, '7. Interpretation and Gap-Filling under the CISG' in Ingeborg Schwenzer, Petra Butler, and Yeşim M Atamer (eds), *Current issues in the CISG and arbitration* (Eleven International Publishing 2014).

Schwenzer, Ingeborg, 'Article 74 CISG: Calculation of Damages in General' in Ingeborg Schwenzer and Ulrich G Schroeter (eds), *Schlechtriem & Schwenzer Commentary on the UN Convention on the International Sale of Goods (CISG)* (5th edn, Oxford University Press 2022).

Schwenzer, Ingeborg, and Muñoz, Edgardo, *Global Sales and Contract Law* (2nd edn, Oxford University Press 2022).

Schwenzer, Ingeborg, and Pereira, Cesar, 'Lost in Translation: Interpreting Diverging but Equally Authentic CISG Texts' (2025) 43 *Journal of Law and Commerce* 129.

UNCITRAL, 'Case Law on UNCITRAL Texts (CLOUT) | United Nations Commission on International Trade Law' <https://uncitral.un.org/en/case_law> accessed 22 October 2024.

UNCITRAL, *Digest of Case Law on the United Nations Convention on the International Sale of Goods* (2016) <https://uncitral.un.org/sites/uncitral.un.org/files/media-documents/uncitral/en/cisg_digest_2016.pdf> accessed 1 November 2025.

UNCITRAL, 'United Nations Commission On International Trade Law' <https://uncitral.un.org/> accessed 22 October 2024.

UNILEX, UNILEX Database <https://www.unilex.info/> accessed 22 October 2024.

Vogenauer, Stefan, 'Article 1.6' in Stefan Vogenauer (ed), *Commentary on the UNIDROIT Principles of International Commercial Contracts (PICC)* (2nd edn, 2015).

Vogenauer, Stefan, 'Introduction' in Stefan Vogenauer (ed), *Commentary on the UNIDROIT Principles of International Commercial Contracts (PICC)* (2nd edn, 2015).

Yalim, Ayse Nihan Karadayi, *Interpretation and Gap Filling in International Commercial Contracts* (Intersentia 2019).

Zeller, Bruno, 'Good Faith—The Scarlet Pimpernel of the CISG' [2000] *International Trade and Business Law Review* Part 2.

Zeller, Bruno, 'Interpretation of the United Nations Convention on Contracts for the International Sale of Goods According to Principles of International Law' (2003) 1 *Journal of International Commercial Law* 273.

Case law

4work SIA v DND Talis UAB [2022] Rīgas pilsētas tiesa (District Court City of Riga) C-2279-22/72, CISG-online 6925.

Asia Telco Technologies v Brightstar Int'l Corp [2015] US District Court for the Southern District of Florida 15-20608-Civ-Scola, CISG-online 3056.

BMW 3 Series case [1995] Oberlandesgericht München (Court of Appeal Munich) 7 U 1720/94, CISG-online 143.

Bois & Matériaux v Ceramiche Marca Corona [2021] Cour d'appel de Bourges (Court of Appeal Bourges) 21/00343, CISG-online 5861.

Brands International Corporation v Reach Companies, LLC [2023] U.S. Court of Appeals (8th Circuit) 23-2164, CISG-online 7006.

BURMS 3D Druck GmbH & Co KG v ROTEC S.a.r.l [2024] Cour d'appel de Rennes (Court of Appeal Rennes) 23/01565, CISG-online 7279.

CeDe Group AB v KAN Sp z.o.o. [2020] Högsta domstolen (Swedish Supreme Court) T 6032-16, CISG-online 5500.

Cold-rolled metal sheets case I [1994] Vienna International Arbitral Centre of the Austrian Federal Economic Chamber (VIAC) SCH-4318, CISG-online 120.

Cozy Casa NV v Vidiled BV [2022] Rechtbank Zeeland-West-Brabant (District Court Zeeland-West-Brabant) C/02/383574 / HA ZA 21-149, CISG-online 5974.

Diammonium phosphate case [2023] Cairo Regional Centre for International Commercial Arbitration (CRCICA) 1527/2021 (Final Award), CISG-online 6272.

Dutch-Italian sales contracts case [2005] Nederlands Arbitrage Instituut (Netherlands Arbitration Institute) Interim Award, CISG-online 1621.

Electronic electricity meters case [2018] Appellationsgericht Basel-Stadt (Court of Appeal Canton Basel-Stadt) ZB.2017.20 (AG.2018.557), CISG-online 3906.

Ets André Bondet SA v Eco Tendance S.a.r.l et al [2021] Cour d'appel de Grenoble (Court of Appeal Grenoble) 18/02617, CISG-online 5780.

Eurasiapatchwork S.p.r.l v […] [2023] Rechtbank Overijssel (District Court Overijssel) C/08/282110 / HA ZA 22-201, CISG-online 6718.

Forestal Guarani SA v Daros Int'l, Inc [2010] US Court of Appeals (3rd Circuit) 08-4488, CISG-online 2112.

Frigera NV v DEC S.r.l [2024] Parket bij het Hof van Cassatie/Parquet près la Cour de Cassation (Advocate General at the Belgian Supreme Court) C.23.0431.N, CISG-online 7066.

Intraval SL v Econ Industries GmbH [2020] Tribunal Supremo (Spanish Supreme Court) 3133/2017 / 398/2020, CISG-online 5370.

Iron molybdenum case [1997] Oberlandesgericht Hamburg (Court of Appeal Hamburg) 1 U 167/95, CISG-online 261.

Italian wooden products case [2019] Okresný súd Dunajská Streda (District Court Dunajska Streda) 19Cb/67/2018 / 6118256517, CISG-online 5661.

Italian-Swiss sales contracts case [2023] Bezirksgericht Willisau (Court of First Instance Willisau) 1C4 23 84, CISG-online 7136.

KT MOTORSPORT spol s r.o v Garage Vandecasteele NV [2022] Court: Nejvyšší soud České republiky (Supreme Court of the Czech Republic) 23 Cdo 1062/2021, CISG-online 6766.

Kumpers Composites GmbH & Co KG v TPI Composites Inc [2025] US District Court for the District of Arizona CV-23-00214-PHX-SMB, CISG-online 7294.

MaRa Medical-Technical-Aid GmbH v Ningbo Laida Automotive Technology Co Ltd [2021] Intermediate People's Court Ningbo, Zhejiang Province (2021)浙 02 民初 824 号, CISG-online 6203.

Mastermedia Cioczek i Wójciak Sp J v MaKaDo Handelsbedrijf BV et al [2022] Rechtbank Den Haag (District Court The Hague) C/09/623157 / HA ZA 22-23, CISG-online 6094.

Metallurgical sand case [2006] Sąd Najwyższy (Supreme Court of Poland) III CSK 103/05, CISG-online 1399.

PVC foil case [2019] Oberlandesgericht Naumburg (Oberlandesgericht des Landes Sachsen-Anhalt) (Court of Appeal Naumburg) 12 U 152/18, CISG-online 4506.

Rock Advertising Limited (Respondent) v MWB Business Exchange Centres Limited (Appellant) [2018] Supreme Court of the United Kingdom UKSC 24, CISG-online 3078.

Scafom International BV v Lorraine Tubes SAS [2009] Hof van Cassatie van België/Cour de cassation de Belgique (Belgian Supreme Court) C.07.0289.N, CISG-online 1963.

SCEA GAEC Des Beauches Bernard Bruno v Teso Ten Elsen GmbH & Co KG [1996] Cour d'appel de Grenoble (Court of Appeal Grenoble) 94/3859, CISG-online 305.

Shenzen Synergy Digital Co, Ltd v Mingtel, Inc [2022] US District Court for the Eastern District of Texas 4:19-cv-00216, CISG-online 5845.

Slovenian-Croatian sales contract (interest) case [2022] Trgovački sud u Splitu (Commercial Court Split) 21. Povrv-607/2020-12, CISG-online 7312.

The North Face t-shirts case [2023] Rechtbank Noord-Holland (District Court Noord-Holland), C/15/331571 / HA ZA 22-544, CISG-online 6736.

Tönnies Lebensmittel GmbH & Co KG v Polarica Oy [2016] Lapin käräjäoikeus (District Court Lapland) 8040, CISG-online 5517.

Turkish-Indian sales contract case [2018] ICC International Court of Arbitration 18981 (Final award), CISG-online 3838.

Used textile cleaning machine case [2003] Bundesgericht/Tribunal fédéral (Swiss Federal Supreme Court) 4C.198/2003, CISG-online 840.

Vanport International, Inc v DFC Wood Products Pty Ltd [2024] US District Court for the District of Oregon 3:22-cv-01041-HZ, CISG-online 6778.

Legislative instruments

UN Convention on the Assignment of Receivables in International Trade 2001.

UNCITRAL Model Law on Commercial Conciliation 2002.

UNCITRAL Model Law on Electronic Signatures 2001.

UNIDROIT Convention on Agency in the International Sale of Goods (Geneva) 1983.

UNIDROIT Convention on International Financial Leasing (Ottawa) 1988, art 6(2); UNIDROIT Convention on International Factoring (Ottawa) 1988.

UNIDROIT Convention on International Interests in Mobile Equipment 2001.

United Nations Convention on the Use of Electronic Communications in International Contracts 2005.

Chapter 6

Advisory Council, 'CISG-AC Opinion No. 3, Parol Evidence Rule, Plain Meaning Rule, Contractual Merger Clause and the CISG', Rapporteur: Professor Richard Hyland, Rutgers Law School, Camden, NJ, USA, 23 October 2004.

Allan Farnsworth, E, *United States Contract Law* (Rev edn, Juris Publishing 1999).

Anderson, Ross G, 'Article 2.1.14' in Stefan Vogenauer (ed), *Commentary on the UNIDROIT Principles of International Commercial Contracts (PICC)* (2nd edn, 2015).

Beale, Hugh G, and others, *Cases, Materials and Text on Contract Law* (3rd edn, Hart Publishing 2018).

Björklund, Andrea A, 'Article 29 CISG' in Stefan M Kröll, Loukas A Mistelis, and Pilar Perales Viscasillas (eds), *UN Convention on Contracts for the International Sale of Goods (CISG): A Commentary* (2nd edn, CH Beck 2018).

Bridge, Michael G, *The International Sale of Goods* (4th edn, Oxford University Press 2017).

Brunner, Christoph, Hurni, Christoph, and Kissling, Michael ,'Commentaries on Articles 8–9 CISG' in Christoph Brunner and Benjamin Gottlieb (eds), *Commentary on the UN Sales Law (CISG)* (Wolters Kluwer Law International 2019).

Brunner, Christoph, Pfisterer, Stefanie, and Köster, Pascale, 'Article 16 (Revocability of Offer)' in Christoph Brunner and Benjamin Gottlieb (eds), *Commentary on the UN Sales Law (CISG)* (Kluwer Law International 2019).

CISG Advisory Council, CISG-AC Opinion No. 1 (Revised), Electronic Communications under CISG, (14 October 2024). Rapporteur: Professor Christina Ramberg, Gothenburg, Sweden. Adopted Unanimously by the CISG Advisory Council during Its 53th Meeting, in Pavia (Italy), 14–17 October 2024.' (2024).

CISG Advisory Council, CISG-AC Opinion No. 13 Inclusion of Standard Terms under the CISG, Rapporteur: Professor Sieg Eiselen, College of Law, University of South Africa, Pretoria, South Africa, 20 January 2013 (2013).

Dannemann, Gerhard, 'Choice of CESL and Conflict of Laws' in Gerhard Dannemann and Stefan Vogenauer (eds), *The Common European Sales Law in Context: Interactions with English and German Law* (Oxford University Press 2013).

del Pilar Perales Viscasillas, María, '"Battle of the Forms" under the 1980 United Nations Convention on Contracts for the International Sale of Goods: A Comparison with Section 2-207 UCC and the UNIDROIT Principles' (1998) 10 *Pace International Law Review* 97.

DiMatteo, Larry A, *The Law of International Contracting* (2nd edn, Kluwer Law International 2009).

Ferrari, Franco, 'Article 14' in Stefan M Kröll, Loukas A Mistelis, and Pilar Perales Viscasillas (eds), *UN Convention on Contracts for the International Sale of Goods (CISG): A Commentary* (2nd edn, CH Beck 2018).

Ferrari, Franco, 'Article 19' in Stefan M Kröll, Loukas A Mistelis, and Pilar Perales Viscasillas (eds), *UN Convention on Contracts for the International Sale of Goods (CISG): A Commentary* (2nd edn, CH Beck 2018).

Ferrari, Franco, and Torsello, Marco, *International Sales Law: CISG in a Nutshell* (Second edition, West Academic Publishing 2018).

Flechtner, Harry M, 'The U.N. Sales Convention (CISG) and MCC-Marble Ceramic Center Inc. v. Ceramica Nuova D'Agostino, S.P.A.: The Eleventh Circuit Weighs in on Interpretation, Subjective Intent, Procedural Limits to the Convention's Scope, and the Parol Evidence Rule' 18 *Journal of Law and Commerce.*

Flechtner, Harry M., *Honnold's Uniform Law for International Sales under the 1980 United Nations Convention* (5th edn, Wolters Kluwer 2021).

Gillette, Clayton P, and Walt, Steven D, *The UN Convention on Contracts for the International Sale of Goods: Theory and Practice* (2nd edn, Cambridge University Press 2016).

Google, 'Request or Return a Read Receipt—Gmail Help' <https://support.google.com/mail/answer/9413651?hl=en> accessed 27 November 2025.

Hachem, Pascal, 'Article 4 CISG: Substantive Scope of Convention' in Ingeborg Schwenzer and Ulrich G Schroeter (eds), *Schlechtriem & Schwenzer Commentary on the UN Convention on the International Sale of Goods (CISG)* (5th edn, Oxford University Press 2022).

Hachem, Pascal, 'Article 7 CISG: Interpretation of the Convention and Gap-Filling' in Ingeborg Schwenzer and Ulrich G Schroeter (eds), *Schlechtriem & Schwenzer Commentary on the UN Convention on the International Sale of Goods (CISG)* (5th edn, Oxford University Press 2022).

International Institute for the Unification of Private Law (ed), *UNIDROIT Principles of International Commercial Contracts* (2016 edn, UNIDROIT International Institute for the Unification of Private Law 2017).

Kritzer, Albert H (ed), 'Pre-contract Formation'. *Pace Law School Institute of International Commercial Law* <https://www.cisg.law.pace.edu/cisg/biblio/kritzer1.html> accessed 28 October 2024.

Magnus, Ulrich, 'Incorporation of Standard Terms' in Larry A DiMatteo and others (eds), *International Sales Law: Contract, Principles & Practice* (CH Beck 2016).

Mohs, Florian, 'Article 55 CISG: Price Determination in Case of Open Price Contracts' in Ingeborg Schwenzer and Ulrich G Schroeter (eds), *Schlechtriem & Schwenzer Commentary on the UN Convention on the International Sale of Goods (CISG)* (5th edn, Oxford University Press 2022).

Naudé, Tjakie, 'Article 2.1.20' in Stefan Vogenauer (ed), *Commentary on the UNIDROIT Principles of International Commercial Contracts (PICC)* (2nd edn, 2015).

Naudé, Tjakie, 'Article 2.1.21' in Stefan Vogenauer (ed), *Commentary on the UNIDROIT Principles of International Commercial Contracts (PICC)* (2nd edn, 2015).

Naudé, Tjakie, 'Article 2.1.22' in Stefan Vogenauer (ed), *Commentary on the UNIDROIT Principles of International Commercial Contracts (PICC)* (2nd edn, 2015).

Naudé, Tjakie, 'Introduction to Arts 2.1.19–2.1.22' in Stefan Vogenauer (ed), *Commentary on the UNIDROIT Principles of International Commercial Contracts (PICC)* (2nd edn, 2015).

Neumann, Thomas, *The Duty to Cooperate in International Sales: The Scope and Role of Article 80 Cisg* (Sellier 2012).

Nottage, Luke, 'Article 2.1.1' in Stefan Vogenauer (ed), *Commentary on the UNIDROIT Principles of International Commercial Contracts (PICC)* (2nd edn, Oxford University Press 2015).

Nottage, Luke, 'Article 2.1.4' in Stefan Vogenauer (ed), *Commentary on the UNIDROIT Principles of International Commercial Contracts (PICC)* (2nd edn, 2015).

Ostendorf, Patrick, *International Sales Terms* (3rd edn, CH Beck 2018).

Perales Viscasillas, Pilar, 'Article 9' in Stefan M Kröll, Loukas A Mistelis, and Pilar Perales Viscasillas (eds), *UN Convention on Contracts for the International Sale of Goods (CISG): A Commentary* (2nd edn, CH Beck 2018).

Pereira, Cesar, and Moniz de Aragão, AJ, 'Electronic Communications: Should the CISG Advisory Council Opinion No. 1 (2003) be Updated?' in *The Electronic CISG: 7th MAA Schlechtriem CISG Conference* (Eleven International Publishing 2017).

Schmidt-Kessel, Martin, 'Article 13 CISG: Definition of "Writing"' in Ulrich Schroeter and Ingeborg Schwenzer (eds), *Schwenzer & Schlechtriem Commentary on the UN Convention on the International Sale of Goods (CISG)* (5th edn, Oxford University Press 2022).

Schmidt-Kessel, Martin, 'Article 8 CISG: Interpretation of Parties' Statements or Conduct' in Ingeborg Schwenzer and Ulrich G Schroeter (eds), *Schwenzer & Schlectriem Commentary on the UN Convention on the International Sale of Goods (CISG)* (5th edn, Oxford University Press 2022).

Schmidt-Kessel, Martin, 'Article 9 CISG: Usages and Practices' in Ingeborg Schwenzer and Ulrich G Schroeter (eds), *Schlechtriem & Schwenzer Commentary on the UN Convention on the International Sale of Goods (CISG)* (5th edn, Oxford University Press 2022).

Schroeter, Ulrich, 'The Cross-Border Freedom of Form Principle under Reservation: The Role of Articles 12 and 96 CISG in Theory and Practice' [2014] *Journal of Law and Commerce*.

Schroeter, Ulrich, 'Article 14 CISG: Offer (Including Incorporation of Standard Terms)' in Ingeborg Schwenzer and Ulrich G Schroeter (eds), *Schlechtriem & Schwenzer Commentary on the UN Convention on the International Sale of Goods (CISG)* (5th edn, Oxford University Press 2022).

Schroeter, Ulrich, 'Article 15 CISG: Effectiveness and Withdrawability of Offer' in Ulrich Schroeter and Ingeborg Schwenzer (eds), *Schlechtriem & Schwenzer Commentary on the UN Convention on the International Sale of Goods (CISG)* (5th edn, Oxford University Press 2022).

Schroeter, Ulrich, 'Article 16: Revocability of Offer' in Ulrich Schroeter and Ingeborg Schwenzer (eds), *Schlechtriem & Schwenzer Commentary on the UN Convention on the International Sale of Goods (CISG)* (5th edn, Oxford University Press 2022).

Schroeter, Ulrich, 'Article 18 CISG: Acceptance and Its Effectiveness' in Ingeborg Schwenzer and Ulrich G Schroeter (eds), *Schlechtriem & Schwenzer Commentary on the UN Convention on the International Sale of Goods (CISG)* (5th edn, Oxford University Press 2022).

Schroeter, Ulrich, 'Article 19 CISG: Acceptance Modifying the Offer (Including 'Battle of Forms')' in Ingeborg Schwenzer and Ulrich G Schroeter (eds), *Schlechtriem & Schwenzer Commentary on the UN Convention on the International Sale of Goods (CISG)* (5th edn, Oxford University Press 2022).

Schroeter, Ulrich, 'Article 24: Definition of "Reaches"' in Ulrich Schroeter and Ingeborg Schwenzer (eds), *Commentary on the UN Convention on the International Sale of Goods (CISG)* (5th edn, Oxford University Press 2022).

Schroeter, Ulrich, 'Introduction to Articles 14–24 CISG' in Ingeborg Schwenzer and Ulrich G Schroeter (eds), *Schlechtriem & Schwenzer Commentary on the UN Convention on the International Sale of Goods (CISG)* (5th edn, Oxford University Press 2022).

Schroeter, Ulrich, 'Article 29: Modifications of Contract: "No Oral Modification" Clauses' in Ingeborg Schwenzer and Ulrich G Schroeter (eds), *Schlechtriem & Schwenzer Commentary on the UN Convention on the International Sale of Goods (CISG)* (5th edn, Oxford University Press 2022).

Schulze, Reiner, in Larry A DiMatteo and others (eds), *International Sales Law: A Handbook* (2nd edn, Nomos 2021).

Schwenzer, Ingeborg, and Mohs, Florian, 'Old Habits Die Hard: Traditional Contract Formation in a Modern World' (2006) 6 *Internationales Handelsrecht*.

Schwenzer, Ingeborg, and Muñoz, Edgardo, *Global Sales and Contract Law* (2nd edn, Oxford University Press 2022).

Schwenzer, Ingeborg, and others, *International Sales Law: A Guide to the CISG* (3rd edn, Zed Books 2019).

Spagnolo, Lisa, 'Opening Pandora's Box: Good Faith and Precontractual Liability in the CISG' (2007) 21 *Temple International and Comparative Law Journal* 261.

United Nations (UN) Conference Official Records, 'Documents of the Conference and Summary Records of the Plenary Meetings and of the Meetings of the Main Committees' (1991) UN Doc A/CONF.97/19.

United Nations (UN) Conference Official Records, 'Documents of the Conference and Summary Records of the Plenary Meetings and of the Meetings of the Main Committees' (1991) UN Doc A/CONF.97/C.1/SR.9

UN Secretariat 'Legal Guide to Uniform Legal Instruments in the Area of International Commercial Contracts (with a Focus on Sales)' (2020) Un Doc A/CN.9/1029.

Vogenauer, Stefan, 'Article 1.9' in Stefan Vogenauer (ed), *Commentary on the UNIDROIT Principles of International Commercial Contracts (PICC)* (2nd edn, 2015).

Vogenauer, Stefan, 'Article 4.2' in Stefan Vogenauer (ed), *Commentary on the UNIDROIT Principles of International Commercial Contracts (PICC)* (2nd edn, 2015).

Vogenauer, Stefan, 'Article 4.3' in Stefan Vogenauer (ed), *Commentary on the UNIDROIT Principles of International Commercial Contracts (PICC)* (2nd edn, 2015).

Zachariasiewicz Maciej, 'Inclusion of Standard Terms in Electronic Form under the CISG' in Ingeborg Schwenzer and others (eds), *The Electronic CISG: 7th MAA Schlechtriem CISG Conference: 26 March 2015, Vienna: Conference in Honour of Peter Schlechtriem 1933–2007* (Eleven International Publishing 2017).

Zeller, Bruno, 'Determining the Contractual Intent of Parties under the CISG and Common Law—a Comparative Analysis' (2002) 4 *European Journal of Law Reform* 629.

Zeller, Bruno, The CISG and the Battle of the Forms' in Larry A DiMatteo (ed), *International Sales Law: A Global Challenge* (Cambridge University Press 2014).

Zuloaga Rios, 'Article 2.1.15' in Stefan Vogenauer (ed), *Commentary on the UNIDROIT Principles of International Commercial Contracts (PICC)* (2nd edn, 2015).

Zuloaga Rios, 'Article 2.1.16' in Stefan Vogenauer (ed), *Commentary on the UNIDROIT Principles of International Commercial Contracts (PICC)* (2nd edn, 2015).

Zuppi, Alberto L, 'Article 8 CISG' in Stefan M Kröll, Loukas A Mistelis, and Pilar Perales Viscasillas (eds), *UN Convention on Contracts for the International Sale of Goods (CISG): A Commentary* (2nd edn, CH Beck 2018).

Case law

2P Commercial Agency s.r.o. v SRT USA, Inc [2013] US District Court for the Middle District of Florida 2:11-cv-652-FtM-29SPC, CISG-online 2395.

Aceros Asuncion SA v Compañia Integral De Construcciones SA [2019] Tribunal de Apelación en lo Civil y Comercial de Asunción, Sexta Sala 63/2019.

Alpha Prime Development Co v Holland Loader Co [2010] US District Court for the District of Colorado 09-cv-01763-WYD-KMT, CISG-online 2111.

Austrian wood case [1998] Oberster Gerichtshof (Austrian Supreme Court) 2 Ob 191/98x, CISG-online 380.

Beijing Metals & Minerals Import/Export Corp v American Business Center, Inc [1993] US Court of Appeals (5th Circuit) 92-2171, CISG-online 89.

Bowling alleys case [2014] Bundesgerichtshof (German Supreme Court) VIII ZR 410/12, CISG-online 2513.

Caiato v Factor France SA [1995] Cour d'appel de Grenoble (Court of Appeal Grenoble) 93/4126, CISG-online 157.

Car phones case [2004] Oberlandesgericht Düsseldorf (Court of Appeal Düsseldorf) I-15 U 88/03, CISG-online 915.

Cobalt sulphate case [1993] Landgericht Hamburg (District Court Hamburg) 404 O 175/92, CISG-online 215.

Concealed line gutters case [2020] Gerechthof 's-Hertogenbosch (Court of Appeal 's-Hertogenbosch) 200.241.641/01, CISG-online 5331.

Concrete slabs case [2002] Oberlandesgericht Koblenz (Court of Appeal Koblenz) 8 U 1909/01, CISG-online 716.

Coöperatieve Federatie van Edelpelsdierenhouders Nederasselt U.A. v Ceva Santé Animale S.A. [2025] Netherlands Commercial Court, NCC C/13/736825, CISG-online 7354.

Demex Pty Ltd v John Holland Pty Ltd [2022] Supreme Court of Queensland QSC 259, CLOUT case 2148.

DG Belgrano SA v Procter & Gamble Argentina SRL [2013] Cámara Nacional de Apelaciones en lo Comercial.

Exclusive distribution contract case [2018] Oberster Gerichtshof (Austrian Supreme Court) 8 Ob 149/18x, CISG-online 3912.

Fauba France FDIS GC Electronique v Fujitsu Mikroelektronik GmbH [1995] Cour de Cassation (French Supreme Court) 92-16.993, CISG-online 138.

Fertilizantes Tocantins SA v TGO Agriculture (USA), Inc [2024] US District Court for the Middle District of Florida 8:21-cv-2884-VMC-JSS, CISG-online 6878.

Filling and packaging plant case [2006] Zivilgericht Basel-Stadt (Court of First Instance Basel-Stadt) P 2004 152, CISG-online 1731.

Ford Escort Cabrio case [1999] 9 Zivilsenat (9th panel for civil matters) 9 U 146/98, CISG-online 512.

French chocolate products case [1995] Oberlandesgericht Frankfurt am Main (Court of Appeal Frankfurt am Main) 9 U 81/94, CISG-online 258.

French prêt-à-porter clothing case [2014] Tribunal de Première Instance de Genève (Court of First Instance Geneva) CISG-online 2714.

Gantry SA v Research Consulting Marketing [1995] Tribunal de Commerce de Nivelles (Commercial Court Nivelles) 1707/93, CISG-online 366.

Geneva Pharmaceuticals Tech v Barr Laboratories [2002] US District Court, SD New York 201 F. Supp. 2d 236 (2002).

Golden Valley Grape Juice and Wine, LLC v Centrys Corporation / Centriys Corporation v Separator Technology Solutions Pty Ltd [2010] US District Court, Eastern District of California CV F 09-1424 LJO GSA.

Hanwha Corp v Cedar Petrochemicals, Inc [2011] US District Court for the Southern District of New York 09 Civ. 10559 (AKH), CISG-online 2178.

Hoffman v Red Owl Stores, Inc [1965] Supreme Court of Wisconsin 26 Wis. 2d 683, 133 NW 2d 267.

ICC Case No 11849 [2003] ICC International Court of Arbitration Final Award.

Insulation material case [2012] Oberster Gerichtshof (Austrian Supreme Court) 1 Ob 215/12t, CISG-online 2438.

Interland Chemie BV v Tessenderlo Chemie BV [2008] Rechtbank Breda (District Court Breda) 160136 / HA ZA 06-826, CISG-online 2252.

Ioannis Kardassopoulos and Ron Fuchs v The Republic of Georgia [2010] International Centre for Settlement of Investment Disputes ARB/05/18 and ARB/07/15.

Italian fashion textiles case III [1990] Landgericht Hamburg (District Court Hamburg) 5 O 543/ 88, CISG-online 21.

Italian marble steps case [1996] Landgericht Kassel (District Court Kassel) 11 O 4185/95, CISG-online 191.

Italian socks case I [1995] Oberlandesgericht Hamm (Court of Appeal Hamm) 11 U 206/93, CISG-online 141.

Italian steel coils (VAT) case [2020] Tribunale d'appello Ticino (Court of Appeal Canton Ticino) 12.2018.110, CISG-online 5493.

Jacques Olle de Cause v Miguel Arturo Vaccheta Boggino y Otros [2020] Corte Suprema de Justicia—Sala Civil y Comercial 104.

Kolmar Petrochemicals Americas, Inc v Idesa Petroquímica SA de CV [2005] Primer Tribunal Colegiado en Materia Civil del Primer Circuito (1st Panel of the Federal Court of Appeal for the 1st Circuit) 127/2005, CISG-online 1004.

Les Verreries de Saint Gobain SA v Martinswerk GmbH [1998] Cour de Cassation (French Supreme Court) 96-11.984, CISG-online 344.

Magellan Int'l Corporation v Salzgitter Handel GmbH [1999] U.S. District Court for the Northern District of Illinois 99 C 5153, CISG-online 439.

Manufactured paint case [2008] Nejvyšší soud České republiky (Supreme Court of the Czech Republic) 32 Odo 824/2007, CISG-online 1848.

Material for metal covers case [2008] Landgericht Landshut (District Court Landshut) 43 O 1748/07, CISG-online 1703.

MCC-Marble Ceramic Center, Inc v Ceramica Nuova D'Agostino S.pA [1998] US Court of Appeals (11th Circuit) 97-4250, CISG-online 342.

Milk powder case [2002] Bundesgerichtshof (German Supreme Court) VIII ZR 304/00. CISG-online 651.

MITEC Automotive AG v Ford Motor Company [2010] Oberlandesgericht Jena (Court of Appeal Jena) 7 U 303/10, CISG-online 2216.

Mixing equipment case [2019] Court of Appeal of Warsaw VII AGa 1093/18, CISG-online 5298.

New Excelsior, Inc v Amut Dolci Bielloni S.r.l [2022] US District Court for the Western District of North Carolina 1:21-cv-193-MOC, CISG-online 6122.

NF Smith & Associates, LP v Karl Kruse GmbH & Co KG [2023] US District Court for the Southern District of Texas 4:22-CV-3877, CISG-online 6627.

Norfolk Southern Railway Co v Power Source Supply, Inc [2008] US District Court for the Western District of Pennsylvania 07-140-JJf, CISG-online 1776.

Oz Optics Ltd v Timbercon Inc [2011] Court of Appeal (Ontario) 2011 ONCA 714.

Paving stones case I [2014] Cour de Cassation (French Supreme Court) 12-27188, CISG-online 2514.

Pig iron case I [1998] China International Economic & Trade Arbitration Commission (CIETAC) CISG/1998/11, CISG-online 1135.

Pork case III [2006] Oberlandesgericht Dresden (Court of Appeal Dresden) 9 U 0982/06, CISG-online 1625.

Prenger v Baumhoer [1997] Missouri Court of Appeals, Western 939 S.W.2d 23.

Production line for the production of cellulose products case [2018] Østre Landsret (Court of Appeal for the Eastern Circuit) B-424-17, CISG-online 4581.

Propane gas case [1996] Oberster Gerichtshof (Austrian Supreme Court) 10 Ob 518/95, CISG-online 224.

Robert Weed Plywood Corp v Canusa Wood Products, Ltd [2023] US District Court for the Northern District of Indiana 3:23-CV-30 RLM-MGG, CISG-online 6675.

Roser Technologies, Inc v Carl Schreiber GmbH [2013] US District Court for the Western District of Pennsylvania 11cv302 ERIE, CISG-online 2490.

Rubber sealing members case [2003] Oberlandesgericht Düsseldorf (Court of Appeal Düsseldorf) I-17 U 22/03, CISG-online 919.

Sunprojuice DK A/S v San Sebastián SCA [2007] Audiencia Provincial de Madrid (Court of Appeal Madrid) 92/2007, CISG-online 1637.

Thompson v Palmer [1933] High Court of Australia [1933] HCA 61, 49 CLR 507.

Tomich v Crosstown Holdings Pty Ltd [2020] Supreme Court of Western Australia Case No. CIV 3054 of 2019, CLOUT case 1911.

Transmar Commodity Group Ltd. v Cooperativa Agraria Industrial Naranjillo Ltda. [2018] U.S. Court of Appeals for the Second Circuit, 16-3532-cv, CISG-online 3060.

Triage Matériel Professionnel S.a.r.l v JGB-2 Sp z o.o [2023] Cour d'appel de Paris (Court of Appeal Paris) 21/19946, CISG-online 6569.

Twisted yarn case [2000] Oberlandesgericht Frankfurt am Main (Court of Appeal Frankfurt am Main) 9 U 13/00, CISG-online 594.

VŠ vs AN, AN [2006] Supreme Court of Lithuania 3K-P-382/2006.

Wall tiles case [1991] Landgericht Baden-Baden (District Court Baden-Baden) 4 O 113/90, CISG-online 24.

Waltons Stores (Interstate) Ltd v Maher [1988] High Court of Australia 164 CLR 387.

Xiamen ITG Group Corp, Ltd v Peace Bird Trading Corp et al [2024] US District Court for the Eastern District of New York 19-CV-6524 (DLI) (ST), CISG-online 7182.

Zodiac Seats US LLC v Synergy Aerospace Corp. [2020] U.S. District Court for the Eastern District of Texas, 4:17-cv-00410, CISG-online 5172.

Legislative instruments

American Law Institute, *Restatement of the Law (2d) of Contracts* (American Law Institute).

ICC Uniform Rules for Collections (URCC) 522.

Principles of European Contract Law (PECL) 2002.

UNIDROIT Principles of International Commercial Contracts 2016 (PICC).

Uniform Commercial Code (UCC) 2018.

United Nations Convention on Contracts for the International Sale of Goods (CISG) 1980.

Chapter 7

Bonell, Michael Joachim, 'The New Provisions on Illegality in the UNIDROIT Principles 2010' 16 *Uniform Law Review* 523.

Brödermann, Eckart, *UNIDROIT Principles of International Commercial Contracts. An Article-by-Article Commentary* (2nd edn, Kluwer Law International 2023).

Brunner, Christoph, Murmann, Thomas, and Stucki, Marius, 'Article 4 (Issues Covered and Excluded; Validity and the Effect on Property Interest in the Goods Sold)' in Christoph Brunner and Benjamin Gottlieb (eds), *Commentary on the UN Sales Law (CISG)* (Kluwer Law International 2019).

Ciacchi, Aurelia Colombi, 'Immortal Contracts in Europe: The First Common Core' in Aurelia Colombi Ciacchi, Chantal Mak, andZeeshan Mansoor (eds), *Immoral Contracts in Europe* (Intersentia 2020).

CISG Advisory Council, 'CISG-AC Opinion No. 23, Mistake, Fraud, Misrepresentation and Initial Impossibility in CISG Contracts, Rapporteur: Professor Hugh Beale, Universities of Warwick (Em.) and Oxford, United Kingdom. Adopted Unanimously by the CISG Advisory Council Following its 47th Meeting, in Kopaonik, Serbia, on December 12–14, 2023' (2023).

Cuniberti, Gilles, 'Article 1.4' in Stefan Vogenauer (ed), *Commentary on the UNIDROIT Principles of International Commercial Contracts (PICC)* (2nd edn, 2015).

Cuniberti, Gilles, 'Article 3.3.1' in Stefan Vogenauer (ed), *Commentary on the UNIDROIT Principles of International Commercial Contracts (PICC)* (2nd edn, 2015).

Djordjević, Milena, 'Article 4' in Stefan M Kröll, Loukas A Mistelis, and Pilar Perales Viscasillas (eds), *UN Convention on Contracts for the International Sale of Goods (CISG): A Commentary* (2nd edn, CH Beck 2018).International Institute for the Unification of Private Law (ed), *UNIDROIT Principles of International Commercial Contracts* (2016 edition, UNIDROIT International Institute for the Unification of Private Law 2017).

Du Plessis, Jacques, 'Article 3.2.15', *Commentary on the UNIDROIT Principles of International Commercial Contracts (PICC)* (2nd edn, 2015).

Du Plessis, Jacques, 'Article 3.2.5', *Commentary on the UNIDROIT Principles of International Commercial Contracts (PICC)* (2nd edn, 2015).

Du Plessis, Jacques, 'Article 3.2.6', *Commentary on the UNIDROIT Principles of International Commercial Contracts (PICC)* (2nd edn, 2015).

Du Plessis, Jacques, 'Article 3.2.7', *Commentary on the UNIDROIT Principles of International Commercial Contracts (PICC)* (2nd edn, 2015).

Hachem, Pascal, 'Article 4 CISG: Substantive Scope of Convention' in Ingeborg Schwenzer and Ulrich G Schroeter (eds), *Schlechtriem & Schwenzer Commentary on the UN Convention on the International Sale of Goods (CISG)* (5th edn, Oxford University Press 2022).

Hachem, Pascal, 'Article 7 CISG: Interpretation of the Convention and Gap-Filling' in Ingeborg Schwenzer and Ulrich G Schroeter (eds), *Schlechtriem & Schwenzer Commentary on the UN Convention on the International Sale of Goods (CISG)* (5th edn, Oxford University Press 2022).

Huber, Peter, 'Article 3.2.10', *Commentary on the UNIDROIT Principles of International Commercial Contracts (PICC)* (2nd edn, 2015).

Huber, Peter, 'Article 3.2.13', *Commentary on the UNIDROIT Principles of International Commercial Contracts (PICC)* (2nd edn, 2015).

Huber, Peter, 'Article 3.2.16', *Commentary on the UNIDROIT Principles of International Commercial Contracts (PICC)* (2nd edn, 2015).

Huber, Peter, 'Article 3.2.2' in Stefan Vogenauer (ed), *Commentary on the UNIDROIT Principles of International Commercial Contracts (PICC)* (2nd edn, 2015).

Huber, Peter, 'Article 3.2.9' in Stefan Vogenauer (ed), *Commentary on the UNIDROIT Principles of International Commercial Contracts (PICC)* (2nd edn, 2015).

Lando, Ole, and others (eds), *Principles of European Contract Law. Parts I–III. Prepared by the Commission on European Contract Law* (Kluwer Law International 2019).

Lohsse, Sebastian, 'Validity' in Nils Jansen and Reinhard Zimmermann (eds), *Commentaries on European Contract Laws* (Oxford University Press 2018).

Meier, Sonja, 'Illegality' in Nils Jansen and Reinhard Zimmermann (eds), *Commentaries on European Contract Laws* (Oxford University Press 2018).

Schroeter, Ulrich G, 'Contract Validity and the CISG' (2017) 22 *Uniform Law Review* 47.

Schroeter, Ulrich, 'Introduction to Articles 14–24 CISG: General Questions Regarding the Formation of the Contract' in Ingeborg Schwenzer and Ulrich G Schroeter (eds), *Schlechtriem & Schwenzer Commentary on the UN Convention on the International Sale of Goods (CISG)* (5th edn, Oxford University Press 2022).

Schwenzer, Ingeborg, and Muñoz, Edgardo, *Global Sales and Contract Law* (2nd edn, Oxford University Press 2022).

von Bar, Christian, and others (eds), *Principles, Definitions and Model Rules of European Private Law: Draft Common Frame of Reference (DCFR)* (Sellier 2009).

Case law

Argentinean company v Chilean company [1997] Ad hoc Arbitration, Buenos Aires Unknown.

Xie Hao v Liu Xiaoyong [2015] Chongqing Wanzhou District People's Court.

Legislative instruments

Council of Europe Warsaw Convention (2005).

Draft Common Frame of Reference (DCFR)

OECD Convention on Combating Bribery of Foreign Public Officials in International Business Transactions (1997)

PICC 2016

United Nations Convention Against Corruption (UNCAC) (2003)

United Nations Convention Against Transnational Organized Crime (UNTOC) (2000)

Chapter 8

Ağaoğlu, Cahit, 'Incoterms® 2020' (2020) 40 *Public and Private International Law Bulletin.*

Brunner, Christoph, and Dimsey, Mariel, 'Article 31 (Place of Delivery)' in Christoph Brunner and Benjamin Gottlieb (eds), *Commentary on the UN Sales Law (CISG)* (Wolters Kluwer Law International 2019).

Brunner, Christoph, and Dimsey, Michael, 'Article 31 (Place of Delivery)' in Stefan M Kröll, Loukas A Mistelis, and Pilar Perales Viscasillas (eds), *UN Convention on Contracts for the International Sale of Goods (CISG): A Commentary* (2nd edn, CH Beck 2018).

Brunner, Christoph, and Dimsey, Mariel, 'Article 30 (Seller's Principal Obligations)' in Christoph Brunner and Benjamin Gottlieb (eds), *Commentary on the UN Sales Law (CISG)* (Wolters Kluwer Law International 2019).

Brunner, Christoph, and Gottlieb, Benjamin, 'Article 34 (Documents Relating to the Goods)' in Christoph Brunner and Benjamin Gottlieb (eds), *Commentary on the UN Sales Law (CISG)* (Wolters Kluwer 2019).

Brunner, Christoph, and Lauterburg, Bernhard, 'Commentaries on Articles 32–34 CISG' in Christoph Brunner and Benjamin Gottlieb (eds), *Commentary on the UN Sales Law (CISG)* (Wolters Kluwer Law International 2019).

CISG Advisory Council, 'CISG-AC Opinion No. 11, Issues Raised by Documents under the CISG Focusing on the Buyer's Payment Duty, Rapporteur: Professor Martin Davies, Tulane University Law School, New Orleans, U.S. August 3, 2012'.

Davies, Martin, 'Documents that Satisfy the Requirements of CISG Art. 58' (2011) 59 *Belgrade Law Review.*

Flechtner, Harry M., *Honnold's Uniform Law for International Sales under the 1980 United Nations Convention* (5th edn, Wolters Kluwer 2021).

ICC (ed), *Incoterms 2020: ICC Rules for the Use of Domestic and International Trade Terms* (International Chamber of Commerce 2019).

International Institute for the Unification of Private Law (ed), *UNIDROIT Principles of International Commercial Contracts* (2016 edn, UNIDROIT International Institute for the Unification of Private Law 2017).

Lima Rego, Margarida, and Gürses, Özlem, 'Chapter 12: Insurance Requirements in Incoterms® 2020' in Özlem Gürses (ed), *Research Handbook on Marine Insurance Law* (Elgar 2024).

Man Kim, Sang, 'Right Choice of DPU in Incoterms 2020' (2021) 16 *Global Trade and Customs Journal.*

Piltz, Burghard, 'Article 33' in Stefan M Kröll, Loukas A Mistelis, and Pilar Perales Viscasillas (eds), *UN Convention on Contracts for the International Sale of Goods (CISG): A Commentary* (2nd edn, CH Beck 2018).

Reid, Hadleigh, 'FCA (Free Carrier) Incoterm Explained' (*DCL Logistics*, 13 May 2022) <https://dclcorp.com/blog/shipping/fca-free-carrier-incoterm/> accessed 24 November 2025.

Samil Demirci, Celal, Burak Yalcin, Kemal, and Sait Okur, Mustaga, 'Incoterms 2020' 23 *GSI Articletter* 33.

Schlechtriem, Peter, 'Interpretation, Gap-Filling and Further Development of the U.N. Sales Convention' (2004) 16 *Pace International Law Review* 279.

Secretariat A/CONF.97/5 Secretariat Commentary on the Draft Convention on Contracts for the International Sale of Goods 1978.

Widmer Lüchinger, Corinne, 'Article 30 CISG: General Obligations of the Seller' in Ingeborg Schwenzer and Ulrich G Schroeter (eds), *Schlechtriem & Schwenzer Commentary on the UN Convention on the International Sale of Goods (CISG)* (5th edn, Oxford University Press 2022).

Widmer Lüchinger, Corinne, 'Article 30 CISG: General Obligations of the Seller' in Ingeborg Schwenzer and Ulrich G Schroeter (eds), *Schlechtriem & Schwenzer Commentary on the UN Convention on the International Sale of Goods (CISG)* (5th edn, Oxford University Press 2022).

Widmer Lüchinger, Corinne, 'Article 31 CISG: Place of Delivery' in Peter Schlechtriem, Ingeborg Schwenzer and Ulrich G Schroeter (eds), *Commentary on the UN Convention on the International Sale of Goods (CISG)* (5th edn, Oxford University Press 2022).

Widmer Lüchinger, Corinne, 'Article 33 CISG: Time of Delivery' in Ingeborg Schwenzer and Ulrich G Schroeter (eds), *Shlectriem & Schwenzer Commentary on the UN Convention on the International Sale of Goods (CISG)* (5th edn, Oxford University Press 2022).

Widmer Lüchinger, Corinne, 'Article 34 CISG: Handing over the Documents by the Seller' in Ingeborg Schwenzer and Ulrich G Schroeter (eds), *Schlechtriem & Schwenzer Commentary on the UN Convention on the International Sale of Goods (CISG)* (5th edn, Oxford University Press 2022).

Widmer Lüchinger, Corinne, 'Delivery of Goods under the CISG' in Ingeborg H Schwenzer, Yeşim M Atamer, and Petra Butler (eds), *Current issues in the CISG and arbitration* (Eleven International Publishing 2014).

Case law

AGES Maut System GmbH & Co KG v Butler Nederland BV [2023] Rechtbank Gelderland (District Court Gelderland) 10562327 CV EXPL 23-4193, CISG-online 6644.

Elettrocanali S.pA v AC Distribution S.a.r.l [2023] Cour d'appel de Pau (Court of Appeal Pau) 22/00579, CISG-online 7063.

Facade panels for mountain lodge case [2020] Tribunal Cantonal du Valais/Kantonsgericht Wallis (Court of Appeal Canton Valais) C1 19 260, CISG-online 5497.

Georgian individual v Georgian joint-stock company [2020] Supreme Court of Georgia AS-1548-2019.

Ghanaian gold case [2023] Obergericht des Kantons Zürich (Court of Appeal Canton Zurich) LB210015-O/U, CISG-online 6759.

Glimm Screens BV v Elos Med SP [2023] Gerechtshof Arnhem-Leeuwarden (Court of Appeal ArnhemLeeuwarden) 200.313.285/01, CISG-online 6449.

Italian wooden products case [2019] Okresný súd Dunajská Streda (District Court Dunajska Streda) 19Cb/67/2018 / 6118256517, CISG-online 5661.

María José Ramírez de Aranda y otros v Hernán Darío Ramírez Almada [2018] Corte Suprema de Paraguay—Sala Civil y Comercial 72/2018.

Protective masks case III [2022] Landgericht Bonn (District Court Bonn) 1 O 188/21, CISG-online 6384.

Ribbon case [2001] Rechtbank van Koophandel Kortrijk (Commercial Court Kortrijk) A.R. 3669/2000, CISG-online 757.

S&P Project Co Ltd v PVE Crane Rental BV [2023] Rechtbank Zeeland-West-Brabant (District Court ZeelandWest-Brabant) C/02/399366 / HA ZA 22-340, CISG-online 6553.

Steinbock-Bjonustan EHF v Duma NV [2004] Rechtbank van Koophandel Kortrijk (Commercial Court Kortrijk) AR 2136/2003, CISG-online 945.

Storage tanks of a fruit processing plant case Oberster Gerichtshof [2017] Austrian Supreme Court) 8 Ob 12/17y, CISG-online 3043.

Uhren Atelier Gehm GmbH v […] [2024] Rechtbank Zeeland-West-Brabant (District Court ZeelandWest-Brabant) 10539076 CV EXPL 23-1326, CISG-online 7195.

Chapter 9

Brunner, Christoph, and Gottlieb, Benjamin, 'Article 35 (Conformity of the Goods)' in Christoph Brunner and Benjamin Gottlieb (eds), *Commentary on the UN Sales Law (CISG)* (Wolters Kluwer 2019).

Brunner, Christoph, and Peter, Flavio, 'Article 38 (Time for Examining the Goods)' in Christoph Brunner and Benjamin Gottlieb (eds), *Commentary on the UN Sales Law (CISG)* (Kluwer Law International 2019).

Brunner, Christoph, and Peter, Flavio, 'Article 39 [Notice of Lack of Conformity]' in Christoph Brunner and Benjamin Gottlieb (eds), *Commentary on the UN Sales Law (CISG)* (Kluwer Law International 2019).

CISG Advisory Council, 'CISG-AC Opinion No. 19, Standards and Conformity of the Goods under Article 35 CISG, Rapporteur: Professor Djakhongir Saidov, King's College London, United Kingdom. Adopted by the CISG Advisory Council, 25 November 2018' (2018).

CISG Advisory Council, 'CISG-AC Opinion No. 22, The Seller's Liability for Goods Infringing Intellectual Property Rights under Article 42 CISG, Rapporteur: Dr. David Tebel, Rothorn Legal, Frankfurt Am Main, Germany, 7–9 August 2022' (2022).

CISG-AC Opinion No 2, Examination of the Goods and Notice of Non-Conformity Articles 38 and 39, 7 June 2004. Rapporteur: Professor Eric E. Bergsten, Emeritus, Pace University School of Law, New York.

Flechtner, Harry M., *Honnold's Uniform Law for International Sales under the 1980 United Nations Convention* (5th edn, Wolters Kluwer 2021).

Flechtner, Harry, 'Conformity of Goods: Inspection and Notice' in Larry A DiMatteo (ed), *International Sales Law: A Global Challenge* (Cambridge University Press 2014).

GAFTA, Arbitration Grain and Free Trade (GAFTA), 'Grain and Feed Trade Contracts' <https://www.gafta.com/All-Contracts> accessed 24 November 2025.

ISO, 'ISO 16162:2012—Cold-Rolled Steel Sheet Products—Dimensional and Shape Tolerances' (*iTeh Standards*) <https://standards.iteh.ai/catalog/standards/iso/74865495-fbc6-4003-ba69-e34e9f158c34/iso-16162-2012> accessed 15 March 2025.

Kröll, Stefan, 'Article 35' in Stefan M Kröll, Loukas A Mistelis, and Pilar Perales Viscasillas (eds), *UN Convention on Contracts for the International Sale of Goods (CISG): A Commentary* (2nd edn, CH Beck 2018).

Kröll, Stefan, 'Article 38' in Stefan M Kröll, Loukas A Mistelis, and Pilar Perales Viscasillas (eds), *UN Convention on Contracts for the International Sale of Goods (CISG): A Commentary* (2nd edn, CH Beck 2018).

Kröll, Stefan, 'Article 39' in Stefan M Kröll, Loukas A Mistelis, and Pilar Perales Viscasillas (eds), *UN Convention on Contracts for the International Sale of Goods (CISG): A Commentary* (2nd edn, CH Beck 2018).

Kröll, Stefan, 'Article 39' in Stefan M Kröll, Loukas A Mistelis, and Pilar Perales Viscasillas (eds), *UN Convention on Contracts for the International Sale of Goods (CISG): A Commentary* (2nd edn, CH Beck 2018).

Kröll, Stefan, 'Article 41' in Stefan M Kröll, Loukas A Mistelis, and Pilar Perales Viscasillas (eds), *UN Convention on Contracts for the International Sale of Goods (CISG): A Commentary* (2nd edn, CH Beck 2018).

Kröll, Stefan, 'Article 42' in Stefan M Kröll, Loukas A Mistelis, and Pilar Perales Viscasillas (eds), *UN Convention on Contracts for the International Sale of Goods (CISG): A Commentary* (2nd edn, CH Beck 2018).Mohs, Florian, 'Anmerkung zu BGer, 13.11.2003 – 4C.198/2003' (2004) *IHR* 219.

Schmidt-Kessel, Martin, 'Article 9 CISG: Usages and Practices' in Ingeborg Schwenzer and Ulrich G Schroeter (eds), *Schlechtriem & Schwenzer Commentary on the UN Convention on the International Sale of Goods (CISG)* (5th edn, Oxford University Press 2022).

Schwenzer, Ingeborg, 'Article 35 CISG: Conformity of Goods' in Ingeborg Schwenzer and Ulrich G Schroeter (eds), *Schlechtriem & Schwenzer Commentary on the UN Convention on the International Sale of Goods (CISG)* (5th edn, Oxford University Press 2022).

Schwenzer, Ingeborg, 'Article 38 CISG: Buyer's examination of the Goods' in Ingeborg Schwenzer and Ulrich G Schroeter (eds), *Schlechtriem & Schwenzer Commentary on the UN Convention on the International Sale of Goods (CISG)* (5th edn, Oxford University Press 2022).

Schwenzer, Ingeborg, 'Article 39 CISG: Buyer's Notice of Non-conformity' in Ingeborg Schwenzer and Ulrich G Schroeter (eds), *Schlechtriem & Schwenzer Commentary on the UN Convention on the International Sale of Goods (CISG)* (5th edn, Oxford University Press 2022).

Schwenzer, Ingeborg, 'Article 41 CISG: Third Party Claims in General' in Ingeborg Schwenzer and Ulrich G Schroeter (eds), *Schlechtriem & Schwenzer Commentary on the UN Convention on the International Sale of Goods (CISG)* (5th edn, Oxford University Press 2022).

Schwenzer, Ingeborg, 'Article 42 CISG: Third party claims based on intellectual property' in Ingeborg Schwenzer and Ulrich G Schroeter (eds), *Schlechtriem & Schwenzer Commentary on the UN Convention on the International Sale of Goods (CISG)* (5th edn, Oxford University Press 2022).

Schwenzer, Ingeborg, 'Article 44 CISG: Buyer's excuse for not giving notice' in Ingeborg Schwenzer and Ulrich G Schroeter (eds), *Schlechtriem & Schwenzer Commentary on the UN Convention on the International Sale of Goods (CISG)* (5th edn, Oxford University Press 2022).

Schwenzer, Ingeborg, and Muñoz, Edgardo, 'Sustainability in Global Supply Chains under the CISG' (2021) 23 *European Journal of Law Reform* 321.

Schwenzer, Ingeborg, and Muñoz, Edgardo, *Global Sales and Contract Law* (2nd edn, Oxford University Press 2022).

Schwenzer, Ingeborg, and Tebel, David, 'Suspicions, mere suspicions: non-conformity of the goods?' (2014) 19 *Uniform Law Review* 1.

Tebel, David, 'Article 41 (Third-Party Claims to Goods)' in Christoph Brunner and Benjamin Gottlieb (eds), *Commentary on the UN Sales Law (CISG)* (Kluwer Law International 2019).

Tebel, David, 'Article 42 (Third-Party Claims Based on a Patent or Other Intellectual Property)' in Christoph Brunner and Benjamin Gottlieb (eds), *Commentary on the UN Sales Law (CISG)* (Kluwer Law International 2019).

United Nations (UN) Conference Official Records, 'Commentary on the Draft Convention on Contracts for the International Sale of Goods, prepared by the Secretariat' (1978) UN Doc A/CONF.97/5.

Case law

[...] v Ed Fruit & Vegatables B.V. [2009] Rechtbank Breda (District Court Breda) 197586 / KG ZA 08-659, CISG-online 1789.

[...] v A.N. International B.V. [2023] Rechtbank Zeeland-West-Brabant (District Court Zeeland-West-Brabant) C/02/390635 / HA ZA 21-595 (E), CISG-online 6283.

4work SIA v DND Talis UAB [2022] Rīgas pilsētas tiesa (District Court City of Riga) C-2279-22/72, CISG-online 6925.

AXA France IARD SA v Actimeat SAS [2024] Cour d'appel de Versailles (Court of Appeal Versailles) 23/04101, CISG-online 7027.

Axarfruit S.L. v Organto Europe B.V. [2024] Gerechthof 's-Hertogenbosch (Court of Appeal 's-Hertogenbosch) 200.326.374_02, CISG-online 7060.

Cables and wires case, Bundesgericht/Tribunal fédéral (Swiss Federal Supreme Court) (2004) 4C.144/2004, CISG-online 848.

Carbomat NV v Pric Advies BV [2020] Gerechtshof Arnhem-Leeuwarden (Court of Appeal ArnhemLeeuwarden) 200.258.522/01, CISG-online 5495.

Carlos Soto S.A. v Don Emiliano [2015] Audiencia Provincial de Pontevedra (Court of Appeal Pontevedra) 681/2014 / 531/2015, CISG-online 2730.

Cehave NV v Bremer Handelsgesellschaft mbH, The Hansa Nord [1976] QB 44.

China North Chemical Industries Corp. v Beston Chemical Corp. [2006] U.S. District Court for the Southern District of Texas, Civ. A. H-04-0912, CISG-online 1177.

Clothes case IV [2003] China International Economic & Trade Arbitration Commission (CIETAC) CISG/2003/01, CISG-online 1451.

Coenegrachts Substraat NV v Shasta B.V. [2020] Ondernemingsrechtbank Antwerpen (Commercial Court Antwerp) A/19/00853/2020/2972, CISG-online 6928.

Coffee machines case, Oberster Gerichtshof (Austrian Supreme Court) (2005) 3 Ob 193/04k, CISG-online 1041.

Dcoop Sociedad Cooperativa Andaluza v Patano S.r.l [2023] Audiencia Provincial de Jaén (Court of Appeal Jaén) 1697/2021 / 1323/2023, CISG-online 6896.

Denim 'New Elite Col' case, Oberlandesgericht Düsseldorf (Court of Appeal Düsseldorf) (2015)—I-21 U 14/15, CISG-online 2731.

Doscha B.V. v Walotex B.V. et al. [2023] Gerechtshof Arnhem-Leeuwarden (Court of Appeal Arnhem-Leeuwarden) 200.317.640/01l, CISG-online 6639.

Facade panels for mountain lodge case, Tribunal Cantonal du Valais/Kantonsgericht Wallis (Court of Appeal Canton Valais)(2020)—C1 19 260, CISG-online 5497.

FBA Plants BV v Ovibell GmbH & Co KG [2023] Rechtbank Gelderland (District Court Gelderland) C/05/401601 / HA ZA 22-126, CISG-online 6360.

Frigera N.V. v D.E.C. S.r.l. [2024] Parket bij het Hof van Cassatie/Parquet près la Cour de Cassation (Advocate General at the Belgian Supreme Court) C.23.0431.N, CISG-online 7066.

Grinding set for hygienic tissues producing machine case, Bundesgerichtshof (German Supreme Court), (1999)—VIII ZR 287/98, CISG-online 475.

Hof van Cassatie van België/Cour de cassation de Belgique (Belgian Supreme Court), CISG-online 7068.

Hoogendik Import/Export B.V. et al. v Bluemarine Fish International, S.L. [2014] Audiencia Provincial de Pontevedra (Court of Appeal Pontevedra) 251/2013 / 569/2014, CISG-online 2576.

Italian shoes case XV [1994] Landgericht Berlin (District Court Berlin) 52 S 247/94, CISG-online 399.

Jet'Sac S.A.S. v Lung Meng Machinery Co. Ltd. [2022] Cour d'appel de Douai (Court of Appeal Douai) 21/01679, CISG-online 6345.

Kitchens case VI Kreisgericht Wil (Court of First Instance Wil) (2016)—VV.2015.33-Wl2ZE-DWE, CISG-online 2936.

Linkafrica Holding BV v Rigo Trading SA [2023] Rechtbank Amsterdam (District Court Amsterdam) C/13/722336 HA ZA 22-699. CISG-online 6387.

MaRa Medical-Technical-Aid GmbH v Ningbo Laida Automotive Technology Co. Ltd. [2021] 浙江省宁波市中级人民法院 (Intermediate People's Court Ningbo, Zhejiang Province), (2021)浙02民初824号. CISG-online 6203.

Mest Prom 3 LLP v S. Avto OAO [2007] судебная коллегия Высшего Арбитражного Суда Российской Федерации (Supreme Arbitrazh (Commercial) Court of the Russian Federation) BAC-12842/2007, CISG-online 2525.

Mitjavila SAS et al v Copaco NV et al [2019] Hof van Beroep Gent (Court of Appeal Ghent) 2017/AR/853, CISG-online 6774.

Musgrave Ltd. v Ceramique Culinaire de France SA. [1995] Cour d'appel de Colmar (Court of Appeal Colmar), 1 B 9400488, CISG-online 226.

New Zealand mussels case, Bundesgerichtshof (German Supreme Court) (1995)—VIII ZR 159/94, CISG-online 144.

Okuma MA-400 machine case [2024] Gerechthof 's-Hertogenbosch (Court of Appeal 's-Hertogenbosch) 200.311.762_01, CISG-online 7017.

Ölflex Solar XLSv cables case [2021] Parket bij de Hoge Raad (Advocate General at the Dutch Supreme Court) 20/00933, CISG-online 5602.

Organic barley case [2002] Oberlandesgericht München (Court of Appeal Munich) 27 U 346/02, CISG-online 786.

Organic rye case [2023] Landgericht Halle (District Court Halle) 8 O 48/22, CISG-online 7197.

Portuguese clogs case [2024] Rechtbank Overijssel (District Court Overijssel) C/08/309410 / HA ZA 24-44, CISG-online 7206.

PVC foil case [2019] Oberlandesgericht Naumburg (Oberlandesgericht des Landes Sachsen-Anhalt) (Court of Appeal Naumburg) 12 U 152/18, CISG-online 2406.

Realturf Systems, S.L. v Eurograss, Inc [2019] 2014-CA-018348, CISG-online 6730.

Rijn Blend oil case [2002] Nederlands Arbitrage Instituut (Netherlands Arbitration Institute) 2319, CISG-online 740.

Salzgitter Flachstahl GmbH v Riveco Generai Sider S.pA [2022] Corte Suprema di Cassazione (Italian Supreme Court) 36144/2022, CISG-online 6009.

Shenzen Synergy Digital Co, Ltd v Mingtel, Inc [2022] US District Court for the Eastern District of Texas 4:19-cv-00216, CISG-online 5845.

Shenzen Synergy Digital Co., Ltd. v Mingtel, Inc. [2023] U.S. Court of Appeals (5th Circuit) 22-40440, CISG-online 6392.

Spanish clothes case [2008] 서울중앙지방법원 (Central District Court Seoul) 2007GaHap19698, CISG-online 2510.

Stolen wheel loader case [2023] Obergericht des Kantons Zug (Court of Appeal Canton Zug) Z1 2022 6, CISG-online 6313.

Sunrise Foods Int'l, Inc v Ryan Hinton Inc [2019] US District Court for the District of Idaho 1:17-CV-00457-CWD, CISG-online 4522.

TCE Diffusion S.a.r.l v Elettrotecnica Ricci [2000] Tribunal de Commerce de Montargis (Commercial Court Montargis) 2000/0788, CISG-online 577.

The North Face t-shirts case, [2023] Rechtbank Noord-Holland (District Court Noord-Holland) C/15/331571 / HA ZA 22-544, CISG-online 6736.

Trinity Metals LLC v Shred-Tech North America et al. [2022] U.S. District Court for the Southern District of Indiana, 1:21-cv-02876-RLY-DML, CISG-online 6258.

Used textile cleaning machine case, Bundesgericht/Tribunal fédéral (Swiss Federal Supreme Court) (2003)—4C.198/2003, CISG-online 840.

VW Crafter case [2019] Oberlandesgericht Celle (Court of Appeal Celle) 7 U 158/18, CISG-online 5381.

White crystal sugar case [2008] Spoljnotrgovinska arbitraža pri Privrednoj komori Srbije (Foreign Trade Court of Arbitration of the Chamber of Commerce and Industry of Serbia) T-9/07, CISG-online 1946.

Legislative instruments

Allgemeines Bürgerliches Gesetzbuch of 1 June 1811 (ABGB).
Argentina, Civil and Commercial Code.
Armenia, Commercial Code.
Azerbaijan, Commercial Code.
Belarus, Commercial Code.
Brazilian Civil Code
Bürgerliches Gesetzbuch (BGB)
Chinese Civil Code
Council Directive (EC) 1999/44 on certain aspects of the sale of consumer goods and associated guarantees [1999] OJ L 171
Council Directive (EU) 2011/83 on the sale of consumer goods [2011] OJ L 304/64
French Code Civile 1804
Guatemala, Commercial Code
Kazakhstan (Kaz) Commercial Code
Kyrgyzstan, Commercial Code
Lithuania, Commercial Code
Lithuanian Civil Code
Russian Civil Code
Russian Federation, Commercial Code
Sale of Goods Act 1979
Schweizerisches Obligationenrecht of 30 March 1911 (OR)
Swiss Code of Obligations
Tajikistan, Commercial Code
U.S. Uniform Commercial Code (UCC)
Ukrainian Civil Code
United Nations Uniform Law on the International Sale of Goods 1964 (ULIS)
Uzbekistan, Commercial Code

Chapter 10

Atamer, Yesim M, 'Article 5.1.7' in Stefan Vogenauer (ed), *Commentary on the UNIDROIT Principles of International Commercial Contracts (PICC)* (2nd edn, Oxford University Press 2015).

Atamer, Yesim M, 'Article 6.1.1' in Stefan Vogenauer (ed), *Commentary on the UNIDROIT Principles of International Commercial Contracts (PICC)* (2nd edn, Oxford University Press 2015).

Atamer, Yesim M, 'Article 6.1.10' in Stefan Vogenauer (ed), *Commentary on the UNIDROIT Principles of International Commercial Contracts (PICC)* (2nd edn, Oxford University Press 2015).

Atamer, Yesim M, 'Article 6.1.11' in Stefan Vogenauer (ed), *Commentary on the UNIDROIT Principles of International Commercial Contracts (PICC)* (2nd edn, Oxford University Press 2015).

Atamer, Yesim M, 'Article 6.1.2' in Stefan Vogenauer (ed), *Commentary on the UNIDROIT Principles of International Commercial Contracts (PICC)* (2nd edn, Oxford University Press 2015).

Atamer, Yesim M, 'Article 6.1.3' in Stefan Vogenauer (ed), *Commentary on the UNIDROIT Principles of International Commercial Contracts (PICC)* (2nd edn, Oxford University Press 2015).

Atamer, Yesim M, 'Article 6.1.7' in Stefan Vogenauer (ed), *Commentary on the UNIDROIT Principles of International Commercial Contracts (PICC)* (2nd edn, Oxford University Press 2015).

Atamer, Yesim M, 'Article 6.1.8' in Stefan Vogenauer (ed), *Commentary on the UNIDROIT Principles of International Commercial Contracts (PICC)* (2nd edn, Oxford University Press 2015).

Atamer, Yesim M, 'Article 6.1.9' in Stefan Vogenauer (ed), *Commentary on the UNIDROIT Principles of International Commercial Contracts (PICC)* (2nd edn, Oxford University Press 2015).

Atamer, Yesim M, 'Article 6.2.1' in Stefan Vogenauer (ed), *Commentary on the UNIDROIT Principles of International Commercial Contracts (PICC)* (2nd edn, Oxford University Press 2015).

Bărnuţ, Andreea, 'Cryptocurrencies as a Payment Method in the Vienna Convention on International Sales of Goods' (2022) *Lawyers Week Juridice* <https://rlw.juridice.ro/21093/cryptocurrencies-as-a-payment-method-in-the-vienna-convention-on-international-sales-of-goods.html> accessed 20 November 2025.

Basedow, Jürgen, 'The State's Private Law and the Economy' (2008) 56 *The American Journal of Comparative Law* 709.

Botoye, Karibi, Ejims Enwukwe, N and Amiesimaka, Tamuno Bassey, 'The Interplay between INCOTERMS and CISG on the International Sale of Goods' (2022) 2 *The Journal of Law and Policy* 102.

Brödermann, Eckart, *UNIDROIT Principles of International Commercial Contracts: An Article-by-Article Commentary* (2nd edn, Kluwer Law International 2023).

Brunner, Christoph, Lerch, Matthias, and Rusch, Lukas, 'Article 55 (Determining the Purchase Price)' in Christoph Brunner and Benjamin Gottlieb (eds), *Commentary on the UN Sales Law (CISG)* (Kluwer Law International 2019).

Brunner, Christoph, Lerch, Matthias, and Rusch, Lukas, 'Article 57 (Place of Payment)' in Christoph Brunner and Benjamin Gottlieb (eds), *Commentary on the UN Sales Law (CISG)* (Kluwer Law International 2019).

Brunner, Christoph, Lerch, Matthias, and Rusch, Lukas, 'Article 60 (Buyer's Obligation to Take Delivery)' in Christoph Brunner and Benjamin Gottlieb (eds), *Commentary on the UN Sales Law (CISG)* (3rd edn, Kluwer Law International 2019).

Butler, Petra, and Harindranath, Arjun, 'Article 53' in Stefan M Kröll, Loukas A Mistelis, and Pilar Perales Viscasillas (eds), *UN Convention on Contracts for the International Sale of Goods (CISG). A Commentary* (2nd edn, CH Beck 2018).

Butler, Petra, and Harindranath, Arjun, 'Article 54' in Stefan M Kröll, Loukas A Mistelis, and Pilar Perales Viscasillas (eds) *UN Convention on Contracts for the International Sale of Goods (CISG). A Commentary* (2nd edn, CH Beck 2018).

Butler, Petra, and Harindranath, Arjun, 'Article 55' in Stefan M Kröll, Loukas A Mistelis, and Pilar Perales Viscasillas (eds) *UN Convention on Contracts for the International Sale of Goods (CISG). A Commentary* (2nd edn, CH Beck 2018).

Butler, Petra, and Harindranath, Arjun, 'Article 56' in Stefan M Kröll, Loukas A Mistelis, and Pilar Perales Viscasillas (eds) *UN Convention on Contracts for the International Sale of Goods (CISG). A Commentary* (2nd edn, CH Beck 2018).

Butler, Petra, and Harindranath, Arjun, 'Article 57' in Stefan M Kröll, Loukas A Mistelis, and Pilar Perales Viscasillas (eds) *UN Convention on Contracts for the International Sale of Goods (CISG). A Commentary* (2nd edn, CH Beck 2018).

Butler, Petra, and Harindranath, Arjun, 'Article 58' in Stefan M Kröll, Loukas A Mistelis, and Pilar Perales Viscasillas (eds) *UN Convention on Contracts for the International Sale of Goods (CISG). A Commentary* (2nd edn, CH Beck 2018).

Butler, Petra, and Harindranath, Arjun, 'Article 60' in Stefan M Kröll, Loukas A Mistelis, and Pilar Perales Viscasillas (eds), *UN Convention on Contracts for the International Sale of Goods (CISG). A Commentary* (2nd edn, CH Beck 2018).

CISG Advisory Council, 'CISG-AC Opinion no 5, The buyer's right to avoid the contract in case of non-conforming goods or documents 7 May 2005, Badenweiler (Germany). Rapporteur: Professor Dr. Ingeborg Schwenzer, LL.M., Professor of Private Law, University of Basel' (2005).

CISG Advisory Council, 'CISG-AC Opinion No. 11, Issues Raised by Documents under the CISG Focusing on the Buyer's Payment Duty, Rapporteur Martin Davies, Tulane University Law School, New Orleans, U.S.A., 3 August 2012' (2012).

CISG Advisory Council, 'CISG-AC Opinion No. 11, Issues Raised by Documents under the CISG Focusing on the Buyer's Payment Duty, Rapporteur: Professor Martin Davies, Tulane University Law School, New Orleans, U.S. August 3, 2012' (2012).

Ferrari, Franco, and Torsello, Marco, *International Sales Law—CISG in a Nutshell* (3rd edn, West Academic Publishing 2022).

Flechtner, Harry M, *Honnold's Uniform Law for International Sales under the 1980 United Nations Convention* (5th edn, Kluwer Law International 2021).

Goode, Roy, 'Rule, Practice, and Pragmatism in Transnational Commercial Law' (2005) 54 *The International and Comparative Law Quarterly* 550.

Hill, Jonathan, 'Choice of Law in Contract under the Rome Convention: The Approach of the UK Courts' (2004) 53 *The International and Comparative Law Quarterly* 334.

ICC (ed), *Incoterms 2020: ICC Rules for the Use of Domestic and International Trade Terms* (International Chamber of Commerce 2019).

International Institute for the Unification of Private Law (ed), *UNIDROIT Principles of International Commercial Contracts* (2016 edn, UNIDROIT International Institute for the Unification of Private Law 2017).

Khan, Ul Islam, and others, 'A Compendious Study of Online Payment Systems: Past Developments, Present Impact, and Future Considerations' (2017) 8 *International Journal of Advanced Computer Science and Applications* 266 ff.

Király, Miklós, 'The Vienna Convention on International Sales of Goods and the Bitcoin' (2019) 16 *US-China Law Review* 181.

Lookofsky, Joseph, *Understanding the CISG* (4th worldwide edn, Law and Business: Wolters Kluwer 2012).

Mohs, Florian, 'Article 34' in Ingeborg Schwenzer and Ulrich Schroeter (eds), *Schlechtriem & Schwenzer: Commentary on the UN Convention on the International Sale of Goods* (5th, Oxford University Press 2022).

Mohs, Florian, 'Article 53 CISG: General obligations of the buyer' in Ingeborg Schwenzer and Ulrich Schroeter (eds), *Schlechtriem & Schwenzer: Commentary on the UN Convention on the International Sale of Goods* (5th edn, Oxford University Press 2022).

Mohs, Florian, 'Article 55 CISG: Price determination in case of open price contracts' in Ingeborg Schwenzer and Ulrich Schroeter (eds), *Schlechtriem & Schwenzer: Commentary on the UN Convention on the International Sale of Goods* (5th edn, Oxford University Press 2022).

Mohs, Florian, 'Article 56 CISG: Price Fixed by Weight' in Ingeborg Schwenzer and Ulrich Schroeter (eds), *Schlechtriem & Schwenzer: Commentary on the UN Convention on the International Sale of Goods* (5th edn, Oxford University Press 2022).

Mohs, Florian, 'Article 57 CISG: Place of payment' in Ingeborg Schwenzer and Ulrich Schroeter (eds), *Schlechtriem & Schwenzer: Commentary on the UN Convention on the International Sale of Goods* (5th edn, Oxford University Press 2022).

Mohs, Florian, 'Article 58 CISG: Time of payment; principle of payment against goods or documents' in Ingeborg Schwenzer (ed), *Schlechtriem & Schwenzer: Commentary on the UN Convention on the International Sale of Goods* (4th edn, Oxford University Press 2016).

Mohs, Florian, 'Article 60' in Ingeborg Schwenzer and Ulrich Schroeter (eds), *Schlechtriem & Schwenzer: Commentary on the UN Convention on the International Sale of Goods* (5th edn, Oxford University Press 2022).

Omlor, Sebastian, 'The CISG and Libra: A Monetary Revolution for International Commercial Transactions?' (2020) *Stanford Journal of Blockchain Law and Policy* <https://stanford-jblp.pubpub.org/pub/cisg-and-libra/release/1> accessed 20 July 2024.

Oxford Reference, 'Documents against Acceptance' (*Oxford Reference*) <https://www.oxfordreference.com/display/10.1093/oi/authority.20110803095724405> accessed 17 November 2025.

Ramberg, Jan, *International Commercial Transactions* (4th edn, International Chamber of Commerce) 142.

Schlechtriem, Peter, 'Interpretation, Gap-Filling and Further Developments of the U. N. Sales Convention' (2004) 16 *Pace International Law Review* 305.

Schroeter, Ulrich G, 'Article 14 CISG: Offer (Including Incorporation of Standard Terms' in Ingeborg Schwenzer and Ulrich Schroeter (eds), *Schlechtriem & Schwenzer: Commentary on the UN Convention on the International Sale of Goods* (5th edn, Oxford University Press 2022).

Schwenzer, Ingeborg, 'The Danger of Domestic Pre-Conceived Views with Respect to the Uniform Interpretation of the CISG: The Question of Avoidance in the Case of Non-Conforming Goods and Documents' (2005) 36 *Victoria University of Wellington Law Review* 805.

Schwenzer, Ingeborg, 'Force Majeure and Hardship in International Sales Contracts' (2008) 39 *Victoria University of Wellington Law Review* 709.

Schwenzer, Ingeborg, 'Article 76' in Ingeborg Schwenzer and Ulrich Schroeter (eds), *Schlechtriem & Schwenzer: Commentary on the UN Convention on the International Sale of Goods* (5th edn, Oxford University Press 2022).

Vogenauer, Stefan, 'Article 5.1.3' in Stefan Vogenauer (ed), *Commentary on the UNIDROIT Principles of International Commercial Contracts (PICC)* (2nd edn, Oxford University Press 2015).

UNCITRAL, *Digest of Case Law on the United Nations Convention on the International Sale of Goods* (2016).

United Nations (UN), 'Report of the First Committee' (1980) UN Doc A/CONF.97/11 (1980).

United Nations (UN), Conference Official Records, 'Commentary on the Draft Convention on Contracts for the International Sale of Goods, prepared by the Secretariat' (1978) UN Doc A/CONF.97/5.

Case law

AMC di Ariotti e Giacomini S.n.c. v Zimm & Söhne GmbH [1998] Corte Suprema di Cassazione (Italian Supreme Court) 7759, CISG-online 538.

Clothes case II [1997] Kantonsgericht St. Gallen (Court of Appeal Canton St Gallen) 3 ZK 96-145, CISG-online 330.

Cobalt sulphate case [1996] Bundesgerichtshof (German Supreme Court) VIII ZR 51/95, CISG-online 135.

Congelados del Cibao v 3 Kids Corp. et al. [2022] U.S. District Court for the Southern District of New York, 19-CV-7596 (LJL), CISG-online 6857.

Cushions case [2000] China International Economic & Trade Arbitration Commission (CIETAC) CISG/2000/15, CISG-online 1592.

Isola P EOOD v Nordmann, Rassmann Handelsgesellschaft mbH [2021] Апелативен съд София (Court of Appeal Sofia) 2139/2020, CISG-online 5583.

Hummer Shoe Industry Co., Ltd. v Specialty Fashion Group Ltd. [2018] 厦门市中级人民法院 (Intermediate People's Court Xiamen, Fujian Province) (2018) Min 02 Min Zhong No. 261, CISG-online 4803.

Iron Ore Case, CIETAC, 5 May 2005, CISG online 1685.

Isola P. EOOD v Nordmann, Rassmann Handelsgesellschaft mbH [2021] Апелативен съд София (Court of Appeal Sofia) 2139/2020. CISG-online 5583.

Italian Textiles Case II [1996] Landgericht Duisburg (District Court Duisburg) 45 (19) O 80/94, CISG-online 186.

Italian Wine Case IV [1994] Kammergericht (Court of Appeal Berlin) 2 U 7418/92, CISG-online 130.

Leather Goods Case [1997] Oberlandesgericht München (Court of Appeal Munich) 7 U 2070/97 CISG-online 282.

Mercedes, Porsche Cayennes and BMW's case [2006] Oberlandesgericht München (Court of Appeal Munich) 23 U 2421/05, CISG-online 1394.

Mixing equipment case [2019] Sąd Apelacyjny w Warszawie (Court of Appeal Warsaw) VII AGa 1093/18, CISG-online 5298.

Mixing equipment case [2019] Sąd Apelacyjny w Warszawie (Court of Appeal Warsaw) VII AGa 1093/18, CISG-online 5298.

Omlat S.r.l v Mecanumeric SA [2023] Cour d'appel de Toulouse (Court of Appeal Toulouse) 18/03969, CISG-online 6647.

Rabobank Nederland v Teppich Fabrik Malans AG [1994] Rechtbank's-Hertogenbosch (District Court 's-Hertogenbosch Netherlands) 2548/43, CISG-Online 453.

Snowchains case [2008] Kantonsgericht St. Gallen (Court of Appeal Canton St. Gallen) BZ.2007.55, CISG-online 1768.

Telecommunication equipment case I [2000] Landgericht Trier (District Court Trier) 7 HKO 155/00, CISG-online 595.

Veal case I [2017] Handelsgericht des Kantons Zürich (Commercial Court Canton Zurich) HG170107-O, CISG-online 3400.

VW Passat and Golf case [1998] Oberlandesgericht München (Court of Appeal Munich) 7 U 3771/97, CISG-online 339.

Zhongshan Ruicheng Clothing Textile Co Ltd v AmeBalance BV [2024] Rechtbank Den Haag (District Court The Hague) C/09/658069 / HA ZA 23-1074, CISG-online 7185.

Legislative instruments

International Chamber of Commerce, *UCP 600: Uniform Customs and Practice for Documentary Credits* (2007 Revision, ICC Publication No 600).

International Standard Banking Practice for the Examination of Documents under Documentary Credits ("ISBP") (ICC Publication No. 681 (2007).

Chapter 11

Bridge, Michael, and Benjamin, Judah P (eds), *Benjamin's Sale of Goods* (8th edn, Sweet Maxwell 2012).

Brunner, Christoph, Klingler, Désirée, and Mauerhofer, Marc André, 'Article 66 (Loss or Damage After Passing of Risk to Buyer)' in Christoph Brunner and Benjamin Gottlieb (eds), *Commentary on the UN Sales Law (CISG)* (Wolters Kluwer Law International 2019).

Brunner, Christoph, Klingler, Désirée, and Mauerhofer, Marc André, 'Article 67 (Risk When the Contract Involves Carriage)' in Christoph Brunner and Benjamin Gottlieb (eds), *Commentary on the UN Sales Law (CISG)* (Wolters Kluwer 2019).

Brunner, Christoph, Klingler, Désirée, and Mauerhofer, Marc André, 'Introductory Remarks to Arts. 66–70' in Christoph Brunner and Benjamin Gottlieb (eds), *Commentary on the UN Sales Law (CISG)* (Wolters Kluwer 2019).

Brunner, Christoph, Klingler, Désirée, and Mauerhofer, Marc André, 'Article 68 (Sale of Goods During Transit)' in Christoph Brunner and Benjamin Gottlieb (eds), *Commentary on the UN Sales Law (CISG)* (Kluwer Law International 2019).

Brunner, Christoph, Klingler, Désirée, and Mauerhofer, Marc André, 'Article 69 (General Residual Rules on Risk)' in Christoph Brunner and Benjamin Gottlieb (eds), *Commentary on the UN Sales Law (CISG)* (Kluwer Law International 2019).

Brunner, Christoph, Klingler, Désirée, and Mauerhofer, Marc André, 'Article 70 (Risk When Seller is in Breach)' in Christoph Brunner and Benjamin Gottlieb (eds), *Commentary on the UN Sales Law (CISG)* (Kluwer Law International 2019).

CISG Advisory Council, 'CISG-AC Opinion No. 17, Limitation and Exclusion Clauses in CISG Contracts, Rapporteur: Prof. Lauro Gama Jr., Pontifical Catholic University of Rio de Janeiro, Brazil, 16 October 2015' (2015).

Erauw, Johan, 'Article 66' in Stefan M Kröll, Loukas A Mistelis, and Pilar Perales Viscasillas (eds), *UN Convention on Contracts for the International Sale of Goods (CISG): A Commentary* (2nd edn, CH Beck 2018).

Erauw, Johan, 'Article 67' in Stefan M Kröll, Loukas A Mistelis, and Pilar Perales Viscasillas (eds), *UN Convention on Contracts for the International Sale of Goods (CISG): A Commentary* (2nd edn, CH Beck 2018).

Erauw, Johan, 'Article 69' in Stefan M Kröll, Loukas A Mistelis, and Pilar Perales Viscasillas (eds), *UN Convention on Contracts for the International Sale of Goods (CISG): A Commentary* (2nd edn, CH Beck 2018).

Erauw, Johan, 'Article 70' in Stefan M Kröll, Loukas A Mistelis, and Pilar Perales Viscasillas (eds), *UN Convention on Contracts for the International Sale of Goods (CISG): A Commentary* (2nd edn, CH Beck 2018).

Feltham, JD, 'C.I.F. and F.O.B. Contracts and the Vienna Convention on Contracts for the International Sale of Goods' [1991] *Journal of Business Law* 416.

Flechtner, Harry M., *Honnold's Uniform Law for International Sales under the 1980 United Nations Convention* (5th edn, Wolters Kluwer 2021).

Galer, Jonas, and Luth, Felix, 'The Passing of Legal Risk under the Vienna Sales Convention: Does Article 66 CISG Cover Acts of State?' (2012) 16 *Vindobona Journal* 19.

Hachem, Pascal, 'Article 6 CISG: Exclusion or Derogation by the Parties (Party Autonomy)' in Ingeborg Schwenzer and Ulrich G Schroeter (eds), *Schlechtriem & Schwenzer Commentary on the UN Convention on the International Sale of Goods (CISG)* (5th edn, Oxford University Press 2022).

Hachem, Pascal, 'Article 66 CISG: Loss after Risk Has Passed' in Ingeborg Schwenzer and Ulrich G Schroeter (eds), *Schlechtriem & Schwenzer Commentary on the UN Convention on the International Sale of Goods (CISG)* (5th edn, Oxford University Press 2022).

Hachem, Pascal, 'Article 67 CISG: Passing of Risk When Sale Involves Carriage' in Ingeborg Schwenzer and Ulrich G Schroeter (eds), *Schlechtriem & Schwenzer Commentary on the UN Convention on the International Sale of Goods (CISG)* (5th edn, Oxford University Press 2022).

Hachem, Pascal, 'Article 68' in Ingeborg Schwenzer and Ulrich G Schroeter (eds), *Schlechtriem & Schwenzer Commentary on the UN Convention on the International Sale of Goods (CISG)* (5th edn, Oxford University Press 2022).

Hachem, Pascal, 'Article 69 CISG: Passing of Risk in Other Cases' in Ingeborg Schwenzer and Ulrich Schroeter (eds), *Schlechtriem & Schwenzer: Commentary on the UN Convention on the International Sale of Goods* (5th edn, Oxford University Press 2016).

Hachem, Pascal, 'Article 70 CISG: Effect of Fundamental Breach on Passing' in Ingeborg Schwenzer and Ulrich Schröter (eds), *Schlechtriem & Schwenzer: Commentary on the UN Convention on the International Sale of Goods* (5th edn, Oxford University Press 2022).

Hachem, Pascal, 'Introduction to Artciles 66–70: General Questions Regarding the Passing of Risk' in Ingeborg Schwenzer and Ulrich G Schroeter (eds), *Schlectriem & Schwenzer*

Commentary on the UN Convention on the International Sale of Goods (CISG) (5th edn, Oxford University Press 2022).

ICC (ed), *Incoterms 2020: ICC Rules for the Use of Domestic and International Trade Terms* (International Chamber of Commerce 2019).

Lookofsky, Joseph, 'The 1980 United Nations Convention on Contracts for the International Sale of Goods' in J Herbots and Roger Blanplain (eds), *International Encyclopaedia of Laws: Contracts* (4th edn, Kluwer Law International 2016).

Lookofsky, Joseph, *Understanding the CISG: A Compact Guide to the 1980 United Nations Convention on Contracts for the International Sale of Goods* (6th edn, Kluwer Law International 2022).

Mackaay, Ejan, *Law and Economics for Civil Law Systems* (2nd edn, Edward Elgar Publishing 2021).

Schwenzer, Ingeborg, and Muñoz, Edgardo, *Global Sales and Contract Law* (2nd edn, Oxford university press 2022).

Schwenzer, Ingeborg, 'Article 36 CISG: Relevant Time for Conformity of Goods' in Ingeborg Schwenzer and Ulrich Schroeter (eds), *Schlechtriem & Schwenzer: Commentary on the UN Convention on the International Sale of Goods (CISG)* (5th edn, Oxford University Press 2022).

UNCITRAL, Digest of Case Law on the United Nations Convention on the International Sale of Goods (2016) art 66, 304 <https://uncitral.un.org/sites/uncitral.un.org/files/media-docume nts/uncitral/en/cisg_digest_2016.pdf> accessed 1 November 2025.

Case law

[…] v Edco Eindhoven BV [2022] Rechtbank Oost-Brabant (District Court Oost-Brabant) C/01/ 364407 / HA ZA 20-720, CISG-online 5906.

AGES Maut System GmbH & Co KG v Butler Nederland BV [2023] Rechtbank Gelderland (District Court Gelderland) 10562327CV EXPL 23-4193, CISG-online 6644.

Business cards case [2006] Cour de Justice de Genève (Court of Appeal Canton Geneva) ACJC/ 47/2006, CISG-online 1504.

CLOUT case 253 [1998] Repubblica e Cantone del Ticino, La seconda Camera civile del Tribunale d'appello 12.97.00193, Issue 25 CLOUT Case 253.

Fertilizantes Tocantins SA v TGO Agriculture (USA), Inc [2024] US District Court for the Middle District of Florida 8:21-cv-2884-VMC-JSS, CISG-online 6878.

Jaxtal Imports Pty Ltd v Shanghai Xinlian Textile Import & Export Co, Ltd [2018] People's Court Shanghai Changning District (2017) Hu 0105 Min Chu No. 19401, CISG-online 4118.

Metal lockers case [2019] ВАРНЕНСКИ ОКРЪЖЕН СЪД (District Court Varna) 972/2016, CISG-online 5588.

Okuma MA-400 machine case [2024] Gerechthof 's-Hertogenbosch (Court of Appeal 's-Hertogenbosch) 200.311.762_01, CISG-online 7017.

Pizza boxes case [2000] Amtsgericht Duisburg (Local Court Duisburg) 49 C 502/00, CISG-online 659.

SMR Automotive Systems Spain, SAU v Bühler Motor GmbH [2013] Juzgado de Primera Instancia e Instrucción No 2 de La Almunia de Dona Godina (Court of First Instance No 2 of La Almunia de Dona Godina) 107/2013, CISG-online 2532.

Legislative instruments

United States Uniform Commercial Code (UCC) 1952.

Chapter 12

Brunner, Christoph, Akikol, Diana, and Bürki, Lucien, 'Article 45 [Remedies Available to Buyer]' in Christoph Brunner and Benjamin Gottlieb (eds), *Commentary on the UN Sales Law (CISG)* (Wolters Kluwer 2019).

Brunner, Christoph, Akikol, Diana, and Bürki, Lucien, 'Article 48 [Cure After Date for Delivery; Requests for Clarification]' in Christoph Brunner and Benjamin Gottlieb (eds), *Commentary on the UN Sales Law (CISG)* (Wolters Kluwer 2019).

CISG Advisory Council, 'CISG-AC Opinion No. 10, Agreed Sums Payable upon Breach of an Obligation in CISG Contracts, Rapporteur: Dr. Pascal Hachem, Bär & Karrer AG, Zurich, Switzerland, 3 August 2012.' (2012).

CISG Advisory Council, 'CISG-AC Opinion No. 17, Limitation and Exclusion Clauses in CISG Contracts, Rapporteur: Prof. Lauro Gama Jr., Pontifical Catholic University of Rio de Janeiro, Brazil, 16 October 2015.' (2015).

CISG Advisory Council, 'CISG-AC Opinion No. 21, Delivery of Substitute Goods and Repair under the CISG, Rapporteurs: Professor (Em.) Dr. Ingeborg Schwenzer, LL.M., University of Basel, Switzerland, and Dr. Ilka H. Beimel, Germany, 3 and 4 February 2020.' (2020).

CISG Advisory Council, 'CISG-AC Opinion No. 23, Mistake, Fraud, Misrepresentation and Initial Impossibility in CISG Contracts, Rapporteur: Professor Hugh Beale, Universities of Warwick (Em.) and Oxford, United Kingdom. Adopted Unanimously by the CISG Advisory Council Following Its 47th Meeting, in Kopaonik, Serbia, on December 12-14, 2023' (2023).

CISG Advisory Council, 'CISG-AC Opinion No. 5, The Buyer's Right to Avoid the Contract in Case of Non-Conforming Goods or Documents, Rapporteur: Professor Dr. Ingeborg Schwenzer, LL.M., Professor of Private Law, University of Basel, 7 May 2005.' (2005).

Cuniberti, Gilles, 'Article 1.5' in Stefan Vogenauer (ed), *Commentary on the UNIDROIT Principles of International Commercial Contracts (PICC)* (2nd edn, 2015).

Djordjević, Milena, 'Article 4' in Stefan M Kröll, Loukas A Mistelis, and Pilar Perales Viscasillas (eds), *UN Convention on Contracts for the International Sale of Goods (CISG): A Commentary* (2nd edn, CH Beck 2018).

Fountoulakis, Christiana, 'Article 71 CISG: Suspension of Performance' in Ingeborg Schwenzer and Ulrich G Schroeter (eds), *Schlechtriem & Schwenzer Commentary on the UN Convention on the International Sale of Goods (CISG)* (5th edn, Oxford University Press 2022).

Hachem, Pascal, 'Article 4 CISG: Substantive Scope of Convention' in Ingeborg Schwenzer and Ulrich G Schroeter (eds), *Schlechtriem & Schwenzer Commentary on the UN Convention on the International Sale of Goods (CISG)* (5th edn, Oxford University Press 2022).

Hachem, Pascal, 'Article 6 CISG: Exclusion or Derogation by the Parties (Party Autonomy)' in Ingeborg Schwenzer and Ulrich G Schroeter (eds), *Schlechtriem & Schwenzer Commentary on the UN Convention on the International Sale of Goods (CISG)* (5th edn, Oxford University Press 2022).

Hachem, Pascal, 'Article 68 CISG: Passing of Risk When Goods Are Sold in Transit' in Ingeborg Schwenzer and Ulrich G Schroeter (eds), *Schlechtriem & Schwenzer Commentary on the UN Convention on the International Sale of Goods (CISG)* (5th edn, Oxford University Press 2022).

Huber, Peter, 'Article 48' in Stefan M Kröll, Loukas A Mistelis, and Pilar Perales Viscasillas (eds), *UN Convention on Contracts for the International Sale of Goods (CISG): A Commentary* (2nd edn, CH Beck 2018).

International Institute for the Unification of Private Law (ed), *UNIDROIT Principles of International Commercial Contracts* (UNIDROIT International Institute for the Unification of Private Law 2017).

Mistelis, Loukas A, 'Article 6' in Stefan M Kröll, Loukas A Mistelis, and Pilar Perales Viscasillas (eds), *UN Convention on Contracts for the International Sale of Goods (CISG): A Commentary* (2nd edn, CH Beck 2018).

Müller-Chen, Markus, 'Article 48 CISG: Seller's Right to Cure after Date for Delivery' in Ingeborg Schwenzer and Ulrich G Schroeter (eds), *Schlechtriem & Schwenzer Commentary on the UN Convention on the International Sale of Goods (CISG)* (5th edn, Oxford University Press 2022).

Schelhaas, Harriet, 'Article 7.1.3' in Stefan Vogenauer (ed), *Commentary on the UNIDROIT Principles of International Commercial Contracts (PICC)* (2nd edn, 2015).

Schelhaas, Harriet, 'Article 7.1.4' in Stefan Vogenauer (ed), *Commentary on the UNIDROIT Principles of International Commercial Contracts (PICC)* (2nd edn, 2015).

Schelhaas, Harriet, 'Article 7.1.5' in Stefan Vogenauer (ed), *Commentary on the UNIDROIT Principles of International Commercial Contracts (PICC)* (2nd edn, 2015).

Schwenzer, Ingeborg, 'Article 35 CISG: Conformity of Goods' in Ingeborg Schwenzer and Ulrich G Schroeter (eds), *Schlechtriem & Schwenzer Commentary on the UN Convention on the International Sale of Goods (CISG)* (5th edn, Oxford University Press 2022).

Schwenzer, Ingeborg, 'Article 37 CISG: Seller's Right to Cure Prior to Date of Delivery' in Ingeborg Schwenzer and Ulrich G Schroeter (eds), *Schlechtriem & Schwenzer Commentary on the UN Convention on the International Sale of Goods (CISG)* (5th edn, Oxford University Press 2022).

Schwenzer, Ingeborg, 'Article 74 CISG: Calculation of Damages in General' in Ingeborg Schwenzer and Ulrich G Schroeter (eds), *Schlechtriem & Schwenzer Commentary on the UN Convention on the International Sale of Goods (CISG)* (5th edn, Oxford University Press 2022).

Schwenzer, Ingeborg, and Muñoz, Edgardo, *Global Sales and Contract Law* (2nd edn, Oxford University Press 2022).

Schmidt-Kessel, Martin, 'Article 8 CISG: Interpretation of Parties' Statements or Conduct' in Ingeborg Schwenzer and Ulrich G Schroeter (eds), *Schwenzer & Schlechtriem Commentary on the UN Convention on the International Sale of Goods (CISG)* (5th edn, Oxford University Press 2022).

Zuppi, Alberto L, 'Article 8 CISG' in Stefan M Kröll, Loukas A Mistelis, and Pilar Perales Viscasillas (eds), *UN Convention on Contracts for the International Sale of Goods (CISG): A Commentary* (2nd edn, CH Beck 2018).

Case law

[…] v Luka Food d.o.o. [2021] Vrhovni kasacioni sud/Врховни касациони суд (Serbian Supreme Court) 135/2021, CISG-online 6859.

Búfalo SA v Alberto Mazzilli [2020] Tribunal de Apelaciones en lo Civil de Segundo Turno 431-622/2018 / 33/2020, CISG-online 5416.

Co-owners […] v Angevine de Construction Bois (ABC) S.a.r.l. et al [2021] Cour d'appel de Rennes (Court of Appeal Rennes) 18/03460 CISG-online 5598.

Dominion Denmark A/S v Polytex Composite s.r.o [2023] Sø- og Handelsretten (Maritime and Commercial Court) BS-48358/2019-SHR, CISG-online 6331.

EPS granules case [2025] Oberlandesgericht Linz (Court of Appeal Linz) 2 R 14/25d, CISG-online 7288.

Facade panels for mountain lodge case [2020] Tribunal Cantonal du Valais/Kantonsgericht Wallis (Court of Appeal Canton Valais) C1 19 260, CISG-online 5497.

Gramercy Holdings I, LLC v Matec S.r.l et al [2023] US District Court for the Southern District of New York 20 Civ. 3937 (JPC), 20 Civ. 4136 (JPC), CISG-online 6477.

Hama GmbH & Co KG v Yongkang Kangteng Film Equipment Co, Ltd [2018] Intermediate People's Court Jinhua, Zhejiang Province (2018) Zhejiang 07 Minzhong No. 361, CISG-online 4782.

Perkins Manufacturing Comp v Haul-All Equipment Ltd [2020] US District Court for the Northern District of Illinois 19 cv 03769, CISG-online 5233.

Protective masks case IV [2025] Oberlandesgericht Köln (Court of Appeal Cologne) U 46/23. CISG-online 7261.

Protective masks case VII [2025] Oberlandesgericht Köln (Court of Appeal Cologne) 8 U 38/23, CISG-Online 7282.

Solea International BVBA v Bassett & Walker International Inc [2019] Court of Appeal of Ontario C66182 / 2019 ONCA 617, CISG-online 4505.

Transportes Peñón Blanco SAPI de CV et al. v Volvo Group North America, LLC et al. [2024] US District Court for the Middle District of North Carolina 1:23CV176, CISG-online 6909.

Triage Matériel Professionnel S.a.r.l v JGB-2 Sp z. o.o. [2023] Cour d'appel de Paris (Court of Appeal Paris) 21/19946, CISG-online 6569.

Vintage Porsche 911 S Targa case [2023] Oberlandesgericht München (Court of Appeal Munich) U 1224/21. CISG-online 6641.

Wiesenhof International GmbH v Estonian Meat House OÜ [2023] Tartu Maakohus (County Court Tartu) 2-22-11320, CISG-online 6648.

Legislative instruments

United States Uniform Commercial Code (UCC) 1952.

Chapter 13

Bell, Gary F, 'Article 62' in Stefan M Kröll, Loukas A Mistelis, and Pilar Perales Viscasillas (eds), *UN Convention on Contracts for the International Sale of Goods (CISG): A Commentary* (2nd edn, CH Beck 2018).

Björklund, Andrea A, 'Article 25' in Stefan M Kröll, Loukas A Mistelis, and Pilar Perales Viscasillas (eds), *UN Convention on Contracts for the International Sale of Goods (CISG): A Commentary* (2nd edn, CH Beck 2018).

Björklund, Andrea A, 'Article 28' in Stefan M Kröll, Loukas A Mistelis, and Pilar Perales Viscasillas (eds), *UN Convention on Contracts for the International Sale of Goods (CISG): A Commentary* (2nd edn, CH Beck 2018).

Bridge, Michael G, *The International Sale of Goods* (4th edn, Oxford University Press 2017).

Brunner, Christoph, and Leisinger, Benjamin, 'Article 25 (Definition of "Fundamental Breach")' in Christoph Brunner and Benjamin Gottlieb (eds), *Commentary on the UN Sales Law (CISG)* (Kluwer Law International 2019).

Brunner, Christoph, and Bodenheimer, Rouven, 'Article 28 (Specific Performance and Rules of the Forum)' in Christoph Brunner and Benjamin Gottlieb (eds), *Commentary on the UN Sales Law (CISG)* (Wolters Kluwer 2019).

Brunner, Christoph, Akikol, Diana, and Bürki, Lucien, 'Article 46 (Buyer's Right to Compel Performance)' in Christoph Brunner and Benjamin Gottlieb (eds), *Commentary on the UN Sales Law (CISG)* (Kluwer Law International 2019).

Brunner, Christoph, Schmidt-Ahrendts, Nils, and Czarnecki, Mark, 'Article 74 (General Rule for Measuring Damages)' in Christoph Brunner and Benjamin Gottlieb (eds), *Commentary on the UN Sales Law (CISG)* (Kluwer Law International 2019).

Burrows, Andrew, *Remedies for Torts, Breach of Contract and Equitable Wrongs* (Oxford University Press 2019).

Burrows, Andrew, 'We Do This at Common Law but That in Equity' (2022) 22 *Oxford Journal of Legal Studies* 1.

CISG Advisory Council, 'CISG-AC Opinion No. 21, Delivery of Substitute Goods and Repair under the CISG, Rapporteurs: Professor (Em.) Dr. Ingeborg Schwenzer, LL.M., University of Basel, Switzerland, and Dr. Ilka H. Beimel, Germany, 3 and 4 February 2020.' (2020).

Dessemontet, Raphael, 'The Non-Conformities, Limitation Periods and Duties of the Buyer in the International Sales of Goods: A Comparison of the CISG, the UNIDROIT Principles, the UCC, and the Swiss, French, and German Laws' (2011) 6 *International Business Law Journal* 603.

Djordjević, Milena, 'Article 74' in Stefan M Kröll, Loukas A Mistelis, and Pilar Perales Viscasillas (eds), *UN Convention on Contracts for the International Sale of Goods (CISG): A Commentary* (2nd edn, CH Beck 2018).

Eisenberg, Theodore, and Miller, Geoffrey P, 'Damages Versus Specific Performance: Lessons from Commercial Contracts' (2015) 12 *Journal of Empirical Legal Studies* 38.

Flechtner, Harry M., *Honnold's Uniform Law for International Sales under the 1980 United Nations Convention* (5th edn, Wolters Kluwer 2021).

Fountoulakis, Christiana, 'Article 82 CISG: Buyer's Loss of Rights Where Restitution of Goods Is Impossible' in Ingeborg Schwenzer and Ulrich G Schroeter (eds), *Schlechtriem & Schwenzer Commentary on the UN Convention on the International Sale of Goods (CISG)* (5th edn, Oxford University Press 2022).

Huber, Peter, 'Article 46' in Stefan M Kröll, Loukas A Mistelis, and Pilar Perales Viscasillas (eds), *UN Convention on Contracts for the International Sale of Goods (CISG): A Commentary* (2nd edn, CH Beck 2018).

International Institute for the Unification of Private Law (ed), *UNIDROIT Principles of International Commercial Contracts* (UNIDROIT International Institute for the Unification of Private Law 2017).

Lobban, Michael, 'What Did the Makers of the Judicature Acts Understand by "Fusion"?' in John CP Goldberg, Henry E Smith, and PG Turner (eds), *Equity and Law: Fusion and Fission* (Cambridge University Press 2019).

Lookofsky, Jospeh M, *Understanding the CISG: A Compact Guide to the 1980 United Nations Convention on Contracts for the International Sale of Goods* (Kluwer Law International BV 2017).

Mohs, Florian, 'Article 62 CISG: Seller's Right to Require Performance' in Ingeborg Schwenzer and Ulrich G Schroeter (eds), *Schlechtriem & Schwenzer Commentary on the UN Convention on the International Sale of Goods (CISG)* (5th edn, Oxford University Press 2022).

Moréteau, Olivier, 'Remedies for Breach of Contract: A Theoretical and Practical Approach to Specific Performance in International Commercial Law' [2017] *International Business Law Journal* 639.

Müller-Chen, Markus, 'Article 28 CISG: Judgement for Specific Performance' in Ingeborg Schwenzer and Ulrich G Schroeter (eds), *Schlechtriem & Schwenzer Commentary on the UN Convention on the International Sale of Goods (CISG)* (5th edn, Oxford University Press 2022).

Müller-Chen, Markus, 'Article 46 CISG: Buyer's Right to Require Performance, Delivery of Substitute Goods or Repair' in Ingeborg Schwenzer and Ulrich G Schroeter (eds), *Schlechtriem & Schwenzer Commentary on the UN Convention on the International Sale of Goods (CISG)* (5th edn, Oxford University Press 2022).

Schelhaas, Harriet, 'Article 7.2.1' in Stefan Vogenauer (ed), *Commentary on the UNIDROIT Principles of International Commercial Contracts (PICC)* (2nd edn, Oxford University Press 2015).

Schelhaas, Harriet, 'Article 7.2.2' in Stefan Vogenauer (ed), *Commentary on the UNIDROIT Principles of International Commercial Contracts (PICC)* (2nd edn, Oxford University Press 2015).

Schelhaas, Harriet, 'Article 7.2.3' in Stefan Vogenauer (ed), *Commentary on the UNIDROIT Principles of International Commercial Contracts (PICC)* (2nd edn, Oxford University Press 2015).

Schelhaas, Harriet, 'Article 7.2.4' in Stefan Vogenauer (ed), *Commentary on the UNIDROIT Principles of International Commercial Contracts (PICC)* (2nd edn, Oxford University Press 2015).

Schwenzer, Ingeborg, 'Specific Performance and Damages According to the 1994 UNIDROIT Principles of International Commercial Contracts' (1998) 1 *European Journal of Reforms* 289.

Schwenzer, Ingeborg, 'Article 37 CISG: Seller's Right to Cure Prior to Date of Delivery' in Ingeborg Schwenzer and Ulrich G Schroeter (eds), *Schlechtriem & Schwenzer Commentary on the UN Convention on the International Sale of Goods (CISG)* (5th edn, Oxford University Press 2022).

Schwenzer, Ingeborg, 'Article 74 CISG: Calculation of Damages in General' in Ingeborg Schwenzer and Ulrich G Schroeter (eds), Schlechtriem & Schwenzer Commentary on the UN Convention on the International Sale of Goods (CISG) (5th edn, Oxford University Press 2022).

Schwenzer, Ingeborg, and Ilka, Beimel, 'Replacement and Repair of Non-Conforming Goods under the CISG' (2017) 17 *Internationales Handelsrecht* 185.

Schwenzer, Ingeborg, and Muñoz, Edgardo, *Global Sales and Contract Law* (2nd edn, Oxford University Press 2022).

Sidhu, Dawinder S, 'The Immorality and Inefficiency of an Efficient Breach' (2006) 8 *The Tennessee Journal Of Business Law* 61.

Schroeter, Ulrich, 'Article 25 CISG: Fundamental Breach of Contract' in Ingeborg Schwenzer and Ulrich G Schroeter (eds), *Schlechtriem & Schwenzer Commentary on the UN Convention on the International Sale of Goods (CISG)* (5th edn, Oxford University Press 2022).

United Nations (UN) Conference Official Records, 'Documents of the Conference and Summary Records of the Plenary Meetings and of the Meetings of the Main Committees' (1991) UN Doc A/CONF.97/19, 305, 1.

Case law

Albrecht & Dill Trading GmbH v ERST Finance AS et al [2023] Tallinna Ringkonnakohus (Court of Appeal Tallinn) 2-21-10111, CISG-online 6841.

Boxmark Leather GmbH & Co KG v Sals Leather Services S.r.l [2024] Tribunal de Apelaciones en lo Civil de Segundo Turno (Court of Appeal for the Second Circuit) 171/2024 / 2-19258/2022, CISG-online 7035.

Capsule filling machine case [2019] İstanbul 9 Asliye Ticaret Mahkemesi (9th Commercial Court Istanbul) 2014/402 / 2019/566, CISG-online 5144.

Consorcio ALYR Berlín SAS v Impala Terminals Barrancabermeja SA [2019] Centro de Arbitraje y Conciliación Mercantil de la Cámara de Comercio de Bogotá (Center of Arbitration and Conciliation of the Chamber of Commerce Bogota) 5332, CISG-online 6700.

Dominion Denmark A/S v Polytex Composite s.r.o. [2023] Sø- og Handelsretten (Maritime and Commercial Court) BS-48358/2019-SHR, CISG-online 6331.

Hungarian injection moulding tools case [2014] VIII Zivilsenat (8th panel for civil matters) Bundesgerichtshof (German Supreme Court) VIII ZR 394/12, CISG-online 2545.

Jura BV v Willemen Infra NV [2020] Gerechthof 's-Hertogenbosch (Court of Appeal 's-Hertogenbosch) 200.241.641_01, CISG-online 5331.

Lamborghini Countach 112 case [2021] Handelsgericht des Kantons Aargau (Commercial Court Canton Aargau) HSU.2021.4, CISG-online 5824.

Lori s.r.l. v Parandian GmbH [1994] Oberlandesgericht Frankfurt am Main (Court of Appeal Frankfurt am Main) 5 U 15/93, CISG-online 123.

Pallets case I [2002] Amtsgericht Viechtach (Local Court Viechtach) C 419/01, CISG-online 755.

Pelliculest S.a.r.l. et al. v Morton International GmbH et al [2000] Cour d'appel de Colmar (Court of Appeal Colmar) 200002525, CISG-online 578.

Prime electrolytic tinplate case [2019] ICC International Court of Arbitration ICC Case No. 23605/DDA/TO (Final Award), CISG-online 5966.

Protective masks case VII [2025] Oberlandesgericht Köln (Court of Appeal Cologne) 8 U 38/23, CISG-online 7282.

Punching line case [2023] Bezirksgericht Willisau (Court of First Instance Willisau) 1A4 18 9, CISG-online 7179.

Realturf Systems, SL v Eurograss, Inc [2019] Circuit Court of the 11th Judicial Circuit (Miami-Dade County) of the State of Florida 2014-CA-018348, CISG-online 6730.

Solea International BVBA v Bassett & Walker International Inc [2019] Court of Appeal of Ontario C66182 / 2019 ONCA 617, CISG-online 4505.

U.S. Uniform Commercial Code (UCC) *AWB v General Company for Silos and Storage* [2020] Court of Cassation (Egyptian Supreme Court) 2490 of Judicial Year 81, CISG-online 5708.

Vaccum cleaners case [1998] Oberlandesgericht Celle (Court of Appeal Celle) 3 U 246/97, CISG-online 506. *Ingredients for ice cream production case* [2013] Oberlandesgericht Koblenz (Court of Appeal Koblenz) 2 U 50/12, CISG-online 2469.

X-ray tubes case [2015] VIII Zivilsenat (8th panel for civil matters), Bundesgerichtshof (German Supreme Court) VIII ZR 352/13, CISG-online 2596.

Zodiac Seats US LLC v Synergy Aerospace Corp [2020] US District Court for the Eastern District of Texas 4:17-cv-00410, CISG-online 5172.

Legislative instruments

Code des procédures civiles d'exécution.
U.S Uniform Commercial Code (UCC).

Chapter 14

Bach, Ivo, 'Article 49' in Stefan M Kröll, Loukas A Mistelis, and Pilar Perales Viscasillas (eds), *UN Convention on Contracts for the International Sale of Goods (CISG): A Commentary* (2nd edn, CH Beck 2018).

Bach, Ivo, 'Article 50' in Stefan M Kröll, Loukas A Mistelis, and Pilar Perales Viscasillas (eds), *UN Convention on Contracts for the International Sale of Goods (CISG): A Commentary* (2nd edn, CH Beck 2018).

Bell, Gary F, 'Article 64' in Stefan M Kröll, Loukas A Mistelis, and Pilar Perales Viscasillas (eds), *UN Convention on Contracts for the International Sale of Goods (CISG): A Commentary* (2nd edn, CH Beck 2018).

Björklund, Andrea A, 'Article 25' in Stefan M Kröll, Loukas A Mistelis, and Pilar Perales Viscasillas (eds), *UN Convention on Contracts for the International Sale of Goods (CISG): A Commentary* (2nd edn, CH Beck 2018).

Bridge, Michael, 'Issues Arising under Articles 64, 72 and 73 of the United Nations Convention on Contracts for the International Sale of Goods' (2005) 25 *Journal of Law & Commerce* 405.

Bridge, Michael, 'The CISG from the Common Lawyer's Point of View' in Peter Mankowski and Wolfgang Wurmnest (eds), *Festschrift für Ulrich Magnus zum 70. Geburtstag* (De Gruyter 2014) 172.

Brunner, Christoph, and Altenkirch, Markus, 'Article 50 [Remedy of Reduction of Price]' in Christoph Brunner and Benjamin Gottlieb (eds), *Commentary on the UN Sales Law* (CISG) (Wolters Kluwer Law International 2019).

Brunner, Christoph, and Altenkirch, Markus, 'Article 72 (Avoidance Prior to Date for Performance)' in Christoph Brunner and Benjamin Gottlieb (eds), *Commentary on the UN Sales Law (CISG)*, (Kluwer Law International 2019).

Brunner, Christoph, and Leisinger, Benjamin, 'Article 25 (Definition of "Fundamental Breach")' in Christoph Brunner and Benjamin Gottlieb (eds), *Commentary on the un Sales Law (CISG)* (Wolters Kluwer Law International 2019).

Brunner, Christoph, and Leisinger, Benjamin, 'Article 49 (Buyer's Right to Avoid the Contract)' in Christoph Brunner and Benjamin Gottlieb (eds), *Commentary on the UN Sales Law (CISG)*, (Kluwer Law International 2019).

Brunner, Christoph, and Leisinger, Benjamin, 'Article 64 (Seller's Right to Avoid the Contract)' in Christoph Brunner and Benjamin Gottlieb (eds), *Commentary on the UN Sales Law (CISG)* (Kluwer Law International 2019).

Brunner, Christoph, and Leisinger, Benjamin, 'Article 71 [Suspension of Performance]' in Christoph Brunner and Benjamin Gottlieb (eds), *Commentary on the UN Sales Law (CISG)*, (Kluwer Law International 2019).

Brunner, Christoph, Schläpfer, Beat, and Boog, Christopher, 'Article 73 (Avoidance in Installment Contracts)' in Christoph Brunner and Benjamin Gottlieb (eds), *Commentary on the UN Sales Law (CISG)* (Wolters Kluwer 2019).

Chitty, Jospeh, *Chitty on Contracts* (35th edn, Sweet & Maxwell 2023).

CISG Advisory Council, 'CISG-AC Opinion No. 22, The Seller's Liability for Goods Infringing Intellectual Property Rights under Article 42 CISG, Rapporteur: Dr. David Tebel, Rothorn Legal, Frankfurt Am Main, Germany, 7–9 August 2022' (2022).

CISG Advisory Council, 'CISG-AC Opinion No. 23, Mistake, Fraud, Misrepresentation and Initial Impossibility in CISG Contracts, Rapporteur: Professor Hugh Beale, Universities of Warwick (Em.) and Oxford, United Kingdom, December 12–14, 2023' (2023).

CISG Advisory Council, 'CISG-AC Opinion No. 5, The Buyer's Right to Avoid the Contract in Case of Non-Conforming Goods or Documents, Rapporteur: Professor Dr. Ingeborg Schwenzer, LL.M., Professor of Private Law, University of Basel, 7 May 2005.' (2005).

dels Sants Mirambell Fargas, Miquel, (ed), *The Seller's Right to Cure under Article 48 CISG* (Eleven International Publishing 2018).

Fountoulakis, Christiana, 'Article 26 CISG: Notice of Avoidance' in Ingeborg Schwenzer and Ulrich G Schroeter (eds), *Schlechtriem & Schwenzer Commentary on the UN Convention on the International Sale of Goods (CISG)* (5th edn, Oxford University Press 2022).

Fountoulakis, Christiana, 'Article 71 CISG: Suspension of Performance' in Ingeborg Schwenzer and Ulrich G Schroeter (eds), *Schlechtriem & Schwenzer Commentary on the UN Convention on the International Sale of Goods (CISG)* (5th edn, Oxford University Press 2022).

Fountoulakis, Christiana, 'Article 72 CISG: Avoidance in Case of Anticipatory Breach of Contract' in Ingeborg Schwenzer and Ulrich G Schroeter (eds), *Schlechtriem & Schwenzer Commentary on the UN Convention on the* Fountoulakis, Christiana, 'Article 73 CISG: Avoidance of Instalment Contracts' in Ingeborg Schwenzer and Ulrich G Schroeter (eds), *Schlechtriem & Schwenzer Commentary on the UN Convention on the International Sale of Goods (CISG)* (5th edn, Oxford University Press 2022).

Fujita, Carlos Eduardo, *The CISG and Commodity Sales* (Eleven International Publishing 2022).

Huber, Peter, 'Article 48' in Stefan M Kröll, Loukas A Mistelis, and Pilar Perales Viscasillas (eds), *UN Convention on Contracts for the International Sale of Goods (CISG): A Commentary* (2nd edn, CH Beck 2018).

Huber, Peter, 'Article 7.3.1' in Stefan Vogenauer (ed), *Commentary on the UNIDROIT Principles of International Commercial Contracts (PICC)* (2nd edn, 2015).

Huber, Peter, 'Article 7.3.3' in Stefan Vogenauer (ed), *Commentary on the UNIDROIT Principles of International Commercial Contracts (PICC)* (2nd edn, 2015).

Huber, Peter, 'Comparative Sales Law' in Mathias Reimann and Reinhard Zimmermann (eds), *The Oxford Handbook of Comparative Law* (Oxford University Press 2019).

Huber, Peter, 'Introduction to Section 7.3 of the PICC' in Stefan Vogenauer (ed), *Commentary on the UNIDROIT Principles of International Commercial Contracts (PICC)* (2nd edn, 2015).

Kröll, Stefan M, 'Article 41' in Stefan M Kröll, Loukas A Mistelis, and Pilar Perales Viscasillas (eds), *UN Convention on Contracts for the International Sale of Goods (CISG): A Commentary* (2nd edn, CH Beck 2018).

International Institute for the Unification of Private Law (ed), UNIDROIT Principles of International Commercial Contracts (UNIDROIT International Institute for the Unification of Private Law 2016).

Mohs, Florian, 'Article 64 CISG: Seller's Right to Avoid Contract' in Ingeborg Schwenzer and Ulrich G Schroeter (eds), *Schlechtriem & Schwenzer Commentary on the UN Convention on the International Sale of Goods (CISG)* (5th edn, Oxford University Press 2022).

Mohs, Florian, 'Article 65 CISG: Seller's Right to Specify Features of Goods' in Ingeborg Schwenzer and Ulrich G Schroeter (eds), *Schlechtriem & Schwenzer Commentary on the UN Convention on the International Sale of Goods (CISG)* (5th edn, Oxford University Press 2022).

Müller-Chen, Markus, 'Article 46 CISG: Buyer's Right to Require Performance, Delivery of Substitute Goods or Repair' in Ingeborg Schwenzer and Ulrich G Schroeter (eds), *Schlechtriem & Schwenzer Commentary on the UN Convention on the International Sale of Goods (CISG)* (5th edn, Oxford University Press 2022).

Müller-Chen, Markus, 'Article 48 CISG: Seller's Right to Cure after Date for Delivery' in Ingeborg Schwenzer and Ulrich G Schroeter (eds), *Schlechtriem & Schwenzer Commentary on the UN Convention on the International Sale of Goods* Müller-Chen, Markus, 'Article 49 CISG: Buyer's Right to Avoid Contract' in Ingeborg Schwenzer and Ulrich G Schroeter (eds), *Schlechtriem & Schwenzer Commentary on the UN Convention on the International Sale of Goods (CISG)* (5th edn, Oxford University Press 2022).

Müller-Chen, Markus, 'Article 50 CISG: Buyer's Right to Reduce Price' in Ingeborg Schwenzer and Ulrich G Schroeter (eds), *Schlechtriem & Schwenzer Commentary on the UN Convention on the International Sale of Goods (CISG)* (5th edn, Oxford University Press 2022).

Saidov, Djakhongir, 'Article 71' in Stefan M Kröll, Loukas A Mistelis, and Pilar Perales Viscasillas (eds), *UN Convention on Contracts for the International Sale of Goods (CISG): A Commentary* (2nd edn, CH Beck 2018).

Saidov, Djakhongir, 'Article 72' in Stefan M Kröll, Loukas A Mistelis, and Pilar Perales Viscasillas (eds), *UN Convention on Contracts for the International Sale of Goods (CISG): A Commentary* (2nd edn, CH Beck 2018).

Saidov, Djakhongir, 'Article 73' in Stefan M Kröll, Loukas A Mistelis, and Pilar Perales Viscasillas (eds), *UN Convention on Contracts for the International Sale of Goods (CISG): A Commentary* (2nd edn, CH Beck 2018).

Schroeter, Ulrich, 'Article 25 CISG: Fundamental Breach of Contract' in Ingeborg Schwenzer and Ulrich G Schroeter (eds), *Schlechtriem & Schwenzer Commentary on the UN Convention on the International Sale of Goods (CISG)* (5th edn, Oxford University Press 2022).

Schroeter, Ulrich, 'Article 27 CISG: Dispatch Principle' in Ingeborg Schwenzer and Ulrich G Schroeter (eds), *Schlechtriem & Schwenzer Commentary on the UN Convention on the International Sale of Goods (CISG)* (5th edn, Oxford University Press 2022).

Schwenzer, Ingeborg, 'Avoidance of the Contract in Case of Non-Conforming Goods (Article 49(1)(a) CISG)' (2005) 25 *Journal of Law and Commerce* 437.

Schwenzer, Ingeborg H, 'Article 74 CISG: Calculation of Damages in General' in Ingeborg Schwenzer and Ulrich G Schroeter (eds), *Schlechtriem & Schwenzer Commentary on the UN Convention on the International Sale of Goods (CISG)* (5th edn, Oxford University Press 2022).

Schwenzer, Ingeborg, 'Article 41 CISG: Third Party Claims in General' in Ingeborg Schwenzer and Ulrich G Schroeter (eds), *Schlechtriem & Schwenzer Commentary on the UN Convention on the International Sale of Goods (CISG)* (5th edn, Oxford University Press 2022).

Schwenzer, Ingeborg, 'Article 42 CISG: Third Party Claims Based on Intellectual Property' in Ingeborg Schwenzer and Ulrich G Schroeter (eds), *Schlechtriem & Schwenzer Commentary on the UN Convention on the International Sale of Goods (CISG)* (5th edn, Oxford University Press 2022).

Schwenzer, Ingeborg, 'Article 79 CISG: Exemption from Liability for Damages' in Ingeborg Schwenzer and Ulrich G Schroeter (eds), *Schlechtriem & Schwenzer Commentary on the UN Convention on the International Sale of Goods (CISG)* (5th edn, Oxford University Press 2022).

Schwenzer, Ingeborg, and Muñoz, Edgardo, *Global Sales and Contract Law* (2nd edn, Oxford University Press 2022).

Tebel, David, 'Article 41 (Third-Party Claims to Goods)' in Christoph Brunner and Benjamin Gottlieb (eds), *Commentary on the UN Sales Law (CISG)*, (Kluwer Law International 2019).

Tebel, David, 'Article 42 [Third-Party Claims to Goods]' in Christoph Brunner and Benjamin Gottlieb (eds), *Commentary on the UN Sales Law (CISG)*, (Kluwer Law International 2019).

Vogenauer, Stefan (ed), 'Article 7.4.13', *Commentary on the UNIDROIT Principles of International Commercial Contracts (PICC)* (2nd edn, 2015).

United Nations (UN) Conference Official Records, 'Documents of the Conference and Summary Records of the Plenary Meetings and of the Meetings of the Main Committees' (1991) UN Doc A/CONF.97/19.

Case law

[…] Sà.r.l. v Emerito SL [2024] Cour d'appel de Montpellier (Court of Appeal Montpellier) 22/01909, CISG-online 6846.

Austrian insulation material (distribution agreement) case [2023] Oberlandesgericht Graz (Court of Appeal Graz) 5 R 73/23d-23, CISG-online 6628. *Chinese wire rod case II* [2015] Bundesgericht/Tribunal fédéral (Swiss Federal Supreme Court) 4A_614/2014, CISG-online 2592.

Auto-Moto Styl S.r.o. v Pedro Boat BV [2005] Gerechtshof Leeuwarden (Court of Appeal Leeuwarden) 0400549, CISG-online 1100.

Bloom Lake General Partner Ltd et al. v Worldlink Resources Ltd [2014] ICC International Court of Arbitration 18209/VRO/AGF/ZF (c. 18251/VRO/AGF) (Final award), CISG-online 5277.

BP Oil International, Ltd v Empresa Estatal Petroleos de Ecuador (PetroEcuador) [2003] US Court of Appeals (5th Circuit) 02-20166, CISG-online 730.

Brands International Corporation v Reach Companies, LLC [2023] US District Court for the District of Minnesota 0:2021cv01026, CISG-online 6279.

BRI Production 'Bonaventure' S.a.r.l. v Pan African Export [1995] Cour d'appel de Grenoble (Court of Appeal Grenoble) 93/3275, CISG-online 151.

Calzaturificio Piceno di Roberto Catinari & Uvaldo Raccosta v Vivace Mode GmbH [1997] Oberlandesgericht Düsseldorf (Court of Appeal Düsseldorf) 6 U 87/96, CISG-online 385.

Car phones case [2004] Oberlandesgericht Düsseldorf (Court of Appeal Düsseldorf) I-15 U 88/03, CISG-online 915.

Czech cheese case [1998] Schiedsgericht der Hamburger freundschaftlichen Arbitrage (Hamburg Friendly Arbitration) CISG-online 638.

Dcoop Sociedad Cooperativa Andaluza v Patano S.r.l. [2023] Audiencia Provincial de Jaén (Court of Appeal Jaén) 1697/2021/1323/2023, CISG-online 6896.

Dingxi Longhai Dairy, Ltd v Becwood Technology Group LLC [2011] US Court of Appeals (8th Circuit) 10-2612, CISG-online 2256.

Dingxi Longhai Dairy, Ltd v Becwood Technology Group, LLC [2008] US District Court for the District of Minnesota 08-762 DSD/SRN, CISG-online 1774.

Diversitel Communications, Inc v Glacier Bay Inc [2003] Superior Court of Justice of Ontario 03-CV-23776 SR, CISG-online 1436.

Downs Invest P/L v Perwaja Steel SDN BHD [2000] Supreme Court of Queensland [2000] QSC 421 / SC No 10680 of 1996, CISG-online 587 859, note 80.

FCF SA v Adriafil Commerciale S.r.l. (Egyptian cotton case II) [2000] Bundesgericht/Tribunal fédéral (Swiss Federal Supreme Court) 4C.105/2000, CISG-online 770.

Frese Biogas GmbH & Co KG v Circular Values BV et al. [2024] Rechtbank Zeeland-West-Brabant (District Court ZeelandWest-Brabant) C/02/367340 / HA ZA 20-1, CISG-online 7014.

Gente Oil Ecuador Pte Ltd v Republic of Ecuador [2022] Permanent Court of Arbitration Case No. 2018-12.

German goods case [1999] ICC International Court of Arbitration 9978 (Final Award), CISG-online 708.

Hearing implants case [1993] Landgericht Aachen (District Court Aachen) 43 O 136/92, CISG-online 86.

Hungarian furniture case [1998] Oberlandesgericht Hamm (Court of Appeal Hamm) 19 U 127/97, CISG-online 434.

Hungarian mushrooms case [1995] Arbitration Court attached to the Hungarian Chamber of Commerce and Industry VB/94124, CISG-online 250.

Iron molybdenum case [1997] Oberlandesgericht Hamburg (Court of Appeal Hamburg) 1 U 167/95, CISG-online 261.

Italdecor s.a.s. v Yiu's Industries (HK) Limited [1998] Corte di Appello di Milano (Court of Appeal Milan) 790, CISG-online 348.

Italian shoes case XV [1994] Landgericht Berlin (District Court Berlin) 52 S 247/94, CISG-online 399.

Italian shoes case XXV [2004] Oberlandesgericht Düsseldorf (Court of Appeal Düsseldorf) I-6 U 210/03, CISG-online 916.

Italian sunflower oil case [1997] Handelsgericht des Kantons Zürich (Commercial Court Canton Zurich) HG 950347, CISG-online 327.

Ketchup bottles case [2003] Oberlandesgericht Rostock (Court of Appeal Rostock) 3 U 19/03, CISG-online 920.

Lentils case [1996] China International Economic & Trade Arbitration Commission (CIETAC) CISG/1996/56, CISG-online 2281.

Macedonian lambskin coats case [1998] Handelsgericht des Kantons Zürich (Commercial Court Canton Zurich) HG 930634, CISG-online 415.

Mansonville Plastics (BC) Ltd v Kurtz GmbH et al [2003] Supreme Court of British Columbia C993594, CISG-online 1017.

Memory modules case [2001] Oberlandesgericht Hamm (Court of Appeal Hamm) 13 U 102/01, CISG-online 1430.

Metal concentrate case [1996] ICC International Court of Arbitration 8574 (Final Award), CISG-online 1293.

OIL Otto International Leasing AG v Zernopererabatyvayuschy kombinat Barnaulskaya melnitsa [2002] Federal Arbitrazh Court for the Western Siberia Circuit F04/2712-494/A03-2002, CISG-online 2282.

Packages for animal food case [1997] Turun hovioikeus (Court of Appeal Turku) S 95/1023, CISG-online 1297.

Paprika powder case I [1995] Landgericht Ellwangen (District Court Ellwangen) 1 KfH O 32/95, CISG-online 279.

Protective masks case IV [2025] Oberlandesgericht Köln (Court of Appeal Cologne) 8 U 46/23, CISG-online 7261.

Protective masks case VII [2025] Oberlandesgericht Köln (Court of Appeal Cologne) 8 U 38/23, CISG-online 7282.

Q-railing glass partition for swimming pool case [2022] Rechtbank Gelderland (District Court Gelderland) C/05/393151 / HA ZA 21-468, CISG-online 5954.

R&R Manufacturing SAS v Everestt International Industries Ltd [2023] Cour d'appel de Besançon (Court of Appeal Besançon) 21/01330, CISG-online 6643.

Shanghai Anlili International Trading Co. Ltd. v J & P Golden Wings Corp. [2008] 上海市第一中级人民法院 (Intermediate People's Court Shanghai No. 1) IPC/34, CISG-online 2059.

Skin care products case [1998] Helsingin hovioikeus (Court of Appeal Helsinki) S 96/1215, CISG-online 1304.

Spanish orange juice case [2010] Oberlandesgericht Düsseldorf (Court of Appeal Düsseldorf) I-17 U 132/08, CISG-online 2171.

Stolen wheel loader case [2023] Obergericht des Kantons Zug (Court of Appeal Canton Zug) Z1 2022 6, CISG-online 6313.

Thai-made emulsion case [1989] China International Economic & Trade Arbitration Commission (CIETAC) CISG-online 1230.

Triage Matériel Professionnel S.a.r.l. v JGB-2 Sp z.o.o. [2023] Cour d'appel de Paris (Court of Appeal Paris) 21/19946, CISG-online 6569.

Used printing machines case I [1995] Oberlandesgericht Celle (Court of Appeal Celle) 20 U 76/94, CISG-online 152.

Valero Marketing & Supply Co v Greeni Oy [2007] US Court of Appeals (3rd Circuit) 06-3390, 06-3525, CISG-online 1510.

Legislative instruments

England Sale of Goods Act 1979.
Hong Kong Sale of Goods Ordinance 1924.
New Zealand Sale of Goods Act 1908.
Scotland Sale of Goods Act 1979.
Singapore Sale of Goods Act 1979.
Swedish Sales Law.
U.S. Uniform Commercial Code (UCC) 2003.

Chapter 15

Atamer, Yesim M, 'Article 78' in Stefan M Kröll, Loukas A Mistelis, and Pilar Perales Viscasillas (eds), *UN Convention on Contracts for the International Sale of Goods (CISG). A Commentary* (2nd edn, CH Beck 2018).

Atamer, Yesim M, 'Article 79' in Stefan M Kröll, Loukas A Mistelis, and Pilar Perales Viscasillas (eds), *UN Convention on Contracts for the International Sale of Goods (CISG). A Commentary* (2nd edn, CH Beck 2018).

Atamer, Yesim M, 'Article 80' in Stefan M Kröll, Loukas A Mistelis, and Pilar Perales Viscasillas (eds), *UN Convention on Contracts for the International Sale of Goods (CISG). A Commentary* (2nd edn, CH Beck 2018).

Bacher, Klaus, 'Article 78 CISG: Obligation to Pay Interest' in Ingeborg Schwenzer Ulrich Shroeter (eds), *Schlechtriem & Schwenzer: Commentary on the UN Convention on the International Sale of Goods* (5th edn, Oxford University Press 2022).

Bridge, Michael, 'The CISG and the UNIDROIT Principles of International Commercial Contracts' (2014) 19 *Uniform Law Review* 623.

Brödermann, Eckart, 'Article 7.4.9' in Eckart Brödermann, *UNIDROIT Principles of International Commercial Contracts: An Article-by-Article Commentary* (2nd edn, Kluwer Law International 2023).

Brödermann, Eckart J, 'Article 7.4.7' in Eckart Brödermann, *UNIDROIT Principles of International Commercial Contracts: An Article-by-Article Commentary* (2nd edn, Kluwer Law International 2023).

Brunner, Christoph, *Force Majeure and Hardship under General Contract Principles: Exemption for Non-Performance in International Arbitration* (Wolters Kluwer 2008) 61

Brunner, Christoph, 'Article 79 [Impediment Excusing a Party From Damages]' in Christoph Brunner and Benjamin Gottlieb (eds), *Commentary on the UN Sales Law (CISG)*, (Kluwer Law International 2019).

Brunner, Christoph, and Feit, Michael, 'Article 78 [Interest on Sums in Arrears]' in Christoph Brunner and Benjamin Gottlieb (eds), *Commentary on the UN Sales Law (CISG)* (3rd edn, Kluwer Law International 2019).

Brunner, Christoph, and Schäfer, Friederike, 'Article 77 [Mitigation of Damages]' in Christoph Brunner and Benjamin Gottlieb (eds), *Commentary on the UN Sales Law (CISG)* (3rd edn, Kluwer Law International 2019).

Brunner, Christoph, Boog, Christopher, and Schläpfer, Beat, 'Article 80' in Christoph Brunner and Benjamin Gottlieb (eds), *Commentary on the UN Sales Law (CISG)* (3rd edn, Kluwer Law International 2019).

Brunner, Christoph, Schmidt-Ahrendts, Nils, and Czarnecki, Mark, 'Article 74' in Christoph Brunner and Benjamin Gottlieb (eds), *Commentary on the UN Sales Law (CISG)* (3rd edn, Kluwer Law International 2019).

Brunner, Christoph, Schmidt-Ahrendts, Nils, and Czarnecki, Marl, 'Article 75 [Calculation of Loss in the Case of Avoidance of the Contract and Substitute Transaction]' in Christoph Brunner and Benjamin Gottlieb (eds), *Commentary on the UN Sales Law (CISG)* (3rd edn, Kluwer Law International 2019).

CISG Advisory Council, 'CISG-AC Opinion No. 10, Agreed Sums Payable upon Breach of an Obligation in CISG Contracts, Rapporteur: Dr. Pascal Hachem, Bär & Karrer AG, Zurich, Switzerland, 3 August 2012' (2012).

CISG Advisory Council, 'CISG-AC Opinion No. 13 Inclusion of Standard Terms under the CISG, Rapporteur: Professor Sieg Eiselen, College of Law, University of South Africa, Pretoria, South Africa, January 20 2013' (2013).

CISG Advisory Council, 'CISG-AC Opinion No. 14, Interest under Article78 CISG, Rapporteur: Professor Doctor Yeşim M. Atamer, Istanbul Bilgi University, Turkey. Adopted unanimously by the CISG Advisory Council following its 18th meeting, in Beijing, China on 21 and 22 October 2013' (2013).

CISG Advisory Council, 'CISG-AC Opinion No. 17, Limitation and Exclusion Clauses in CISG Contracts, Rapporteur: Prof. Lauro Gama Jr., Pontifical Catholic University of Rio de Janeiro, Brazil, 16 October 2015' (2015).

CISG Advisory Council, 'CISG-AC Opinion No. 20, Hardship under the CISG, Rapporteur: Prof. Dr. Edgardo Muñoz, Universidad Panamericana, Guadalajara, Mexico. Adopted by the CISG Advisory Council following its 27th meeting, in Puerto Vallarta, Mexico on 2–5 February 2020' (2020).

CISG Advisory Council, 'CISG-AC Opinion No. 6, Calculation of Damages under CISG Article 74, Rapporteur: Professor John Y. Gotanda, Villanova University School of Law, Villanova, Pennsylvania, USA, 2006' (2006).

CISG Advisory Council, 'CISG-AC Opinion No. 7, Exemption of Liability for Damages under Article 79 of the CISG, Rapporteur: Professor Alejandro M. Garro, Columbia University School of Law, New York, N.Y. 12 October 2007' (2007).

CISG Advisory Council, 'CISG-AC Opinion No. 8 Calculation of Damages under CISG Articles 75 and 76. Rapporteur: Professor John Y. Gotanda, Villanova University School of Law, Villanova, Pennsylvania, USA. Adopted by the CISG-AC following its 12th meeting in Tokyo, Japan, on 15 November 2008' (2008).

CISG Advisory Council, 'CISG-AC, Opinion no. 12, Liability of the Seller for Damages Arising Out of Personal Injuries and Property Damage Caused by Goods and Services under the CISG, Rapporteur: Professor Hiroo Sono, School of Law, Hokkaido University, Sapporo, Japan, 20 January 2013' (2013).

Czarnecki, Mark, Brunner, Christoph, and Schmidt-Ahrendts, Nils, 'Article 76 (Calculation of Loss in Case of Goods With Market Prices)' in Christoph Brunner and Benjamin Gottlieb (eds), *Commentary on the UN Sales Law (CISG)*, (Kluwer Law International 2019).

Davies, Martin, and Snyder, David, *International Transactions in Goods: Global Sales in Comparative Context* (Oxford University Press 2014).

Djordjević, Milena, 'Article 74' in Stefan M Kröll, Loukas A Mistelis, and Pilar Perales Viscasillas (eds), *UN Convention on Contracts for the International Sale of Goods (CISG). A Commentary* (2nd edn, CH Beck 2018).

Djordjević, Milena, 'Article 75' in Stefan M Kröll, Loukas A Mistelis, and Pilar Perales Viscasillas (eds), *UN convention on Contracts for the International Sale of Goods (CISG): A commentary* (2nd edn, CH Beck 2018.

Djordjević, Milena, 'Article 76' in Stefan M Kröll, Loukas A Mistelis, and Pilar Perales Viscasillas (eds), *UN Convention on Contracts for the International Sale of Goods (CISG). A Commentary* (2nd edn, CH Beck 2018).

Djordjević, Milena, 'Article 77' in Stefan M Kröll, Loukas A Mistelis, and Pilar Perales Viscasillas (eds), *UN Convention on Contracts for the International Sale of Goods (CISG). A Commentary* (2nd edn, CH Beck 2018).

Eisenberg Formula; Melvin Eisenberg, 'Impossibility, Impracticability, and Frustration' (2009) 1 *Journal of Legal Analysis* 207.

Erauw, Johan, 'Article 67' in Stefan M Kröll, Loukas A Mistelis, and Pilar Perales Viscasillas (eds), *UN Convention on Contracts for the International Sale of Goods (CISG). A Commentary* (2nd edn, CH Beck 2018).

Flechtner, Harry M., *Honnold's Uniform Law for International Sales under the 1980 United Nations Convention* (5th edn, Wolters Kluwer 2021).

Gillette, Clayton P, and Walt, Steven D, *The UN Convention on Contracts for the International Sale of Goods: Theory and Practice* (2nd edn, Cambridge University Press 2016).

Graves, Jack, 'Penalty Clauses as Remedies: Exploring Comparative Approaches to Enforceability' (2013) 29 *Touro Law Review* 681, 684.

Hachem, Pascal, 'Article 4 CISG: Substantive Scope of Convention' in Ingeborg Schwenzer and Ulrich G Schroeter (eds), *Schlechtriem & Schwenzer Commentary on the UN Convention on the International Sale of Goods (CISG)* (5th edn, Oxford University Press 2022).

Hachem, Pascal, 'Article 5 CISG: Liability for Death or Personal Injury' in Ingeborg Schwenzer and Ulrich Shroeter (eds), *Schlechtriem & Schwenzer: Commentary on the UN Convention on the International Sale of Goods* (5th edn, Oxford University Press 2022).

Ishida, Yasutoshi, 'CISG Article 79: Exemption of Performance, and Adaptation of Contract through Interpretation of Reasonableness - Full of Sound and Fury, but Signifying Something' (2018) 30 *Pace International Law Review* 331.

Hondius, Ewoud, and Janssen, André, 'Chapter 26: Disgorgement of Profits: Gain-Based Remedies throughout the World' in Ewoud Hondius and André Janssen (eds), *Disgorgement of Profits: Gain-Based Remedies throughout the World*, 8 (Springer 2015).

ICC Force Majeure Clause 2003, ICC publication 650; ICC Force Majeure Clause 2020.

International Chamber of Commerce (ICC), Force Majeure Clause 1985 ICC publication 421.

International Institute for the Unification of Private Law (ed), *UNIDROIT Principles of International Commercial Contracts* (UNIDROIT International Institute for the Unification of Private Law 2017).

McKendrick, Ewan, 'Article 6.2.2' in Stefan Vogenauer (ed), *Commentary on the UNIDROIT Principles of International Commercial Contracts (PICC)* (2nd edn, Oxford University Press 2015).

McKendrick, Ewan, 'Article 6.2.3' in Stefan Vogenauer (ed), *Commentary on the UNIDROIT Principles of International Commercial Contracts (PICC)* (2nd edn, Oxford University Press 2015).

McKendrick, Ewan, 'Article 7.4.10' in Stefan Vogenauer (ed), *Commentary on the UNIDROIT Principles of International Commercial Contracts (PICC)* (2nd edn, Oxford University Press 2015).

McKendrick, Ewan, 'Article 7.4.13' in Stefan Vogenauer (ed), *Commentary on the UNIDROIT Principles of International Commercial Contracts (PICC)* (2nd edn, Oxford University Press 2015).

McKendrick, Ewan, 'Article 7.4.2 in Stefan Vogenauer (ed), *Commentary on the UNIDROIT Principles of International Commercial Contracts (PICC)* (2nd edn, Oxford University Press 2015) para 19.

McKendrick, Ewan, 'Article 7.4.3' in Stefan Vogenauer (ed), *Commentary on the UNIDROIT Principles of International Commercial Contracts (PICC)* (2nd edn, Oxford University Press 2015).

McKendrick, Ewan, 'Article 7.4.4' in Stefan Vogenauer (ed), *Commentary on the UNIDROIT Principles of International Commercial Contracts (PICC)* (2nd edn, Oxford University Press 2015).

McKendrick, Ewan, 'Article 7.4.5' in Stefan Vogenauer (ed), *Commentary on the UNIDROIT Principles of International Commercial Contracts (PICC)* (2nd edn, Oxford University Press 2015) paras 1–2.

McKendrick, Ewan, 'Article 7.4.6' in Stefan Vogenauer (ed), *Commentary on the UNIDROIT Principles of International Commercial Contracts (PICC)* (2nd edn, Oxford University Press 2015) paras 1-2.

McKendrick, Ewan, 'Article 7.4.8' in Stefan Vogenauer (ed), *Commentary on the UNIDROIT Principles of International Commercial Contracts (PICC)* (2nd edn, Oxford University Press 2015).

Muñoz, Edgardo, and Ament-Guemez, David Obey, 'Calculation of Damages on the Basis of the Breaching Party's Profits under the CISG' (2017) 8 *The George Mason Journal of International Commercial Law* 201.

Mohs, Florian, 'Introduction to Articles 66–70' in Ingeborg Schwenzer and Ulrich Schroeter (eds), *Schlechtriem & Schwenzer: Commentary on the UN Convention on the International Sale of Goods* (5th edn, Oxford University Press 2022).

Müller-Chen, Markus, 'Article 50' in Ingeborg Schwenzer and Ulrich Shroeter (eds), *Schlechtriem & Schwenzer: Commentary on the UN Convention on the International Sale of Goods* (5th edn, Oxford University Press 2022).

Neumann, Thomas, 'Shared Responsibility under Article 80 CISG' (2009) *Nordic Journal of Commercial Law* 1.

Neumann, Thomas, *The Duty to Cooperate in International Sales: The Scope and Role of Article 80 CISG* (Sellier 2012).

Pichonnaz, Pascal, 'Article 7.1.7' in Stefan Vogenauer (ed), *Commentary on the UNIDROIT Principles of International Commercial Contracts (PICC)* (2nd edn, Oxford University Press 2015).

Saidov, Djakhongir, 'Damages: The Need for Uniformity' (2005) 25 *Journal of Law and Commerce* 393.

Saidov, Djakhongir, *The Law of Damages in International Sales: The CISG and Other International Instruments* (Bloomsbury Academic 2008).

Schelhaas, Harriet, 'Article 7.1.1' in Stefan Vogenauer (ed), *Commentary on the UNIDROIT Principles of International Commercial Contracts (PICC)* (2nd edn, Oxford University Press 2015).

Schelhaas, Harriet, 'Article 7.1.2' in Stefan Vogenauer (ed), *Commentary on the UNIDROIT Principles of International Commercial Contracts (PICC)* (2nd edn, Oxford University Press 2015).

Schmidt, Mareike, 'Profiting from Substitute Transactions? Offsetting Losses and Benefits under the CISG' in Andrea Buechler and Markus Müller-Chen (eds), *Private Law, National—Global—Comparative: Festschrift für Ingeborg Schwenzer zum 60. Geburtstag* (Stämpfli 2011).

Schmidt-Ahrendts, Nils, 'Disgorgement of Profits under the CISG' in Ingeborg Schwenzer and Lisa Spagnolo (eds), *State of Play: The 3rd Annual MAA Schlechtriem CISG Conference* (Eleven International Publishing 2010).

Schroeter, Ulrich, 'Article 14 CISG: Offer (Including Incorporation of Standard Terms)' in Ingeborg Schwenzer and Ulrich G Schroeter (eds), *Schlechtriem & Schwenzer Commentary on the UN Convention on the International Sale of Goods (CISG)* (5th edn, Oxford University Press 2022).

Schwenzer, Ingeborg, and B Leisinger, 'Ethical Values and International Sales Contracts' in Ross Cranston, Jan Ramberg and Jacob Ziegler (eds), *Commercial Law Challenges in the 21st Century – Jan Hellner in memoriam* (Stockholm Centre for Commercial Law 2007).

Schwenzer, Ingeborg, and Muñoz, Edgardo, 'Duty to Renegotiate and Contract Adaptation in Case of Hardship' (2019) 24 *Uniform Law Review* 149.

Schwenzer, Ingeborg, and Muñoz, Edgardo, *Global Sales and Contract Law* (2nd ed, Oxford university press 2022).

Schwenzer, Ingeborg, and Pascal Hachem, 'The CISG - Successes and Pitfalls' (2009) 57 *American Journal of Comparative Law* 457.

Schwenzer, Ingeborg, and Pascal Hachem, 'The Scope of the CISG Provisions on Damages' in Djakhongir Saidov and Ralph Cunnington (eds), *Contract Damages: Domestic and International Perspectives* (Bloomsbury Publishing 2008).

Schwenzer, Ingeborg, 'Article 74 CISG: Calculation of Damages in General' in Ingeborg Schwenzer and Ulrich Schroeter (eds), *Schlechtriem & Schwenzer: Commentary on the UN Convention on the International Sale of Goods* (4th edn, Oxford University Press 2016).

Schwenzer, Ingeborg, 'Article 75 CISG: Calculation of Damages in Case of Avoidance and Substitute Transaction' in Ingeborg Schwenzer and Ulrich G Schroeter (eds), *Schlechtriem & Schwenzer Commentary on the UN Convention on the International Sale of Goods (CISG)* (5th edn, Oxford University Press 2022).

Schwenzer, Ingeborg, 'Article 76 CISG: Calculation of Damages in Case of Avoidance without Substitute Transaction' in Ingeborg Schwenzer and Ulrich Schroeter (eds), *Schlechtriem & Schwenzer: Commentary on the UN Convention on the International Sale of Goods* (5th edn, Oxford University Press 2022).

Schwenzer, Ingeborg, 'Article 77 CISG: Mitigation of Damages' in Ingeborg Schwenzer and Ulrich Schroeter (eds), *Schlechtriem & Schwenzer: Commentary on the UN Convention on the International Sale of Goods* (5th edn, Oxford University Press 2022).

Schwenzer, Ingeborg, 'Article 79 CISG: Exemption from Liability for Damages' in Ingeborg Schwenzer and Ulrich Schroeter (eds), *Schlechtriem & Schwenzer: Commentary on the UN Convention on the International Sale of Goods* (5th edn, Oxford University Press 2022).

Schwenzer, Ingeborg, 'Article 80 CISG: Breach Caused by Creditor' in Ingeborg Schwenzer and Ulrich Schroeter (eds), *Schlechtriem & Schwenzer: Commentary on the UN Convention on the International Sale of Goods* (5th edn, Oxford University Press 2022)

Schwenzer, Ingeborg, 'Force Majeure and Hardship in International Sales Contracts' (2008) 39 *Victoria University of Wellington Law Review* 709.

Vogenauer, Stefan (ed), *Commentary on the UNIDROIT Principles of International Commercial Contracts (PICC)* (2nd edn, Oxford University Press 2015).

Vogenauer, Stefan, 'Article 5.1.4' in Stefan Vogenauer (ed) *Commentary on the UNIDROIT Principles of International Commercial Contracts (PICC)* (2nd edn, Oxford University Press 2015).

Watterson, Stephen, 'Gain-Based Remedies for Civil Wrongs in England and Wales' in Ewoud Hondius and André Janssen (eds), *Disgorgement of Profits: Gain-Based Remedies throughout the World*, 8 (Springer 2015).

UNCITRAL, Digest of Case Law on the United Nations Convention on the International Sale of Goods (2016).

United Nations (UN), Conference Official Records, 'Commentary on the Draft Convention on Contracts for the International Sale of Goods, prepared by the Secretariat' (1978) UN Doc A/CONF.97/5.

Zeller, Bruno, 'Penalty Clauses: Are They Governed by the CISG' (2011) 23 *Pace International Law Review* 1.

Case law

Amalgamated Investment & Property Co Ltd v John Walker & Sons Ltd [1977] 1 WLR 164, CA.

Art books case [1999] Handelsgericht des Kantons Zürich (Commercial Court Canton Zurich) HG 970238.1, CISG-online 488.

Artem v Gray Fox Logistics [2020] Arbitration Institute of the Stockholm Chamber of Commerce (SCC) V 2019/066, CISG-online 5548.

Attianese S.p.A. v P. S. Import ApS [2024] Sø- og Handelsretten (Maritime and Commercial Court) BS-40411/2023-SHR, CISG-online 7177.

Attorney General v Blake [2001] 1 AC 268 (HL).

Audiencia Provincial de Valladolid, Dry Top N.V. v Sociedad Cooperativa Piñón-Sol [2015] Audiencia Provincial de Valladolid (Court of Appeal Valladolid) 69/2015, CISG-online 2619.

Automatic diffractometer case [1995] Международный коммерческий арбитражный суд при Торгово–промышленной палате Российской Федерации (Tribunal of International Commercial Arbitration at the Russian Federation Chamber of Commerce and Industry (MKAC)) 123/1992, CISG-online 207.

Bacon case I [1992] Oberlandesgericht Hamm (Court of Appeal Hamm) 19 U 97/91, CISG-online 57.

Beer case I [2013] Oberlandesgericht Brandenburg (Court of Appeal Brandenburg) 6 U 5/12, CISG-online 2400.

Behr France S.a.r.l. v Romay AG [2004] Cour de Cassation (French Supreme Court) Y 01-15.964, CISG-online 870.

Berrycare Group d.o.o. v ABB Growers B.V. [2024] Gerechthof 's-Hertogenbosch (Court of Appeal's-Hertogenbosch) 200.318.359_01, CISG-online 6881.

Brands International Corporation v Reach Companies, LLC [2024] US Court of Appeals (8th Circuit) 23-2164, CISG-online 7006.

Brands International Corporation v Reach Companies, LLC, No 23-2164 (8th Cir, 30 May 2024).

Brassiere cups case [2008], Cour d'appel de Rennes (Court of Appeal Rennes) R.G. 07/03098, CISG-online 1746.

BRI Production 'Bonaventure' S.a.r.l. v Pan African Export [1995] Cour d'appel de Grenoble (Court of Appeal Grenoble) 93/3275, CISG-online 151.

Bulbs for four-leaf clover case [2019] Oberlandesgericht Düsseldorf (Court of Appeal Düsseldorf) . I-6 U 2/19, CISG-online 4614 *[...] v Luka Food d.o.o.* [2021] Vrhovni kasacioni sud/Врховни касациони суд (Serbian Supreme Court) 135/2021, CISG-online 685.

Butter case [1997] Helsingin hovioikeus (Court of Appeal Helsinki) S 96/605, CISG-online 782.

Italian shoes case III [1989] Landgericht Stuttgart (District Court Stuttgart) 3 KfH O 97/89, CISG-online 11.

Castel Electronics Pty Ltd v Toshiba Singapore Pte Ltd [2010] Federal Court of Australia [2010] FCA 1028, CISG-online 2158.

China Railway No. 10 Engineering Group Co. Ltd. v Triorient LLC [2020] American Arbitration Association—International Centre for Dispute Resolution (AAA/ICDR) 01-19-0003-0137, CISG-online 5639.

Chinese graphite electrodes case [2024] Oberlandesgericht Stuttgart (Court of Appeal Stuttgart) 5 U 65/23, CISG-online 6942.

Clay case [2011] Oberlandesgericht Koblenz (Court of Appeal Koblenz) 6 U 555/07, CISG-online 2301.

Clay case [2012] Bundesgerichtshof (German Supreme Court) VIII ZR 100/11, CISG-Online 2348.

Cold-rolled metal sheets case I [1994] Vienna International Arbitral Centre of the Austrian Federal Economic Chamber (VIAC) SCH-4318, CISG-online 120.

Cooling machine case [2002] Oberster Gerichtshof (Austrian Supreme Court) 7 Ob 301/01t, CISG-online 643.

Coöperatieve Federatie van Edelpelsdierenhouders Nederasselt U.A. v Ceva Santé Animale S.A. [2025] Netherlands Commercial Court, NCC C/13/736825, CISG-online 7354.

Delchi Carrier, SpA v Rotorex Corp [1995] US Court of Appeals (2nd Circuit) 95-7182, 95-7186, CISG-online 140.

Diammonium phosphate case [2023] Cairo Regional Centre for International Commercial Arbitration (CRCICA), 1527/2021 (Final Award), CISG-online 6272.

Dunlop Pneumatic Tyre Co. Ltd v New Garage and Motor Co, Ltd [1915] AC 79.

Dye for clothes case [1997] Audiencia Provincial de Barcelona (Court of Appeal Barcelona) 755/95-C, CISG-online 338.

Failure to open letter of credit and penalty clause case [1992] ICC International Court of Arbitration 7197, CISG-online 36.

Fashion products case [2003] ICC International Court of Arbitration 11849, CISG-Online 1421.

FHR European Ventures LLP v Cedar Capital Partners LLC [2014] UKSC 45.

Final award in ICC Case No. 9466, Y.B. Com. Arb. 2002.

Fundiciones Balaguer, S.A. v Ferrell-Ross Roll Mfg. [2024] U.S. District Court for the Southern District of Texas, 4:23-cv-4437, CISG-online 7229.

Gasum Oy, v Gazprom Export LLC [2022] Ad hoc Arbitral Tribunal, CISG-online 7151.

Glimm Screens B.V. v Elos Med S.P. [2023] Gerechtshof Arnhem-Leeuwarden (Court of Appeal ArnhemLeeuwarden) 200.313.285/01, CISG-online 6449.

Goodman Food Products, Inc. v Sunrise Foods Int'l Inc. [2022] U.S. District Court for the Central District of California, 2:21-cv-06518-SB-ADS, CISG-online 6047.

Greenyard Fresh France v Banaland, LLC [2021] Cour d'appel de Paris (Court of Appeal Paris) 19/21002, CISG-online 5795.

Hearing implants case [1993] Landgericht Aachen (District Court Aachen) 43 O 136/92, CISG-online 86.

Hefei Ziking Steel Pipe Co., Ltd. v Meever & Meever et al. [2021] U.S. District Court for the Southern District of Texas, 4:20-CV-00425, CISG-online 5685.

Hewlett-Packard France v Matrox Graphics Inc. [2020] Cour supérieure du Québec/Superior Court of Québec, 2020 QCCS 78 / 500-05-070786-023, CISG-online 4876.

Hiking guidebooks case [2013] Oberlandesgericht Köln (Court of Appeal Cologne) 16 U 106/12, CISG-online 2480.

Hungarian T-shirts case [2006] Oberlandesgericht Koblenz (Court of Appeal Koblenz) 6 U 113/06, CISG-online 1407.

Hungarian wheat case [2006] Oberlandesgericht Karlsruhe (Court of Appeal Karlsruhe) 7 U 1001/04, CISG-online 1328.

IBS Engineering GmbH v Holland Filter B.V. [2024] Gerechthof's-Hertogenbosch (Court of Appeal's-Hertogenbosch) 200.332.839/01, CISG-online 7158.

ICC Award [1999] No 5953 Clunet 1990, 1056 *Hannaford v Australian Farmlink Pty Ltd* [2008] Federal Court of Australia [2008] FCA 1591 / ACN 087 011 541, CISG-online 1782.

ICC Case 4462 of 1985 and 1987, *Yb.Com.Arb. 1991* 54 Collection of ICC Arbitral Awards III 3.

ICC Case No. 17768 [2013] ICC International Court of Arbitration 17768 *VSL Middle East LLC v Trenzas y Cables de Acero PSC SL* [2013] Audiencia Provincial de Cantabria (Court of Appeal Cantabria) 400/2013, CISG-online 2487.

Indian glass mosaic tiles case [2013] Oberster Gerichtshof (Austrian Supreme Court) 4 Ob 208/12k, CISG-online 2398.

Indian-Russian sales contract case I [2004] MKAC 97/2004, CISG-online 1188.

Inmed v Etablissements JR Maruani [2019] Cour de Cassation (French Supreme Court) 18-10969, CISG-online 4631.

Iritecna S.pA v Marc Rich & Co AG [1993] Tribunale di Genova (District Court Genova) 1912, CISG-online 540.

Italian fashion textiles case II [1990] Amtsgericht Oldenburg in Holstein (Local Court Oldenburg in Holstein) 5 C 73/89, CISG-online 20.

Italian fashion textiles case III [1990] Landgericht Hamburg (District Court Hamburg) 5 O 543/88, CISG-online 21.

Italian shoes case XIII [1994] Oberlandesgericht Düsseldorf (Court of Appeal Düsseldorf) 17 U 146/93, CISG-online 119.

Italian shoes case XXV [2004] Oberlandesgericht Düsseldorf (Court of Appeal Düsseldorf) I-6 U 210/03, CISG-online 916.

Italian tiles case III [1995] Amtsgericht Alsfeld (Local Court Alsfeld) 31 C 534/94, CISG-online 170.

Jiangsu Taiping Rubber Co., Ltd. v Kumwoo Investment Co., Ltd. [2018] Intermediate People's Court Zhenjiang, Jiangsu Province (2016) Su 11 Min Chu No. 337, CISG-online 4120.

Key press case [1995] Bundesgerichtshof (German Supreme Court) VIII ZR 18/94, CISG-online 149 (previous instances [1992] Landgericht Düsseldorf (District Court Düsseldorf) 31 O 223/91.

Krane-Maschinen-Service GmbH & Co Handels-KG v Grúas Andaluza, SA [2010] Audiencia Provincial de Murcia (Court of Appeal Murcia) 408/2010, CISG-online 2130.

Lamborghini hauler case [2013] Oberlandesgericht Koblenz (Court of Appeal Koblenz) 3 U 223/13, CISG-online 2472 note II.1.b]cc).

Macromex Srl v Globex International Inc [2007] American Arbitration Association – International Centre for Dispute Resolution (AAA/ICDR) 50181T 0036406 (Interim Award), CISG-online 1645.

Medical-Technical-Aid GmbH v Ningbo Automotive Technology Co. Ltd. [2021] 浙江省宁波市中级人民法院 (Intermediate People's Court Ningbo, Zhejiang Province) (2021)浙 02 民初 824 号, CISG-online 6203.

Minh Dung Aluminum Company, Ltd v Aluminum Alloys MFG LLC [2021] U.S. District Court for the Middle District of Pennsylvania, 1:20-cv-01764, CISG-online 5633.

Natural stones case III [2010] Oberster Gerichtshof (Austrian Supreme Court) 8 Ob 30/10k, CISG-online 2296.

Pharmaceutical glycerin case [2017] Oberlandesgericht Wien (Court of Appeal Vienna) Austria, CISG-online 2814.

Ponte Vecchio Beheer BV v DST Global Solutions (Realty) Limited [2024] Parket bij de Hoge Raad (Advocate General at the Dutch Supreme Court) 23/02925, CISG-online 7028.

Portuguese clogs case [2024] Rechtbank Overijssel (District Court Overijssel) C/08/309410 / HA ZA 24-44, CISG-online 7206.

Prakasa Indústria e Comércio de Utilidades do Lar Ltda v Mercomáquinas Indústria Comércio e Representações Ltda [2009] Tribunal de Justiça do Estado do Rio Grande do Sul (Court of Appeal of the State of Rio Grande do Sul) 70025609579, CISG-online 2368.

Pressure sensors case [2007] Arbitration Institute of the Stockholm Chamber of Commerce (SCC) CISG-online 1521.

Printed circuit boards case [2019] Cour d'appel de Paris (Court of Appeal Paris) 18/04137, CISG-online 5765.

Production line for foamed boards case [1992] ICC International Court of Arbitration 7585, CISG-online 105.

Propane gas case [1996] Oberster Gerichtshof (Austrian Supreme Court) 10 Ob 518/95, CISG-online 224.

Protective masks case IV [2025] Oberlandesgericht Köln (Court of Appeal Cologne) 8 U 46/23, CISG-online 7261.

Realturf Systems, S.L. v Eurograss, Inc. [2019] Circuit Court of the 11th Judicial Circuit (Miami-Dade County) of the State of Florida, 2014-CA-018348, CISG-online 6730.

REC Solar Grade Silicon Co., Ltd. v Hairun Photovoltaic Technology Co., Ltd [2018] Intermediate People's Court Wuxi, Jiangsu Province (2018) Su 02 Min Chu No. 131, CISG-online 4107.

Scafom International BV v Lorraine Tubes SAS [2009] Hof van Cassatie van België/Cour de cassation de Belgique (Belgian Supreme Court) C.07.0289.N, CISG-online 1963.

Shamo jeans case [1999] Oberlandesgericht Hamburg (Court of Appeal Hamburg) 1 U 31/99, CISG-online 515.

Ski wear and sportswear case [2010] Handelsgericht des Kantons Zürich (Commercial Court Canton Zurich) HG070223/U/dz, CISG-online 2160.

Shenzen Synergy Digital Co., Ltd. v Mingtel, Inc. [2022] U.S. District Court for the Eastern District of Texas, 4:19-cv-00216, CISG-online 5845.

Sofas case [2024] Rechtbank Zeeland-West-Brabant (District Court ZeelandWest-Brabant) 10251115 \ CV EXPL 22-3954 (E), CISG-online 7254.

Solarpower GmbH v Servis FVE a. s. et al. [2018] Nejvyšší soud České republiky (Supreme Court of the Czech Republic) 32 Cdo 2978/2016, CISG-online 4197.

Solea International BVBA v Bassett & Walker International Inc. [2018] Superior Court of Justice of Ontario, CV-15-527848 / 2018 ONSC 4261, CISG-online 4194.

South Korean stainless wire case [1997] Bundesgerichtshof (German Supreme Court) VIII ZR 300/96, CISG-online 277.

Steel bars case I Steel bars case I [1989] ICC International Court of Arbitration 6281 (Final Award), CISG-online 8.

Suministros industriales diversos, S. A. v Hunan Pulaili Pipe Co., Ltd. (Welded Carbon Steel Pipe Case) [2019] Hunan Changsha Tianxin District People's Court, (2018) Xiang 0103 Min Chu No. 3578, CISG-online 5504.

Sunrise Foods Int'l, Inc. v Ryan Hinton Inc. [2019] U.S. District Court for the District of Idaho, 1:17-CV-00457-CWD, CISG-online 4522.

Suspension of delivery case [2010] 대구지방법원 (District Court Daegu) 2007GaHap11525, CISG-Online 2505.

Tex-Isle Supply, Inc. v Tecnotubi S.p.A. et al. [2023] American Arbitration Association – International Centre for Dispute Resolution (AAA/ICDR), 01-20-0015-5404 (Final Award), CISG-online 6682.

THI Medical, S.A.C. v Filmore Management Trading, LLC et al. [2023] U.S. District Court for the Southern District of Florida, 21-21632-Civ-GAYLES/TORRES, CISG-online 6489

Urangesellschaft GmbH v Nynco Trading Ltd. [2021] ICC International Court of Arbitration, ICC Case 23069/GR (Final Award), CISG-online 6665.

KRAPE S.A. v LIK Supply, Corp. [2022] U.S. District Court for the Eastern District of New York, 21-CV-03742-AMD-JRC, CISG-online 6024.

Vine wax case [1999] Bundesgerichtshof (German Supreme Court) VIII ZR 121/98, CISG-online 396.

VÚB a.s. v LITOZ s.r.o. [2019] Nejvyšší soud České republiky (Supreme Court of the Czech Republic) 23 Cdo 427/2017-336, CISG-online 4867.

Xiamen Suncare Medical Device Ltd. v Bunnik Creations B.V. [2025] Rechtbank Rotterdam (District Court Rotterdam) C/10/631379 / HA ZA 22-2, CISG-online 7332.

Zapata Hermanos Sucesores, SA v Hearthside Baking Comp [2002] US Court of Appeals (7th Circuit) 01-3402, 02-1867, 02-1915 CISG-online 684.

Zhongshan Ruicheng Clothing Textile Co. Ltd v AmeBalance B.V. [2024] Rechtbank Den Haag (District Court The Hague) C/09/658069 / HA ZA 23-1074, CISG-online 7185.

Chapter 16

Bacher, Klaus, 'Article 88 CISG: Self-help and Emergency Sale of Preserved Goods' in Ingeborg Schwenzer and Ulrich G Schroeter (eds), *Schlechtriem & Schwenzer: Commentary on the UN Convention on the International Sale of Goods* (5th edn, Oxford University Press 2022).

Bacher, Klaus, 'Introduction to Articles 85–88 CISG: General Questions Regarding the Preservation of the Goods' in Ingeborg Schwenzer and Ulrich Schroeter (eds), *Schlechtriem & Schwenzer: Commentary on the UN Convention on the International Sale of Goods* (5th edn, Oxford University Press 2022).

Bonell, Joachim, 'The New Provisions on Illegality in the UNIDROIT Principles 2010' (2011) *Uniform Law Review—Revue de droit uniforme* 517.

Bridge, Michael, 'Article 81' in Stefan M Kröll, Loukas A Mistelis, and Pilar Perales Viscasillas (eds), *UN Convention on Contracts for the International Sale of Goods (CISG): A Commentary* (2nd edn, CH Beck 2018).

CISG Advisory Council, 'CISG-AC Opinion No. 14, Interest under Article78 CISG, Rapporteur: Professor Doctor Yeşim M. Atamer, Istanbul Bilgi University, Turkey. Adopted unanimously by the CISG Advisory Council following its 18th meeting, in Beijing, China on 21 and 22 October 2013' (2013).

CISG Advisory Council, 'CISG-AC Opinion No. 23, Mistake, Fraud, Misrepresentation and Initial Impossibility in CISG Contracts, Rapporteur: Professor Hugh Beale, Universities of Warwick (Em.) and Oxford, United Kingdom, December 12–14, 2023' (2023).

CISG Advisory Council, 'CISG-AC Opinion No. 9, Consequences of Avoidance of the Contract, Rapporteur: Professor Michael Bridge, London School of Economics, London, United Kingdom. Adopted by the CISG-AC following its 12th meeting in Tokyo, Japan on 15 November 2008' (2008).

Cuniberti, Gilles, 'Article 3.3.1' in Stefan Vogenauer (ed), *Commentary on the UNIDROIT Principles of International Commercial Contracts (PICC)* (2nd edn, Oxford University Press 2015).

Cuniberti, Gilles, 'Article 3.3.2' in Stefan Vogenauer (ed), *Commentary on the UNIDROIT Principles of International Commercial Contracts (PICC)* (2nd edn, Oxford University Press 2015).

Flechtner, Harry M., *Honnold's Uniform Law for International Sales under the 1980 United Nations Convention* (5th edn, Wolters Kluwer 2021).

Fountoulakis, Christiana, 'Article 81 CISG: Parties' Release from Obligations; Restriction' in Ingeborg Schwenzer and Ulrich Schroeter (eds), *Schlechtriem & Schwenzer: Commentary on the UN Convention on the International Sale of Goods* (5th edn, Oxford University Press 2022).

Huber, Peter, 'Article 7.3.6' in Stefan Vogenauer (ed), *Commentary on the UNIDROIT Principles of International Commercial Contracts (PICC)* (2nd edn, Oxford University Press 2015).

Huber, Peter, 'Article 7.3.7' in Stefan Vogenauer (ed), *Commentary on the UNIDROIT Principles of International Commercial Contracts (PICC)* (2nd edn, Oxford University Press 2015).

International Institute for the Unification of Private Law (ed), *UNIDROIT Principles of International Commercial Contracts* (UNIDROIT International Institute for the Unification of Private Law 2017).

Magnus, Ulrich, 'The Remedy of Avoidance of Contract under CISG—General Remarks And Special Cases' (2005) 25 *Journal of Law & Commerce*.

Mohs, Florian, 'Effects of Avoidance and Restitution of the Goods: Remarks on the Manner in which Articles 7.3.5 and 7.3.6 of the UNIDROIT Principles Compare with Articles 81 and 82 of the CISG' in John Felemegas (ed), *An International Approach to the Interpretation of the United Nations Convention on Contracts for the International Sale of Goods (1980) as uniform sales law* (Cambridge University Press 2007).

Schwenzer, Ingeborg, and Muñoz, Edgardo, *Global Sales and Contract Law* (2nd edn, Oxford University Press 2022).

Schwenzer, Ingeborg, 'Article 74 CISG: Calculation of Damages in General' in Ingeborg Schwenzer and Ulrich G Schroeter (eds), *Schlechtriem & Schwenzer Commentary on the UN Convention on the International Sale of Goods (CISG)* (5th edn, Oxford University Press 2022).

Sono, Hiroo, 'Article 86 CISG' in Stefan M Kröll, Loukas A Mistelis, and Pilar Perales Viscasillas (eds), *UN Convention on Contracts for the International Sale of Goods (CISG): A Commentary* (2nd edn, CH Beck 2018).

Sono, Hiroo, 'Article 88 CISG' in Stefan M Kröll, Loukas A Mistelis, and Pilar Perales Viscasillas (eds), *UN Convention on Contracts for the International Sale of Goods (CISG): A Commentary* (2nd edn, CH Beck 2018).

Storme, Michael, 'Harmonisation of the Law on (Substantive) Validity of Contracts (Illegality and Immorality)' in Jürgen Basedow, Klaus J Hopt, and Hein Kötz (eds) *Festschrift für Ulrich Drobnig zum siebzigsten Geburtstag* (Mohr Siebeck 2024).

Vogenauer, Stefan, 'The UNIDROIT Principles of International Commercial Contracts at Twenty: Experiences to Date, the 2010 Edition, and Future Prospects' (2014) 19(4) *Uniform Law Review—Revue de droit uniforme* 496.

Zimmermann, Reinhard, 'The Unwinding of Failed Contracts in the UNIDROIT Principles 2010' (2011) 25 *Uniform Law Review* 570.

Case law

[1995] Landgericht Düsseldorf 2 O 506/94, Unilex.

Chinese goods case [1996] Schiedsgericht der Handelskammer Hamburg (Court of Arbitration of the Hamburg Chamber of Commerce) Partial Award (on the merits) CISG-online 187.

Dimur Fruits SL v Fairtrasa Holland BV [2021] Rechtbank Den Haag (District Court The Hague) C/09/592683 / HA ZA 20-472, CISG-online 5564.

DSM Dyneema B.V. v Electromichaniki Kimis EPE [2009] Polimeles Protodikio Athinon (Multi-member Court of First Instance Athens) 4505/2009, CISG-online 2228.

Filanto, S.pA v Chilewich International Corp [1992] US [Federal] District Court for the Southern District of New York 91 Civ. 3253 (CLB), CISG-online 45.

German goods case [1999] ICC International Court of Arbitration 9978 (Final Award), CISG-online 708.

Gimex, SA v Basque Imagen Grafica y Textil, SL [2003] Audiencia Provincial de Navarra (Court of Appeal Navarra) 73/2002, CISG-online 811.

Mercedes Maybach case [2019] Oberster Gerichtshof (Austrian Supreme Court) 4 Ob 110/19h, CISG-online 4509.

Shamo jeans case [1999] Oberlandesgericht Hamburg (Court of Appeal Hamburg) 1 U 31/99, CISG-online 515.

Solmed Supplies SL v Dieha Capital BV [2023] Rechtbank Zeeland-West-Brabant (District Court Zeeland-WestBrabant) C/02/383910 / HA ZA 21-168 (E), CISG-online 6434.

Venison case [1999] Oberlandesgericht Braunschweig (Court of Appeal Braunschweig) 2 U 27/99, CISG-online 510.

Legislative instruments

American Law Institute, *Restatement of the Law (2d) of Contracts* (American Law Institute).

Chapter 17

Brödermann, Eckart, *UNIDROIT Principles of International Commercial Contracts. An Article-by-Article Commentary* (2nd edn, Kluwer Law International 2023).

International Institute for the Unification of Private Law (ed), *UNIDROIT Principles of International Commercial Contracts* (UNIDROIT International Institute for the Unification of Private Law 2017).

Schwenzer, Ingeborg, 'Article 39 CISG: Buyer's Notice of Non-conformity' in Ingeborg Schwenzer and Ulrich G Schroeter (eds), *Schlechtriem & Schwenzer Commentary on the UN Convention on the International Sale of Goods (CISG)* (5th edn, Oxford University Press 2022).

Schwenzer, Ingeborg, and Hachem, Pascal, 'The CISG—Successes and Pitfalls' (2009) 57 *American Journal of Comparative Law* 457.

Schwenzer, Ingeborg, and Muñoz, Edgardo, *Global Sales and Contract Law* (2nd edn, Oxford University Press 2022).

Wintgen, Robert, 'Article 10.3' in Stefan Vogenauer (ed), *Commentary on the UNIDROIT Principles of International Commercial Contracts (PICC)* (2nd edn, 2015).

Case law

Corsetti S.r.l. v Préfac Béton Environnement S.A.S. [2025] Cour d'appel de Riom (Court of Appeal Riom), 23/00524, CISG-online 7367.

Hubstaplerfall [2005] Bundesgericht (Swiss Federal Supreme Court) 121 III 453.

MMA IARD SA et al. v Inter Mutuelles Entreprises SA et al [2024] Cour d'appel de Toulouse (Court of Appeal Toulouse) 18/05127, CISG-online 6920; *OKWIND v TGB Group Technologies, S.L.* [2024] Audiencia Provincial de Barcelona (Court of Appeal Barcelona), 749/2022 / 981/2024, CISG-online 7300.

Park Plus Inc. v Sotefin SA [2023] Swiss Arbitration Centre, 500146-2022 (Final Award), CISG-online 7020.

Legislative instruments

Convention on the Limitation Period in the International Sale of Goods 1974.

Index

For the benefit of digital users, indexed terms that span two pages (e.g., 52–53) may, on occasion, appear on only one of those pages.